2 ANATOMY AND PHYSIOLOGY OF SPEECH

2nd EDITION

HAROLD M. KAPLAN

Department of Physiology
Southern Illinois University
Carbondale, Illinois

McGRAW-HILL BOOK COMPANY

New York   St. Louis   San Francisco   Düsseldorf   Johannesburg
Kuala Lumpur   London   Mexico   Montreal   New Delhi   Panama
Rio de Janeiro   Singapore   Sydney   Toronto

This book was set in Baskerville by Monotype Composition Company, Inc.,
and printed on permanent paper and bound by The Maple Press Company.
The designer was Jo Jones; the drawings were done by BMA
Associates, Inc. The editors were Robert Fry and Ellen Simon.
John A. Sabella supervised production.

To my wife

CONTENTS

PREFACE

Rapid progress in the fields of anatomy, physiology, and speech pathology has necessitated a new edition, making it possible to rearrange and restate the subject material and present new theories.

Some illustrations have been revised and new ones added. More frequent chapter and paragraph headings facilitate isolation and retrieval of the material.

The general organization of the material is arbitrary and follows the pattern of the course which the author has given for many years to senior college and graduate students.

Selected pathophysiologic material has been included because of the writer's conviction that some knowledge of the applications of anatomy and physiology will better motivate the student. This material appears to be readily comprehended at the level of training expected, and it provides an incentive for further study.

The text attempts to unify anatomic and physiologic data into an orderly account of the normal sensory and motor aspects of speech. It is hoped that the book will provide an adequate account of those separate but integrated parts of the human structure which are called the speech apparatus.

The text is directed chiefly to students of speech who may need a relatively detailed description of the pertinent structures and bodily processes involved. It is also addressed to anatomists and physiologists who are interested in this aspect of human function.

The subject matter is adapted to fit into the needs and limitations of a basic course. No single work that is short of encyclopedic can hope to encompass the information in this field both extensively and intensively, and collateral reading is expected.

Harold M. Kaplan

Anatomy and Physiology of Speech

A SURVEY OF THE SPEECH MECHANISM

Plan and Scope of the Study

Some textbooks of physiology have energy as the central theme; others revolve around homeostasis, or the preservation of the dynamic steady state of an organism. The emphasis in this text is upon the search for correlating structure and function with the acoustic signals (symbols). By what operational methods is communication achieved?

Transmission of information through speech involves (1) the structures and processes by which signals are produced, e.g., phonation and articulation; (2) the nature of the acoustic signals produced by these activities; and (3) the mechanism of conversion of the signals by a listener into meaningful sound. The first and third of these interdependent chain reactions will be especially stressed in this text, from an anatomic and physiologic point of view.

The organs which are correlated in vocal activity are not structures primarily formed for speech. They are the inherited products of our ancestral history, and most of the primitive members in this historical sequence were by structural necessity notably silent. The organs subserving speech in man develop a sophistication far beyond the needs of the biologic functions they serve. The biologist turns to comparative anatomy to shed some light upon the intermediate aspects of this racial story.

Speech is a behavioral activity, and the metabolic and mechanical influences upon its gradual emergence and differentiation during and after fetal life are of interest. The analysis through embryology contributes to an understanding of the personal history of behavior.

To produce sound in man, not only have the brain and sense organs specialized but the respiratory and digestive systems in particular have developed regional modifications. The anatomic machinery then acquired differential functions, and it is these great divisions of function which are discussed in the text.

A nervous system and an adjunctive set of chemical messengers, or hormones, set the speech structures into motion and integrate all the processes involved. The respiratory system generates the air blast, and the vocal folds vibrate with, or respond in some fashion to, the exhaled stream of air. There is above the folds a series of resonating chambers which serve to modulate the vibrations. Structures for articulation mold the resonated waves into meaningful speech sounds. Finally, there is the auditory mechanism which provides for reception, transmission, and even crude analysis of the incident sound. The degree of auditory acuity and cerebral interpretation has much to do with the ability to form and modulate sounds correctly.

The Acoustic Signal

Speech is a varied and complex multidimensional signal whose acoustic properties include energy, frequency, and time. Some brief attention is given to these parameters at the outset of the text. The sound spectrograph is a convenient method of displaying the spectrum of the signal and has made possible the observation of the time parameter.

Acoustic signals are emitted by most vertebrates, and the sensory receptors of each species are especially responsive to such airborne messages from their own kind. Animal communication, although of great interest, is not emphasized in this text.

Neural Control

A primary cerebral motor area may initiate and immediately direct the action of the discrete groups of skeletal muscles which energize the speech structures. Since no meaningful series of sounds seems possible simply as a result of many isolated although delicate movements, other areas of the brain appear to be necessary for an overall command. Thus we note the action of the premotor cortex and secondary cerebral motor areas.

The cerebellum is also necessary as a distribution and timing center. It monitors the impulses from the cerebrum and the muscles and fires them back into the muscles much as the distributor of an auto engine sends high-voltage electric current from the spark coil into the separate spark plugs just at the right time.

The basal ganglia, which are islands of cells lying principally within the white matter of the cerebral hemispheres and downstream from the cerebral cortex, come into play adjunctively with the cerebellum to regulate the tone, rhythm, and directiveness of the nerve impulses which are firing into the muscles as a consequence of cerebral activation. Lower centers in the brainstem and in the core of the brain, called the reticular formation, are similarly kept busy correcting the nature of the stream of neural impulses which are funneling into the effectors.

The muscles, by self-contained devices called stretch receptors, feed information back into the central nervous system concerning what has happened to them with respect to tension, tone, position in space, force, rhythm, or other characteristics. This is truly automation, and it permits the whole circuit to be hypothetically subject to considerable mathematical analysis by the methods of cybernetics. This does not necessarily mean that the analysis is in the traditional aspects of binary digital or analog structures.

Great association areas are additional elements of the regulatory apparatus. They are needed for the synthesis of the ideas to be expressed and for the automatic selection of the words to be used in syntax. In an early localization theory, Broca's area, which is one of the association areas, is considered to be necessary to integrate the speech musculature. If destroyed on both cerebral hemispheres, the individual speech muscles may not be paralyzed but they cannot be coordinated.

The timing of execution of the motor events is essential to the proper formation of speech sounds. Just as the muscles of expiration start their contraction earlier than that of the muscles of the larynx, so do all the muscles of the successively higher chambers relate to one another in orderly sequence. Timing and rhythm are prime functions of the neural regulators of speech structures.

Respiration

The energy for sound originates in the lungs, and the intensity of the sound is related to the force of contraction of the chest muscles. At this stage we are dealing in generalizations. For example, intensity is a physical determinant of loudness, and the latter is related to the amplitude of excursion of the vocal folds and to any amplification of tone by the resonators.

Although it is possible to produce sounds upon inhalation, it is the exhalation which normally drives air up through the glottal opening between the vocal folds. The vocal folds, in consequence, respond in different ways, depending upon many factors.

While the lung pressure is increasing, the vocal folds tend to be approximated, and they remain so until they are forced apart by the pressure of the exhaled air. The breath stream is converted by the vibrations excited in the vocal folds to a sound stream. The function of the respiratory air in speech is to provide adequate expiratory pressures to vibrate the vocal folds and an airstream from which vowel and consonant sounds are produced. This activity demands a precise coordination of activity between the structures for breathing and the events occurring at and above the vocal folds. Expiration is controlled to match the tension and resistance of the vocal folds.

The chest does not maintain a steady pressure during phonation but may produce pulses of pressure corresponding to the syllables while retaining an overall posture to keep up an adequate respiratory volume and supply of air for phonation.

The Vocal Folds and Phonation

The larynx, or voice box, is the upper part of the air passage, specially modified for the production of sound. It is a system of cartilages, capable of being acted upon readily and with great mobility by voluntary muscles. In speech, it can move as a whole, while localized internal regions move or vibrate directly and with precision.

The basic component of the larynx is the pair of true vocal folds. The action of the folds is essentially that of a valve, and sound production has developed from reflex closure of the glottis, or space between the folds. Sound is produced by events relating the exhaled air to vibrations of the vocal folds and changing contours of the glottal margins. In this process the larynx breaks the exhaled breath stream into a series of puffs which are converted to laryngeal, or glottal, tones.

The exact mechanism of phonation is still to be determined, but it is best described by a myoelastic-aerodynamic theory in which the folds respond to the subglottic pressures of the exhaled air. The tone produced by the effect of the vocal fold vibrations on the airstream contains parameters that are expressed in such terms as pitch, intensity, and quality.

The true folds are mobile structures whose length, mass, position, and tension are readily altered. Although the intensity of sound is importantly related to chest muscles and pulmonary pressures, the pitch and to a certain extent the quality or timbre are related to the vocal folds, particularly to their tension and length.

The Resonators and Resonance

The original tone produced by the activity of the vocal folds is called the glottal tone. The complex waveform contains musical tones consisting of a fundamental and overtones whose frequencies are integral multiples of the fundamental frequency. The waveform also contains nonmusical, or aperiodic (nonperiodic), tones involving noises of no definite pitch. The glottal tone is monotonous and unlike the final speech sounds that are uttered.

All the regions of the larynx are capable of physically acting upon both the behavior of the laryngeal vibrator and the transmitted sound vibrations. The quality of the voice is thus changed. Some of the waves are weakened, others are reinforced, and still others remain unchanged. The distribution of energy is altered, being increased for the most part. Amplification resulting from a high efficiency of the conversion of the kinetic energy of the airstream to the acoustic energy of the sound stream is called resonance.

The subglottic resonators are the trachea and thoracic cavities. The supraglottic resonators are the cavities of the larynx above the vocal folds, the pharynx, and oral and nasal chambers. Other resonators are being identified. For example, even dentition is considered a factor in resonance. All these resonators have a differential importance in their effect on the quality of tone. The manner of coupling of the oral and pharyngeal spaces is especially significant.

A tube with uniform cross-sectional area has regularly spaced resonant frequencies, and if nonuniform, it has irregularly spaced resonant frequencies. If closed at one end only, the lowest resonant frequency is that of a wave whose length is 4 times the tube length. The successively higher resonant frequencies are odd-numbered multiples of the lowest one. If the human vocal tract is considered (as a simplification only) to be uniform, 17 cm in length, and closed below, its resonant frequencies occur at 500, 1,500, 2,500, 3,500 Hz and so on. Because the vocal tract has so many resonant frequencies, it can intensify the harmonics of the glottal tone at several frequency regions. The vocal tract resonances are formants, and the corresponding frequencies are formant frequencies. These are characteristic for every change in shape taken by regions of the vocal tract, and the possibilities of resonances are enormous. The spectrum of speech expresses the frequency and intensity of each harmonic (overtone) of the speech waveforms. The intelligibility of speech is highly dependent upon these factors. Vowel recognition is especially (but not exclusively) dependent upon the frequencies of the lower formants.

All told, resonance gives a pleasing quality, richness, and carrying power to the voice while minimizing the incident energy demanded.

Articulation

The vocal folds vibrate to produce voiced sounds, but there are also so-called voiceless (unvoiced) sounds which are produced without vocal fold vibration. Vowels are voiced, but consonants are voiced or unvoiced. The complex sound stream, in traveling upward through the supraglottic passages, eventually reaches structures which act as valves to stop the stream completely or to narrow the spaces for its passage. The sounds are shaped, fused, and separated. The articulators give quality to the consonants and assist in forming some of the vowel-sound families. Articulators include the lips, tongue, mandible, velum, posterior pharyngeal wall, hyoid bone, and the inner edges of the vocal folds. The hard palate and teeth belong in this category in that they act as walls against which the articulators move.

Articulation involves accuracy in placement of structures, timing, direction of movements, force exerted, speed of response, and neural integration of all the events. It is no wonder that articulation problems are the most prevalent of all the speech disorders. From the standpoint of speech pathology the prevalence of articulation problems is particularly obvious because there are fairly precise standards for comparison.

There is a rhythm in speech which may be a timing mechanism for articulation as well as serving to order, or organize, speech events. The syllable, whose physiologic correlate may be a breath pulse, expressed in the variations of subglottic pressure, has a predictable rate and rhythm for an individual.

The rhythm and speed of articulation involve the neural integration of such a large number of muscles that it would appear necessary for automatic control mechanisms to exist below the level of consciousness and release an organized store of information.

6   The results of articulation are the vocal utterances, composed of elementary sounds, the consonants and vowels, which are combined into words. Words are the symbols for concepts, and words are the basis for speech. The process of speech is a highly developed form of communication, or language, because it is the articulate expression of thought.

The intelligibility of speech sounds necessitates an adequate intensity of tones, an adequate band of frequencies, and a minimal reverberation (reflections that decrease in intensity within a short time). There are linguistic, semantic, and psychologic cues in addition to the information provided by the acoustic features.

The Auditory Mechanism

Since speech is transmitted by sound waves, much can be learned by examining the physical properties of sound waves and by studying the ear as an organ for the reception and analysis of sound waves. Sound, itself, acts like a feedback mechanism, which significantly influences voice and articulation.

The ear fulfills the essential conditions of good resonance and damping, which means that it can reproduce a tone faithfully while preventing its persistence.

The mechanisms of hearing have been the subject of exhaustive investigation. Time and three-dimensional space enter the concepts.

The external ear offers few problems. The problem solved by the middle ear is that of transferring sound energy from air to a liquid medium without significant loss. It manages to accomplish this by a tympanic membrane and chain of bones which amplify the incident pressures through leverage and a hydraulic-press action. Unaided transfer of vibratory energy from air to water is not efficient. The mechanical advantage gained only by leverage is inadequate, however, and the more important factor in facilitating the critical step from air to fluid is the fact that the drum membrane has a cross-sectional area of about 90 mm² and the energy falling there can be concentrated upon the stapes with an area of only about 30 mm².

The analytic receptors for sound are in the inner ear. The spiral organ of Corti, which lies on the basilar membrane in the floor of the cochlear duct within the inner ear, is of special interest because it is the primary sensor and analytic structure and also because its mode of reaction lends itself to investigative technics.

The inner ear apparently can serve for the crude analysis of the complex form of the incident sound waves. This involves, among other responses, a place of maximum excitability along the basilar membrane which shifts progressively with frequency. During the shift different auditory nerve fibers correspondingly undergo maximal excitation. The nerve impulses remain canalized within the auditory tract so that a given tone produces a peak of activity in a localized area of the temporal cortex. Within the framework of this "place" theory there are resonance and traveling-wave theories concerning how the basilar membrane responds to different sound frequencies. In the resonance view the basilar membrane acts selectively as a series of tuned resonators. In the traveling-wave theory the waves grow in size and subside by damping, short wavelengths dying out more quickly. A definite time is needed for conduction of the wave. At one region the basilar membrane is maximally deflected, the region differing with frequency and recognizable by the cerebrum.

7

The organ of Corti does not act like the diaphragm in a telephone, transmitting vibrations without alteration to the brain, as proposed in the last century and later supported erroneously by the Wever-Bray volley theory, whose tenets held that asynchronous firing of impulses could bring up to 30,000 impulses to the brain in 1 sec. The discovery of concomitant by-products of the effects of sounds called cochlear potentials explained the asynchronous firing and militated against the telephone view.

The volley theory may be thought of as one version of the so-called frequency theories. In these, the frequencies of the incident waves are said to be reproduced in the frequencies of the nerve discharges, and these frequencies are cerebrally interpreted as different pitches. In a compromise modification proposed by Wever and Bray, called the resonance-volley theory, pitch has a twofold representation; i.e., low tones are represented by frequency, high tones by place, and other tones by a combination of the two.

The waves that are now believed to be capable of crude analysis by the peripheral mechanisms are transduced to coded information, which is transmitted through a four-neuron pathway to the temporary cerebrum. At every synaptic level there may be some synthesis of the information into more discrete aspects of the parameters of sound. The final perception of all the qualities of sound is most likely accomplished in the associative areas of the cerebrum.

8

2 THE PHYSICAL NATURE OF SOUND

If sound were defined as a sensation produced through the organs of hearing, there would be no sound in the absence of a living organism. If it is defined as that which is capable of producing an auditory sensation, then there is sound in the physical sense. We are concerned with the physical causes and with the physiologic or psychologic responses.

Sound is produced by matter in motion, by vibrating bodies of various kinds which set up a disturbance in an elastic medium, usually air. Sound will also travel in solids and liquids but not in a vacuum. A sound is a propagated change in the density and therefore in the pressure of an elastic medium. To a degree sound disappears as it travels. Its free energy is dissipated in heating the air through which it passes. Sound decays with time and distance.

Sound waves undergo reflection (change of direction in the original medium at a bounding surface), refraction (change of direction due to a change in the properties of the medium), and diffraction (change of direction due to the wave's striking a sharp edge or opening that is of the order of magnitude of the wavelength).

The organic generator of speech sounds is the vocal fold, and emphasis must be placed on understanding its *vibrations* and the ensuing propagated disturbances, which are longitudinal, mechanical *waves*.

Vibratory Motion

Vibratory motion is the motion of a body, having the property of inertia, which upon displacement from equilibrium position is acted upon by a restoring force whose effective component is directed toward the equilibrium position.

Mass, elasticity, and *energy* are fundamental to vibratory motion. If an elastic spring is clamped at its lower end with a lead ball attached to its upper end (Figure 2-1) and the spring then pulled to right position *A*, upon release it first swings back past its equilibrium position *B* to left position *C*.

The driving force lies in the fact that the work performed in bringing the spring to *A* gives it potential energy. This is gradually changed to kinetic energy, becoming all kinetic when the spring reaches its mean position at *B*. As a result of its *inertia,* the kinetic energy is increasingly transformed to potential energy as the spring travels toward *C*. If there were no resistance the swing would *vibrate* (oscillate) to and fro indefinitely. Due to energy losses it becomes *damped* and eventually stops in the equilibrium position.

Terminology

The *displacement* of a vibrating body at any instant is its distance from the equilibrium position.

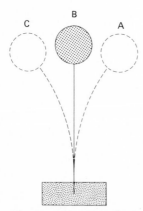

Figure 2-1 An elastic spring pendulum. Energy is entirely potential at *A* and *C* and entirely kinetic at *B*.

The *amplitude* is the maximum displacement, or distance between the equilibrium position and either extremity of its swing.

The *cycle* is the movement of the body from *B* to *A* to *C* to *B* again (Figure 2-1).

The *frequency* is the number of cycles in a unit of time, usually 1 sec. The frequency range which can stimulate the human ear spreads from about 20 to 20,000 Hz and is called the *audible range*. A longitudinal mechanical wave whose frequency is below this is an *infrasonic* (subsonic) wave, and one whose frequency is above it is an *ultrasonic* wave

A point may be made about the use of abbreviations for frequency units. In the older physiologic literature, dv/sec (double vibrations per second) was a common expression because of the employment of tuning forks. The terms c/s and cps (cycles per second) are in common though passing use. The term hertz (Hz) coined to honor Hertz, has now been officially adopted. Ordinarily, the use of eponyms is deplored in the biomedical literature.

The *period* is the time required for the body to execute one cycle. The period and frequency are reciprocals.

Simple Harmonic Motion
This describes the periodic pendular or oscillatory motion of the tuning fork and is the commonest type of motion produced in air particles by vibrating bodies. The simple harmonic, or sinusoidal, wave is the simplest periodic waveform. All musical tones involve such motions.

If a particle vibrates about an equilibrium position (at which no net force acts on the particle) under the influence of a force that is proportional to the distance of the particle from the equilibrium position, the particle has simple harmonic motion. The *displacement* is the distance of the particle from equilibrium at any instant, and the *amplitude* is the maximum displacement. A *restoring force* always directs the particle back to equilibrium position. The kinetic and potential energy vary during oscillation, as explained previously.

Simple harmonic motion may be expressed as the projection of a uniform circular movement upon the diameter of a circle. The symmetrical wave described is called a sinusoidal or *sine wave*. If one watches a particle moving with a constant velocity in a circle, with the eye in the plane of the circle, the particle appears to oscillate back and forth along the diameter of the circle. This can be illustrated by suspending a ball from the ceiling by a long string and setting the ball moving in a circle parallel to the floor so that the string describes the surface of a cone. Look at the ball from a distant point in the plane of the circle. The ball approaches and recedes, but it appears to move at right angles to the line of sight.

To fix the position of the particle at a given time, another particle, which is imaginary, may be considered to be traveling in a circle and always staying vertically above the first one. The orbit of the imaginary particle is called the *circle of*

11

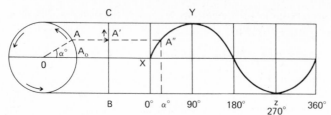

Figure 2-2 Simple harmonic motion. If a point A describes a circle about an origin O, with uniform angular velocity, then A', which is the projection of A on the vertical line BC, will travel up and down in simple harmonic motion. The oscillating A' may move toward the right at constant speed to describe the curve running from 0 to 360°. In this course, called a sine wave, one wavelength is the distance between 0 and 360°. The definition of points along the abscissa is seen in terms of the degrees A has rotated from the A_0 position.

reference. The distance traveled by the particle from its equilibrium point (center of its linear path), or half a full excursion, is proportional to the radius of the circle, and it expresses the *amplitude* of the vibration. The position of the particle in the circle of reference is called the *phase* of the motion. Motion from one phase to the next corresponding phase is *one cycle*. The distance from one particle to the next one in the same phase indicates the *wavelength*.

 12

The usefulness of the concept of simple harmonic motion is that it describes and analyzes wave motions. The reader is referred to standard textbooks of physics.

Waves

Nature
A wave is a disturbance, traveling through any medium in which there is a restoring force acting upon a displaced particle.

Leonardo da Vinci in the fifteenth century observed waves moving across a wind-swept field of wheat and noted that the forward motion of the grain was an illusion and that each stalk merely vibrated back and forth as the wave passed on. It is only the *form* of the disturbance that moves on as one part after another of the medium receives energy and transmits it.

In deep water there are waves that roll toward the shore, but the water does not. The wave motion is an up-and-down displacement. Although any wave is propagated through its medium, the medium does not move along with the wave.

The propagation of large water waves results from the tendency of water to "seek its level" and is caused by gravity. The restoring force for large water waves is gravity, but that for ripples is chiefly surface tension. Although, in considering the situation in water, gravitational waves are produced only on the free surface of the water, sound waves are different in that they usually travel through air, which has no free surface. Therefore, sound waves must have different forces underlying their propagation. This will be considered later.

Kinds of Waves

Classifications differ according to the manner of production (radio waves, tidal waves), to the medium in which they move (air, water, earth), and in other ways. The classification below emphasizes the direction in which the particles are vibrating relative to the direction in which the wave is traveling.

If a particle oscillates in a line parallel to the direction in which the wave is moving, the wave is *longitudinal.*

If a particle oscillates at right angles to the direction in which a wave is moving, the wave is *transverse.*

If a particle oscillates in a curve whose plane is at right angles to the direction in which a wave is moving, the wave is *torsional.*

For a wave (other than a surface wave) to move through a medium, the medium must have elasticity. A solid medium has shearing elasticity; i.e., when any particle within it moves in any direction, neighboring particles are dragged along with it and therefore neither a transverse nor a torsional wave can be produced in it. Gases and liquids have only volume elasticity, and they can transmit only longitudinal (compressional) waves. Since sound waves are transmitted not only in air but also in fluids and solids, sound waves must be longitudinal waves.

Waves passing in a rope illustrate transverse waves (Figure 2-3). One end of a rope is tied to a support, and with the other end held in the hand the rope is pulled fairly taut. If the hand is moved suddenly upward, a pulse seen as a hump travels down the rope at uniform velocity. One particle after another is raised by the passing hump, falling back as the pulse travels on.

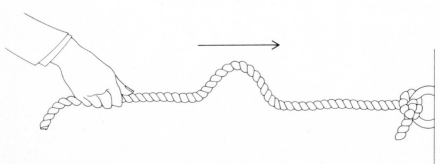

Figure 2-3 Pulse in a rope.

13

The Generation of Sound Waves in Air

Vibrating particles compress the surrounding air on a forward movement and rarefy the air on a backward movement. The air transmits these disturbances away from the source as a series of waves. If unimpeded, they spread out in all directions from the source. For simplicity we usually deal with one-dimensional propagation.

Consider this in terms of the generation of pure tones by a tuning fork. If a tuning fork vibrates (Figure 2-4), the right-hand prong moves from *a* to *b* while the left prong moves from *a'* to *b'*. Let us consider the right prong only.

When moving from *a* to *b*, the air molecules in front are compressed. This motion is transmitted from one molecule to the next, generating a pulse of *compression,* or *condensation,* which travels at about 1,100 ft/sec at sea level, or the velocity of sound in air. The speed of the wave is determined by the properties of the medium, (e.g., temperature or molecular weight of the gaseous medium).

When the prong swings back from *b* to *a*, it leaves a vacuum behind it. This causes the air molecules to generate impulses traveling to the left to fill the vacuum. Or a *rarefaction* is set up which moves forward just behind and with the same velocity as the condensation. For every complete vibration of the tuning fork, a condensation and rarefaction are generated. In Figure 2-4 one wavelength is the distance from a condensation to a condensation (*c* to *c'*) or from a rarefaction to a rarefaction (*r* to *r'*). Wavelengths are customarily designated by the Greek letter λ (lambda).

Wavelength relates frequency to the velocity of sound

$$\lambda = \frac{\text{velocity of sound}}{\text{frequency}}$$

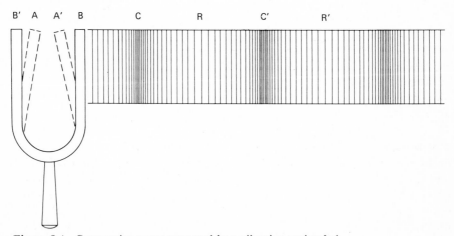

Figure 2-4   Compression waves generated by a vibrating tuning fork.

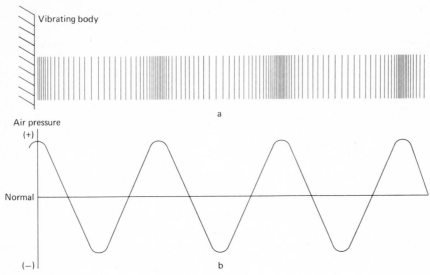

Figure 2-5   Representation of sound waves.

A pure tone whose frequency is 1,100 Hz has a wavelength in air of 1 ft (1,100/ 1,100).

Since vibratory motion is communicated from particle to particle, each particle vibrates a little later than the preceding one from which it received the energy and a little earlier than the one to which it gives energy. Particles in a wave are thus vibrating in different phases. The phase indicates the stage of progress in the cycle of a particle.

Figure 2-5 represents a series of sound waves, relating the phases to the compressions and rarefactions. The motion of the particles is forward at the regions of greatest compression and backward toward the source at the regions of greatest expansion. The wavy line serves only to show graphically either pressure variations or longitudinal displacements. Actually, the particle motions are entirely in the direction of the waves and the pressure variations have no directional properties at all.

Modification of Sound Waves in the Ear
As long as the density and elasticity remain constant throughout the medium, a wave that has begun will continue to move without change of direction. If these properties change, there may ensue a turning back (reflection) of part of the wave system and a transmission of part with a change in direction (refraction) and usually with absorption and dissipation of energy. Since the media within the ear are heterogeneous, the energy changes are appreciable.

Stationary (Standing) Waves

Transverse waves in a string are reflected at its ends, and longitudinal waves traveling along a tube are reflected at the ends of the tube. An incident wave and the reflected wave traveling back along the same path may produce a state called *interference*. This implies the addition of pressures to give regions of high and low pressure. Interference between the waves traveling in opposite directions produces standing waves. Consider this for a string.

If a string attached to the prong of a tuning fork is kept taut at the other end *s* (Figure 2-6), vibrations set up travel to *s* and are reflected with a change of phase.

If the cord length is changed by moving *s*, a point is found where the cord is put into a stationary waveform, as illustrated by Figure 2-6. At given points n_1 and n_2, called *nodes*, the cord appears at rest. Halfway between each node, there are maximal displacements (a_1, a_2, a_3), called *antinodes*.

Since n_2 to *s* and *s* to n_2 are constant, the time required for vibrational travel each way is constant. That is, any phase difference between the wave just passing n_2 and the one reflected back to n_2 is constant. If the two waves meet in opposition at a point, the point is a node. If the forward and reflected wave are in conjunction, the point is an antinode. Stationary waves and their properties thus involve the combination of two similar wave trains moving in opposite directions.

The discussion can be extended to standing longitudinal waves in a tube and will then have application to conditions underlying the phenomenon called *resonance,* which occurs in air columns such as the supraglottic passages. Just as the operation of stringed instruments depends on the production of stationary waves along the string, so wind instruments employ standing compressional waves in a tube. Consider a tube which is closed at one end (opposite).

Resonance of an Air Column

If a sounded tuning fork is held over a tall narrow jar and the length of the air column varied by slowly adding water (*w*), the sound at a certain point of filling

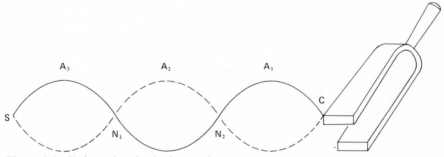

Figure 2-6 Nodes and antinodes in a stationary wave.

16

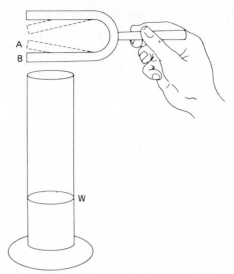

Figure 2-7 Resonance of an air column.

is amplified much more than if the fork were sounded in a room. Measurements show that the air column is one-fourth the wavelength of the sound emitted by the fork.

If we examine the movements of one prong through *ab* (Figure 2-7), when the prong descends, it initiates a condensation, which travels down to the water surface and is reflected as a condensation from the denser medium. If the air-column length is one-fourth of the wavelength, the wave travels one-half the wavelength upon returning to *b*. The fork has at this point completed one-half of a complete vibration and will swing upward to produce an upward condensation. There are now two condensations starting upward in the same phase. This produces *reinforcement,* with increase in sound intensity. Similar reasoning holds for the rarefaction occurring under the fork when swinging in the reverse order.

There is still a second and far more important reason for sound amplification (called *resonance*) in this system. This lies in the establishment of standing waves in the tube. In the instance above, the jar cannot cause any increase in the original energy, but its walls do serve to prevent the waves from spreading out as they do in air.

In the second instance, which involves standing waves, the waves on leaving the open end of the tube can spread out. The open end acts as a rarer medium causing a small part of the wave energy to be reflected back without change of phase into the tube. The direct wave and reflected wave are thus in about the same phase, producing an antinode, or reinforcement. The air column acts this way on all entering waves, producing an intense standing wave in the tube.

The nature of the reflection at the open end of the tube depends on whether the tube is wide or narrow relative to the wavelength. If narrow, as in most musical instruments, the reflected wave has almost the same phase as the incident wave. This makes the open end approximately an antinode.

An organ pipe contains a resonating air column. When air reaches the lip of the pipe, part of it enters and initiates a compressional wave in the enclosed air. The wave travels back and forth, but whenever it returns to the starting area, it reacts on the incident air to produce *sympathetic vibration* (to be explained later). Stationary waves are established. The vibrating incident air produces an antinode at or near the pipe orifice. The open end must be an antinode and the closed end a node. The vocal tract may be regarded as a tube closed below and open above at the lips.

Vibrating Systems as Sources of Sound

Complex Tones

A string can vibrate at a number of different frequencies. The lowest is the *fundamental* frequency, and the higher ones are *overtones*. Overtones whose frequencies are integral multiples of the fundamental form a harmonic series, in which the fundamental is the first *harmonic*.

Sounds at the larynx consist of a fundamental frequency and many harmonics which are whole-numbered multiples of that fundamental. If the fundamental is 125 Hz, the second harmonic is 250, the third harmonic is 375, and the progression continues. An adult male voice can contain 40 to 50 harmonics, as visualized in a sound spectrogram.

Fourier (1768–1830), a French mathematician, showed that a complex *periodic* (repeating the same basic shapes) waveform can be analyzed into many simple sine curves. Each sine wave corresponds to a simple tone, and each such component tone is a harmonic.

In listening to ordinary speech, one may sense the low and high tones. If the overtones have frequencies 2, 3, 4, 5, . . . times that of the fundamental, i.e., integral multiples of the fundamental, they may properly be called harmonics (as well as overtones). The term partial is used for both the fundamental and its overtones. In a fundamental of 100 Hz and an overtone of 200 Hz, the fundamental is the first partial and 200 Hz is the second partial (or first overtone). The partial is the segmental vibration, and the overtone is the sound resulting from segmental vibration above the first partial.

The simplest but not necessarily the correct explanation of the origin of the complex waveform in speech is that the vocal folds are behaving as a set of vibrating strings. In accordance with this simplified assumption, the fibers of the vocalis muscles of the folds vibrate not only as a whole but also in localized groups. This action simultaneously produces sounds of different frequencies. If a string, as a model, vibrates as a whole, the wave produced is a fundamental note. If each half vibrates, the first overtone is produced. If each third vibrates, the next overtone is produced. In these instances the wavelength decreases from 1 to ½ to ⅓, whereas the frequency increases reciprocally from 1 to 2 to 3.

An early method of analyzing complex sounds employed a set of Helmholtz resonators, which are distorted spheres, each enclosing a given volume of air. If a complex sound is produced, only specific resonators vibrate at given amplitudes. The sounded frequencies are thus analyzed.

The frequencies and relative amplitudes of a complex sound can be sorted out by a graphic specification called the *spectrum* of a sound, which relates the amplitudes and frequencies present. This is a logical procedure since a sound may be visualized in more than one waveform but still be sensed as the same sound if the wave components are identical.

A waveform is readily visualized by a *cathode-ray oscilloscope* and the spectrum of sounds by the *sound spectrograph*. Other important instruments include the *spectral analyzer* and *wave analyzer*. The reader is referred to Denes and Pinson (1963) for a brief review. Ladefoged (1962) has a clear discussion of wave analysis and Potter et al. (1966) of the sound spectrograph.

19

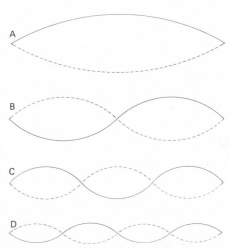

Figure 2-8 Diagrammatic displacement of a string vibrating as a whole, in halves, in thirds, and in fourths. A string in vibration could execute all these movements simultaneously to produce a complex waveform.

The acoustic properties of speech sounds, which express the qualities of the voice, include amplitude; periodicity, i.e., tones having a definite pitch; duration; and spectral composition, i.e., the distribution of sound energy among the frequency components of a complex sound.

Many speech sounds are *aperiodic,* having overtones at all frequencies. A distinction between tones and noise arises in complex speech waveshapes. In tones, the frequencies have well-defined mutual relationships. The lowest frequency is the fundamental, and it generally determines the pitch sensed.

If the sound waves are not regular and periodic, noise rather than tone is produced. Noise may be defined as a sound to which no definite pitch can be assigned. It is a waveform having a number of frequencies combined in a random manner (Bogert and Peterson, 1957). The waveform is compounded from pure tones, and the elements of the total waveform can be differentiated by harmonic analysis. The distinction between noise and tone is frequently a matter of psychology and training. Even physically, the distinction between degrees of periodicity and complexity may be a relative one.

Noise and tone are simultaneously emitted in speech. The relatively pure tones are vowels, which are normally of laryngeal origin. The sounds that are largely noise include the voiceless consonants, such as /s/ or /k/, which originate in the organs of articulation. Examples of sounds that are usually considered as noise include taps, hisses, shrieks, bangs, and squeaks.

A presentation and reemphasis of some definitions follow. A *frequency component* is one of several sine waves in a complex wave. The *basic frequency* is the most important frequency component and usually the one with the largest amplitude. The *fundamental frequency* is the lowest frequency of the several frequency components of a complex wave. It is produced when a sounding body vibrates as a whole. Its amplitude may be large or small.

The *formants* (spectral peaks) are areas of the speech spectrum containing relatively large frequency components. They depend upon the shape of the vocal tract, they correspond to the basic frequencies of air vibrations in the vocal tract, and they are the prime factors underlying the quality of the sound. The formants do not correspond to the fundamental frequencies.

The term formant is used with two different meanings (Curtis, 1968). In one sense it is a property of the acoustic spectrum, referring to concentrations of energy, as seen in the spectrographic analyses of vowels. It also refers to a resonant mode of the vocal tract. The two concepts are not synonymous.

The *pitch* of a sound depends chiefly upon the fundamental frequency. The latter varies with the rate at which the vocal tract produces pulses. The pitch does not depend upon the formants, and thus the pitch of a vowel can be changed without altering its quality.

Sound Spectrograph

The *sound spectrograph* converts the rapidly occurring sounds of speech into visible, continually changing spectral patterns, or *spectrograms*. This technic developed by the Bell Telephone Laboratories during World War II, is now extremely important. The method applies the principle of Fourier analysis to the complex speech waveform.

The spectrograms of spoken words constitute visible speech since they are records of the speech spectrum and are pictures of sound, showing the patterns of voice energy. Frequency appears on the ordinate of the graph and time on the abscissa; the amplitude or intensity used in making a speech sound is projected as density of black marks on the record.

The subject speaks into a high-fidelity magnetic tape recorder, and the audiosignal is stored on tape. The audiosignal is very short. The signal is reproduced a large number of times by playing back the tape. Each time it is played back, the data recorded are passed through a continuously variable bandpass filter. This permits a different range of the spectrum to be scanned for each revolution. The ouput of the filter for the wave band that is analyzed drives a pen which reproduces the wave pattern on recording paper. The pen usually produces an electric spark, which burns the paper. The spark discharge eliminates any pen lag and allows faithful reproduction of the signals. This explains the intensity-blackness by-product. The paper is on a drum, whose speed of revolution equals that of the loop of magnetic tape, so that points in the record can be matched with the speech sound.

21

A given darkness in the record expresses the intensity of the sound. Thus, wherever there is energy in a given frequency range, a black mark is burned onto the record. A horizontal black mark indicates that the incident wave lasted so many milliseconds, during which sinusoids of certain frequencies were expressed and an amplitude above a certain threshold was attained.

The records bring out all the varieties of acoustic modulation involved. That due to the vocal folds is expressed by fine vertical striation. Modulation caused by constriction of the air tunnel, as for example in sounding /s/, is seen as random marks across a range of frequencies. Modulation by resonance, involving the production of vowels, is shown by heavy horizontal lines, with up and down movements reflecting diphthongs. Modulation by interrupting the airstream, e.g., "stops," appears as vertical gaps with subsequent characteristic vertical smears.

It has been claimed that each pattern is distinctive as are those of fingerprints. In this view the shape and size of an individual's mouth, throat, and nasal cavities cause his voice energy to be concentrated into frequency bands, and the pattern of such bands remains constant despite such factors as age, tonsil removal, or loss of teeth. Although it is supposedly possible to correlate "voice prints" with people as fingerprints now do, strong evidence has been presented against the use of spectrograms as voice prints for personal identification (Bolt et al., 1969). Whereas fingerprint patterns are a direct representation of anatomic traits, vocal anatomy is not represented in any direct way in voice spectrograms.

Resonance of Complex Tones Generated by Vibrating Systems in the Vocal Tract

Resonance may be thought of as the production of motion in the air-filled vocal tract by sound. It involves the relationships among several vibrating bodies and tubes, each affecting the others.

Definitions

If two pendulums of equal length are supported at their upper ends and are free below, and if one pendulum is made to swing, the other may acquire a vibratory motion equal to the first. The first will continue to supply energy to the second and will stop, at which point the second will swing through an arc having (except for friction) the original amplitude of the first.

If the experiment is repeated with two pendulums of dissimilar length, the second pendulum may not respond at all. A vibrating pendulum produces vibrations in another pendulum only if they have equal periods (as in the two with equal lengths). This is *sympathetic vibration,* or *resonance.* In the early resonance concept of hearing, structures in the inner ear were said to act as a series of selective *resonators* which respond to incident frequencies corresponding with their own natural periods.

The term *natural period* means that a body which is free to vibrate will do so at a characteristic frequency determined by its inherent properties. In a so-called *free vibration,* the waves may be regularly repeated and are then called *sinusoidal.* The amplitude of the displacement gradually decays from the initial value, due to friction.

In the instance of one vibrating body driving another, *forced vibration* is said to occur. The driven body tends to follow the form of the driving motion and is dependent upon both its amplitude and frequency. If the driving motion is at a frequency equal to that of the natural period of the "slave" system, the amplitude of response is maximal and even greater than the applied motion. The frequency at maximum is the *resonant* (or *formant*) *frequency.* Close to the maximum, *resonance* may still occur, though the response has less amplitude.

To illustrate the above, a *resonance curve* may be constructed (Figure 2-9) relating the amplitude of forced vibrations to the frequencies of a driving source. If a vibrating tuning fork drives one of the same natural period, the amplitudes of response are greatest at the *resonant frequency.* As the ratios of frequencies between driver and slave increasingly change, above or below this point, the amplitudes become increasingly lower on either side. The frequency range within which a resonator will respond effectively is the *bandwidth.*

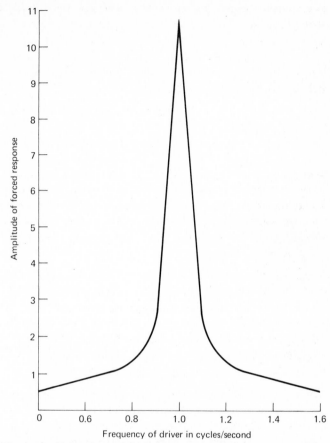

Figure 2-9 Resonance curve relating the amplitude of response (forced vibrations) to the frequency of a driving source. The amplitude of the applied motion is constant. At 1 Hz, the natural period of the resonating body, the response exceeds the driving motion.

Due to friction, the amplitude of vibrations of any nondriven vibrating system will decrease. This is called *damping*. The term *decrement* is a quantitative measure of the effect and is the natural logarithm of the ratio of two consecutive vibrations. The mouth and pharynx are strongly damped because of their soft mucous membranes (Winckel, 1965). This prevents marked changes in loudness in a sound produced at resonant and other frequencies.

Resonance of Complex Tones in the Vocal Tract Acting as a Tube

Resonance depends on many factors including length, diameters, and whether the tubes are open or closed. The vocal tract is a tube that can be closed both above and below (or opened above under certain circumstances).

Tubes Open at One End In the human vocal tract, if one end is closed, it is a place of no air motion, or node. The open end is an antinode. Such a system resonates naturally to given frequencies of the sound generator (Judson and Weaver, 1965). An infinite number of resonances is possible. It was once thought that a system of simple resonators existed and that each resonance acted independently of others. However, the vocal tract behaves more like an acoustic transmission line in which the resonant characteristics are related to, and interdependent with the characteristics of the system as a whole (Curtis, 1968).

The human voice may be considered much like the sound of an organ pipe. A stream of air is forced through a slit between the vocal folds, which can vibrate. Certain frequencies are strengthened in the supraglottic space. In this tube, considered closed at the vocal fold end, the lowest resonant frequency corresponds to the frequency of the sound wave whose wavelength is 4 times the length of the tube. The overtones present are those that give a displacement node at the closed end and an antinode at the open end. The even harmonics will be missing, only the odd harmonics being present.

In such a tube the frequencies of the overtones are 3, 5, 7, . . . (always an odd number) times the frequencies of the fundamental tone. As with a vibrating string, the fundamental and overtones are excited at the same time. In an approximate 17-cm-long human vocal tract the lowest resonant frequency is 500 Hz, and the successive resonant frequencies are 1,500, 2,500 3,500, and up, in odd-number multiples. The resonances have a spacing of 1,000 Hz. If the vocal tract is longer, there are lower frequencies for all resonances.

Tubes Open at Both Ends An antinode occurs at both ends of such tubes. The tube length L equals one-half the wavelength λ, or $\lambda = 2L$, of the sound produced, and the fundamental frequency in cycles per second equals 1,100 ft/sec (approximate velocity of sound in air)/(twice the length, in feet). In such tubes all odd- or even-numbered partials can be produced. In other words, the open pipe resonates at all harmonics of the fundamental frequency.

The abundant capacity for variation of the vocal tract greatly enriches the possibilities for resonance. When the size and shape of the cavities change, the resonant (formant) frequencies also change. This has a great effect on the quality and exactness of vowels (Murphy, 1964).

Energy in Sound Waves

Units of Expression

Energy is the capacity to do work and is numerically identical with work. Since energy is transmitted with and by waves, it provides a measure of the strength of a sound in air.

The strength may be considered in terms of particle displacement, particle velocity, or sound pressure. A traveling sound wave has all these parameters. *Displacement,* measured in centimeters, is difficult to evaluate because of the small dimensions involved. *Velocity* expresses the displacement per unit of time, usually noted as centimeters per second. It is often most convenient to consider the *pressure* variations in a sound wave. Just as there are displacements from equilibrium position, there are changes from the undisturbed pressure. The ear reacts predominantly to alterations in pressure (Winckel, 1965).

Although it is difficult to measure the small forces needed to displace a single molecule, one might get around this by measuring the force acting on a large surface; then by dividing this force by the area of the surface, the force per unit area, or pressure, is derived.

A tuning fork need produce only very small pressures to move particles of air in the form of a vibratory motion resulting in sound. The pressure acts over a unit area, and is expressed in dynes per square centimeter (or microbars). One dyne is the force which acting on a mass of 1 gram for 1 second produces an acceleration of 1 cm/sec. The range of pressures between just audible sounds to loud traumatic ones is 0.0002 to 2,000 dynes/cm^2, at a frequency of 1,000 Hz. This range is difficult to represent in a linear scale and requires a logarithmic scale, involving the use of *decibels*.

In the process of moving an air particle, work is done, expressed as force times the distance moved. If 1 dyne moves the particle 1 cm, 1 erg of work is accomplished. Work is often considered on a basis of time needed for accomplishment, or rate. The ratio of work to time can be expressed in ergs per second, which is a unit of *power*. By increasing the factor 1 million times, 10^6 ergs/sec is 1 watt/sec. Power may also be expressed in microwatts, or 10^{-6} watt/sec.

Whatever the units, the energy involved in the vibratory motion becomes dissipated with distance, and the sound gets weaker. Actually, the energy does not change, but the energy per unit area decreases because the same energy becomes more thinly spread. This is often expressed as the inverse-square law, in which the energy per unit of area per unit of time decreases inversely with the square of the distance from the sound source.

The *intensity* is a convenient way of expressing the statements above and is commonly used to indicate the power transmitted along the wave. The intensity involves the flow of energy (in ergs) carried by the sound waves through a unit area (square centimeters) in a unit time (seconds). The intensity may be expressed in bels or more conveniently in decibels (0.1 bel or 1 dB).

The Decibel
The bel is the logarithm of the ratio of the energy of two sounds. The logarithm is used to avoid large numbers. The bel (and also the decibel) state by what ratio one value is greater or lesser than another. For example, a sound is 1 bel greater than another if its energy is 10 times greater than the other (or the logarithm of the ratio is 1); a sound of 3 bels (30 dB) is 1,000 times greater in power.

The bel is an impractically large unit. A power ratio of 1 bel expresses an increment from 100,000 to 1 million or from 1 million to 10 million. The decibel specifies a smaller ratio, i.e., one-tenth the power ratio in bels.

Although the power of a sound wave could be expressed in a unit such as watts per square centimeter, the decibel, which is an intensity ratio, allows us to use small numbers to express the intensity of the loudest sounds. Fortuitously, 1 dB is approximately the least discernible difference in loudness from the subjective standpoint.

In reemphasizing the usefulness of the decibel, one might consider that although loudness is related to the relative amplitudes of sounds, it is necessary for ready quantitation of the differences to relate loudness to other units of measurement. This involves a knowledge that the *power* varies with the square of the amplitude. Because power is generally thought of relatively, a reference level for a 1,000-Hz tone is established, where the sound (as noted above) has an amplitude of 0.0002 dyne/cm^2, which is a unit of sound pressure, or a power of 10^{-16} watt/cm^2. Because the loudest but not painful sound has 1,000,000 times more amplitude and 1,000,000,000,000 times more power, a more convenient unit, based on the ratio of powers, had to be sought.

A sound at a given pressure can have several different decibel values, depending on the choice of the pressure chosen as the zero, or baseline, level. Although in one system the base line is 0.0002 dyne/cm^2, in another system it is the average normal hearing threshold. In a third system the reference pressure is 1 microbar (1 dyne/cm^2).

The scale whose starting point is 0.0002 dyne/cm^2 is termed the *sound pressure level* scale (SPL). A 50-dB SPL implies a pressure 50 dB above 0.0002 dyne/cm^2. The scale whose starting level is at average normal hearing is termed the *hearing threshold* level or *hearing level* scale (HL). This has applications in audiometric testing. In an audiometric chart following the recommendations of the International Standards Organization, the decibel markings for "hearing loss" (hearing threshold level) represent an HL scale.

Intensity Levels of Speech

Only a fraction of the respiratory breath stream is converted to sound energy. In work units the energy output in ordinary speech is only about 100 to 200 ergs/sec. In loud speech the power output might be about 2,000 ergs/sec. These are very small quantities.

As already anticipated, sound energy may be expressed in intensity. A standard reference sound that has been adopted is called the *intensity level* and states that a 1,000-Hz tone, which is close to the just audible level, has an intensity of 10^{-16} watt/cm^2 (0.0002 dynes/cm^2). If a similar sound were expressed in decibels, the decibel value would be termed the *sensation level* and would have no absolute physical meaning. A sound intensity that is expressed in decibels has meaning only in relation to the standard physical reference. Thus, the average sound intensity stated to be 60 dB represents a value that is so much greater than a sound of 10^{-16} watts/cm². This is a 1 million to 1 ratio.

The listing of a few intensity ratios can illustrate the discussion.

RATIO	LOG OF RATIO	DIFFERENCE IN DECIBELS
1 to 1	0	0
10 to 1	1	10
100 to 1	2	20
1000 to 1	3	30
10,000 to 1	4	40

Also, the relationship of certain parameters already discussed may be noted. The intensity is proportional to the square of the pressure. Therefore a 100-fold in-

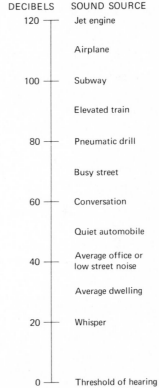

DECIBELS	SOUND SOURCE
120	Jet engine
	Airplane
100	Subway
	Elevated train
80	Pneumatic drill
	Busy street
60	Conversation
	Quiet automobile
40	Average office or low street noise
	Average dwelling
20	Whisper
0	Threshold of hearing

Figure 2-10 Crude decibel values of nonspecific environmental sounds.

crease in intensity produces a 10,000-fold increase in pressure. Or, if 20 dB is a 100 to 1 intensity ratio, this equals a 10 to 1 pressure ratio.

If a reference level is taken as 0 dB for the intensity of the faintest sound audible to a normal ear, then the intensity of lively speech is perhaps as high as 60 dB. Ordinary speech is a mixture of sounds of various intensities, and the weaker sounds may be about 30 dB less than the stronger ones. The vowels are the sounds of greatest intensity.

Gray and Wise (1959) describe intensity differences as follows. If very loud speech is 60 dB greater than a very soft whisper, and if the number of decibels is 10 times the logarithm of the numerical ratio between these two intensities, then the logarithm itself is 6, or the corresponding number is 10^6 (1 million). That is, very loud speech is 1 million times greater than a soft whisper. If we arbitrarily ascribe a value of zero to the power of average speech, then very loud speech has a power of plus 20 dB, weak speech minus 20 dB, and a whisper minus 40 dB.

Judson and Weaver (1965) consider the definition of intensity in terms such as the average speech power, or the totality of all speech sound energy emitted in a complete speech divided by the total time for that activity. They note an estimate of 15 microwatts for the average speech power of the average person in this country. This estimate rises to 1,000 in extremely loud speech and falls to 0.001 microwatt in soft whispering. The greatest range of intensity one would expect would vary from 0.01 to 5,000 microwatts, which would correspond to a range of about 60 dB. Houssay (1955) states that the whole range of intensities perceptible to the human ear is expressed by 120 dB. Figure 2-10 illustrates the discussion.

3 ANATOMIC CONCEPTS AND BODILY ORGANIZATION

The Relationships of Anatomy

Anatomy is the science describing the architecture of the body. Its subdivisions are:

Gross, or macroscopic, anatomy: the study of structures visible to the eye.

Microscopic anatomy, or *histology*: the study of the microscopic structure of tissues and organs. The study of the cell is *cytology*.

Developmental anatomy: the study of the growth and development of an organism throughout its life.

Embryology: an aspect of developmental anatomy dealing with development from origin to birth.

Comparative anatomy: the evolutionary relationships among animals and the racial (phylogenetic) history of man.

Classification

An understanding of the human body is made clearer by a study of man's racial history (phylogeny). The comparative approach to the speech mechanism has a logical basis. It suffices here to point out the universal system employed when classifying any animal, including man. This is a starting point for any discussion of the evolutionary relationships (homologies) between two organisms or their similarly functioning structures or processes.

Carolus von Linné (Linnaeus) proposed his natural system of classification in 1758. All organisms are designated by two names and placed in a basic unit called a *species*. These are grouped in turn into a genus, family, order, class, phylum and kingdom. Keys can be drawn up for any organism by which it is classified and its proper name given. This system is based on structure, and is known as the binomial system of nomenclature.

The organism (animal or plant) is named in Latin because that language is not subject to continual variations in meanings and it was the language of scholarship in Europe in the time of Linnaeus. The organism's first name (genus) is always a capitalized noun, and the second name (species) is a lowercase adjective. Both names are italicized.

As an example, let us classify man.

KINGDOM	Animalia
PHYLUM	Chordata
SUBPHYLUM	Vertebrata
CLASS	Mammalia
ORDER	Carnivora
FAMILY	Homidae
GENUS	*Homo*
SPECIES	*sapiens*

The science of classification is *taxonomy*. Although Linnaeus thought of the species as an unchanging unit, systematists regard a species as a taxonomic unit (taxon) or population that is influenced by ecologic and genetic factors. The species is a taxon that has the greatest number of homologous structures in common. The genus has fewer such structures in common.

Anatomic Terminology

The terminology first adopted in anatomy was called the BNA (*Basle Nomina Anatomica*), which was a result of a series of international meetings in Basle,

Switzerland. The meetings were begun by anatomists in 1895 to adopt a universal anatomic language.

In 1950 the Fifth International Congress of Anatomists, held at Oxford, appointed an International Anatomical Nomenclature Committee to revise gross anatomic terminology. Their revisions were approved in 1955 in Paris. The list of terms adopted there, known as the *Nomina Anatomica* (NA, or NAIC) is now the official terminology. It was agreed that (1) structures shall be designated by one term only; (2) every term in the official list shall be in Latin, each country to be at liberty to translate the official term into its own vernacular; (3) each term shall, as far as possible, be short and simple; (4) the terms shall preferably have an informative or descriptive value; (5) structures closely related in space shall as far as possible have similar names, e.g., arteria femoralis, vena femoralis, nervus femoralis; (6) differentiating adjectives shall generally be arranged as opposites, i.e., major and minor, superficialis and profundus; and (6) eponyms shall not be used in official nomenclature.

The student is advised to consult sourcebooks of Greek and Latin roots (Henderson and Henderson, 1949; Robbins, 1951; Hough, 1953; MacNalty, 1965; Graham, 1966; and Thomson, 1967).

Terminology of Spatial Relations

Because of man's erect position, confusion arises at times in the usage of terms that describe corresponding structures in man and animals. In man, the anatomic position is one in which the individual stands erect with his face toward the observer, his arms hanging at the sides, and the palms of his hands turned forward. All references to parts are based upon this arbitrary posture.

In man, the terms dorsal and posterior are synonyms for the region of the body toward the back, whereas ventral and anterior refer to the front or belly side. The terms superior and cranial refer to the uppermost region in the standing position, but, on the contrary, inferior and caudal refer to the lowest region. In comparative or animal anatomy, the head end is said to be anterior and the tail end posterior; the region toward the back is dorsal and the belly side is ventral. A part above another part is superior in man and cranial in animals; a part below another is inferior in man and caudal in animals. The term cephalic means cranial in all cases. Rostral means directed toward the head end, as opposed to caudal.

Median is toward the midline, and lateral is away from the midline. Internal means the center of mass of the structure described, and external is the opposite. These terms are used most frequently in describing the walls of cavities and hollow, soft organs (viscera). Cutaneous vs. deep is used to refer to body surface in contrast to that region just within the surface. Proximal means nearer the point of attachment, and distal means farther away. Thus, the wrist is distal to the elbow.

Adverbs are formed from these adjectives by substituting for the ending *-al,* the ending *-ad* or *-ally,* e.g., proximad or proximally. Central is a term referring to the principal part found internally, but peripheral indicates an extension toward the surface. The central and peripheral nervous systems are examples. Parietal describes the walls enclosing the body cavity or surrounding the organs, whereas visceral refers to the organs within the body cavities.

Several planes of reference are used. The median longitudinal or sagittal plane passes anteroposteriorly only through the center of the body, and it divides the body into right and left halves. Any other similarly directed cut produces a longitudinal plane that is off center, and it is thus not a median or sagittal plane. Some

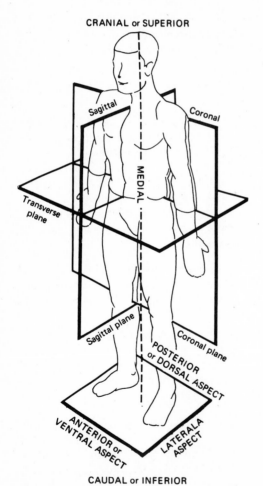

Figure 3-1 Planes and axes of the human body.

writers use the terms sagittal for any plane parallel to the sagittal suture of the skull. A vertical cut at right angles to the sagittal, passing in a transverse or right to left direction through the body, divides the body into anterior, or ventral, and posterior, or dorsal, parts, and is called a frontal plane. A transverse plane is a crosscut at any level that divides the body into cranial and caudal parts.

The Architectural Plan of the Body

Vertebrate animals, including man, develop as a tube within a tube; the outer one is the framework of the body wall, and the inner one is the digestive tube. The space between the two tubes is the body cavity, or coelom. The primitive nervous system runs longitudinally down the entire body, just dorsal to the coelom.

The coelom in mammals becomes a ventral cavity enclosed by the body wall. In development it is divided into the thoracic and abdominal cavities by a partition called the diaphragm. The thoracic cavity is subdivided into two lateral or pleural cavities between which there is a central region, or mediastinum; the pericardial cavity which encloses the heart takes up a sizable portion of the central medias-tinum.

The abdominal cavity is only arbitrarily but not actually subdivided into an upper abdominal and a lower pelvic cavity. The abdominal cavity acquires a lining which is called the peritoneum. The space and all the soft organs lying within the lin-ing are said to be in the peritoneal cavity. Some organs lie behind the peritoneum. An organ such as the kidney may lie behind the peritoneum (or be retroperitoneal) but still lie within the greater abdominal cavity. The pelvic chamber is that por-tion of the abdominal cavity located inferior to an imaginary line stretched across the crests of the hipbones.

The different body cavities hold the soft internal organs called the viscera.

Protoplasm

A complex multicellular vertebrate animal is highly organized into progressively complex building blocks called cells, tissues, organs, and systems, in that order. Athough the cell has been classically considered to be the structural and functional unit, the electron microscope reveals many subcellular organelles that are special-ized units of activity.

Robert Hooke in 1665 first used the term cell. He described the structure of cork as a series of empty spaces, resembling the cells in a honeycomb. The material in the spaces was described by Dujardin in 1835 and termed sarcode. Purkinje in 1839 used the word *protoplasm* instead of sarcode. In 1838, Schleiden and Schwann proposed the *cell theory* that all plants and animals are composed of cells.

Protoplasm is the living material of which cells are composed. In the living state the ground structure of protoplasm may not be clearly outlined, but upon fixation and staining it is characteristically granular, fibrillar, or alveolar. Its living secrets are unknown because chemical analysis makes it lifeless.

The elementary analysis of protoplasm shows that 95 percent by weight is carbon, hydrogen, oxygen, and nitrogen and that almost 30 other elements constitute the remaining 5 percent. All these elements may also be found in inorganic matter, indicating that the materials alone of protoplasm do not endow it with the properties of life. These properties are a result of the integrative pattern in which the elements are brought together.

The elements combine to characteristic compounds so that protoplasm contains about three-fourths water, many inorganic salts, and organic compounds classified as proteins, fats, and carbohydrates. The inorganic salts are remarkably similar in concentrations to those of the same salts in seawater, and these relative concentrations stay fairly constant among diverse organisms in the face of widely different environmental conditions.

Protoplasm presents the picture of a colorless, viscous, slimy substance or colloidal mass that may change with activity from a fluid, or sol, state to a viscous, or gel, state. For example, muscle contraction may represent a reversible gelation of the colloids of protoplasm. Sol–gel changes are generally reversible processes, and life ceases with any tendency toward irreversibility.

34 The vital attributes of protoplasm include irritability, growth, metabolism, contractility, conduction and reproduction. Irritability denotes the power to respond to stimuli. Growth means an increase in size by multiplication of cells. Metabolism implies all the energy exchanges within the organism at a given time. Contractility refers to the power of motion and locomotion. Conduction implies the propagation of impulses, which are usually nervous. Reproduction is based on the capacity to produce new protoplasm.

The Cell

The cell is an organized mass of protoplasm surrounded by a limiting membrane. It typically contains a central nucleus and the outer cytoplasm.

Nucleus

The nucleus of the resting (nondividing) cell is generally spherical and is enclosed by a relatively porous double membrane. The nucleoplasm fills the space within the membrane and contains long slender bodies called *chromosomes*. The chromosomes carry the genes that are needed to transmit parental characters to the offspring. The genes are composed primarily of DNA (deoxyribonucleic acid).

The nucleus also contains one or more sharply demarcated spherical bodies called nucleoli (karyosomes). The nucleolus contains RNA (ribonucleic acid) and pro-

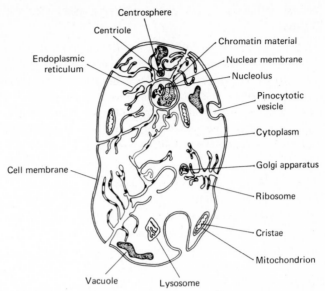

Figure 3-2 Ultrastructure of a typical animal cell.

teins. There is evidence that all the RNA appearing in the cell cytoplasm comes from the nucleus, using DNA as a template (primer) for its formation. The formation of RNA may be the principal function of the nucleus in the resting cell. Because DNA does not leave the nucleus, it appears to be RNA that transmits the information coded by DNA for use in the cytoplasm. The present evidence is that RNA is employed for the synthesis of proteins. The sites of synthesis are the ribosomes, which are bodies usually located on the outer surface of cytoplasmic canals termed the endoplasmic reticulum.

There are three forms of RNA. *Messenger* RNA is the form that transports the coded information for protein synthesis out of the nucleus. It makes temporary contact with the ribosomes. *Transport* RNA attaches specific amino acids to itself and carries them to the ribosomal place of protein synthesis, depositing the amino acids in the polypeptide chain of the developing protein. *Ribosomal* RNA is the main component of the ribosomes, whether the latter are free in the cytoplasm or line the endoplasmic reticulum.

Because the useful life of messenger RNA molecules is limited, frequent replacements are essential, which makes the nucleus vital to the existence of the cell.

The nucleus is the controlling or informational center for the entire cell. It is necessary for cell division, which occurs by an orderly process called mitosis. This process involves activities of the chromosomes and their genes.

Chromosomes are composed of protein and DNA. The constancy of DNA in each set of chromosomes for a given species is such that DNA is considered to be the material that determines the hereditary pattern. DNA carries the genetic information.

The importance of DNA led to intensive investigation to understand its structure. Watson and Crick in 1953 were the first workers to demonstrate conclusively by a model that the DNA molecule is a double helix consisting of two parallel polynucleotide chains. This is similar to a spiral staircase whose two handrails are alternating molecules of sugar and phosphate and whose steps are base pairs. In these pairs, adenine and thymine are linked together by hydrogen bonds, and guanine and cytosine are similarly joined.

There are thousands of turns in the spiral, and the base pairs may be arranged in a multitude of orders. The enormous possibilities for variations confirm the view that the sequence of base pairs is the key to the heredity-determining qualities of DNA. Also, the DNA can in some way control the coding for the synthesis of proteins.

DNA duplicates itself in cell division by a split between the paired bases that allows the helices to separate. Each nucleotide of the single chain acquires a new complementary nucleotide. The bases pair again, and when subsequently the phosphate and sugar moieties are united enzymatically, duplication is complete.

Cytoplasm

Under the electron microscope the cytoplasm is seen to contain many organelles (living subunits) and inclusions (products of cell activity or substances that have passed through the cell membranes). The outer membrane is double, protein and lipid in composition, and selectively permeable.

The groundwork appears to contain a clear fluid, the hyaloplasm. Lying within the hyaloplasm is an interconnecting network of canals, the endoplasmic reticulum. They extend to the cell surface, where they become continuous with the thin plasma membrane.

The mitochondria are rods, filaments, or spheres scattered throughout the cytoplasm. They have a double-layered outer membrane, which extends in multiple fashion toward the center. Within the mitochondria oxidative metabolism and energy transfers occur, during which the food energy is transduced to high-energy compounds as adenosine triphosphate. Considerable enzyme activity occurs in these powerhouses of the cell.

The Golgi apparatus is typically a fibrillar network close to the nucleus. This net is especially abundant in cells of the liver or other organs that have a secretory activity.

Associated with cell division is a centrosome, which consists of a granule or centriole surrounded by a centrosphere. Figure 3-4 illustrates cell division.

All the above structures may be classified as organelles. Other bodies in the cytoplasm represent food, pigment, secretory particles, or products of cellular metabo-

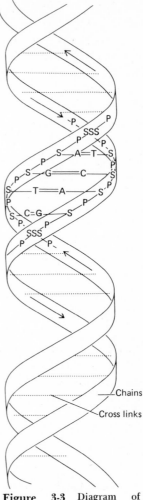

Chains

Cross links

Figure 3-3 Diagram of DNA helix. S=Sugar, P= phosphate group, G=guanine, C=cytosine, T=thymine, and A=adenine.

lism. There are also vacuoles, which appear as single spaces, droplets, or a fine canal system.

Cells are usually microscopic and are measured in microns, the order of which is a thousandth of a millimeter. The largest single cell in the human body is the ovum, or egg cell, whose diameter is 130 to 140 μm (10^{-6} meter). In the protozoans the entire organism is one cell, but in the multicellular organisms there are billions of cells.

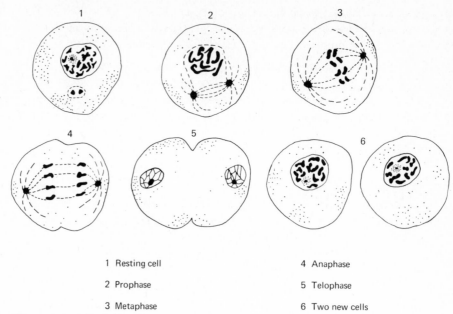

1 Resting cell	4 Anaphase
2 Prophase	5 Telophase
3 Metaphase	6 Two new cells

Figure 3-4 Cell division by mitosis.

38 All cells have a life span varying with their position and function. The human red blood cell lives 4 months, but the white blood cell lives only a few weeks or less. A nerve cell may live as long as the individual. Cells of glands and skin are continually perishing and always being replaced. Many kinds of changes indicate cell senescence, including enlargement or shrinkage, opacity, fragmentation, and loss of function. There are mechanisms, such as chemical solution or ingestion by other phagocytic scavenging cells, to clear the resulting cellular debris.

Tissues: General Nature

With increase in the complexity of the organism, cells lost total self-sufficiency, and they specialized for specific functions. A community of interdependent cells became characteristic of the metazoan animals.

When groups of similar cells and their intercellular products combine for particular functions, they form a tissue. Tissues may be classified by embryologic origin, such as from one of the three primary germ layers of the embryo called ectoderm, mesoderm, or entoderm. They may also be classified more commonly by function, in which case there are four fundamental types called the epithelial, connective, muscular, and nervous tissues. Blood and lymph are often added as a fifth, fluid tissue.

Tissues have three components, the cells, the intercellular medium, and the intercellular products of cellular metabolism.

All cells of a tissue are surrounded by fluid. This provides for interchanges and ensures an internal constancy. In blood and lymph the intercellular medium is the plasma, which is the predominating characteristic of fluid tissue.

Although secretory products of cells may appear transiently in the intercellular medium as they diffuse to the blood or lymphatic capillaries, other intercellular products of cell metabolism remain permanently in the medium. It is in this way that fibers, cartilage, and bone develop and determine the characteristic nature of the tissue.

Epithelium

This covers the outer surface of the body, and it lines the walls of internal cavities. It also forms glands and parts of the sense organs. It guards the underlying structures against dehydration, chemical assaults, and pathogenic organisms. In the alimentary canal, for example, it acts as a selectively permeable membrane which controls the directional flow of water and other substances.

Epithelium is essentially cellular, with a very small intercellular medium and few intercellular products. The cells are closely packed to form a continuous sheet, or membrane. Some fluid between the cells provides for exchange of nutritive and excretory substances. Blood capillaries are in adjacent tissues and may be considered as absent from epithelium.

The epithelial cells come from any of the germinal layers of the embryo. The ectoderm produces outer coverings, such as the epidermis of the skin or the linings

39

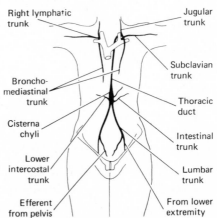

Figure 3-5 Schematic of major lymphatic collecting systems. (From *O. C. Brantigan, Clinical Anatomy. Copyright 1963. McGraw-Hill Book Company. Used by permission.*)

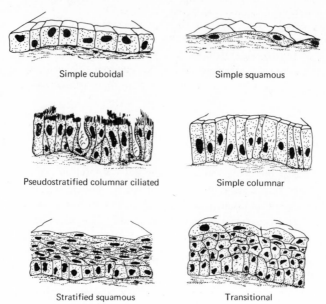

Figure 3-6 The shapes of epithelial cells.

of the nose, mouth, and anus. The entoderm forms inner linings, such as those of the digestive and respiratory tracts. The mesoderm produces the linings of the heart, blood vessels, lymph vessels, and ducts of a great part of the urogenital system as well as the linings of the peritoneal, pleural, and pericardial cavities.

The term epithelium is a general one, and specialized terms are also used. For example, the endothelium refers to the single layer of cells which forms the internal wall (intima) of blood and lymph vessels as well as the internal wall (endocardium) of the heart. The surface covering of the peritoneum, pleura, and pericardium is called mesothelium. The single layer of cells lining the spaces of the brain and cord sheaths is called mesenchymal epithelium. Mesenchyme lines the internal surface of small sacs and cavities. It produces lubricating sheaths around tendons, it lines joint cavities, and it lines sacs, called bursae, which relieve friction where muscles or tendons pass over bony prominences.

Epithelium is of three kinds, depending upon the shape of the cells. It may be squamous (flat), columnar (in which the height exceeds the width), or cuboidal (in which the height and width are about equal).

There may be one or more layers of cells in a given type of epithelium. If one layer, it is simple, and if several layers, it is stratified. In stratified epithelia new cells are continually produced by cell division in the deepest cell layers. This replaces aged or injured surface cells.

The layers are correlated with function, e.g., a blood capillary requires only a one-layered wall to permit maximum interchange of substances across it, but the skin needs several cell layers for mechanical and antibacterial protection. The epithelium may need many glands to lubricate it against mechanical injury, as in the digestive tract, and it may need the power to push out foreign bodies, as in the respiratory tract. In the latter region the cells contain hairlike processes, or cilia, which move in synchronism to expel unidirectionally any mucous film or foreign particle.

Some epithelia, as in the respiratory tract, contain cells which falsely appear to be stratified. These are said to be pseudostratified.

Glands

These are specialized epithelial structures which produce and discharge fluids. If the material discharged is useful, it is called a secretion; otherwise it is an excretion. The gland may resemble a tube with an opening or duct, in which case it is an exocrine gland. It may have other shapes and no duct so that its products are delivered to the surrounding blood or lymph capillaries. In this instance it is an endocrine gland, and its products are hormones.

Unicellular glands on mucous membranes are goblet cells, and they secrete a gelatinous substance called mucus. This is to be distinguished from a watery or serous fluid put out by serous glands. Mixed glands secrete both fluids and are seromucinous.

41

The mucous membranes and their glands form the linings of the digestive, respiratory, and genitourinary tracts. They have one or several layers of epithelial cells resting upon a foundation of connective tissue called the submucosa. Although a certain proportion of the epithelial cells produce mucus continually, secretion increases with infections or irritations, as in the running nose of the common

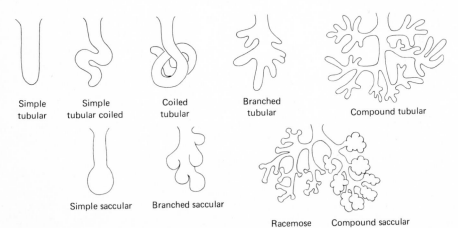

Simple tubular

Simple tubular coiled

Coiled tubular

Branched tubular

Compound tubular

Simple saccular

Branched saccular

Racemose

Compound saccular

Figure 3-7 Simple and compound exocrine glands.

cold and the accumulation of mucus in tracheal or bronchial infections. The protein or mucin component of the mucus develops in the goblet type of epithelial cell, and such cells when filled burst to discharge their contents. The mucus is a protection against irritants, and it traps foreign substances.

The typical gland is multicellular. Its cells invaginate (sink below the surface) like a recessed test tube into whose lumen they discharge their secretions. The secretion reaches the surface through a pore. In the simple glands there is one test-tube-like sac. In the compound tubular or alveolar (round) glands there are many sacs which eventually deliver their secretion to a common stem.

Membranes
These are sheets which cover surfaces, line cavities, or partition segments of the body. Most membranes are epithelial, although some of a protective nature may be fibrous connective tissue.

The *serous* membranes form the internal lining of closed body cavities. When strengthened by fibrous tissue they are called a *serosa*.

The *mucous* membranes form the internal linings of cavities or organs that have a passageway to the external environment. When strengthened by connective tissue, they are called a *mucosa*.

42   Connective Tissue

This tissue is widespread throughout the body and takes many forms. It binds or connects structures, packs and fills spaces, resists physical forces, supports the body, and aids in bodily defense, repair, nutrition, and regeneration. Its origin is from mesenchyme, which is embryonic connective tissue, or that part of the mesoderm which forms the connective tissues and also the blood and lymph vessels. For a discussion of connective tissues with an extensive bibliography, the reader is referred to Chvapil (1967).

The three main components of connective tissues are cells, fibers, and a matrix. Connective tissue has relatively few cells compared with other tissues, but it has a large amount of intercellular substance, or matrix. There is generally a rich blood supply. The matrix looks different in each variety of connective tissue. This difference is correlated with the special functions of the tissue, as in cartilage or bone. In all connective tissues intercellular products are dominant and take the form of fibers. The cells produce the fibers and regulate the activity of the tissue.

Connective Tissue Cells
There are several varieties of connective tissue cells. The most numerous are *fibroblasts,* occurring in all kinds of connective tissue. These produce fibers and are descendants of the mesenchyme. They can become phagocytes or scavengers, and they can also differentiate into osteocytes (bone cells). When a fibroblast

produces modifications in its medium, it becomes fixed in position as an adult cell termed a *fibrocyte.*

Mast cells are a less frequent variety. Their function is uncertain. *Histiocytes* are numerous and act as scavengers, having the power to move like an ameba toward particulate matter. There are other scavenging cells similar to histiocytes whose main function is phagocytosis. They occur in the spleen, liver, lymph nodes, bone marrow, and elsewhere. Collectively, they form a reticuloendothelial system which is indispensable in bodily defense and immunity. A rare cell in the connective tissue is the *plasma cell,* whose numbers increase in certain diseases. The eosinophils, lymphocytes, and neutrophils of the blood represent the wandering cells of the connective tissues. They leave the blood especially during an infection.

The Intercellular Medium
The simplest form of the medium is tissue fluid, which resembles blood plasma. This form is seen in *mesenchyme,* in which the cells are bathed in a nutritive medium. This embryonic type can evolve into many varieties of connective tissues, such as fat, cartilage, and bone.

In the more specialized modifications of mesenchyme, a denser ground substance, or matrix, appears. Mucopolysaccharides are the predominant chemical compounds of the ground substance. These turn the tissue fluid to a colloidal mixture whose viscosity is increased. Hyaluronic acid is a mucopolysaccharide that binds water into its colloidal structure, producing a firmness in the medium. Considerable attention is given to the matrix of connective tissues in certain regions. For example, the permeabilities and spreading activities of ground substance have been correlated with nasal infections (Hopp and Burns, 1958; Weisskopf and Burns, 1958).

43

Connective Tissue Fibers
The fibers, which are protein in nature, are the characteristic substance of the connective tissues. They are always present, although obscured in some instances.

Collagenous fibers are typical of all kinds of connective tissue, and they yield a gelatinous substance, called collagen, upon boiling. The fibers are long, flexible, wavy threads, and they form bundles which travel in any direction through the intercellular framework. Although the bundles are strong and pliable, they lack extensibility. This group includes the strong but not particularly stretchable muscle tendons and the ligaments, which show a more irregular fiber arrangement. Sometimes the dense white fibers are arranged into broad sheets called *aponeuroses.* Their presence will be considered later in structures such as the palatine aponeurosis, or framework of the soft palate, and in the abdominal aponeurosis, or framework of the anterior abdominal wall.

The elastic type of fiber, unlike the collagenous type, contains elastin. It shows a high degree of elasticity, which decreases with age, as in the blood vessels. Elastic fibers are not so numerous as collagenous fibers, and they appear as delicate threads which may branch repeatedly to form a network. Hollow organs subject to internal pressure variations contain membranes built of elastic tissue. This is characteristic of such speech structures as the trachea, bronchioles, and larynx.

Reticular fibers contain a scleroprotein known as reticulin. These fibers form the reticular or networklike architecture of lymphoid and myeloid tissue. They are found also in the interstitial tissue of glandular organs, the papillary layer of the skin, and elsewhere.

Types of Connective Tissue

Adult connective tissues are classified into three types by the nature of the cells and matrix. Fibrous tissue is connective tissue proper. Fluid tissue is a special type which includes blood and lymph. Supporting tissue includes cartilage and bone.

The embryonic connective tissue has been described as mesenchyme, or a network of branching cells with long processes within an abundant fluid intercellular substance. It fills the spaces between developing organs and it differentiates to adult connective tissues and smooth muscle. There is a second embryonic type called mucous connective tissue, which is found in the umbilical cord as Wharton's jelly.

In the adult the fibrous tissue, or connective tissue proper, takes many forms. These types are adipose, areolar, collagenous, elastic, reticular, and others.

44

The most widely distributed is the areolar type, which has the appearance of delicate interlacing strands, simulating a dense cobweb. It is found in the lower layers of the skin, around blood vessels and nerves, under mucous and serous membranes, and in any unoccupied region. Within the semifluid or amorphous matrix there are many kinds of cells, such as fibroblasts, histiocytes, and others. The fibers are yellow (elastic) and white (collagenous). This loose connective tissue in the region of muscles and beneath the skin stores water, sugar, and salt (sodium chloride). It connects the skin and membranes with the deeper structures, and it serves as a packing between organs. Although this tissue serves for loose wrapping, it can provide general regional support and strength. The fibers of areolar tissue come from the fibroblasts, which represent the typical cells. Areolar tissue contains many cells, in contrast to tendons or ligaments, where cells are relatively scarce.

The areolar tissue lying below the skin and covering the muscles and organs is called *fascia*. The superficial fascia, or tela subcutanea, is the loose tissue directly beneath the skin. Because of a high fat content it is insulating as well as binding. The deep fascia, which invests muscles, loses its fat and is predominantly collagenous for strength.

Adipose or fatty connective tissue is a second or modified type. Certain cells of areolar tissue obtain the power to absorb fat from the blood vessels and to deposit it in their cytoplasm. These cells come from the mesenchyme and are called *adipoblasts* or *steatoblasts*. The liquid fat or oil fills the cell and displaces the nu-

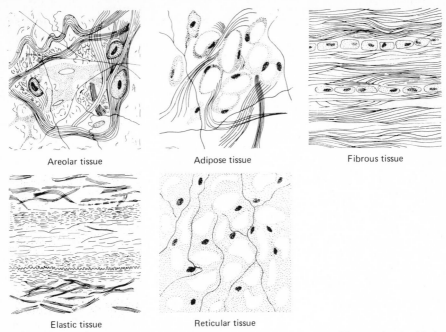

Areolar tissue Adipose tissue Fibrous tissue

Elastic tissue Reticular tissue

Figure 3-8 The major varieties of connective tissues. Note the difference in the kinds and arrangements of the fibers.

cleus so that it is flattened against the cell membrane. This tissue is much more cellular than fibrous or intercellular. It occurs chiefly in the subcutaneous structures called superficial fascias, in mesenteries, in the axillary and inguinal regions, and around the heart and kidneys. It pads the joints and occurs in the marrow of the long bones. It supports and protects organs like the kidney, acts as a heat insulator, serves as a reserve source of food, and gives the body its contours.

The third type is reticular connective tissue. It forms a network of cells with numerous fine fibers traveling in all directions. This tissue provides the framework of the lymph nodes, liver, bone marrow, and spleen. It lies just inside the lining of the digestive tract.

Membranes Although the covering membranes are constructed from epithelium, they also have an underlying layer of connective tissue. In the mucous membranes the connective tissue underlying the epithelium is called the lamina propria. In the serous membranes such as the peritoneum, pleura, and pericardium, the free surface is loose mesothelium, and the deeper surface is loose connective tissue. The connective tissue component not only cements the epithelium to structures below but also allows the passage of blood and nerves to the epithelium.

Another major type of membrane is called fibrous. This is made up entirely of fibrous connective tissue. It exists to connect adjacent structures or to form capsules around organs. Thus, for example, the periosteum surrounds bone, the interosseous membranes connect adjacent bones such as the radius and ulna, and the synovial membranes line joint cavities.

Tendons (Sinews) These are white glistening cords, or bands, which attach muscles to bones. When the end of the muscle is approached, the connective tissue framework increases in quantity and extends beyond the muscle fibers as a dense cord, or tendon, or as a flattened tendon called an *aponeurosis.* Tendons have considerable tensile strength while being flexible and at the same time inextensible.

Aponeuroses These are flat wide bands of fibrous tissue which interconnect muscles or a muscle with the periosteum of a bone. As an example, the abdominal aponeurosis almost wholly covers the anterior abdominal region. Dense collagenous fibers are arranged in parallel, separated at intervals by areolar tissue, which allows the passage of blood vessels.

Ligaments These are strong flexible bands, or capsules, of fibrous tissue that hold bones together at joints. The tensile strength is provided by a parallel arrangement of closely packed collagenous fibers.

Cartilage

The connective tissues harden to cartilage or bone in specific regions. Cells of the mesenchyme divide and cluster into compact cellular masses. They separate and function temporarily as fibroblasts, laying down fibers in the medium. The cells also add products directly to the medium or else regulate the deposition of products from precursors originating in the capillaries. These products absorb and incorporate the fibers into the matrix which is becoming firmer.

The matrix imprisons the cells, now called *chondroblasts,* in cavities termed lacunae. The adult cells, termed *chondrocytes,* divide into several cells within the enlarging lacunae and in turn produce more of the matrix. When the matrix is firm, further growth is made possible only by activity of mesenchymal cells at the periphery. Since the cells usually have no processes and the substrate is compact and devoid of blood vessels, lymphatics, and nerves, the fluid from the outer blood vessels must penetrate the interstitial substance to reach the cells. Metabolism is therefore low, and repair of injury is slow.

Cartilage becomes enclosed by a vascular sheath called the perichondrium. This is dense fibrous tissue that contains mesenchyme cells which are potential cartilage producers. The perichondrium is absent in joint cavities.

Three types of cartilage occur, each subserving specific functions.

The most common type is *hyaline,* which is modified areolar connective tissue. The collagenous and elastic fibers in it are masked by the matrix. It occurs in the costal cartilages of the ribs, in the covering over bone surfaces within joints, and in the cartilages of the nose, larynx, and respiratory passages. In the embryo it forms most of the temporary skeleton. Hyaline cartilage is flexible, slightly elastic, and semitransparent. Its cells, which are typically spherical, divide several times within the solidifying matrix. It has a tendency to calcify and ossify with age; this fact is important for the voice.

Elastic cartilage is more flexible, elastic, and opaque than hyaline cartilage. Its cells are spherical and become encapsulated singly or in groups. It contains a predominance of elastic fibers, which form a network that is not visible in the masking matrix.

This variety is found where movement of the cartilage is necessary and thus where calcification and ossification would interfere with function. Thus the elasticity of the epiglottic cartilage ensures closure of the inlet when it is apposed to the elastic cartilage occurring in the apices of the arytenoids. The pliability of the pharyngeal ostium of the Eustachian tube facilitates opening of the tube during swallowing to equalize atmospheric and tympanic pressures. Elastic cartilage is found also in the auricular cartilage, which does not tend to calcify although it has for the most part lost its function.

Fibrocartilage is found in the intervertebral disks, in the interarticular cartilages of many joints, and elsewhere. It is a strong and flexible variety which is transitional between cartilage and connective tissue. It contains many collagenous fiber bundles arranged in rows, as in tendons. The capsules containing the cells are located in the narrow spaces between the bundles. It has the tendency of hyaline cartilage to calcify with age and develop into bone.

47

Bone

Bone is the densest variety of connective tissue, calcium salts being responsible for its rigidity. The totality of mineral salts constitutes about two-thirds of the weight of any bone.

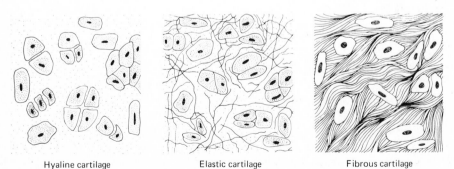

Hyaline cartilage   Elastic cartilage   Fibrous cartilage

Figure 3-9 Varieties of cartilage showing the arrangement of cells and fibers.

Gross Structure

A typical long bone has a shaft, or diaphysis, and two ends, or epiphyses. The diaphysis is almost wholly a dense substance called compact bone, but its innermost layer is spongy, or cancellous, bone. There is a large space in the center of the shaft, termed the medullary cavity, which is filled with bone marrow. The marrow develops from mesenchyme and invades the cartilage as it is being replaced by bone.

Yellow marrow occurs in the medullary cavity of long bones and is mainly adipose tissue. Red marrow occurs in the bodies of vertebrae, the tables of the cranial bones, the sternum, ribs, clavicle, scapula, and the proximal ends of the femur and humerus. The red marrow has many cells within the connective tissue and has a rich vascular supply. This marrow forms red blood cells, platelets, and most leucocytes, and it helps destroy worn-out red cells by phagocytosis.

A fibrous membrane called the periosteum covers the external surface of a bone except at its joint surfaces and sends perforating fibers into the underlying bone. The periosteum allows tendons and ligaments to gain attachment to the bone. It contains an inner layer which produces bone cells, or osteoblasts, particularly in youth. Blood vessels penetrate the periosteum as a rich network from which minute branches go into the underlying compact layer through spaces called Volkmann's canals. The vessels communicate with an inner system of Haversian canals and also independently supply the spongy bone. Bones may have an adjunctive blood supply through an artery which enters a nutrient foramen in the outer compact layer and then enters the inner medullary cavity. Arterial branches reach the internal cancellous substance in the region of the bone where the blood cells are being produced, and veins then return from this area.

A single-layered membrane called the endosteum lines the narrow cavities of bones and the Haversian canals of compact bone. Its cells have osteoblastic activity.

Types of Bones

Long bones occur in the upper and lower extremities. *Short* bones are essentially spongy bones wrapped in a thin layer of compact bone. The wrist bones are examples. *Flat* bones have two plates of compact bone sandwiching spongy bone

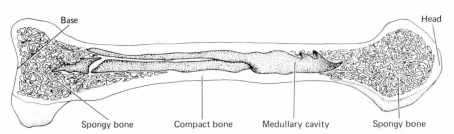

Figure 3-10 Longitudinal section of typical bone.

between them. The skull bones, ribs, and scapula are examples. *Irregular* bones include those of various shapes not included in the preceding categories. They include vertebrae and some skull bones. *Sesamoid* bones are small round bones (except for the kneecap) developing in tendons or in the capsules of joints and serving to eliminate friction.

Terminology of Osseous Structures
Anatomic terms used frequently in describing bony structures belonging to the vocal mechanism are defined below.

Canal: a bony passageway produced by structures traveling a considerable distance through a bone

Crest: a prominent ridge

Condyle: a rounded or knucklelike process for articulation

Facet: a small smooth region found between projections or roughed regions

Fossa: a pit or hollow

Foramen: an opening in a bone

Groove: a furrow

Head: an enlargement at one end of the bone beyond its neck

Meatus: a tube or passage

49

Process: a bony prominence

Sinus: a cavity inside a bone; a groove on the inside of the skull (includes cerebral sinuses)

Spine: a sharp projection

Sulcus: a furrow

Trochanter: a very large bony process

Tubercle: a small round projection

Tuberosity: a large roughened projection

Development of Bone
Some bones develop by direct mineralization of membranous tissue (membrane bones), but others develop by depositing minerals in preexisting cartilage, which is removed as new bone is formed (cartilage bones). The processes of development are very similar in either case. The cartilage bones make up most of the skeleton.

Long bones grow in circumference by deposition of bone inside the periosteum, whose deeper layer contains osteoblasts. When new bone forms peripherally, cells termed osteoclasts dissolve the bone nearest the medullary cavity. This enlarges the cavity adaptively with the increasing circumference of the shaft.

Long bones grow in length by osteoblasts' replacing cartilage in the epiphyses. New cartilage cells then form at the ends of the bone. When all cartilage is eventually replaced by bone, growth in length ceases. This occurs at about twenty years of age in the male and about eighteen years in the female.

Histology of Bone

In the microscopic anatomy of compact bone the structural unit is the osteon, or Haversian system. This unit has a central lumen called the Haversian canal, in which capillaries and venules run. Around each canal are concentric layers, or Haversian lamellae. Although the osteons generally travel longitudinally, the Haversian lamellae run spirally to the axis of the canal. In a long bone there are circumferential lamellae, which run parallel to the surface of the bone on the exterior and interior. Also, there are interstitial lamellae, which occupy the intervals between the Haversian lamellae.

Any single osteon contains, in addition to its central canal and fibrillar structure, many spaces, or lacunae. These lie between the Haversian lamellae and are therefore arranged in circular fashion. The lacunae contain the bone cells (osteocytes).

The bone cells which are trapped in such spaces in the compact bone can be nourished through a system of microscopic intercommunicating channels. Such a system radiates everywhere from the lacunae as canaliculi. The innermost canaliculi run into the Haversian canals, which travel almost longitudinally through the compact bone. This allows interchanges between the vessels in the Haversian canals and the bone cells in the circular lacunae around the canals. The fluid from the blood vessels of the Haversian canals reaches all parts of the Haversian system through the circulatory tract involving the lacunae and their extending canaliculi. In the spongy, or cancellous, bone the Haversian systems are deficient, and the lamellar arrangement differs.

The canaliculi of the lacunae communicate with Volkmann's canals and thus with the blood vessels of the vascular periosteum. They are also in contact with the

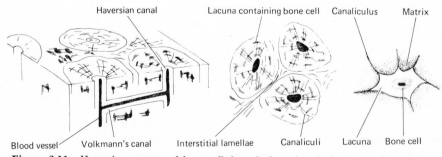

Figure 3-11 Haversian systems of bone. Enlarged view of a single bone cell.

internal lining, or endosteum, of the marrow cavity if it is present. The periosteum sends nerve fibers as well as arteries into the bone. These fibers are afferent myelinated and autonomic unmyelinated.

The Joints

The bones, cartilages, and softer connective tissues are assembled in given areas to form joints. The joints, or articulations, are connections between two separate segments or parts of the skeleton.

Types of Joints

The *synarthrosis* is the immovable or slightly movable joint found in the union of bones of the skull, in the insertion of teeth into sockets in the mandible and maxilla, in the joining of ribs with costal cartilages, and elsewhere. There is no joint cavity, so that motion is limited or absent.

In newer terminology the joints called synarthroses are placed in two categories. The *fibrous joints* are those in which the bones are joined by fibers. The *cartilaginous joints* are those in which the binding occurs by cartilage.

Fibrous joints are subdivided to *sutures, syndesmoses,* and *gomphoses.* In sutures, as in the skull, the bone ends are serrated and approximated by fibrous tissue. In syndesmoses, as between the spinous processes and laminae of adjacent vertebrae, the connection is made by dense fibrous connective tissue which is deposited in the form of ligaments. In the gomphosis, exemplified by a tooth and its socket, irregularly arranged fibrous tissue holds the tooth firmly in the socket while allowing reactivity to biting and grinding.

Cartilaginous joints are subdivided into *symphyses* and *synchondroses.* In symphyses, as between the bodies of adjacent vertebrae, the ends of the bones are covered by cartilage and are separated by an intercartilage disk. In this instance the approximation is through a fibrous capsule. Flexibility is provided. In synchondroses, as between ribs and costal cartilages, the bone ends are approximated by cartilages.

Most of the bodily joints are *diarthroses*, or *synovial joints,* and these have variable degrees and directions of free motion. The bones are joined by fibrous tissue called the articular capsule, within which is a joint cavity. The internal layer of the capsule secretes a minute amount of synovial fluid into the joint cavity to nourish and lubricate the articulation. The opposed ends of the bones in a diarthrosis are covered by hyaline or articular cartilage.

Types of Movements in Synovial Joints The simplest movement is gliding, in which one part moves or glides over another. In the movement called flexion there is a bending or a decrease in the angle between parts of the body, but in extension there is a stretching or an increase in the angle. Adduction implies

51

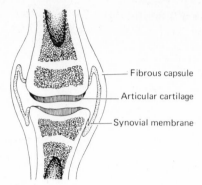

Fibrous capsule

Articular cartilage

Synovial membrane

Figure 3-12 A typical freely movable joint.

movement toward the median line, whereas abduction is the opposite. Rotation involves turning a part about a fixed axis. The arytenoid cartilages, which are important agents in the movements of the vocal folds, are capable of rotating clockwise or counterclockwise. The exact effect of such movements upon the vocal folds and the glottis is still inconclusive. In circumduction the end of a structure describes a circle while the structure itself describes the base of a cone. In the shoulder joint the apex in the socket describes the circle while the hand describes the base of the cone.

The diarthroses are classified into groups by their varieties of motion. In the hinge joint, or ginglymus, motion is in one plane, usually forward or backward. The pivot, or trochoid, is limited to rotation. In the condyloid joint, a condyle or ovoid surface fits into an elliptical cavity, and all movements except rotation are permitted. This is illustrated in the wrist joint. In the ball and socket joint, or enarthrosis, a rounded head of one bone moves in a cuplike cavity of another, as in the hip joint, and motion occurs around an indefinite number of axes. In the saddle joint, opposing surfaces are alternately concave and convex, as in the carpometacarpal joint of the thumb, and a great freedom of motion is permitted. In the gliding joints, or arthrodia, where plane surfaces or those alternately and slightly concave and convex meet, only gliding motion is permitted. This occurs between the articular processes of vertebrae.

In the areas about joints in which friction occurs, *bursae,* or sacs, which contain synovial fluid appear. These sacs smooth over the gaps in the joint and facilitate the sliding of muscle and tendons over prominences of bones or ligaments.

Muscular Tissue

Motion is an important activity of many parts of the speech apparatus and it is made possible by the specialization of muscle cells for the function of *contractility.* This is the property that allows a muscle to change its shape, by becoming shorter and thicker. Muscles, like other cells, also possess the related properties of *irritability* (or *excitability*), *extensibility*, and *elasticity*.

Types of Muscle

There are three types of muscles, differentiated through structure and function. They are smooth (plain, unstriated), skeletal (striated, voluntary), and cardiac (heart). All have contractility, or the power to shorten, and this is expressed in a direction parallel to the long axis of their cells. The contractile element of the cells is a myofibril. The fibrils tend to aggregate as fine parallel filaments into fibers which are long slender threads.

Smooth muscle cells are spindle-shaped, thick in the center, and tapering at each end, with cytoplasmic myofibrils and a central nucleus. Such muscles are found in the walls of visceral tubes. Their general occurrence in the speech apparatus is not extensive. They regulate the diameter of the blood vessels, determine the caliber of the bronchioles, and are generally essential to the movements of the internal organs. They are innervated by the autonomic nervous system.

Cardiac muscle forms the major portion of the heart wall. The fibers branch and interlace into a syncytium, or netlike structure. Myofibrils are present, and the sacroplasm is abundant. There is a rich coronary blood supply. The nerve supply is autonomic. This kind of muscle is a pump to aid the circulation of the blood.

Striated muscle is concerned with the voluntary movements of skeletal structures. It is especially involved in the speech apparatus, where it adjusts many localized speech structures to specific demands. It occurs in the vocal mechanism as muscles attached to cartilages or bones which form the skeletal framework of the larynx, respiratory system, face, and other speech structures. It permits communication of one's wishes, thoughts, or reactions to one's fellows by speech, signal, facial expression, or body attitude.

53

Gross and Fine Structure of Skeletal Muscle

An entire skeletal muscle mass is covered by a connective tissue called *epimysium*. This is a fibrous membrane which may be considered as the *deep fascia* binding the

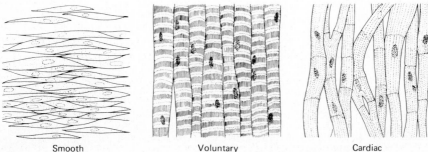

Smooth   Voluntary   Cardiac

Figure 3-13 Comparison of fiber arrangements in the different kinds of muscle tissues.

muscle. At each end of the muscle the fibrous sheath merges into *tendons* that insert usually into bones.

The more fixed attachment of a muscle, which functions as a basis of action, is termed the *origin*. The movable attachment, where the effects are exerted, is termed the *insertion*. These can be reversed. As an example, the thyrohyoid can depress the hyoid or elevate the thyroid cartilage, depending on the relative fixations of the parts to be moved. Generally, the origin is near the spinal axis, and the insertion is peripheral. The fibers of origin are often very short, and the muscle appears to arise in a fleshy rather than a fibrous manner from the bone. The insertion is generally smaller and more precisely limited than the origin is to the area of attachment. The portion of muscle between the origin and the insertion is called the *body* or *belly* of the muscle.

The epimysium sends partitions of connective tissue called *perimysium* into the muscle to subdivide it into bundles called *fasciculi*. There are also fine strands of

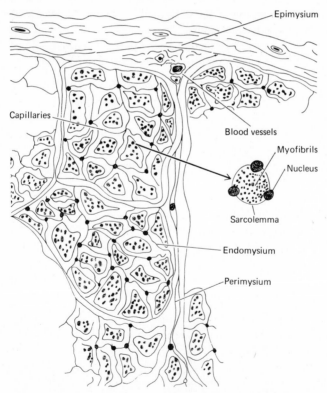

Figure 3-14 Cross section of striated muscle (diagrammatic), showing connective tissues. The endomysium encloses single muscle fibers, the perimysium encloses bundles of fibers, and the epimysium ensheathes the whole mass.

tissue called *endomysium*, which extend from the perimysium into the interior of the fasciculi and penetrate the spaces between the individual fibers. A thin membrane, the *sarcolemma*, covers each fiber. The sarcolemma blends into the strands of the larger connective tissue units of the muscle.

Skeletal muscle is composed essentially of thousands of cylindrical fibers that run in parallel. Each fiber is developed from a cell that elongates from 1 to 40 mm. The fiber is multinucleated and contains protoplasm, called sarcoplasm, in which long contractile filaments, called myofibrils, are embedded. Each myofibril is striped periodically by alternate transverse dark and light bands. This makes the fibers look cross-striated. Changes in the relative thickness of the dark and light bands are associated with contraction.

Blood and Nerve Supply Each skeletal muscle receives blood from one or more arteries which break up into a rich capillary network in the connective tissues around the fibers. The fibrous interior is separated from the blood only by a thin sarcolemma and a one-layered capillary membrane. This allows ready interchange of solutes and water. The veins correspond with the general arrangement of the arteries and are equipped everywhere in the muscle with valves. This provides for return of impure blood, without backflow.

Lymphatic capillaries do not appear between individual muscle fibers but are located between fasciculi. The intercellular fluid travels out of the connective tissue of the muscle at a slow rate until it reaches the lymphatic capillary.

Each fiber receives nerve twigs, which penetrate the sarcolemma. This arrangement will be described under the nervous system. The machinery involves (1) motor nerve fibers, which run through a myoneural junction, or motor end plate, to collections of muscle fibers, and (2) afferent nerve fibers, which run from specific receptors in the muscles and their tendons to the central nervous system.

Mechanism of Skeletal Muscle Contraction

It was once thought that the contraction of a muscle occurred by folding of its contractile proteins, actin and myosin. Data from electron microscopy and x-ray diffraction studies have lent support to a sliding-filament theory of contraction. Striated muscles contain two types of fibrils, of different diameters. The larger type is A and the smaller is I. The A fibers are composed of myosin and the I fibers of actin. The two kinds of fibers interdigitate with each other.

When the muscle fiber shortens, the A band remains unchanged in length but the I band decreases in width, i.e., its ends come closer together, by sliding in between the A bands. The so-called H gap is decreased. The result is to shorten the sarcomere, or unit of structure, of a fiber confined between two Z lines. The actin filaments slide farther into the A bands between the larger myosin filaments. Since actin filaments are attached to the Z disks, these are pulled closer together. The Z line may be a membrane running transversely through the myofibrils, attached to the sarcolemma, and having some relationship to the irritability of the muscle.

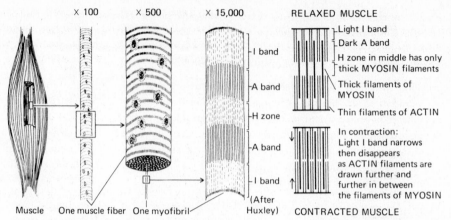

Figure 3-15 Skeletal muscle and the mechanism of contraction. (*By permission from A. B. McNaught and R. Callander, Illustrated Physiology, rev. ed. The Williams & Wilkins Company, Baltimore, 1965.*)

In regard to forces that produce the sliding oblique bridges existing between actin and myosin, filaments may pull the actin filaments a short distance then detach and form again. This cycle is repeated often in a single contraction, under the influence of energy probably derived from the chemical breakdown of adenosine triphosphate.

The Problem of Muscle Tone

Electromyography is a method for recording electrical activity and responses of muscles. Electromyographic evidence indicates that normal human muscle at rest is relaxed. This is contrary to the classical view that all resting muscles are in a low-energy state of partial tension, called tone, involving neuromuscular activity. The absence of a resting potential may be due to instrumental limitations, however, rather than to complete muscle relaxation.

The current thinking demands a redefinition, in which tone is a function of the natural passive elasticity, or turgor, of muscle and also of the active, intermittent contraction of muscle in response to the reaction of the nervous system to stimuli (Basmajian, 1962). A limb muscle involved in maintaining upright posture is truly active, but not all the muscles of the lower extremity need be active when a person stands.

The evaluation of normal tone is entirely a matter of judgment since quantitative measures are lacking. The most important criterion is the resistance of muscles to *passive* manipulation (DeJong, 1967). That is, the subject allows his muscles to be relaxed, and there is no voluntary motion. To test tone, it is passive and not active movement that is examined, with attention directed to the degree of tension present on passive stretching of the muscles and also to their extensibility and range of motion. In the muscles of an extremity, where tone is most easily detected, the subject is requested to relax completely, avoid all tension, and "give" the extremity to the examiner. The part is moved passively and slowly through its range of motion and then at varying speeds, with observation of resistance to movement, ability to maintain postures against external forces, limitation of range, and many other responses.

Muscles as Levers

The cooperative function of muscles and bones produces a mechanical advantage called leverage. A simple lever may be thought of as a rigid bar that moves freely about an intermediate fixed point call the fulcrum. On one side of the fulcrum the bar is acted upon by a weight or resistance. On the opposite side of the fulcrum the bar is acted upon by a force or effort needed to overcome the resistance. In the human body the bones are the levers, the resistance is the body or some other weight to be moved, and the effort to overcome the resistance is the muscular work applied by the muscle at its insertion to the bone.

To maintain a lever in equilibrium, the effort times its distance from the fulcrum must equal the resistance times its distance from the fulcrum.

Three classes of levers are recognized. In a lever of the first class, the effort and resistance are on either side of the fulcrum. If the effort is applied in one direction, the resistance is made to move in the opposite direction. Thus, to raise one's head, assuming the atlantooccipital joint to be the fulcrum, the effort of the back muscles downward raises the facial aspect of the skull upward.

In levers of the second class, the fulcrum is at one end, the effort is at the other end, and the resistance is between them. The effort and resistance are made to move in the same direction. A second-class lever is said to be exemplified in the action by which one rises to stand on tiptoe. The fulcrum is the ball of the foot, the resistance is the weight of the body applied at the joint between the tibia and ankle bones, and the effort is the upward force of the gastrocnemius muscle at its insertion on the calcaneus (Grollman, 1964).

In a lever of the third class, the effort is exerted between the fulcrum and the resistance. Most body levers fall in this category. When a person flexes his forearm with a weight acting downward in his hand, the fulcrum is at the proximal end, or elbow, while the effort is exerted upward by the more distal forearm muscles, which are between the fulcrum and the weight. Following the principle stated above, when the distance to the resistance is greater than the distance to the place of effort, the effort used must be greater than the resistance.

Since the mechanical advantage of a lever is the ratio of the effort arm to the resistance arm, individuals whose muscles are inserted farther from the joints about which levers move have greater mechanical advantage than those whose muscles insert closer to the fulcrum. This has application in comparing extrinsic and intrinsic muscles in the larynx.

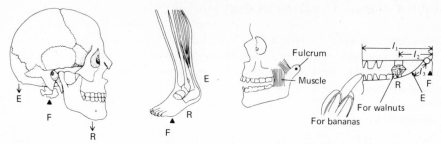

Figure 3-16 Three classes of muscle levers in man. *Left:* class I, the fulcrum is between the resistance and the effort when elevating the face at the atlantooccipital joint. *Second from left:* class II, the fulcrum is at one end and the effort at the other in elevating the foot at the metatarsophalangeal joint. *Right two figures:* class III, the fulcrum is at one end and the resistance at the other in elevating the mandible for crushing food.

Nervous Tissue

This is described in Chapter 4. The cells specialize to neurons, which become the microscopic units of structure and function.

Organs

The tissues combine to form organs. Each organ is built up from two or more tissues which are associated to perform some special function. The tongue and larynx are organs, but their next simpler constituents are tissues. The larynx contains epithelium, connective tissue, muscles, nerves, and blood vessels. Any organ generally has a characteristic or predominant tissue and accessory supporting tissues.

Systems

Systems are arrangements of closely allied organs which unite for a common function. This category includes the nervous, muscular, integumentary, skeletal, circulatory, respiratory, endocrine, excretory, digestive, and reproductive systems.

The systems themselves work in close coordination to produce specific bodily activity. In speech, muscular and skeletal activity under nervous and endocrine control simultaneously comes into play with adjunctive respiratory, circulatory, and other system activity.

In the study called systematic anatomy, the body is divided into a set of functional systems which are studied one at a time. This text is concerned with the activities of specific regions, and the method of regional anatomy is used. All systems or parts lying within the localized region are collectively considered at the same time. The gross regions which concern us most are the head, neck, thorax, and abdomen.

Applied Anatomy and Physiology

Chromosome Aberrations and Speech

It may be appropriate to discuss some conditions involving the integrity of the chromosomes which affect the speech mechanism. Cleft palate and mongolism, which have some overlapping aspects, are illustrative of two types of chromosome defects. Mongolism emphasizes the relevance of *cytogenetics,* or the study of the nature and variations of the chromosomes.

All human cells have 46 chromosomes. These include 22 pairs of autosomes that are entirely unlike one another in genetic material and often in shape. There are also X and Y chromosomes, the male possessing one X and one Y type and the female two X types.

Blood samples can be taken from an individual and leucocytic blood cells therein so processed that a photograph can be obtained of all the chromosomes within a single blood cell of the male or female. The chromosomes can be arranged in pairs which decrease progressively in size, and are so numbered, from 1 to 22, plus the X and Y chromosomes. Such a picture is called a *karyotype.*

In mongolism (Down's syndrome), the chromosome group numbered 21 in the series shows three chromosomes in the one group rather than the expected pair. The condition is thus called *trisomy* 21. The error occurs in cell division. It is probable that the members of a chromosome pair did not separate as they should have during the production of sperm or egg cells. One cell then contained two

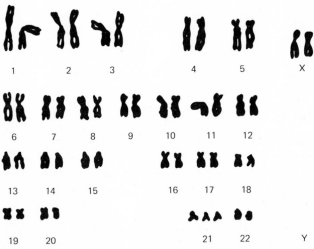

Figure 3-17. Trisomy 21 in a female (the Y chromosome is missing). Except for the abnormality of three chromosomes in group 21, the karyotype is normal. The resulting symptomatology is called sporadic mongolism (Down's syndrome).

members of a pair of chromosomes and a second cell had none. Upon subsequent union of the cell containing the two chromosomes with a normal cell, the developing zygote had 47 chromosomes. One cell obtained three chromosomes. The other cell had only 45 chromosomes, a condition termed *monosomy*.

The particular chromosome aberration of trisomy described above is associated with mental retardation, an enlarged tongue, and often slanted eyes that give the disease its name of mongolism. Trisomies occurring in chromosome groups other than pair 21 produce different syndromes. There are also other kinds of chromosomal abnormalities, e.g., *deletions* and *translocations,* involving losses of chromosomal parts or the breaking and exchange of parts.

The reader is referred to Luchsinger and Arnold (1965) and West and Ansberry (1968) for brief accounts and some literature citations, and to Burns (1969) for a general exposition. Lenneberg (1967) discusses language from the standpoint of evolution and genetics and cites literature concerning the familial occurrence of a variety of speech disorders.

4 NEURAL REGULATION OF SPEECH

Animals and man express their "states of mind" by a pattern of behavior or language that takes many diverse forms in the various phylogenetic groups. In man the articulate sounds emitted in the form of vowels and consonants are shaped into words, each of which is an expression or symbol of a thought or idea. In the development of speech the units, or words, are each progressively associated with all possible stimuli arising in the external and internal environment, both in receiving the sound message and in responding to it. An enormously complicated associating structure, the brain, is developed to receive, channelize, and interpret the incoming messages and to form concepts by which meaningful expressive sounds may be adaptively produced at will. In the speech function the nature of the associations between the incoming impulses from tactile, visual, auditory, and other receptors and the manner of response to these by adequate control of the effective devices is important. On the expressive side alone of sound an enormous integrative faculty is needed to articulate a single idea, since many bodily structures and processes have to be activated in coordination at one time.

The action of the central nervous system upon a specific effector may seem to lend itself to ready inspection and analysis in terms of anatomic and physiologic correlates, but the relationship between the nervous system and specific behavior is extremely complex. The nervous system does not simply move a muscle of speech or cause a gland to lubricate the vocal folds. The orderly performance of speech or other behavior involves the proper balance, timing, and distribution of energy into a large number of muscles and glands. Coordination must occur between various parts of the brain and all the peripheral structures that constitute the speech mechanism. At least hundreds of discrete messages must be sent in rapid-fire sequence. Whether one event triggers others in succession or whether many independent events occur simultaneously is obscure. In any case, the central nervous system must be looked upon more in terms of its regulatory function than as a device to trigger a specific discharge. In this regulatory capacity, the property of modulation of the central regulators by feedback from the effectors under control must never be overlooked.

As Lenneberg (1967) has pointed out, the interplay of activity in the nervous system goes on continuously, and the results of stimulation are not expressed as a change from a passive to an active state but as an alteration of such factors as rate and rhythm in the discharges of cells. In this sense speech like other behavior might be thought of in terms of modulation of activity in active neuron nets.

Lenneberg emphasizes that the essence of language is structure and pattern and that the dimensions of the patterns are temporal. To a great degree, central nervous disorders of speech and language should be considered as disorders of timing mechanisms. This does not deny that such disorders may reflect a disordered balance, e.g., excitation and inhibition.

The control of speech by the nervous system was emphasized by Broca (1861) and Wernicke (1874), but these investigators were concerned with cortical localization. Although their ideas were later disputed by Pierre Marie (1906), Head (1926), and Goldstein (1926), the involvement of the nervous system was conclusively demonstrated.

The neural regulators of speech are divided into (1) the central nervous system, consisting of the brain and spinal cord; (2) the peripheral nervous system, including the cranial and spinal nerves; and (3) the autonomic nervous system, innervating organs not under voluntary control, such as smooth muscles and glands.

The Structural Unit of Behavior

The neurons are the units of which the entire nervous system is composed. According to the *neuron doctrine,* established since the beginning of this century, there are no other elements within the nervous system that participate in the basic neural functions of this system. Some speculation exists, however, about a neural function for the glial cells.

A neuron is a cell that comes from the outermost embryonic tissue called the ectoderm. It is derived from a neuroblast.

The neuron assumes an elongated form best adapted to its function of conducting impulses by the sprouting out of various processes from its centralized cell body. Any single process may become enormously attenuated on one side of its parent cell body, thus forming the axon, or nerve fiber. In man one nerve fiber may extend from the lower spinal cord to the tip of the toe, a span of about 3 ft. On the opposite side of the cell body the processes called dendrites are considerably shorter and more numerous, and they serve to collect impulses from the axon of the preceding neuron.

The typical neuron, which has one axon and several dendrites, is called multipolar. It is characteristic of the efferent cranial and spinal nerves. In distinction, the afferent fiber of the peripheral nerves is bipolar. It has a centripetal dendrite and a centrifugal axon, both arising from a cell body that helps form a dorsal-root ganglion.

The cell bodies of neurons lie in the gray matter of the central nervous system or in outlying ganglia. Each cell body has a nucleus and nucleolus, and its cytoplasm

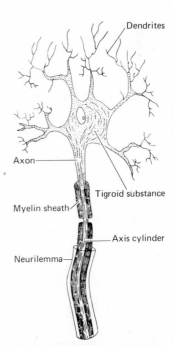

Figure 4-1 A single multipolar neuron showing axon, dendrites, and cell body.

contains neurofibrils, Nissl bodies (tigroid substance), and the internal reticular apparatus of Golgi.

The Nissl bodies extend from the cell body into the dendrites but not into the typical axon. They are granular masses which give the cell a striped appearance. Since they decrease in size during conduction, it has been claimed that they contribute material for the conduction process. In some diseases they disappear, a process called chromatolysis, and there is a concomitant loss in neuron conduction. When a neuron fires an impulse, the related uptake of oxygen and release of carbon dioxide appear to be related to the amount of Nissl substance present.

The neurofibrils are fine filaments which extend through the whole length of the cytoplasm of the neuron. They can be readily visualized in the core, or axis cylinder, of the axon. The fibrils are probably concerned in the transmission of nerve impulses.

Axons, or nerve fibers, differ in their coverings. Fibers without sheaths are found in the gray matter of the central nervous system. The typical cranial or spinal nerve contains a fatty myelin (medullated) sheath within a neurilemma (Schwann's sheath). The myelin sheath is periodically constricted by nodes of Ranvier, and each internode is associated with a single neurilemma cell. The neurilemma is necessary for regeneration if a nerve is injured. Unmyelinated fibers found in certain varieties of peripheral nerves have only a neurilemma, whereas the fibers of the white matter of the central nervous system contain only myelin.

64

The Nerve Impulse

Neurons are uniquely adapted to control and direct the activity spreading through them as a reaction to a stimulus. The propagated disturbance is the nerve impulse. The activity is expressed by such manifestations as oxygen and carbon dioxide interchange, heat production, and the flow of electric currents. In the classical theory the nerve impulse was thought to be identical with a wave of axon potential called the action current inasmuch as the velocities of the nerve impulse and the action current were identical. The velocity in medullated fibers varies

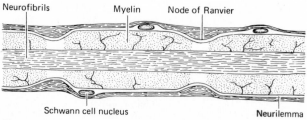

Figure 4-2 Enlarged section of myelinated axon (nerve fiber).

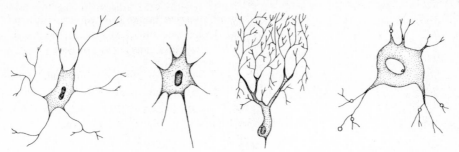

Figure 4-3   Some representative **neurons** showing variations in form.

from 100 to 125 m/sec and **in nonmedul**lated fibers from 65 to 100 m/sec.   With
the discovery that specific **chemicals** are liberated along the trunks of active nerve
fibers, diffusing across synapses **and** entering the cells of the final effectors, the
nerve impulse has come to be **considered** as electrochemical.   Each cell or segment
receives the impulse and transmits it in an all-or-none fashion to the next segment
of the fiber, the energy for **transmission** coming from the fiber itself.

Substances lying inside and **outside** of the nerve fiber are dissolved in a polar
medium, water, and can ordinarily **dissociate** from the molecular form to positively
and negatively charged particles **called** *ions*.   In the resting nerve fiber the selectively permeable surface **membrane** separates positive ions on the outer surface
from negative ions on the **inner surface**.   The membrane is therefore polarized,
with the inner surface negative **to the** exterior by 50 to 100 millivolts.

The concentration of sodium **ions** outside the membrane is about 10 times greater
than that within.   The **concentration** of potassium ions inside the membrane is
20 to 50 times that outside.   **There is** a great pressure for sodium ions to flow in,
except that the resting membrane **is** impermeable to sodium ions.

One of the marked effects of **a stimulus** is to depolarize the membrane, which permits a rapid movement of **sodium ions** inward; this so reverses the potential that
the external surface becomes **negative** to the interior.   The alteration in potential
difference is expressed as the **spike** potential of an action current that once begun
spreads automatically along the **fibers**, independently of the initial stimulus.   The
excited region acts as a "sink" **to stimulate** currents in adjacent parts of the axon.

At the height of the potential **shift** there is a decrease in the inward passage of
sodium ions, but permeability **to the** exit of potassium increases.   Following this, a
so-called sodium pump is **responsible** for transporting sodium to the outside of the
membrane.   A slower diffusion **of** potassium ions occurs in an inner direction.
The sodium pump is energized **by** adenosine triphosphate changes and perhaps
also by creatine phosphate, **but these** compounds do not influence the movements
of sodium and potassium ions **during** the spiking process (Scheer, 1963).

Immediately after the passage of the nerve impulse the excitability of the fiber drops to zero and then rises, producing absolute and relative refractory periods. The absolute refractory period (about 0.5 msec) is one in which no stimulus, however strong, can reexcite the fiber until the traveling peak of potential, or spike, is nearly completed. The time interval for excitability to gradually return to normal is the relative refractory period (about 2 to 3 msec). The impulses thus cannot be transmitted continuously like a stream of water from a hose, but they resemble more the discontinuous yet repetitive volley of bullets from a machine gun.

Nerve Impulses at Synapses
The region of interneuronal contact is called a synapse. This area is not one of actual fusion but rather one of microscopically close contact that nevertheless allows the passage of nerve impulses. Any disruption of this functional linkage interferes with the operation of the pool of neurons involved in a given activity. The synapses act as valves to ensure a forced polarity in conduction from dendrite to cell body to axon and thence to the next neuron.

The synapse is not just a directional valve. In the cybernetic point of view its importance in "choice" is emphasized. Switching operations involving differential routing of impulses go on in the synapse, and changes in output strength are also made possible.

In a two-neuron connection, the preceding axon is seen, in the electron microscope, to possess many feet, or "buttons," on the apex of its terminal branches. These buttons establish the functional connection between the neurons. Actually, there are other varieties of terminals, or telodendrites.

Spatial summation occurs if two or more axons or several of the buttons discharge at one time into the next neuron. An ineffective stimulus can thus be made to produce an impulse whose strength is great enough to allow it to be propagated across the synapse. A similar effect is obtained by a fast repetitive discharge of sub-threshold impulses into the buttons; this is called *temporal summation*.

Whereas conduction in a neuron is essentially electrical, conduction across a synapse is essentially chemical and is carried out by ions. This accounts for a synaptic delay. Where the tip of each axonic branch enlarges to an end button, there are tiny vesicles. The vesicles respond to incoming impulses by releasing a chemical transmitter which increases the permeability of the next neuron. The excitatory transmitter is acetylcholine (ACh) at all synaptic junctions except the neuroeffector synapses of sympathetic (thoracolumbar) autonomics. ACh is catalyzed from choline and acetic acid in the presence of the enzyme cholinacetylase. It is hydrolyzed in milliseconds by the enzyme cholinesterase. The lost vesicles are replaced by the activity of mitochondria in the terminal neuron region.

ACh activity facilitates the flow of ions, such as sodium, across the junction, with lowering of electrical resistance and the production of a discharge in the succeeding neuron.

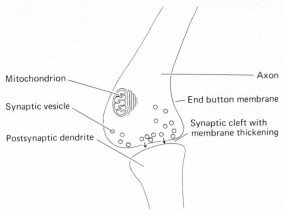

Figure 4-4 Schematic representation of a synaptic ending and its constituents. The mitochondrion is exaggerated to give an idea of length.

Inhibition at Synapses There are two varieties of inhibition at synapses, *presynaptic* and *postsynaptic*. In the presynaptic region inhibitory terminals are thought to release an inhibitor substance into the presynaptic nerve fibrils. The latter are then prevented from releasing their excitatory transmitter substance.

The impulses producing inhibition in somatic motor neurons travel in a special kind of internuncial or inhibitory neuron called the Renshaw cell, found in the gray matter of the cord. Their dendrites receive the incoming impulses from collaterals of the afferent fibers. One of the blocking agents found only in inhibitory neurons is gamma aminobutyric acid. This may be the main inhibitory transmitter.

Postsynaptic inhibition is thought to come about as a result of the action of the inhibitory transmitter. Special inhibitory terminals may make the postsynaptic membranes more permeable to ions such as potassium or chloride but not to sodium. The potassium ions move out of the neuron, and chloride ions move in. The result is to reproduce and magnify the resting condition of the fiber; i.e., the outside is more positive and the inside more negative. This is called *hyperpolarization*, and it prevents depolarization of the membrane.

The Peripheral Nerves

Nearly all nerves contain both afferent and efferent fibers so that they conduct impulses toward as well as away from the centers. We not only produce motion, secretion, or changed blood supply in our speech effectors, but we in turn receive considerable information from these organs concerning their general status and vitality.

Spinal Nerves

There are typically in man thirty-one pairs of spinal nerves differentiated to eight cervical, twelve thoracic, five lumbar, five sacral, and one caudal (coccygeal). Each pair, except for the cervicals, is named for the vertebra above its exit.

The spinal nerves, as well as the cranial, constitute the lower motor neurons, or final common paths, into which impulses are funneled from both the pyramidal and extrapyramidal systems. The muscles of speech which are innervated by the spinal neurons are in the neck, thorax, and abdomen. These muscles receive their innervation through cervical and thoracic nerves.

The anterior divisions of the upper four cervical nerves intertwine to form a cervical plexus. Nerves going out from this plexus are the chief source of innervation for the muscles of the neck which are concerned in speech.

The last four cervical plus the first and usually the second thoracic nerves produce a brachial plexus. Nerves branch out from this plexus to innervate the upper extremity and the upper muscles of respiration.

The nerves leaving the thoracic sector of the spinal cord below T-2 do not intermix to form a plexus. They leave the cord as individual pairs of nerve trunks. These nerves innervate thoracic and abdominal structures, including the respiratory muscles in these regions.

68   Most of the largest peripheral nerves contain fibers which have originated from several spinal nerve roots. The phrenic nerve to the diaphragmatic muscle of breathing originates typically from three roots in the cervical plexus. A lesion in a single peripheral nerve trunk may thus involve fibers belonging to more than one spinal nerve.

Cranial Nerves

The cranial nerves arise from the brain as twelve pairs. Some authorities also list number 0, the nervus terminalis, from the nasal septum. Unlike the spinal nerves they originate at irregular intervals. The cranial nerves are not all concerned with speech; all, however, will be briefly characterized. They are conventionally designated by roman numerals I to XII.

I *Olfactory Nerve* It arises in the mucous membranes of the upper nasal cavity, and it ends in the olfactory bulb. From there the olfactory tract passes to the rhinencephalon. The nerve is purely sensory and serves for smell. Olfaction does have a significant relationship to taste, and persons with loss of smell suffer reduction in taste.

II *Optic Nerve* The visual fibers originate in the retina of each eye, and they travel toward the brain in the paired optic nerves. At a region called the optic chiasm the fibers from the nasal half of each retina cross over to become a part of the opposite tract. This allows two retinal images, formed on corresponding

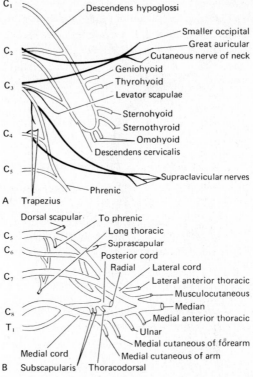

C_1 — Descendens hypoglossi
C_2 — Smaller occipital
— Great auricular
— Cutaneous nerve of neck
C_3 — Geniohyoid
— Thyrohyoid
— Levator scapulae
— Sternohyoid
— Sternothyroid
C_4 — Omohyoid
Descendens cervicalis
C_5
Supraclavicular nerves
— Phrenic
A   Trapezius

Dorsal scapular   To phrenic
C_5 Long thoracic
C_6 Suprascapular
Posterior cord
Radial   Lateral cord
C_7 Lateral anterior thoracic
— Musculocutaneous
— Median
C_8 Medial anterior thoracic
T_1 Ulnar
Medial cutaneous of forearm
Medial cord   Medial cutaneous of arm
B   Subscapularis   Thoracodorsal

Figure 4-5 (*a*) The cervical plexus and its nerves of distribution; (*b*) the brachial plexus and its nerves of distribution.

69

retinal points, to be fused to a single stereoscopic sensation in one cerebral hemisphere.

The first-order neurons end in lower visual centers, mainly the lateral geniculate bodies. The second-order neurons travel in the geniculocalcarine tract to the occipital cortex.

III *Oculomotor Nerve* It passes as a motor nerve from the midbrain to several eyeball muscles.

IV *Trochlear Nerve* It passes as a motor nerve from the midbrain to a single eyeball muscle.

V *Trigeminal Nerve* This is important to speech. It is sensory to the muscles of the face and tongue, and it is motor to the muscles of chewing. It has three great divisions, the ophthalmic, maxillary, and mandibular. The sensory ophthalmic innervates the nose, orbit, forehead, and cranium. The sensory maxillary inner-vates the upper row of teeth, the upper lips, and the cheek. The mandibular is

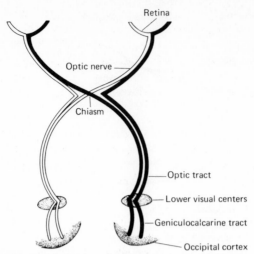

Figure 4-6 The neurons and their manner of crossing in the optic tract.

sensory from the teeth and skin of the lower jaw and also from the skin on the side of the cranium; it sends motor fibers to the muscles of mastication while it receives proprioceptive impulses of movement from these muscles.

70

VI *Abducens Nerve* It passes as a motor nerve from the pons to a single eyeball muscle.

VII *Facial Nerve* It travels as a mixed nerve from the medulla; its sensory fibers innervate the taste buds of the anterior two-thirds of the tongue. Its main distribution is motor to the facial muscles of expression situated about the scalp, forehead, eyes, nose, and mouth. Lesions produce ipsilateral facial paralysis involving disorders of facial expression and movement. There may be faulty control of jaw movements in a motor-root involvement.

VIII *Auditory Nerve* This goes between the auditory and nonauditory labyrinth of the internal ear and the medulla. It has cochlear and vestibular divisions, and both sections are sensory. The former is for hearing, and the latter for postural reactions of the head. Lesions of the cochlear division lead to hearing defects. Lesions of the vestibular division lead to disturbances in bodily equilibrium and orientation in space.

IX *Glossopharyngeal Nerve* This is a mixed nerve of the medulla. Its motor branches innervate pharyngeal muscles. Lesions of these fibers produce variable degrees of paralysis of the palate, pharynx, and larynx. Its sensory branches include taste fibers from the root of the tongue as well as from the mucous membranes of the mouth and pharynx. Paralysis of sensory fibers affects taste and also proprioception of movements in the tongue root.

X *Vagus Nerve* This will be described in detail under laryngeal innervation. It is a mixed nerve from the medulla, supplying sensory and motor fibers to the vocal organs, pharynx, lungs, esophagus, alimentary canal, and the heart. The terminal branches to the larynx have crossed and uncrossed fibers. There are two great divisions which are pertinent to phonation, the superior and inferior laryngeal nerves. Lesions of either trunk produce specific phonatory disorders.

XI *Spinal Accessory Nerve* This is a motor nerve from the medulla to the palate, neck muscles, and trapezius. It has a cranial branch which joins the superior laryngeal and pharyngeal branches of the vagus. It also has a spinal branch to the sternocleidomastoid muscle, and this branch joins with cervical nerves. Impairment of muscle action following lesions in this nerve leads to faulty articulation and to difficulty with guttural sounds.

XII *Hypoglossal Nerve* This is a motor nerve from the medulla to the muscles of the tongue. The upper motor neurons are chiefly crossed. The nerve also innervates muscles connecting the tongue with the mandible and hyoid bone. In lesions of the nerve the tongue deviates, and it may become paralyzed and atrophied. With failure to control the tongue many sounds are slurred.

Receptors

The sense organs are divided into exteroceptors, proprioceptors, and interoceptors. Exteroceptors respond to cutaneous stimuli. Proprioceptors carry information about the status of the body muscles and position in space. Interoceptors respond to conditions within the body. Textbooks of histology may be consulted for details of structure, and only the proprioceptors will be emphasized here.

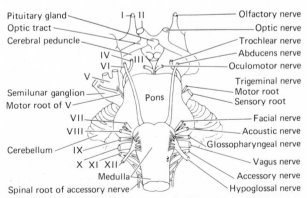

Figure 4-7 Ventral view of brain showing emergence of cranial nerves. (*By permission from J. G. Chusid and J. J. McDonald, Correlative Neuratomy and Functional Neurology, 13th ed., Lange Medical Publications, Los Altos, Calif., 1967.*)

NUMBER, NAME, SENSORY OR MOTOR TYPE	LOCUS OF EXIT FROM SKULL	STRUCTURES SUPPLIED BY AFFERENT FIBERS (FUNCTION)	STRUCTURES SUPPLIED BY EFFERENT FIBERS (FUNCTION)	POSSIBLE GENERAL EFFECTS OF A LESION
I—Olfactory, sensory	Cribriform plate	Mucosa of upper third of nose (smell)	None	Impairment or loss of sense of smell
II—Optic, sensory	Optic foramen	Retina (vision)	None	Dysfunction of pupil; blindness; hemianopsia; word blindness
III—Oculomotor, motor	Supraorbital fissure	Superior rectus; medial rectus; inferior rectus; inferior oblique; levator palpebrae; (proprioception)	Same eye muscles (eyeball movements); ciliary muscle (accommodation); iris muscles (pupillary movements)	Paralysis impairs eyeball movements or focusing or light reflex
IV—Trochlear, motor	Supraorbital fissure	Superior oblique (proprioception)	Superior oblique (eyeball movement downward and outward)	Paralysis impairs muscle function and proper directional movement of eyeball
V—Trigeminal, mixed	Ophthalmic from supraorbital fissure; maxillary from foramen rotundum; mandibular from foramen ovale	Skin of anterior half of scalp and of face; mucous membranes of structures in head; general sensation from anterior two-thirds of tongue; pain from cornea of eye; reflexes involving lacrimal gland; sensations from teeth; proprioception from muscles of mastication	Muscles of mastication (chewing and speech articulation)	Neuritis or neuralgic pains; facial hemiatrophy; faulty control of mandibular movements
VI—Abducens, motor	Supraorbital fissure	Lateral rectus (proprioception)	Lateral rectus (eyeball movement, primarily outward)	Impairment of outward movement of eyeball

72

NUMBER, NAME, SENSORY OR MOTOR TYPE	LOCUS OF EXIT FROM SKULL	STRUCTURES SUPPLIED BY AFFERENT FIBERS (FUNCTION)	STRUCTURES SUPPLIED BY EFFERENT FIBERS (FUNCTION)	POSSIBLE GENERAL EFFECTS OF A LESION
VII—Facial, mixed	Internal auditory canal; stylomastoid foramen	Mimetic musculature (proprioception); taste receptors of anterior two-thirds of tongue (taste)	Muscles of expression (movements); lacrimal system (secretion of tears); submaxillary and sublingual glands (secretion of saliva)	Facial paralysis; Bell's palsy; hemiplegia; dysarthria; speech disorders; impairment of secretory fluid production and delivery
VIII—Auditory, sensory	Internal auditory canal for cochlear and vestibular branches	Cochlea for the cochlear branch (hearing); utricle, saccule, and semicircular canals for vestibular branch (equilibrium)	None	Impairment of hearing; disturbance of postural equilibrium
IX—Glosso-pharyngeal, mixed	Jugular foramen	Taste buds of posterior third of tongue (taste); mucous membranes of posterior third of tongue, pharynx, soft palate, tonsils (swallowing); carotid sinus (control of blood pressure)	Muscles of pharynx (swallowing); parotid gland (secretion of saliva)	Paralysis affects taste, possible sensory loss from root of tongue; palsy of palate, pharynx, and larynx, depending upon nature and extent of the injury
X—Vagus, mixed	Jugular foramen	Mucous membranes of larynx, trachea, bronchi (respiratory reflexes); lungs (stretch reflexes to control respiration); arch of aorta (reflex inhibition of heart); stomach (hunger)	Muscles of palate, pharynx, esophagus (swallowing); muscles of larynx (phonation); muscle of heart (inhibition); muscles of respiratory tree (constriction); glands of stomach, pancreas, intestines	In superior laryngeal paralysis there is inability of the vocal folds to tense; voice low and unsteady; anesthesia of the upper larynx and epiglottis may occur; in recurrent nerve paralysis there is loss of adduction or

73

NUMBER, NAME, SENSORY OR MOTOR TYPE	LOCUS OF EXIT FROM SKULL	STRUCTURES SUPPLIED BY AFFERENT FIBERS (FUNCTION)	STRUCTURES SUPPLIED BY EFFERENT FIBERS (FUNCTION)	POSSIBLE GENERAL EFFECTS OF A LESION
			(secretion of fluids)	abduction; there may be defects in tensing or relaxing or loss of sphincteric action
XI—Spinal accessory, motor	Jugular foramen	Palate and neck muscles, trapezius (proprioception)	Muscles of palate, trapezius, sternocleidomastoid (movements)	Impairment of action of muscles, depending upon nature and extent of injury; faulty articulation and difficulty with guttural sounds
XII—Hypoglossal, motor	Hypoglossal foramen	Muscles of tongue (proprioception)	Muscles of tongue and those connecting tongue with mandible and hyoid bone (movements)	Tongue deviates and may become paralyzed and atrophied; palatine paresis; many sounds are slurred

Receptors, or end organs, act as transducers, converting one form of energy into another. If a muscle is stretched, a local current is set up. Mechanical energy is converted into electrical energy, the generator current. This does not become a nerve impulse but triggers it when the generator current reaches the first node of Ranvier in the axonic part of the neuron. Once the nerve impulse begins, it is all-or-none, and this is independent of the intensity of the generator current. The generator current, however, is graded in intensity to the strength of the mechanical stimulus. This is reflected in the nerve impulse as an increase in the frequency but not in the amplitude of the action currents.

Proprioceptors

Stretching a muscle produces a contraction which tends to restore the muscle to its previous length. This is one aspect of the so-called stretch (proprioceptive) reflex, and it involves receptors called muscle spindles (proprioceptors), which react by generating action potentials. These receptors thus behave as transducers that measure muscle length. They minimize the changes in muscle length produced by forces such as gravity.

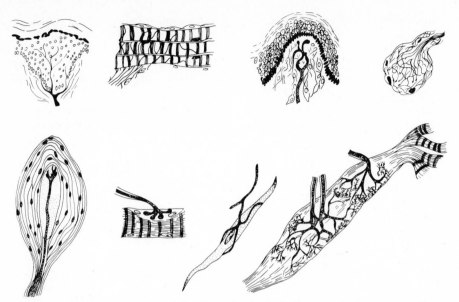

Figure 4-8 Some varieties of peripheral terminations of afferent and efferent nerve fibers: (*a*) "free termination" in epithelium (*after Retzius*); (*b*) Krause's corpuscle from conjunctiva (*after Dogiel*); (*c*) Meissner's corpuscle from skin (*after Dogiel*); (*d*) Pacinian corpuscle (*after Ruffini*); (*e*) termination upon tendon sheath (*Huber and DeWitt*); (*f*) neuromuscular spindle (*after Dogiel*); (*g*) motor termination upon smooth muscle fiber; (*h*) motor end plate on skeletal muscle fiber (*after Bohm and von Dabidoff*). (*From L. F. Edwards, Concise Anatomy, 2d ed. Copyright 1956. McGraw-Hill Book Company. Used by permission.*)

75

There is an additional proprioceptive feedback from tendon receptors (Golgi tendon apparatus). The tendon spindle detects the stretch of a tendon (or measures the forces produced by the contracting fibers). The tendon spindle is less sensitive than the muscle spindle, and it responds to overloading, resulting in the inhibition of contraction, thus protecting the muscle and its tendon. In addition to the protective function, the tendon spindle is a transducer in a continuous feedback system that regulates muscle tension, just as the muscle spindle regulates muscle length (Mountcastle, 1968).

The two varieties of stretch receptors in muscles are claimed in most recent theories not to contribute to conscious proprioception; i.e., they do not give information about the position of a limb but function essentially for the subconscious control of muscles, in the ways stated above.

Muscle Spindles Although tendon spindles appear at the junctions of muscle fibers and their tendons and are in series with the contractile parts of the muscle, muscle spindles occur within the belly of a muscle, and being attached in parallel with the other muscle fibers, they are stretched whenever the muscle is stretched.

Muscle spindles are attached at both ends to the ordinary muscle fibers (which are called *extrafusal fibers*).

Each muscle spindle consists of a connective tissue sheath containing 2 to 10 thin muscle fibers called *intrafusal fibers*. These fibers attach to the sheaths of the surrounding extrafusal skeletal muscle fibers. At about the middle of the intrafusal fiber mass there is a nucleated region which is noncontractile but which stretches whenever the whole spindle stretches. This central region is enveloped by an *annulospiral receptor*, which discharges into a nerve fiber that goes to the spinal cord.

There is a second type of receptive device within the muscle spindle. Termed a *flower-spray receptor*, it lies on either side of the annulospiral receptor. The flower-spray mechanism excites its own type of afferent nerve fiber.

The stimulus that usually sets off the muscle spindle is the stretch of its middle section. When the muscle stretches, the annulospiral endings respond quickly and then adapt. The flower-spray endings, however, respond only to far greater degrees of stretch or deformation.

Alpha and Gamma Motor Systems The response of the muscle involves two kinds of efferent neurons. One kind is the *alpha* fiber to the extrafusal fibers of the muscle. One such nerve fiber may control 100 to 300 extrafusal muscle fibers, and

76

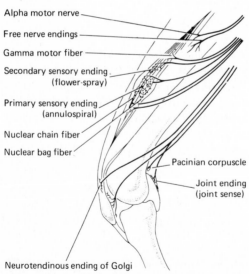

Alpha motor nerve
Free nerve endings
Gamma motor fiber
Secondary sensory ending (flower-spray)
Primary sensory ending (annulospiral)
Nuclear chain fiber
Nuclear bag fiber
Pacinian corpuscle
Joint ending (joint sense)
Neurotendinous ending of Golgi

Figure 4-9 Nerve endings in voluntary muscles, tendons, and joints. The muscle spindle. (*From C. R. Noback, The Human Nervous System. Copyright 1967. McGraw-Hill Book Company. Used by permission.*)

this constitutes a *motor unit*. A second kind of neuron is the *gamma* fiber. This innervates the intrafusal muscle fibers within the muscle spindle. Almost one-third of all motor fibers to muscle are gamma in type.

In function, the annulospiral endings respond to muscle stretch and discharge into their specific afferent systems which reach the spinal cord. In return, the gamma efferent fibers send impulses back directly to the intrafusal fibers within the muscle spindle. The two end sections of the intrafusal fibers contract and decrease the length of the spindle. This in turn excites the annulospiral, or flower-spray, endings, and they fire again, sustaining the contraction. Thus, the gamma motor nerves change the length of the muscle spindle. The feedback to the cord adjusts the length of the surrounding mass of muscle to the length of the spindle. The muscle spindle thus functions as a comparator.

The system just described is a servomechanism and is adjunctive to the efferent alpha nerve fiber. The separate purpose of the alpha system, which begins in large spinal ventral horn cells, is to bring about muscle contraction of the main mass of extrafusal muscle fibers and to do this without regard to limits of action. The gamma system is more regulatory, and the muscle is made to contract to a predetermined length. Muscles thus have two distinct types of neural control mechanisms.

Information from the tendons involving tension and the reflex responses thereto utilize mechanisms very similar to those of the muscle spindles. Tension control is a modifier of length regulation and compensates for imperfections occurring in the system.

These so-called *stretch reflexes* are essential to maintain muscle tone without voluntary direction.

The Spinal Cord

The spinal cord is a center of reflex activity and also a region for the transmission of impulses to and from the brain.

External and Internal Structure

The true nervous part of the cord extends from the foramen magnum at the base of the skull to the first lumbar vertebra at the small of the back, a distance of about 18 in. Although the cord is so shortened that it does not extend through the whole length of the vertebral column, the spinal nerves maintain their intervertebral exit positions, so that the lowest nerves continue vertically inside the neural canal for some distance before emerging. This produces a horsetail appearance, called the cauda equina, at the hind end of the cord. Only the upper nerves leave the cord at right angles; the lower ones exit at increasingly acute angles. The non-nervous continuation of the cord, which ties it down to the lowest vertebrae, or coccyx, is called the filum terminale.

The cord has the same sheaths as the brain. These are the outer dura mater, the middle arachnoid membrane, and the inner pia mater. Cerebrospinal fluid flows within the subarachnoid spaces.

There is a gross swelling at the level of the arms and of the legs. These cervicobrachial and lumbrosacral enlargements are associated with the increased nerve supply to the limbs. In these regions the ventral roots of the segmented nerves form an interlacing network, or plexus, so that the nerves which exit have a complex composition. The respiratory and some other muscles active in speech are energized from branches of the cervical and brachial plexes.

A transverse section at any level of the spinal cord shows its internal structure. The gray or nuclear matter is internal and arranged like the letter H with a dorsal and a ventral horn in each half of the cord. Each horn is cross-connected by a transverse gray band. The center of this band contains a central canal which is continuous with the brain ventricles. The white matter forms columns, or funiculi, which are dorsal (posterior), lateral, and ventral (anterior). Within each funiculus there are tracts whose fibers have the same origin and ending and fasciculi which contain fibers belonging to two or more tracts.

The tracts are ascending or descending, and they may be long or short. The short tracts begin and end in the cord and are ascending, descending, or mixed. The short tracts connect the activities of one spinal segment with another, and they are association tracts, or ground bundles. The long tracts connect the brain and the

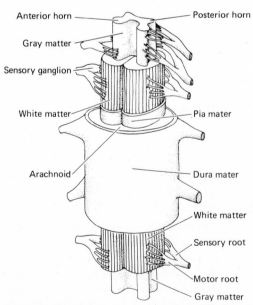

Figure 4-10 The layers and sheaths of the spinal cord.

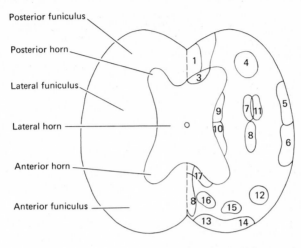

Posterior funiculus

Posterior horn

Lateral funiculus

Lateral horn

Anterior horn

Anterior funiculus

Figure 4-11 Diagrammatic section of the spinal cord showing the major ascending and descending tracts.

1. Goll	7. Lateral corticospinal	13. Ventral spinothalamic
2. Burdach	8. Rubrospinal	14. Vestibulospinal
3. Posterior ground bundle	9. Lateral ground bundle	15. Ventral reticulospinal
4. Lissauer	10. Lateral spinothalamic	16. Tectospinal
5. Flechsig	11. Lateral reticulospinal	17. Anterior ground bundle
6. Gowers	12. Olivospinal	18. Direct corticospinal

cord, but they also contain individual fibers which are actually short association neurons.

The Ascending Spinal Pathways

The sensations synthesized in the brain are either general or special. General sensations include such modalities as pain, heat, cold, touch, and proprioception. Special sensations include vision, hearing, taste, and smell. Each modality is carried from its own distinct peripheral sense organ through specific pathways in the spinal cord and brain up to its cortical terminus.

There are various levels of termination so that all impulses generated from the receptors do not reach consciousness but establish lower reflex connections for essential but unconscious bodily reactions to the stimulus. Many reflexes operate through a localized segmental level of the cord, as do the stretch reflexes.

The ascending spinal pathways carry general sense impulses. Those for special senses are carried by cranial nerves.

Cutaneous Senses

The sensations include touch and pressure, pain, hot, and cold. Several histologic kinds of receptors are involved. Those for pain are free nerve endings. The receptor for heat is Ruffini's end organ, and that for cold is Krause's end bulb. The touch and pressure receptors include Meissner's corpuscles, hair end organs, and other less-defined terminations.

The first-order neurons for discriminative touch travel up the dorsal columns of Goll and Burdach to reach the hindbrain. Then second-order neurons decussate and travel up as the internal arcuate fibers of the medial lemniscus. The lemniscus terminates in the thalamus. From there, third-order neurons reach the somesthetic (parietal) cortex. This is the pathway for general touch sensation, touch localization, and two-point discrimination (of compass points).

Cruder impulses for touch and pressure are sent up a few segments by the tract of Lissauer in the posterolateral funiculus, then pass across the cord to the ventral spinothalamic tract. This tract intermingles with the medial lemniscus and reaches the thalamus. The thalamic radiations in turn pass to the somesthetic cortex.

Pain, heat, and cold impulses are transmitted a few segments up the tract of Lissauer. Then they decussate to enter the lateral spinothalamic tract. This tract also joins the medial lemniscus and reaches the thalamus. The final thalamic radiation goes to the somesthetic cortex.

Proprioception

Deep receptors, called proprioceptors, include muscle spindles, Golgi tendon spindles, and the Pacinian corpuscles located between muscles and around the joints. These receptors respond to stretch or deformation.

The first-order neurons travel to the hindbrain. The second-order fibers decussate and are found in the internal arcuate system of the medial lemniscus. These terminate in the thalamus. The third-order neurons reach the somesthetic cerebral cortex.

By this route, which carries information about deep pressure and muscular sensibility, we recognize the position of our muscles and the extent of their movements. Stereognosis is the sensation that results when the tridimensional qualities of a stimulus are perceived. This sensation is also described as conscious proprioception.

The dorsal columns mediate still other sensations. We perceive the rapid oscillations of a tuning fork (vibration sense) through these fibers.

Some of the muscle impulses from the proprioceptive end organs, including some impulses from the speech musculature, go primarily to the cerebellum. These nonsensory afferent impulses travel ipsilaterally in the tracts of Flechsig and of Gowers (dorsal and ventral spinocerebellar tracts). Some of the nonsensory afferent impulses ascend to the cerebellum in the external arcuate system, which contains ipsilateral fibers originating in the columns of Burdach and of Goll. The cerebellar activity, which is described as unconscious proprioception, may serve to regulate the rapid and rhythmic movements of the muscles.

The Descending Spinal Pathways

The afferent impulses are integrated in cerebral association areas for coordinated response. If we may set up a hypothetical model, we can postulate a master center of correlation, located in the angular gyrus of the cerebral cortex. It is situated at the approximate center of the association areas belonging to each of the general and special senses.

Impulses for the adaptive responses are sent from the angular centers to the ideomotor area just in front of it in the supramarginal gyrus of the dominant parietal lobe. This area quickly selects the course of action, although it is under the inhibitory influence of decisions formulated in the prefrontal lobe. The ideomotor area, once fully activated, works through the motor and premotor cortex.

The Corticospinal (Pyramidal) Tracts

These originate chiefly in the precentral motor cortex, area 4. Some of the fibers may begin in the premotor cortex (area 6) and even in the postcentral parietal region. Lassek (1939; 1940) dissected the human pyramidal tract and showed that the histologic units called Betz cells are not the only neurons making up the pyramidal system. Of approximately 1 million pyramidal fibers, there are only 25,000 to 30,000 Betz cells on each side.

81

Those pyramidal fibers which synapse with cranial nerve nuclei are called *corticobulbar,* and those which pass into the spinal cord are *corticospinal.* All the pyramidal fibers form a bundle running through an area called the internal capsule that is surrounded by the corpus striatum. At the upper end of the midbrain the corticobulbar fibers begin to separate from the internal capsule, and they synapse with the nuclei of the cranial nerves III, IV, and VI to the eyeball muscles. Some of the fiber bundles terminate in the basilar pons and are called *corticopontine* fibers.

The remainder of the corticobulbar fibers pass through the ventral, or motor, aspect of the crura and pons, and they course into the medulla, where they synapse with nuclei of cranial nerves V, VII, IX, X, XI, and XII. These fibers decussate to a variable extent at the level of the nuclei they supply. The corticobulbar tract has an important control over the speech muscles of the head and neck through the intermediation of the cranial nerves.

The greater corticospinal tract descends to the pyramids of the medulla where 80 percent or more of the fibers decussate to form the lateral corticospinal tract. The remaining fibers continue ipsilaterally down the anterior funiculus of the cord as the anterior corticospinal tract. There is considerable decussation even in the ipsilateral tract so that for the most part one side of the brain controls the other side of the body. The anterior tract does not pass below the thoracic cord. At every level of the cord the fibers of the lateral tract synapse upon internuncial neurons. The pyramidal (corticospinal) fibers constitute the upper motor neuron whereas the anterior horn cell and its axonal nerve fiber form the lower motor neuron. It takes two neurons in this total path to innervate the muscle effectors.

The pyramidal fibers give the energy for contraction. This is expressed in the form of isolated, delicate, and graded movements. If the upper motor pyramidal neuron is interrupted, the muscles go into flaccid (atonic) paralysis. The pyramidal fibers must normally have a tonic or facilitative effect upon the spinal centers. This facilitation is not powerful; if area 4 is destroyed along with suppressor area 4-S, the muscles become spastic. Even following a simple hypotonia associated with an area 4 lesion, spasticity may develop, suggesting that the motor organization is more complicated than the conventional views hold.

A flaccid paralysis is produced when the lower motor neuron circuit is interrupted. This is caused by the loss of nerve impulses from the nutritive central motor nuclei. A progressing peripheral, or Wallerian, degeneration follows.

The Extrapyramidal Tracts

The premotor cortex works chiefly through the basal ganglia and the extrapyramidal tracts. It also sends into the motor area impulses which excite the Betz cells and the associated nuclei. In this way it influences the motor area. Both premotor and motor cortex are necessary in skilled movements. The premotor area establishes the background for activity in the muscles by putting them into a correct postural pattern, and the motor cortex provides the delicate adaptive movements. The premotor cortex controls groups rather than individual muscles. Such suppressor areas as 4-S, 8-S, and others in the premotor cortex inhibit muscles. In this way activity such as respiratory movements can be suppressed with demand during phonation.

There are many descending routes from the premotor cortex and basal ganglia, and any estimate of their relative importance is still tentative. All the tracts taking part in this system are called extrapyramidal. Until recently the *rubrospinal* tract was thought to be of considerable significance. This tract originates in the red nucleus into which impulses funnel from the cerebellum and upper basal ganglia. It then crosses over in the pons and descends through the lateral cord to the sacrum, and it synapses at every level with the anterior horn cells.

The reticular formation of the brainstem and the *reticulospinal* tract have assumed an increasing importance. A considerable number of frontal cortex fibers end in the reticular formation. There is an uncrossed reticulospinal tract in the anterior funiculus and a crossed one in the lateral funiculus. Before the motor cortex energizes a muscle, inhibitory impulses are sent down through the reticular substance to the cord to suppress the segmental facilitation which could disturb the proposed motion. The reticular formation also contains centers for facilitation, which, on occasion, increase the excitability of the anterior horn cells. The red nucleus may work chiefly through the reticular formation by way of the rubro-reticular tract.

The *vestibulospinal* tract lies chiefly in the anterior cord, and it runs ipsilaterally from the vestibular nucleus down to the sacrum. It adjusts the body muscles to postural changes first occurring in the head.

The *tectospinal* tract runs contralaterally from the midbrain to the thoracic region in the anterior cord. It is a path from the retina and the auditory receptors to the muscles of the head and neck.

The *olivospinal* tract in the lateral cord runs from the inferior olivary nucleus to the cervical cord. It is of uncertain function.

Just as there is a corticobulbar separation from the corticospinal fiber system, so the extrapyramidal tracts tend to project to the motor neurons of the brainstem as well as to those of the spinal cord.

The Separateness of the Descending Tracts

The discussion above, which seems to dichotomize the pyramidal and extrapyramidal systems, may need some reevaluation. Peele (1961) says that many cerebral cortical areas are probably associated in part with extrapyramidal activity. Area 4 is said to supply extrapyramidal fibers which descend with the pyramidal tract in the internal capsule and the pyramidal system in the brainstem (Ochs, 1965). This explains the fact that a "stroke" which occurs following a lesion in the internal capsule may be associated with marked *spasticity*.

Meyers (1955; 1956) questions the conventional view that voluntary movements are the unique function of the pyramidal system. He challenges the concept of the dichotomy of the pyramidal and extrapyramidal tracts, stating that their separateness has never been operationally demonstrable. He also states that the composition of the pyramidal tract or system is for the most part unknown. Moreover, he objects to equating voluntary phasic activities with the pyramidal tract and involuntary tonic-postural behavior with the extrapyramidal system.

We are actually in an era of revolutionary thought in neurology. Bucy (1957) asserts that there is no single pyramidal tract arising in the precentral gyrus which is responsible for the control of voluntary muscular activity. The origin of many of the pyramidal fibers is in doubt, and probably not all the fibers originate in the cerebral cortex. Bucy urges that the term pyramidal tract and the concept which it represents should both be discarded. Instead of a pyramidal system there are fibers of diverse origin passing from the brain to the spinal cord. He seems to be even more opposed to the concept of the existence of an extrapyramidal system. This is said to have no unity whatsoever except that it is not a part of the pyramidal system. Even the term premotor cortex may have to be discarded. There is some evidence that it does not give the cumbersome mass movements described in the literature. It has also been stated by Schaltenbrand and Woolsey (1964) that we can no longer think of a motor area and a premotor area, or of an area 4 related to a pyramidal tract and an area 6 related to an extrapyramidal system. All these systems exist but perhaps should not be related to separate parts of the precentral motor cortex.

The Reflex Arc

The reflex arc is the basic unit of neural function, and it brings about a response to a stimulus, always mediated through the central nervous system except for axon reflexes.

The reflex arc contains (1) a receptor; (2) an afferent neuron; (3) a synaptic connection, at least in the anterior, or ventral, gray horn of the cord; (4) an efferent neuron whose cell body is in the anterior gray horn of the cord; (5) an effector; and (6) a collateral fiber to connect with cells that inhibit antagonistic muscles.

Very few reflexes are localized to a single spinal segment (monosynaptic reflexes). In the knee kick, a common example, it appears that only one synapse is involved. If the entering impulses are not confined to their segmental level but ascend to reach the cerebrum or any other brain area in which they can attain consciousness, the afferent neuron or impulse is called sensory. Impulses not producing consciousness are nonsensory. If the outgoing impulses energize a muscle, the efferent neuron is motor. Using this terminology, secretory fibers activate glands, vasomotor fibers regulate the caliber of blood vessels, and so on.

Reflexes intermediated through centers in the spinal cord are relatively fixed in character, and they function as though an operational groove or "path of least resistance" between the receptor and effector had been laid down constitutionally in the cord. Such reflexes are unlearned or unconditioned. They are not com-

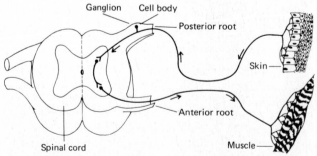

Figure 4-12 A reflex arc showing afferent and efferent neurons and an internuncial connector. Classical concept.

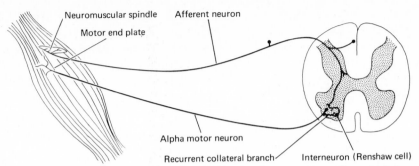

Neuromuscular spindle   Afferent neuron

Motor end plate

Alpha motor neuron

Recurrent collateral branch   Interneuron (Renshaw cell)

Figure 4-13 The knee jerk. This is an example of an extensor reflex which involves a two-neuron path, utilizing transmission on the same side, within a single segment of the spinal cord. Impulses generated in the annulospiral ending of the muscle spindle travel up the afferent neuron. The integrated central response uses the alpha motor neuron to the muscle, via the motor end plate.

pletely fixed, since they may be reinforced (facilitated) or inhibited (suppressed) with circumstances.

Inhibition is an important property of reflex conduction, especially reciprocal inhibition in which the afferent neurons so dichotomize (divide) that they may excite certain motor neurons while inhibiting their immediate antagonists. In this way purposeful behavior is obtained. If we energize the elevator muscles of the mandible or the hyoid bone, we should inhibit the antagonistic depressors. If we abduct (open) the vocal folds, we should inhibit the adductor (closing) action.

85

Through reciprocal innervation, muscle proprioceptors modulate the speed of a movement and produce smoothness in the effort. There is an explosiveness to muscle contraction in the ataxia of tabes dorsalis, where proprioceptive impulses are not transmitted.

The Internuncial System of the Cord
Internuncial cells and their associated synaptic junctions are important elements of the reflex arc and explain much of central behavior.

For one thing, the internuncial system provides for convergence of motor discharges from diverse sources. Along with the anterior motoneurons, this system is the final level for integration of all the motor impulses.

There is in the gray matter of the cord a set of internuncial cells called *Renshaw cells*. Certain impulses entering the gray matter may be directed into collaterals of motor neurons and travel from them to the dendrites of the Renshaw cells in the medial part of the anterior gray horn. The Renshaw cells in turn send axons to motor neurons which are inhibitory to those muscles which are the antagonists in a reaction. This provides for reciprocal inhibition and orderliness of action, already described above.

Stretch (Myotactic) Reflex

This has been considered before, implicating the annulospiral and flower-spray endings in the spindles as the proprioceptive end organs and the alpha and gamma efferents as the motor neurons. The alpha neurons energize the main muscle mass, and the gamma neurons change the tension on the slack intrafusal muscle fibers, which allows the proprioceptive end organs to fire again.

The stimulation of proprioceptors in a muscle or tendon sends impulses into a localized segment of the central nervous system, and the impulses returning through the motor neurons increase the tone of the same muscle. By this action a muscle responds adaptively to any force which tends to stretch it or to change its shape. The tension so imparted to the muscles through their segmental spinal nerve centers is ordinarily regulated by central fibers that come down from higher centers to synapse upon the cell bodies of the motor neurons (final common path).

The muscles are able to send back to the central nervous system from their proprioceptors information concerning their tensions and positions in space. This is the principle of feedback, whose essential machinery is the stretch reflex and whose governing centers are, to an appreciable extent, below the cerebrum, making these reflexes basically unconscious. The speech muscles are examples of such reflex machines. Much of speech is automatic or self-regulating, although always susceptible to diversional or antagonistic influences from many sources. Thus, speech is readily subject to interruptions and breakdowns, particularly in central disturbances of an emotional nature.

There is a difference in the intensity of the stretch reflex according to the nature of the stimulation. A sudden increase in stretch causes a powerful reaction, called

86

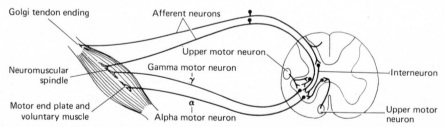

Figure 4-14 Gamma reflex loop. Following the phasic extensor reflex, continuous stretch of the extensor muscles is sustained by activities in a gamma reflex loop. This loop includes the gamma motor neuron, muscle spindle, afferent neuron, alpha motor neuron, and muscle. Upper motor neurons facilitate gamma neurons, causing intrafusal spindle muscles to contract. This stretches structures of the muscle spindle bag region such that afferent neurons discharge into the cord. In response, the alpha motor neurons maintain extensor fiber contraction. The Golgi tendon endings monitor the increasing tension and in turn discharge via the central nervous system into inhibitory (interneuron) fibers of the alpha motor neuron pool. This inhibits the excitatory effects of the gamma loop, thus promoting integration and timing.

the *phasic stretch reflex*. A slow, continuous stretch is followed by weak reaction, called the *tonic stretch reflex*. Subsequent to a sudden shortening of a muscle, the stretch reflex becomes involved in relaxing the muscle tone and preventing further shortening. This is brought about by a decrease in the rate of stimulation of the annulospiral end organ of the muscle spindle. The spindle adapts to the smaller length, and the tone reappears. This is known as the shortening reaction. The stretch reflex thus has the function of damping abrupt changes in muscle length. A smooth movement results.

Stretch reflexes are used to evaluate the degree of facilitation in the centers. An increase in facilitatory impulses produces exaggerated responses, and a decrease causes weakening or loss of the stretch reflexes.

If a muscle is suddenly stretched and the stretching force is sustained, stretch reflexes involving the cord can produce more phasic contractions in the muscle. The repeated oscillations of the effector are known as *clonus*. Observation of clonus indicates the degree of facilitation that is occurring.

The response of a muscle in continuing to contract following a single strong stretch stimulus has been known as *afterdischarge*. There are two reasonable explanations. For one thing, the branching of the afferent fibers may allow the impulses to travel at different times through paths containing many internuncial neurons. As a second possibility, some of the internuncial neurons form closed or reverberating circuits so that the impulses travel circularly through such neuron pools, firing at intervals into the motor neuron even after the afferent impulses have ceased to enter the cord. These reverberating or cybernetic circuits characterize every level of the central nervous system, and they are considered to be important in all kinds of behavior. Memory is an illustration of this in that we recall the same thought over and over again, implying that the nerve impulses traverse the same neuronal circuits repeatedly.

The state of the stretch reflex at any one time is seen to be the resultant of excitatory, facilitatory, and inhibitory forces. If there is partial or full obliteration of the stretch reflex by cumulative inhibitory action, a "clasp-knife" effect may be observed as follows. Upon attempting to flex a rigid extended joint in a human patient with spasticity, resistance is encountered throughout the initial part of the bending. Upon forcibly continuing to produce flexion the extensor muscles yield unduly, and then any degree of flexion can be put upon the joint. Because the stretched muscle elongates freely, this is a *lengthening reaction*.

Another example of altered inhibitory control over the stretch reflex is seen in "cogwheeling." In this reaction the limb does not offer resistance evenly throughout the full range of a passive movement but responds as a series of "catches and gives." There is a jerkiness sensed by the observer when he passively extends or flexes muscles at various joints. The neural mechanisms are uncertain but may involve the globus pallidus (Ruch and Fulton, 1960).

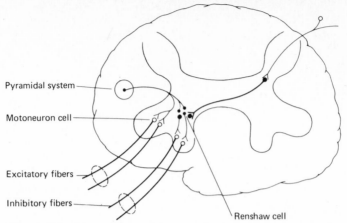

Pyramidal system

Motoneuron cell

Excitatory fibers

Inhibitory fibers

Renshaw cell

Figure 4-15 Cross section of spinal cord showing motoneurons and Renshaw cells and indicating how excitation or inhibition are produced by the efferent alpha motor system.

Spasticity is another distinct state, claimed to indicate a release of the segmental stretch reflex. The exaggeration is expressed as an increase in muscle tension, an increase in resistance to manipulation, clonus, and a lowered threshold of the spinal stretch reflex.

In the classical view, spasticity in cerebral palsy may occur because the higher centers no longer brake the relatively intense activity of the segmental stretch reflexes. Antagonists do not relax when the agonists are active. Ruch and Fulton (1960) note, however, that in man the spinal reflexes are not intrinsically very strong. Therefore, for spasticity to develop, some facilitatory tract in the brainstem must remain functional following damage above and maintain the stretch reflexes. This could be the reticulospinal system.

The kinesthetic sensibility, which expresses for the stretch reflex the quantitative consciousness of the movement, position, and tension of muscles, has been investigated in the speech literature. Fairbanks and Bebout (1950) studied the amount of error in trying to duplicate a tongue position. College students with superior and inferior articulation showed no real differences. Earlier Patton (1942) had studied general body muscles and concluded that speech defectives have an inferior kinesthetic sensibility. Critchley (1967) notes that the initiation of words is based upon kinesthetic memory, in which various patterns of neuromuscular responses are elicited. Even in a deafened individual, a muscular memory for words remains.

Conditioned Reflexes

Many of the reflexes concerned in speech are not inherited but are conditioned or developed through associations. The conditioned reflexes involve the cerebrum primarily but not exclusively, since they have been produced in decorticate animals. These responses occur when an indifferent stimulus is given for a period of time along with the stimulus that ordinarily evokes a fixed response. The indifferent stimulus then becomes adequate to elicit the same response. Thus ringing a bell while placing food in the mouth soon causes salivation even when the bell is sounded in the absence of food. Man or animals can be progressively conditioned to respond only to a certain note. This selectivity requires an internal inhibition which is very slowly developed in the cortical and perhaps the subcortical regions.

All learning involves the conditioning of reflexes, and this includes the development of speech. In the historical origin of speech there are views implying that speech is primitively an unconditioned response, in that man spontaneously produces sounds through irregularities in respiratory movements when excited by external stimuli. The conditioning of speech is illustrated in man when he begins to make sounds for directive purposes. Given environmental symbols become associated with specific sounds.

In the development of a single individual, the random or aimless activities occurring in the speech apparatus progressively drop out. The child can express what it wishes, using the neuromuscular machinery with increasing efficiency until all the essential reflexes become automatic and subconscious. The random unconditioned responses that first elicit the sounds occur in the tongue, lips, jaws, throat, and respiratory system. Such chance sounds come to be associated with success in the fulfillment of needs. If the sound when given alone also obtains a successful result, the stage is set to use it independently of the other generalized bodily activity previously employed.

The Brain

All levels of the central nervous system do not equally receive the impulses for speech or equally control the expressive mechanisms of speech. The centers of seemingly greatest importance are in the highest level, or cerebrum, but there are diverse adjunctive subcortical regions of considerable regulatory importance.

Developmental Anatomy
The neural tube is derived from the ectoderm. This is first seen in the eighteenth embryonic day as a thickening to form a neural plate along the midline of the future back. In the head region the ectoderm thickens and forms the placodes, or primordia, of the organs of special sense.

The neural plate elongates, and its lateral margins rise to form the neural folds. By continuation of this process, the elevated margins grow medially to meet and fuse in the midline. Thus, the neural tube is produced, initially at the cervical level, and then progressing cranially and caudally until it is closed over fully near the end of the first month. The tube then becomes depressed below the surface. Its cavity forms the ventricles of the brain and the central canal of the spinal cord.

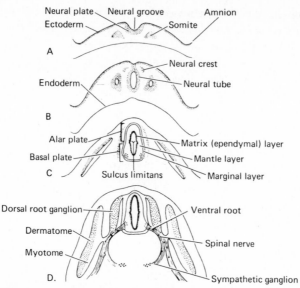

Figure 4-16 Development of the spinal cord, neural crests, and spinal nerves in human embryos of (*a*) about nineteen days; (*b*) about twenty days; (*c*) about twenty-six days; and (*d*) about one month of age. (*From C. R. Noback, The Human Nervous System. Copyright 1967. McGraw-Hill Book Company. Used by permission.*)

90

By the close of the first month the cranial end of the tube has formed the primordium of the brain, seen as three vesicles, prosencephalon, mesencephalon and rhombencephalon, which will eventually form the forebrain, midbrain, and hindbrain, respectively.

A layer of cells, called the matrix or ependymal layer, which lines the central canal, proliferates mitotically and forms neuroblasts and glioblasts. The neuroblasts differentiate into neurons. Those from the basal region develop into lower motor neurons to muscles and glands.

At the original junction of the ectoderm of the skin and the edges of the neural plate, a paired column of cells called the neural crests differentiate. These cells produce neuroblasts which will form afferent (dorsal root) neurons and their processes.

Neuroblasts from both the neural crest and the basal plate migrate outward from the neural tube and on each side form ganglia of the autonomic nervous system. These retain a connection, called the preganglionic fiber, with the neural tube (central nervous system).

Other cells of the neural crest form satellite cells of the ganglia and neurilemma cells of the peripheral nerves.

By the sixth week of embryonic life the prosencephalon has divided to a telencephalon and diencephalon. The rhombencephalon has divided to a metencephalon and myelencephalon.

The brain then changes from a five-vesicle tubular form to a complex and contorted form. This occurs by flexures, by differential enlargements, by growth of the cerebral hemispheres caudally to cover over most other structures, and by formation of convolutions in the cerebrum and folia in the cerebellum. The ultimate form of the brain is outlined by the close of the third month.

The cerebral hemispheres develop from the telencephalon. The sylvian fissure is seen in the third month, and the cortical lobes develop rapidly thereafter, the temporal lobe being the slowest. The rolandic, calcarine and parietooccipital sulci are seen in the fifth month, and the main gyri and sulci are prominent in the seventh month.

The motor and sensory areas, in front of and behind the rolandic fissure, respectively, are differentiated during the fifth and sixth months, and the cerebral cortex expands at this time. A cortex having six depth layers is recognizable by the seventh month. The pyramidal cells appear in the third month.

The ventricles of the brain, which are derived as modifications of its lumen, develop simultaneously with the tube itself. The cranial nerves, except for the olfactory and optic, are present by the sixth week.

91

The white fibers below the cortex begin to acquire myelin in the fifth month, and this process continues during the eighteenth to the thirtieth postnatal months, varying with the location of the fibers. At term, the brain has a gelatinous consistency because some of the somatic afferent tracts in the subcortical white matter are unmyelinated. At two years of age the brain is firmer, and the relative proportions of its subdivisions are similar to those of the adult.

The brain of the neonate is about 10 percent of the body weight whereas it is about 2 percent in the adult. The absolute weight increases from about 350 g to about 1,000 g at the close of the first year. The brain weighs about 1,380 g (48.6 oz) in the adult male and 1,250 g (44 oz) in the adult female. There is rapid growth to the fifth year and a practical cessation of growth after the twentieth year. The brain loses weight in old age. The number of neurons at birth progressively decreases. Noback (1967) cites an estimate of 50,000 neurons lost daily from twenty to seventy years of age.

After development, the forebrain includes such structures as the cerebral hemispheres and their commissures, the first, second, and third ventricles, the corpus striatum, thalamus, and hypothalamus.

The midbrain, which is the smallest of the three vesicles, includes among its important bodies the corpora quadrigemina, red nuclei, substantia nigra, cerebral peduncles, and cerebral aqueduct.

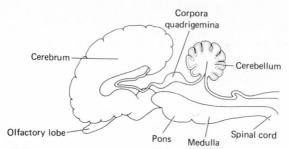

Figure 4·17 Diagram of major structures developed from the three embryonic brain vesicles.

The hindbrain contains in its anterior section the cerebellum above and the pons varolii below. It contains in its posterior section the medulla oblongata (bulb) and the fourth ventricle.

Blood Supply of the Brain

The blood supply to the brain is of practical interest to the speech pathologist. As Brain (1965) observes, the location of a lesion within the cerebral hemisphere influences the prognosis of certain conditions, such as aphasia. In the instances of "Broca's aphasia" and "pure word dumbness" the prognosis is better with increasing distance of a vascular lesion from the central fissure. Brain used the term *pure word dumbness* to indicate an apraxic anarthria and *Broca's aphasia* to indicate a predominantly expressive, cortical motor (or verbal) aphasia.

The internal carotid artery ascends to enter the base of the skull at the level of the optic chiasm. It then branches to anterior and middle cerebral arteries.

The anterior cerebral artery supplies the medial aspect of the frontal lobe and also the medial aspect of the brain to the preoccipital notch and then travels superiorly over the brain surface.

The middle cerebral artery supplies the basal aspect of the frontal lobe and the frontal portion of the temporal lobe. It travels in the fissure of Sylvius and is distributed profusely over the lateral aspects of the frontal, parietal, and temporal lobes. A branch of the middle vessel, the lenticulostriate artery, goes to the basal ganglia and internal capsule. This is an "artery of sudden death" in that it may rupture, especially in a hypertensive individual. A contralateral paralysis, or hemiplegia, often follows such rupture. This can involve the muscles participating in the expressive aspects of speech.

The carotid system ascending anteriorly is supplemented by the vertebral arteries, which branch from the subclavians and ascend in the transverse processes of the upper six cervical vertebrae. Upon entering the skull through the foramen magnum, the vertebral arteries join to form the basilar artery. Just prior to this union the vertebral arteries produce the posterior inferior cerebellar artery.

The basilar artery travels forward within the skull and gives off anterior inferior cerebellar and superior cerebellar arteries. The basilar vessel then ends in the posterior cerebral artery, which supplies the inferior aspect of the temporal cortex and the medial aspects of the occipital and temporal lobes.

The carotid and vertebral systems fuse to a circular structure, called the circle of Willis, at the base of the brain, surrounding the optic chiasm and pituitary gland. This equalizes the distribution of blood in the brain. Also if one of the major arteries is destroyed, provision for blood flow is allowed through other vessels.

Cerebrospinal Fluid

The brain contains internal chambers called ventricles. The large lateral ventricles lie within the cerebral hemispheres. They connect with the third ventricle by the foramen of Monro, and the third connects with the fourth ventricle by the aqueduct of Sylvius. The fourth ventricle narrows and continues as the central canal through the spinal cord.

The brain and cord are covered by three connective tissue layers, called meninges. From outside in these are (1) the dura mater, or tough fibrous coat; (2) the arachnoid, a very thin, weblike membrane; and (3) the pia mater, a membrane intimately

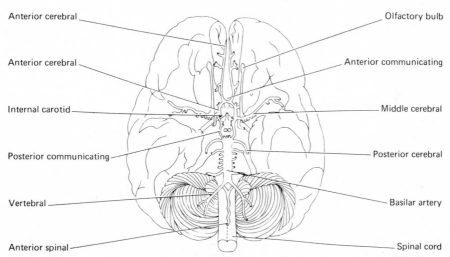

Anterior cerebral — Olfactory bulb

Anterior cerebral — Anterior communicating

Internal carotid — Middle cerebral

Posterior communicating — Posterior cerebral

Vertebral — Basilar artery

Anterior spinal — Spinal cord

Figure 4-18 The arterial circulation at the base of the brain. The circle of Willis. From this circle the anterior, middle, and posterior cerebral arteries supply the cerebral hemispheres. The anterior spinal artery goes to the cord.

adherent to the brain and cord. A relatively spacious area exists between the arachnoid and pia mater, called the subarachnoid space.

The cerebrospinal fluid flows within the entire neural canal system. The fluid is secreted ultimately from the blood which gains access to the ventricles by filtration and diffusion across specialized blood vessels called choroid plexes. The passage occurs especially into the lateral ventricles. All the substances of the blood plasma can gain access to the cerebrospinal fluid, although there are considerable differences in concentration.

The cerebrospinal fluid travels from the lateral ventricles via the foramina of Monro into the third ventricle and then through the aqueduct of Sylvius into the fourth ventricle.

The fourth ventricle is continuous with the central canal of the spinal cord, and it is also an area containing three foramina through which the fluid can gain access into the subarachnoid space. These are the medial foramen of Magendie and the two lateral foramina of Luschka.

Active circulation of the fluid ensues in the subarachnoid space, so that the liquid spreads over the entire surface of the brain and the cord. Eventually the excess fluid is drained back to the bloodstream by leaving the subarachnoid space through specialized arachnoid tufts and entering spaces called the dural venous sinuses, located in the outermost brain covering (dura mater). The fluid within these dural sinuses continuously drains downward and out of the skull and finally returns to the right side of the heart. The force behind the cerebral circulation is a continuous gradient of pressure between the capillaries at the formation and absorption

94

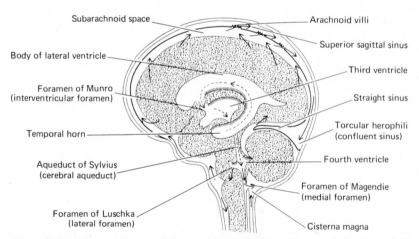

Figure 4-19 The circulation of the cerebrospinal fluid. (*By permission from J. T. Manter and A. J. Gatz, Clinical Neuroanatomy and Neurophysiology, 2d ed., F. A. Davis Company, Philadelphia, 1961.*)

sites. The normal pressure is 8 to 10 mm of mercury in the recumbent posture, and the volume at a given time is 100 to 120 ml.

The cerebrospinal fluid protects the brain against injury because of the external and internal water cushions. There is considerable evidence that it also has a nutritive function.

The cerebrospinal circulation is intimately related to many kinds of brain damage caused by fluid-pressure alterations or by fluid-volume and chemistry changes following infectious diseases. The consequence of such damage could be manifested as a disorder of symbolization or the general capacity to use language. In the condition called internal hydrocephalus, the foramina permitting passage of cerebrospinal fluid to the subarachnoid space are missing. In external hydrocephalus the villi leading to the arachnoid may be ill developed, so that fluid accumulates in the subarachnoid space.

The Cerebrum

Developmental Relationships
The cerebrum is the major derivative of the telencephalon, or anterior portion of the forebrain. It arises as lateral outgrowths that form the paired cerebral hemispheres. These become larger than all other parts of the brain, practically enclosing the other structures. Each hemisphere differentiates to a corpus striatum, olfactory lobe, and pallium. The corpus striatum is in the anterolateral region of the hemisphere. The olfactory lobe is an outgrowth of the floor in front of the corpus striatum, and it forms the smell brain, or rhinencephalon. The pallium constitutes the great remainder of the hemisphere, which differentiates to an outer cellular or gray layer called the cerebral cortex and an inner white or medullated nerve-fiber core called the medulla.

In the higher vertebrates the cerebrum forms a larger proportion of the central nervous system than it does in the lower forms. In animals that appear especially capable of learning, the cerebrum is relatively large.

Surface Topography
The paired cerebral hemispheres are almost completely separated by the longitudinal cerebral fissure. Each hemisphere has a lateral, medial, and inferior surface. The rostral tip is the frontal pole, and the caudal tip is the occipital pole. The temporal lobe has a projecting anterior tip called the temporal pole.

The surface of the cortex is increased in area by the formation of folds, or convolutions, and appear as hills, or gyri, and valleys, or sulci. The deep sulci are called fissures; the paired cerebral hemispheres are thus divided by the great longitudinal fissure. The fissures also subdivide each hemisphere into regions called lobes, which are useful in the rough localization of structures and functions. The frontal lobe is anterior to the fissure of Rolando (central sulcus) and superior to the fissure of Sylvius (lateral cerebral fissure). The parietal lobe is above the sylvian fissure and between the rolandic and parietooccipital fissures. The temporal lobe is below the sylvian fissure and in front of the parietooccipital fissure. The occipital lobe is behind the parietooccipital fissure. The lobes correspond roughly to the cranial bones that overlie them.

There is an additional lobe not visible on the hemisphere surface because it lies within the lateral cerebral fissure of Sylvius. This is the insula, or island of Reil, and it is obscured by the overlying convolutions of the frontal and parietal lobes.

The lobes are not units of function. The more basic gross units are called areas. Most of the motor areas are in front of the central fissure of Rolando, and most of the sensory areas are behind it.

Microscopic Anatomy

Most of the cerebral cortex has six depth layers. The hippocampal gyrus, which may be phylogenetically the oldest part of the cortex, is hidden medial to the temporal lobe and has only three depth layers. There are about 10 to 12 billion neurons and nonnervous kinds of fibers distributed within these layers.

Layer 1, the most superficial, appears to receive the diffuse projection of fibers from the thalamus. Layer 2, the outer granular layer, contains pyramidal and granular cells. Layer 3, still deeper, has a less populated concentration of pyramidal cells, and there are intercortical association fibers. Layer 4, the inner granular, is composed of sensory fibers ascending in the thalamic radiations. Layer 5 is composed mainly of pyramidal cells, but there are intercortical association fibers. Layer 6 has many spindle-shaped cells. In general, the superficial cortical layers have no marked influence on motor reactions, unlike layer 5.

There is a differentiation of the white matter, or medulla, that lies in the interior of the cerebrum. The white fibers form a network connecting various regions of

96

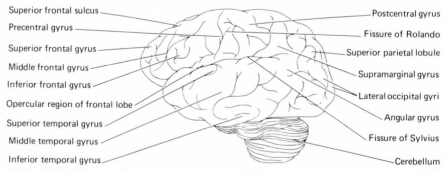

Superior frontal sulcus
Precentral gyrus
Superior frontal gyrus
Middle frontal gyrus
Inferior frontal gyrus
Opercular region of frontal lobe
Superior temporal gyrus
Middle temporal gyrus
Inferior temporal gyrus

Postcentral gyrus
Fissure of Rolando
Superior parietal lobule
Supramarginal gyrus
Lateral occipital gyri
Angular gyrus
Fissure of Sylvius
Cerebellum

Figure 4-20 The major divisions of the cerebrum, external lateral view.

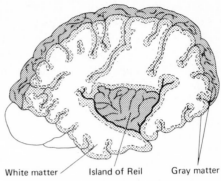

White matter   Island of Reil   Gray matter

Figure 4-21 The insula, or island of Reil.

the cortex with one another and with other parts of the brain and providing for intercommunication and association.

Some white fibers form great crossbands, or *commissures,* that interconnect the paired hemispheres. Thus, the corpus callosum connects the paired nonolfactory regions called the neocortex, and the anterior commissure connects the paired olfactory regions called the archipallium.

The corpus callosum, or great cerebral commissure, allows the two cerebral hemispheres to share learning and memory (Sperry, 1967). One viewpoint is that engrams, or memory traces, are established in one hemisphere, and are available to the other hemisphere when required. The corpus callosum helps (1) correlate

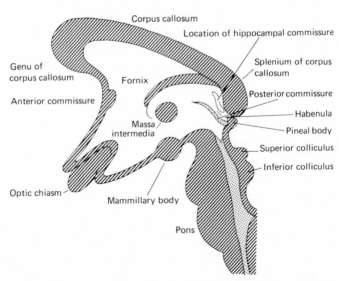

Corpus callosum

Location of hippocampal commissure

Genu of corpus callosum

Fornix

Splenium of corpus callosum

Anterior commissure

Posterior commissure

Habenula

Massa intermedia

Pineal body

Superior colliculus

Inferior colliculus

Optic chiasm

Mammillary body

Pons

Figure 4-22 Sagittal diagrammatic view of diencephalic and midbrain regions. White commissures are emphasized.

images in the left and right halves of the **visual field,** (2) integrate sensations from paired limbs, (3) unify cerebral processes of **attention** and awareness, and (4) engage in any number of activities in which the **hemispheres** interact. It may have a tonic **effect** on the brain cells into which it delivers **impulses.** Sperry (1967) notes that if the corpus callosum fails to develop, centers **for language** and other functions develop in compensation on both sides of the **brain.**

A second kind of fiber in the cerebral white **matter** is the *projection fiber,* which travels vertically and connects the cerebrum **with other** parts of the brain and with the spinal cord.

A third variety, the *association fiber,* travels **between** rostral and caudal aspects and connects regions on the same side of the **cerebrum.** An example of an important variety of association fiber is seen in the *external capsule.* The posterior half of the left cerebral hemisphere, which helps **elaborate** meanings in response to auditory and visual stimuli, is linked by the **external** capsule to the lowest part of the precentral convolution, which regulates **articulatory** movements. In this way articulated speech becomes the expression of **meanings.** The external capsule extends from the tip of the temporal lobe, beneath **the cortex** of the island of Reil, to the lower portion of the precentral convolution **and** to the posterior section of the second and third frontal convolutions.

Methods of Analyzing Cerebral Cortical Function

The effects of extirpation of the cerebral **hemispheres** have been studied most completely in the dog. In the classic **work of Goltz** (1834–1902), such a dog was studied for 1½ years postoperatively, and **later experiments** have periods of observation extended to several years.

Decorticated dogs can run and jump with **agility,** sleep as usual, and growl if disturbed. They retain a sense of pain and **ingest food** and water brought into contact with the snout but are without sight **or smell.** They lose memory for ac-

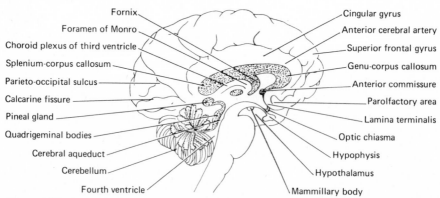

Figure 4-23 Internal view of the cerebrum **showing major** structures and the ventricles.

quired habits and are not capable of learning. There is no interest in the environment and no recognition of known objects.

A more recent procedure is to excise a limited cortical region and observe the effects on behavior. Similar operations have been extended to human patients. Frontal, parietal, and temporal lobe sections and ablations, known as lobotomies and lobectomies, have been performed extensively in man. There is considerable application to the neurology of speech. For example, the results of temporal lobe ablations indicate that much of this lobe is concerned with understanding present experience and with memory.

A second variety of study is by electrical stimulation of the exposed cortex. A third method is to apply a drug such as strychnine to the cortical surface and map out the areas that fire. A fourth method, applicable to the intact organism, is to tap off the spontaneous electrical currents and analyze the brain-wave patterns. This is electroencephalography. A fifth method, utilizing the intact subject, is the method of conditioned reflexes for analysis of behavior. The technics of neurochemistry are also evolving as still another approach.

The procedures show that the cerebrum is the highest neural integrative region. It is the seat of such psychic functions as sensation, perception, memory, consciousness, judgment, and volition.

Cerebral Dominance

Hemispheric dominance, or lateralization, has been a concept of considerable importance and controversy in speech pathology. In the course of evolution many important functions have shifted to the cerebrum, a process called encephalization. The cerebrum has become more complex in structure and function, and the areas in it that are needed for associations have been greatly increased. The differentiation of speech has come to be linked with the development of the highest cerebral centers and with an increasing importance of the descending tracts controlling the speech effectors. It may be necessary to note that language and speech are not the exclusive properties of the cerebral cortex but involve subcortical and midbrain activities.

In man encephalization is associated with the dominance of a single cerebral hemisphere. At birth the hemispheres seem to have about equal potentialities, but this is controversial. The angular gyrus, located close to the junction of the parietal, occipital, and temporal lobes, appears to be bilaterally functional. This gyrus is an area in which the brain may synthesize many diverse impulses to integrated concepts. Many sensations appear to be simultaneously associated within it, and the composite meaning of such sensations is lost if a sizable lesion develops in the angular gyrus of the dominant hemisphere. The patient, for example, may develop an agnosia, i.e., failure to comprehend the meaning of the written or the spoken word.

The term hemisphere dominance is applicable when the anatomic basis of a given function is resident solely or chiefly in one hemisphere. Speech appears to fit into this category, since its higher control is generally located in the left cerebral hemisphere in right-handed individuals. This does not imply that the right hemisphere is excluded from some subordinate control.

Hemispheric dominance may be a unique property of the human brain. The reasons for one hemisphere to take control are obscure, but it may be difficult or impossible to synthesize meaningful concepts about the same stimulus simultaneously in both hemispheres, and therefore one side somehow gains ascendancy. Berry and Eisenson (1956) state that the midline organs subserving speech, such as the jaw, lips, tongue, and larynx, have a bilateral cortical representation but that only the neurons in the primary motor-projection area in one hemisphere are essential for speech. Although the mechanisms of voice are bilaterally present, the skills needed to organize and express speech are restricted to a dominant hemisphere. Luchsinger and Arnold (1965) state that specialized cerebral function is the prime requisite for the development of all human communicative abilities.

According to Brain (1965), speech necessitates a precise integration of many bilateral muscles so that they contract synchronously. This requires that the right and left cerebral motor cortices be under the control of a single coordinating speech center.

Dominance usually implies that most or all functions will be governed by one hemisphere, but this is not always so. The premotor and parietal functions may be mutually contralateral (on opposite sides). Ambidextrous and left-handed individuals may show right dominance in the premotor cortex and left dominance in the angular-gyrus and ideomotor areas. Such facts may be disturbing in mapping out speech therapy or in rehabilitation after neurosurgery. Dominance may thus be pure or mixed; the latter is common in the same person. It need not be all-or-none, as exemplified by ambidexterity. There is always the problem of whether it is congenital or acquired.

As evidenced by present tests, the left hemisphere of the cerebrum is dominant in approximately 90 percent of the population, and the left angular gyrus is the more important integrative center. Guyton (1966) states that destruction of the dominant temporal lobe and angular gyrus produces in an adult a marked loss in intellect and the capacity to interpret the meaning of sensory experiences. Attempts to develop the interpretative functions of the corresponding nondominant regions meet with very little success. According to Guyton, compensation with the nondominant hemisphere readily occurs, however, in a child under six years of age.

Speech is not the only activity which is predominantly represented in one hemisphere. Handedness is another. Most individuals are right-handed and left-cerebral-dominant.

There is an indistinct relationship among cerebral dominance, handedness, and speech. Speech centers, however, become established in the left hemisphere, somewhat independently of handedness. Apparently laterality for language and handedness are not directly associated, and one does not necessarily determine the other.

The polarization of language function is seen not only in right and left cerebral hemisphere disparities but also in an anteroposterior manner within the single left hemisphere (Lenneberg, 1967). Whereas anterior lesions are followed chiefly by motor disturbances of language, posterior lesions are related chiefly to sensory disturbances.

Another lateralized function may be that of hearing. Although the auditory tract projects to both temporal cortices, a right-handed individual may recognize the sound in the left hemisphere, and the reverse may hold true for the left-handed person. Certain auditory stimuli are more efficiently reported when they stimulate the ear contralateral to the dominant hemisphere for speech. The reader is referred to the discussion by Milner (1962) of laterality effects in audition and also to discussions edited by Mountcastle (1962) on interhemispheric relations and cerebral dominance.

Other cerebral areas are also unilateralized. The premotor cortex is generally dominant on the same side as the angular gyrus. The speech areas located in the premotor region which control the larynx, jaw, and tongue are strongly left-dominant. There is an ideomotor area just in front of the angular gyrus that is more functional on the generally dominant hemisphere.

Cerebral Localization

Localization was suggested over a century ago by the anatomist Franz Joseph Gall (1758–1828), who associated specific functions in man with definite cortical areas. Since then the existence of localization has been abundantly demonstrated. An early proof of a specific motor area was that of Fritsch and Hitzig in 1870. They applied a galvanic current to the exposed cerebrum of a wounded soldier and observed a strictly localized muscular response. Much of the later work has been based upon observations of responses in the electrically stimulated cortex and upon the bodily effects of artificial and natural cortical lesions.

The study of changes in function as a result of injury has been the technic most widely used throughout the history of neurophysiology. Experiments on dogs and monkeys suggest that localization is a general phenomenon in higher animals (Luchsinger and Arnold, 1965).

The antilocalizationist point of view was first presented by Flourens (1794–1867) and Goltz, who discerned no differences when lesions were made in various regions of the cerebrum of animals.

A single functional area of the cortex may extend into diverse histologic areas. Subcortical regions have yet to be explored. The cause-and-effect relations among a bodily defect, a cortical lesion, and the assumptions as to the normal function of the part of the cortex suffer upon logical analysis of the argument. Speech as a function is not analyzable into motion or sensation but is based upon integrated processes involving the entire brain, and its disturbance is expressed in terms of the highest psychic activities. As Wilson (1966) points out, the brain does not consist of separate organs, and any behavior will depend upon the state of activity throughout the whole brain. Also, one area may participate in many different aspects of behavior, and the nature of the most prominent symptom that follows a lesion is only one clue to the contribution that area makes to the total mental response.

In spite of the uncertainty that any behavior is elaborated in a fixed topographical place on the cortex, the theory has provided a tangible working basis for the analysis of cerebral function.

Cortical Function Maps
The cortex is no longer considered in terms of lobes but is divided into functional areas. The original system of Brodmann had nine general areas in the neocortex subdivided into perhaps fifty secondary areas, each designated by a numeral. Over 200 secondary areas are now numbered.

There are several cerebral motor areas. The principal motor area, 4, is in the precentral convolution of the frontal lobe, just in front of the fissure of Rolando. This contains the neurons that control the voluntary muscles, such as those of the lips, jaw, tongue, pharynx, and larynx.

Different parts of the body are represented in specific regions of the precentral convolution. Motor reactions occurring in order from toe to head are controlled by discrete centers running from the rolandic fissure down into the sylvian fissure. The movements are isolated and delicate. The response with prolonged stimulation spreads. This is seen in Jacksonian epilepsy where there is a "march" of the symptoms.

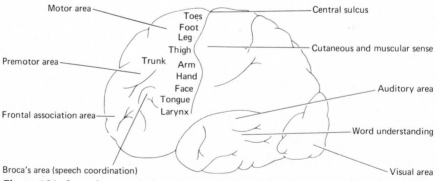

Figure 4-24 Lateral external view of the left cerebral hemisphere, indicating some functional areas.

Rasmussen and Penfield (1947) describe the bodily representation as follows. Centers for laryngeal and pharyngeal movement are located at the inferior end of the precentral convolution. When one cortex is stimulated, the pharynx is bilaterally contracted and both vocal folds are adducted. Above these cerebral centers there are motor nuclei for the palate, mandible, and tongue in successive order. Above in succession there are centers for movements of the lower face, neck muscles, thumb and fingers, wrist, forearm, arm, shoulder, and the upper and lower trunk. Anterior to the upper trunk is a center for the diaphragm. Above the centers for the lower-trunk muscles there are centers for the thigh, leg, foot, and toes.

Area 4 is not purely motor since lesions there weaken muscular sensibility. Either the motor and sensory areas overlap or they are connected by association tracts. Actually, all areas are activated in behavior. Area 4 has a relatively great cellular representation for the speech muscles.

There are several secondary motor areas. Area 8 in the frontal lobe and area 19 in the parietal lobe can produce eye movements independently of area 4. There are areas, such as 4S just in front of the motor area, called suppressor areas in that they inhibit motor activity. Other areas in the parietal lobe act similarly.

Some secondary regions such as area 6 of the premotor cortex control voluntary motion. Area 6 works in part through the motor cortex, but it also projects downward into relay systems called the basal ganglia. Stimulation of the premotor cortex has a greater influence over the mass movements of groups of muscles than it does over the delicate movements of single muscles. The mass movements, like the swinging of a limb in walking, are postural, and they relate the individual to his position in space.

The motor areas for controlling speech are well developed in both the premotor and motor cortex. Area 44 (Peele, 1961), located in the frontal lobe in the left inferior frontal convolution above the union of the fissures of Rolando and Sylvius, controls the formation of words, and it shows marked unilateral dominance. This is called Broca's area after a French surgeon, Paul Broca (1824–1880). It has connections to and from every part of the cortex so that all varieties of conscious experiences are potentially associated with speech. Broca's area was claimed in the earlier literature to act as a special correlation center funneling impulses to that part of the motor cortex which will control the bodily effectors of speech. The impulses are transmitted down to the motor nuclei of cranial and spinal nerves. In 1861 Broca first read his now famous paper on speech loss from pathologic disturbance of the cerebral cortex before the Académie de la Société d'Anthropologie. Broca's contribution lies more in the controversies and research he stirred up than in the accuracy of his observations and conclusions. His sample was too small, no dissection was performed, and his specimens (still at the Sorbonne) show wide variations in their lesions. Bastian (1880) found still other localized areas, and he related cerebral lesions to language defects.

Other speech areas, such as area 7B along Rolando's fissure in the frontal lobe and area 7A behind and beneath the great sensory areas of the parietal lobe, have been proposed. Area 7C in the frontal-orbital region is said to associate the emotional components of speech, originating in the thalamus, with ordinary muscular speech movements. Penfield and Rasmussen (1950) describe at least three areas that control the formation of words; one is frontal, one parietal, and one temporal.

A writing center was postulated by a Frenchman named Charcot in 1883. He also described a center for *ideation,* and he proposed a concept of visual- and auditory-minded individuals. Mills (1904) spoke of motor centers, a visual center, a graphic center, and an auditory center.

Electrical stimulation of certain cortical areas has produced vocalization in which the individual does not produce words but utters a sound which is usually a vowel. Penfield and Rasmussen (1950) produced vocalization by stimulating the precentral or postcentral "face" field in either hemisphere and by stimulating the medial aspect of the superior frontal convolution in either hemisphere in front of the central fissure. By stimulating these rolandic and superior frontal areas, speech has also been arrested. Penfield and Roberts (1959) proposed a cortical map in which stimulation of discrete points of the exposed cortex during surgery was stated to influence the motor aspects of speech.

The *prefrontal* cortex, areas 9, 10, 11, and 12, at the anterior-apical end of the frontal lobe, is important in speech and in general intellectual activities. Prefrontal-lobe lesions and prefrontal destruction subsequent to bilateral section called lobotomy are not followed by distinct defects. Personality changes such as disinterest, change in social attitudes, and intellectual deterioration occur. The prefrontal cortex has been called an ideational association area in which the bases of abstract thinking are evolved. In this sense it is a significant determinant for speech which depends upon memory and abstractions.

Oddly enough, much work on this region was begun in the last century when in 1848 a man named Phineas Gage had a crowbar blown through his head by an explosion. The motor cortex was not penetrated, but the prefrontal areas were destroyed. The patient recovered but displayed obvious personality changes. Such alterations in behavior eventually suggested the possibility of prefrontal lobotomy.

There seems to be little or no localization in the prefrontal areas. These areas connect to an ideomotor center in the supramarginal gyrus of the predominant parietal lobe. When the ideomotor area receives impulses, it is probable that it consciously and automatically decides upon a course of action; in this sense it reflexly selects the words and sentences of a conversation.

The ideomotor area is inhibited by the prefrontal cortex so that the rapid reflex activity of the former may be subjected to censor. This monitoring and selection of ideas may be a function of the prefrontal cortex. The pattern is illustrated in speech. The prefrontal area plans the speech in its own time by calling upon memory and associations, and then the ideomotor area decides upon the sequence of the words. The ideomotor area in turn sends this information to motor areas, after which the laryngeal and associated organ patterns are placed into integrated motion.

Investigators such as von Monakow, Head, and many others have denied that there are any strict centers for speech (Wepman, 1951). One argument is that various areas of cortical damage can effectively destroy the speech function. Lenneberg (1967), in reviewing the methods and arguments used to substantiate speech localization, concludes that there is no evidence for an absolute language area. There are, however, some regions which are frequently involved in language disturbances, and there are other regions which are never involved in speech or language. There is no decisive evidence that Broca's area has any more relationship to speech than areas adjacent to it.

Although it is customary for the writer to offer a commentary following a recital of conflicting theories, this is not always in the best interest. Even at best, the so-called truth is as evanescent as the technic from which it is derived.

Sensory Areas of the Cerebral Cortex

We have so far described the correlating and expressive areas of the cerebral cortex, but we have not yet considered the afferent or receptive areas that receive the impulses. Information is received from any of the bodily receptors and ascending tracts, and it is also received as a feedback from the very muscles that have been activated.

The parietal cortex, including areas 3, 1, 2, 5, and 7, is called the somesthetic area. It receives and integrates general senses such as pressure, pain, hot, cold, and muscle sensations. The bodily periphery is represented spatially on the contralateral somesthetic cortex. Areas 5 and 7 allow tridimensional reasoning about the projected sensations. Thus we recognize form, texture, weight, etc., a faculty called stereognosis. Speech is an example of such stereognostic activity. The proprioceptive muscle impulses from the speech muscles and elsewhere, which are fed back into the postrolandic region, reflexly stimulate a continuous and orderly pattern of behavior in the very same muscles. Cutaneous as well as deep pressure impulses can by association initiate a flow of responsive speech.

The temporal cortex and perhaps a portion of the parietal lobe are concerned with auditory sensations. The auditory projection endings in the temporal cortex are in Heschl's convolution, which is in the superior temporal gyrus. About one-half of the impulses from each ear end in each superior temporal gyrus so that the total removal of one temporal lobe hardly impairs hearing. Removal of the temporal lobe on the dominant side, however, decreases the meaning of sounds. This results from loss of the auditory association areas, 41 and 42, located in the hind part of the superior temporal convolution. Speech responses are greatly dependent upon the meaning of sounds.

Speech is also related to impulses arriving in other sensory cortical areas, such as those dealing with vision, taste, or smell; but these relationships are more indirect, and the cortical areas in question will not be described.

The concept of sensory centers of speech historically followed the localization views for the motor cortex. Carl Wernicke (1848–1905) in Germany described in 1874 an auditory center in the temporal convolution. This is now called Wernicke's area. It includes a region in the left superior temporal gyrus called area 22. This is directly behind areas 41 and 42, and it also includes the adjacent part of the middle temporal gyrus. Its destruction is followed by the failure to understand the spoken word (acoustic verbal agnosia) and occasionally by inability to comprehend the written word (visual verbal agnosia).

Dejerine (1906) describes a form of sensory aphasia which is a word blindness, or alexia, resulting from impairment of that part of the left cortex in which the angular gyrus and the parietal, temporal, and occipital lobes meet.

Basal Ganglia

Many subcortical centers, or nuclei, cooperate with the cerebrum to control the voluntary muscles, including those of speech. Basal ganglia is a collective term for several subcortical nuclear masses in the forebrain and midbrain. These masses connect directly or indirectly to the premotor cortex above and project down to a midbrain structure called the red nucleus or to the reticular formation of the brainstem. These structures have decussating fibers traveling down the spinal cord, so that the basal ganglia have a contralateral control over the muscles.

The term basal ganglia is used variably by different writers. Peele (1961) says that it includes the caudate, putamen, globus pallidus, and the amygdaloid nuclei. It would secondarily embrace other nuclei in the diencephalon, midbrain, pons, and medulla. These would include the subthalamus, red nuclei, substantia nigra, and certain nuclei of the brain tegmentum and reticular formation. The thalamus and hypothalamus are only remotely included in that they connect as the others with parts of the extrapyramidal system. West (1957) classifies the thalamus as a basal ganglion, although he agrees with conventional views in excluding the hypothalamus. In much of the current literature the thalamus is also treated apart from the basal ganglia because it is a great center for afferent rather than efferent impulses.

For convenience in the present discussion, the basal ganglia are discussed as including the corpus striatum, red nucleus, subthalamus, and substantia nigra. The anatomy of the basal ganglia is complex and poorly known. The system may operate as a unit.

Corpus Striatum
This is divided into the caudate and lenticular nucleus, the latter being subdivided into the putamen and globus pallidus.

The *striate body proper,* which includes the caudate nucleus and putamen, can initiate and control voluntary movements that are gross rather than discriminative. The delicate precise movements are controlled by the cerebral motor cortex. Whereas the cerebrum appears to regulate movements that require considerable attention, the striate body is concerned with those which are performed unconsciously.

The striate body may utilize two different efferent pathways. One is via the globus pallidus to the thalamus to the cerebrum, and thence downward by the pyramidal and extrapyramidal paths. The other is via the substantia nigra to the reticular formation, and thence downward by the reticulospinal or other extrapyramidal tracts.

The *globus pallidus* increases muscle tone and can also excite the cerebral cortex. It is thus facilitatory. It can establish a background tone for subsequent movements.

The globus may utilize two different efferent pathways. On is through the thalamus to the cerebral motor cortex, and thence downward by pyramidal and extrapyramidal systems. The other is by short tracts to the reticular formation, and thence downward.

Red Nucleus

This midbrain structure has two distinct parts, the magnocellular and parvocellular nuclei. The magnocelluar nuclei receive impulses from the striate bodies and other structures. They send reorganized impulses down through the rubrospinal tract or else into the reticular formation and thence into the reticulospinal tract. The action is to produce flexion and extension of the body axis. The parvocellular nuclei receive cerebellar impulses from the cerebellorubral tracts and send impulses downward chiefly through the reticular formation. They are adjunctive to the cerebellum in the control of muscular activity.

Substantia Nigra

This body receives impulses from the striate body and reticular formation. It may control the gamma activating system of the muscle spindles before the alpha motor neurons to the muscles are activated. This establishes the proper background tone for subsequent motor activity.

Subthalamus

These nuclei may be concerned in crude walking reflexes, and any failure is associated with a breakdown of purposefulness of locomotion.

Much of the function described for the basal ganglia is derived by correlating postmortem studies with prior clinical syndromes. The basal ganglia have become primarily suppressor over motor function. Inhibitory circuits lead from the cortex to the basal ganglia, and there are suppressor fibers returning to the cortex. Lesions

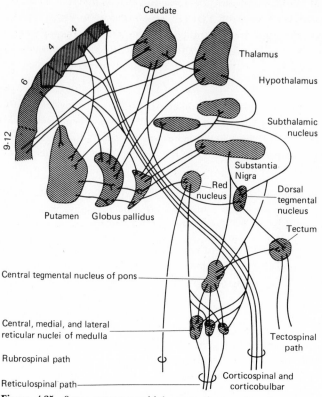

Figure 4-25 Some extrapyramidal connections and pathways.

Labels in figure: Caudate; Thalamus; Hypothalamus; Subthalamic nucleus; Substantia Nigra; Red nucleus; Dorsal tegmental nucleus; Tectum; Putamen; Globus pallidus; Central tegmental nucleus of pons; Central, medial, and lateral reticular nuclei of medulla; Tectospinal path; Rubrospinal path; Reticulospinal path; Corticospinal and corticobulbar; 4; 6; 9-12

in such circuits may produce continual writhing. The latter is exemplified in athetoid movements, particularly in the limbs. Such movements are normally inhibited by the premotor cortex working through the basal ganglia. The speech may be feeble and slurred.

The basal ganglia help to control muscle tone. If they are destroyed, certain facilitative structures such as the motor cortex, as well as the bulboreticular centers of the brainstem, become more excitable. This produces muscular hypertonicity and rigidity.

In sequential motor acts initiated by the motor cortex, it is necessary to inhibit active muscles while exciting other muscle groups. In this activity the suppressor circuits involving the basal ganglia and the cerebrum may play a role. If such inhibition is lacking, unsuppressed oscillations, as in athetosis, could occur.

There is a damping function of the basal ganglia which prevents oscillations between muscle agonists and antagonists when the muscles are at rest. This prevents the muscles from abruptly changing their state and entering into oscillatory contractions. Basal ganglia lesions remove the damping mechanism, and tremors may result. This may be the basis of the resting tremors seen in Parkinson's disease In this syndrome there is widespread destruction of the globus pallidus, substantia nigra, or associated regions.

It is difficult to ascertain which of the basal ganglia are responsible for a specific function or dysfunction. The striate bodies, including the caudate, lenticular, and amygdaloid nuclei, have descending axons that synapse with brainstem nuclei. The latter in turn innervate the muscles of the face, tongue, pharynx, and larynx. The athetoid patient shows disorders of articulation, facial grimaces, and other symptoms indicating trouble somewhere in the complex striate circuits.

The red nucleus and substantia nigra, which lie in the midbrain, are circularly connected with the corpus striatum and the premotor cortex. The cerebellum sends many of its impulses to the muscles by way of the red nucleus. Muscular rigidity and tremor can result from lesions in these bodies.

Thalamus

Anatomic Considerations
The thalamus represents the dorsal aspect of the diencephalon. Still above it is the epithalamus, which is made up of the pineal gland and habenular nucleus (an olfactory reflex center). Below the thalamus are the hypothalamus and subthalamus. The thalamus is on either side of the median third ventricle of the forebrain, and it is bounded laterally by the internal capsule.

Thalamic nuclei Several separate nuclei constitute the thalamus, and there is some variation in how they are classified. Most if not all of the nuclei intercommunicate, but the details are obscure. Many of the fibers from thalamus to cerebral cortex are well traced, however, and a point-to-point connection has been determined in many instances.

The cerebral cortex and thalamic nuclei send fibers to each other, all passing through the internal capsule. This indicates that the cerebrum and thalamus influence one another.

The *lateral geniculate body* is a bilateral structure in the caudal part of the thalamus. It receives the optic tracts and projects to the visual areas of the cerebral cortex. The cortex returns fibers by a corticothalamic tract.

The *medial geniculate body* is a bilateral structure in the caudal part of the thalamus. It receives the lateral lemniscus and projects fibers for hearing to the anterior transverse temporal gyrus of the cerebral cortex.

The *posterior ventral nucleus* is a bilateral structure in the ventral lateral part of the thalamus. It is the chief sensory nucleus of the thalamus, receiving impulses

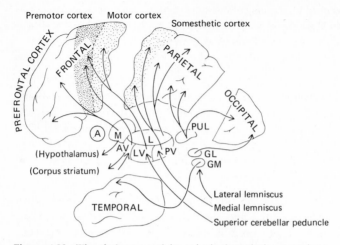

Figure 4-26 The thalamus and its principal cortical connections: A=anterior nucleus, M=medial nucleus, L=lateral nucleus, AV= anteroventral nucleus, LV=ventral intermediate nucleus, PV= posteroventral nucleus, PUL=pulvinar, GL=lateral geniculate, GM=medial geniculate. (*By permission from J. T. Manter and A. J. Gatz, Clinical Neuroanatomy and Neurophysiology, 2d ed., F. A. Davis Company, Philadelphia, 1961.*)

110

from the medial lemniscus and spinothalamic tracts. This nucleus is in mutual interconnection with the somesthetic cortex.

The *anterior nucleus* is a small region that receives a mammillothalamic tract and projects up to the gyrus cinguli. This serves to connect the activities of the hypothalamus with the limbic lobe.

The *medial nucleus* is a small central region which sends fibers to the frontal lobe of the cerebral cortex and also to the hypothalamus. It is a way station between the hypothalamus and frontal cortex.

The *anterior ventral nucleus* is a bilateral structure in the ventrolateral thalamus that mutually interconnects with the corpus striatum and also with the premotor cerebral cortex.

The *ventral intermediate nucleus* is a bilateral structure in the ventrolateral thalamus. It receives fibers from the dentate nucleus of the cerebellum and from the globus pallidus. It projects to the cerebral motor and premotor cortex. This nucleus thus appears to represent a region of motor coordination.

The *lateral nucleus* is a single nucleus that lies in the dorsal lateral area of the thalamus. It receives fibers from other thalamic nuclei, thus perhaps acting as an association nucleus. It is also reciprocally connected with the parietal cerebrum.

The *pulvinar* is a prominent swelling dorsally overhanging the caudally situated geniculate bodies. It reciprocally connects with the junction areas of the parietal, temporal, and occipital cortex. Its functions are obscure.

Epithalamus This is an extra part of the thalamus, containing the *habenular nuclei*, at the base of the pineal body. It is possibly a relay center carrying olfactory impulses to the midbrain.

Thalamic Reticular System This resembles, and has some obscure relationship to, the reticular activating system of the midbrain and hypothalamus. It may produce recruitment or increasing excitement in widespread areas of the cerebral cortex, thus being somehow involved in consciousness, attention, and learning.

Functions
The thalamus perhaps plays some part in every cortical activity, since it sends many tracts up to the cortex and in turn receives some cortical tracts. In its own right it is an organ of crude consciousness. It has a high threshold of stimulation, however, and an exaggerated capacity to respond when this threshold is exceeded. The thalamus deals with the affective qualities of a sensation, i.e., the pleasant or unpleasant qualities associated with the stimulus. Emotional experiences are constructed in this organ and then brought to full consciousness probably in the prefrontal cortex. The physiologic manifestations of the emotion are expressed through the hypothalamus, which is the center of the sympathetic sector of the autonomic nervous system.

The emotional parameters of speech are probably synthesized in the thalamus as affects of the diverse stimuli entering it from many sources. Facial expression and the quality of the voice have thalamic as well as cerebral components in their organization.

In the *thalamic syndrome,* which may follow a cerebral hemorrhage or a thrombosis, the threshold is blunted or raised for all forms of sensation on the opposite side of the body, but there is no true anesthesia. The damage predominates in the ventral posterolateral nucleus, or there is interruption of the pathways from the thalamus to the cerebral cortex (Vinken and Bruyn, 1969). The limbs and trunk are especially affected. There is usually a permanent disturbance of deep sensibility, whereas there is more likely a transient disturbance of the cutaneous sensations. All stimuli, when effective, evoke unpleasant sensations, and even the lightest stimulus may evoke a disagreeable burning type of pain response. Extremes of hot and cold and also scraping and tickling evoke marked discomfort. The overreaction is called *hyperpathia* and may be a result either of irritation of the thalamus or release from higher cortical control. Pleasurable stimulation, as in applying a warm hand to the affected area, may be greatly accentuated. Every stimulus produces an excessive effect on the abnormal half of the body, particularly with regard to the affective aspect, i.e., the unpleasant nature of the stimulus.

The clinical manifestations of lesions of other parts of the thalamus are poorly understood. Unmotivated crying or laughter may be related to lesions of the anterior thalamic peduncle. Severe dementia and choreoathetoid movements have been reported with symmetrical degeneration affecting chiefly the anterior, medial, and lateral nuclei (DeJong, 1967).

Internal Capsule

This is a V-shaped area lateral to the thalamus and medial to the putamen and globus on each side. It is the main road by which the cerebral cortex and the lower centers intercommunicate.

The fiber bundles in the capsule are discrete. The posterior limb of the V near its knee contains fibers traveling from the cerebral motor cortex to nuclei of the cranial nerves. Posterior to these fibers are those from the cortex to upper spinal cord nuclei. Successively posterior are fibers from cortex to red nuclei and then fibers to the lumbar spinal cord nuclei. The most posterior fibers are upward radiations from the thalamus to the sensory cerebral cortex, dealing particularly with hearing and vision. The anterior limb of the V carries anterior thalamic radiations up to the frontal cortex and frontal lobe pathways down to the nuclei of the pons. The medial part of the capsule contains chiefly somesthetic and cerebellar radiations which have previously entered the thalamic way station.

112

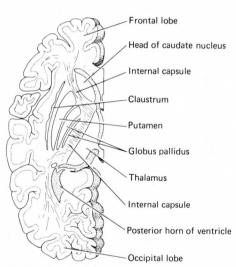

— Frontal lobe

— Head of caudate nucleus

— Internal capsule

— Claustrum

— Putamen

— Globus pallidus

— Thalamus

— Internal capsule

— Posterior horn of ventricle

— Occipital lobe

Figure 4-27 Internal capsule. An anteroposterior section through the left cerebral hemisphere below the level of the ventricle. (*By permission from G. M. Wyburn, The Nervous System, Academic Press Inc., New York, 1960.*)

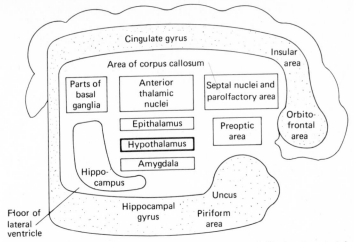

Figure 4-28 The limbic system viewed digrammatically in the mesial aspect of the left cerebral hemisphere.

The descending fibers from the internal capsule converge ventrally into two great fibrous bands at the base of the midbrain. These bands form the *cerebral peduncles.* Fibers within the peduncles are again dispersed as they travel caudally into the pons. Below the pons the fibers reconverge to the pyramidal tracts.

The internal capsule has a susceptibility to thromboses and tumors. Hemorrhage in this area is a likely occurrence in a markedly hypertensive individual, with consequent paralysis of muscle action, including the muscles of speech.

The Limbic System

The limbic system comprises (1) structures on the ventral surface of the temporal lobe which are separate from the neocortex, (2) parts of the olfactory and gustatory systems, and (3) many subcortical centers.

The *hypothalamus* is the central subcortical structure in this system. Other subcortical elements include the *septum, parolfactory area, epithalamus, amygdala, anterior nuclei of the thalamus, preoptic area, hippocampus,* and portions of the *basal ganglia.*

The cortical elements lie on the medioventral surface of each hemisphere. These structures extend as a circumferential ring around the subcortical masses. The ring includes such regions of the cortex as the orbitofrontal area, insular area, cingulate gyrus, hippocampal gyrus, piriform area, and the uncus.

The limbic system is involved in such behavior as pain and pleasure, motor and sensory drives, memory, and the emotions. This is a very old system phylogenet-

113

ically, developed before the thalamocortical relationships appeared. The relationships of the limbic system and peripheral structures are very diffuse, unlike the discreteness of the relationships between the neocortex and its projection systems.

Discharges from parts of the limbic system may be transmitted through the (1) hypothalamus, (2) reticular activating system, (3) basal ganglia, or (4) nonlimbic parts of the cerebral cortex.

Hypothalamus

This is the basal part of the diencephalon, or interbrain. It forms the walls and floor of the third ventricle below the thalamus, continues rostrally to the preoptic area, and blends caudally with the reticular activating system of the midbrain.

The hypothalamus is responsible for the regulation of many of the subconscious vegetative functions of the body, e.g., arterial blood pressure, fluid balance, and some endocrine secretions. It is responsible for certain behavioral functions, as *pain* and *pleasure, punishment* and *reward.* These attributes are highly important to behavior, reinforcing or inhibiting an action.

The hypothalamus is involved in establishing the defensive reaction of *rage* when its punishment areas are activated or *docility* and *tameness* when its reward centers are stimulated.

The anterior hypothalamus is involved predominantly in parasympathetic activity and the posterior hypothalamus in sympathetic activity, but this is only approximately the case (Luhman, 1968). Widespread hyperactivity of the hypothalamus can bring about psychosomatic effects, generalized in sympathetic activity but more localized to a given organ in parasympathetic activity.

The hypothalamus can affect behavior through the anterior lobe of the hypophysis which in turn influences adrenocortical hormones. The hypothalamus controls the reticular activating system in a positive or negative way, bringing about alertness, excitement, wakefulness, or, on the contrary, somnolence and sleep.

Hippocampus

This structure, which results from an inward fold of the cerebral cortex, forms the ventral surface of the inferior horn of the lateral ventricle. It has connections with practically all other parts of the limbic system and distributes impulses via the fornix particularly to the hypothalamus. It may be a switching agent between afferent inputs and appropriate hypothalamic responses. It is claimed to be involved in attention, rage, sexual activities, and in involuntary clonic or tonic movements. Hallucinations have followed electrical stimulation. The reader is referred to the MIT Neurosciences Research Symposium Summaries for a review of the memory functions of the hippocampal area.

Amygdala

This consists of many nuclei below the ventral surface of the cerebral cortex in the pole of each temporal lobe. The amygdala receives its input from all other parts of the limbic system, from the cingulate and hippocampal gyrus, and from the frontal lobes of the cerebrum. It sends impulses back to the same cortical regions and also into the hippocampus and particularly into the hypothalamus.

The amygdaloid nuclei appear to regulate the same functions ascribed to the hypothalamus but in addition regulate a variety of involuntary movements and produce certain responses associated with reproduction both in the male and female. The amygdaloid nuclei are also thought of as a thalamuslike relay center for olfactory and other visceral impulses to the cerebral cortex.

These nuclei represent an important correlating center of the limbic system.

Cerebellum

The cerebellum, or "little brain," is the largest part of the hindbrain and is located in the dorsal metencephalon surrounding the anterior section of the fourth ventricle. It overlies both the pons and medulla and is itself overlapped by the occipital lobe of the cerebral cortex.

The cerebellum contains (1) the flocculonodular lobe, or archicerebellum; and (2) the corpus, which is subdivided into a segmented anterior lobe, or vermis, and a large posterior lobe. The latter is in turn divided to the hemispheres, or neocerebellum, and to the pyramis and uvula, which with the vermis form the paleocerebellum.

The cerebellum is divided into an outer cortex and an inner white matter, which contains subcortical nuclei. The surface of the gray matter is increased by

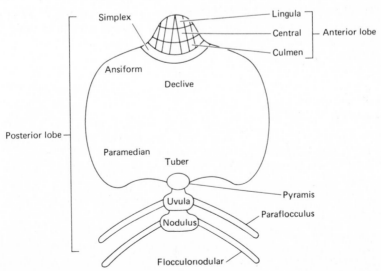

Figure 4-29 The cerebellum extended to a plane to show its major divisions.

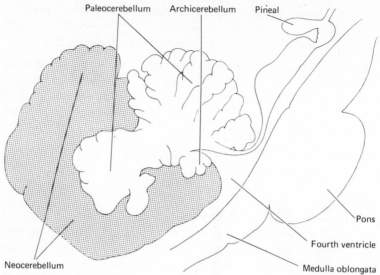

Figure 4-30 Outline sketch of a median section of the brainstem and cerebellum.

Paleocerebellum **Archicerebellum** **Pineal**

Neocerebellum

Pons

Fourth ventricle

Medulla oblongata

leaflike folds called folia. The subcortical nuclei, which are relay stations from the cortex, are the dentate, emboliform, fastigii, and globose nuclei.

The cerebellum connects with other brain regions through its paired stalks, or peduncles. The superior stalks are chiefly efferent to the thalamus or red nucleus. The middle ones are afferent from the pons. The inferior pair are afferent and efferent with the medulla. These stalks are also called brachium conjunctivum superior), brachium pontis (middle), and brachium ad medullam or restiform bodies (inferior).

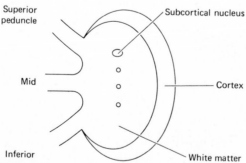

Superior peduncle

Subcortical nucleus

Mid

Cortex

Inferior

White matter

Figure 4-31 Lateral diagrammatic view of the cerebellum to show its subcortical nuclei and its peduncles.

The cerebrum connects with the cerebellum through the corticopontocerebellar tract. The latter is a crossed motor pathway from the frontal or temporal lobes of the cerebral cortex, traveling by way of the pons and the middle peduncle.

The cerebellum sends a cerebellorubral tract out through the superior peduncles to the red nucleus, and this tract is interrupted in the cerebellar subcortical relay nuclei. The path continues down to the spinal cord from the red nucleus through the rubrospinal tract or, more importantly, through the rubroreticular system into the reticular formation of the brainstem. Thence it descends through the reticulospinal tract into the cord, where it synapses with the motor nuclei of the skeletal muscles at every spinal level. The cerebellar neurons decussate to the red nucleus, but the lower neurons decussate back again so that the cerebellar muscle control is ipsilateral (on the same side).

Some efferent neurons of the superior cerebellar stalk rise to the thalamus. This organ in turn sends fibers to the cerebral cortex, thus providing a closed circuit between the cerebrum and the cerebellum. The superior stalk also receives proprioceptive muscle impulses from Gowers' tract of the cord.

The cerebellum receives through its inferior stalks proprioceptive impulses from Flechsig's tract and from the columns of Goll and Burdach of the spinal cord. It accepts impulses through the inferior stalks from the vestibulocerebellar and olivocerebellar tracts and from cranial nerves V, VII, IX, and X. Impulses travel out of this stalk through the cerebellovestibular and cerebelloolivary tracts. These descending tracts first terminate in brainstem relay nuclei. These nuclei in turn send extrapyramidal tracts down the cord to synapse with the nuclei of the anterior horn cells.

The cerebellum is involved in voluntary muscle coordination and in the timing of muscle impulses. It thus coordinates breathing and speaking, gestures, and facial expression. It regulates the strength of the voice and the inspiratory speech pauses to correspond with the meaning of the spoken words. It moderates and improves tone and strengthens neuromuscular activity.

Voluntary movement requires prime movers (agonists or protagonists), oppositional muscles (antagonists), and adjunctive muscles (synergists). Movements are initiated by the protagonists while the antagonists must be simultaneously caused to relax. To increase the efficiency of the action, the joint may be fixated by one or more synergists. In phonation, if the protagonists are acting as vocal fold adductors, the antagonists are abductors, and the synergists may fix the arytenoid cartilages in position. This necessitates (1) coordination, involving a balance between tension and relaxation, and (2) rhythm, or the timing and manner of delivering the energy.

In an afferent sense the cerebellum is the head ganglion of the proprioceptive system. The cerebellum is an assistant to the cerebrum. The latter initiates the discharges while the cerebellum distributes them by exciting or inhibiting lower centers. The cerebellar action is ipsilateral and devoid of consciousness.

In human cerebellar lesions, coordination but not sensation is lost. The primary ill effects decrease perhaps because the premotor cerebral cortex takes over. Certain symptoms are retained. One is asthenia, or loss of muscle force; another is atonia, or loss of tone. Still another is ataxia, or asynergia, which is the loss of the direction and regularity of a movement. Precise movement is impossible as seen in past pointing, in which the patient cannot bring a finger to a predesignated point such as his nose. There is astasia, or loss of steadiness, so that the individual develops an intention tremor when he tries to perform a movement. Alternate acts such as rapidly thrusting out and retracting the tongue become difficult. This failure of timing is called adiadochokinesia.

The cerebellum is extremely important for normal speech. The ataxic individual has an unmodulated and cluttered speech since the timing of alternate movements necessary for modulation and integration is lacking. The overall rhythm fails, and speech occurs in sudden starts. In severe cerebellar injury speech is explosive. The voice apparatus may lose its dominance over respiration. The patient starts to talk with normal intensity, but the voice is soon expended.

There is a cerebellar localization. The flocculonodular lobes (archicerebellum) deal primarily with information from the postural areas of the internal ear. The adjusted impulses are sent into the facilitative and inhibitory regions of the brainstem through which they regulate extensor muscle tone.

The paleocerebellum receives chiefly the tracts of Flechsig and of Gowers, and it sends out responses to the reticular formation, the red nucleus, and the thalamus. It may be primarily an inhibitory center. The impulses from both archi- and paleocerebellum, which travel into the reticular formation, maintain equilibrium even while the muscles are in rapid movement.

The neocerebellum controls rapid, skilled movements. It facilitates by tonic (continuous) feedback the action of the motor and premotor cortex. This quickly increases or decreases the tone in muscle agonists or antagonists according to the need. The basal ganglia differ in that they control the muscles by inhibition and not by excitation. The neocerebellum is able to judge the status of peripheral movements through its extensive proprioceptive reception. It can give this information to the cerebrum, which can then modify its own action adaptively. The neocerebellum is said to be able to predict the result of a movement in space and to brake the action at the appropriate time, thus, for example, preventing past pointing or tremors.

Brainstem

The midbrain, pons, and medulla constitute the brainstem. Some writers include the diencephalon (Noback, 1967). The cerebellum is usually excluded.

Midbrain

This region, the mesencephalon of the embryo, lies caudal to the thalamus and cranial to the cerebellum and pons. Its dorsal surface comprises the four colliculi, and its ventral surface comprises the cerebral peduncles. Between these dorsal and ventral structures there are the ascending and descending pathways and also important nuclear bodies, i.e., red nucleus, substantia nigra, and cranial nerve nuclei III and IV. There is also the cerebral aqueduct and the surrounding reticular formation.

Of the four colliculi, the superior pair represents the chief lower reflex centers in the visual pathway from the retina and it also transmits reorganized visual impulses forward to the lateral geniculate nuclei of the thalamus.

The inferior colliculi are the chief lower reflex centers in the auditory pathway from the organ of Corti. They send reorganized auditory impulses to the medial geniculate nuclei of the thalamus.

The colliculi constitute the tectum, or roof, of the midbrain. The tectum is the region of origin of the tectospinal path as well as of connections for transmitting auditory and visual impulses.

The cerebral peduncles take up the largest part of the ventral midbrain. The peduncles carry fibers from the cerebral cortex and the internal capsule downward to pontile, medullary, and spinal centers.

Pons

This lies ventral to the cerebellum and forms a bridge between the midbrain and the medulla. The basilar part of the pons is mostly concerned with tracts between the cerebral cortex and the cerebellum, but it also carries the descending corticospinal tracts and contains pontine nuclei. Axons of fibers that synapse with these nuclei decussate to form the middle cerebellar peduncles, which pass into the cerebellar hemispheres. This is a two-neuron system by which one hemisphere of the cerebrum controls the opposite hemisphere of the cerebellum. The corticospinal tract fibers become more compact as they leave the pons and become the pyramids of the ventral medulla.

The dorsal part of the pons, called its *tegmental* section, contains the tracts of ascending and descending nerve fibers which pass between the spinal cord and the brain.

The rostral part of the pons contains fibers that form the lateral wall of the fourth ventricle. The fiber mass on each side is the superior cerebellar peduncle. Its efferent components pass from the cerebellar cortex to such structures as the red nucleus, thalamus, and cerebral cortex. This peduncle contains only one incoming tract, the ventral spinocerebellar tract from proprioceptors.

The pons also contains the nuclei of cranial nerves V, VI, VII, and VIII.

The relation of the pons to speech lies in its connections with the basal ganglia and the cerebellum. It forms a part of the extrapyramidal system which controls the muscles. It also contains breathing centers for regulating the respiratory rhythm essential to phonation.

Medulla

The caudal part of the hindbrain, the myelencephalon of the embryo, forms the medulla oblongata.

The medulla is pyramidal in shape, tapering from rostral to caudal ends. The medullary pyramids form large bulges on the ventral surface on either side of the midline. Bulges above, and lateral to, each pyramid also indicate the locations of the inferior olivary nuclei.

The medulla (oblongata) is thought to be an embryologic expansion of the spinal cord (medulla spinalis), but its internal structure and its functions are unlike those of the cord. The medulla contains all the ascending and descending tracts and fibrous systems.

The nerve cells in the medulla form nuclei, some of which produce cranial nerves IX, X, XI, and XII. Others produce such vital centers as the cardiac, respiratory, and vasomotor. Still other nuclei act as relay stations for tracts traveling from the spinal cord to the brain.

A small lesion in the medulla may impair many functions. The integrity of the muscles of speech depends upon the vitality of medullary centers and cranial nerves.

120

Reticular Formation

This "system" is a network of cells and fibers forming a central core of much of the brain. It extends caudally from the reticular nuclei of the thalamus through the

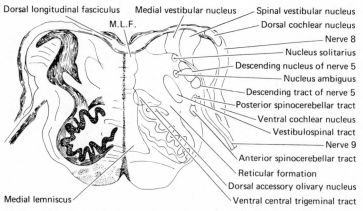

Figure 4-32 Cross section of the upper medulla; MLF=medial longitudinal fasciculus.

center of the midbrain and pons and terminates just rostral to the decussation of the pyramids of the medulla. There is disagreement about the exact boundaries of the reticular formation.

The reticular formation is generalized and undifferentiated, so that its functions are indicated essentially by its afferent and efferent relationships. The long ascending tracts of the cord send collaterals (branches) into the reticular formation as they pass forward to the thalamus. Eventually the afferent impulses terminate in all areas of the cerebral cortex by way of the thalamic projection fibers.

It may not be so much the projection fibers from the main sensory tracts that arouse the cortex as it is the impulses that have originated in the reticular formation. For this reason the mechanism is termed the *reticular activating system* (RAS). It is said to help produce consciousness by bombarding the cerebrum with impulses. The cerebrum returns impulses to it, thus producing a reverberating circuit. The cortex cannot perceive unless it is awake. A signal reaching the sleeping cortex is unrecognized. The RAS thus acts as a general alarm system and if it is destroyed, a coma ensues ending in death (French, 1967).

There is an activation theory of emotion (Lindsley, 1951) which holds that extremes of emotion, e.g., great excitement and rage as opposed to relaxation and sleep, are dependent upon activity in the reticular core.

The *descending* activity of the RAS involves either facilitation or inhibition of motor activity through the spinal nerves. These effects are brought about through the internuncial neurons to the motor cells, and a maintained reticular activation recruits more and more of the interneurons. This in turn brings increasing numbers of motor neurons into the response, in either an excitatory or inhibitory fashion. The RAS perhaps regulates all the motor activities of the body.

121

The reticular formation is fed by the basal ganglia and the cerebellum. Through this reticular way station the premotor cortex and the cerebellum project down to the motor nuclei of the muscles. Perhaps all the suppressor areas of the cerebrum and cerebellum act through an inhibitory mechanism located in the bulbar reticular formation. Even the inhibition of spinal activity due to the corpus striatum suppressors may be mediated in the same way.

The chief tract of the reticular formation is the reticulospinal tract. This is an important extrapyramidal system.

The reticular formation contains a facilitative (as well as an inhibitory) mechanism acting with the cerebellum. Similar influences come from the motor cortex via the pyramidal tracts. Pathologic spasticity of muscles may be maintained chiefly by the excessive facilitation of spinal stretch reflexes, by impulses descending from the facilitative mechanism and the reticulospinal tract. This is at variance with the view that spasticity is mostly related to pyramidal disturbances.

The reticular formation is a key area since the vital centers of breathing as well as the cardiovascular centers are in its caudal sector.

The nervous system is not a collection of separate units with distinct functions. All the sensory and motor apparatus may be pressed into service to focus on the problem at hand, and this demands integrating devices. French (1967) states that the RAS can be the regulator of these diverse activities in that it keeps the brain alert, routes the messages into appropriate channels, monitors the afferent impulses, accepting or rejecting what is relevant or irrelevant, and tempers muscular activity.

O'Leary and Coben (1958) claim that the conceptual importance of the reticular core and other subcortical structures has so increased that the cerebral cortex is on the brink of becoming a dependency. They present an extensive review of the brainstem literature, bringing up a dynamics that minimizes specific neural centers and emphasizes overall integration and multimodal activation of units.

Applied Anatomy and Physiology

Certain selected conditions are brought to attention here as elsewhere through this text because they emphasize the correlative significance of the functional anatomy. For a general survey of topics of considerable interest in clinical neurology, the reader is directed to the six volumes edited by Vinken and Bruyn (1969).

Electroencephalography

The action currents occurring during conduction in peripheral fibers can be visibly recorded by the cathode-ray oscilloscope. In 1924 a German psychiatrist, Hans Berger, emphasized the possibility of visualizing and measuring electric currents produced by the living brain in the intact human organism. He observed that a human being at rest with his eyes closed produced from the occipital and parietal brain regions a rhythmical series of waves, with a frequency of 10 per second and with an amplitude of about 50 microvolts. These were the first waves Berger saw, and he termed them *alpha waves*. The waves disappeared when the subject's eyes were opened, and a different wave appeared, with a frequency of 18 to 20 per second at an amplitude of 20 to 30 microvolts. Called *beta waves*, they occurred in the motor region of the brain as well as in the occipital and parietal regions. Berger introduced the term *electroencephalogram* (EEG) for what he believed to be normal expressions of impulse firings in the brain.

Beginning in 1934, Hallowell Davis and Frederick Gibbs, in Boston, related the specific form of the EEG to brain disorders and correlated epilepsy with characteristic deviations in the electrical records. The EEG procedure is currently a routine portion of a neuropsychiatric examination.

The EEG is a recording of the electrical activity of the brain, obtained from electrodes attached to the scalp. From eight to twenty electrodes are used, twelve being a routine number. Leading from each electrode is a long fine wire running to a junction box. The recording electrodes are of several varieties:

Needle electrodes are very small hypodermic needles.

Disk electrodes are concave silver disks. Electrical contact with the head is made by filling the disk with a conducting paste. These are commonly used on the earlobes and for grounding.

Wet saline electrodes are chlorided silver rods, one end of which is covered with a pad wetted with sodium chloride solution for electrical contact. They are held in contact with the scalp by a rubber net placed over the head and tied under the chin.

The machine is calibrated to relate the standard microvolt input to the displacement of the pen. The tracings may be written by pens on a moving strip of paper or recorded on a cathode-ray oscilloscope, on magnetic tape, or otherwise. The activity thus observed is only a small part of the total activity of the brain, and the ultimate origin of the electrical potentials is obscure. The waves may not all come from the cerebral cortex (Brock and Krieger, 1963).

There are many sources of artifacts in the records. The patient eliminates those due to blinking and eye movements by keeping his eyes closed and motionless. Body movement must not occur. Muscle potential is minimized by making the subject comfortable. There are artifacts from loose electrodes, sweating, drowsiness, 60-Hz currents, pulse waves, and other factors.

The EEG waves of a normal adult are composed of a variety of combinations of alpha and beta waves. About 10 percent of the total record in adult "normals" are theta waves, between 4 to 7 Hz and 10 to 100 microvolts. They are seen particularly in drowsiness and in the early stages of sleep. They are also seen in pathology.

Delta frequencies are from 0.5 to 3.5 Hz and 30 to 150 microvolts. They occur normally only during deep sleep or following hyperventilation. If present during the waking state, they indicate pathology.

The waveforms called spikes are associated with an epileptic seizure, when they occur diffusely and in large numbers.

Whether electroencephalographic visualization may be a useful tool in speech is controversial. It would be useful if the brain waves varied in a characteristic and predictable direction in a given speech disorder associated with brain damage. However, minimally brain-damaged children may show an acceptable EEG. Also, some work on reading problems in school, randomly selected, purports to find abnormal EEG tracings. Roberts (1966), in a study of aphasic children, cautioned against lumping all the "poor readers" or those with little or no speech and finding EEG abnormalities in them.

The reader is referred to the *Index to Current Literature*, published as a quarterly supplement to *Electroencephalography and Clinical Neurophysiology (EEG Journal)*; also to *Progress in Neurology and Psychiatry*, published annually.

Electromyography

Electromyography is the analysis of electrical activity associated with muscle contraction (Baker, 1962). Although its history can be traced to Galvani, clinical electromyography really began with the classical review of Denny-Brown and Pennybacker (1938).

The activity is detected by needle or surface electrodes in electrical contact with muscle. Surface electrodes are usually placed on the skin over a muscle. These small disks are adequate where large volumes of muscles are to be sampled.

The needle electrodes are of several types. A very common one is the Adrian-Bronk type, which is a hypodermic needle of small bore through which an insulated wire is inserted until exposed at the beveled tip end. The wire core serves as the local electrode. It can be led into the amplifier either against the shaft that is in diffuse contact with muscle or against a distant "indifferent" electrode.

All types of electrodes have severe limitations, e.g., the number of electrode placements in a muscle, the reaction of the patient, or change in the relative position of the recording electrode.

The potentials of active muscle are amplified, then visualized on a cathode-ray oscilloscope and simultaneously heard over a loudspeaker. The sounds produced are correlated with the oscillographic "picture." The sounds have the singular advantage of assessing the duration and rhythm of the potentials. The picture and sound can be recorded on tape and later reviewed and photographed. A multi-channeled ink-writing instrument can be used to record events simultaneously from many areas. This is of advantage when summed potentials from large areas of muscles are recorded, as by surface electrodes.

The electromyogram (EMG) is the brief propagated all-or-none action potential of muscle fibers. Normal motor-unit potentials range in amplitude from 0.1 to as many as 3 millivolts, usually 0.2 to 1 millivolt. Durations vary from 2 to 10 msec. The potential and amplitude configurations are functions of electrode placement that is random in relation to any motor unit.

The electrical record (EMG) of muscle activity is obtained with relative ease because the firing of a motor neuron makes a relatively large number of muscle fibers in a *motor unit* discharge simultaneously. The motor unit includes a lower motor neuron, its axon, and the muscle fibers to which the neuron connects. The record can be analyzed in terms of duration, frequency, form and peak voltage, all of which vary in specific muscles and diseases.

The muscle does not show electrical activity at rest, but upon reflex or voluntary stimulation individual motor units fire asynchronously, although each at a regular rate, and an irregular volley is seen. The rate of discharge in a motor nerve increases with greater strength of muscle contraction.

Whereas the EEG expresses the summation of action potentials in the brain, the EMG gives information about sensory and motor nerves, spinal reflexes, and particularly muscles. If a sensory nerve is stimulated, information can be obtained about the afferent system and the spinal reflexes.

In general, the EMG is especially valuable in localizing lesions in the central nervous system which produce dysfunction in the neuromuscular structures. The most important clinical use may be the study and differential diagnosis of lesions of the lower motor neurons. The technic yields information only in regard to electrical correlates of neuromuscular activity, and few types of changes in the EMG are specific for varieties of neural disorder. The EMG only helps to confirm clinical observation but does not substitute for neurologic examination.

Electromyography has received considerable attention in the speech pathology literature. Although it has seemed very promising, its validity in the clinical diagnosis of specific speech disorders is still open to serious argument.

Cerebral Dominance, Localization, and Aphasia

The relationships of dominance, localization, and aphasia are illustrated in disorders following lesions in the major hemisphere. The aphasias constitute a class of such disorders.

Aphasia is a defect or loss of the power of expression by speech, writing, or signs or of comprehending spoken or written language, resulting from injury or disease of brain centers.

125

Aphasia refers to a heterogeneous collection of disorders with different causes and pathologies. The disorder is one of speech and thought. It may arise in association with any lesion in the speech areas of the cerebrum. The most frequent causative disturbances are hemorrhages, stationary clots (thrombi), and moving clots (emboli). Wounds, tumors, and infectious diseases such as encephalitis and meningitis are occasionally involved, as are epilepsy and some of the degenerative diseases of the brain. Such pathologic processes do not necessarily give evidence for the doctrine of localization.

In a motor aphasia the individual may not be able to speak, and if lesions should occur, they are often found in the dominant Broca's area. There are several varieties of the expressive types of aphasia, and all are correlated by variable evidence with some area of the motor or premotor cortex. A pathologic inability to decide what to do, such as to choose meaningful words in speech, has been correlated with lesions in the ideomotor area and classified with the aphasias.

The importance of dominance is illustrated in the sensory aphasias. The failure to recognize spoken words (word deafness) is usually associated with lesions in the dominant superior temporal gyrus. Lesions in the dominant visual-association areas may be associated with failure to recognize written words (alexia) or objects in general (visual agnosia). Wepman (1951) suggests that aphasia may result from cerebral damage on the left side alone and that only the left cerebral hemisphere in all people is concerned with language on the symbolic level. On the articulatory or dysarthric level, language disturbances may result from damage of either hemisphere.

It is said that aphasics retain lower language functions, such as emotional expressions and memorized language content. This occurs supposedly because these faculties are mediated by the nondominant cortex (Eisenson, 1957).

Penfield and Rasmussen (1950) claim that perceptual auditory illusions and receptive auditory aphasia, involving alteration of judgment and of interpretation of sounds, may result from lesions in the superior part of the first temporal gyrus. Solomon (1957) says that the angular gyrus, dealing with the recognition of the visual image of words, and Wernicke's area, dealing with the recognition and interpretation of language sounds, are mutually dependent for correct association of words and sound; the usual clinical picture of a major lesion between both of these areas is a total receptive aphasia characterized by incorrect speech and writing and the inability to understand speech and writing. Solomon notes the existence of a hypothetical relationship between these areas which allows an internal language that is a necessary step to rational speaking or writing.

Aphasias are not always associated with organic lesions in localized cortical areas. Hughlings Jackson (1834–1911) refused to accept the doctrine of localization and stated that the aphasic suffers from a change in the whole personality. He wrote his first paper on speech disorders in 1864. His view became important because he introduced a dynamic concept of aphasia. He distinguished *propositional* or meaningful speech from emotional speech, and he recognized the failure of propositional speech in aphasia.

Henry Head in 1910 began to formulate tests to show that aphasia involves not just a loss or impairment of speech or language but embraces the functions responsible for the recognition and use of numbers, of music, of colors, and of drawings. The whole personality becomes involved (Eldridge, 1968). In 1926, Head proposed a functional, or psychologic approach in which aphasic disorders must not be viewed as isolated affections of speaking, reading, and writing. Each clinical type is an affection of symbolic formulation and expression. Head recognized four forms of such disturbance and called them verbal, nominal, syntactical, and semantic.

Verbal aphasia is a disorder in using words singly or in combination, and in severe cases the patient may be almost speechless. There may be associated lesions found in the region anterior to the motor area for the head and neck.

Nominal aphasia involves the lack of ability to comprehend specific words and particularly names, letters, and numbers. Lesions may occur in the angular gyrus.

Syntactical aphasia implies the inability to place words in an intelligible sequence, resulting in jargon. There may be lesions in the center of the first temporal gyrus.

Semantic aphasia is of the highest order and involves a failure to recognize the true meaning of language. Although a word or phrase is understood, a story is not comprehended nor can it be repeated in its true sense.

Although Head emphasized the psychologic approach as the above classification illustrates, he nevertheless correlated the loss of a specific psychologic function with a circumscribed lesion.

Among other investigators after Head, Kurt Goldstein (1942; 1948) emphasizes the gestalt theory, in which localization is denied but integration as a unit is disturbed. The language difficulty is only one symptom of aphasia. Wepman (1951) states that better prognosis is possible for aphasics through a nonlocalizationist standpoint in which recovery follows reintegration of residual cortical tissue into a functioning whole. Bay (1964) claims that from the clinical point of view one must begin with the stress on the psychologic aspect. Speech is primarily a psychologic phenomenon, and the immediate approach should be by psychologic methods.

Neurophysiology and Stuttering

Stuttering is a variety of faltering or interrupted speech which involves difficulty often with the enunciation of the first letter of a word, usually a consonant. There is marked difficulty with dentals and labials. Stuttering does not differ etiologically or therapeutically from *stammering*, which consists of a difficulty with speaking characterized by a repetition of sounds or syllables. According to DeJong (1967), stammering often indicates embarrassment or hesitation whereas stuttering suggests a more marked emotional quality. Brain (1965) states that stuttering is readily diagnosed and differentiated from all forms of aphasia by the fact that the structure of words and their use to express meanings are unaffected. It differs from other varieties of dysarthria by the characteristic repetitive element plus a distinctive clonus and tonus. It differs from dyslalia by the absence of mispronunciation of consonants because of replacement by faulty sounds. It differs from the related syndrome termed *cluttering*, which refers to sudden irregular accelerations of speech with shifting of stress and syllable division.

127

The etiology of stuttering may be variable. The symptoms nearly always appear in childhood or adolescence, and boys are affected far more often than girls. Stuttering is usually thought of as a disorder not of speech-producing organs proper but of the processes that integrate the activities of these organs (Brutton and Shoemaker, 1967).

The physiogenic school emphasizes neurologic and physical causes. The psychogenic school emphasizes differences in personality structure and behavior; the stutterer has formed attitudes and needs related to speech which interfere with speech. Psychoanalysts relate the condition to emotional conflicts of childhood. A third, or interactionist school, combines the above approaches and usually holds that a functional weakness precipitates a failure in speech production when fear or tension becomes involved. Since 1960 there has been a trend toward emphasizing biologic, hereditary, and neurologic factors as the important etiologic agents. Freund (1966) notes that there is much interest in the direction of learning theory, depth psychology, environmentalism, and experimental psychology. He also notes the attempt to systematize existing theories into (1) constitutional, (2) learning, and (3) neurosis theories. Falck (1969) states that stuttering is learned behavior and follows the rules of learning.

In reviewing the neurophysiologic approach, the failure of, or interference with, an established dominance has been a prominent tenet in theories of the cause of stuttering. The speech and writing areas are closely associated in the dominant hemisphere, and the dissociation of the writing area from the speech area by, for instance, retraining a left-handed person to use his right hand, was widely considered in the past to be sufficient cause to provoke stuttering. The theory of stuttering associated with conflict between two sides of the brain has lost currency.

Stuttering has also been explained neurologically on the basis of a failure in the timing action of the integrative centers located in the cortical or subcortical regions. This results in distorted rhythms.

There is the hypothesis (Karlin, 1950) that stuttering is associated with a delay in the acquisition of the myelin sheaths which ordinarily cover spinal nerve fibers and which also cover the fibers constituting the white matter of the brain. Girls are said to develop the necessary cortical myelin earlier than boys, and they show a lesser incidence of stuttering.

Actually, any attempt to explain stuttering only through anatomy or physiology could meet with objection. The organicists have changed the choice of organ to which they have referred the causative factor. Aristotle thought the tongue was too hard and thick. Hippocrates applied medications to the neck and throat. Celsus emphasized the respiratory aspect.

In reviewing the psychologic theories, stuttering is explained as a symptom of an emotional difficulty, as an aberrant social response, as an inhibition before the conditioned reflex is firmly established, as an expression of certain psychoneuroses, and in other ways. Barbara (1965) stresses the factors of interpersonal relationships and the whole personality as sources of the disorder.

Wyatt (1969) historically reviews the theories of the origin of stuttering, classifying the present ones into genogenic, psychogenic, developmental, and the diverse recent approaches. She proposes a developmental crisis theory in which stuttering is a preventable disorder arising as a disturbance in language learning, coincident with a disruption of the relationship between mother and child. Where rigid defenses have been developed, as in older children, stuttering is said to be not only a personality disorder but also a disturbance in interpersonal relations.

Although there is a view that there may be no obvious common denominators in the causes of stuttering or even that there is no single syndrome of stuttering, evidence for a common conflict does exist (Perkins, 1965).

Pathophysiology of the Basal Ganglia

Among the neurologic disturbances, those related to the control of voluntary movements are of importance. The basal ganglia can play a significant part in such disorders, and the possible mechanisms have been discussed previously.

The dyskinesias called *athetosis* and *chorea* may occur without typical changes in muscle *tonus*. In athetosis the movements are slow, writhing, involuntary, and ceaseless, seen particularly in the hands. The corpus striatum may be the area of the brain most affected. In chorea the movements are involuntary, brief, sudden, jerky, ceaseless, and although purposeless they are well coordinated.

Another dyskinesia is *ballismus,* which may be caused by destruction of the subthalamus (body of Luys) or its fiber tracts. The movements are ballistic (flinging) and violent and are seen in the proximal limb muscles. The term hemiballismus refers to this process occurring on one side.

Parkinson's Disease (Paralysis Agitans) This disease is characterized by a disabling reduction in voluntary movements, by poverty of movement (akinesia), and by postural disorder. Movement is difficult to initiate, and an immobility results. There is no real paralysis. The brain damage is diffuse, and more than one of the basal ganglia appear to be involved.

129

The postural disturbance is expressed by the term *rigidity* (hypertonia), which applies to all varieties of hypertonia that are not of pyramidal origin. There are several types of rigidity, with certain features common to all. Rigidity involves an increase of tone that is present throughout the full range of motion around a joint, thus producing resistance to an applied force. The resistance may be steady and uniform (lead pipe), or intermittent (cogwheel). Thus, in Parkinsonism, a limb typically shows resistance throughout the entire extent of a passive movement, and this occurs both in the extensor muscles and even stronger in the flexors. The lead pipe and cogwheel reactions to bending can both be expressed. In extrapyramidal disorders the rigidity depends upon the integrity of the stretch reflexes. The globus pallidus contributes, although in an obscure manner, to the mechanisms underlying the rigidity.

In Parkinson's disease, *tremor* (hyperkinesia) is an outstanding sign. It occurs during rest as fine, regular, rapid oscillations, most obvious in the distal aspects of the limbs. Interruption of higher descending pathways apparently allows some lower brainstem mechanism, probably the reticulospinal system, to oscillate. The lesion is in some undetermined nuclei, the substantia nigra and globus pallidus being suspected.

Speech becomes indistinct, with loss of meter (prosody), and there may be chewing difficulty because of the rigidity.

Spasticity

This state is expressed as an increase in muscle tone and is found in upper motor neuron disease. It is the most common abnormality of tone. Spasticity is often referred to as pyramidal hypertonia, even though the association of "pyramidal" and "hypertonia" appear physiologically to be in conflict in the sense that pure pyramidal lesions do not produce hypertonia.

Spasticity is to be differentiated from rigidity. The basic character of spasticity is the exaggerated contraction of a muscle when subjected to stretch. If suddenly elongated, it contracts with a vigor related to the degree of spasticity. In clinical parlance this response has been called the stretch reflex (which should be compared with the strict physiologic use of the term stretch reflex).

In spasticity there is resistance to passive movement of muscles, especially marked in the flexors of the arms and extensors of the legs. The tone grades from normal as one rapidly extends or flexes a joint to a marked increase as full extension or flexion is approached. In the classical variety of spasticity, the resistance finally collapses. This is called the *lengthening* or *clasp-knife* response, and it characterizes spasticity rather than rigidity.

Spasticity is said to be a "release phenomenon," which appears at first glance to be due to a release from governance of the segmental stretch reflex. The cause may lie more probably, however, in the predominance of activity in a facilitatory brainstem mechanism such as the reticulospinal system.

130

Cerebral Palsy and Neuromotor Pathophysiology

Cerebral palsy is a disorder of movement and posture resulting from a defect or lesion of the brain and expressed as paralysis, weakness, dyscoordination, or other aberration of motor function. Carrell (1968) states that the most prominent symptom is incorrect movement rather than weakness or absence of motion. There are differences in defining this syndrome.

Five types of motor disturbance are usually described: athetosis (dyskinesia), ataxia, rigidity, tremor, and spasticity. Mixed types occur.

The pathologic basis has been ascribed to dysfunction of the motor control circuitry of the brain (Denhoff, 1966), and damage to the descending systems. In many ways the disease transcends the limited definition of a neuromuscular derangement, since a variety of intellectual and behavioral signs and symptoms may occur, singly or in combinations. The various forms of the disease express the effects of varying and diffuse pathologic processes upon different parts of the brain. At one time all the manifestations of such palsies were classified as Little's disease.

Opinions vary about the etiology of cerebral palsy. Heredity does not seem to be important. Factors related to birth injury and postnatal developmental problems account for over 50 percent of the known cases (Cruickshank, 1966).

The types of neuromuscular disorders are related to the locus of the lesion. The loci may involve the pyramidal tract, extrapyramidal tract, or cerebellar system. According to Denhoff (1966), "pyramidal" involvement is associated with spastic paralysis. Damage to the basal ganglia is associated with athetosis, chorea, tremor, disturbances of tone, or rigidity. Damage to the cerebellum or its peduncles is associated with ataxia, atonia, or intention tremor. Ataxia is expressed by awkwardness or inability in maintaining balance or coordination; these patients find it difficult to coordinate the speech muscles, and articulation may be slurred.

There is no speech or language disorder that is unique to cerebral palsy (Lencione, 1966). Characteristically, the speech patterns are slow, labored, and distorted and are often a result of dysfunction of muscles acting in articulation, breathing, and phonation.

Brainstem Damage
The importance of the brainstem is brought out in bulbar palsy (poliomyelitis), in which the motor nerve cells of the brainstem and the spinal cord are attacked by a virus. Any of the cranial nuclei in the medulla may be destroyed with subsequent atrophy of their axons. The breathing centers of the reticular formation may be damaged, with resulting paralysis of the diaphragm and intercostal muscles. When the vagus nerve nuclei are attacked, weakness or paralysis of the pharynx, soft palate, and vocal folds may result.

When the muscles controlling the soft palate are paralyzed, an adequate nasopharyngeal port closure is lacking, and nasality becomes chronically sustained.

131

Damage to medullary nuclei or an injury to both corticobulbar tracts can produce a thick speech, in which the patient seems to have a mouthful of soft food while he is talking.

The age of incidence of bulbar palsy is highest in the first ten years, and the onset of symptoms is more abrupt in children. A fatal peripheral respiratory failure is common. Fortunately, poliomyelitis is becoming rare, and very few therapists will ever work with a patient having this disease.

5 AUTONOMIC AND ENDOCRINE REGULATORS OF SPEECH

We have seen that the central nervous system functions in part for the reception and storage of information with the capacity to associate the information into complex concepts. The action of the centers upon the peripheral effectors such as muscles and glands is volitional, rapid, and usually precise.

The autonomic and endocrine regulators play a supporting role, which is none the less important. The endocrines come into action relatively slowly, but their effect is strong and sustained. The autonomic and endocrine agencies help establish the background conditions of speech, and they are especially significant in determining the individuality or emotional coloring of the voice.

The autonomic nervous system and the endocrine glands are closely associated in function. This is especially true for the thoracolumbar, or sympathetic, section of the autonomics which acts functionally with the medulla of the adrenal gland to form a *sympatheticoadrenal* system. The linkage is seen in the fact that the hypothalamus is the head center of the sympathetic (and probably the parasympathetic) autonomic nerves and is also the organ in which emotional reactions gain expression. Such behavior intimately involves the activity of both autonomic nerves and endocrine glands.

Nervous and endocrine mechanisms function cooperatively to integrate the organism. Both systems synthesize and release special chemicals. Many endocrine glands, through their hormones, act on the nervous system and are in turn stimulated or inhibited by products of the nervous system. Since many processes are under the control of both hormones and nerves, the term *neuroendocrine system* has a logical basis.

Emotions and Neuroendocrine Involvement

Much of the motivation for speech is emotional. Although phonation appears first as purposeless sounds, it comes to be used in struggle situations, as in hunger, pain, or anger.

The voice is the medium for expressing the emotions, and it is linked with such emotional aspects of personality as stability, friendliness, sympathy, and aggressiveness. The machinery of the emotional responses is located primarily in the hypothalamus. This is evidenced by the sympathetic nervous concomitants of an emotion. Stage fright, for example, produces not only speech aberration but also occasional sympatheticoadrenal responses, including a rapid pulse, cold sweat, and muscle trembling.

Neural coordination appears to break down in strong emotional experiences, and vocal tremors and abnormal muscular rhythms can be produced. The sequelae of the alterations in muscle tone may be reflected in throat tensions and a harsh, strained voice. The autonomic changes have an influence upon breathing and lead to a lack of reserve breath and the disruption of smooth speech flow. Not only do emotions affect respiration, but even the recollections of emotions do so.

Holmes (1940) presents an interesting and provocative hypothesis concerning the role of emotions in poor phonation. Efficient voice production is said to require the matching of an optimal pressure by the breath stream with an optimal resistance by the laryngeal valve. The laryngeal musculature is claimed to operate first for struggle reactions, and such behavior involves a maximum resistance of the laryngeal valve to the passage of the breath stream. This conflict presents the greatest single problem influencing correct voice sounds. The conflict is exaggerated in strong emotional states, in which the voluntary muscles may enter a generalized hypertonic condition. If the emotional changes persist, the approximated vocal folds may become too resistant for correct phonation.

Endocrines and the Larynx

The larynx is changeable at puberty and subject to complex endocrine control. Similarly, the status of the nasal mucosa and its subsequent contribution to voice resonance are under endocrine control. In this sense the voice may be thought of as a barometer of psychic function.

At puberty gonadotropic hormones help shape the voice registers. In the male and female climacteric, which is under strong endocrine control, the characteristics of the voice are again subject to change.

Much of our behavior is endocrine-controlled, although this factor can be over-emphasized. Before birth the endocrines partly determine growth and differentiation. Prenatal influence of the endocrines in the development of the vocal mechanisms is obscure.

Anatomy of the Autonomic Nervous System

The autonomic nervous system innervates all the smooth muscles, glands, and the cardiac muscle. It controls vital functions not under voluntary control. The system is not causative but regulative for functions that are essentially automatic. Thus, the heart will beat in a coordinated manner, the smooth muscles of the alimentary canal can resume normal tone, rhythm, and peristalsis, and the muscles of the arterioles can regain adequate tone, all following complete denervation of the extrinsic nerves.

Usually only the efferent autonomic nerves are described because of their high degree of anatomic organization. The visceral afferents are difficult to consider as an integral unit because they arise from voluntary (somatic) as well as autonomic receptors, and they are not necessarily an exclusive part of the autonomic system. The term visceral afferent is much more appropriate than autonomic afferent for the incoming fibers.

The autonomic system is relatively independent of the central nervous system in its functioning. The system is derived from the central system by the proliferation of neuroblast cells, which maintain contact through nerve fibers with the brain or spinal cord. The typical connections and outflows involve at least two neurons; the first, called preganglionic, connects the central nervous system with the autonomic ganglion (group of cells outside the brain or cord), and the second, called postganglionic, travels from the ganglion to the visceral effector. The preganglionic, or white ramus, has a myelin sheath which is not present in the postganglionic, or gray ramus.

Visceral cell bodies distinct from the somatic cell bodies in the lateral horn of the gray matter of the spinal cord send medullated (white) fibers out of the ventral root. These are efferent preganglionic autonomics. They leave the mixed spinal nerve as a ramus which terminates either in a paravertebral ganglion on each side of the spinal cord or goes out to a collateral ganglion (plexus) distal to the straight chain of paravertebral ganglia. A second neuron, called the gray or postganglionic fiber, leaves the ganglion and either rejoins a spinal nerve or travels directly from the collateral ganglion to the end organ.

In those spinal nerve trunks which carry the visceral efferent fibers, somatic efferent fibers are also carried, which do not synapse in intermediate ganglia but travel directly to a voluntary muscle. Such trunks are actually mixed and carry both somatic afferent fibers and both visceral afferent and visceral efferent fibers. The different fibers of the trunk are called *neuron components* and show that a nerve is very heterogeneous in composition and function.

136

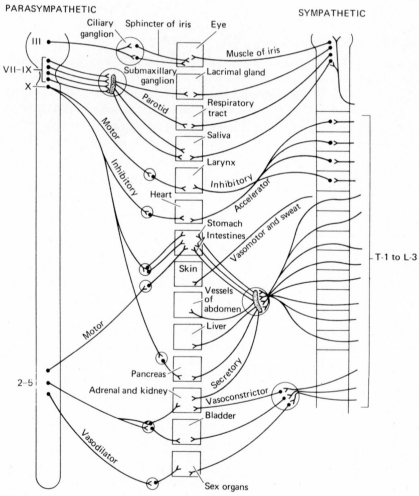

Figure 5-1 Diagrammatic representation of the parasympathetic and sympathetic outflows.

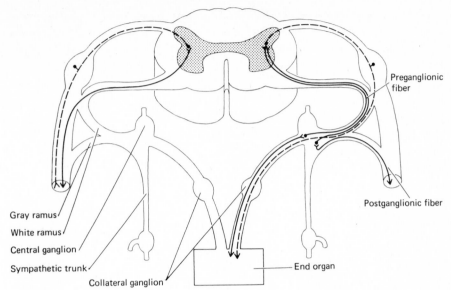

Figure 5-2 Relationship of the sympathetic autonomic ganglia to the spinal cord.

Whereas the cells producing cerebrospinal fibers are found at every segmental level of the spinal cord and also at twelve levels in the brain for the cranial nerve outflow, the entire autonomic preganglionic outflow involves four general levels: the midbrain, hindbrain, and thoracolumbar and sacral segments of the spinal cord.

The thoracolumbar efferents constitute the sympathetic nervous system, while the two cranial plus the one sacral outflows constitute the parasympathetic system. The entire mass is termed the autonomic nervous system. A brief survey of the segmental outflows follows.

Sympathetic Nerves

The preganglionics leave the spinal cord in the anterior roots of all twelve thoracic segments and in those of the first two or three lumbar segments. The postganglionic fibers eventually supply almost every region of the body.

The paired preganglionics terminate just in front of the spinal cord in the sympathetic cell bodies or ganglia. This system forms a kind of stepladder or paired chain of perhaps twenty-two vertebral ganglia anterior to the cord. Each ganglion is cross-connected to its mate like the horizontal rung of a ladder. Each ganglion extends fibers to the ganglia above and below it like the vertical runners of the ladder. The postganglionics leaving each ganglion run peripherally toward the effector. The uppermost part of the ganglionic chain is in the neck at the level of the thyroid cartilage angle, and this portion contains the paired superior, middle, and inferior cervical ganglia.

137

The superior cervical ganglion, which is at the level of the second cervical vertebra, gives off several branches. The most superior, or internal carotid, nerve constitutes the cephalic sector of the system. It enters the cranial cavity with the internal carotid artery. The great cardiac nerve is a second branch and goes to the deep and superficial cardiac plexes of the heart. The ganglion also gives off rami which travel with the first four cervical nerves.

The middle cervical ganglion sends postganglionic fibers to 5-C and 6-C, and it also gives off the middle cardiac nerve. The inferior cervical ganglion sends fibers into 7-C and 8-C, and it is the origin of the inferior cardiac nerve. The cervical ganglia have no direct connection to the cervical cord by white rami, but they are upward extensions of the thoracic part of the stepladderlike chain and receive their preganglionics by upward proliferation of fibers from this chain. By means of the efferent postganglionic outflows from the three pairs of cervical ganglia, a sympathetic control is afforded for all secretory and vasomotor phenomena in the head and neck. The organs of phonation, resonance, and articulation are significantly involved.

The thoracic sympathetics are typically one pair to each spinal segment. The first cervical fuses with the inferior cervical ganglion to produce the stellate ganglion. This ganglion is important, since it can be reached by injection of anesthetics for blocking sympathetic impulses from localized bodily areas. Every thoracic ganglion is connected to the cord by a white ramus.

138

The upper five gray, or postganglionic, rami supply the thoracic aorta and its branches. If there are three splanchnic nerves, 5 to 8-T form the great splanchnic, 9 to 10-T the middle splanchnic, and 11 to 12-T the least splanchnic. These penetrate the abdomen behind the crura of the diaphragm, and they enter the celiac plexus or its branches at 1-L.

In the abdomen there are four lumbar ganglia; the first three are connected to the cord by white rami, and the fourth is an inferior extension of the straight chain. The postganglionics travel into the superior mesenteric, aortic, and hypogastric plexes from which additional sympathetic fibers go to the abdominal and pelvic visceral effectors.

The lowest extensions of the chain are four or five sacral ganglia which have no direct white rami connections to the cord. Their gray postganglionic fibers go to the pelvic plexus and to the coccygeal ganglion.

There are usually many more postganglionic fibers leaving the sympathetic ganglia than there are preganglionics entering them. The numerous synaptic connections in the sympathetic system allow an extensive dissemination of impulses.

Plexes
Within the thorax, abdomen, and pelvis there are several great collections of ganglia, or plexes (also called prevertebral or collateral ganglia). These are outly-

ing way stations for the readjustment of impulses, and they receive fibers not only from sympathetic but also from parasympathetic fibers. The nerve trunks that leave any plexus to the effectors are thus heterogeneous.

The cardiac plexes, superficial and deep, lie at the base of the heart. They collect from the three cervical sympathetic ganglia and from the superior and inferior cardiac branches of the vagus nerve.

The celiac (solar or epigastric) plexus is composed of right and left celiac ganglia behind the stomach. It receives the right vagus and the splanchnic nerves. It in turn sends out branches which follow the celiac artery to its visceral endings. The plexus also sends fibers down the descending aorta. These fibers help form lower plexes which receive reinforcing fibers from lumbar and sacral segments and supply the abdominal and pelvic viscera.

Parasympathetic Nerves

The preganglionics do not go to a straight chain, as in the sympathetic system, but travel greater distances to terminate in plexes or ganglia, some of which lie upon the visceral effector and require only a short postganglionic terminal trunk.

The termination of the preganglionics within or close to the end organ is the most distinctive morphologic characteristic of parasympathetic nerves. Another property is their restricted distribution, which allows this system to exert effects upon a single organ without simultaneously exciting widespread and unrelated changes.

139

The tectal or midbrain outflow includes autonomic nuclei belonging to the oculo-motor cranial nerve. It controls the sphincter of the iris and the ciliary muscle of accommodation.

The bulbar or hindbrain outflow includes several cranial nerves. The facial nerve carries vasodilator and secretory impulses. Some of these impulses travel from the superior salivatory nucleus through the chorda tympani to the tongue and salivary glands. Others pass through the greater superficial petrosal and vidian nerve via the sphenopalatine ganglion to the palate, nasopharynx, and parotid and orbital glands. Similar impulses belonging to the glossopharyngeal nerve go from the inferior salivatory nucleus through the lesser superficial petrosal nerve via the otic ganglion to the parotid gland and oral regions. Another nerve carrying similar impulses is the vagus to the thoracic and abdominal viscera.

The general rule that organs receive double innervation from sympathetic and parasympathetic nerves has exceptions. The sweat glands have only sympathetics, which behave like parasympathetics. Woodburne (1967) states that possibly the vasomotor supply to peripheral blood vessels has no parasympathetics, and Mount-castle (1968) adds the pilomotor muscles, the smooth muscle of the nictitating membrane and of the spleen, and the blood vessels of the skeletal muscles. In such cases increased or decreased activity is effected through a single innervation that is *tonically* active.

Autonomic Control Centers

The hypothalamus is said to control the sympathetic nerve outflow. Lesions in the hypothalamic region indicate that descending fibers run from it to the visceral nuclei of the spinal cord. The hypothalamus is connected to the cerebrum so that any affective experience can have an autonomic effect.

The head centers of the parasympathetic system are more obscure, although evidence points to other bodies in the diencephalon and the hypothalamus is also involved.

The hypothalamus and other diencephalic centers must be regarded as higher autonomic regulators which control lower centers. The latter exist in the midbrain, pons, and medulla. The medullary nuclei control many *vegetative* functions, i.e., those essential to life, including heart rate, blood pressure, and alimentary and urinary processes. Respiration (an involuntary but not an autonomic activity) is also controlled in the hindbrain. These facts indicate that the hypothalamus is not essential to the various sympathetic reflexes and tonic discharges and that they can be managed by bulbospinal mechanisms (Mountcastle, 1968). Also, the hypothalamus is not exclusively concerned with autonomic functions.

The manner in which the hypothalamus influences autonomic functions is complex. Most of the fibers do not travel down in tight, discrete bundles but are diffuse and short and there are many synapses in the pathways.

140

The cerebral cortex is also in control of autonomic responses. A change in arterial pressure is the autonomic response most often elicited.

Chemical Mediators

The differences in the effects of sympathetic and parasympathetic nerves are explainable by the fact that unlike chemical substances are liberated through the postganglionic terminals into the end organs. The actual substances were originally investigated by Cannon and by Loewi. Dale classified parasympathetic fibers as cholinergic and sympathetic fibers as adrenergic.

All preganglionic fibers release acetylcholine (ACh), and the same is true of cerebrospinal nerve endings. These fibers are cholinergic.

Parasympathetic postganglionics release ACh. Most sympathetic postganglionics release norepinephrine and a lesser amount of epinephrine and are adrenergic.

Extracts of nerves produce the same effect as stimulation of the nerves; the substances are thus called *mediators*. The vagus slows the heart by sending ACh into the cardiac cells, and the sympathetics accelerate the heart through transmission of epinephrinelike substances. Cannon originally called the latter sympathin E or I to explain differential excitation or inhibition, but the nature of sympathin has been subjected to various interpretations. Sympathin E had been thought to be norepinephrine, and sympathin I has been called epinephrine (or sympathin A). Both epinephrine and norepinephrine belong to a class of substances called catechol amines.

The ACh released is destroyed by cholinesterase, an enzyme present in all effectors and in the fluids surrounding the cholinergic nerve endings. The epinephrine compounds released at nerve endings are also destroyed, by reabsorption into the sympathetic nerves, and by methylation accelerated by the enzyme catechol O-methyl transferase. The sympathetic autonomics differ from the parasympathetics in that there is substantial persistence of the effective action.

The medulla of the adrenal gland releases epinephrine and norepinephrine at the same time that they are released by nerve action. These are supportive and sub-stitutive actions. The endocrine gland can promote activity not directly influenced by sympathetic nerves.

Autonomic Functions

The autonomic system deals with adaptations to the environment. It innervates structures that are automatic but need be regulated only by a relatively simple control.

Most bodily organs have a double autonomic innervation with few exceptions. The two kinds of nerves are in one sense mutually antagonistic, but in another sense they are complementary. Each division may excite or inhibit depending upon the end organ in question. Thus the vagus may cause active secretion in the vocal folds but it slows the heart. The autonomic system is not essential to life. In the early experiments of Cannon, a totally sympathectomized cat was kept alive for 3½ years, although it lost its power of adaptation to external changes and had to be kept under uniform environmental conditions.

Claude Bernard and later Cannon elaborated on the importance of the constancy of conditions in the immediate environment of the organism. Cannon suggested the term *homeostasis* to define the steady state of the internal medium. Many of the regulatory mechanisms involve the sympathetic autonomics. The activities are usually generalized rather than local. This is called a *mass discharge* and ex-presses an alarm or stress reaction. The parasympathetic nerves have more local-ized activities, such as control only of the heart or of oral secretion.

The Endocrine Glands

The endocrines are specialized glands without a duct system for carrying their secretory products or hormones away. The secretions must therefore be liberated into the surrounding hemal or lymph systems. These glands do not always accel-erate a reaction, but they may prevent it. Hormones usually excite target organs that are situated at variable distances from the site of the hormonal production. The target may be a specific area or process, or the target may be every cell of the body.

Some of the glands producing hormones have both an external (duct) secretion as well as an internal (ductless) secretion. In a few cases the endocrines may be found not as discrete organs but as areas in an organ serving other purposes. This is seen in the pancreas, the small intestine, and the kidney.

A principle called *negative feedback* is involved in the control of hormonal secretion. An endocrine gland tends to oversecrete. When the desired function has been achieved, information is fed back to depress additional secretion. The specific control mechanism for each hormone is a subject of marked interest to physiologists. Also, negative feedback in general is of great importance to the body, e.g., for auditory feedback in the modulation of speech.

In chemical composition, hormones are (1) steroids, as exemplified by those of the adrenal cortex, ovary, and testis, or (2) proteins or amino acids or derivatives of proteins.

The influence of the endocrines upon speech is perhaps most vividly seen in speech under tension. The highly irregular rhythm of breathing, the arrhythmic pulse, and the tremors in the voice are some of the indicators of excess hormone output. The regulatory substances are secreted from more than one gland, and they act in synergism with the sympathetic nervous system.

142

In general, whenever there are alterations in such qualities as the depth, height, timbre, and power of the voice, endocrine dysfunction may be suspected. The signs

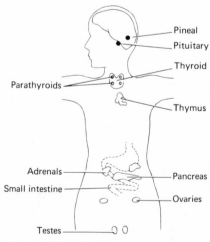

Figure 5-3 Endocrine glands.

of such imbalance are not always prominent. Thus, in early youth a persistent high voice or an excessively deep voice may be the only obvious indications.

Thyroid Gland

This consists of two lateral lobes and an inconstant inferior connecting portion called the isthmus. All the parts are situated upon the anterior surface of the trachea and loosely attached thereto. The nerve supply is autonomic, consisting of the parasympathetic thyroid branch of the superior laryngeal division of the vagus and sympathetic nerves from the superior and middle cervical ganglia. These nerves are vasomotor rather than secretory, and the gland is normally regulated by the thyrotropic hormone from the anterior lobe of the pituitary gland.

A note is inserted here about the usage of tropin instead of trophin as a suffix. Trophin implies a nutritional state, as in atrophic or hypertrophic. Tropin means a substance which has a specific affinity for given tissues, and it is the proper suffix to use for thyrotropin.

The thyroid is interrelated with the gonads. Thus, the thyroid enlarges at puberty, menstruation, and pregnancy, whereas its activity is depressed upon castration. The thyroid is inhibited by the activity of both the adrenal cortex and the medulla.

There are several hormones secreted into the central lumen or colloid of the acini, which are the histophysiologic units of function. The major inorganic component of all the secretions is iodine, and this is essential to the endocrine function.

143

The active hormone is probably thyroxine, which is a cyclic amino acid built from tyrosine; this hormone has been synthesized. Free thyroxine may not in itself be the true thyroid hormone, but perhaps it builds up to a more active polypeptide. The stages of thyroxine synthesis have been found with a tracer called radioactive iodine (iodine 131). Tyrosine is first built to the relatively inactive diiodotyrosine, which is the principal precursor of thyroxine.

Thyroglobulin, which is the specific material of the colloid, has also been thought to be the true hormone. It may be a storage form in which thyroxine conjugates with a protein.

Radioactive iodine compounds in the gland have been separated by chromatography, and by this means another active compound has been discovered called triiodothyronine.

The action of the active principle is to increase tissue oxidation and the standard metabolism (BMR). Accessory actions involve increase in the mental activity, heart rate, blood circulation, heat production, and sweat gland function.

Thyroid deficiency, or hypothyroidism, takes many forms. If iodine is lacking in the diet, the gland swells to compensate, and this produces a simple goiter, which is amenable to iodine replacement. Deficiency or absence of the secretion in the infant produces infantile myxedema, or cretinism, in which growth is slowed and

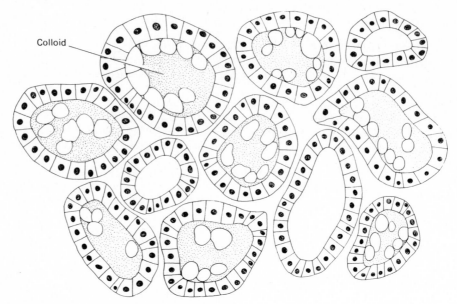

Colloid

Figure 5-4 Follicles of the thyroid gland.

144

dwarfism results. There is depression of the metabolism, sluggish mentality, and arrested somatic and sexual development. In the adult type of myxedema similar but less severe symptomatology occurs.

Hypometabolism of endocrine origin, ascribable to hypothyroidism, is a common clinical condition. It produces many nonspecific symptoms, such as fatigability and intolerance to cold.

The skeletal muscles in hypothyroidism often become torpid and relaxed. Berry and Eisenson (1956) write of a husky, unmodulated voice and slow, clumsy speech in myxedema. Cecil and Loeb (1955) describe a thick speech resulting from an enlarged tongue and swollen lips. In reviewing the "cretin voice" (Luchsinger, 1962), twenty-six of thirty-six cretins studied showed a restricted voice range, poor voice quality, and ill-developed or missing head register. The larynx in all cases showed hypoplasia.

The cretin may have a small larynx, with delayed laryngeal ossification. Levin (1962) describes the voice as low and hoarse, with a small vocal range. The cretin voice may simulate the voice of senility.

In adult myxedema there may be atrophy of the vocalis muscle, incomplete glottal closure, and frequent hoarseness.

In cretinism there may be inner ear deafness, and in myxedema there may be a hearing loss. The external ear is sometimes dry and itching because of reduced ceruminous gland activity.

In excessive secretion the body is flooded with hormone, although the thyroid becomes depleted. The symptoms include raised metabolism, tachycardia, sweating, hypertension, tenseness, nervousness, and exophthalmos (protruding eyeballs).

The skeletal muscles in hyperthyroidism may develop a tenseness which leads to an unpleasant, high pitched, rapid voice displaying breathiness, fine tremors, and irregularities in pitch (Berry and Eisenson, 1956). In Grave's disease there may be tremulous intonation and vocal fatigue, due to lowered vital capacity and rapid, shallow breathing.

The processes of development, which include both growth and differentiation, are upset in hyper- and hypothyroidism. Speech, however, need not be significantly disturbed in an endocrine disorder. This is a problem of the individual case.

145

Parathyroid Glands

These glands are less directly related to speech functions. There are generally two small glands on each side, very close to or embedded in the thyroid glands. Their total excision leads to death. In an experimental animal, total extirpation produces, after a day or more, involuntary muscle twitching which becomes coarser and more severe until it terminates in convulsions. Death occurs from respiratory failure through spasms of the muscles of breathing. The condition is called parathyroid tetany, and it is a result of a decrease in the calcium concentration of the blood. The parathyroids maintain the blood calcium level, as well as that of phosphorus, by releasing parathormone. This hormone draws calcium into the blood from its storage reservoirs such as the bones. Too little secretion results in decreased serum calcium, but excessive hormone raises the serum calcium concentration. A balance is preserved between the blood calcium, the calcium in the bones, and the total excretion of calcium from the body.

The blood calcium is related to neuromuscular irritability, and in this regard the vocal mechanism becomes involved. When calcium decreases excessively, nerve and muscle irritability increases, but when calcium increases, irritability is decreased. In the pathologic state of decreased blood calcium, a rapid and overly nervous speech may be observable.

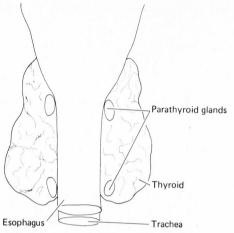

Figure 5-5 The thyroid gland viewed diagrammatically from behind to show the positions of the embedded parathyroid glands.

A by-product of these facts involves the possibility of a real basis for blood-chemistry studies in speech disorders, and this line of endeavor has been pursued. Caution is advised in overemphasizing this line of attack. Speech is an extremely complex function, involving the whole psychic as well as the biologic machinery of behavior. Deviation in the serum concentrations of given substances may be only remotely related to the diagnosis of a given disturbance or to the proper way of treatment.

Thymus Gland

This organ lies in the neck, anterior and lateral to the trachea and deep to the sternohyoid and sternothyroid muscles. It descends into the superior mediastinal area of the thorax behind the sternum and in front of the great vessels of the heart. It is composed of two lobes, supplied with blood from the internal mammary and superior thyroid arteries. The vagus and sympathetic autonomics constitute its innervation. The structure is prominent in the infant and grows in size and weight to eleven or twelve years of age. At about fifteen years it begins to involute, and in old age it is hardly recognizable.

There are numerous hypotheses concerning thymus function. Its control over growth and secondary sexual characters, as well as its capacity to produce lymphocytes, has been frequently emphasized. Its role in speech is purely one of pathology. If the thymus does not regress, it exerts undue pressure upon the structures of the throat. Speech may become infantile and mechanically clumsy. Fortunately, the gland is susceptible to x-rays, which produce shrinkage. In thymus hypertrophy or tumor formation, irradiation or thymectomy has in many instances improved the status of the affected individual. An enlarged thymus with excessively developed lymphoid tissue occurs in status lymphaticus.

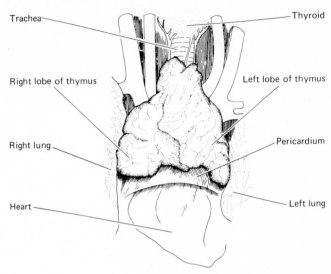

Trachea—
Thyroid

Right lobe of thymus
Left lobe of thymus

Right lung
Pericardium

Heart
Left lung

Figure 5-6 Location of the thymus gland.

Adrenal Glands

These lie above the kidney and consist of a central medulla and peripheral cortex. Both parts are independent functional units joined together in development.

147

Medulla The actions resemble those caused by stimulation of the sympathetic sector of the autonomic nervous system except that the effects are greatly prolonged. The gland is important in helping to shape the emotional tone of the voice and the background conditions for speech. The speech of stage fright and of other fear responses is analyzable on an organic basis by chemical endocrine changes, especially those involving the sympatheticoadrenal system.

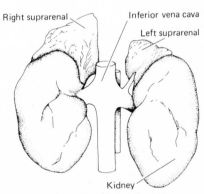

Right suprarenal
Inferior vena cava
Left suprarenal

Kidney

Figure 5-7 Relationships of the suprarenal glands to other structures.

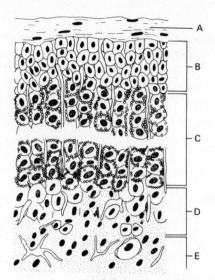

Figure 5-8. Section through a portion of the suprarenal gland: (*a*) capsule, (*b*) zona glomerulosa, (*c*) zona fasciculata, (*d*) zona reticularis, (*e*) medulla.

Histologically, the medulla consists of neuroblasts which are identical with the ganglion cells of the sympathetic nervous system. The medulla is innervated only by preganglionic fibers from the splanchnic nerves, while its secreting cells are morphologically homologous with postganglionic fibers of the sympathetic nervous system. This emphasizes the logical use of the term sympatheticoadrenal system.

The active hormones of the medulla are epinephrine and norepinephrine. About 75 percent of the secretion is norepinephrine. The hormones are carried to all tissues of the body.

Norepinephrine injection produces a more lasting effect than sympathetic nerve stimulation does because of its slow removal from the blood.

Epinephrine has fast but transitory effects. It has a stronger effect on the heart than norepinephrine does, but it has a weaker constricting effect on the blood vessels in the skeletal muscles.

Epinephrine is much the better drug to increase the metabolic rate, raising the activity and excitability of the whole body. It produces liver glycogenolysis and thus raises the blood sugar. It relaxes smooth muscle.

The general function of the medullary hormones is to aid in the adaptation to conditions demanding vigorous neuromuscular activity. Ordinarily, the amounts of circulating hormones are very small, but they increase demonstrably during states of stress or emergency.

Unlike the adrenal cortex, whose actions involve adjustments to nonspecific stress, the medulla may be regarded as a part of the sympathetic nervous system, and its hormones participate in specific reactions (Turner, 1966).

The hormones also serve to stimulate structures not innervated by sympathetic fibers. This is exemplified by the endocrine control of the metabolic rate, which involves all cells. Sympathetic nerves innervate only a small proportion of the body cells.

The vasomotor and secretory activities of the vocal mechanism are simply localized counterparts of the general bodily effects produced by sympatheticoadrenal stimulation.

Cortex The cortex is vital to life, but the medulla is not. The cortex has almost thirty hormones. All are steroids, and they have the same basic structural nucleus as cholesterol. They are chemically related to the sex hormones, some of which are synthesized in the adrenal cortex as well as in the sex glands.

The active adrenal steroids fall into three groups according to physiologic activity. The mineralocorticoids bring about the reabsorption of sodium and chloride from the kidney to the blood. Important examples are deoxycorticosterone and aldosterone. Electrolyte balance of the blood is preserved.

The glucocorticoids do not markedly affect electrolyte balance but produce sugar breakdown in carbohydrate metabolism. Important examples are compound E, or cortisone, and compound F, or hydrocortisone. These have the capacity of being anti-inflammatory drugs.

149

The hormones of the third group are of great interest in vocal physiology. They include the androgens, estrogens, and progesterone. They are variably involved in secondary sexual development. In tumor formation they are excessively secreted, and masculinizing effects occur. Rarely are there femininizing tumors. One may see precocious sexual and somatic development in children or virilism and hirsutism in females (as with the bearded lady of the circus). The effects can be exerted upon or expressed through the qualities of the voice. Thus, in Addison's disease, where widespread cortical destruction may occur, the voice may weaken and become hoarse and cracking.

The voice in many ways expresses the general bodily status, and it is involved in the general adaptation to the environment. The adrenal cortex facilitates such adaptation. Hans Selye postulated the nature of the machinery used by pointing up what occurs upon exposure to stress. He called the forces *stressors* and the reactions the *adaptation syndrome*. The schema of Selye's concept follows. Any alarming stimulus, or stressor, excites the central nervous system, particularly the hypothalamus, which then stimulates a secretion of epinephrine from the adrenal medulla. This causes the anterior lobe of the pituitary gland to liberate adrenocorticotropic hormone (ACTH). This in turn specifically influences the adrenal cortex to liberate hormones of adaptation, which underlie the bodily effects.

The Selye concept has been challenged. It is denied, for example, that the non-specific mechanism described above can account for the evolvement of a given specific reaction.

Pituitary Gland (Hypophysis)

This gland sits in the sella turcica, or saddlelike depression in the body of the sphenoid bone, located in the central part of the floor of the skull. It consists of anterior and posterior lobes which are unlike each other in origin and in function. Neither lobe is vital, and a total hypophysectomy can be survived. An intermediate lobe, having the same origin as the anterior lobe, secretes a hormone which regulates skin pigmentation. The control of pituitary secretions is obscure; it may be neural.

The posterior lobe has no apparent relation to the vocal mechanism. It secretes pitocin, which is involved in the contraction of the muscles of the uterus, and pitressin, which (1) constricts smooth muscles of all arterioles and (2) increases the renal absorption of water.

The anterior lobe is a master gland which controls many other endocrine glands and bodily processes. It controls several kinds of activity, but not all of its hormones are known or capable of being correlated with specific activities. Only selected hormones are touched upon below.

The somatotropic, or growth, hormone acts directly upon tissue cells. If early in life there is marked somatotropic deficiency, dwarfism results. There may be lack of development of the bony and cartilaginous structures comprising the speech machinery. The voice may be weak and the speech infantile.

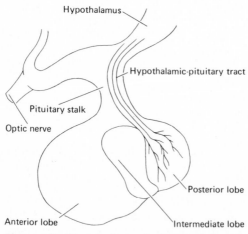

Figure 5-9 The pituitary gland in relation to other structures in the floor of the diencephalon.

Hyperpituitarism, involving particularly the growth hormone, can cause giantism if the overactivity occurs in youth. In an adult, overall growth is not the problem, but there is excessive bone thickening, swelling, and deformation called acromegaly. The mandible and skull bones are involved. Other structures, including the tongue, hyoid bone, larynx, and vocal folds overgrow. The laryngeal cartilages enlarge, in some cases obstructing the laryngeal vestibule, which produces stridor and dyspnea. The ventricular folds of the larynx thicken. A deepening of the voice, especially in females, occurs because the arytenoids and epiglottis enlarge.

Speech disorders may be associated with changes in bony and cartilaginous structures. Speech can be altered by too long a mandible. The male larynx may simulate the high-pitched vocal quality of the female. The motor patterns of gesture, vocal inflection, and facial expression may resemble those of the opposite sex. Berry and Eisenson (1956) write of the indistinct articulation and the hoarse quality of the voice in acromegaly.

The thyrotropic hormone has already been discussed. Thyrotropin has been prepared but only in fairly pure state. The pituitary stimulates the thyroid by secreting thyrotropin. The thyroid gland in turn produces its characteristic effects upon the general metabolism of the body.

The adrenocorticotropic hormone of the pituitary has been discussed. ACTH stimulates the adrenal cortex to produce its characteristic effects.

The pituitary gonadotropic hormones are important in speech. They act only   151
indirectly by stimulating the gonads to produce sex hormones. Thus, they have no effect in castrates. There are three gonadotropins, follicle-stimulating hormone (FSH), luteinizing hormone or interstitial-cell-stimulating hormone (LH or ICSH), and prolactin (luteotropin).

In the male, FSH is gametogenic, and it induces sperm production and the development of the semen-carrying tubules. ICSH stimulates the production of testosterone in the testis. The pituitary hormones are essential in sexual development. Thus, after experimental hypophysectomy the male does not attain sexual maturity and acts like a castrate.

In the female, FSH stimulates maturation of the follicles and growth of the ova. LH converts the ripened follicles into a corpus luteum. Prolactin maintains the corpus luteum and stimulates it to secrete the hormone called progesterone. Prolactin initiates milk secretion in developed mammary glands. After childbirth it depresses the maternal sexual cycles and their associated estrogenic-hormone secretion. In hypophysectomy before puberty, the sexual cycles and sexual maturity fail to occur. In hypophysectomy after puberty the cycles are abolished, and the secondary sexual characteristics are weakened.

In a condition called Fröhlich's syndrome, or dystrophia adiposogenitalis, there is hypofunction of both anterior and posterior lobes, resulting in obesity of the feminine type of distribution and sexual infantilism. The voice in many cases may be infantile in quality.

The Gonads

Disorders of the gonads in either sex may cause profound changes in (1) physiologic control of essential processes or (2) the personality. In either case the changes can be directly or remotely reflected in the qualities of the voice.

Sex hormones exercise a marked control over the secondary sexual characteristics, i.e., sex differences except for those which involve production or movement of the sperm or eggs. Secondary sexual characteristics include differences in body build, distribution of fat, mammary gland development, hair, pigment, and physical differences in the larynx.

The Male The male sex hormones, or androgens, are derived from the interstitial cells of the testis, under the influence of the pituitary ICSH. Testosterone and androstenedione (Turner, 1966) are the main testis hormones. There are also adrenal cortex androgens and synthetic androgens.

Some testosterone is secreted in the embryo, and it produces early initial differentiation of secondary sexual characteristics, e.g., descent of the testes. At puberty, ICSH produces permanent growth of the interstitial cells and maintains testosterone secretion. The latter hormone has many actions; it stimulates spermatogenesis, develops the reproductive organs, and expresses the secondary sexual characteristics, including skeletal configurations and voice changes. The androgens also promote protein anabolism, apparently by influencing gene-controlled mechanisms.

Hypogonadism, or testicular insufficiency, and an associated involvement of the larynx may be produced by changes in the testes or in the anterior pituitary. The opposite condition of hypergonadism, which leads to precocious puberty and voice changes, is often ascribed to tumors of the interstitial cells or of the anterior pituitary.

The voice changes or fails to mature in eunuchism, or total castration, and eunuchoidism, or testicular insufficiency. Castration before puberty causes the most marked disturbances. In the prepuberal male castrate the voice tends to rise in pitch, and the range and registers simulate those of the female. According to Luchsinger and Arnold (1965), castration of the male is followed by a decrease in vocal fold length, regression of the thyroid cartilage angle (Adam's apple), and assumption of a false soprano voice, or falsetto.

In eunuchoidism, when expressed in the very young male, there may be delayed maturation of the larynx, involving retarded ossification. The voice of the adult eunuchoid has the timbre of that of a young boy. The pitch is that of a female.

The Female The sex hormones are produced in the ovaries. By acting in conjunction with the pituitary gonadotropins, they regulate reproductive activities,

152

especially from puberty to the menopause. Ovarian function includes (1) growth and differentiation of the reproductive tract; (2) oogenesis; (3) development of secondary sexual characteristics; (4) control of the menstrual and ovarian cycles; (5) implantation of the ovum in the uterus and the development of the placenta; and (6) control of growth and milk secretion in the mammary glands.

The ovum develops within a follicle that produces estrogens, steroid hormones. Among the active estrogenic hormones are estrone and the more powerful estradiol. The chief function of the estrogens is to stimulate the development of the sexual tract and mammary glands. They also maintain cyclic processes and help express the secondary sexual characteristics. The voice mirrors these changes in a limited area.

In ovariectomy before puberty all maturation, gametogenesis, and sexual cycles stop, and the secondary sexual characteristics fail to develop. Genital tract atrophy, no cycles, sterility, obesity, and considerable emotional disturbance occur in post-puberal ovariectomy, but, the voice, as a secondary sexual activity, need not be markedly disturbed. In many instances, however, there are vocal changes in the prepuberal female castrate. The vocal range and speaking level may be lowered, and the vocal timbre may assume a harshness. It is possible for changes in the voice to take place in postpuberal castration, as in a panhysterectomy, where the ovaries are also removed.

Gonadal endocrine control may be lowered in some clinical conditions, rather than eliminated as in castration. This may be associated with virilizing laryngeal changes. Edema, hyperemia, and thickening of the vocal folds may occur. The voice becomes lower.

153

Voice Changes in Physiologic Processes
Changes related to the activity of gonadal, pituitary gonadotropic, and adrenal cortical hormones occur in normal functional processes and development. The process of general voice change during puberty is called *mutation*. It involves a more capacious breathing, a wider range of tone, and a more pronounced resonance and power of the voice. The speaking voice of the boy may drop one octave, and that of the girl one-third of an octave.

Changes in the menopause are very gradual and much less obvious. They characteristically involve a reduction in the brilliance and range of the voice.

There is correspondingly a voice of the male climacteric that loses volume and strength (Moses, 1954). The range becomes narrower and often higher.

Voice changes may occur in normal processes other than in puberty and menopause. Thus, in the menstrual period, Luchsinger and Arnold (1965) describe changes such as flatness in the singing voice because of hyperemia, slight edema, and lessened mucus secretion in the vocal folds. Levin (1962) discusses a tendency for lowering of the voice during pregnancy. Vascular changes, congestion, and excessive mucus production in the upper respiratory tract lead to coughing and hoarseness. If these symptoms are related to the conditions underlying the pregnant state, they may disappear when the pregnancy is terminated.

The voice changes of age are endocrine-based (Levin, 1962). The voice becomes soft, weak, and limited in range. The pitch may waver. Structural changes in the larynx involve calcification and ossification of the hyaline cartilage, decrease of elasticity, increase in mucus secretion, and general laryngeal atrophy.

Pineal Gland

This is claimed to be an endocrine gland, although no distinct hormone has been extracted in man. There are, however, endocrinelike effects. The gland is said to produce a substance that acts as a brake upon maturation and development of the child before puberty. Where there is a pineal tumor in the child, physical and sexual maturation are precocious and speech is disturbed. Ordinarily, the pineal becomes inactive by puberty.

Melatonin, a substance found only in the pineal gland, is synthesized from serotonin with the help of a catalyst, hydroxyindole-O-methyl transferase. The catalyst also occurs only in the pineal gland. This organ may help regulate photoperiodic influences on the gonads.

154

6 THE RESPIRATORY SYSTEM IN SPEECH

Respiration is a process used primarily for gas-and-energy exchange between an organism and its environment, and breathing for speech is secondary. Nevertheless, respiration is very importantly involved in speech. It provides the air that will be phonated, resonated, and articulated into meaningful sounds.

Breathing is involved in speech not only because of the use made of the exhaled air but also in the negative sense that abnormal breathing is usually associated with certain speech disturbances.

Respiratory physiology has had a long history, with remarkable advances in this century. Hippocrates (460–377 B.C.) suggested that the purpose of breathing is to cool the heart, and Galen (A.D. 130–201) continued to believe in that concept. Rapid progress followed the discovery of oxygen by Joseph Priestly (1733–1804) and the establishment of the chemical identity of respiration with combustion by Antoine Lavoisier (1743–1794).

Respiration originally meant breathing, or to breathe again, and in common usage it still means just that. The meaning has been extended to include the transportation of gases to and from the cells and the utilization of oxygen within the cell. Only problems pertinent to the speech function will be considered in this chapter.

Organismic Basis of External Respiration

Organs Involved

The organs involved in external respiration are (1) the conducting portion, or upper respiratory tree, and (2) the respiratory portion, or lungs.

The conducting portion consists of the nose, pharynx, larynx, trachea, and bronchi. The nose, pharynx, larynx, and trachea will be described in later chapters.

Bronchi   The trachea divides into right and left primary bronchi, which enter the hilus, or root of the lungs.   The right bronchus is more vertical, shorter, and wider than the left and divides into three branches, supplying the upper, middle, and lower lobes, respectively, of the right lung.   The left bronchus divides into two branches, one supplying the upper lobe and the other the lower lobe of the left lung.

The walls of the bronchi are semirigid because they contain cartilaginous rings bound together by membranes.   In the lungs the rings become replaced by irregular cartilage plates.   As the stem bronchi divide into many collaterals ending in bronchioles, the cartilages progressively disappear.   When the bronchiole diameter is about 1 mm, no cartilage persists.

Lungs   These are the essential organs of respiration, situated on either side of the mediastinum in the thorax.   They lie fairly free, being attached by the root and the pulmonary ligament.   They are roughly conical masses of porous, spongy, highly

156

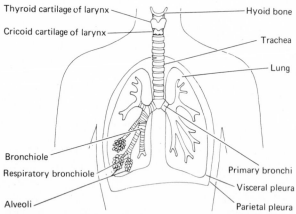

Figure 6-1 Diagrammatic anterior view of the respiratory passages.

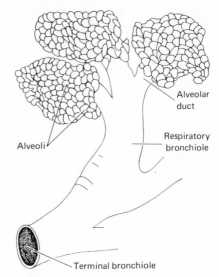

Alveolar
duct

Respiratory
bronchiole

Alveoli

Terminal bronchiole

Figure 6-2 Structure of a respiratory unit, or lobule, which includes a terminal bronchiole and its subdivisions.

elastic material, covered by serous pleural membranes. The apex of each lung projects into the root of the neck, and the base rests upon the diaphragm.

Each lung has a costal, mediastinal, and diaphragmatic surface. The costal surface is convex, and it comes into contact with the inner surfaces of the ribs and their intercostal muscles. The mediastinal surface is medial and concave. It contains the root, or hilus, through which pass the bronchus, bronchial and pulmonary blood vessels, lymphatics, and the autonomic regulatory nerves. The mediastinal surface of the left lung has a decided cardiac notch to receive the heart. The diaphragmatic surface lies at the base of each lung, and it is concave to fit over the diaphragm.

The right lung is divided by two fissures into superior, middle, and inferior lobes. The left lung is divided by a single fissure into superior and inferior lobes.

A lung is composed of the terminal aspects of the bronchi, bronchioles, and their subdivisions, alveoli, blood vessels, lymphatics, nerves and connective tissue.

The bronchioles are tubes having an inner epithelial lining and a middle muscular layer but no outer coat (serosa). They present an exposed smooth muscular layer for the action of the vagal bronchoconstrictor fibers and the thoracolumbar or sympathetic bronchodilator fibers.

Bronchioles divide into terminal bronchioles, each of which leads into respiratory bronchioles. The latter open into long passageways, or alveolar ducts. There are also cross corridors, or atria, which empty into alveoli. Each bronchiole eventually terminates in several alveoli, or air sacs.

The alveoli are the units of structure and function. The alveolar wall is a one-layered selectively permeable epithelium, which is intimately surrounded by a blood capillary. The capillaries have a one-cell-layered endothelium. The interchange of gases takes place in both directions between the alveolar epithelium and the capillary endothelium. The direction and extent of the exchange are determined by the gradient of pressure for any given gas between the air and the blood.

There are about 700 million alveoli in the human lungs, and they present about 70 m^2 of diffusion surface. The lungs consist essentially of the minute elastic alveoli and an open system of tubes leading into them. The mass of tissue is small and assumes a known normal appearance only because the alveoli are distended by their contained air.

The bronchi and lungs are nourished by the bronchial arteries. The bronchial veins bring the blood back. The pulmonary arteries bring impure blood from the right ventricle of the heart to the pulmonary capillaries in a separate circuit, and the purified blood is returned by the pulmonary veins to the left atrium of the heart. It is then pumped into the systemic or general vascular system by the left ventricle.

The only muscle fibers in the lungs are in the walls of the bronchi and bronchioles. The muscles alter the diameters of these tubes so that the regulation of the air volume in the pulmonary passages is effected proximal to the alveoli.

The *lobule* of a lung is an anatomic unit of much more complexity than an alveolus and includes a terminal bronchiole, a respiratory bronchiole, the alveolar ducts, atria, alveoli, blood vessels, and nerves.

Thoracic Cavity   The lungs are situated in the thoracic cavity, a completely closed space within the walls of the chest, or thorax, bounded below by the diaphragm, anterolaterally and posterolaterally by the rib cage, and above by the tissues of the neck.

The cavity has a central space called the mediastinum, filled principally by the heart and great vessels, and two lateral spaces, or pleural cavities, each surrounding a lung.

Each pleural cavity is a closed serous sac, whose walls are fibroelastic membranes. Each pleura has two layers, a visceral one that intimately surrounds the lung and a parietal one that lines the walls of the cavities in which the lungs are situated. The two layers are normally in close contact, so that there is no real pleural cavity on each side. A small amount of fluid between the two layers serves for lubrication.

The Dead Space   There is an *anatomic dead space,* which includes the volume of all airways from the exterior to but not including the respiratory bronchioles since some gas exchange occurs in these bronchioles. This space is about 150 ml in the male and 100 ml in the female, the values changing with age, activity, and posture. The body weight in pounds roughly approximates the dead space in milliliters.

There is a *physiologic dead space* which includes not only the anatomic dead space but also an alveolar volume that may be overventilated or underperfused. Many alveoli are ventilated but do not participate in gas exchange to a material degree. Air is not necessarily distributed uniformly to all alveoli, and blood does not perfuse all alveoli equally. During quiet inspiration the upper lobes expand first, but the lower lobes are adequately ventilated at the close of the phase. In the erect posture the apices of the lungs may not be perfused.

General Activity of Thorax and Air Passages during Exchange of Air

External respiration involves the action primarily of voluntary or skeletal muscles energized by spinal nerves and moving a skeletal framework composing the thorax. The active muscles are usually thought of as being localized in the thorax and abdomen, but depending upon the character of the breathing they may also include some muscles of the neck. Accessory respiratory movements involve smooth, or nonstriated, muscles, such as those in the walls of the bronchial system of tubes. These muscles are energized by autonomic nerves, and they keep the tubes ordinarily in a protective state of partial closure. For a discussion of the regulation of bronchial caliber, the reader is referred to Widdicombe (1966).

159

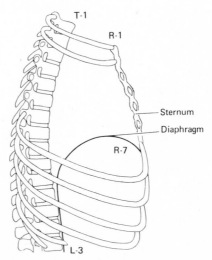

Figure 6-3 Relationships in lateral view of the vertebrae, ribs, sternum, and diaphragm; R=ribs, T=thoracic vertebrae, and L=lumbar vertebrae.

The basic movement in respiration is an upward expanding movement of the thorax. The upward motion of the ribs increases chiefly the anteroposterior and lateral thoracic diameters. The sternum moves upward and forward during inspiration and, by working in conjunction with the ribs, increases the vertical as well as the other two thoracic dimensions. Every rib travels up at the same time during inspiration and down at the same time in expiration. The effect of the ribs in inspiration is more pronounced with the longer lower ribs than with the shorter upper ones. Although the thoracic expansion is not of equal amplitude in all directions, the conical shape of the thorax is maintained during breathing.

According to Rossier et al. (1960), the first six ribs move by torsion about an axis that leads through the neck of each rib, with the net effect of increasing the anteroposterior diameter of the thorax. For the lower ribs, the axis about which rib torsion occurs is displaced anteriorly and leads through the costal cartilages and sternum. Torsion through this axis produces an outward movement of the seventh to tenth ribs, increasing the transverse diameter of the thorax in inspiration. The last two ribs act as a fixation point for the abdominal muscles.

The vertebral column increases in length during inspiration, although as a simplification it may be considered rigid. Because of its relative immobility, the spine serves as the chief fixation point for the breathing mechanism, but the effects of the mechanics are distributed unevenly (Rossier et al., 1960). Although the clavicle and scapula are parts of the pectoral, or shoulder, girdle, which serves to support

160

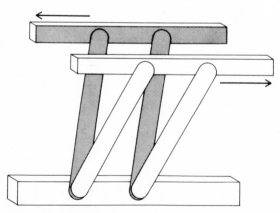

Figure 6-4 Diagrammatic representation of the upward and forward expansion of the thorax during inspiration.

the upper extremity, they also act as points of attachment for several muscles that can elevate the ribs.

The movements of the thoracic framework change the dimensions of the thoracic cavity and permit the exchange of air in breathing. The lungs expand primarily because the thorax expands. In a closed space the pressure is inversely proportional to the volume, other things being equal. As the thoracic pressure decreases with its expanding volume, the lungs expand into the partially evacuated thorax, and the intrapulmonic pressure decreases. Atmospheric air is then drawn into the lung passages through a gradient of pressure. The lungs operate with the changing pressures of the thorax. This is the physical theory of respiration. Actually, the lungs do, to a certain degree, influence their own operation through a stretch-reflex feedback system connected with the control centers of breathing.

The recoil of the inflated lung, which furnishes the force for expiration, is provided in part by its elasticity but also by the surface tension of the fluid lining the air sacs. Because the surface tension of the air sacs would increase with decreasing diameters, the small air sacs would be inflated with difficulty and would empty into the larger air sacs that have less surface tension. This could result in alveolar closure and pulmonary collapse. However, a surface-tension reductant in the lungs, called *pulmonary surfactant,* adds to the retractive force of the lung during inspiration, reduces surface tension to stabilize the lung, and prevents alveolar collapse at low pressure. The lung is thus active metabolically and not just involved in passive transfers of gases.

161

The flow of gases through the air passages is related to velocity. During slow passage in a large smooth single tube, the wall offers resistance to the gas nearest the wall. Friction also exists between this peripheral layer and the next proximal layer of gas. Because of these sliding frictions, the gases in the center move fastest, with progressive decrease in the velocities of the more peripheral layers. There is a central leading tip and a trailing edge. Such flow is called *streamlined* or *laminar.*

Above a certain velocity, layers of gas no longer slide over one another but move as a wall because eddy currents arise. This is called *turbulent* flow, and it depends upon the density and not the viscosity of the gas. Because of the dimensions of the respiratory tract, there is turbulence in the trachea even during quiet breathing and elsewhere in the tract except in the smallest air passages.

In space, as the density of air lowers, the gases are exchanged more easily. Speech is also affected in that the pitch rises, among other changes. This is observed in subjects exposed to a helium environment, in which turbulence is decreased. Under high pressures and increased turbulence, as in diving, speech becomes unintelligible. In normal speech, turbulence is imposed upon the expired air and thus occurs as air is forced through the larynx. For problems involving flow, the reader is referred to Caro (1966).

To a great extent the contraction and expansion of the lungs follow the movements of the thorax. Structural zones within the lung respond differently, however, to thoracic changes. The central portion contains such relatively rigid structures as the bronchi and large blood vessels and can expand only minimally. The peripheral areas, which consist mostly of lung lobules, are highly distensible. Between these extremes, there is a zone of intermediate distensibility, maintaining a degree of rigidity because of connective tissues, bronchi, and vessels.

The Skeletal Framework for Breathing

The bony thorax is composed of twelve thoracic vertebrae posteriorly, the sternum anteriorly, and the twelve pairs of ribs laterally.

Vertebral Column

The vertebral column of the adult is a flexible, multijointed pillar of twenty-six vertebrae. Each vertebra is separated from the others by a cartilaginous intervertebral disk. The joints between the vertebrae are held sturdily in place by complex ligaments. The uppermost seven vertebrae, situated in the neck, are cervical. The next twelve, to which the ribs attach, are thoracic. These are followed by five lumbar vertebrae of the lower back and then by five fused vertebrae forming the single sacrum. The lowest end of the column contains variably four rudimentary vertebrae, usually considered as one structure called the coccyx.

A typical thoracic vertebra has the following features. The body is the unpaired anterior cylindrical part. From this a pair of legs, or pedicles, stems dorsally. Two broad plates called laminae project backward from the pedicles. The laminae fuse in the posterior median line and thus complete an arch which encloses a space

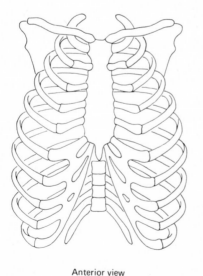
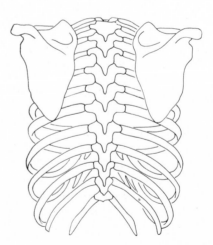

Anterior view   Posterior view

Figure 6-5 Bony framework of the thoracic cage.

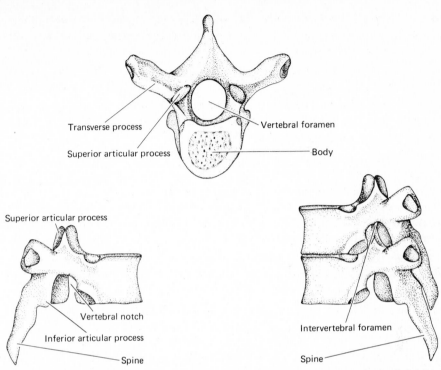

Figure 6-6 Superior and lateral views of thoracic vertebrae and method of joining vertebrae.

called the vertebral foramen. The arch protects the spinal cord, which is inside the vertebral foramen.

Each arch supports several processes. The spinal process is the single dorsal projection. There are two superior and two inferior articular processes for connecting adjacent vertebrae. These form freely movable joints. Less movable connections are also provided by the bodies of the vertebrae piling on top of one another with an intervening intervertebral disk. There are also paired transverse processes that jut out laterally on either side for muscle attachment.

Sternum

The sternum, or breastbone, is a somewhat oblong plate of bone which forms the midanterior portion of the thorax. It is subcutaneous and readily palpable. Its anterior surface is rough, and its posterior surface is smooth.

The sternum not only protects the soft structures within but offers articulation for the upper seven pairs of ribs laterally and provides spaciousness for the thoracic cavity by its anterior convexity and by its forward inclination as it goes downward.

The sternum is composed of three parts, the manubrium, body, and xiphoid (ensiform) process.

The manubrium is the uppermost and widest segment. Its inferior border is fused to the body, or corpus sterni, by fibrocartilage. This joint forms a palpable protuberance, the sternal angle.

The central portion of the superior manubrial border contains a suprasternal notch. Each supralateral region has a clavicular notch, which receives the head of the clavicle. Each sternoclavicular joint is a two-chambered synovial or diarthrodial joint with an articular disk between the two chambers. Each chamber is ordinarily distinct and separate from the other.

Each lateral border of the manubrium receives in a notch the costal cartilages of the first two ribs. The costal cartilage of the second rib is received in a notch at the sternal angle. The upper border of the manubrium is at the level of the lower border of the body of the second thoracic vertebra. The sternal angle is at the upper border of the body of the fifth thoracic vertebra, and the xiphoid process is at the level of the ninth thoracic vertebra.

The body and manubrium ordinarily fuse only in old age, and the body and xiphoid fuse at about forty years of age (Meschan, 1959). This allows plasticity in thoracic movements.

The body, or corpus sterni, comprises about two-thirds of the sternum. It is two or three times wider than it is thick and it is typically composed of three transverse

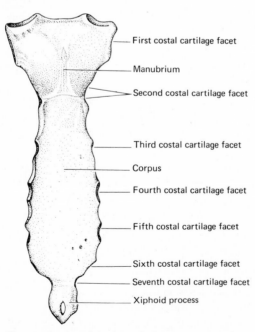

First costal cartilage facet

Manubrium

Second costal cartilage facet

Third costal cartilage facet

Corpus

Fourth costal cartilage facet

Fifth costal cartilage facet

Sixth costal cartilage facet

Seventh costal cartilage facet

Xiphoid process

Figure 6-7 Anterior view of the sternum to show its sections and their landmarks.

ridges that result from fusion of four separate bony pieces. The cartilages of the second to the seventh ribs fit into facets on either lateral border of the body. The seventh costal cartilage is received by a notch common to both the body and the xiphoid process.

The lowest part of the sternum is the easily palpable xiphoid cartilage. This is a small spatula-shaped structure, which is thinner than the sternum and lies on a level with the posterior surface of the bone. This produces an infrasternal depression at the lower end of the sternum. The prominent xiphisternal junction marks the union of the body and xiphoid process. The xiphoid tends to ossify to a bone of many shapes and sizes with advancing years.

Ribs

The twelve pairs of ribs constitute a series of curved elastic bones that make up most of the skeletal framework of the thorax. The upper seven pairs have their cartilages joined directly to the sternum and are "true" ribs. The next three pairs are indirectly connected with the sternum by long costal cartilages and are "false" ribs. The lowest two pairs are too short to be attached anteriorly, but they have their front ends embedded in the abdominal musculature and are "floating" (false) ribs. Sometimes the tenth rib is also floating (Brantigan, 1963).

The costal cartilages and their ribs do not always have the same direction as they travel medially to the sternum. The first cartilage continues the downward course of the first rib. The second cartilage is entirely transverse. The third to the tenth cartilages travel away from their ribs in an obliquely upward direction.

The greatest space of the thorax lies between the third to the eighth ribs, and the greatest amplitude of rib movements occurs there. The ribs above and below that region are shorter and move considerably less.

The curves of a typical rib in the middle of the series are important in respiration. Such a rib has a head, neck, tubercle, and shaft. The head has two facets to articulate with two vertebrae and their intervening disk. The neck is attached by ligaments to the transverse process of the lower of the two vertebrae associated with it. A tubercle at the end of the neck articulates with the facet on the transverse process. The rib thus forms a costocentral and costotransverse joint with the vertebral column, and respiratory elevation and depression are permitted by these joints. It is the heads of the upper nine ribs that articulate with two thoracic vertebrae, the one with which each rib is in numerical correspondence and the vertebra above. The last three ribs have a single articulation and are joined to only one vertebral body. The shaft distal to the tubercle bends laterally and posteriorly to the rib angle, thus giving more space to the posterior thoracic cavity. The angle marks the point where the rib abruptly changes its direction to run anteriorly and inferiorly. Its bend is then such that its inferior border tilts outward and its outer surface is both outward and upward. This eversion of the inferior aspect augments the transverse diameter of the thorax between successive

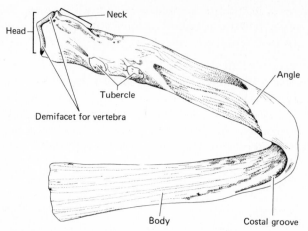

Figure 6-8 A typical rib, excessively turned to show its parts.

ribs, thus increasing the lung space during respiration. The transverse diameter of the thorax is greatest at the level of the eighth rib.

In the lateral and posterior aspects of the thorax all ribs have an oblique direction downward and forward, and the ninth rib has the greatest obliquity. Because of the obliquity of the ribs, higher posteriorly and lower anteriorly, their elevation by muscles increases the anteroposterior diameter of the thorax. That is, when the sternum is raised by cervical muscles, the attached ribs are forced to extend almost directly forward, rather than sloping downward, as is the case in expiration. This makes the anteroposterior diameter considerably greater during inspiration than during expiration.

Judson and Weaver (1965) point out the changing relationship with age of the angle between the ribs and the axis of the body. In the fetus and at birth it averages 90°. At four years of age it is 82°. In the adult it is 64°. The horizontal disposition of the ribs in a baby (Fulton, 1955) makes costal breathing to enlarge the thorax less efficient and explains why babies breathe in a predominantly abdominal manner.

Although specific numbers of vertebrae, ribs, and muscles are listed in these sections, the placement of muscles and of their origins and insertions is highly individualized. Anatomy should emphasize a living, evolving organism rather than lend itself to the conclusion that an organism represents a completed developmental process.

The Muscles of External Respiration

Although muscles are treated in isolation here, the orderly execution of any movement involves the interplay of a considerable number of muscles. Most voluntary muscles are set into agonist-antagonist pairs, such that if one contracts, the other relaxes. This involves quick changes in the distribution of tonus (tone). Interference with the timing may lead to tonic rigidity.

Inspiration requires muscular effort, but expiration is to a large extent passive, although there are expiratory muscles. Even in inspiration very few muscles are required, except during a deep inspiration. There is some doubt whether certain muscles are inspiratory or expiratory. An inspiratory muscle may be defined as one that contracts when the diaphragm contracts whereas an expiratory muscle contracts when the diaphragm relaxes. Both inspiration and expiration constitute a respiratory cycle whose frequency varies with age, size and sex. There are about sixteen cycles per minute in the adult male, and seventeen to eighteen in the female.

Two interpretations are given here of the generalized muscle actions during inspiration. First, it may be held that in quiet inspiration the first two ribs are fixated by neck muscles. The third to the sixth ribs, constituting the upper costal series, are elevated to this fixed region. This activity involves the external and internal intercostal muscles, aided by the serratus posterior superior, serratus anterior, levatores costarum, and other muscles. Concomitantly, the seventh to the tenth ribs, constituting the lower costal series, rotate outward and forward, widening the subcostal angle and increasing chiefly the transverse diameter of the lower thorax. Ribs 11 and 12 are not effective in inspiration but follow the movements of the anterior abdominal wall. There are many other accessory muscles, chiefly on the back and pectoral region, which can help to raise the ribs even higher, particularly in deep inspiration.

167

A second view of inspiratory muscle action is given by Campbell (1958). Movement about the axis of the neck of the first rib raises the sternum, producing an elevated point of fixation. The second through the sixth ribs move about two axes. In one instance movement about the axis of the neck of the rib raises or lowers the sternal

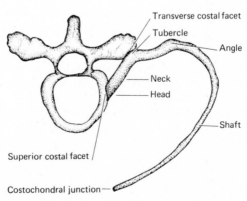

Figure 6-9 Relationship of a vertebra and rib.

end and elevation of the rib sloping downward and forward increases the antero-posterior (AP) thoracic diameter. This is a "pump-handle" effect. In the other instance an axis is said to run through the angle of the rib and the costosternal joint. Movement then raises or lowers the middle of the rib. Since the middle section lies in a plane below the axis, elevation results in an outward movement which increases the lateral diameter of the thorax. This is a "bucket-handle" effect.

Following Campbell, the axes of rotation of the seventh through the tenth ribs are the same as those of the vertebrosternal ribs, but differences in the rib shapes and directions lead to variations in movements. When the anterior ends of ribs 7 to 10 are elevated, the sternum moves posteriorly and the AP thoracic diameter is slightly decreased. Elevation, however, about the AP axis makes the middle of the rib move both laterally and posteriorly, which increases the transverse diameter and the depth of the paravertebral gutter.

Expiration, although involving considerable elastic recoil, includes muscles which not only force the diaphragm back up from the abdomen into the thorax but which also depress the ribs. These include the anterior abdominal wall muscles, trans-versus thoracis, and others. The contraction of the abdominal muscles raises the intra-abdominal pressure and forces the diaphragm upward. In prolonged expira-tion, as in sustaining a note during singing, the abdominal muscles gradually con-tract while the diaphragm slowly relaxes, with the intercostal muscles maintaining a normal contour of the thoracic walls (Crafts, 1966). Quiet breathing is primarily of the abdominal variety with relatively little movement of the thoracic cage.

168

Muscles of the Thorax
These include the diaphragm, external and internal intercostals, subcostals, trans-versus thoracis, levatores costarum, and serratus posterior superior and inferior. Accessory respiratory muscles in the thoracic region include the pectoralis major and minor, the serratus anterior, and the subclavius.

The diaphragm is a musculotendinous partition which completely separates the thoracic and abdominal cavities. It may be regarded as having right and left parts. Its fibers arch the structure into a dome-shaped mass, and all the fibers insert above into a common aponeurotic central tendon.

The dome shape of the diaphragm is produced because the abdominal viscera press up against it as a result of meeting resistance ventrally from the walls of the abdomen which are in tone. The shape is also due to the elastic properties of the lungs. Mountcastle (1968) states that by reducing the resting intrathoracic pressure by about 3 mm of mercury per square centimeter over the 250 cm^2 area of the diaphragm, the lungs bring about an upward force of about 1 kg to bring the dia-phragm into the thorax.

The central tendon is located at the center of the vault, although nearer the ventral aspect of the thorax, which makes the dorsal muscle fibers travel a longer path.

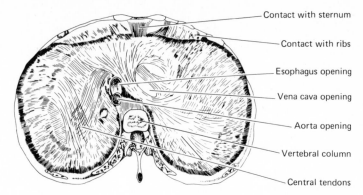

Contact with sternum

Contact with ribs

Esophagus opening

Vena cava opening

Aorta opening

Vertebral column

Central tendons

Figure 6-10 Cross section of the diaphragm.

The shape of the central tendon is like a three-part leaf, of which the right section is the largest, the middle one intermediate, and the left section smallest in size. The varied directions of the fiber systems produce great tensile strength.

In regard to the muscular fibers of origin, the posterior, or vertebral, fibers are two elongated musculotendinous bundles, or crura, which arise on each side of the aorta and are firmly attached on the right to the upper three vertebrae and on the left to the upper two. The sternal fibers originate on the inner aspect of the xiphoid process of the sternum. The paired costal sections originate from the inner surface of the anterior ends of the lowest six ribs and from the costal cartilages of these ribs.

Contraction draws the central tendon down and slightly forward. This enlarges the chest chiefly in the vertical plane. The lungs then expand into the partially evacuated thorax. The central tendon presses upon the abdominal viscera, pushing them downward and forward, so that the anterior abdominal wall protrudes with each inspiration. This activity, which is called abdominal or diaphragmatic breathing, has been claimed to characterize the male in contrast with a type called costal or rib breathing, which characterizes the female. Teleologically explained, the action at a higher level is an adaptation to prevent undue pressure on a rising uterus in the gravid female. The concept has been challenged, and there appears to be no such sexual difference, except in late pregnancy, when high intra-abdominal pressure interferes with diaphragmatic action and puts the major load of inspiration upon the intercostal muscles (Slonim and Chapin, 1967).

The return of the diaphragm in expiration is brought about by contraction of the expiratory muscles of the anterior abdominal wall, by the recoil of the viscera formerly compressed by the diaphragm down into a region of increased intra-abdominal pressure, and by the fact that the musculotendinous tissues of the diaphragm are elastic.

The excursions of the diaphragm are not extensive, the ordinary movements for breathing or speech having a range of 1 to 2 cm, which increases to 3 to 5 cm in deep breathing. The greatest movements are not in the relatively fixed central tendon but in the more peripheral regions. Occasionally one half of the diaphragm will move somewhat more than the other, or even in slightly different sequence, but any marked difference suggests an abnormality.

The degree of movement differs with positioning of the body. The largest quiet breathing excursions take place when the individual is supine. In the erect posture the diaphragmatic dome falls lower, and the excursions are less. In the sitting position the dome is at its lowest, and the movements are minimal. The especially low position of the dome in sitting is due to a relaxation of the abdominal muscles and subsequent decrease of the intra-abdominal pressure below the diaphragm. The right and left leaflets do not necessarily descend equally in inspiration in any bodily position.

The downward pull of gravity in the erect position, which increases the size of the chest cavity, is mostly removed in the recumbent position, and the chest cavity decreases in size.

The diaphragm has been said to account for about two-thirds of the alteration of chest volume in quiet breathing (Blewett and Rackow, 1966). This statement is challenged by Guyton (1966), who claims that about 70 percent of the expansion and contraction of the lungs is caused by the anteroposterior movement of the chest cage and 30 percent by the diaphragm.

170

In man the diaphragm is the chief inspiratory muscle. It is innervated through the paired phrenic nerves which come from the cervical plexus roots C-3, C-4, and

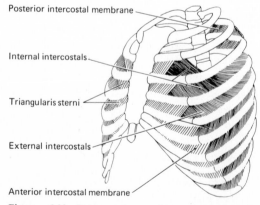

Posterior intercostal membrane

Internal intercostals

Triangularis sterni

External intercostals

Anterior intercostal membrane

Figure 6-11 Intercostal muscles. Anterolateral view. (*By permission from S. M. Friedman, Visual Anatomy, Thorax and Abdomen, Charles C Thomas, Publisher, Springfield, Ill., 1952.*)

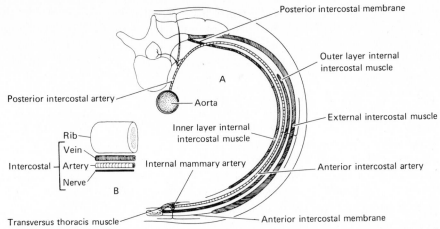

Figure 6-12 Half cross section of the chest wall. The external intercostal muscle is deficient close to the sternum, and the space is closed by the anterior intercostal membrane. (*From O. C. Brantigan, Clinical Anatomy, Copyright 1963. McGraw-Hill Book Company. Used by permission.*)

C-5. Unilateral phrenicectomy paralyzes the corresponding side of the diaphragm. Since the intercostals and most of the accessory inspiratory and all the expiratory muscles are innervated from thoracic and lumbar spinal roots, the diaphragm can stay active even after complete paralysis of the other muscles.

Luchsinger and Arnold (1965) state that the diaphragm differs from all other voluntary muscles in having no proprioceptive nerve endings. Thus, the individual cannot be aware of the position of the diaphragm at any time. From this, these authors conclude that there is no basis for diaphragmatic exercises or for teaching a patient to speak with his diaphragm. Cotes (1965) asserts that there is little objective evidence that breathing exercises can improve the function of the diaphragm, increase the strength of the accessory muscles of respiration, or assist expiration. Its position is not affected by abdominal breathing or other training methods.

The diaphragm functions not only in breathing but in many other activities, such as coughing, defecation, laughing, lifting objects, sneezing, and urination.

The *external intercostal* muscles (paired) contain thin layers of oblique fibers which fill the intercostal spaces. There are eleven pairs, and each extends within its own intercostal space from the vertebral column to the lateral ends of the costal cartilages. The central region that continues medially to the sternum is filled in by the anterior intercostal membrane. The course of each segmental muscle slip is from the lower margin of one rib to the upper margin of the rib below. The direction of the fibers is downward and medialward anteriorly but downward and lateralward posteriorly.

In the classical view, which now appears too restricted, these muscles elevate the ribs and add to the diaphragmatic effect of increasing the vertical dimension of the thorax. They enlarge especially the lateral and the anteroposterior dimensions. The muscle fibers prevent an alternate sucking in and bulging out of intercostal tissues during respiration. Their innervation is through spinal intercostal nerves.

The *internal intercostals* (paired) are somewhat weaker, and they are covered by the external intercostals. They travel from the lower border of one rib to the upper border of the rib below. Although the eleven pairs begin anteriorly at the sternum or between the costal cartilages, they do not extend more posteromedially than the angles of the ribs. The deficient muscular space in back is filled in by the aponeurotic posterior intercostal membrane. The direction of the muscle fibers is at about right angles to that of the external intercostal muscle, and this cross lattice strengthens the thoracic wall.

The internal muscles also elevate the ribs, but this is inconclusive. According to Cotes (1965), the internal intercostals may be either inspiratory or expiratory, depending upon the incline of the structure to which they are attached. The parasternal fibers lie between the costal cartilages, which slope upward, and the direction of these fibers resembles that of the external intercostals. Like the latter, they contract during inspiration. The interosseous fibers lie between the ribs, where they slope downward and forward. During moderate lung inflation these fibers contract during expiration and also during speech.

172   The internal intercostals are supplied by spinal intercostal nerves.

According to Lippold (1968), electromyographic evidence indicates that the anterior fibers of the external and internal intercostal muscles raise the ribs and the posterior

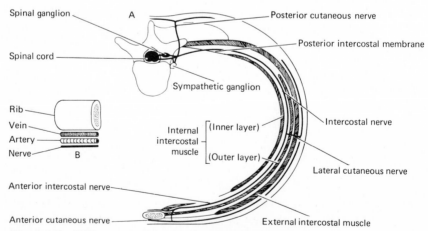

Figure 6-13 Half cross section of the chest wall. The internal intercostal muscle is deficient between the rib angle and the vertebral column, and the space is closed by the posterior intercostal membrane. (*From O. C. Brantigan, Clinical Anatomy. Copyright 1963. McGraw-Hill Book Company. Used by permission.*)

fibers depress the ribs. The external intercostals and part of the internal intercostals contract during quiet and forced inspiration. Both sets of muscles also contract during voluntary expiratory acts, e.g., coughing. Intercostal activity is present during most of the respiratory cycle in that expiratory recoil is checked and slowed down by the intercostals, which relax completely only at the end of expiration. This is in agreement with the statement of Arnold (1968) that controlled expiration, e.g., speaking or singing, is produced by slowing the recoil of the stretched pulmonary tissues and musculoskeletal wall, through the regulated contraction of the intercostal muscles. The diaphragm relaxes fractionally, and the abdominal muscles gradually contract.

There are still other views. It has been stated that in normal breathing the intercostals may simply maintain the ribs a constant distance apart while the thorax is being enlarged superoinferiorly. They are also said to tighten the intercostal spaces. This would occur during inspiration to prevent drawing in of the spaces and during expiration to prevent bulging out of the spaces. Basmajian (1962) states that we must change our concepts about the nature and actions of the muscles of respiration. Thus the intercostals may possibly be used to significantly increase the intrathoracic pressure (as in activities demanding sucking and blowing power) rather than to elevate the ribs. It is also probable that the intercostals are postural muscles.

Draper et al. (1959) have attempted by electromyography to relate intercostal, diaphragmatic, and abdominal muscle activity with lung volumes and subglottic pressures. They state that the external intercostals have a checking activity in the early part of an utterance, opposing the pressures which expel air from the lungs. Upon the termination of the pressures involved in relaxation, the internal intercostals and subsequently the abdominal muscles maintain the pulmonary volume and pressure necessary to activate the vocal folds. The technics and findings of this study are open to question.

Using electromyography, Hoshiko (1960) suggested that the intercostals cooperate to release the syllable. The controversies and notations about the limitations of electromyographic evidence are discussed by Rieber and Brubaker (1966).

All told, the functions of the intercostal muscles, particularly the internal intercostals, have been controversial throughout medical history.

The intercostal spaces are filled in not only by the external and internal intercostal muscles but in addition by a still deeper, or inner, complex of three muscles, the transversus thoracis, intercostalis intimus, and subcostals.

The *transversus thoracis,* or triangularis sterni (paired), lies inside the thoracic cavity, in the anterior aspect. It originates from the inner surface of the body and xiphoid process of the sternum. It runs obliquely lateralward and upward to insert into the posterior surfaces of the second or third to the sixth costal cartilages. This is the only truly thoracic muscle which is definitely expiratory, and it may act essentially in forced expiration, depressing the ribs. The innervation is through intercostal nerves.

There has been a long controversy over whether the transversus thoracis is a muscle of inspiration, expiration, or both. Thus, for example, Arnold (1968) states that (1) its function is speculative; and (2) it works with the intercostals and subcostals to tighten the intercostal spaces in both phases of breathing.

The *intercostalis intimus* muscle begins at the lateral borders of the transversus thoracis, where the two muscles are connected by a thin membrane, then runs posteriorly to the angle of the ribs. This muscle has the same attachments, action, and innervation as the transversus thoracis.

The *subcostals* (paired) are small muscles, variable in number, occurring near the angles of the ribs, and developed best in the lower thorax. They run parallel to the internal intercostals but span two or more intercostal spaces. Each originates from the inner aspect of a rib near its angle, then travels down to the insert on the inner surface of the second or third rib below. According to Crafts (1966), their main action is to aid in inspiration, but Gray (1966) states that they draw adjacent ribs together, and when the last rib is fixed by the quadratus lumborum the subcostals lower the ribs and decrease the volume of the thoracic cavity. Their innervation is through intercostal nerves.

The following three muscles (levatores costarum, serratus posterior superior, and serratus posterior inferior) are usually thought of as back muscles, but will be included here.

174

The *levatores costarum* are twelve pairs of muscles originating from the transverse processes of the seventh cervical and first eleven thoracic vertebrae. The fibers travel laterally and inferiorly parallel to the external intercostal fibers. They insert into the ribs just below their vertebrae of origin and end between the angle and

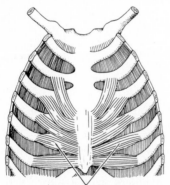

Transverse thoracic

Figure 6-14 Transverse thoracic muscle (triangularis sterni).

the tubercle of each rib. The four lower muscle segments insert, in addition, into ribs two segments below their origin. The muscle fibers can elevate the ribs, and they also act to rotate, extend, or laterally flex the vertebral column. The innervation is through the spinal intercostal nerves.

The *serratus posterior superior* (paired) is on the upper posterior aspect of the thorax, originating variably from the vertebral spines of C-7, T-1, and T-2 and from the ligamentum nuchae. The fibers travel down and laterally to insert distal to the angles of the first three or four ribs. The muscle elevates the upper ribs, acting mainly on their posterior sections. The innervation is through the first three or four thoracic nerves.

The *serratus posterior inferior* (paired), situated between the thoracic and lumbar regions, is as much a muscle of the lower back as it is of the thorax. It originates variably from the spinous processes of vertebrae T-11, T-12, L-1, and L-2. Its fibers course laterally and upward to insert into the last four ribs distal to their angles. It may depress the lower four ribs and pull them laterally in expiration. This holds the ribs fixed against the upward pull of the diaphragm. The innervation is through the last four thoracic nerves. There is some uncertainty about the action of this muscle as there is about most other respiratory muscles. It may possibly assist the diaphragm in forced inhalation by fixation of the lower ribs.

Accessory respiratory action is brought about in the thoracic region through elevation of the ribs by muscles that serve primarily to connect the upper extremity with the anterior and lateral thoracic walls. The four muscles described below can all help to elevate the ribs during inspiration. All except the serratus anterior are classified as pectoral muscles.

The *pectoralis major* (paired) is a fan-shaped muscle superficially located on the anterior and superior aspects of the chest wall. Its clavicular portion originates from the medial half of the clavicle, a costosternal section from the anterior surface of the sternum and the second to the seventh costal cartilages, and an abdominal part from the aponeurosis of the external abdominal oblique muscle. Its fibers course lateralward, forming the anterior axillary fold that terminates on the crest of the greater tubercle of the humerus. Although the main action is to flex, adduct, and medially rotate the arm, it can elevate the ribs if the shoulder girdle is fixed. The respiratory activity may occur only at the end of a maximum inspiration (Campbell, 1958). The innervation is through the medial and lateral anterior thoracic nerves from the brachial plexus

The *pectoralis minor* (paired) is a thin, triangular muscle found deep to the pectoralis major. It originates between the second or third through the fifth ribs near the costal cartilages. The fibers go laterally and upward to insert upon the coracoid process of the scapula. Its main action is to lower the shoulder, but if the shoulder girdle is fixed, the muscle assists the pectoralis major in elevating the ribs. It is innervated by the medial anterior thoracic nerve.

The *subclavius* (paired) is a narrow, cylindrical muscle stretching between the clavicle and the first rib. It originates from the anterior surface of the first rib and its cartilage, and goes laterally and upward to the inferior surface of the clavicle. Its main action is to lower the clavicle, but if the clavicle is fixed the muscle may elevate the first rib. It would appear to be a weak action. The muscle is innervated by nerves C-5 and C-6 emerging from the lateral trunk of the brachial plexus.

The *serratus anterior* (paired) could properly be classified with muscles of the axilla and shoulder. It is a thin quadrangular muscle that forms the medial wall of the axilla and lies on the posterolateral surface of the thorax. It originates along the ventral aspect of the vertebral border of the scapula. It runs downward and forward to insert by several individual slips into the outer surfaces of the upper eight or nine ribs. Although generally considered to have an action upon the scapula and arm, it elevates the ribs when the shoulder girdle is fixed by the rhomboids. It has not been regarded as important in the mechanics of breathing. Basmajian (1962) states that all the upper limb muscles, including the serratus anterior, may play no part in quiet or forced respiration, but this view departs from established concepts. The serratus anterior is innervated by the long thoracic nerve from the brachial plexus.

Muscles of the Neck

At times certain muscles in the neck region elevate the sternum or the uppermost ribs. This action aids the vertical expansion of the thorax and provides a fixation point toward which the superior ribs may be drawn by the activity of the upper costal series of muscles.

The *sternocleidomastoid* (paired) is a strong, cylindrical muscle going upward and laterally along the side of the neck. It has a sternal origin from the manubrium and another origin from the medial third of the clavicle. These unite to one belly that inserts upon the mastoid process and the superior nuchal line of the occipital bone.

The main action of the muscle is to pull the head so that the chin turns to the opposite side. The action of importance in respiration is elevation of the sternum which increases the AP diameter of the thorax. According to Campbell (1958), the muscle contracts only during deep breaths, but it is, along with the scalenes, one of the most important accessory muscles of inspiration. The participation in breathing of the sternomastoid in dyspnea is a common clinical observation.

The innervation is from the spinal part of the spinal accessory nerve (XI) plus branches from C-2 and C-3.

The sternomastoid and perhaps the other neck muscles are active in clavicular breathing, or raising the sternum and clavicle. This is a practice discouraged in breathing for speech. It seems to produce an unsteadiness in tone because of the fluctuations in the rise and fall of the clavicles. It may also produce insufficient air intake, resulting in a loss of strength in the vocal tones.

The *scalenus anterior* (paired) is part of a triangular group of scalene muscles in the anterolateral region of the neck. The most anterior muscle is on the side of the neck deep to the sternocleidomastoid. Its origin is from the transverse processes of the third through the sixth cervical vertebrae. The fibers descend nearly vertically and insert along the upper border of the first rib. The main action is to elevate the first rib in inspiration, with the cervical spine fixed. The innervation is from the ventral rami of C-4 to C-7.

The *scalenus medius* (paired), just posterior to the scalenus anterior, is the longest scalene muscle. It originates from the transverse processes of the lower six cervical vertebrae, travels down the side of the vertebral column, and inserts along the superior border of the first rib. Its main action is to elevate the first rib. The innervation is from the ventral rami of C-3 to C-7.

The *scalenus posterior* (paired) is the smallest muscle and most internal of the group, located in the floor of the posterior triangle of the neck, immediately behind the scalenus medius. It originates from the transverse processes of the lowest two or three cervical vertebrae and inserts into the outer surface of the second rib. Upon fixation of the cervical spine, it elevates the second rib. The innervation is from the ventral rami of C-5, C-6, and C-7.

The scalenes are important accessory muscles of inspiration. Their contribution to the force of inspiration, however, is relatively small. They contract during quiet breathing but not in all individuals. The scalenes may fix the upper ribs and support the apex of the lungs during coughing.

177

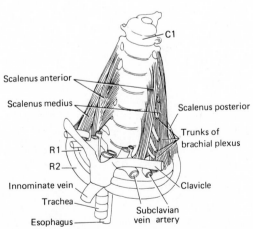

Figure 6-15 The scalene muscles. (*From O. C. Brantigan, Clinical Anatomy, Copyright 1963. McGraw-Hill Book Company. Used by permission.*)

Muscles of the Back Proper

The serratus posterior superior and inferior muscles, forming the third depth layer of back muscles, have already been described.

The *latissimus dorsi* (paired) is a superficial or first-layer back muscle whose primary function is to move the arm and shoulder. The arm may be extended, rotated medially, or pulled posteriorly. This broad flat triangular muscle has several origins, from (1) the spinous processes of the lowest six or seven thoracic vertebrae and all the lumbar and upper sacral vertebrae, (2) the thoracolumbar fascia, (3) the external surfaces of the lowest three or four ribs, and (4) the iliac crest. Its fibers all converge in going laterally and upward to form the palpable posterior axillary fold that inserts by a long tendon into the intertubercular groove on the humerus.

When the arm is fixed, the latissimus dorsi fibers associated with the ribs might be able to elevate those ribs and facilitate inspiration. It is claimed that contraction of the muscle as a whole compresses the lower thorax and facilitates expiration (Campbell, 1958). Innervation is through the thoracodorsal nerve from the brachial plexus.

The *quadratus lumborum* (paired) is a flat muscular sheet deeply placed in the dorsal abdominal wall between the last rib and the iliac crest (upper surface of the hipbone). The length of this space is only 3 to 4 in. The muscle originates along the iliac crest and iliolumbar ligament and travels upward and somewhat medially to insert along the last rib and the upper four lumbar vertebrae. It may depress the last rib, anchor it against the pull of the diaphragm, and fix the last two ribs in forced expiration.

178

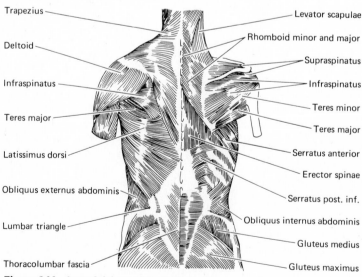

Figure 6-16 Superficial muscles of the back.

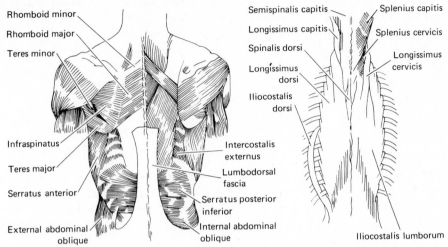

Figure 6-17 Deep muscles of the back.

The small attachments of this muscle to the thorax and its relatively small size minimize its importance in breathing. It is, questionably, a muscle of expiration. The innervation is from T-12 and L-1, although innervation from L-1 through L-4 has also been described (Crafts, 1966).

179

Trapezius (Paired) This is a superficial muscle of the back, originating from the superior nuchal line, external occipital protuberance, ligamentum nuchae, and the spines of vertebrae C-7 through T-12. The lowest section inserts on the spine of the scapula, the middle section on the spine of the scapula and the acromion process, and the highest section on the lateral third of the clavicle.

The muscle fixes the upper extremity to the trunk, adducts the scapulae, raises or lowers the scapulae, or rotates the scapulae such that the inferior angle is moved laterally.

The trapezius is a muscle of inspiration because (1) its superior fibers extend the neck and assist the action of the sternomastoid and (2) the muscle fixes the shoulder girdle and assists the pectoral muscles.

The innervation is from the spinal accessory nerve and from ventral rami of C-3 and C-4. It is thought that only the spinal accessory carries the motor fibers (Crafts, 1966).

Sacrospinalis (Paired) Also known in most recent terminology as the *erector spinae,* this is a strong cordlike muscle running along the whole length of the back from the occiput to the sacrum in the vertebral groove on either side of the spinous processes of all the vertebrae. It forms the fourth or deepest layer of the back muscles. The muscle is thickest in the lower thoracic and in the lumbar regions, where it becomes enclosed within the fibrous thoracolumbar fascia.

The muscle has a common origin below from the spines of all the lumbar vertebrae, the sacrum, the posterior sacroiliac ligament, the iliac crest, and the thoracolumbar fascia. In passing upward it splits into three parallel columns, the medial spinalis, the middle longissimus, and the lateral iliocostalis. Each of these is in turn divided from below upward generally into three sections. To illustrate, the iliocostalis lumborum inserts into the angles of the lower six or seven ribs, the iliocostalis dorsi inserts into the angles of the upper six ribs, and the iliocostalis cervicis inserts into the transverse processes of the lower three or four cervical vertebrae. Where the iliocostalis lumborum fibers travel up and depress their ribs of insertion during expiration, the cervicis section may be thought of as traveling down from lower cervical vertebrae to upper ribs and thus elevating these ribs during inspiration. The iliocostalis dorsi travels upward from the lower six ribs to the angles of the upper six ribs, and it may typically depress these structures. The respiratory actions of the separate vertical divisions of a single muscle column are thus variable with the segmental location of the division.

The longissimus and spinalis muscles are also variably concerned with action upon the ribs and therefore with respiration. The main activity of this entire group of muscles is postural and adapted to maintaining man's gravitational position. These

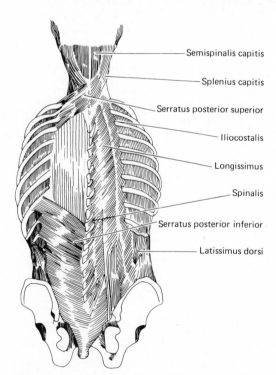

Semispinalis capitis

Splenius capitis

Serratus posterior superior

Iliocostalis

Longissimus

Spinalis

Serratus posterior inferior

Latissimus dorsi

Figure 6-18 Deepest muscles of the back, emphasizing the erector spinae (sacrospinalis) system.

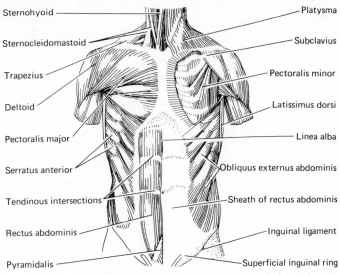

Sternohyoid

Sternocleidomastoid

Trapezius

Deltoid

Pectoralis major

Serratus anterior

Tendinous intersections

Rectus abdominis

Pyramidalis

Platysma

Subclavius

Pectoralis minor

Latissimus dorsi

Linea alba

Obliquus externus abdominis

Sheath of rectus abdominis

Inguinal ligament

Superficial inguinal ring

Figure 6-19 Superficial muscles of the abdomen.

muscles are also responsible for flexion and extension and for rotational movements of the trunk. The nerve supply is from posterior rami of the spinal nerves at different levels of the spinal cord.

Muscles of the Abdomen

This group includes four muscles on the anterior abdominal wall which are expiratory and thrust the descended diaphragm back into the thoracic cavity.

A small, inconstant structure, the pyramidalis, although a muscle of the anterior abdominal wall, will not be described because its function is not respiratory but one that tightens a midline fascia called the *linea alba*, when the muscle contracts. The linea alba extends from the xiphoid to the pubic symphysis and is formed by the intertwining aponeuroses of the external and internal abdominal oblique muscles plus the transverse muscle.

The abdominal wall includes a great expanse whose superior boundaries are the xiphoid process and costal margins, whose inferior boundaries are the pubis and iliac crest, and whose posterior boundary is a large sector of the vertebral column. The abdominal muscles fill in the entire area.

Unless the ribs are fixed by other muscles, the four large abdominal wall muscles draw the ribs downward and thereby help to lower and to decrease the volume of the thorax. They form a wall that encloses and supports in position the abdominal viscera. They assist in defecation, voiding of urine, vomiting, delivery of the fetus, and other activities involving increased intra-abdominal pressure. When the vertebral column is not made rigid, they act in corresponding pairs to flex the body, or singly to bend it lateralward, or with one another (as the external oblique of one side with the opposite internal oblique) for rotation.

The nerve supply of the four muscles is by the seventh to the twelfth intercostals and the iliohypogastric and ilioinguinal nerves.

The *external abdominal oblique* (paired) is the most superficial member. It is a flat broad structure covering the surface of the lower thoracic and abdominal walls. It originates from the outer surfaces and inferior borders of the lower eight ribs. Its fibers course downward and medialward to a threefold insertion. Most of the fibers join the most superficial layer of the tendinous abdominal aponeurosis, which covers the whole front of the abdomen. Through this aponeurosis the muscle inserts into the linea alba, which is a system of interlacing fibers in the midline of the abdomen. A second set of fibers travels downward and forms a strong *inguinal* (Poupart's) *ligament*. This is a cord palpable in the groin between the anterior superior iliac spine above and the pubic tubercle below. The ligament divides the abdominal wall and the thigh. A third set of fibers, which is the lowest and most posterior, travels almost vertically downward and ends along the external aspect of the iliac crest.

The *internal abdominal oblique* (paired) is deep to the external oblique in the anterolateral abdominal wall. It arises from the thoracolumbar fascia, the anterior two-thirds of the iliac crest, and from the lateral two-thirds of the inguinal ligament. Many of its fibers go vertically up and end in the cartilages of the lower three or four ribs. The main mass of fibers passes from the iliac crest forward around the abdomen and eventually inserts into the linea alba by first entering the abdominal aponeurosis. The most inferior fibers, which arise from the inguinal ligament, run downward and forward to the pubis.

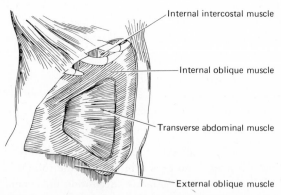

Figure 6-20 Abdominal wall muscles in depth, observed by cutting sections out of the overlying muscles.

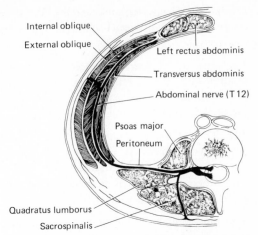

Internal oblique

External oblique

Left rectus abdominis

Transversus abdominis

Abdominal nerve (T 12)

Psoas major

Peritoneum

Quadratus lumborus

Sacrospinalis

Figure 6-21 Half cross section of the abdominal wall to show the relationships of the muscle layers. (*From Brantigan, Clinical Anatomy, Copyright 1963. McGraw-Hill Book Company. Used by permission.*)

The *transverse abdominal* (paired) is the deepest of the anterior abdominal muscles. It originates from (1) the inner surfaces of the lower six ribs, (2) the thoracolumbar fascia, (3) the inner edge of the iliac crest, and (4) the inguinal ligament. Its fibers run horizontally forward and around the abdomen. Some insert into the deepest layer of the abdominal aponeurosis and from there extend to the linea alba. A few of the lowest fibers go to the pubis and the inguinal ligament.

The *rectus abdominis* (paired) is a long flat muscle longitudinally placed in the anterior abdominal wall. It parallels the midline on either side, just lateral to the linea alba. Its origin is the outer surface of the xiphoid process and also the fifth, sixth, and seventh costal cartilages. It courses vertically downward to insert into the body of the pubic bone and into the symphysis pubis. The muscle is crossed by three or more fibrous bands, or tendinous inscriptions, which represent the septa between the original embryonic muscle building blocks called myotomes.

The contracting rectus fibers push inward upon the abdominal viscera and in turn force the diaphragm upward. They may also assist in depressing the ribs by pulling the sternum downward. These are expiratory functions.

The Abdominal Aponeurosis This is one of several fascias that are important in the abdominal, back, pelvic, and inguinal regions. The extensive abdominal, or central, aponeurosis is composed of three pairs of aponeuroses, more or less adherent to each other, and the strength of the total structure is due chiefly to this arrangement. Each of the three aponeuroses that produce the central structure is bilateral. Traced laterally, each is seen to be continuous with one of three bilateral

183

flat abdominal muscles, and therefore the three aponeuroses have been named the external oblique, internal oblique, and transverse abdominal aponeurosis, respectively.

The crisscross of fibers that occurs when the three aponeuroses are in anatomic position gives great strength to the entire structure. This interlacement of fibers is very prominent in the midline, where the right and left fibers meet and fuse to produce the linea alba.

The Thoracolumbar Aponeurosis The older terminology refers to this as the lumbodorsal fascia. It is a strong membrane which attaches to the vertebral column, especially in the lumbar region, and to the dorsal margin of the iliac bone. The structure provides an extremely strong base which extends the surface area for muscle attachments beyond that which the bones can provide.

The thoracolumbar fascia has two parts, thoracic and lumbar. The lumbar part is the dorsal fascial attachment of the transverse abdominal muscle. It splits to form a sheath for the deep dorsal muscles. The thoracic section of the thoracolumbar fascia is a delicate sheet that extends from the vertebral spines to the angles of the ribs, and it spans the deep dorsal muscles.

The Rectus Sheath In connection with the anterior abdominal musculature, a fibrous sheath encloses the rectus muscle and covers a large portion of the anterior wall. The sheath is formed by the aponeuroses of the external oblique, internal oblique, and transversus muscles. In the upper two-thirds of the abdomen the anterior and posterior sections of the rectus sheath are of equal thickness. In the lower third the anterior sheath consists of all three aponeuroses and is considerably thicker than the posterior sheath. The posterior (deep) rectus sheath in the lower third consists solely of transversalis fascia. This is a layer of connective tissue that lines the entire interior of the abdomen, and is seen deep to the transverse abdominal muscle. Also deep to the sheath is a loose layer of connective tissue called the subserous fascia, and still more internal is the peritoneum.

Crafts (1966) compares the abdominal muscles with those forming the thoracic wall. The external intercostals are said to be the analog of the external abdominal

184

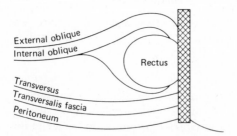

Figure 6-22 Schematic of the rectus sheath and its components in the upper abdomen.

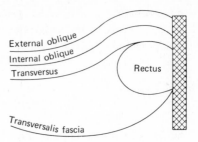

Figure 6-23 Schematic of the rectus sheath and its components in the lower abdomen.

oblique. The internal intercostals are the analog of the internal abdominal oblique. The transversus thoracis plus the intercostalis intimus plus the subcostals are the analogs of the transverse abdominal muscle.

The Regulation of Breathing

Central and Peripheral (Afferent) Neural Mechanisms

Knowledge of the central nervous control of breathing originated with the observations of Legallois in 1812 and Flourens in 1824 that a lesion in a small area of the medulla oblongata results in cessation of breathing. It is now known that breathing is controlled by centers located in various parts of the brain, including the cerebrum, pons, reticular formation of the medulla, and in the brainstem near the fourth ventricle. All these centers are closely integrated.

The conscious centers of control of the voluntary muscles of respiration, which alter the thoracic volume to produce interchange of gases and more pertinently to provide the air blast necessary for speech, are in the motor and associated areas of the cerebrum. None of these cortical centers is required to maintain vegetative breathing, and the muscular apparatus is ordinarily turned over to the unconscious control of the bilateral pontine and medullary centers.

The medullary centers are in the ventral wall of the medulla. Each cell group is cross-connected and controls both sides of the body. Each lateral area is made up of an inspiratory center and a separate expiratory center. The centers control many muscles. All those for inspiration contract together, and all those for expiration contract alternately.

The inspiratory center is well defined caudally in the ventral part of the medullary reticular formation. The expiratory center does not have a well-defined anatomic area but is represented by cell bodies of neurons in the dorsal part of the medullary reticular formation somewhat more cranial than the inspiratory center.

A third pair of centers, called *pneumotaxic* centers, is located in the upper half of the pons, at about the same level as the inferior colliculus. This center is well defined anatomically and is often referred to as the pontine expiratory center. It works in conjunction with the medullary centers, as will be seen later.

The respiratory centers of the hindbrain are always under the potential control of the higher brain centers, and respiration can thus be modified at will. In speech we can spend the air blast in accordance with the need. We can vary the location in the body where the respiratory activity is most emphasized. We can change the parameters of sound, such as loudness, pitch, quality, and duration, although respiration may not be primary in this activity.

The voluntary changes impressed upon biologic, or vegetative, breathing are temporary. The chemical status of the blood is a prime factor in preserving a steady state, particularly in regard to a continuity of respiratory rhythm.

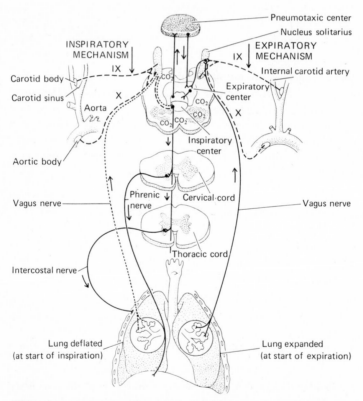

Figure 6-24 Interconnections of the control centers and structures for breathing. (*From L. L. Langley, E. Cheraskin, and R. Sleeper, Dynamic Anatomy and Physiology, 2d ed. Copyright 1958. McGraw-Hill Book Company. Used by permission.*)

Although the statement can be challenged, it may be considered that the respiratory centers display tone or automatic rhythm even when isolated. The nature of their responses, however, depends upon continuous bombardment, chiefly by chemical and nervous stimuli. The centers operate the thoracic machinery adaptively through efferent nerve impulses. The regulation of breathing is thus reflex in nature. At rest, the most important reflex influences originate in the lungs and also in the carotid and aortic regions.

The respiratory centers of the medulla are influenced by impulses generated directly in the lungs, whose alveoli contain *inflation* (stretch) *receptors*. Upon inflation of the alveoli, afferent proprioceptive impulses travel through the vagus nerve to the expiratory center. This in turn discharges inhibitory impulses to the inspiratory center, and inspiration is cut short.

The collapse of the lung may be passive and requires no action from the expiratory center (Tuttle and Schottelius, 1965). At a given degree of deformation the inspiratory center regains power of spontaneous activity and discharges impulses for the subsequent inspiration. The rhythmic afferent vagal impulses are termed the Hering-Breuer reflex. The normal, or eupneic, rhythm is thus maintained. This is a self-regulating mechanism, whereby the lung feedback controls the lung movements, and it does so somewhat independently of the intrathoracic pressures.

There is a set of *deflation receptors* in the lung which are stimulated perhaps only under the stress of labored breathing. They stimulate vagal afferents which terminate directly in the medullary inspiratory centers. This activity is not an aspect of eupnea, or quiet breathing.

187

The pneumotaxic centers in the pons receive their impulses from the inspiratory centers of the medulla. In turn, the pontine centers relay impulses to the expiratory centers, and subsequently the inspiratory centers are inhibited. The result of inspiratory center inhibition is to cut off impulses to the pneumotaxic centers. The inspiratory centers are then freed from inhibition and operate to initiate the next inspiration.

The pneumotaxic centers have a low order of irritability and are perhaps put into the central neural regulatory circuit only during labored breathing. In essence, the inflation receptor to the expiratory center pathway appears to be of greatest importance to normal quiet breathing.

According to Wright (1961), the function of the pneumotaxic center is periodically to inhibit the inspiratory center, thus converting its spontaneous continuous discharge into a rhythmic pattern of discharge. In this view these two centers may be regarded as forming a mutually reacting closed circuit which converts the steady discharge of the inspiratory center into an alternating pattern of activity (inspiration) and rest (expiration).

The respiratory centers are influenced by nerve impulses arising in specialized receptors within the walls of blood vessels. Impulses from pressure receptors in the arch of the aorta and in the carotid sinus at the beginning of the internal carotid artery travel up to the centers through the sinus nerve and other nerves. These impulses generally act to inhibit the centers. Thus, a rise in blood pressure depresses respiration.

Afferent nervous impulses come to the centers from any part of the body. Certain afferent nerves excite the centers, and they are designated as pressor fibers; other fibers, which are depressors, inhibit the centers. The centers are, for example, excited by cold but inhibited in swallowing. In the latter activity the bolus of food reaching the throat sets up inhibitory impulses in the glossopharyngeal nerve fibers leaving that region for the respiratory centers, and the thoracic cage is temporarily held in suspended animation.

Respiratory fibers go to the centers from accessory respiratory structures, and such impulses usually protect these accessory structures against the entrance of foreign bodies. The trigeminal nerve supplies the nasal mucosa, the glossopharyngeal supplies the pharynx, and the vagus supplies the larynx.

Chemical Regulation of Breathing

Impulses from chemoreceptors, located in the carotid and aortic bodies, stimulate the centers. Acids thus adaptively increase respiration. The carotid bodies are at the bifurcation of the common carotid artery and are innervated by Hering's nerve, a branch of the glossopharyngeal. The aortic bodies are located above the aortic arch and are innervated by the nerve of Cyon, a branch of the vagus. Both receptors are sensitive to hypoxia and, to a lesser extent, to hydrogen ion increase.

The peripheral chemoreceptors may be involved in normal breathing but apparently have their major function during hypoxia. They are a valuable mechanism to help maintain arterial oxygen concentration. Changes in arterial oxygen concentration have almost no direct effect on the respiratory center itself.

The primary chemical (humoral) regulatory control of the respiratory centers appears to be central not peripheral. The centers are influenced by local alterations in blood chemistry, and the most important stimulus may be the carbon dioxide in the blood of the brain. The centers are so sensitive to minute changes in the pressure and concentration of carbon dioxide that this gas has been called the respiratory hormone. As the carbon dioxide concentration rises, it activates the medullary inspiratory center. With a further rise the expiratory center may be activated, which blocks the activity of the inspiratory center.

Slonim and Chapin (1967) state that the local control resides in central chemoreceptors. These receptors have been identified in dogs and cats in the medulla and are thought to be present in man. Unlike the peripheral chemoreceptors, the central ones do not respond to hypoxia but rather to the concentrations of carbon dioxide and hydrogen ions in the tissue fluids of the respiratory center.

Guyton (1966) notes that the carbon dioxide concentration and the pH of the cerebrospinal fluid are of great importance in respiratory regulation. There is a small bilateral area in the medulla that is sensitive to changes in the hydrogen ion concentration of the cerebrospinal fluid. Although the pH of the blood below the brain does not affect the pH of the cerebrospinal fluid because of an impermeability to hydrogen ions of the blood–cerebrospinal fluid barrier, the carbon dioxide pressure of the blood readily affects the pH of the cerebrospinal fluid because of great permeability of carbon dioxide in the barrier. Also, upon crossing the barrier, carbon dioxide forms carbonic acid, which in turn changes the local pH. The cerebrospinal fluid as a mechanism to control breathing does so therefore in response to changes in blood carbon dioxide concentration rather than to changes in blood pH. The effect of hydrogen ions may be one that stimulates the respiratory center directly as a result of pH changes in the interstitial fluids surrounding the centers.

Motor Outflows to Maintain Breathing
We have described the breathing centers and their modes of stimulation. We have yet to consider the motor nerves that are influenced by the centers. The discharge during inspiration stimulates those neurons in the cervical and thoracic spinal cord which innervate the inspiratory muscles. The discharge during expiration appears to inhibit the activity of the inspiratory cells. Motor neurons to the muscles of expiration may be relatively inactive during quiet breathing, becoming active during hyperventilation or where there is a demand for active contraction of the expiratory muscles.

The motor nerves have already been listed for each of the respiratory muscles so far described. The cranial nerves are hardly involved, and the spinal nerves belong to the cervical, thoracic, and lumbar segments of the spinal cord.

There are eight pairs of cervical nerves, and the anterior rami of the first four plus the hypoglossal form the cervical plexus. The last four cervical plus the first two thoracic nerves form the brachial plexus. Many of the respiratory nerves come from these plexes. Examples include (1) the phrenic from C-3, C-4, and C-5 to the diaphragm; (2) the anterior thoracic from C-5, C-6, C-7, C-8, and T-1 to the pectoralis major and minor; (3) the long thoracic from C-5, C-6, C-7, and C-8 to the serratus anterior; and (4) the thoracodorsal nerve from C-6, C-7, and C-8 to the latissimus dorsi muscle.

There is no plexus formation for the thoracic nerves from T-2 through T-12. The anterior rami of the upper six pairs produce the intercostal nerves to the thoracic musculature, and those of the lower six produce the thoracoabdominal nerves to the abdominal as well as to the thoracic musculature. The true back muscles involved in respiration and situated in the deeper regions of the back are innervated by the posterior rather than the anterior rami of the cervical, thoracic, and lumbar nerves.

Accessory motor nerves to the muscles of breathing include cranial nerves, such as the vagus nerve to the larynx and the facial nerve to the nose.

Structures Used in Breathing for Speech

The muscles used in quiet inspiration are mostly thoracic. The muscles used in quiet expiration are primarily abdominal. Actually, quiet expiration is predominantly passive. The muscles are active, however, in forced expiration.

In speech the situation changes. Since expiration must be controlled, the expiratory muscles of the abdomen become tensed to regulate the expenditure of air. The thoracic and abdominal muscles are unequally active. The contraction of the abdominal muscles just prior to phonation sets the form of the thoracic and abdominal walls.

The upper and lower chest muscles may be activated almost independently in breathing, and historically arguments arose over which type was preferable for speech. Many French workers of the early nineteenth century emphasized upper-chest breathing. In 1855 Mandl, a French physician, attacked this view, and his counterproposal for abdominal breathing was carried to an extreme by English investigators. There are also advocates of a medial breathing between the chest and abdominal types. There are claims that air volumes are important, which has given strength to the proponents of exercises for deep breathing.

Descriptive terms, such as clavicular, thoracic, and abdominal breathing are in use (Akin, 1953). In clavicular breathing there is an elevation of the shoulders which raises the abdominal musculature and interferes with the descent of the diaphragm. Not enough air for speech or singing is taken in.

190

Darley (1964) cites literature claiming that in clavicular breathing there are excessive neck and throat tensions, an unavoidable unsteadiness, and overly frequent inhalation resulting in interruption of phonation and inappropriate phrasing. Darley states that clinicians often fail to examine the respiratory behavior in speech disorders but that breathing drives the utterance and its influence upon speech disorders should not be disregarded.

Thoracic breathing emphasizes inhalation, or the initial phase of the respiratory cycle, and by itself does not exist. Abdominal breathing emphasizes exhalation through the local activity of muscles activating the abdominal region; this is also unlikely to occur in isolation.

There is the current view that speakers have just as effective a voice with acceptable quality no matter how they breathe. It is not necessary to change a person's way of breathing so long as it is normal. The exception to this may be in singing but not in speech.

There is also said to be no significant relation between lung volume and normal or acceptable tone. This view implies that ordinary speech does not require deep breathing. The pressure and volume of air must of course be adequate and not subliminal. Voices do not fail because of insufficient air intake but because not enough is taken in at the proper time or the air is not used correctly.

Berry and Eisenson (1956) claim that changes in sound intensity are less dependent upon the pressure and volume of the exhaled air than they are upon a process which involves a balance among contracting respiratory muscles. To effect speech, the lower ribs become fixed in an elevated postion in exhalation while the abdominal muscles compress the abdomen. Tension from the thoracic activity increases the diaphragmatic tension, which in turn opposes the abdominal activity. The breath stream is delicately controlled by this unstable equilibration of forces.

Judson and Weaver (1965) write that the expenditure of air has a specific relation to the intensity of the sound produced and a definite rate of expenditure of air is associated with each sound. The volume expended is related to the sound, its position in the word, the position of the body, the status of the person's health, his age, and other factors, including psychologic ones. The expenditure of the exhaled air is controlled to a fine degree at the larynx and with more crudeness by the muscles of breathing.

Stetson (1951) discusses breathing with respect to the syllable. In rest breathing, air is expelled through pressure caused by the weight and elasticity of the structures displaced by inspiratory muscles. Forced expiration is effected chiefly by the contraction of the abdominal wall musculature. In breathing for speech where more than 2.5 to 4 syllables per second are uttered, the abdominal muscles are held rigid and fixate the inferior border of the rib cage. In this way they afford resistance for the muscular pulses accomplished by the internal intercostal muscles.

While abdominal muscles are said to posture the ribs and the abdominal walls such that breath pressure movements can be properly effected, certain thoracic muscles produce more rapid breath pulse movements, called *chest pulses*. Such pulses are said to be the motions that really produce the air pressure required to set up vocal tones.

191

Stetson (1951) relates chest pulses to normal phonation. These pulses, or specialized breathing movements, allow the development of the air pressure needed just prior to vocalization (see Johnson et al., 1956). Any failure in timing between the chest pulses and muscular activity at the glottis may produce phonatory disorders. Van Riper and Irwin (1958) refer to the synchronism between glottal closure and the chest pulse as the *vocal attack*.

Stetson provided great impetus to the study of respiratory muscle activity during speech, and his contributions are numerous. His conclusions, however, drawn from kymographic recordings of body wall movements and from recordings of the air pressure in the trachea and lungs, are now considered inadequate and faulty.

Ladefoged (1967) stresses the importance of analyzing respiratory muscle activity during speech by electromyography. Testing Stetson's conclusions by the EMG, plus pressure and volume recording, he found that the amount and kind of respiratory muscle activity during speech depend on both the volume of air in the lungs and the subglottal (tracheal) pressure.

According to Ladefoged, the muscles adapting the air pressure to phonation must keep up a certain level of pressure in the lungs despite a constant decrease of *relaxation pressure,* i.e., the totality of forces exerted by the abdomen, stretched lung tissues, and elastic costal structures. If phonation follows a deep inspiration, the external intercostals check the costal depression to regulate the subglottal air pressure. When the volume of lung air has decreased below that after a normal inspiration, the external intercostals cease activity. The internal intercostals then gradually increase their activity to maintain the subglottal pressure up to a value just below that at the end of normal expiration, whereupon supplementary muscles aid the internal intercostal action. Ladefoged states that proper investigation of respiratory muscle activity during speech demands a realization of the importance of the relation between the respiratory muscles and the relaxation pressure.

Physiologic Respiratory Changes during Speech

There are physiologic as well as morphologic correlates of speech. Moses (1954) points out that in speaking several respiratory parameters must be coordinated, including (1) the depth and volume of breathing, (2) the frequency of breathing, (3) the relation of expiration to inspiration, (4) the relation between the quantity of air used and the intended tone, (5) the relation between thoracic and abdominal activities, and (6) the rhythm of breathing.

192

Respiration during speech involves muscular work. This is expressed in heightened thoracic and abdominal muscular activities, a rising subglottal pressure, and the expulsion of air against the resistance of tubes. A person can speak for extremely long periods of time, however, despite the work performed, without any demonstrable respiratory distress.

Work is done in vegetative breathing, without speech. The configuration of the thorax for ventilation is always changing, which implies a force of muscle contraction times a distance of movement of thoracic structures. The work may also be expressed as pressure times volume. In another perspective, force is needed to stretch all the elastic tissues involved, to set tissues in motion, and to move respiratory gases through the air passages. Mountcastle (1968) cites values of 0.6 kilogram meters per minute for the overall work of quiet breathing at rest. He also notes that the work done, expressed in terms of metabolic cost, is 0.5 to 1 ml of oxygen per liter of plumonary ventilation. If one takes the ratio between the work per liter and the oxygen cost per liter, the *efficiency* of breathing averages no greater than 8 percent. Slonim and Chapin (1967) observe that the muscular work of breathing is measurable in terms of its oxygen cost, and they may be consulted for a brief discussion of the oxygen cost of breathing in health and disease.

In the inspiratory phase the work is performed by the respiratory muscles. During expiration the muscles can be relatively passive, and the work is done by the release of energy which was stored up in the collagen and elastic tissue of the lung while it was being expanded (Cotes, 1965). The collagen fibers uncurl and the elastic fibers lengthen on inspiration. Since they embrace the air sacs, larger airways, and blood vessels, all these structures participate in the expansion of the lung.

The respiratory muscles must exert force to move the thorax and to overcome several types of resistance to exchange of gases in the airways. There is also the problem of the ability of the lungs and thorax to be expanded. The term *compliance* is used to indicate the degree to which lung volume can be changed by imposed changes of intrapulmonary pressure. Compliance is expressed in liters per centimeter of water and has a normal value of about 0.23 liter/cm.

The role played by carbon dioxide as a respiratory hormone has already been considered. The rate of exchange of carbon dioxide in the blood is adjusted to metabolic needs, but it also varies with speech. According to Lenneberg (1967), the gas may be retained somewhat longer at the start of an utterance than during quiet breathing and then expelled slightly faster than ordinary. There may be controlling mechanisms to adaptively relate ventilation and speech.

The locus of the neural regulation of breathing during speech is speculative. Because speech and breathing are somehow integrated, and because speech involves cortical centers, there is an inference that the breathing rhythm during speech is modulated by cortical processes.

There is clinical evidence that neuroendocrine agencies coordinate breathing with speaking and that this coordination becomes automatic with conditioning. The integrated responses can break down in emotional disturbances. Respiratory processes are readily altered by fear and anxiety. The respiratory system is one of the most sensitive indicators of emotion. Changes in the rate and depth of breathing, in connection with blood-pressure deviations, constitute the basis of lie-detector tests.

Fear changes diaphragmatic physiology with subsequent dyscoordination between diaphragmatic and laryngeal pressures. If the pulmonary pressure is less than the pressure needed at the glottis to approximate the vocal folds, the tone contains quavering tremors. If the pulmonary pressure is disproportionately high, however, an excessive flow of "wild air" can escape. In neurosis, vocal disturbances are characteristically accompanied by respiratory disturbances. In heart and lung diseases and in other maladies with altered respiration, symptomatic speech patterns may occur.

Instrumental Recording of Respiratory Processes

Pneumography

In normal breathing without speech the inspiratory and expiratory phases of a breathing cycle are almost equal. This was made subject to visualization in 1895 with the use of the early model of the pneumograph. This device is still used in student teaching laboratories to obtain crude records of external thoracic movements. The record, or pneumogram, is obtained by strapping a rubber tube containing a helical spring around the chest and leading off the varying air volumes within the tube through one open end to an expansible tambour. A pen seated upon the tambour writes a record on special paper. The paper is mounted on a drum that commonly has a rotary movement. The instrument, with its provisions for the mechanical or electrical movement of the drum, is a kymograph.

Much more sophisticated instruments are available. Polypneumographs, in which several variables are simultaneously related, can be obtained by substituting for the conventional but progressively more archaic kymograph, polygraphs, or channel recorders. The reader is referred to Steer and Hanley (1957) for some of the later pneumographic instrumentation, but even these writings have been outdated by rapid advances. A list of comprehensive references describing current methods and instruments is available in the text series called *Annual Review of Physiology* in the section on Respiration.

The pneumograph can be used to obtain records showing frequency, amplitude, and rhythms of breathing, duration of inspiration and expiration and differences in their patterns, and signs of activity in antagonistic muscle groups.

The pneumograph was used by many of the earlier investigators to visualize breathing patterns in speech disorders. As examples, Steer (1935) showed that there was considerable asynchrony of breathing in stutterers, with marked duration of inspiration and expiration during a spasm and with thoracic and abdominal opposition occurring both in vegetative breathing and in breathing during speech. Hull and Bryngelson (1941) observed that in speech by certain spastics, the thorax expanded for an abnormally long period and also that thoracic and abdominal opposition occurred both in their vegetative breathing and breathing during speech. These investigators thought that abdominal compensation might in part have accounted for the ability to talk while the thorax was expanded. Starbuck and Steer (1954) listed from pneumographic studies the significant and nonsignificant differences they found between stutterers and nonstutterers. All these early investigations suffer from instrumental faults.

In general, pneumograms allow a comparison of breathing with and without speech. The following differences may be visualized.

194

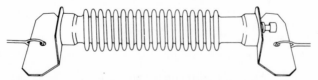

Figure 6-25 A conventional pneumograph, prototype of those used in channel recorders. (*Harvard Apparatus Company, Dover, Mass.*)

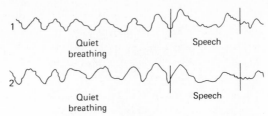

Quiet
breathing

Speech

Quiet
breathing

Speech

Figure 6-26 Polypneumogram. Quiet breathing compared with breathing during speech. Curve A shows thoracic breathing, and curve *B* shows abdominal breathing. Whereas both regions are synchronized in quiet breathing, they are slightly out of phase during speech.

The Rate and Rhythm If the subject talks, the inspiratory phase is shortened and the expiratory phase prolonged. Nonspeaking phases of about 1-¾ sec each for inspiration and expiration change in speaking to ¼ to ½ sec for inspiration and 3 to 4 sec for expiration. The expiration phase may be even more prolonged in trained speakers and in singers.

Van Riper and Irwin (1958) compared the relative durations of inspiration and expiration in speech. Whereas in quiet breathing the duration of inhalation divided by the duration of the whole breathing cycle is 0.40 to 0.45, this ratio decreases to 0.16 during speech. They also stated that the amount of air used in speech exceeds that used in quiet respiration.

During speech the rhythm of breathing changes from smooth, regular and periodic to one that follows the rhythm and purposes of thinking for phonation.

The Depth Exhalation is more forceful and controlled. The inspiratory slope becomes steep because of a rapid intake of breath preceding speech. The diaphragm has a greater excursion.

Spirometry

Whereas pneumography is concerned with the movements of breathing, spirometry is concerned with the volumes of air interchanged.

The *wet spirometer* is a gas meter in which a cylinder that floats in water can be raised upon forcing air into it, the degree of rise being calibrated in terms of volumes of air put into the cylinder. The Hutchinson cylinder, developed in 1846 and containing about 6 liters of air, is the prototype. The functional capacities of the lungs in relation to many environmental factors and also to normal and pathologic speech have been studied by this procedure. The machine is especially pertinent to speech physiology in the determination of volumetric measurements, including *vital capacity*.

An instrument called the *dry spirometer* is also available to measure the volume of air exhaled. This is much less used, its advantage residing in its being less

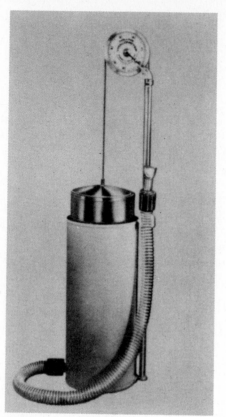

Figure 6-27 Wet spirometer. (*Warren E. Collins, Inc., Braintree, Mass.*)

cumbersome, and its disadvantages in an uncertain reliability and its dependency upon the force of exhalation. The instrument resembles an anemometer, in which the volume of air exhaled causes vanes to rotate, a needle on a calibrated dial being used to read the volume.

For a discussion of spirometry, the reader is referred to Knowles (1959), Rossier et al. (1960), and Cotes (1965).

Respiratory Volumes Air in the lungs may be considered in terms of volumes or else in combinations of volumes that are termed *capacities*. The numerical values cited herein do not accurately represent those found in any given individual.

The *tidal volume* is that air which enters and leaves the pulmonary passages with each quiet inspiration or expiration. It is about 500 cm³.

The *inspiratory reserve volume* is the extra air that can be inspired in excess of the tide. It equals at least 1,500 cm³, and twice this amount has been obtained in young male adults.

The *expiratory reserve volume* is the extra air that can be expired in excess of the tide. It equals about 1,500 cm³ and often less.

The *residual volume* is the amount of air left in the lungs following the most forceful expiration. It equals about 1,500 cm³. It is important to provide air in the alveoli under any circumstances.

The *inspiratory capacity* is the tidal volume plus the inspiratory reserve volume. It represents a maximum forced inspiration following a quiet expiration. It varies from about 2,000 (above) to 3,500 cm³.

The *functional residual capacity* is the expiratory reserve volume plus the residual volume. It equals about 3,000 cm³ and represents a "stationary" reserve that could remain in the lungs at the end of a normal expiration.

The *total lung capacity* is the maximum volume which the lungs can hold with the greatest inspiratory effort. It is at least 5,000 cm³ in the young male adult, being made up of a tide, an inspiratory reserve volume, and the stationary reserve.

The *vital capacity* represents the amount of air that can be expelled by an individual after as deep an inspiration as possible. If the numerical values above are employed, the vital capacity might average 3,500 cm³, or the sum of the tidal air plus the inspiratory and expiratory reserves. Vital capacity measurements are usually reduced to standards based on an individual's surface area (obtained from

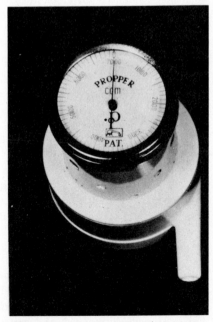

Figure 6-28 Dry spirometer. (*Propper Manufacturing Company, Long Island City, N.Y.*)

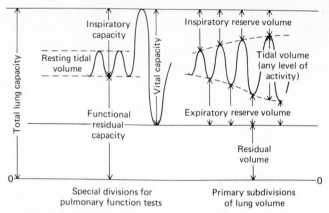

Figure 6-29 Subdivisions of the lung volume. (*By permission from J. R. Pappenheimer (Chairman), Standardization of Definitions and Symbols in Respiratory Physiology, Fed. Proc., 9: 602–605, 1950.*)

tables computed from height and weight). As an approximation, the standard is 2,600 cm³/m² for adult males and 2,000 cm³/m² for adult females. A reduction exceeding 15 percent of the norm for a given group may be suggestive of pathology.

198

The vital capacity in man is significantly lowered in certain cardiac and pulmonary conditions, and it is therefore used in the diagnosis and prognosis of cardiac decompensation and pulmonary tuberculosis. Pulmonary diseases may lower the vital capacity for a number of years. In a healthy person the vital capacity has been widely used as an approximate measure of lung capacity and therefore of respiratory physical fitness. This relationship with physical fitness is now being denied (Lippold, 1968) because several factors alter vital capacity, such as posture, training, or disease. Even advanced disease can sometimes exist in the lungs without any alteration in vital capacity.

The vital capacity has been variably emphasized in the physiology of speech on the theory that ample lung volumes are essential to normal tone quality. This has been qualified. Even when one speaks loudly, more breath is not necessarily used, and the adjustments may involve changes in resonance. In fact, respiratory defects in disease are very often compensated with regard to speech. A person with a collapsed lung and low vital capacity need not have any inadequacy of voice. Barnes (1926) obtained statistical data to show that vital capacity and ability in oral reading are not correlated.

In a study of defective and normal speech groups among children, Carrell (1936) claims to observe a difference in vital capacity. He concludes that the speech-defective children are physically inferior, and they also make poor use of their structural possibilities. All the early studies are of questionable validity, due partly to instrumentation factors and also to the limitations of making "normal" measurements on subjects.

The *respirometer* is a modified spirometer attached to a kymograph drum that rotates at known speeds. The use of calibrated paper allows determination of the respiratory rate, tidal volume and lung volumes. The record, or spirogram, is useful for analyzing vegetative breathing, vital capacity, and breathing in controlled speech.

Oral Manometry

Instruments are available to measure oral breath pressure. The amount of pressure exerted upon blowing forces a liquid up a tube, with a known relation between cause and effect. Instruments with a moving needle on a dial can measure the pressure (Spriestersbach and Powers, 1959).

The *pneumotachograph* can measure the rate of airflow through the nasal and oral cavities during speech by transmission through a face mask and transduction of pressure to an electric signal that can be recorded.

Electromyography

Hoshiko (1960) picked up action currents from respiratory muscles during speech, amplifying and recording them. This now common method provides a means of exploring the less accessible parts of the apparatus for speech production.

Fluoroscopy

The x-ray fluoroscope visualizes especially the thoracic structures in action.

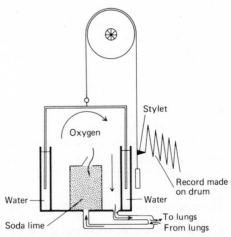

Figure 6-30 Section through a metabolimeter, which is used in spirometric and related pulmonary function tests.

Cinefluorography

Motion picture photography of the fluoroscopic image, demanding only very short exposure times because of image intensifiers, is useful in the study of breathing.

Recording of Pressures during Breathing

The pulmonary or intrapulmonic pressure is the pressure of air within the lungs and respiratory passages. It is measured most simply by inserting a tube connected to a mercury manometer into a single nostril. The pressure at rest is atmospheric, since the respiratory passages communicate freely with the air. A negative pressure of 2 to 3 mm (below 760) develops during inspiration, and a positive pressure of 2 to 3 mm develops during expiration. If there is obstruction to the air passages, the variations in pressure are much greater. Expiratory pressures as high as 10 to 40 mm are attained in coughing, in which the pressure is built up by inhaling deeply, closing the glottis, and producing a forced expiration against the closed glottis. In speech, variable expiratory pressures are built up against the closed or partly closed glottis, and these events help determine the qualities of the voice. Usually the blast pressures employed in speech are not very great. Some of the highest expiratory pressures are produced in certain pathology, as in bronchial asthma, where it could take 100 mm of pressure to force the lung air up through the functionally closed passages.

The second kind of respiratory pressure is the intrapleural, or intrathoracic, which is the pressure in the pleural cavities and in the mediastinum. The pleural cavities are potential spaces within the double-walled sac that surrounds and encloses each lung. The mediastinum is the central region of the thorax. It lies between the two lungs and their pleural investments.

The intrathoracic pressure is always negative because the thorax, which is a closed chamber, expands at birth and permanently reduces its internal pressure. Moreover, the lungs stretch and, being elastic, tend to produce a continuous pull away from the chest wall. These factors explain a permanent negative pressure, which is about 5 mm at the end of expiration. With each inspiration the thorax expands more than the lungs do, and the intrathoracic negativity increases to about 10 mm below atmospheric pressure.

This changing negativity prevents collapse of the lungs, and it is also responsible for the rhythmic expansion and compression of the lungs. For the most part the lungs are controlled by the thoracic movements. We have previously called this the physical theory of respiration.

Applied Anatomy and Physiology of Breathing and Speech

Although respiration is ordinarily turned over to centers below consciousness in the hindbrain, voluntary control again takes over, even though subconsciously, in respiration during speech. The column of air must be controlled (breath control) so that inhalation is quick, with a larger amount of air inhaled, and exhalation is prolonged. Ventilation becomes more active than in the purely respiratory rhythm. The regularity is changed because of sentence patterns.

The most efficient sounds, in the sense that they require the least breath expenditure, are vowels. The voiceless fricatives, such as /f/ and /s/ use considerable breath output, and one must learn to sound these with minimal exhalation.

Faulty breath control characterizes many speech deviations. In the condition of breathiness there is too little tension in the region of the vocal folds and insufficient resistance to exhalation; the wasted breath therefore contributes to an unpleasant, mousy tone. The loss of energy in wasted breath could necessitate a hyperventilation which may be ameliorated through a learned reduction of respiratory movements. The breathy or husky voice may result either from disorders of respiration or disorders of phonation.

The harsh voice may also show both respiratory and phonatory deviations. There is not only an excessive general bodily as well as laryngeal tension, but also in many cases abnormal respiratory movements, including marked abdominal contractions.

In the hoarse voice, which has both husky and harsh qualities, an individual may voluntarily force his breathing in addition to overtensing his larynx.

The residual breather takes too little breath for speech, and his voice is hard to hear. People who are subbreathers, or hypothyroid, or in poor health may release the air in insufficient bubbles to a larynx that gets too tense. They sound as if they were ill, and the condition is described as unsustained phonation. Cerebral palsy may affect breathing so that the tone may not be sustained.

The reader is referred to Darley (1964) for literature on the respiratory activities during speech in cerebral palsy and other neurologic disorders, as well as in palatal dysfunction and in stuttering (see also Luchsinger and Arnold, 1965).

7 THE STRUCTURE FOR PHONATION

The larynx is the phonating mechanism. Through movements of its cartilages, which are activated by voluntary muscles and controlled by cerebrospinal nerves, it produces sounds.

The larynx is roughly triangular above and tapered to a narrow cylindrical portion below. It is located in the neck directly anterior to the esophagus and is in continuity with the pharynx above and the trachea below. The paired lobes of the thyroid gland lie on either side of it. The transverse isthmus that connects the two thyroid lobes crosses in front of the larynx at the lower section of that organ. Behind the larynx are the fourth, fifth, and sixth cervical vertebrae, from which it is separated by the laryngeal portion of the pharynx. The larynx should be considered a specialized part of the respiratory system.

The Laryngeal Framework

The supporting structures of the larynx consist of cartilages and membranes.

Hyoid Bone

The unpaired hyoid bone is just above the larynx. Although it is primarily a support for the tongue, it may be considered a part of the laryngeal framework. The larynx is suspended from the hyoid, and many of the laryngeal muscles have a hyoid attachment.

The hyoid bone is unique in having no direct attachments to any other bone. It is held in position by muscles and ligaments. These supports go into it from the bones of the skull above and from the laryngeal cartilages below.

The hyoid is slender and U-shaped. It lies in a horizontal plane with the limbs of the U pointing posteriorly. The outer surface of the bone can be felt through the skin at the junction of the front of the neck and the floor of the mouth.

The anterior section of the hyoid bone is the body. The posteriorly directed limbs are the major horns, or greater cornua. The posterior tip of each limb has a tubercle to which the lateral thyrohyoid ligament connects. This ligament provides stability to a joint in which the major horns of the hyoid articulate with the superior horns of the thyroid cartilage.

At the junction between the body and each horn, a small conical spike juts upward. These spikes are the paired minor horns, or lesser cornua. They allow hyoid suspension to the temporal bones of the skull by the stylohyoid ligament.

The hyoid bone has an alimentary function in swallowing, a speech function involving support of phonatory and articulatory structures, and perhaps even a respiratory

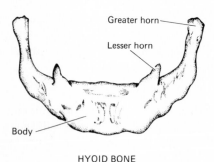

HYOID BONE

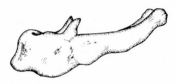

Lateral view

Figure 7-1 Anterior and lateral views of the hyoid bone.

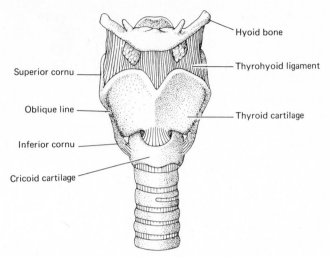

Figure 7-2 Laryngeal cartilages seen in anterior view.

function in separating the airway from the food passage. This bone is sometimes called the hitching post because it is the attachment for membranes, ligaments, and a number of muscles.

Thyroid Cartilage

205

The larynx proper has nine cartilages. The most prominent is the unpaired thyroid cartilage. The thyroid cartilage is made up of right and left quadrilateral plates, or laminae. These are easily palpated in the anterior and lateral walls of the neck. The laminae fuse to form a thyroid angle in the median ventral line. The superior aspect of the fused plates is the especially prominent Adam's apple (laryngeal prominence). The upper border of each lamina drops sharply in the central anterior region above the prominence to produce a V-shaped superior thyroid notch.

The laminae diverge in back so that they enclose a wide space. The posterior border of each lamina is prolonged above and below into superior and inferior horns, respectively. The superior horn is the longer one. It is directed upward with a slight dorsomedial inclination, and it terminates in a rounded extremity which joins the extremity of the great cornu of the hyoid bone by the lateral thyrohyoid ligament. This ligament is a round elastic cord, which frequently contains a nodule called the triticeous cartilage. The junction of thyroid and hyoid on each side is the thyrohyoid joint.

The inferior horn on each side is shorter and stouter than the superior and curves somewhat medially in its downward course. The medial aspect of its tip has a circular flat facet through which it articulates with a facet on the lateral aspect of the cricoid cartilage. This is the cricothyroid joint. The presence of joints indicates the flexibility of the laryngeal cartilages.

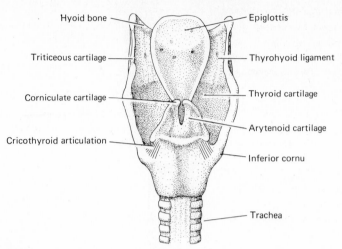

Hyoid bone

Triticeous cartilage

Corniculate cartilage

Cricothyroid articulation

Epiglottis

Thyrohyoid ligament

Thyroid cartilage

Arytenoid cartilage

Inferior cornu

Trachea

Figure 7-3 Posterior view of larynx to show the cartilages and their connecting ligaments.

The lateral surface of each lamina is divided by a ridge called the oblique line into two unequal areas. The oblique line originates above at the superior thyroid tubercle, which is a prominence just below the superior border of the lamina. The oblique line goes forward and downward and terminates in the inferior tubercle on the lower border of the lamina. The thyrohyoid, sternothyroid, and inferior pharyngeal constrictor muscles use the oblique line as a place of attachment.

The internal surface of each thyroid lamina is smooth and somewhat concave. Several structures are attached internally at the angle formed by the union of the two laminae. These include the thyroepiglottic, ventricular, and vocal ligaments, the stem of the epiglottis, and also the thyroarytenoid, thyroepiglottic, and vocalis muscles.

When the larynx rises, the thyroid cartilage slips up under cover of the hyoid with a synovial bursa between them.

Cricoid Cartilage

The unpaired cricoid cartilage lies in front of the sixth cervical vertebra, between the thyroid cartilage above and the trachea below, being partly included within the curvature of the thyroid laminae. With the head extended it is easily visible in a lean neck and can be palpated in the normal neck.

The cricoid has the shape of a signet ring whose lumen is elliptical above and more circular below. It is smaller than the thyroid cartilage but thicker and stronger. Its inner surface is smooth and lined by mucous membrane continuous with the laryngeal cavity above and the trachea below.

The cricoid is the only complete ring of cartilage in the respiratory tract. The front and sides of the ring form the cricoid arch. The posterior section of the ring is a flattened hexagonal plate, or signet (posterior quadrate lamina), which extends upward to fill the region not occupied by the divergent thyroid laminae. The signet is about 25 mm in height, and the arch is about 8 mm in height.

The signet has a median vertical ridge on its posterior external surface. The longitudinal muscle fibers of the esophagus attach to the lower part of this ridge. A shallow depression on each side of the ridge allows attachment of the posterior cricoarytenoid muscle.

The arch of the cricoid provides for attachment of muscles to its external surface. The cricothyroid muscles attach in front and at the sides A portion of the inferior pharyngeal constrictor muscle attaches more posteriorly. The inferior cornu of the thyroid cartilage connects with the cricoid on each side at the junction of the cricoid arch with the signet.

The lower border of the cricoid is fairly horizontal and forms the base and circumference of the larynx. It allows attachment to the first ring of the trachea through the cricotracheal ligament.

The upper cricoid border provides attachment anteriorly for the median cricothyroid ligament and the more lateral paired conus elasticus ligaments. Rising posteriorly, the upper border is received between the spreading laminae of the thyroid cartilage. The upper border has a posterior central notch, on each side of which is a smooth surface that faces upward and outward. This arrangement provides for the paired cricoarytenoid joints. The joints are on the downward-sloping portion of the cricoid, lateral to the horizontal section. The arytenoid cartilages must not be thought of as resting upon the horizontal section of the superior border of the cricoid.

Arytenoid Cartilages

The paired arytenoid cartilages are in the posterior section of the larynx. They are approximately three-sided pyramids. Since each has a triangular base as well as

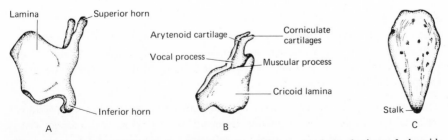

Figure 7-4 Individual disarticulated laryngeal cartilages: (*a*) Lateral view of thyroid; (*b*) the cricoid, arytenoids, and corniculates; (*c*) anterior view of the epiglottis.

three triangular sides, each could be considered tetrahedral (Cates and Basmajian, 1955). Palmer and LaRusso (1965) list four surfaces and three important angles.

The surfaces of the triangular sides of each arytenoid are medial, posterior, and anterolateral. The medial surface is almost vertical. The posterior surface is concave and smooth, and it is covered by the oblique and transverse arytenoid muscles. The anterolateral surface is the largest. It presents two pits, a triangular fovea above, which contains mucous glands, and an oblong fovea below for the vocalis muscle. An arcuate crest horizontally separates the two pits. The anterolateral surface has in its upper part an eminence called the colliculus.

Each arytenoid has an apex and base. The apex is pointed, and it curves medially and posteriorly. The apex articulates with the claw-shaped corniculate cartilage. An angular crest projects inferomedially from the apex to end in the vocal process (see below).

The base is concave. It joins the facet of the cricoid cartilage to produce a mobile synovial articulation. A posterolateral projection called the *muscular process* is at the lateral angle of the base. The lateral and posterior cricoarytenoid muscles insert at the lateral angle. A *vocal process,* which gives attachment to the vocal ligament, forms the prominent anterior angle.

Corniculate Cartilage

The corniculate cartilages (of Santorini) are small paired conical elastic-tissue nodules, each capping the arytenoid apex and prolonging it posteromedially. Occasionally they are fused with the arytenoid cartilages. The paired corniculates resemble two tiny hooks curved inwardly. Possibly they protect the arytenoids. Muscle fibers are inserted into them.

Cuneiform Cartilage

The paired rodlike cuneiform cartilages (of Wrisberg) are yellow elastic cartilages located in the posterior parts of the aryepiglottic folds, which are membranes stretching between the epiglottis above and the arytenoids below. The cartilages are not always present, and they are said to be degenerate structures that may have served historically to support the aryepiglottic folds.

Epiglottis

The highest laryngeal cartilage is the unpaired epiglottis. This is elastic cartilage resembling a leaf. It lies in the front of the larynx just behind the root of the tongue. The epiglottis forms the oblique anterior wall of that section of the larynx which is the entrance, or vestibule.

There are two surfaces, anterior, or lingual, and posterior, or laryngeal. The anterior surface curves forward. A mucous membrane covers its upper aspect and is extended onto the sides and root of the tongue as the median and paired glossoepiglottic folds. A space between the base of the tongue and the lingual surface of the epiglottis is called the *vallecula.*

The posterior or laryngeal surface of the epiglottis is concavoconvex in passing downward. The lower posterior aspect has a prominent epiglottic tubercle, or cushion, which lies over the upper part of the thyroepiglottic ligament. The cushion is visible in a laryngoscopic examination. Mucous glands lie in recessed pits in the surface of the cartilage.

The stem, or petiole, of the epiglottis is long and narrow. It is attached anteriorly to (1) the thyroepiglottic ligament, which meets the angle of the thyroid cartilage just below the superior thyroid notch, and (2) the hyoepiglottic ligament, which connects the epiglottis with the superior border of the body of the hyoid bone.

The epiglottis is related to the partition of air and food during swallowing. The food, or bolus, in passing into the pharynx is reflected upon the upper surface of the epiglottis and it is then sent down the posterior part of the pharynx into the esophagus. If inhalation is at the same time reflexly inhibited and the pharynx actively elevated, the glottis will be narrowed and no food will be taken into the windpipe. According to Boies et al. (1964), it is not the epiglottis that is important in protecting against material entering the windpipe but rather the constrictor action of the ventricular folds.

The epiglottis in the early literature was claimed to act as a movable lid which protected the larynx. It apparently does not descend over the entrance of the larynx in the manner of a trapdoor since this would be hindered by the hyoepiglottic ligament. More recently, the epiglottis has been considered to be a fairly rigid, semi-upright structure which deflects the bolus to the esophagus. Its movements have been analyzed by fluoroscopy, through a surgical pharyngostome, in cinefluorography, by spotting its dorsal surface with ink and observing the imprints that reflect its oppositions during swallowing, and by other methods.

There is radiological evidence from a subject who had a silver clip placed on the tip of his epiglottis that this structure does turn down during swallowing (Jenkins, 1960). The situation was not entirely definite inasmuch as the movements were very rapid. There is confirmatory evidence of movement in another subject whose pharynx could be observed from the exterior. Also, by the use of high-speed cineradiography (Saunders et al., 1951), the epiglottis has been seen to act as a trapdoor which bends backward and seals the larynx during swallowing. At the same time, the aryepiglottic folds shorten, to assist in pulling the epiglottis down and back.

We may assume the correctness of the statements of Crafts (1966) summarizing the movements of the epiglottis in swallowing. The larynx is raised by the digastric, mylohyoid, geniohyoid, stylohyoid, and hyoglossus muscles elevating the hyoid bone and the thyrohyoid, stylopharyngeus, palatopharyngeus, and salpingopharyngeus muscles elevating the larynx proper. This pushes the larynx against the epiglottis, the latter being forced against the base of the tongue. The tip of the epiglottis is brought downward by the aryepiglottic and thyroepiglottic muscles. The entrance closure into the larynx is completed by an adductive action of the transverse arytenoid and lateral cricoarytenoid muscles upon the rima glottidis.

The epiglottis is not a vital organ since the removal of a large part of it does not prevent swallowing. It may serve chiefly for respiration. Bosma (1957) discusses these problems.

Negus (1949) claims that the epiglottis evolved primarily in association with the nasopharynx and soft palate for olfaction. The structure is almost universally absent in amphibians, reptiles, and birds, and these animals have in general a poorly developed sense of smell. All mammals possessing a keen sense of smell have a well-developed epiglottis, which lies in contact with the soft palate. There is also the view that this organ is concerned phylogenetically with taste.

The epiglottis may develop cysts. In the newborn these can produce laryngeal stridor or death from laryngeal obstruction (Asherson, 1957). In adults the cysts may vary from a painless and harmless type to those associated with infection or obstruction. They can interfere with deglutition and phonation.

The epiglottis may add to resonance by producing changes in the size of the laryngeal cavity. Judson and Weaver (1965) point out that many workers place great emphasis on the tubercle of the epiglottis, a prominence near the inferior end of the petiole, but that, all told, the importance of the epiglottis to the voice is speculative.

Other Laryngeal Cartilages

There are inconstant or supernumerary cartilages in the larynx. Small paired *sesamoid* cartilages occur at the lateral edges of the arytenoids. Small paired *triticeous* cartilages are found in the posterolateral margins of the thyrohyoid membrane. A tiny single *interarytenoid* cartilage is enveloped by the cricopharyngeal ligament and underlies the mucous membrane of the pharynx.

There are histologic differences in the cartilages. The arytenoid, cricoid, and thyroid cartilages contain hyaline cartilage. The apices of the arytenoids, the corniculate, cuneiform, and epiglottis contain elastic tissue. These differences have importance in that the hyaline tissues usually ossify progressively with age, beginning in early adulthood (Palmer and LaRusso, 1965).

The Laryngeal Joints

The laryngeal cartilages are united by joints. Two very important articulations include the cricoarytenoid and cricothyroid joints. The fact that they are synovial provides for the mobility of cartilage necessary for phonation.

Cricoarytenoid Joint

The arytenoids and cricoid form a pair of cricoarytenoid joints. Grant (1965) says that the under surface of each arytenoid and the lateral sloping parts of the superior border of the cricoid lamina have oval articular facets. The long axes of the ovals are at right angles to each other, which allows the arytenoid to glide medially and laterally, forward and backward, and to rotate.

Grant's statements are essentially followed by Woodburne (1965), who claims that each cricoarytenoid joint has two oval facets, convex on the upper border of the cricoid and concave on the base of the arytenoid. The long axis of the arytenoid facet is anteroposterior and that of the cricoid facet is transverse. This arrangement determines the types of movement. The arytenoids can glide medially and laterally and also forward and backward. The backward motion tilts the vocal process of the arytenoid upward. The forward motion brings it downward. This action is a result of the curvature and slope of the cricoid facet. There is also a rotary motion which brings the vocal processes together or pulls them apart to variable degrees.

Morris (1966) states that the cricoarytenoid joint is a typical arthrodial, or gliding, joint and that motion is very free. A posterior cricoarytenoid ligament is important in keeping the arytenoid upon the sloping articular surface of the cricoid and in limiting its movements.

Gray (1966) states that two movements of the diarthrodial cricoarytenoid joint are allowed. The arytenoid can rotate on a vertical axis and move the vocal process medially or laterally, which narrows or widens the glottis. In the second movement the arytenoids glide toward or away from each other. The direction and slope of the approximating cricoid surface cause the lateral motion to have also a forward and downward direction. Both rotation and gliding are so associated that medial gliding and medial rotation occur together, and the same holds for lateral gliding and lateral rotation.

According to Ballenger (1969), there are two main types of motion: (1) a rocking motion around the axis of the joint and (2) a gliding motion parallel to the long axis of the cricoid facet. He claims that there is no gross rotation around a vertical plane but there is a slight rotary motion pivoting around the posterior cricoarytenoid ligament.

As in all synovial joints, the capsule is thickened by accessory ligaments, which are relatively unimportant, except for the posterior cricoarytenoid ligament (Jackson and Jackson, 1959). It runs from the posteromedial aspect of the capsule to the base of the arytenoid cartilage and terminates just lateral to the midpoint of the superior margin of the cricoid lamina. When the cricoid is tilted such that its superior border moves posteriorly, the ligament pulls the arytenoid posteriorly. It causes the cricoid to be tilted in the opposite direction when the arytenoid is pulled forward.

Cricothyroid Joint
A joint is formed on each side between the round lateral facet on the cricoid and a facet on the medial aspect of the inferior horn of the thyroid cartilage. This is arthrodial. There are a joint capsule, synovial membrane, and accessory ligaments posteriorly. The cartilages may glide anteroposteriorly against one another. Gray (1966) says that in gliding there is a limited shift of the cricoid on the thyroid in different directions. The cricoid may also rotate upon the inferior thyroid horn

around an axis passing transversely through both joints. Ballenger (1969) admits rotatory motion in the sagittal plane only.

Because this joint is the fulcrum for the cricothyroid muscle, destruction or fixation of the joint lessens the effect of the muscle on the tension of the vocal folds.

The Laryngeal Membranes

Several membranes and ligaments unite the cartilages and by limiting the extent and direction of their movements contribute to orderly laryngeal activity. The membranes divide the larynx into three vertical compartments. Some enter into the construction of the ventricular and the vocal folds.

The unpaired *thyrohyoid* membrane suspends the larynx from the hyoid bone. The membrane is attached above to the superior margin and greater horns of the hyoid. It passes downward behind the hyoid and ends upon the superior border and superior horns of the thyroid cartilage. The median section of this membrane is thick and is called the *medial thyrohyoid* ligament. The posterolateral sections of the membrane connect the greater horns of the hyoid with the superior horns of the thyroid cartilage. This section is the *lateral thyrohyoid* ligament.

Between the central thick portion and the cordlike lateral portions, the membrane is thin and weak. It is pierced by the superior laryngeal nerve and the superior laryngeal vessels.

The thyrohyoid membrane and the hyoid are separated by a mucous bursa, which facilitates upward movement of the larynx, as during swallowing.

We have noted that the epiglottis is connected to the hyoid bone by the *hyoepiglottic* ligament and to the thyroid cartilage by the *thyroepiglottic* ligament. At the lower end of the larynx, the cricoid is connected to the uppermost tracheal ring by the *cricotracheal* ligament.

The *cricothyroid* membrane is important. It becomes involved in the construction of the vocal folds. This membrane has a central and paired lateral sections. The central section, or *middle cricothyroid* ligament, travels as a vertical anterior band between the cricoid arch and the lower border of the central part of the thyroid cartilage. It closes the interval in front between the thyroid and cricoid cartilages.

The paired lateral sections are known as the *conus elasticus* (synonyms are the elastic cone and the cricovocal membrane). The term conus elasticus derives from the fact that the ligaments form a cone as they slant superiorly and medially.

The lateral sections have free cephalic margins; i.e., they are not attached above to the inferior border of the thyroid cartilage. They slope upward and medially on the inner aspect of the thyroid lamina, and their free upper border becomes somewhat thickened from front to back to form the *vocal ligaments*.

The vocal ligaments form the medial part of each vocal fold. They have a thick layer of elastic tissue and are the chief support of the folds.

Each vocal ligament is attached ventrally to a perichondral process at the posterior surface of the thyroid angle. At its dorsal end each vocal ligament has a broad insertion to the upper and medial surfaces of the vocal process of the corresponding arytenoid cartilage.

The paired *quadrangular* membranes appear as irregular vertical folds. The membrane, a loose elastic tissue, arises anteriorly from the lateral border of the epiglottis and the posterior surface of the thyroid angle. The membrane on either side extends posteriorly in a downward slope to the corniculate cartilage and the medial margin of each arytenoid.

The lateral parts of the quadrangular membrane are widely separated superiorly. As the membrane on each side descends somewhat vertically, it also turns medially. The paired membranes thus tend to converge inferiorly. The terminal inferior borders are free and thickened and are called the *ventricular* (vestibular) *ligaments*. The ligaments are horizontal and well developed ventrally. They are attached close to the thyroid angle ventrally. At their dorsal ends they are attached to the medial border of the triangular fovea of the arytenoid cartilages.

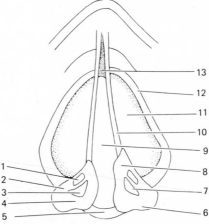

Figure 7-5 The vocal fold area looking down from above (diagrammatic): 1, oblong fovea; 2, muscular process of arytenoid cartilage; 3, triangular fovea; 4, apex of arytenoid cartilage; 5, posterior aspect of cricoid cartilage; 6, arytenoid; 7, anterolateral aspect of arytenoid; 8, vocal process of arytenoid; 9, rima glottidis; 10, vocal ligament; 11, conus elasticus; 12, anterosuperior aspect of cricoid arch; 13, cricothyroid ligament.

The paired ventricular ligaments constitute the framework of the *ventricular, or false, vocal folds.* The ligaments also help support the aryepiglottic folds which bound the laryngeal entrance.

The term *vestibular membrane* is occasionally used to describe the structure which forms the ventricular ligaments. The vestibular membrane is the quadrangular membrane. Woodburne (1965) says that the vestibular membrane is a weak submucosal sheet of connective tissue. It is covered posteriorly by the aryepiglottic and thyroepiglottic muscles.

The paired *aryepiglottic folds* form the superior aperture of the larynx. These folds begin at the sides of the epiglottis. They slope downward as they are extended backward. The folds envelope the supporting cartilages of Wrisberg posteriorly and terminate at the cartilages of Santorini and the arytenoids. When the posterior cricoarytenoid muscles act to open the laryngeal aperture, the aryepiglottic folds are pulled backward.

The aryepiglottic folds help form lateral channels on each side. Fluid can travel down from the tongue base and be channeled into the troughs between these folds and the lateral wall of the pharynx. The sphincter muscles within the aryepiglottic folds close the laryngeal aperture during swallowing to prevent inundation of the windpipe by solid and liquid food. Collins (1966) states that in speaking, the aryepiglottic folds become high, smooth, and taut. This produces a deep supraglottic cavity for the regulation of resonance.

Cleary (1954) gives a description of the aryepiglottic folds with particular reference to the otolaryngologist. The muscles of these folds were called the constrictor vestibuli muscles by Luschka in 1871. At that time the folds were thought to contribute to phonatory movements. It now appears that their main function is related to the epiglottis in swallowing. Pressman (1954) suggests that they constrict the larynx in swallowing.

Cleary asserts that the aryepiglottic folds are of paramount importance in the active closure of the larynx. If there is swelling of these folds, choking may occur because the edema prevents adequate muscular closure of the folds and the water gets into the windpipe. Although susceptible to swelling, the aryepiglottic folds are rarely the cause of obstruction, the ventricular folds being more often at fault.

Internal Divisions of the Larynx

The cavity of the larynx (cavum laryngis) is continuous below with the cavity of the trachea. Superiorly, the cavity is an anterior diverticulum of the lowest part of the pharynx. The laryngeal interior is somewhat funnel-shaped, and it has three divisions from above downward.

Vestibule (Supraglottic Region)
The superior division, or *vestibule,* includes the space between the entrance to the larynx above (aditus laryngis) and the ventricular folds below. The entrance is

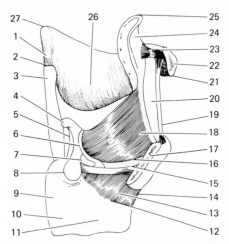

Figure 7-6 The internal aspect of the right side of the larynx to show membranes and ligaments: 1, corniculate cartilage; 2, lateral thyrohyoid ligament; 3, posterior section of thyroid cartilage; 4, apex of arytenoid cartilage; 5, posterior border of arytenoid; 6, arcuate crest; 7, oblong fovea; 8, muscular process of arytenoid; 9 and 10, posterior and inferior aspects of cricoid cartilage; 11 and 12, cricoid arch and its superior aspect; 13, conus elasticus; 14, cricothyroid ligament; 15, vocal ligament; 16, vestibular ligament; 17, part of thyroid plate; 18, quadrangular membrane; 19, median thyrohyoid ligament; 20. fat pad anterior to epiglottis; 21, bursa posterior to the hyoid; 22, body of hyoid bone; 23, hyoepiglottic ligament; 24, anterior aspect of epiglottis; 25, superior aspect of epiglottis; 26, lateral thyrohyoid ligament; 27, superior aspect of greater cornu of hyoid bone.

215

shaped like a triangle, wide in front, narrow behind, and sloping down from front to back. The vestibular cavity is wide above, but it narrows from side to side as it approaches the glottis. The tubercle of the epiglottis is on the anterior wall of the vestibule. The term *paraglottis* is often used for the intralaryngeal portion of the epiglottis with the preglottic body of fat tissue. The term *supraglottis* includes the entire region above the inferior margins of the false vocal folds. These fleshy folds bulge upward into the vestibule.

Ventricle (Glottic Region: Ventriculus Laryngis; Sinus of the Ventricle)
The middle division is a spindle-shaped cavity which extends from the ventricular folds above to the flat superior surface of the vocal folds below. It is 12 to 20 mm long by 4 to 8 mm high, being about twice as large in the male as in the female.

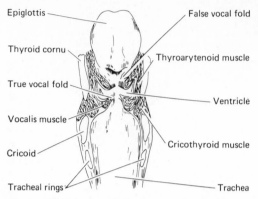

Epiglottis

Thyroid cornu

True vocal fold

Vocalis muscle

Cricoid

Tracheal rings

False vocal fold

Thyroarytenoid muscle

Ventricle

Cricothyroid muscle

Trachea

Figure 7-7 Interior of the larynx, showing its vertical divisions and some internal structures.

The ventricle provides a space for free vibration of the vocal folds, and it functions perhaps as a resonator. The space was known to Galen in A.D. 300, and it was described by Morgagni in 1741—thus the name, ventricle of Morgagni. This area is well described by Freedman (1938), and Gray (1966).

Anteriorly, the sinus, or ventricle, on each side is prolonged upward. This produces a pair of culs-de-sac, each of which is a *laryngeal sacculus,* or *appendix of the ventricle.* Each sacculus projects between the ventricular fold and the thyroid cartilage. The sac goes as high as the upper border of the thyroid cartilage.

The sacculus represents an atavistic (throwback) structure which is better developed in monkeys and other anthropoids than in man. According to Freedman (1938), the sacculi exist in the orangutan and chimpanzee as huge air sacs which extend down the neck even as far as the axillae. When breathing is suspended, as during use of the forelegs, the air sacs become a useful source of oxygen.

The mucous membrane of the sacculus contains many glands. Their secretion is expressed by muscular fasciculi upon the vocal folds for lubrication.

Inferior Division (Infraglottic Region)

The lowest division of the larynx includes the space between the vocal folds above (rima glottidis) and the inferior border of the cricoid cartilage below.

Some writers refer to everything in the larynx above the vocal folds as supraglottic (hyperglottic) and everything below as infraglottic (hypoglottic; subglottic). The narrowest part of the laryngeal cavity is at the rima glottidis, the width varying with the type of activity.

The lowest subglottic region has a narrow cross section. In the infant the diameter of the subglottic lumen is 6 to 8 mm, and this is easily blocked by edema of the mucosa lining the rigid cricoid ring (Lewis et al., 1967).

Ventricular Folds

The true and the false folds are normally visible in technics to visualize the interior of the larynx.

The paired ventricular or false vocal folds (plicae ventriculares; vestibular folds) are thick rounded folds of mucous membrane developed around the ventricular (vestibular) ligaments. They are soft and somewhat flaccid. Each contains the lower portion of the quadrangular membrane, including the ventricular ligaments. Each also contains some fat cells, a few muscle fibers from the thyroarytenoid muscle, and many mucous glands. The framework is elastic connective tissue. The mucous membrane is continuous anteriorly with that lining the base of the epiglottis and laterally with that lining the aryepiglottic folds; posteriorly it is continuous with the anterior aspect of the arytenoid swelling.

The ventricular folds reach the angle of the thyroid laminae anteriorly, where they are most prominent. They do not reach the dorsal laryngeal wall posteriorly. They are attached posteriorly to the arytenoids, and, like the true folds, they can move with the arytenoids. In forced closure of the glottis they may contract with the true folds (Van Riper and Irwin, 1958).

The opening between the edges of the false folds is the false glottis (glottis spuria, rima vestibuli). The size and shape of the aperture are variable with circumstances. The separation is wider than that of the true glottis; this is particularly true in trained singers.

217

The ventricular folds can be brought together and serve as a valve to build up air pressure within the deeper lung passages when excess intrapulmonary pressure is needed (Boies, 1964).

Sound production is related to the ventricular folds, although rarely under ordinary circumstances. These folds can be approximated and separated, and this can occur with, or independently of, the activity of the true folds. The tone is unpleasant because of interference with the upward passage of the sound waves. Vibrations can be reflected downward. Closure of the ventricular folds may be fleeting and unpredictable.

If the true folds are excised, the false ones can substitute, a condition called dysphonia plicae ventricularis. The voice is husky, and the pitch is low (Chiba and Kajiyama, 1958). The false folds do not vibrate during the production of a vowel, and they are not required to perform a special function in the production of any consonant. They do not descend and come into contact with the true folds in ordinary speaking or pronunciation. This denies a view that they can modify the vibration of the true folds as a kind of damper and as loads or nodal supports.

An opposite point of view may be presented. The false folds can alter the resonance function of the vestibule by the effect of their closure upon the shape of the vestibule. Berry and Eisenson (1956) cite evidence that during very high frequencies the false folds influence the vibration of the true folds, since they just impinge upon the true folds. As a result they give enough pressure to the upper surface of the latter to restrict the width of the vibrating sector; this could increase the vibrational frequency.

According to Meano and Khoury (1967), the function of the false vocal folds lies solely in their direct contribution to the formation of the supplementary harmonic overtones, which originate, acoustically speaking, in the superior resonating tube.

An important function of the false folds is to lubricate the true folds (Gray and Wise, 1959). By the use of cinematography during speech, drops of mucus have been traced in passage from the false folds to the true folds. This action is likely to facilitate the rapid alterations in shape and tension which the true folds undergo.

Chiba and Kajiyama (1958) state that the primary function of the false folds is during swallowing. They serve as an airtight cover for the true folds, act as a cushion for the epiglottis in cooperation with the arytenoids, and protect the vocal folds.

Vocal Folds

The paired vocal or true folds (plicae vocales) lie parallel and inferior to the ventricular folds and extend from the posterior surface of the thyroid angle to the vocal processes of the arytenoids. They diverge from a common anterior fixation point (the vocal tendon of Broyles), and each band then becomes attached like a shelf of tissue to the lateral wall of the larynx. Each vocal fold contains the vocal ligament, the vocalis and thyroarytenoid muscles, and a covering of mucous membrane.

The vocal folds are occasionally called cords or bands, and at times the free fibrous borders of the folds are called the bands. Cords suggest vibrational strings. The term folds is descriptive, since the structures are actually prominent folds which project from the inner walls of the larynx.

When viewed from above, the true folds are seen as paired strips of muscle with inner or medial borders of connective tissue. When seen from below, they are arched structures. The arching is produced by the relatively great thickness of the muscles at the lateral borders in contrast with the thin medial borders. The mass or thickness of the folds is important since it appears to be one of the determinants of the fundamental frequency of phonation (Hollien, 1962).

There is a sex difference in the structure of the vocal folds, apparent in coronal section. The folds of the male are heavier and more rounded.

The varying descriptions of the vibrating edges of the folds as being rounded or else sharp and thin are related to the kind of activity in which the folds are being engaged.

The anterior two-thirds to three-fifths of the vocal folds is membranous, and the remaining posterior section is cartilaginous. Only the membranous portion can vibrate. The cartilage sector produces approximation of the nonvibratory structures.

The middle of the vibrating membranous region is the place of maximal impact when the folds meet. This explains the frequency of nodules (probably inflammatory tumors) and polyps (irritative responses to mechanical injury) in that area. (It is probable that polyps can collapse into the nodule form.)

Mucous Membrane

Each true fold is nonvascular and displays a pale mucous membrane. The free edge appears white except at the anterior terminal, where there is a yellow spot produced by the presence of cartilage or elastic tissue.

The mucous membrane is firmly adherent about the vocal folds and the laryngeal aspect of the epiglottis. Its looseness elsewhere in the larynx facilitates swelling with subsequent dysfunction in breathing and speaking.

The mucosa covering the apposed surfaces of the folds is stratified squamous, while it is ciliated columnar in other parts of the folds. According to Gray (1966), squamous epithelium is characteristic of the upper posterior surface of the epiglottis and the upper part of the aryepiglottic folds. It also covers the anterior or pharyngeal surface of the epiglottis. Ciliated columnar epithelium covers the remainder of the laryngeal surface. This respiratory kind of epithelium extends down into the trachea and bronchi. The cilia beat toward the pharynx.

219

Histologic structure should be regarded as having correlation with function. Thus a squamous covering is advantageous over the free border of each fold because it resists the severe trauma produced by the repeated contact of the opposite fold. A columnar ciliated covering is most advantageous near the inpocketing of the ventricle inasmuch as cilia are needed to drive away foreign matter and the mucus globules which normally collect in that region.

There are differences of opinion about the nature of the epithelium of the larynx. Hopp (1955) reviews the literature. In his opinion the embryonic epithelium of the vocal folds becomes cuboidal and then stratified, and this includes the region extending into the ventricle. The other areas of the larynx, except where the vocal folds extend into the interarytenoid region, develop ciliated epithelium of a columnar and pseudostratified type. Hopp claims that islands of squamous epithelium occur rarely in the adult larynx and may be a result of pathologic changes.

The larynx is variably supplied with glands. A rich supply of mucous glands is found in the lower epiglottis, the aryepiglottic folds, ventricular folds, ventricles, and in the areas below the glottis. Such glands are missing on the upper epiglottis and on the parts of the vocal folds that meet. Morris (1966) writes of the tendency of the glands to form clusters. An anterior group belongs to the epiglottis. A middle group is in the ventricular folds, in the triangular fovea of the arytenoid cartilages, and about the cuneiform cartilages. A posterior set is located about the transverse arytenoid muscle.

The glands keep the vocal folds well lubricated, especially in the active regions. A few drops of mucus are characteristically present on the inner margin of each fold. Mucus flows to the folds particularly from the paired saccules, which are membranous reservoirs. The submucous coat of the saccule contains sixty to seventy glands which open onto the mucous membrane.

The saccular glands are emptied by the action of intrinsic laryngeal muscles. This action includes the compression exerted by muscle fibers originating in the apex of the arytenoids and running into the aryepiglottic fold of mucous membrane. Freedman (1938) states that the mucus is periodically squirted as a thin stream from the ventricles upon the true folds, and he calls the sacculus the "oilcan" of the vocal folds.

Submucosal Histology

The tissues of this layer have a loose fibrous stroma except over the epiglottis and true vocal folds. The loose arrangement facilitates accumulation of edema fluid or inflammatory exudates. In the areas where there is more adherence, edema occurs much more slowly.

There is a potential subepithelial space (Rienke's space) at the margin of each true vocal fold between the epithelium and the conus elasticus. This space, which extends along the length of each fold, is limited above and below by the linea arcuata. The latter defines the boundary of the squamous epithelium covering the true folds, and it lies 2 to 3 mm from the free margin of each fold. Inflammatory and neoplastic processes may spread in Rienke's space but are restricted in their extension.

The Glottis and Its Changing Contour

The glottis (rima glottidis) is the variable opening between the vocal folds. The anterior section, which is bounded by the folds, is membranous and is the vocal glottis. This comprises about three-fifths of the total length. The posterior section,

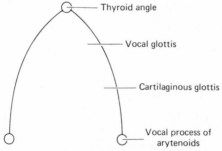

Figure 7-8 Diagrammatic anteroposterior view of the glottis, showing its vocal (membranous) and cartilaginous sections.

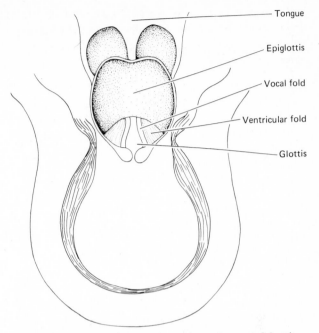

Figure 7-9 Glottal area seen from above, in normal inspiration. (*By permission from* **H. L. Dawson**, *Basic Human Anatomy, Appleton-Century-Crofts, Educational Division, Meredith Corporation, New York, 1966.*)

221

which is bounded by the medial surfaces of the arytenoid cartilages and posteriorly by the transverse arytenoid muscle, is the cartilaginous glottis.

In the quiet state the average length of the membranous glottis is 15.5 mm in the male and 11.5 mm in the female. The length of the cartilaginous glottis is 7.5 mm in the male and 5.5 mm in the female (Morris, 1966). These portions can be elongated by stretching the vocal folds. The widest part of the glottis in the male can increase to about 12 mm, depending on conditions.

According to Ballenger (1969), the term glottis denotes vertically an area of the larynx from the superior surface of the vocal fold to an arbitrary line about 3 mm below. The infraglottis is subjacent to this line. The division is made because of the different lymphatic supply to the two regions.

The variations in the shape of the glottis are involved in the production of the complex waveform of sound. The width and general shape of the glottis are changed primarily by movements of the arytenoid cartilages through muscle action. There are many degrees of the open and even of the closed position.

When the larynx is at rest and quiet breathing prevails, the glottis is open but narrow and has the shape of a long triangle. The vocal folds move slightly toward and away from each other. The aperture is wider during inhalation, and it is narrower during exhalation. In forced respiration the glottic chink can practically attain the capacity of the trachea, the widest part of the opening being at the extremities of the vocal processes of the arytenoids (Woodburne, 1969); Morris (1966) says it becomes lozenge-shaped.

The glottis can be closed at will or automatically by reflex. The reflex action is protective, occurring with eating, drinking, and other conditions, and prevents aspiration of material into the trachea. Reflex closure is so strong that in drowning involuntary control may keep the trachea occluded until death (Brantigan, 1963).

When the arytenoids glide toward each other, the glottic opening, or chink, is narrowed. The same result is possible by rotation of the arytenoids such that their anterior vocal processes are brought closer together. The tendency to close the glottic margins is called adduction, whereas the opposite motion constitutes abduction. There is a statement made by Fink and Basek (1956), based on evidence from motion pictures, that the opening and closing of the glottis are accompanied by sliding movements of the arytenoids to and from the midline, with no evidence that rotation of cartilages occurs. This has never been conclusively demonstrated and can be argued against.

When the arytenoids are tilted backward, the vocal folds may be stretched. This can increase the tension. Relaxation can be produced by forward tilting. The tension is influenced by rotary movements at the cricothyroid joint and also by changes in the mode of contraction of the intrinsic muscles in the vocal folds. The relationships between movements and tension are not all clear-cut.

Any section of the glottal edge can be adducted or abducted without necessarily relating to any other part (Pressman and Kelemen, 1955). This is because the paired thyroarytenoid and vocalis muscles of the vocal folds seem to be capable of differential or segmental contraction. This activity can occur independently of the arytenoid movements. Confirmation of this statement by the effects on phonation in pure abductor paralysis seems to be lacking.

The Laryngeal Muscles

The larynx is operated by skeletal muscles innervated by cerebrospinal nerves. There is adjunctive glandular and vascular machinery, regulated by the autonomic system.

Although the voluntary mechanism has been well described by anatomists, its exact functioning in speech is still to a considerable extent inconclusively known. This is illustrated, for example, in the changing ideas of the muscle relationships in the movements of the vocal folds. To what extent does rotation or any other movement of the arytenoid cartilages explain the opening and closing of the glottal margins?

Laryngeal muscles have been classified in different ways. Grollman (1964) speaks

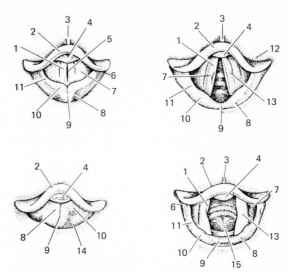

Figure 7-10 Various forms of the larynx in action, as seen with the laryngoscope: *upper left:* position of vocal folds in high-pitched tones; *upper right:* shape of glottis in inspiration; *lower left:* tightly closed position of folds when lifting a weight; *lower right:* deep quiet breathing, in which the laryngeal inlet is widely opened; 1, true vocal folds; 2, epiglottis; 3, glossoepiglottic fold; 4, tubercle of epiglottis; 5, rima glottidis, or vocal cleft; 6, pharyngoepiglottic fold; 7, false vocal folds; 8, corniculate tubercles; 9, interarytenoid incisure; 10, cuneiform tubercles; 11, aryepiglottic folds; 12, epiglottic vallecules; 13, dents in vocal folds indicating point of attachment of vocal ligaments to vocal processes of arytenoid cartilages; 14, pharynx; 15, tracheal bifurcation. (*By permission from S. L. Polyak, G. McHugh, and D. K. Judd, The Human Ear, Sonotone Corporation, Elmsford, N.Y., 1946.*)

223

of respiratory laryngeal muscles, which can draw the vocal folds away from the midline, thereby permitting the free passage of air. Other muscles are phonatory.

In most descriptions the laryngeal muscles are also divided into two groups, extrinsic and intrinsic, but with other divisions of function. The extrinsic muscles support the larynx and change its spatial relationships. They have at least one attachment to some structure outside the larynx. The intrinsic muscles control phonation and have both their origins and insertions within the larynx.

Extrinsic Muscles
Elevators of the Hyoid and Larynx The elevators are called suprahyoid muscles. The entire larynx including the hyoid bone may be raised, or the larynx proper may be raised toward a fixed hyoid.

If the larynx is elevated while the hyoid bone is fixed, the thyrohyoid would be the chief muscle concerned. The hyoid could be fixed in position chiefly by the hyoglossus, geniohyoid, mylohyoid, and the middle pharyngeal constrictor muscles. Others are also involved.

The elevation of the larynx tends to decrease the length and caliber of the laryngopharynx. This affects resonance. There are views that changes of pitch from lower to higher are associated with a cranial movement of the larynx. However, Keenan and Barrett (1962) state that pitch is dependent upon the length of the vocal folds but not upon the vertical position of the larynx. Basically, laryngeal elevation is related more to swallowing than to phonation.

The chief elevator muscles are described individually below.

The *digastric* muscle (paired) has two bellies. The posterior one originates on the mastoid process of the skull and passes downward and forward to an intermediate tendon, which gains an attachment to the body of the hyoid bone. It draws the hyoid upward and backward, and it also tilts the bone. This belly is innervated by the facial nerve.

The anterior belly descends from the inner surface of the mandible, near the symphysis, to the intermediate tendon and body of the hyoid bone. With the mandible fixed, it brings the hyoid upward and forward. It is innervated by the mylohyoid nerve, which is a derivative of the inferior alveolar branch of the mandibular division of the trigeminal nerve.

The *stylohyoid* (paired) is a slender muscle located along the upper border of, and roughly parallel to, the posterior belly of the digastric muscle. It originates from the styloid process of the temporal skull bone and runs downward and forward to the greater cornu of the hyoid bone, which it elevates and retracts. It may also tilt the bone. It is innervated by the facial nerve.

The *mylohyoid* (unpaired) forms the muscular floor of the mouth. It originates from the inner aspect of the mandible along the mylohyoid line, which runs forward from the last molar tooth to the point of the jaw (mental symphysis). It goes medialward and downward and fuses with the fibers on the other side in a median line (raphe) that extends from a point near the symphysis back to the hyoid bone. The most posterior fibers attach directly to the body of the hyoid. With a fixed mandible, the muscle elevates and draws forward the hyoid, and it also "raises" the tongue, whose root is attached to the hyoid. This action is typical of the initial phase of swallowing. Acting reversely from the hyoid, it can depress the lower jaw, as in chewing or speech. The muscle is innervated by the mylohyoid nerve.

The *geniohyoid* (paired) is a cylindrical muscle situated on the upper (buccal) surface of the mylohyoid. The paired fibers lie in contact on either side of the midline. The muscle originates at the symphysis of the mandible and runs backward and downward to insert upon the body of the hyoid. With a fixed mandible, it elevates the hyoid and tongue and also protrudes these structures. Acting from below, it assists in depressing the mandible. The muscle is innervated by the hypoglossal nerve plus nerve fibers from C-1.

There are three muscles, described below, which might also be classified with the suprahyoid musculature.

The *genioglossus* originates on the superior ventral spine on the inner surface of the mandibular symphysis. Its lower fibers insert upon the hyoid. Its middle and upper fibers have a broad insertion upon the under side of the tongue from root to apex.

The *hyoglossus* arises from the body and greater cornua of the hyoid and travels almost straight upward to insert upon the posterolateral areas of the tongue.

The *middle pharyngeal constrictor* muscle could be classified as a weak elevator, although its chief action on the hyoid bone is to pull it backward. It may be considered to travel from the posterior median septum of the pharynx to the greater cornua of the hyoid and to the stylohyoid ligament.

Depressors of the Hyoid and Larynx These are the infrahyoid muscles, and they depress the larynx. The sternothyroid muscle is perhaps the most significant.

The *sternohyoid* (paired) is a flat muscle located on the deep anterior surface of the neck. Just above their origin the paired sternohyoids may lie in contact. Each arises on the manubrium sterni, on the clavicle, and also along the sternoclavicular ligament and runs upward to attach to the inferior border of the hyoid body. The muscle depresses the hyoid bone. It is innervated by the ansa hypoglossi, containing fibers from C-1, C-2, and C-3.

225

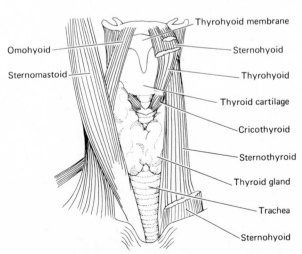

Figure 7-11 Extrinsic muscles and the superficial relations of the larynx viewed from the anterior aspect of the neck.

The *omohyoid* (paired) is a long, narrow muscle with two bellies. The inferior belly originates from the scapula and goes almost horizontally forward to terminate at an intermediate tendon that is held fixed chiefly by cervical fascia. The superior belly passes vertically and medially upward from the tendon and inserts along the lower border of the hyoid lateral to the sternohyoid insertion. Acting from the scapula, it depresses and retracts the hyoid. The muscle is innervated by the ansa hypoglossi, containing fibers from C-1, C-2, and C-3.

The *sternothyroid* (paired) is a long ribbonlike muscle deep to the omohyoid and sternohyoid on the anterior surface of the neck. It originates on the sternum and goes upward to insert upon the corresponding thyroid lamina. A few fibers continue superiorly to end in the thyrohyoid and the inferior pharyngeal constrictor muscles. The sternothyroid depresses the thyroid cartilage. It is innervated by the ansa hypoglossi, containing fibers from C-1, C-2, and C-3.

The *thyrohyoid* muscle (paired) arises on each side from the thyroid lamina and goes vertically upward to insert on the major cornu and body of the hyoid bone. It depresses the hyoid or, with a fixed hyoid, elevates the thyroid cartilage. It may tilt the hyoid backward. The muscle is innervated by the descendens hypoglossi and the first two cervical nerves.

Intrinsic Muscles

The intrinsic muscles may be grouped according to their general effects upon the glottis.

226

The abductor opens the glottis. Only one muscle is involved, the *posterior crico-arytenoid* (paired). This arises as a flat, triangular structure on the posterior surface of the cricoid and goes upward and lateralward to the muscular process of each arytenoid. It rotates each arytenoid outward so that the muscular process is drawn posteriorly and the vocal process laterally, thus widening the glottic space. The more lateral fibers draw the arytenoids laterally. The muscle may also tilt the

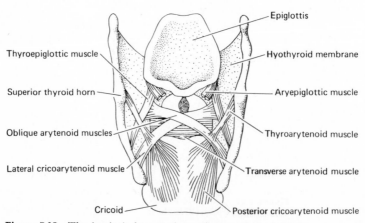

Thyroepiglottic muscle

Superior thyroid horn

Oblique arytenoid muscles

Lateral cricoarytenoid muscle

Cricoid

Epiglottis

Hyothyroid membrane

Aryepiglottic muscle

Thyroarytenoid muscle

Transverse arytenoid muscle

Posterior cricoarytenoid muscle

Figure 7-12 The intrinsic laryngeal muscles seen from behind.

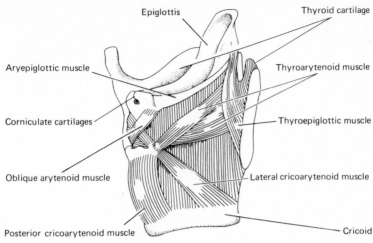

Figure 7-13 The intrinsic muscles along the sides of the larynx.

vocal processes backward. This muscle is especially active during inspiration and is said to be primarily respiratory (Hast, 1967).

The adductors narrow the glottis. Four muscles are involved.

The *transverse arytenoid* (unpaired) is a thick, rectangular mass covering the entire deep posterior surface of both arytenoids. It may be considered to originate along the muscular process and lateral border of one arytenoid and to cross over to the lateral edge of the other arytenoid. It draws the arytenoids medially by a gliding action (without rotation), which adducts the vocal folds. The activity of this muscle is said to precede phonation.

The *oblique arytenoid* muscle (paired) is placed externally upon the transverse arytenoid, and its two limbs form the letter X. Each member arises on the lower posterior surface of one arytenoid and goes upward and across the midline to insert at the summit of the other arytenoid. The muscle adducts the vocal folds, and it acts as a weak sphincter for the superior opening of the larynx. There is a view that the oblique arytenoids may tilt the apices of the arytenoid cartilages toward one another.

Some of the muscle fibers, in rising to their insertion, continue upward and forward, as the *aryepiglottic* muscle of the aryepiglottic fold. These fibers insert upon the lateral edge of the epiglottis and upon the quadrangular membrane. The aryepiglottic muscles act with the oblique arytenoids to bring together the aryepiglottic folds and to approximate the arytenoid cartilages to the tubercle of the epiglottis. It may be noted that the oblique and transverse arytenoids are given the collective name of arytenoideus, or interarytenoid muscle.

The *lateral cricoarytenoid* (paired) is a small, rectangular muscle in the lateral wall of the larynx, deep to the thyroid cartilage. Its own deep surface is seated upon the conus elasticus. It originates from the arch of the cricoid and goes upward and

227

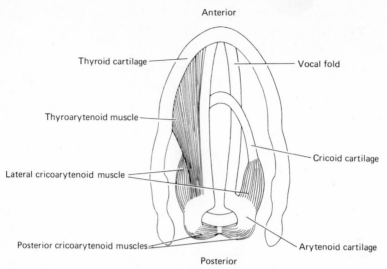

Anterior

Thyroid cartilage

Vocal fold

Thyroarytenoid muscle

Cricoid cartilage

Lateral cricoarytenoid muscle

Posterior cricoarytenoid muscles

Arytenoid cartilage

Posterior

Figure 7-14 Cross-sectional view of some intrinsic laryngeal muscles, viewed from above.

backward to insert upon the front part of the muscular process of the corresponding arytenoid. In the conventional view the muscle rotates each muscular process forward and inward and brings the vocal processes toward each other. It has been noted (Greene, 1964) that the lateral fibers are practically in line with the long axis of the cricoarytenoid joint and must pull the arytenoid cartilage laterally and *outward*. The more medial fibers act conventionally. If these actions are as described, the lateral cricoarytenoids and posterior cricoarytenoids are synergists that maintain the arytenoid cartilages in readiness for action. If the oblique fibers of the lateral cricoarytenoids predominate, both muscles function as abductors.

The *thyroarytenoid* muscle (paired) lies parallel to each vocal fold. It arises on the posterior surface of the thyroid cartilage, and its lateral fibers insert on the lateral edge and muscular process of each arytenoid.

In the thyroarytenoid mass there is a question about fibers which may run perpendicular to the main stream of fibers and which could control the length of the segment that is vibrating.

The thyroarytenoid could pull the thyroid cartilage upward and backward, but this would be likely only if the arytenoids were fixed, which is possible. This action would decrease the tension on the folds. The muscle may help in the formation of a sphincter ring around the superior aspect of the larynx. It has been said to be an adductor in that it helps to rotate and draw forward the muscular processes of the arytenoids. Van Riper and Irwin (1958) state that it can alter the loudness of tones. If it relaxed slightly while the cricothyroid and lateral cricoarytenoid pulled constantly, the pitch would fall and the loudness would rise. The relaxed thyroarytenoids would permit the folds to be blown further apart with the same amount of air pressure. Woodburne (1969) notes that the thickening of the muscle which accompanies its shortening also contributes to sealing the glottis.

According to Greene (1964), the thyroarytenoid muscles upon contraction oppose the lengthening of the vocal folds produced by cricothyroid muscle action. The thyroarytenoids thus determine the degree of tension and the bulk of the main body of the folds. The thyroarytenoids are occasionally termed the *internal tensor* of the folds, chiefly because of the muscle elasticity.

The lengthening of the folds does not mean an increase in tension, and the shortening of the folds does not mean a decrease in tension. In explanation, the vocal fold has fibers running in all directions. Squares of this network can be converted into diamonds by lengthening the folds, and the tension need not increase.

The *vocalis* muscle (paired) forms the main mass of the vocal folds, and it importantly influences their mode of vibration. It is enclosed within each fold, bounded medially by the conus elasticus and laterally by the thyroarytenoid muscles. It originates chiefly from the posterior aspects of the thyroid angle and to a small extent from the upper section of the conus elasticus. It goes horizontally back to each vocal process and to the lateral surface of the corresponding arytenoid.

The vocalis muscle is considered by some investigators to be the medial part of the thyroarytenoid (Houssay, 1955; Gray, 1966). In this sense there is an external and an internal thyroarytenoid. The latter fibers insert upon the vocal processes of the arytenoids. Zenker (1964) states that the thyroarytenoid muscle as a whole should be considered as the "vocal muscle" because a separation of an external and internal part cannot be made anatomically or histologically.

The characteristic action of the vocalis muscle is to increase tension. By partial or differential contraction it may change the vibrational mode of the folds and determine the register. It can possibly shorten the folds and reduce the tension by bringing the arytenoids toward the thyroid angle. The ability of its fibers to contract in separate bundles brings about modifications of the inner margin of the folds and the contour of the glottis.

Luchsinger and Arnold (1965) describe the vocalis muscle as the internal vocal fold tensor which functions chiefly for fine isometric tension of the folds. When the arytenoids move the folds grossly to a median position of phonation, the vocalis muscles then determine precisely the width, length, and shape of the glottis.

Greene (1964) states that the vocalis muscle can bunch up the conus elasticus, thus augmenting the vertical depths of the opposing surfaces of the folds. This influences pitch.

The term *aryvocalis* muscle refers to shorter fascicles of the vocalis muscle running from and into the vocal ligament. This muscle is said to bring about the tiny adjustments of the vocal ligament occurring in phonation. It may regulate pitch by varying the length of the vibrating sector of the vocal folds.

The *cricothyroid* (paired) is a broad muscle superficially placed upon the larynx. The anterior section originates along the lower border and outer surface of the cricoid arch and runs almost vertically up to the thyroid laminae. The posterior section, which has the same origin, goes upward and backward to the inferior cornu of the thyroid.

The vertical anterior section approximates the anterior portions of the cricoid and thyroid cartilages. Arnold (1961) claims that it is only the cricoid that can move, because the thyroid is fixed by its external strap muscles to the hyoid and sternum.

The posterior section pulls the thyroid cartilage forward and increases the distance between the thyroid and arytenoids. The vocal folds are elongated and tensed (Gray, 1966). In another interpretation of the action, there is a rocking effect at the cricothyroid joint, with the cricoid being tilted backward and downward. Since the attached arytenoids are involved in the movement, the result is to lengthen the distance between the anterior insertion of the vocal folds on the thyroid cartilage and their posterior insertion on the vocal processes.

Luchsinger and Arnold (1965) say that the muscle produces crude isotonic tension of the folds, and it is the chief vocal fold elongator and tensor to effect production of high tones.

The cricothyroid may act secondarily as an external adductor of the arytenoids.

Several muscles exert their main effect upon the aryepiglottic folds, the ventricular folds, or the epiglottis. The *ventricularis* muscle (paired) goes from the lateral border of the arytenoid to the side of the epiglottis. The *aryepiglottic* muscles, which are in this category, have already been described. The *thyroepiglottic* (paired) is a thin and variable muscle directly above the thyroarytenoid muscle, arising on the inner surface of the thyroid close to its angle and going upward and backward to the aryepiglottic fold and margin of the epiglottis. This muscle may depress the epiglottis, widen the upper laryngeal port, or perhaps be part of the sphincter ring in that area.

Relationships of the Muscles to the Activities of the Larynx
The larynx has many functions, and the muscles are involved frequently in accomplishing those functions.

Respiratory Activity Fink and Basek (1956) have studied laryngeal movements through electromyography, roentgenograms, and motion pictures. Their findings follow. In quiet respiration some activity was found in all the muscles of the larynx, in both inspiration and expiration. The activity of all the muscles increased with strong respiratory efforts, but the pattern of action changed with the phase of respiration. Thus sternothyroid activity was prominent during inspiration, and the thyrohyoid was relatively quiet. During expiration there was greater activity in both muscles, especially in the thyrohyoid, while the cricothyroid and vocalis activity heightened.

In forced respiration muscle tone increased in both phases of breathing, but in the inspiratory phase the increase affected the sternothyroid more than the thyrohyoid.

230

At this time the larynx was descending. With deep expiration the thyrohyoid activity increased, and at this time the larynx was ascending.

The rhythmic rise and fall of the larynx with respiration produce folding and unfolding of the laryngeal soft tissues. This action resembles that of a bellows whose folds are the vestibular and vocal folds, and it places a mediolateral sliding motion on the arytenoids.

From observations that respiration always involves laryngeal activity, the question may be asked whether the larynx can ever be rested. In the therapy of voice abuse, silence is usually effective, but the time needed for a cure is influenced by the continuous biologic activity of the larynx.

Valvular Activity   In response to a foreign body, both the laryngeal entrance (laryngeal aditus) and the rima glottidis must close, probably at the same time.

The laryngeal entrance is closed by (1) elevation of the larynx by extrinsic muscles, (2) muscular sphincter action in the aryepiglottic folds, (3) adduction of the arytenoid cartilages by appropriate muscles, and (4) pulling the arytenoid cartilages forward by the thyroarytenoid muscles.

The rima glottidis is closed by approximation of the arytenoid cartilages and of the vocal folds.

The larynx uses valvular activity to build up intrathoracic pressure by preventing the escape of air from the lungs. To do this, both the ventricular and vocal folds are closed. The ventricular folds may be adducted by the arytenoid, thyroarytenoid, and perhaps also the lateral cricoarytenoid muscles.

Phonation   This involves adduction and abduction of the vocal folds and other activities considered previously and to be discussed later. The adductors, abductors, tensors, and relaxers are variably brought into the action.

Neural Control of the Larynx

The nerve supply of the larynx includes (1) a sensory distribution from general sense receptors in the mucous membranes, (2) an afferent set of nerves from mechanoreceptors in the muscles, mucous membranes and joints, (3) a motor nerve supply to energize the extrinsic and intrinsic laryngeal muscles, and (4) an autonomic system of efferents to regulate blood and secretion.

Sensory Nerves
Sensory fibers transmit impulses dealing with the condition of the mucous membrane. They are responsible for consciousness of dryness, irritation, and pain.

Sensory afferents from the supraglottic region, which travel in the superior laryngeal nerve, are essential to sensation at the laryngeal inlet. This information prevents inhalation of food and secretions by initiating reflex closure of the larynx. A bilateral sensory failure may lead to aspiration pneumonia, just as this may occur in a comatose person who has no reflex response (Lewis et al., 1967).

Afferent Nerves Involving Mechanoreceptors

There is a triple system of reflexes (articular, mucosal, and myotactic) that are operated from mechanoreceptors located within the tissues of the larynx (Kirchner and Wyke, 1964; 1965a; 1965b; Wyke, 1968).

Muscle Proprioception The intrinsic muscles of the larynx have a myotactic (proprioceptive) reflex system originating in mechanoreceptors analogous to those in other skeletal muscles. This is contrary to the earlier views of Sherrington. A similar system exists in the extrinsic laryngeal muscles. Such receptor systems signal position, movement and tension in the vocal folds and are adjunctive to voice modulation by the hearing mechanisms.

Proprioceptive innervation of the muscles is by way of the superior laryngeal nerves (Crosby, 1964). The cells of the origin of the proprioceptive fibers are presumably in the jugular (or superior) ganglia of the vagus nerves. It is uncertain whether there are gamma (small motor) fibers to the proprioceptive endings in the larynx and if they run in the superior laryngeal nerves.

The Laryngeal Joints The joints are an additional source of proprioceptive activity. Mechanoreceptors are identifiable in the joint capsules. Passive stretch of the capsule by movement in specific directions of the joint produces afferent discharges from the low-threshold receptors. These evoke transient changes of motor unit activity in all the laryngeal muscles. Such reflexes are part of the normal coordination of the laryngeal muscles during respiration and phonation. The articular reflexes are distinct but supplementary to the tonic myotactic reflexes operated from muscle mechanoreceptors.

Pressure Receptors in the Mucosal Walls Low-threshold mechanoreceptors embedded in the supraglottic and infraglottic laryngeal mucosa are stimulated by changes in air pressure, especially during the phases of breathing. They contribute reflexly to the coordinated changes of tone in the laryngeal muscles. The afferent fibers travel in the laryngeal nerves.

The articular mechanoreceptors along with air pressure–sensitive receptors in the mucosal walls of the laryngopharynx and sensors in the intrinsic musculature all make a significant contribution to feedback and reflex actions of the larynx.

Autonomic Nerves

Autonomic fibers reach the larynx through the superior and inferior laryngeal nerves and also by way of the vasomotor system traveling with the superior thyroid and the superior and inferior laryngeal arteries. Fibers from the superior cervical ganglion may join the superior laryngeal nerve or its external branch, but they more often travel through the pharyngeal plexus to arrive at the larynx. Some fibers travel a short distance with the superior cervical sympathetic nerve and then join the superior laryngeal nerve. Other fibers from the plexus around the external carotid artery travel with the superior thyroid arteries and twigs from the corresponding plexus on the subclavian artery.

Autonomic fibers control the caliber of blood vessels and laryngeal secretions. Among the vasomotor structures, a cushion formation in the form of vascular mounds or protruding rings has been described in the larynx (Pressman and Kelemen, 1955). Its purpose is to control blood flow.

MOTOR NERVES TO THE LARYNGEAL MUSCLES

MUSCLE	NERVE INNERVATION
Extrinsic:	
1 Suprahyoid:	
Digastric (anterior belly)	V Mylohyoid branch
Digastric (posterior belly)	VII Digastric branch
Stylohyoid	VII Stylohyoid branch
Mylohyoid	V Mylohyoid branch
Geniohyoid	XII Geniohyoid branch plus C-1
2 Infrahyoid:	
Sternohyoid	XII Branch of ansa hypoglossi plus C-1, C-2, C-3
Omohyoid	XII Branch of ansa hypoglossi plus C-1, C-2, C-3
Sternothyroid	XII Branch of ansa hypoglossi plus C-1, C-2, C-3
Thyrohyoid	XII C-1 and C-2 communicating with descendens hypoglossi
Intrinsic:	
Posterior cricoarytenoid	
Oblique arytenoid	
Transverse arytenoid	
Lateral cricoarytenoid	X Inferior (recurrent) laryngeal branch of the vagus
Thyroarytenoid	
Vocalis	
Thyroepiglottic	
Cricothyroid	X Superior laryngeal branch of the vagus

233

As noted in the table, the extrinsic muscles are innervated by cranial nerves V, VII and XII and also by the upper cervical spinal nerves. The intrinsic muscles are innervated by the Xth cranial, or vagus, nerve.

The Vagus Nerve The importance of the vagus nerve in laryngeal physiology warrants a somewhat detailed discussion (see Holt, 1968).

The vagal nuclei are in the hindbrain. They mediate impulses that are motor, sensory, or mixed. Sensory fibers originate from cells in the jugular ganglion and ganglion nodosum. Somatic motor fibers arise from the nucleus ambiguus and from the ganglion nodosum. Parasympathetic efferent fibers originate from the dorsal nucleus.

The cells of the jugular ganglion mediate general sensation from the cutaneous parts of the external ear. The ganglion also has connections with nerves other than the vagus.

The dorsal nucleus sends fibers to the parasympathetic vagal plexes that supply thoracic and abdominal viscera.

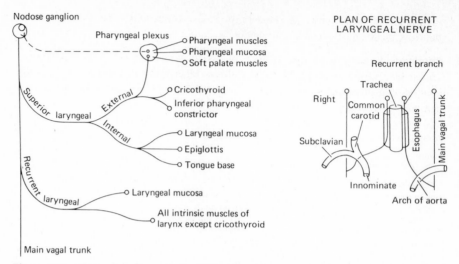

Figure 7-15 Upper branches of the vagus nerve that energize laryngeal and associated structures (diagrammatic).

The cells of the ganglion nodosum connect with fibers related to the pharynx, larynx, trachea, esophagus, and soft organs in the thorax and abdomen.

The *ganglion nodosum* has a pharyngeal branch, which joins with pharyngeal branches of the glossopharyngeal and with the superior cervical ganglion of the sympathetic. This union produces the pharyngeal plexus. To this plexus the vagus contributes motor fibers for the muscles of the pharynx and the soft palate, excluding the stylopharyngeus and tensor veli palatini.

At the lower end of the ganglion nodosum the superior laryngeal branch of the vagus separates from the main trunk. It travels downward and forward to the greater horn of the hyoid, where it splits into two branches, external and internal.

The external branch descends vertically to the cricothyroid muscle. This branch contains both motor and sensory fibers. The internal branch, primarily sensory, enters the larynx by penetrating the thyrohyoid membrane, and it divides into three terminal trunks. One of these innervates the mucous membrane of the aryepiglottic fold, the second supplies the mucous membrane of the lateral laryngeal walls, and the third goes to the pharyngeal mucous membrane behind the cricoid and arytenoid cartilages.

The sensory fibers are responsible for the sensation of irritation and pain. In the cough reflex, which adaptively protects the lungs, these sensory impulses represent the afferent limb of a reflex arc whose efferent limb is represented by motor impulses to thoracic and laryngeal muscles. Since the superior laryngeal branch transmits impulses for general sensation from the upper laryngeal areas, it may become involved in laryngeal carcinoma, tuberculosis, and other conditions. Because of the superficial location of the nerve, it can be anesthetized topically. Such

234

anesthesia, however, prevents the patient from sensing collected secretions in the local area.

The main trunk of the vagus at the ganglion nodosum descends through the neck and thorax, and it gives off the recurrent (inferior) laryngeal nerve. On the right side the recurrent nerve loops around the subclavian artery, but on the left it arises in the thorax and loops under the aortic arch. On both sides the recurrent nerve ascends in a groove between the trachea and the esophagus, and, lateral to the cricoid cartilage, each nerve bifurcates to terminal anterior and posterior divisions.

The recurrent nerve is chiefly motor, but it contains sensory fibers to the mucosa of (1) the glottis, (2) the larynx below the vocal folds, (3) the trachea, and (4) the esophagus. Hollinshead (1954) denies any significant sensory components in the recurrent nerve. Gillilan (1954) restates the hypothesis that the recurrent laryngeal nerve originates in the spinal accessory part of the nucleus ambiguus and that the superior laryngeal branch is the one of true vagal origin. In this view the vagus innervates the upper pharyngeal muscles while the accessory nerve innervates the lower muscles of both the pharynx and the esophagus. The bulbar portion of the spinal accessory, which is represented in the recurrent laryngeal, is said to supply all intrinsic laryngeal muscles except the cricothyroid. It is stated that there is no recurrent laryngeal nerve when the right subclavian artery originates from the descending aorta.

There is controversy about the muscles energized by the superior and inferior laryngeal branches of the vagus nerve. Conventionally, the motor fibers of the superior laryngeal branch are said to go only to the cricothyroid muscle. All other intrinsic muscles are said to be regulated by the inferior laryngeal or recurrent branch. According to Vogel (1952), however, the superior laryngeal nerve, through its internal branch, also supplies the interarytenoid (transverse arytenoid) muscle.

Faaborg-Andersen (1957) says that the cricothyroid muscle is innervated by the external branch of the superior laryngeal nerve, but he holds that the interarytenoid muscle is energized by the internal branch of the superior laryngeal nerve and also by the recurrent nerve. Campbell and Murtagh (1956) note that the cricothyroid muscle may be supplied by both the superior and inferior laryngeal nerves.

This citation of differing opinions does have functional meaning. For example, it helps explain the fact that the rima glottidis tends to close if both recurrent laryngeal nerves are accidentally cut during surgery (Crafts, 1966). The remaining cricothyroid tensors and transverse arytenoid adductors should theoretically prevail in action.

The last nucleus to be considered is the *nucleus ambiguus*. According to Krieg (1942), the lowest fibers from the nucleus ambiguus unite with the upper part of the spinal accessory and travel with it into the jugular foramen, where they join the vagus. This bundle is termed the vagal accessory to distinguish it from the spinal accessory. It is actually a part of the vagus, although it is usually stated to be a part of the spinal accessory. Krieg states that the nucleus ambiguus is the motor nucleus for deglutition and phonation and that a lesion therein would affect phonation.

Gray (1966) defines the nucleus ambiguus as the nucleus of the special visceral motor fibers of the glossopharyngeal, vagal, and the cranial part of the spinal accessory nerves which innervate the voluntary muscles of the pharynx and larynx. It represents an extension of the dorsolateral cells of the anterior column of the spinal cord up into the medulla, where it forms a slender column in the reticular formation. Krieg (1942) says that the corresponding cells in gill-breathing vertebrates supply muscles which move the third (glossopharyngeal) branchial arch and also the more caudal (vagal) arches. He calls these cells the branchial motor column, and he notes that all the muscles innervated are derivatives of the gill muscles of primitive vertebrates. Although there was originally one nerve for each arch, the nerves of all arches below the third appear to have joined into one. The muscles of the lower arches become the muscles of the larynx, and the nerve supply is from the vagus.

The nucleus ambiguus of the vagus receives fibers from the contiguous sensory nuclei, from the spinal nucleus of the trigeminal nerve, and from the nucleus of the tractus solitarius. These fibers correlate the laryngeal machinery and help complete swallowing reflexes. The nucleus ambiguus is also reached by corticobulbar fibers from the right and left precentral convolutions, and this connection helps complete voluntary control of the pharynx and larynx.

236 Furstenberg and Magielski (1955) describe a motor pattern of movements in the nucleus ambiguus. This nucleus supplies motor fibers to the voluntary muscles of the pharynx, larynx, and esophagus. In the cat the cricothyroid muscle is energized from the rostral area of the nucleus, and the following muscles are energized more caudally in the order listed: dorsal cricoarytenoid, thyroarytenoid, lateral cricoarytenoid, and arytenoid. The order is essentially similar in monkeys, and it is probable that the pattern holds in man. While the cricothyroid is energized from the most cranial of the cells, the adductor muscles are from the most caudal.

In such a pattern, central lesions can produce disturbed functions in some laryngeal muscles without involving all of them. This explains the observations of Pressman (1953) in a patient who had a central lesion and concomitant closure of the ventricular folds due to bilateral recurrent nerve paralysis, with no corresponding disturbance of the vocal folds.

Laryngeal Blood Supply

The various components of the larynx are supplied with blood vessels chiefly from branches that originate in the superior and inferior thyroid arteries.

The superior laryngeal branch of the superior thyroid artery follows the internal laryngeal branch of the superior laryngeal nerve. It goes beneath the thyrohyoid muscle, penetrates the thyrohyoid membrane, and gives blood to the laryngeal

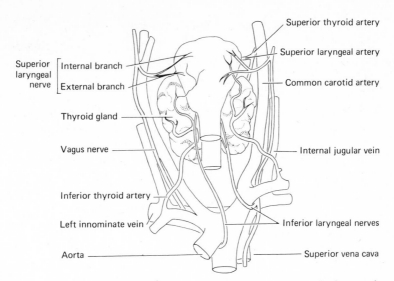

Figure 7-16 View from behind of the main blood vessels to the laryngeal area; the vagus nerve is also seen.

muscles, mucous membranes, and glands. The superior thyroid artery also gives off a cricothyroid artery that passes across the cricothyroid membrane.

The inferior laryngeal branch of the inferior thyroid artery (from the thyrocervical trunk of the subclavian artery) reaches the posterior aspect of the larynx by traveling with the inferior laryngeal nerve upward upon the trachea and beneath the inferior pharyngeal constrictor muscle. It gives blood to the muscles and mucous membranes of this region, and it anastomoses with the superior laryngeal artery.

The inferior thyroid vessel also produces an ascending cervical artery whose muscular branches supply the infrahyoid muscles.

The description has been for the vascular supply chiefly to the interior of the larynx. The exterior parts are supplied mainly by the infrahyoid and cricothyroid branches of the superior thyroid artery.

In regard to the venous return, the superior laryngeal veins empty into the superior thyroid veins. The latter drain into the internal jugular veins. The inferior laryngeal veins empty into the inferior thyroid veins, and the latter drain into the innominate vein.

Lymphatic Drainage

The lymphatic drainage of the laryngeal mucosa has been investigated in detail, but much less is known about the lymph vessels of the laryngeal cartilages and musculature. The brief description that follows is for the mucosa.

237

The vessels may be few in number or missing in parts of the true vocal folds, as along their free borders. The sparseness may be due to a paucity of subepithelial tissue in this area. The drainage pathways are sharply divided by the true folds, into a fairly independent upper and lower lymphatic system. The systems are especially developed in infants and children and regress with age.

The superior, or supraglottic, vessels are extensive and drain outward via the thyrohyoid membrane and superior thyroid veins. Before leaving the larynx they combine with lymph vessels from the hypopharynx. The superior vessels empty into several regions, including the subdigastric node and other nodes around or along the internal jugular vein.

The inferior, or infraglottic, vessels follow two or more paths. One set, which drains the infraglottic area, leaves through the cricothyroid membrane. It may enter nodes anterior to the membrane or in front of the upper trachea. Other lymphatics travel to deep cervical nodes and also to those accompanying the inferior thyroid vessels.

The scarcity of lymphatics in the true vocal folds and the density of the lymph vessels in all the extrinsic structures are responsible for the characteristic behavior of laryngeal cancer (Rogers et al., 1966). A lesion occurring on the true fold (intrinsic cancer) tends to remain localized. If the lesion occurs above or below the true folds (extrinsic cancer), it tends to metastasize.

238

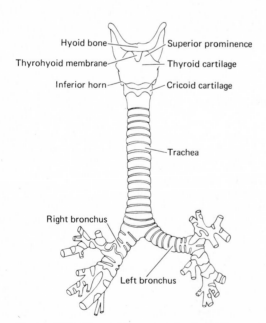

Figure 7-17 The trachea seen from in front.

The Trachea

The trachea is below and continuous with the larynx. It is an elastic tube, about 4 in. long and 1 in. in diameter, extending from approximately the sixth cervical vertebra to the fourth or fifth thoracic vertebra, where it divides into the right and left bronchial tubes. Its length in the male is about ½ in. longer than in the female.

Its outer walls contain sixteen to twenty alternate rings of cartilage and fibrous tissue. The cartilages are deficient posteriorly, and this space contains muscles which can change the bore of the tube. Calcification of the rings may occur normally in an adult as an aspect of aging. The cartilages ordinarily present marked irregularities, and they occasionally fuse with adjoining cartilages.

The organ lies in the midline, except at the lowest end, where it inclines slightly to the right. It is more superficial in the upper portion. The anterior neck muscles overlap its lateral edges, but they leave an exposed midline strip of fascia. Additional anterior tissue, which contains a rich venous network, is found above the jugular notch. The isthmus of the thyroid gland crosses the organ anteriorly between the third and fourth cartilage rings. Only seven or eight rings are palpable above the jugular notch.

The internal lining is a pseudostratified, columnar, ciliated mucous membrane. A submucous layer contains many mucous and serous glands.

239

The blood supply is from the inferior thyroid arteries and veins. The nerves are sympathetic and also from the vagus and its recurrent division.

In the human infant the trachea is small, but in the adult it is wide and can transmit more air than the larynx can allow to pass.

The trachea is protected from the entrance of foreign bodies by several devices. The epiglottis partly covers it. Moreover, inhalation is reflexly inhibited during swallowing. The larynx may be closed above the trachea by approximating the true and false vocal folds. The cricopharyngeal sphincter at the esophageal entrance, which is normally closed, is opened reflexly when the bolus stimulates the pharynx; the bolus then passes into the esophagus rather than into the trachea. The trachea moves upward in swallowing and downward especially in deep inspiration.

Judson and Weaver (1965) lean to the view that the trachea is a resonator for certain pitches. The cartilage framework and the factor of length give the trachea the necessary qualities of a resonator. The effectiveness of the trachea and perhaps even of the bronchi as resonators extends through a narrow range, since they have a fairly constant shape and size, which make it impossible to voluntarily adjust them adaptively.

According to Holmes (1940), the resonance of the trachea influences the vibratory rate of the vocal folds. At given pitches phonation is better if it is tuned to the tracheal resonator.

Not all investigators agree that the trachea has a resonance function. Akin (1958) asserts that it is a breath-supply tube and not a resonator.

Comparative Anatomy of the Larynx

From a biologic standpoint, the larynx is not primarily an organ of voice. Most aquatic animals close the glottis except during brief periods of respiration, and this closure is adequate for excluding water. The larynx appears to be a device to prevent the entrance of foreign bodies. In man there may be an additional protective closure at the level of the sphincteric aryepiglottic folds. The human glottis is importantly concerned with breathing in that it has an obstructive influence upon the air current and regulates the pressure and volume of air in the lungs and pulmonary tree. The voice is a by-product of these laryngeal activities, and it has developed along with the human brain and man's needs as a social organism.

Negus (1949) has made a detailed study of the biology of the laryngeal structures and in a 1957 paper he makes a plea for emphasizing the study of comparative anatomy and physiology because of their aid in interpreting the functions of the larynx. Negus's early study (1929) is monumental.

240

Negus describes a larynx in the bichir (*Polypterus*), a fish that has an air bladder shut off from the alimentary canal by a muscular sphincterlike valve. He contends that in certain "air-breathing" fishes, water and noxious substances must be prevented from getting into the structures which are acting like lungs. An opening into the floor of the pharynx modifies to become a valve. This develops sphincteric muscle fibers, which contract when the fish is in water but relax when air is breathed out of water.

The next stage in evolution is the development of fibers to dilate the opening, or glottis, and the origin of these fibers is the pharyngeal floor. Lateral cartilages develop for muscle attachment and facilitate the pull upon the edges of the glottis. This is seen in the axolotl (*Ambystoma*). These larynges are very small. They are situated in the pharyngeal floor, where they do not obstruct the digestive passage and where they can serve the needs of a simple respiratory device. In salamanders each lateral cartilage has a cephalic segment corresponding to the arytenoid of higher animals and pulled apart by muscles. Although the caudal segments are separated in the amphibians, they fuse in the higher vertebrates to produce a cartilage ring around the breathing tube.

Among the amphibians a urodele called *Necturus* is a good type form to show the rudiments of a larynx. There are two lateral cartilages on either side of a glottal opening to the lungs.

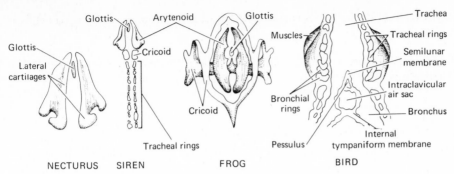

Glottis Arytenoid Glottis Trachea

Glottis Cricoid Muscles Tracheal rings

Lateral Semilunar
cartilages membrane

Intraclavicular
air sac

Bronchial Cricoid
rings Bronchus

Internal
Tracheal rings Pessulus tympaniform membrane

NECTURUS SIREN FROG BIRD

Figure 7-18 Outline of the larynx in some lower vertebrates.

In the higher, or anuran, amphibians, such as the frog, the development is more complex. The lungs produce the pressure for sound. There is a pair of arytenoid cartilages and also a cricoid cartilage modified from the upper tracheal rings. The arytenoids are operated by dilator and adductor muscles. A pair of vocal folds develop as two folds parallel with the glottis on the inner wall of the laryngotracheal chamber. In the anurans, the males, especially, develop accessory resonating chambers, or vocal sacs, in the throat.

Among the reptiles and birds the larynx is more deficient than in amphibians, but the trachea is better developed. In the alligator (*Crocodilia*) another ringlike cartilage, or fused cricothyroid, appears. This will become the thyroid cartilage of higher animals. This cartilage separates into a thyroid and a cricoid cartilage by a joint forming between them. The articulation facilitates opening and closing of the laryngeal cavity.

241

The birds develop a secondary larynx, called the syrinx. This forms below the larynx at the junction of the trachea and bronchi as an adaptation to centralize weight for flying. The reduced primary avian larynx has no vocal folds, and sound is produced by vibration of membranes in the syrinx. At the opening of each bronchus in the median wall there is a thin internal tympaniform membrane that vibrates with the exhaled air. Singing birds have an additional unpaired semilunar membrane stretching from front to back near the union of the trachea and bronchi. This membrane is supported by a bony ridge called the pessulus. The bird can change the shape of its tracheobronchial chamber, and it can activate the modified tracheobronchial rings which build up the syrinx. It combines such a structure with intercartilages, membranes, and muscles to form an efficient phonating device.

Although in man the arrangement of the vocal folds presents difficulties to inspiratory speech, the folds of some singing birds react with equal ease to the inspiratory or expiratory stream of air. A canary or lark may warble for minutes with obvious inspiration, and its voice is produced both during inspiration and expiration. Bocock and Haines (1954) state that vibrations of the human vocal folds during inhalation occur in the intake sound of stertorous breathing or in such involuntary efforts as the first sound of a sneeze.

The major cartilages of the human larynx correspond with those in aquatic vertebrates which support the fourth and fifth branchial (visceral) arches and serve a respiratory function. The muscles of these arches produce the muscles of the human larynx.

A great diversity of air sacs occurs in connection with the larynx of many animals. Most sacs develop muscles which expel the trapped air. The air is pushed into the lungs for greater respiratory utilization. The buccal air sacs of frogs, the laryngeal sacs of apes, and the abdominal sacs of birds function in this manner in the rebreathing of air. This may be advantageous for conserving energy or even air where a fresh supply is difficult to obtain.

The air sacs occur not only as diverticula of the larynx but also in connection with other parts of the respiratory system. The lateral buccal air sacs of the tree frog are supralaryngeal. The tracheal sacs of chameleons, the syringeal sacs of certain ducks, and the pulmonary air sacs in birds are infralaryngeal.

In mammals, where the ventricule first appears as a chamber, air sacs are produced that may serve for the rebreathing of air. Thus when muscle activity is employed as in climbing, the thoracic structure becomes fixed to allow maximal pectoral muscle play and the air sacs can be temporarily used in place of the lungs for rebreathing air. The sacs are large among anthropoid apes but small in man.

It has been thought that air sacs provide a mechanism for voice production, but the evidence does not bear this out. An adult male gorilla with large sacs is usually silent, while the young gorilla with small or no sacs may be noisy. Some of the noisiest gibbons have no sacs. The presence of sacs, however, is thought in many instances to influence or improve the quality of the voice.

In regard to the vocal folds proper, a wide range of tones necessitates relatively long vocal folds (Pressman and Kelemen, 1955). This is achieved more in some animals (such as the lemur and monkey) than in man.

The *quality* of the laryngeal tones depends considerably on the contours of the vocal folds. Sharp folds, as in the lemur and monkey, favor shrill rather than pleasant tones. Very widely rounded folds, as in the cow and reindeer, bring about inefficient control of pitch and volume. The human vocal folds are intermediate in form, the margins being neither too thin nor too rounded.

The margins of the human folds, unlike those of deer and oxen, are freely movable, an important factor in permitting efficient *vibratory* action.

The reader is referred to Walter and Sayles (1949) for a classical description of the comparative anatomy of the larynx.

Developmental Anatomy

Holinger and Johnson (1954) review the congenital anomalies of the larynx and state that they can be understood through developmental anatomy. They classify the anomalies into five groups: (1) laryngeal stridor, (2) webs, (3) atresia, (4) subglottic stenosis, and (5) cysts and laryngoceles. The reader is also referred to Jackson and Jackson (1959) and Ballenger (1969).

The larynx differentiates in the embryo of about 3 mm as a laryngotracheal groove in the anterior midline of the pharyngeal floor of the foregut. This stage corresponds to the third week, but most of the subsequent development occurs between the fourth and tenth weeks. Malformations occur readily during this period. The hind part of the groove becomes the esophagus while the front part proliferates to a larynx and to the respiratory system below the larynx (Haines and Mohiuddin, 1968).

The primordium is entoderm. At 4 mm the entoderm has produced lung buds, which are beginning to bifurcate. The respiratory organs at that stage are represented by a laryngeal slit, a tracheal tube, and two primary bronchi. The bronchi will branch repeatedly and produce all the peripheral divisions of the respiratory tree.

The upper and lower sections of the larynx develop somewhat differently. The upper part comes from the pharyngeal floor. The lower part develops around the tracheal stem.

The epiglottis appears at 5 mm. It is a rounded prominence that arises as a midventral mass condensing from the material of the third and fourth arches. This

243

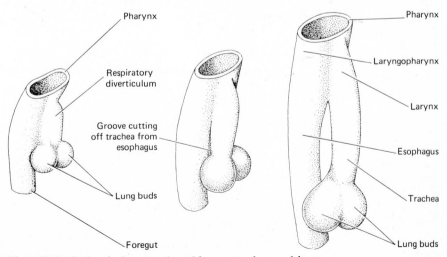

Figure 7-19 Embryologic separation of larynx, trachea, and lungs.

mass becomes a valvelike structure placed transversely in front and above the entrance to the larynx. Cartilage develops within it.

The original slit that opens into the trachea from the pharynx is the glottis. Material from the fourth and fifth arches swell upon each side of the glottis. These protuberances are the beginnings of the arytenoid cartilages. They appear in the fifth or sixth week and are well defined by the early third month.

The arytenoid swellings proliferate tongueward and meet the epiglottis primordium, against which they arch upward and forward. In the seventh week this activity adds a transverse groove to the original sagittal slit and makes the laryngeal opening T-shaped. Because of epithelial blocking, the laryngeal entrance is at first blind, but at ten weeks the opening is more evident. Lateral recesses called laryngeal ventricles appear, and each becomes bounded by lateral shelves, of which the vocal folds are the caudal pair.

The thyroid cartilage condenses from lateral masses within the fourth arches sometime during the first month, and it chondrifies considerably by the seventh week. Cartilages from the mesenchyme of the fourth and fifth arches are added to the epithelial larynx also in the seventh week.

The cricoid cartilage appears paired in the sixth arch at the sixth week. By the end of the second month both halves have fused and chondrified.

244

Laryngeal muscles develop from the fourth and fifth arches. The vagus nerve to the muscles and other elements of the primitive arches remains constant, and the nerve continues to supply the laryngeal muscles and the other derivatives of the arches. The outer musculature surrounding the foregut produces the paired cricothyroid muscles.

Morris (1966) raises the question whether the arytenoid, epiglottic, and other lesser cartilages of the larynx are derivatives of the branchial arches, but he admits that the evidence is strong.

By the close of the second month the internal laryngeal structures, including the vocal and ventricular folds, have been laid down. Patten (1968) states that the later details are added slowly and the larynx takes on a definitive configuration only in the last trimester of gestation.

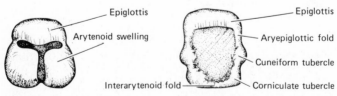

Figure 7-20 Early embryologic appearance of some laryngeal cartilages.

Positional changes in the larynx occur early in development. The larynx of the 14-mm embryo, which is five or six weeks of age, is opposite the basiocciput. By the fourth month it has descended so that the inferior boundary of the cricoid is opposite the superior boundary of the fourth cervical vertebra. This boundary shifts by the fifth month to the inferior boundary of the fourth cervical vertebra. At term, the reference line is at the level of the body of the sixth vertebra, and the descent has not ended since in the adult the lower border of the sixth vertebra has been reached. The highest laryngeal structure, the epiglottis, eventually comes to lie opposite the inferior border of the third cervical vertebra.

Age and Sex Changes in the Larynx

The larynx at birth is relatively larger than in the adult, although it is smaller in actuality; the vocal folds are both actually and relatively shorter in length. The infant larynx is softer and more pliable. The thyroid alae first resemble a semicircle; then they become angulated and especially so in the male. The epiglottis, aryepiglottic folds, and arytenoid cartilages forming the laryngeal inlet are less rigid than in the adult, and their supporting muscles are weaker.

As the infant grows, the larynx descends, and its lumen is displaced posteriorly from the vertical. It appears that the development of the hind part of the tongue depresses the larynx and pushes its inlet posteriorly.

The laryngeal descent is ascribed to a recession of the jaws along with alterations in the pituitary and vertebrooccipital angles. This explanation is questionable (Morris, 1966).

245

The positional changes away from the nasopharynx have some important consequences. The angulation of the airway that follows decreases the volume of air that could be exchanged in a straight tube (Pressman and Kelemen, 1955). The final laryngeal position allows for a large tongue.

Knowledge of the level of the larynx during childhood is important in endotracheal anesthesia and in some traumatic and surgical conditions. Roche and Barkla (1965) tabulate the expected mean levels during the ages 2.25 to 11 years.

The larynx grows to about the third year and then shows no marked development until puberty. Prior to about the twelfth year there are no major laryngeal sex differences.

At puberty, especially in the male, the walls become strengthened, the cavity larger, the vocal folds thicker and heavier, and the laryngeal prominence, or Adam's apple, becomes conspicuous. The progressive laryngeal development continues in many instances up to twenty-five years of age.

In the adult male the angle between the paired thyroid laminae, or alae, is approximately a right angle, but in the adult female the alae are more divergent and form an angle of approximately 120°.

The length of the vocal folds increases gradually in both sexes to puberty; then there is an abrupt increase in the male. The accompanying table illustrates the change with time. The values of 23 mm in the adult male compared with 17 mm in the adult female are common in the literature.

AGE	LENGTH, MM
Three days	3
Two weeks	4
Two months	5
Nine months	5.2
One year	5.5
Five years	7.5
Six and one-half years	8
Fifteen years	9.5
Adult male	17–23
Adult female	12.5–17

There is a sex difference in the dimensions of the adult larynx as a whole. The vertical diameter, from the upper border of the epiglottis to the lower border of the cricoid, is 70 mm in the adult male and 48 mm in the adult female. The transverse measurement is 40 mm in the male and 35 mm in the female. The greatest antero-posterior diameter is 40 mm in the male and 35 mm in the female.

The vocal folds of the adult female have a smaller cross section than those of the adult male because of a lesser amount of fat, muscle, and other tissue. The vocal folds of the female, due to their smaller length and width, vibrate more rapidly than in the male, thus accounting for the higher pitch of the female voice.

246

Structural modifications in the larynx change the voice at many stages of life. The frequency range of the newborn is a few semitones, and it increases chiefly by adding higher tones until a maximum frequency is reached at about the eleventh year. Structural changes at puberty are rapid, and the pitch lowers by an octave in boys and generally by two notes in girls. The voice in eunuchs remains infantile in puberty. Yet, in comparison with the female, the voice power of the male castrate remains relatively strong. The causes of this are obscure. Perhaps they are related to lung capacity and a genetic difference in the body form and structure.

The puberal changes are associated with the production especially in the male of tenor, baritone, and bass voices, although females show a similar pattern of voice range. The more abrupt changes at puberty occurring in the male are associated with a disproportionate slowness of development in control. The voice may break, or the pitch may be variable. The changes in both sexes are considered under the term *mutation.*

The thyroid, cricoid, and most of the arytenoids are derived from branchial cartilages and are composed of hyaline cartilage (Grant and Basmajian, 1965). A variable calcification and ossification occurs with age, beginning at about twenty-five years in the thyroid cartilage and later in the others. The hyaline cartilages may be entirely bone at about sixty-five years of age. The most common sites of early calcification are the posterior and inferior sections of the thyroid and cricoid laminae (Jackson and Jackson, 1959).

Calcification and ossification are not the same process, and calcification does not always precede ossification. The process of calcification often differs in men and women.

As calcification proceeds, there is a decrease in the range of the voice, particularly for the high frequencies, along with a decrease in resonance and steadiness.

Not all laryngeal cartilages calcify or ossify. The vocal processes and the apices of the arytenoid are yellow elastic cartilage which tends to escape these particular degenerative changes.

In senescence there is fatty infiltration and reduction in the number of lymph vessels. The muscles and vocal folds undergo atrophy. Control weakens, and the pitch rises, the voice typically becoming shrill and tremulous.

8 LARYNX AND VOCAL FOLDS: FUNCTIONS AND THEORIES

Functions of the Larynx

The larynx has several functions, and of these the biologic, or vegetative, ones arose early in animal evolution. This is not to take the narrow view that the function of phonation is secondary and that man's structure and activities would be unaffected even if the vocal structures were to disappear. So many correlative activities exist between the brain, the forelimbs, and the larynx that one must conclude that these structures are all mutually interactive in directing human development.

Protective

This function is seen in all vertebrates with pulmonary breathing. The laryngeal orifice may close, assisted by epiglottic coverage and elevation of the larynx, to prevent food or foreign bodies from entering a system necessarily patent for the exchange of environmental and pulmonary gases. In activities such as the cough reflex, the glottis closes in the early expiratory phase so that the rising subglottic pressure can abruptly open this valve and expel any noxious agent.

Fixative

Lifting a weight is preceded by glottal closure to fix the thorax. The retention of air in the lungs allows the forelimbs to exert greater force. One may compare one's arm force isometrically with and without holding the breath. Fixation is needed by animals with powerful forelimbs, and tree-climbing mammals have a well-developed larynx that appears to be associated with strong forelimb action. Glottal closure is not indispensable, since it is possible for laryngectomized persons to lift and carry heavy weights. It is known, however, that loss of fixative power is a vocational handicap to laryngectomees.

As a highly related activity, the glottis is closed to support the activity of the abdominal wall muscles as in defecation, urination, or parturition. This is the essential component of the Valsalva maneuver.

Deglutitory

In swallowing, the larynx rises to grasp the bolus and force it downward through the esophagus.

Tussive and Expectorative

This protective activity allows expulsion of material that has succeeded in passing through the glottis. Such activity expels endogenous material, such as pus, secretions, or sequestra, from the lungs.

Respiratory

The larynx is a part of the upper respiratory system and is thus involved with the exchange of gases. In pathology such as laryngeal edema, where obstruction to gas transfer occurs, the importance of the respiratory function is seen. The larynx is not altogether passive, since the changing contours and diameters of the glottic valve can influence air volume, pressure, and even chemistry.

Circulatory

A strong voluntary occlusive action of the larynx against a free exit of air during expiration plus a buildup of pressure within a contracted thorax (as in the Valsalva maneuver) has the effect of compressing the large veins entering the heart. This impedes blood circulation in the thorax. The effect is worsened by the absence of the normal sucking effect that ordinarily returns venous blood to the heart. The subject may suffer vertigo or loss of consciousness, following sustained cerebral control over such activity, although medullary respiratory centers can take over and abduct the folds.

Emotional

Laryngeal activity is involved in crying, moaning, shuddering, distress, and terror. There have been attempts at psychiatric classifications by voice. Friedhoff et al. (1964) note that the voice appears to contain information in its loudness variations and changes in emphasis and register which may be clues to emotional states. The voice in many ways reflects such states more directly than blood pressure or skin resistance does.

Greene (1964) stresses that hysterical aphonia and dysphonia are disorders of interpersonal relationships, expressable by vocal changes.

Rousey and Moriarty (1965), in a psychiatric approach, attribute hoarseness and phonation at too low a pitch in a patient to the demands for assertion of masculinity or for premature attempts at expressions of sexuality. Deviations in sounds described as breathy are ascribed to repression or denial of sexuality. The sounds of harshness and nasality are claimed to express aggression.

Phonatory

The larynx is an instrument for producing sounds. It is not the sole organ of voice since crows, parrots, and laryngectomized individuals "talk" without a sound-producing larynx. Even the vocal folds proper are not essential for producing sound, as evidenced by the cat, in which sound is produced with good quality despite the fact that the vocal folds are represented only by a thin layer of sub-mucosal connective tissue.

Theories of Sound Production

Historical Review

Some individuals in the field have little interest in a historical survey of the theories of phonation, basing their objection upon the fact that present thinking centers mostly around one view, the myoelastic-aerodynamic theory. The present writer takes a middle road, presenting the material because history is an important and integral part of any scientific field but omitting the details of pros and cons, which are available from many sources.

Aristotle (384–322 B.C.) compared the larynx to a flute and he regarded the trachea as the body of the instrument. The voice was said to be produced in the trachea, and speech occurred through modulation of the voice by movements of the tongue and lips. Aristotle believed that the sounds of animals were produced by the impingement of air on the walls of the trachea. The Roman physician Galen (A.D. 130–200) had essentially the same views.

The reader is directed to Eldridge (1968) for a historical account of persons contributing to the knowledge of speech disorders from the pre-Renaissance to the present time. Eldridge noted that in the fifteenth century Leonardo da Vinci in Rome demonstrated the production of voice, using the lungs, trachea, and larynx of a human cadaver and even of a goose.

There were no further significant advances in phonatory views until the eighteenth century. In 1700, Dodart expanded on Aristotle's theory, although still comparing the larynx to a flute. Dodart stated that eddy currents in the glottis produced sound as a whisper does. The glottis was said to be the generator of vowels, whose pitch depended upon the glottic area. The function of the vocal folds was to control the area of the glottis.

An objection to the flute-pipe theory is that the pitch in this kind of instrument is governed by the length of the tube. It would, however, require an open tube of about 6 ft to produce the low G of a bass voice, so that the comparison breaks down.

Antoine Ferrein was the next investigator of note, probably the first to bring animal experimentation into the field, and he may be said to be a founder of the science of voice physiology. In 1741, before the Paris Academy of Sciences, he produced intelligible sound in the larynx of a sacrificed dog by approximating the folds and blowing through the trachea. This showed that the vibrations of the folds are essential to phonation. He later repeated these experiments on the larynx of a human cadaver. Ferrein introduced the term *vocal cords*. He compared the ligaments of the glottis (vocal cords) to the strings of a violin that could be set into motion by air currents, and he said that the muscles were the powers designed to stretch or relax the folds.

Objections to Ferrein's views eventually arose. Ferrein had overstressed the importance of the folds in claiming that sound was a direct result of their vibrations.

Johannes Müller in 1835 experimented with the excised human larynx and demonstrated that vibrations of the adducted folds produce sound whose pitch rises as the fold tension increases. His experiments (in 1837) showed that there were differences in the vibrations of strings and the human vocal folds.

Guilmette in 1877 protested against Ferrein's theory, "for it has a tendency to bring on physical disease by concentrating the mind on the throat, instead of fixing it on the diaphragm as the grand propelling agent." In Guilmette's theory the respiratory mucous membranes are the phonators that emit the sound. The larynx by lengthening and shortening the so-called vocal tunnel modifies the sound in respect to pitch only and makes it high or low. The mind was conceived by Guilmette as the engineer that directs, controls, and governs this complicated mechanism at will. He unduly emphasized the diaphragm.

Another objection to the Ferrein view is that the scale of changes produced by the tension of strings is not the same as that produced by the tension of the vocal folds. Also, it does not seem possible for strings as short as those of the vocal ligaments to produce the resonant low tones of the deep bass voice.

In general, a vibrating-string theory holds that a blast of air passing between the true folds sets them into vibration. The folds are regarded as cords or as strings which are the individual fibers of the vocalis muscle. These may be sounded in whole, which produces the fundamental tone, or in part, which produces the overtones. Pitch can be changed by altering the tension in the folds. This is analogous to raising the pitch in a violin by increasing the tautness of its strings. There can be a damping effect of foreshortening the vocal folds. The segments left free to vibrate produce a higher-pitched sound. In the violin the length of the strings is shortened with the fingers.

One objection to the string theory is that in a direct blast, certain tones would submit the folds to excessively high tensions.

Prior to those investigators of the nineteenth century who cited evidence against Ferrein's string theory, Savart in 1825 likened the larynx to a kind of whistle. He attempted to account for the presence of the ventricles of the larynx and the superior ligaments not mentioned in previous theories; the ligaments of the glottis and the ventricles that open between them play an essential role in the primitive formation of sound. Air passing through the glottis strikes the superior ligaments. These ligaments bind the upper opening and have the same function as the stopper that apportions the wind in an organ pipe. Then the air within the larynx vibrates, giving out a sound that increases in intensity because the sonorous waves that form within it are prolonged into the pharynx, mouth, and nasal cavities.

Helmholtz deserves emphasis among the mid-nineteenth-century investigators because he turned attention to the glottis and the role of air passing through it. In 1863 he stated that puffs of air escaping through the glottis are the primary source of the sound. A glottis generator exists in the larynx. Magendie confirmed the view of Helmholtz that the vocal ligaments cut up the air column into a rapid and regular succession of puffs. The escape of the puffs through a variable laryngeal opening that alternately opens and closes produces the sound. The proponents of this view in its limited form regarded the folds as behaving like the reed of a musical instrument. In fact, the most popular historical view was to compare the vocal folds to a reed instrument. Reeds temporarily come together and then open, allowing air to escape in puffs. The rapid escape of puffs produces the sound. Pitch is changed by varying the size of the opening, its shape and rigidity, and the force of the exhaled air.

253

Pressman (1942) calls the reed theory faulty in that pitch in a reed instrument changes with the action of the resonating cavities whereas in the body the alterations in pitch are highly dependent upon the length, tension, and shape of the vocal folds.

One could add considerably more history to the period between Helmholtz in 1863 and a theory proposed by Husson in 1950. Many investigators in the nineteenth and early twentieth centuries produced mechanical models, usually animal membranes, to imitate the activity of the vocal folds. These models were inferior to the larynx in vivo, but they advanced the experimental science. The core of the twentieth-century history is the conflict between the neurochronaxic and the myoelastic-aerodynamic theories.

Neurochronaxic (Neuromuscular; Clonic) Theory

Husson in 1950 proposed in Paris a neuromuscular theory in which the vibrational frequency of the folds at a given pitch results directly from the nerves energizing the muscles involved. The thyroarytenoids rhythmically contract and relax because of repetitive nervous discharges into them. The active agent is the glottic margin, which allows tracheal air to be released in a series of puffs. The rhythmic impulses of the thyroarytenoid muscle are produced by nerve action with the same rhythm as that of the recurrent laryngeal nerve and with a frequency corresponding to the emitted sound. To state it another way, the vocal folds are stimulated by the recurrent laryngeal nerve at a frequency reflecting the frequency produced by the vocal folds. The origin of the vibrations must be sought for in the rhythmic activity of the brain cells governing the recurrent nerve fibers.

The brain-controlled vibrations set the vocal folds into activity, and this in turn activates the air column. It is denied that the air column sets the vocal folds into motion; rather the air increases the opening amplitude. The statement that airflow is responsible for amplitude but not frequency was later modified to the view that air has no dynamic role but is passively altered by the fold vibrations and thus aids in the production of audible sound.

The rhythmic phonatory impulses are said to be ordinarily of cerebral origin but may arise from different levels of the brain, depending upon the nature of the sound.

Another tenet of the theory deals with the way in which high-frequency impulses are transmitted by the recurrent laryngeal nerve. The highest frequency is limited by the refractory period of the nerves, which Husson takes to be 2 msec. The folds are said to vibrate maximally at 500 Hz. For frequencies between 500 and 1,000, single muscle fibers receive impulses at alternate movements of the folds. At still higher frequencies, single muscle fibers may be similarly activated at every third or higher movement of the folds. The bundle of fibers is thus able to transmit higher frequencies than a single fiber can. This explanation resembles the resonance-volley theory of hearing.

The arguments against the theory are more compelling than those supposedly supporting it. The role of the vocalis (thyroarytenoid) muscle is said to be overestimated. Also, because the left recurrent nerve is longer than the right, there should be phase differences between the right and left vocal folds.

The electromyographic data supposed to support Husson's theory do not confirm it. Studies in cats brought out the lack of relationship between electromyographic potentials and the frequency of stimulation of the folds.

Faaborg-Andersen (1957) points out that it is the refractory period of the muscles (3 to 4 msec) and not that of the nerve which determines the maximal tone frequency at which the muscle fibers are energized with each movement of the folds.

It has also been demonstrated in dogs that the fold vibrational frequency follows the stimulating frequency only up to 7 Hz and that the muscles tetanize (convulse) at 25 Hz.

Negus (1957) states that the demonstration of action potentials in laryngeal muscles during phonation is not valid evidence that the muscles are contracting rhythmically. The muscles may contract rhythmically at low stimulation frequencies, but at higher frequencies they go into tetanic or tonic contraction. Also, according to Negus, the human pitch rises as high as 2,048 Hz and to produce this would throw an impossible burden on the clonic theory.

The question was raised by van den Berg (1958) why a certain minimal volume of air is needed to initiate vocal fold vibrations.

Husson based his theory partly on anatomic studies first made by Goerttler (1951), who claimed that the muscle fibers of the folds do not run parallel with the vocal ligament but insert as a complex pattern of fingers in the vocal ligament. The oblique insertions open the glottis when the muscles contract. Later investigators could find no vocal fold fibers running in the oblique direction described. Negus (1957) remarks that Husson's contention that the margins of the glottis are pulled aside by oblique fibers inserted into the conus elasticus is practically impossible to accomplish in man.

Much of the evidence that was adduced for the theory was based originally on stroboscopic observations (Husson et al., 1950; Husson, 1951). However, stroboscopic examination of tracheostomized patients showed no movements of the vocal folds in the open tubes (van den Berg, 1958) and high-speed films of patients with pharyngeal stomas showed no vocal fold movement when the airstream was directed away from the larynx (Ruedi, 1959). In Husson's theory the folds should vibrate independently of the air column.

255

Rubin (1960) found no evidence by motion pictures that the folds could respond to recurrent nerve stimulation by transverse contractions, which the theory proposed.

Convincing arguments against the theory are summarized by van den Berg (1958) and Weiss (1959). Some of these arguments become less pointed in the light of newer discoveries. For example, van den Berg notes that the frequency shifts upward in a less dense medium, e.g., after inhaled helium, and claims that this is normal in the myoelastic-aerodynamic view but not explicable in the neurochronaxic view. However, with the discovery of mechanoreceptors sensitive to air pressure in the glottal areas, shift pitch may be feasible in either theory. The same may apply where van den Berg noted that persons with tracheal stomas phonated when the stoma was occluded but vocal fold vibrations ceased when the stoma was uncovered. Again, sensory feedback of air pressure loss may have altered or inhibited the neural innervation implicit in Husson's views.

Classical Myoelastic, or Tonic, Theory

In the tonic theory sounds are associated with the rhythmic opening and closing of the glottis. The vocal folds are opened by the variable intratracheal pressures. The subsequent loss of pressure allows the folds to close again because of their elasticity. The active agent is the tracheal pressure which produces a series of puffs through a tonically closed glottis.

The vocal folds vibrate transversely under the pressure of the tracheal bellows. The frequency corresponds with the equilibrium between the force and volume of the airstream and the tension of the myoelastic contraction. Nerves are essential only for glottic contraction and to control the tension of the vocal folds. The term myoelastic was apt and referred to the importance of muscle elasticity in phonation.

This view was formulated more than a century ago by Johannes Müller (1839) and was widely accepted. Müller collected data from excised cadaver larynges. Earlier results leading to the theory were obtained by Ferrein in 1731 from human cadavers. Experiments on human cadavers were also performed by Lermoyez in 1886.

In explaining laryngeal effects on pitch, Müller showed on the excised larynx that an increase in subglottic pressure led to a higher frequency of vibration. To keep the pitch at constant lower levels he had to decrease the tension of the vocal folds. He called this the law of compensation of forces in the larynx. Contradictions to this have been observed in singing, in that the law is followed in the head voice but in the chest voice pitch is decreased as the subglottic pressure rises.

Portmann (1957), who favors the clonic theory of Husson, cites objections to the tonic theory as follows:

1 The myoelastic theory is based on experiments with cadavers and artificial larynges. Such results are not fully transferable to the living larynx because it is necessary to use an airstream and a vocal fold tension that are so extreme that they are incompatible with physiologic possibilities.

2 A singer using a falsetto should have a sensation of thoracic strength and great laryngeal tension, but instead he may feel relaxed.

3 The vocal folds can vibrate without being closely approximated, and they fail to vibrate when tensely adducted in spite of a strong subglottal pressure.

4 A probe placed on the active fold does not stop the vibrations, although it should if the subglottic pressure produced the disturbance.

5 The head register is not as tiring as the chest register.

Aerodynamic Theory

Guthrie and Milner (1939) express the opinion that vocal fold vibrations are an aerodynamic process, resulting from the pressure of expired air. Pressman (1942)

256

expounds these views more fully. The laryngeal muscles do not produce the vocal note but only adjust and hold the vocal folds in a given position, at a certain tension and with a certain contour. The pulmonary air does the rest. Changes in the shape of the glottic chink plus changes in the elasticity of its margins produce variations in pitch.

The first step in producing the tone is loose approximation of the vocal folds, due to arytenoid movements, followed by an increase in fold tension. From the adducted position finely detailed movements occur.

The final position of the vocal folds in producing a tone is the result of two muscular forces: (1) the adductor muscles approximate the folds and place them under varying tensions, and (2) a finely regulated pull of certain thyroarytenoid fibers counterpulls against the adductors over a varying portion of the folds.

The everted edges of the vocal folds spring back because of inherent elasticity. The rapid repetition of eversion and falling back of the *margins* of the folds in a wave-like manner constitutes the vibrations of the folds.

The aerodynamic view is consistent with and supports the essential propositions of the myoelastic theory. The aerodynamic aspects of the latter view are stressed by Tonndorf (1925), who describes a suction effect during the approximation of the vocal folds in analogy to Bernoulli's theorem. Vibration cannot be ascribed only to lateral elastic pressure. There is an inward sucking movement produced by a negative pressure, and this exists where the walls of a tube with a narrow passage are elastic. The vibrations start and continue under the influence of a sucking effect. Smith (1954) agrees that adduction is brought about by a sucking effect which follows the plosion of the upper edges of the vocal lips and produces a subglottal closure. Smith also states that insufficient attention is paid to subglottal events.

The aerodynamic principle referred to above is the famous theorem of Daniel Bernoulli. It applies to steady motion of fluids or gases along any channel, straight or curved, and of constant or variable bore, provided that the velocity and pressure are constant over each cross section of the channel. There is an extension of this theorem to unsteady motion, but it is not applicable to the present discussion.

The law states, in one form, that

$$\Sigma \ [d \ + \ \tfrac{1}{2}(v^2 p] \ = \ C$$

where d = density, v = velocity, p = pressure, and C has a constant value all along the streamline (but in general will have different values in different streamlines).

In a fluid the pressure varies inversely with the velocity if the total energy is constant. With constant volume, if the cross section decreases, the velocity increases and the pressure decreases. In the application to air flow through the true vocal folds, a constant-velocity subglottic airstream will increase in velocity during passage through the narrow glottis, and the concomitant negative pressure will suck the partly adducted vocal folds medialward.

Von Leden (1961) states that the myoelastic theory is weak unless aerodynamic processes are admitted to support it. He prefers the term aerodynamic to myoelastic theory, to emphasize the relative importance of the phenomena involved.

There have been objections to the concept of a suction effect (Luchsinger and Arnold, 1965). It is said that suction plays no important role with ordinary sound pressures. Further, instead of a continuous streaming process during phonation, the impulses are produced intermittently.

Myoelastic-Aerodynamic Theory
The theory is a fusion of myoelastic and aerodynamic concepts and is the most generally accepted view. As originally proposed, it held that phonation involves balancing the force of air pressure against the elasticity, mass, and tension of the vocal folds.

Starting from the approximated (median) position of the vocal folds, a sufficient subglottic, or tracheal, pressure is built up to force them to open. In the subsequent phase of reduced pressure, it may be primarily the elasticity of the contracted muscles that drives the folds back to the "resting" position. The vocal folds themselves are largely passive in that the aerodynamics of the flowing air constitutes the basic source of energy for the phonatory events.

The recoil of the folds may result secondarily from the fact that the rapid flow of air through their margins creates a negative pressure between them, which pulls them together. In addition, adductor muscle activity can enter into the final closure, depending upon the type of phonation. The process is repeated with every puff of exhaled air.

The static restoring force resulting from the stretch of the vocal muscles and the Bernoulli force which is a consequence of the negative pressure created by high-speed air flow tend to alter in relative importance with change in register (Lieberman, 1968). The Bernoulli restoring force is said to be dominant in the chest register.

The mechanism of closure of the glottis is a point of controversy. Van den Berg (1958) says it involves at least three determinants: (1) the decrease of subglottic pressure as the air escapes, (2) the shortening of the folds as a result of their tension, and (3) a sucking action of the escaping air in proportion to its velocity.

The larynx handles the moving exhaled pulmonary air flow and breaks it into a series of discrete puffs. The pressures involved constitute the forces that set the vocal folds into vibration. These vibrations are independent of the frequencies of the nerve–muscle motor unit activities. The amplitude and frequency of the vibrations depend upon factors to be considered later.

The "sound" stream is not the same as the original "breath" stream. The latter is relatively very slow and is not perceived, being used only to activate the vocal folds. The resulting sound waves are minute pressure changes in the surrounding air. The vibrations modulate the air, resulting in pulselike variations in volume and velocity. The pulses travel in the supraglottic chamber at the speed of sound, and this constitutes the phonated excitation.

The Subglottal System This area, which influences the activities of the vocal folds, has been partly neglected in research because it is hidden and data from the living subject are difficult to obtain. Subglottal resonances (formants) caused by the behavior of this system have been found and partly located on the dog and in human cadavers (van den Berg, 1964). Subglottal resonance helps to explain certain amplified partials.

The air pressure below the vocal folds is determined particularly by four factors (Ladefoged, 1967): (1) an inspiratory muscular effort decreases the pressure; (2) an expiratory muscular effort increases the pressure; (3) the resistance to the air-stream at the glottis or elsewhere in the tract affects the pressure and also the rate of air flow; (4) the *relaxation pressure* (sum of forces due to abdomen, stretched lung tissues, and elasticity of rib cage) can increase the pressure. The net effect of these forces is to maintain a constant level of background pressure in the lungs, which can be made available for speech.

Moving the air, by pressure effects, is not a major problem in normal phonation. The control of the moving air, however, is very important. This involves proprioceptive mechanisms in the respiratory muscles. There is a view that the role of the muscle spindle lies more in the control of motion than in the perception of the spatial position of the muscles involved.

Muco-undulatory Theory

This is associated with Perello (quoted from Greene, 1964), who observed that the mucous lining of the larynx is only loosely attached by areolar connective tissue to the underlying muscle and may therefore be capable of independent undulations. Such activity is claimed to play a part in determining the quality, or harmonic structure, of the phonated sound, although not its fundamental pitch.

Even in the absence of muscular activity, mucosal changes are said to cause pitch variations. The mucosal activity may be more important than the pressure-vacuum effects described as an aspect of the Bernoulli effect. The undulations travel upward and also from front to back over the folds and thence to the laryngeal ventricles.

Other Views

Many acoustic analyses have treated the larynx as a high impedance generator (Bogert and Peterson, 1957). The tone emitted from the larynx has a complex frequency composition. The fundamental frequency corresponds with the rate of glottal opening and closing, and it is determined by the bursts of periodically expelled air. The oscillations within the vocal tract do not essentially bear an integral relationship to the vocal fold frequencies. The term formant frequencies is used for the resonant frequencies. The upper formant frequencies are considerably dependent upon the details of cavity shape, but the shape is less important for the lower formant frequencies.

Perkins (1957) says that phonation occurs when the dynamics between subglottal air pressure and the resistance of the glottal margins are such that a slight subglottal pressure is favored. The tension and thickness of the vocal folds are important in this dynamic balance, since they hold the subglottal pressure at a given value. The tension and thickness are determined by the extent to which the folds are stretched. It takes more pressure to displace thick vocal folds than thin ones. In turn the folds yield to the greater force with a greater displacement.

The vocal fold displacement in Perkins's view should not be equated with vocal intensity, since displacement only partially accounts for the dynamics affecting volume. It is not true per se that abducting the folds raises the sound volume by increasing the amount of the breath stream. In phonation the air is compressed above the folds when they are abducted, and the degree of supraglottic compression is important.

The two most important events in phonation, according to Perkins, are the force with which the folds are abducted and the degree to which the glottal edges billow. They are observed to billow when they are thickened in emitting low tones, and this may hold true when they are thickened for high, heavy tones. In high, thin tones the glottal edges are thin.

Classification of Positions of the Vocal Folds under Varying Conditions

Greene (1964) emphasizes six positions classically described for the vocal folds according to their status or activity:

The *median* position is the midline, adductor, or phonatory attitude.

The *paramedian* position is one in which the folds are slightly abducted.

The *glottic chink* is the position in which the folds are adducted, but a small degree of separation is permitted during breathing.

The *cadaveric* position exists when the folds are slack, or between paramedian and gentle abduction.

The *gentle abduction* position is one in which the folds are separated more widely than in the cadaveric state but not maximally. It is expressed in quiet breathing.

The *full abduction* state involves maximal separation of the folds and is expressed in forced inspiration.

Responses of the Larynx and Vocal Folds
in Vegetative Activities

The vocal folds are never "silent" since they do not normally stay in a fixed position even in the absence of phonation. However, they may be considered as silent in the sense that they do not *vibrate* except during phonatory activity involving voiced sounds.

Resting Position

The vocal folds are slightly abducted. The anterior intermembranous sector is triangular, whereas the intercartilaginous part tends to be rectangular.

Breathing

In *quiet* breathing the muscles are relatively relaxed, and the glottis is open. The vocal folds are widely separated during inspiration but narrow somewhat during expiration. The opening is roughly triangular in either phase. There are no vibratory phenomena and no sound.

The ventricular folds and the laryngeal port (vestibular sphincter area) are open. The subglottic walls just below the folds are irregularly shaped, which may favor turbulence. There are no significant movements in the soft palatal structures.

During inspiration the larynx lowers, in many persons it travels backward, and it usually deviates to the left. All these movements are of small amplitude. The circular fibers of the cricopharyngeal pinchcock remain closed; otherwise more air would be swallowed into the esophagus than through the relatively narrow glottic chink.

In *forced* breathing (which can be normal or abnormal) the abductors are contracted to open all parts of the glottis widely, while the adductors are inhibited, during inspiration. The vocal folds may be drawn so far apart that the glottic chink is almost as wide as the tracheal lumen. The glottis may become lozenge-shaped because of marked contraction of the posterior cricoarytenoid muscle.

Swallowing

The vocal folds, ventricular folds, and vestibular-epiglottic parts of the larynx tend to close. The entire larynx is elevated appreciably toward the base of the tongue by the action of the palatopharyngeus, stylopharyngeus, and inferior constrictors of the pharynx. The cricoid and arytenoid cartilages are displaced anteriorly.

Coughing, Gagging, Laughing

The folds are closed abruptly and firmly and are then explosively opened. In the early phase of the cough reflex the larynx opens widely to increase the inspiratory volume of air. The subsequent valvular closure first involves simple glottic closure (shutter mechanism) and then includes closure of both the true and false folds, particularly the latter. Analogous to a ball-valve mechanism, the paraglottis is squeezed by ascent of the larynx. It is the great increase in subglottic pressure along with forced expiration that violently opens all the sphincters. Coughing, like throat clearing, is an injurious activity in that the entire larynx goes into stressful movements.

There are other vegetative activities accompanied by sounds. In *yawning*, the mouth opens widely, a large volume of air is inhaled, and the vocal folds are widely abducted. In *hiccup*, a deep inspiration occurs with the vocal folds being widely abducted, but this phase is abruptly terminated by a violent contraction of the diaphragm and sharp closure of the vocal folds.

Activity of the Larynx and Vocal Folds in Normal Phonation

Ordinary Phonation (Conversational Level)

To produce varied tones under average conditions of voice production, the vocal folds are gently adducted to a median position all along their length just prior to phonation. The adduction is such that the folds can resist the exhaled air but not prevent its upward passage or the ability of folds to vibrate. The capacity to vibrate depends upon (1) the air pressure, (2) the elasticity of the folds, (3) the maintenance of a proper muscle tone upon which moderate muscle contraction can be superimposed, and (4) sufficiently regular fold margins so that they can be brought into precise parallel approximation.

The buildup of air pressure opens the folds, which in turn leads to an abrupt lowering of the pressure in the glottic area. It was once widely thought that these physical events cause the folds to be sucked back to the median closed position, where they just make contact. This *Bernoulli effect,* which indicates that air escapes in pulses, may not be the significant mechanism for the periodic expansion and contraction of the glottis. More probably, the vocal folds are pushed back to median position primarily because of their elasticity. In addition, the folds are always subject to different degrees of tension and elongation by muscle action. They open to variable degrees with the pulmonary air blast, depending upon the tone to be produced.

Following approximation and tension, a countertension mechanism involving muscles can be set into action. When the tone is emitted, the internal margins of the folds engage in fine vibratory movements.

In ordinary phonation the upper, or vestibular, area of the larynx and the ventricular folds stay open. The subglottal space just below the vocal folds may (it is controversial) become more regular in shape, which promotes the aerodynamics of sound production by reducing turbulence and increasing the efficiency of air flow (Lenneberg, 1967).

262

During adduction of the folds, their medial edges sharpen, their upper surface flattens, and their lower surface arches. These changes are thought to allow the air pressure to open the folds more readily.

The folds do not move as stiff bands. The opening may develop from front to back or from back to front in an undulating or wavelike progression. Pressman and Keleman (1955) state that regardless of pitch, the anteriormost segments of the folds come to approximation first, then the middle segments, and finally the posterior segments. However, in the moderate voice range, evidence is strong that approximation first occurs posteriorly and then proceeds anteriorly.

The vocal folds vibrate in a characteristically altered manner with specific conditions. At a low frequency they seem relaxed. The entire fold vibrates, and the main mass of the muscles of the fold participates in the activity. In this wavelike motion the movement progresses from underneath to on top, and there is eversion of the vocal lips.

The vibration of the folds is chiefly horizontal, with a maximum displacement of about 4 mm, which is in contrast with a vertical displacement of 0.2 to 0.5 mm.

In a balanced right and left vocal muscular system the movements of the folds are synchronous and in phase. In lack of balance, out-of-phase motion is possible, and the folds may display unequal frequencies and amplitudes of motion. In the condition termed *diplophonia,* there are inequalities in elasticity and mass, accompanied by unilateral differences in the vibratory patterns of the vocal folds. Double tones are heard.

The original classification of the vocal fold activity was as a cycle having two phases. The activity may be classified as a three-phase process. There is a period of approximation, an opening phase (abduction), and a closing phase (adduction).

In the 1937 high-speed motion pictures at the Bell-Telephone Laboratories, with subjects using sounds ranging from 120 to 350 Hz, the vocal folds were thought to be closed for nearly half a two-phase cycle. Timcke et al. (1958), using synchron-stroboscopic measurements, found that the opening phase of the glottic activity is shorter than the closing phase. Timcke computed the *open quotient,* which is a ratio of the fraction of the cycle during which the glottis is open compared with the duration of the entire cycle. In normal voice production the open quotient changes very little with respect to the frequency of vibration, with a tendency to increase slightly with a rise in pitch. The quotient decreases with increasing intensity and increases with decreasing intensity.

Muscles Used in Ordinary Phonation The relationships of muscle contraction to vocal fold activity are still experimental (Michel, 1954). The extrinsic muscles adjust the laryngeal framework. They are involved in topical adjustments between the cricoid and thyroid cartilages during pitch adjustments. The intrinsic

263

muscles more directly and intimately influence the shape of the glottis and determine the tension of the vocal folds.

The arytenoid muscles come into play early to approximate the arytenoid cartilages. The lateral cricoarytenoid muscles simultaneously aid in adducting the vocal folds to close the glottis. All cricoarytenoid muscles then act to fix the arytenoid cartilages in position. If the opposing contraction of the cricothyroid and thyroarytenoid muscles are well balanced, the elasticity of the folds is increased and can be finely adjusted to changing demands.

The length of the folds is determined chiefly by the opposition between the thyroarytenoid and cricothyroid muscles, and approximation is regulated additionally by the lateral cricoarytenoids in conjunction with the lateral parts of the thyroarytenoids (Huntington, 1968). The last two pairs of muscles can also exert a medial compression to more precisely determine the *effective* length.

The thyroarytenoid-vocalis musculature is an important determinant of the shape and tension of the folds. The cricothyroids may serve for crude control of the increase in tension and for elongation of the folds in producing high tones.

The abductor muscle (posterior cricoarytenoid) has essentially a respiratory function. The folds need only the pressure of the subglottic air to be opened.

The Laryngeal Tone The basic laryngeal tone that results at the outset is apparently weak and unrecognizable as speech.

The laryngeal tone is partly musical and partly nonmusical. The musical component comprises a fundamental tone and overtones. The nonmusical vibrations do not have a fundamental or any definite pitch, but they can nevertheless activate the resonating chambers.

The vocal fold vibrational frequency determines the frequency of the fundamental tone. Its production is through conversion of the energy of the airstream into acoustic energy (sound), and its usual range is from 100 to 400 Hz.

Van den Berg (1958) states that the fundamental frequency (which importantly characterizes the individual voice and which is at the basis of *habitual pitch*) is determined by (1) the vibrating vocal fold mass, (2) the tension in the vibrating portion, (3) the effective glottal area, (4) the damping effect on the vocal folds, and (5) the value of the subglottic pressure. These are mutually dependent factors.

Although the larynx is coupled to other structures in the vocal tract, the fundamental frequency is usually determined by the larynx in accordance with the principle that the frequency is governed by the organ with the smallest damping. The myoelastic-aerodynamic theory is claimed to account for any of the effects of coupling on vibratory behavior, regardless of the types of coupling that may occur.

Normal Laryngeal Activity in Vowel Formation In the *harmonic* theory, the waves produced at the larynx are composed of fundamentals and overtones. Certain of these frequencies correspond to the resonant characteristics of resonators in the vocal tract, and it is only these frequencies which will be amplified. The quality of the vowel will depend on the frequencies amplified. In this view the resonators do not add tones of their own.

In the *inharmonic* theory the resonators respond to the exhaled puffs of air by producing their own tones, which are not necessarily in harmonic relation to the laryngeal frequencies. The vowels are claimed to be chiefly dependent upon the resonated tones of the vocal tract and also, although less so, on the laryngeal frequencies.

There may be very little contradiction between the two concepts. The vowels begin to be differentiated in the larynx, but the supraglottic cavities (coupled mouth and pharynx) enrich and specify them with a characteristic quality. This view suggests an interaction in the formation of sounds among all parts of the vocal mechanism. It may be that the energy lost by supraglottic damping of the formants of the vowels permits a predominance of the fundamental tone set up by the vocal fold vibrations.

Vocal Fold Activity Following Training The manner of vibration of the folds seems to vary with environmental factors, as training. Closure time is greater for the trained speaker, and the amplitude of vibration is less. A trained voice produces a given sound intensity with less volume of air, and it covers a wider range of pitch and intensity than the untrained voice does.

265

Although the positioning of the larynx with pitch is variable, depending upon the individual's training and experience, the positioning influences the dimensions of the resonating chambers and thus affects the quality of the voice.

Vocal Parameters: Pitch

Range of Pitch

The entire range of all human voices may cover about five octaves, varying in frequency from about 50 to 2,000 Hz. These values are for laryngeal fundamentals and first harmonics, but one should also consider the higher harmonics (formants) with a central range of 500 to 2,000 Hz that are necessary to intelligible speech, i.e., in the *audiologic speech range*. The pitch of the voice as finally heard by a listener implies not only a laryngeal component but that due to resonances in other parts of the vocal tract.

Although the range of pitch in ordinary conversation for a single individual may be less than one octave, he might have a potential voice range of about two octaves, and by training this might be extended to at least three octaves.

In regard to sex differences, the adult male's conversational voice is about 128 Hz, and that of the adult female is about 256 Hz. For any given male or female, the average range of conversational voice extends above and below these values in a characteristic manner.

The range of the voice and the artificially classified voice types (bass, baritone, and tenor in the adult male; contralto, mezzosoprano, and soprano in the adult female) are determined by the dimensions of the larynx, but they are also dependent upon such other factors as cultural influences, training, and the body type. There is an optimum, or natural pitch, for each individual, which is most appropriate for him. It is determined by the efficient activity of the larynx in conjunction with that of the resonators. The optimum pitch is not necessarily the same as the habitual pitch used by the individual.

The common terms applied to pitch levels that are inappropriate to the age and sex are *eunuchoid, high, castrato, shrill,* or *treble.*

Factors Influencing Pitch

The pitch of the vibrating phonatory air column, as produced at the glottic level and related to laryngeal mechanisms, is directly related to the frequency of movement of the vocal folds. The frequency is itself determined by the mass of the vocal folds and their stiffness, or elasticity, in relation to their length. The tension of the folds, the subglottal air pressure, and the shape of the glottis all enter as determinants of pitch. A vibrational frequency F can be halved by doubling the vocal fold length L, or multiplying the mass M by 4, or dividing the tension T by 4 in accordance with the equation

$$ F = \frac{1}{2L} \sqrt{\frac{T}{M}} $$

Length This is an important factor. If two sets of folds have the same cross section and tension but unequal lengths, the longer one will vibrate more slowly. The male vocal folds are about one-third longer than those of the female. This difference in length partly accounts for the lower pitch of the male voice. By shortening the length of the vibrating folds, i.e., limiting the vibrant portion, the "height" of the sound is augmented. In high pitches the vibrations of the folds can be restricted to the anterior part, whereas in lower pitches the vibrations may involve their entire length.

It is to be emphasized that the pitch can rise if the folds are actively elongated, depending on a simultaneous thinning of the cross section of the muscle mass being stretched. The elasticity of the thinner folds is greater, and they return faster to their position of adduction. This increases the frequency and raises the pitch. Therefore, the statements above about the influence of resting length should not a priori suggest that the pitch lowers as the folds are actively stretched. There is need to differentiate between structurally longer folds and actively elongated folds, keeping in mind the effects due to the alteration of other dimensions and contour changes during the stretching process.

266

The structural length of the quiet folds is determined to an important degree by inheritance and also by endocrine activity. Glandular immaturity or imbalance before puberty is a causative factor in vocal folds that are too short. Gonadal and pituitary hormones are involved, as witnessed by the fact that in Fröhlich's syndrome laryngeal immaturity is common. During puberty the length of the male glottis nearly doubles.

The pathologically shortened glottis is accompanied by a reduction in the vocal range. The chest voice may be lost, and high pitches are prevalent.

Mass The chief mass of the true folds is the paired vocalis muscles, which are an inner part of the larger thyroarytenoid muscles. The more massive the folds, the lower will be their vibrational frequency and the pitch. The male has heavier folds than the female. Mass, or thickness, is an important determinant of the fundamental frequency of phonation (Hollien, 1962).

Tension The effect of increasing the tension is to increase the frequency and the resulting pitch. By altering string tension on a violin without changing the mass or length, the instrument can be tuned. It is possible to alter the tension of the vocal folds at relatively constant length by variations in the shape of the folds brought about by muscle action. The thickness of the parts is changed. An increase in the so-called isotonic tension of the muscles makes the folds stiffer and increases the vibrational frequency. The edges of the folds can vary from round and thick to sharp-pointed and thin. If the attachments of the vocalis and thyroarytenoid muscles are fixed by other laryngeal muscles, their contractions increase the fold tension. Fixation anteriorly is accomplished by the infrahyoid muscles and posteriorly by the posterior cricoarytenoid muscles. The external laryngeal muscles may increase their contractile power and pull outward upon the fold attachments. Since the motion is highly limited, the folds are tensed rather than elongated.

267

The central nervous system can maintain or alter the tension. The effector muscles that are well equipped for fine adjustment and thus regulation of tension of the vocal folds include the cricothyroid and thyroarytenoid.

Excessively flaccid folds are associated with lowering of the speaking voice.

Subglottic Air Pressure If the elasticity of the vocal fold margins and all other factors stay constant, an increase in the subglottic pressure raises the pitch of the laryngeal tone. (The amplitude and loudness are also raised.)

Elasticity The effect of increasing the elasticity of the vocal fold margins, with subglottic pressure constant, is to increase the pitch. In this type of activity the glottic margins will have less excursion, less air will be used in a given time, and the tone intensity will decrease.

Position and Size of the Larynx The effect of the positioning of the larynx upon pitch is controversial. Vocal pitch alterations from lower to higher are generally thought to be accompanied by elevation of the larynx and a tightening of the vocal folds. There is an opposite view that pitch may not be dependent upon the vertical position of the larynx (Keenan and Barrett, 1962).

A systematic relationship between vocal pitch and laryngeal size is reported (Hollien, 1960), smaller larynges having high pitch ranges. Hollien and Curtis (1960) report an association between low pitch, large vocal fold area, and large vocal fold thickness.

Supraglottic Effects on Pitch   Events occurring in the supraglottic region may affect pitch and intensity. This involves effects upon the tension of the vibrating folds and also upon the size, shape, and tension of the resonators. As West and Ansberry (1968) note, the resonators are integral parts of the same tube containing the vibrating folds. Thus not only can they react to the waves produced by the folds, but they may partly determine the very behavior of the folds. When the resonators respond efficiently to transduce kinetic energy into tones, *resonance,* which implies amplification, occurs. If the soft supraglottic structures interfere with transduction and some energy is lost, this constitutes *impedance.* A loss can result from absorption of waves or from the difference between the frequency of response of the vocal folds and the supraglottic chambers.

Changes in the Vocal Tract with Rising Pitch

Brewer (1964) lists three physiologic correlates of increasing pitch: (1) there is variable elongation of the folds with a change in mass; (2) the tension of the intrinsic muscles is varied concomitantly with changes in stiffness or elasticity of the folds; and (3) there can be shortening of the vibrating segment by damping or stopping of the posterior sections of the folds.

In the lowest tone, of the guttural type, which is generally below the speaking range, the vocal folds are shortened and relaxed. The folds are bowed outward, and there is a gap between them (less wide than in ordinary inspiration). The folds are relatively thick and vibrate with relative slowness. There is an increase in the relative duration of the closure phase of the cycle, but a systematic relationship has not been demonstrated between closure duration and pitch (Huntington, 1968).

With increasing pitch, the vocal folds seem to lengthen and stiffen. They change shape from round and thick to wedge-shaped. The margins of the folds sharpen and are the only parts that vibrate. The glottis is a narrow slit.

In very high pitches, when the vocal folds reach maximum elongation and tautness, the pitch can be raised further by a *damping process* in which appropriate portions of the folds come into firm adduction, such that one fold segment damps the activity of the opposite one. The foreshortened segments, anterior to the damped segments, may undergo no changes in tension or thickness, and they vibrate very rapidly.

Adjunctive to firming the margins of the vocal folds to control the resiliency, which in turn determines the frequency of puffs of air passing through the glottis, the tracheal air pressure is increased and the supraglottic air column is shortened by raising the larynx and pushing upward all tissues attached to the hyoid bone. The ventricles and pharynx tend to be constricted, the tongue and associated tissues are elevated, and the oral lips are separated.

Vocal Parameters: Vibrato

The vibrato is a rhythmic variation in pitch of the voice occurring with an average frequency of six or seven times per second. There is also a rhythmic intensity change of 2 or 3 dB. These values are associated with a pleasant voice quality. The vibrato is ordinarily emphasized in the singing voice, but even the normal conversational voice has a slight vibrato. When completely lacking where expected, the voice is described as *flat, hard,* or *metallic.*

When the vibrato increases in frequency to about twelve per second, it is called *tremulo* (tremulous) or palsied. The tones are irregular, quivering, or uncontrolled and are sensed as unpleasant. The tremulo suggests a deterioration of the voice, seen acutely in fear and chronically in senility or debility.

Vocal Parameters: Intensity

The contours of the glottis and the manner of vibration of the vocal folds are altered not only for and with changes in *frequency* but also for and with changes in the physical and measurable attribute of sound called *vocal intensity,* or the energy generated by the vocal folds. The final intensity of the tone indicates the energy carried by the sound waves and perceived by the listener.

Determinants of Vocal Intensity

Several factors determine intensity. They include the value of the subglottic air pressure produced by the respiratory apparatus, the rate of air flow through the vocal folds, the elasticity of the vocal folds, the excursion of the folds associated with the amplitude of vibration, changes in positioning of the larynx as a whole, and lesser-known influences.

The factors are related. (1) If the subglottic air pressure increases, with the fold elasticity constant, the glottic space increases and the amplitude of vibration increases. The intensity of the laryngeal tone, which depends upon the amplitude of vibration (or the volume and velocity of the air flow), increases. Within limits, the vocal intensity is proportional to the square of the vocal fold vibrational amplitude (Luchsinger and Arnold, 1965). In the case of the listener, there are greater excursions of the ear mechanism, and the sound is sensed as louder. (2) If the elasticity of the folds increases, with the pressure constant, a decrease in the excursion of the fold lips will be associated with a decrease in the amplitude of vibration. The intensity of the laryngeal tone decreases.

The expiratory blast, with its effect on the amplitude of fold vibrations, may be the chief factor affecting intensity. It would be incorrect, however, to regard the specific value of the pressure below the vocal folds as the determinant of amplitude. The emphasis should be placed rather on the differential in pressure between the upper and lower surfaces of the folds (West and Ansberry, 1968). Factors increasing this differential increase the amplitude of vibration and therefore the intensity of the tone.

Among the clinical conditions that prevent the buildup of sufficient pressure to produce ample vibration of the folds there are (1) pneumothorax, in which collapse of the lung reduces the air spaces; (2) paralysis of the diaphragm; (3) low vital capacity, from many causes; and (4) enlarged heart, which prevents adequate thoracic expansion.

Adequate pulmonary pressure and its manner of modification by the vocal folds are to be stressed rather than the *amount* of air as a determinant of intensity. The amount exhaled must attain a minimum value, but an excess is unnecessary. In fact, the amount of air used should be small in comparison with the perceived intensity, and this ratio varies with different sounds, bringing in the concept of the efficiency of producing sounds.

270   *Loudness,* commonly measured in decibels, is a psychologic effect, representing the response of the listener to the strength of tones. Loudness is related to the final intensity of the phonated and resonated tones and is also influenced by the frequencies of the waves. The physiologic correlates at the laryngeal level involve the vocal fold responses in amplitude and configuration to greater subglottic pressures. There are concomitant changes in the elasticity of the folds and in the vibrational frequency. Loud phonation also involves a lowering of the entire larynx.

Voices lacking adequate loudness are commonly termed *asthenic, thin,* or *weak.* A weak voice may not always express a disorder of structure or function but may represent a personality disorder (West and Ansberry, 1968).

The term *volume* is not synonymous with loudness but refers to the extensiveness or space-filling characteristic of tone and has some relationship with the extensiveness of stimulation of the cochlea of the ear (Murphy, 1964).

Vocal Parameters: Clarity (Quality) of Tone

Voice, like other sounds (coughing, grunting, sighing, etc.), has three common attributes; pitch, intensity, and quality. Clarity, which is not a scientific term, is an aspect of quality (timbre). The quality as finally perceived will depend in the main on the frequency and character of the overtones that accompany any fundamental tone sounded.

Clarity is a desirable quality of the voice, and any departure from the expected is described in such terms as *hoarse, husky,* or *strident* voice.

The clarity of the laryngeal tone will depend greatly on the absence of irregularities, edema, or other pathology on the vibrating parts of the vocal folds and therefore on the proper adduction of the folds. In instances of irregularities on the edges of the vocal folds, the glottis may close only incompletely, and the opening quotient of each vibrational cycle increases. An excess of air escapes instead of being transduced to sound, and a noisy, rough quality ensues.

There is an aberration of clarity called harshness, or *glottal fry,* which Moore and von Leden (1958) consider as a physiologic rather than a pathologic phenomenon. It occurs as an unpleasant, rough, rasping sound. The functional correlates involve hypertensive activity of the extrinsic and intrinsic laryngeal muscles and a deviating vibratory pattern of the vocal folds, in which the folds separate usually twice in quick succession and then adduct firmly in a relatively long closed phase. Moore and von Leden deny any involvement of the ventricular folds and suggest the term *dicrotic dysphonia* for the voice quality. Luchsinger and Arnold (1965) describe this as a habitual hyperkinetic dysphonia.

In pathology, the *site* of a lesion on the vocal folds importantly determines the clarity of the tone. Those lesions which are nearest the anterior commissure produce the severest symptoms, e.g., hoarseness.

271

Laryngeal Activity in Phonation Other than Normal Speaking

Vocal Attack

To initiate the act of phonation the vocal folds have to assume a specific position. This may be normal or abnormal, so that different types of positional attitude are recognized.

In the *soft vocal attack,* which is the normal, the vocal fold adduction is gentle and moderate. There is a narrow glottal slit just before phonation. The subglottal pressure increases and gradually incites the fold vibrations. The listener hears this as a smooth flow of sounds.

In the *hard vocal attack* the folds adduct forcefully prior to phonation. The subglottic pressure rises and is then markedly lowered upon forcing the folds apart. This produces an unpleasant clicking noise. This *glottal stop* is potentially damaging.

In the *aspirate* or *breathy attack* the vocal folds are adducted, but the glottal closure is not firm and the posterior one-third of the glottis is open. The listener hears a soft blowing sound.

Whispering

This is an aphonic laryngeal activity, and it can take place without the intervention of the larynx by appropriate movements of oral structures.

Considerable confusion can arise in the analysis of whispering unless the terms movement and vibration are differentiated. Although, in a physical sense, muscular movements might be thought of as involving vibratory phenomena, the two concepts should ordinarily be considered independent processes in laryngeal terminology. The vocal folds can move without necessarily vibrating. It is the consensus that the vocal folds do not vibrate in true whispering. The statement is said to hold even if the whisper is lively (Bocock and Haines, 1954), but this is controversial. At any rate, in moderate whispering there is language without phonation.

In ordinary whispering, the vocal folds are closed to varying degrees. The anterior two-thirds are gently approximated, but the cartilaginous posterior one-third remains open, leaving a wide gap for air leakage. Pressman and Keleman (1955) attribute the space to the fact that the gliding movements of the arytenoids fail to occur. A hissing sound occurs as air passes through the whisper triangle. There is no tonal pitch. Irregular vibration of the folds occurs, and friction noises constitute the tone. Despite the absence of fundamental and overtones, identifiable vowels are heard because of the sufficiency of nonperiodic noises. There is no individuality, however, in the utterances, since the uniqueness of a given voice depends on the presence of the fundamental and harmonic overtones.

272

If the whisper is intense (stage whisper), the folds may be firmly adducted in the anterior two-thirds (Greene, 1964), and significant vibratory movements might very well then occur anteriorly, despite little or no visible activity at the still open posterior cartilaginous region. Considerable air volume is used. The subglottic air pressure remains lower than in the conversational voice. The false vocal folds may be partially adducted and the sphincteric girdle contracted.

The movements of the true folds in whispering are of clinical interest in discussing whether the voice can be rested by whispering. The laryngeal movements differ in speaking and whispering, but traumatization from fold movements, as well as from the subglottal air blasts, is possible in both activities (Morrison, 1955). Apparently the voice cannot be rested with confidence by resorting to whispering when hoarse, and there are stresses attending strong whispering.

Singing

Although speaking and singing may not basically involve unlike laryngeal mechanisms, they have been differentiated. In singing, the motion for inhalation and exhalation is said to be determined by the subglottal pressure and by the duration and maintenance of this pressure. In speaking, the subglottal pressure is weak and often repetitive.

In singing, the energy needed is much greater, and the concomitant sensations can be localized. Freund (1958) says that speech is controlled chiefly in the diencephalon while singing requires cortical control. The cortex is essential for regulation of the pitch, the tone intervals, and the emotional expression.

The voice of the singer is influenced by several factors. One is an air-impedance effect, or resonance phenomenon, in which reflection into the larynx from the pharyngeal, nasal, and oral chambers hinders vocal fold vibration. To restore the stability of the exhaled airstream, the glottic sphincter contracts. Proprioceptive impulses that give information about the positions and tensions of the active muscles are transmitted through the trigeminal, glossopharyngeal, and vagus nerves.

In singing, laryngeal elevation is very small in persons with well-trained voices, and it may be positioned low prior to singing (Luchsinger and Arnold, 1965).

The voice range in music or in the phonation of musical tones can be divided arbitrarily into *registers,* whose characteristics have been studied especially by cinematography and stroboscopy. At one time two registers were thought to exist, the chest and the head, or falsetto. Many investigators divide the registers into chest, middle, and head, but there are others who add the falsetto (male) and whistle (female) types.

The chest register is referred to the chest subjectively, and it includes low tones with many overtones. The glottis may be slightly open, and the entire mass of the folds vibrates.

Over the range of the middle register the folds are almost parallel, and with rising pitch they become increasingly elongated and tensed.

273

The head register includes the high tones with few overtones, and the vibrations are subjectively referred to the head. The elongation and tension of the folds may become maximal, after which the pitch can be raised only by shortening (damping) the vibrating glottis. The vibrations become limited to the tensed and sharpened inner margins of the folds.

Human beings, unlike animals with a restricted range, have a capacity for making the transition more easily from one range to another. The tones of the conversational voice may be said usually to encompass the chest voice and the lower part of what may be called the middle register.

The Falsetto Rubin et al. (1960) define the falsetto as that part of the voice which encompasses the upper singing range and in which basic alterations occur in the mechanics of phonation. A *break,* or abrupt change, occurs in the quality of the voice in passing from the lower register to the falsetto and vice versa. This is especially marked in the untrained voice. Rubin studied the falsetto with motion pictures taken by indirect laryngoscopy at 6,000 to 8,000 frames per second.

There is variation of opinion about the physiologic activity of the larynx in the falsetto. Greene (1964) states that the folds are firmly adducted except in a part of the anterior section. In this less tensed area, vibrations occur at high speed.

The smaller the length of this freely vibrating section, the higher the pitch. The fold margins are elongated and thinned out.

Van Riper and Irwin (1958) cite evidence that it is not true that only a part of the folds vibrates in the falsetto. The entire edges of the folds are said to be displaced.

Rubin et al. (1960) state that confusion exists because there are three basic patterns of vibrations in falsettos, and each or all of them can be present in any one voice. The common feature is that a lesser amount of thyroarytenoid substance is set into vibration. The main mass of the muscle no longer vibrates, and only its margins vibrate, at high frequency.

In one pattern, the open-chink reaction, the fold margins may not touch each other, or do so only occasionally. In a second pattern, the closed-chink reaction, the folds make contact. The third pattern, called *stop closure* or *damping,* occurs in the highest reaches of the falsetto in some voices. This mechanism, which allows the pitch to rise beyond that realizable by any other laryngeal pattern, has been discussed earlier. Often, only a pinpoint opening may remain at the anterior commissure.

Judson and Weaver (1965) state that the air pressure produces an inconstant elliptic glottal opening in the middle or anterior third of the length of the vocal folds and that the resulting continual inefficient escape of air represents the greatest difference between the falsetto and normal phonation. Also, the falsetto is much more dependent upon air pressure than upon increased fold elasticity.

Silent Speech

An interesting question is whether the intrinsic muscles move during silent speech. In 1924, Watson, a behaviorist, described thinking as subvocal talking, but Wertheimer in 1945 denied that silent speech is necessary to the thinking process. Faaborg-Andersen found increased action potentials in the vocal muscles of subjects thinking without audible phonation. It has been stated that in silent reading the eye movements of stutterers tended to show the same types of perseverations, retrials, etc., that one hears in audible stuttered speech.

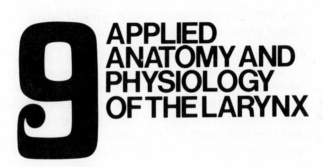

9 APPLIED ANATOMY AND PHYSIOLOGY OF THE LARYNX

There are diverse kinds of phonatory disorders, the causes being chiefly anatomic, physiologic, or psychologic. In many instances the disorder represents a mixture of categories. The abnormalities are divided by some into two categories, organic and functional.

Many periodicals devote considerable attention to these problems. The student should become aware of the expanding literature, and the following journals may be consulted. The list is far from complete.

Annals of Otology, Rhinology and Laryngology

Acta Oto-Laryngologica

Archives of Otolaryngology

Folia Phoniatrica

Journal of the Acoustical Society of America

Journal of Auditory Research

Journal of Laryngology and Otology

Journal of Neurophysiology

Journal of Speech and Hearing Disorders

Journal of Speech and Hearing Research

Laryngoscope

Quarterly Journal of Speech

Speech Monographs

Transactions, American Academy of Ophthalmology and Otolaryngology

Transactions, American Laryngological Association

Transactions, American Laryngological, Rhinological and Otological Society

The *DSH* (Deafness, Speech and Hearing) *Abstracts* has very comprehensive coverage of pertinent American and foreign journals.

The clinical literature is voluminous, and only a rigid selection of applied problems can be fleetingly presented, especially in a biologically oriented text. Milisen (1957) points up the importance of the problem in his estimate that about 1 percent of the people of this country have phonatory defects and that such defects comprise about 5 to 15 percent of the defective speech population. He differentiates speech deviations from speech defects. The former include any demarcations from an assumed normal speech pattern, whereas the latter signify extreme deviations or those which significantly interfere with communication.

276

Instrumentation

Indirect Mirror Examination of the Larynx

This method employs the head mirror along with the laryngeal mirror (invented by Garcia in 1854). The operator faces a good light source that shines into a head, or frontal, mirror held over his left eye. The mirror is adjusted to reflect the light into the subject's throat, both members being seated and facing each other. The operator uses a dry, warm, previously sterilized laryngeal (guttural) mirror, and with his right hand he inserts the mirror into the subject's mouth directly above the lower incisors, with the back of the mirror just contacting the velum. The subject's tongue may be kept lowered and out of the field by pressure of a tongue depressor held in the operator's left hand. The gag reflex caused by the contact of the laryngeal mirror with the borders of the fauces has to be controlled. The laryngeal mirror is illuminated by reflected light from the frontal mirror, and the image of the vocal folds is inversely reflected to the operator's eyes by the laryngeal mirror.

Visualization of the vocal folds is facilitated by making the subject issue the long /a/ sound. If the individual takes a slow and deep inspiration, then sounds /i/, the behavior of the vocal folds can be watched.

Direct Laryngoscopy

The direct laryngoscope is a speculum, or tube, with a distal light. It pulls aside the obstructing tissues and permits the viewing of a direct, undistorted image of the larynx. This is distinguished from indirect, or mirror, laryngoscopy which yields a reflected image of the larynx.

The examination is a delicate endoscopic procedure best performed in an operating room with the subject under mucosal anesthesia. The reader is referred to Jackson and Jackson (1959) and Ballenger (1969) for details. Through the use of binocular eyepieces and general anesthesia, endolaryngeal microsurgery is facilitated.

Taub (1966) has designed an oral panendoscope that permits simultaneous visual observation and audiovisual recording of the operation of vocal structures during the production of laryngeal speech sounds in normal and abnormal subjects. The image of structures at the distal end is transmitted through lenses to the eyepiece in normal rather than upside-down position. The effect is as though the viewer's eye were actually in the mouth. Illumination is adequate for color motion photography. The instrument has been used to examine the superior surface of the palate, to evaluate pharyngeal flap operation results posteriorly, and for palatal surgery.

Transillumination

An apparatus enclosing a light source of high intensity is applied to the neck at the thyroid region. The examiner inserts a laryngeal mirror into the oral cavity, with the room darkened, and can visualize the transilluminated topographical aspects of the laryngeal interior. The vocal folds become evident, and any localized change in thickness along them is detectable by differential opacity (Meano and Khoury, 1967).

Cinematography

It is possible to photograph the larynx by positioning a mirror in the throat so that it reflects a light beam down into the larynx and also reflects the image of the laryngeal structures back to a camera. Since the vocal folds vibrate at the frequency of a tone of a given pitch, even the slowest vibrations are too fast to be optically visualized. A movie camera which attains high speeds, e.g., 4,000 exposures per second, can solve the problem of optical analysis. Still higher speeds have been used to analyze high-frequency vibrations such as in the falsetto.

Farnsworth (1940) at the Bell Telephone Laboratories successfully introduced high-speed motion-picture technics for research on the larynx. A large number of films have since appeared, some ultra-high-speed, showing how the larynx operates under diverse conditions.

In high-speed cinematography the laryngeal vibrations can be slowed sufficiently for them to be visualized. This result can also be accomplished by stroboscopy, but the latter is useful where the movements are periodic and not irregular. If by high-speed cinematography vocal fold vibrations are recorded at 4,000 frames per second but reproduced at 16 frames per second, the reduction of 250 times allows a 100-Hz vibration to be seen as 0.4 Hz or a 1,000-Hz vibration as 4 Hz (Brewer, 1964).

Stroboscopic Analysis

This technic also permits the vocal folds to be visualized during their vibration. The folds can be seen slowed down by selecting single exposures of successive phases of the activity. The positions of the vocal movements for various sounds can be seen.

The examiner and subject relate to each other as in laryngoscopic examination, but an intense light is projected via the examiner's head mirror into the subject's throat. The incident light ray is intercepted at exact, controlled times.

In theory, if light to an object is interrupted a few times every second, there is a consciousness of light flickering. In the principle of positive afterimage sensations, the eye continues to sense the object from $\frac{1}{7}$ to $\frac{1}{5}$ sec following the absence of illumination to the object. If the light to an object is interrupted at least twenty times per second, the observer believes that the object is continuously illuminated.

One may place a perforated disk, with holes equidistant from each other and from the disk center, between a light source and a head mirror on the examiner. Suppose that while the examiner is visualizing the vocal folds, the folds are vibrating at 100 Hz. Each fold is then being deviated from the center $\frac{1}{200}$ sec, and returning the next $\frac{1}{200}$ sec. If the disk is made to revolve so that it interrupts the light 100 times per second, then only the outward or inward phase of the vocal fold movement will be seen in the recording laryngeal mirror and the folds will not appear to be moving.

278

A vibrating fold appears immobile because it is illuminated by each light stimulus in the same phase of its vibration. Every complete rotation of the disk (at a certain velocity) corresponds to a complete vibration of the vocal fold.

Stroboscopes are usually equipped with a device for phase shift. If the disk is operated out of phase with the folds, different phases of the successive fold periods are illuminated. The continuous shift of the visible phases can be accelerated or retarded, and because of ocular fusion a harmonic vibration in slow motion is sensed.

When stroboscopy was first used to study the larynx by Oertel in 1879, the rotating perforated disk was introduced to interrupt the incident light beam. Later research produced the electron stroboscope, which uses gas discharge tubes to produce discrete light impulses.

Although in theory a subject may be said to phonate a vowel on a constant pitch, in practice the pitch level varies and a synchronism between vocal fold frequency and light flashes must then be achieved by additional instrumentation in the circuit. In the laryngeal *synchronstroboscope* the frequency of intermittence of the luminous source is regulated electronically by the voice of the subject being examined (Timcke et al., 1958; Meano and Khoury, 1967).

Roentgenography

The fluoroscope can visualize the arytenoid cartilages or the larynx under varying conditions of phonation. Conventional flat plates can reveal any calcification in the cricoid or thyroid cartilages. The elongation of the vocal folds with rising pitch is seen in lateral radiographs. Planigraphy (or tomography) aids in visualizing the coronal plane view and permits separate study of the right and left sides. It brings out the subglottic region and the contours of the ventricle (Ardran et al., 1953).

X-ray cinematography refers to motion studies of body structures. Cinefluorography is an inclusive term for studies of motion obtained by radiologic means regardless of the augmenting system (Potsaid, 1961). The images are obtained through the use of an x-ray-activated fluorescent screen. Cinefluorography shows the relative form and positions of the vocal structures during their action. Films are made while the subject pronounces selected sounds, and simultaneous tape recordings of the sounds may be made. From movements of the barium-coated structures, clues to anatomic defects contributing to speech difficulty can be obtained. A supplementary instrument, the x-ray image intensifier, which electronically amplifies the x-ray images on fluorescent screens, is very significant in research as well as in the diagnosis of laryngeal pathology.

279

Electromyography

Many investigators have studied the laryngeal muscles electromyographically (Faaborg-Andersen, 1964). Data have been provided about activity during quiet and forced breathing, whispering and ordinary phonation, and in disturbances of the voice. The reader is referred back to chapter 4 for a discussion of this technic.

Evaluation of Muscle Function

The possibility of accurately testing the status and activity of the intrinsic laryngeal muscles may ultimately be fully realized and made routine. Attempts to date have mostly involved electromyography, laryngoscopy, high-speed photography, and stroboscopy, but these instrumental technics themselves need to be progressively refined. Hiroto et al. (1968) state that by their technic of transcutaneous approach to the intrinsic laryngeal muscles with needle electrodes, electromyography is made a feasible routine method of examination in laryngeal paralysis.

The data from instruments are not all-inclusive but need to be correlated with symptomatology related to muscle dysfunction. Such symptoms include oral dryness, throat clearing, swallowing difficulty, swelling of the cervical muscles and glands, episodes of aphonia, throat tickling or rawness or burning or scratchiness, cough, choking spells, and the quality of the voice (Brewer, 1964). Digital palpation of the laryngeal region gives significant information about form, texture, mobility, and the elicitation of tenderness (which itself is revealing of pathology).

Anomalies of Development

The larynx is a midline structure and obliquity is a constitutional disorder, possibly hereditary. The consequence is that the external and internal muscles are not parallel or symmetrical, and the muscles of one vocal fold exert a disproportionate force (for which compensation is possible). Congenital lack of symmetry is not unexpected since bilaterality is not accompanied by perfect duplication of paired structures.

Embryologic malformations of the entire larynx are rare, and the more frequent ones are those of the epiglottis. Apart from distortions of its shape, there are the bifid epiglottis and the failure of the epiglottis to appear.

In the bifid organ there is variable splitting in the midline, which ranges from a slight indentation of the free border to a complete split. Montreuil (1949) explains the bifid anomaly on the assumption that there is a bilateral origin of the epiglottis from a large swelling on the laryngotracheal duct called the furcula of His. An absence or incomplete fusion of the paired primordia could occur. The furcula helps form the tongue anteriorly and the epiglottis posteriorly.

Triboletti (1958) presents a case in which incomplete separation of the laryngotracheal groove from the primitive gut produced a common laryngotracheoesophageal tract. Ordinarily, this groove appears on the ventral surface of the gut in the 3-mm fetus.

280

The larynx may be variably closed by membranes called webs, or by adherence of the vocal folds, or by stenosis resulting from thickening of subglottal structures. There can be a complete congenital closure (atresia), incompatible with life.

Positional Maladjustments of the Vocal Folds or of the Larynx

Tone purity depends upon the evenness and regularity of the vibrations on the edges of the folds. Anything interfering with the free vibrations of the folds or allowing unused breath to escape between them can add noise elements.

Any growth on the folds can prevent them from being closed. This results in the escape of unvocalized air. The condition is called *breathiness* or pneumophonia. The voice is said to have an aspirate quality, and the effect is as though a whisper were added to the normal tone. The extra rush of air which is not modulated by the vocal folds superimposes friction noises upon the tones produced by vocal fold vibrations. Breathiness may also be brought on as a result of faulty breathing, poor vocal habits, or even general weakness. An inability to approximate the folds is also at times ascribable to weakness or paralysis of the folds.

Where the folds are drawn too tightly together during phonation, a shrill, harsh, creaking noise, which is called *stridency* or stridor, enters the tone. Some causes include general tension, spastic paralysis, or often a throat strain or "pinched throat." There is excessive constriction of muscles all through the vocal tract. The vibrations of the vocal folds are hindered, and supraglottal friction noises are introduced.

In the condition known as *glottal stop,* or *hard vocal attack,* there may be extreme glottal closure prior to phonation. This has already been described.

A positional maladjustment involving an abnormal elevation of the entire larynx occurs in the condition called *ventricular phonation* (ventricular dysphonia), in which the false folds phonate. This disorder may originate from an acute laryngitis in which speech is forced during temporary dysfunction of the true folds. The false folds may also assume this function if the true folds are separated, as by a tumor. The disorder may also be congenital. Sometimes this substituted vocal activity of the false folds is desirable, as in surgical deficiencies of the vocal folds.

Positional maladjustments may involve the joints of the larynx. Arthrology does not seem to enter the speech literature often mainly because of the infrequency of joint pathology. The most flexible joint in the larynx is the cricoarytenoid articulation (Gisselsson, 1950), and rare cases of dislocation preferentially involve this area. The cricothyroid joint is dislocated with extreme rarity, because the joint is firmly bound.

In the rare condition of *rheumatic laryngeal arthritis,* progression of the inflammatory process may lead to complete permanent fusion (ankylosis) of the cricoarytenoid joint. The vocal folds are usually fixed in the midline, the condition resembling a recurrent laryngeal nerve abductor paralysis.

281

Hyperactivity of the Mucosa

The volume of mucus secretion in the larynx and vocal folds particularly is adaptively regulated to demand. Excess fluid facilitates an adherence of the folds that results in damping of their excursions, plus an uneven weighting effect that interferes with the normal undulating movements. The clinging mucus slows the rate of vibration and lowers the pitch. Accumulated mucus globules on the folds can act as secondary vibrators set into action by the ordinary fold vibrations, the result being the production of transients, or extraneous noises (Moore, 1957).

Hoarseness

Hoarseness is a rough, harsh quality of the voice, and the pitch is relatively low. It is not a disease, but it is a very important symptom of throat disorders. Its chronic form often indicates serious pathology. Although it does not exist unless the vocal folds are involved, other areas, such as the pharynx, may contribute to its duration and general pathology.

Hoarseness is an aspect of *dysphonia,* which refers to a voice deviating from an acceptable norm. A definition should be broad and include alterations in tonal quality that range all the way from a slight drop of pitch to practically complete aphonia (loss of voice). The tonal variations are usually produced by changes in the shape, tension, or motility of the vocal folds. The causes may be congenital, infectious, mechanical, psychologic, hormonal, traumatic, functional, or neoplastic.

The ability of the vocal folds to approximate each other is decreased. Air leaking through a deformed glottis or through a widened space between the folds can produce rasping tones. The thyroid cartilage may be tilted upward, there may be a hard glottal attack, and the voice frequently "breaks," requiring throat clearing. If the vocal fold vibrations have three components, i.e., each cycle has an opening, closing, and closed phase, then during hoarseness the differential timing of the phases may be disturbed and the duration of the cycles may be irregular.

Acute simple laryngitis is the most common cause of hoarseness, and the vocal folds temporarily swell and thicken. There is also an acute laryngitis accompanying upper respiratory infections associated with streptococci and other virulent organisms. The vocal folds can thicken and swell in acute allergic and vasomotor disturbances.

Hoarseness in a child may also reflect vocal abuse, psychologic changes, or precocious puberty. In the infant, congenital causes should be suspected, including laryngeal cysts, flaccid cartilages, edema from tracheal aspiration, and paralysis from disturbances of the recurrent laryngeal nerve or of the central nervous system. The control of the recurrent nerve over the laryngeal muscles is so great that any disturbance of these nerve fibers can change the mobility of the vocal folds and produce hoarseness. In surgical removal of the thyroid gland, hoarseness may result from concomitant damage not only to the recurrent nerve but also to the external branch of the superior laryngeal branch of the vagus nerve.

Endocrine derangements may set up background conditions for hoarseness. In the thyroid deficiency called myxedema the voice can become hoarse and low-pitched. Women with the adrenogenital syndrome may develop a deep and harsh voice; they also tend to develop a temporary huskiness during treatment with large doses of the male sex hormone testosterone.

Much hoarseness results from abuse of the vocal folds. In the advanced stage of irritative responses to mechanical trauma, fibrous nodes can develop, particularly in the center of the vibrating fold. At this point the vibrations have the widest amplitude, and the mechanical impact between the two folds is maximal. The benign nodular growths are called vocal nodules, screamer's nodes, singer's nodes, or in clinical terms chorditis nodosa.

Nodules vary histopathologically, some having fibrous inflammatory tissue and others loose vascular tissue. They are usually covered with a thickened epithelium. In the stroma there are leucocytes, fibrous connective tissue, and inflammatory tissue.

Nodules develop when the vocal folds are overly active, and they are usually bilateral. They interfere with the ability of the vocal folds to be correctly approximated.

There may be other benign laryngeal growths associated with hoarseness. The most common is a *papilloma*, which is an epithelial tumor with a core of vascular connective tissue. Papillomas may occur in any part of the larynx and may recur.

Polyps are common tumors that are not true neoplasms. They are constituted of loose connective tissue with branched star-shaped cells in a matrix of viscous mucoid substance. Polyps are usually limited in adults to the anterior region of one fold. In general, growths associated with hoarseness are benign, but if hoarseness is persistent, malignancy should be considered.

Paralysis of the Vocal Folds

Effects Involving the Central and Peripheral Nervous System

Laryngeal paralysis (or palsy) may be sensory or motor. A sensory paralysis involves loss of sensation and reflex function and most often is caused by impairment of the trunk or internal branch of the superior laryngeal nerve. Lesions of the trunk above the separation of the superior laryngeal nerve usually produce both sensory and motor losses.

A motor paralysis involves loss of laryngeal movements and may follow lesions of the upper or lower motor neurons. Since the muscles of phonation and articulation seem to be controlled by fibers from the upper motor corticospinal tracts of both cerebral hemispheres, paralysis of the vocal folds from upper motor lesions ensues only upon bilateral destruction of the upper motor systems. Speech is markedly affected. The imperfect articulation is called dysarthria.

283

Lesions may occur in the vagus nerve, which is the lower motor neuron. Depending upon the level of the lesion, the superior or inferior laryngeal branch of the vagus or both branches may be involved.

If the superior laryngeal nerve is involved, anesthesia of the upper larynx and epiglottis may accompany paralysis of the cricothyroid muscle. The vocal fold becomes slack, and although phonation may not be seriously impaired, the voice fatigues readily. Paralysis of this nerve alone is rare.

If the inferior laryngeal nerve is at fault, one or more of the other laryngeal muscles may become paralyzed. This involves defects in tensing or relaxing, adduction or abduction, or loss of sphincteric action resulting from paralysis of muscles of the aryepiglottic folds along with the adductor muscles. The principal defect is usually the loss of adductor or abductor motion. Recurrent laryngeal lesions may not significantly influence sensation from the larynx. Brain (1955) states that the <u>left recurrent nerve is more exposed to damage because of a longer course.</u>

Paralysis may be unilateral or bilateral, partial or complete. Speech disturbance is not an essential sequel to partial paralysis. If one fold is paralyzed, hoarseness is typical. If both are paralyzed, speech is lost.

Unilateral paralysis may be caused by damage to, or pressure upon, the recurrent laryngeal nerve on the same side. It can occur, for example, in mediastinal tumor, or aneurysm, in goiter, and in cervical lymph node enlargement. The causes of bilateral paralysis may be the same as the above, but more often they involve post-diphtheric neuritis or disease processes affecting the hindbrain nuclei of the vagus nerve, e.g., progressive bulbar paralysis, anterior poliomyelitis.

Individuals with hysteria may simulate an organic picture of aphonia in which there is an apparent paralysis of the folds closely resembling a true paralysis.

The term paralysis usually implies disturbance in the nerve supply. In this sense it would not be the proper designation for lack of movement caused by disorders originating in the laryngeal muscles and joints.

Semon's Law

Felix Semon in 1881 was the proposer of the widely known concept that attempts to explain why in a slowly progressing limited injury or disease of the recurrent laryngeal nerve the adductor muscles are more apt than the abductors to remain functional. Semon said that the nerve trunk contains separate abductor and adductor fibers and the former are more susceptible. In partial paralysis of the nerve the functional adductors are the cause of the assumption of a fixed midline position of the folds. In complete paralysis the cadaveric position (semiabducted) is assumed.

The evidence for Semon's law is not only clinical but also agrees with a principle of comparative anatomy that primitive functions (i.e., adductors are necessary for the preservation of life) survive better than more recently acquired ones.

Although the postulates provide a good rule of thumb for the clinician, they do not explain all the positions observed in paralyzed folds. Such positions are determined by the interaction of many factors, rather than being subject to a fixed law. Also, there is no proof that abductor fibers are more susceptible to degeneration. The position of adduction may not be due to persistence of adductor function but to the unbalanced action of the cricothyroid muscle.

Involvement of the Intrinsic Muscles

From a standpoint of the muscle groups affected, there are three main groups of paralysis, the adductor, abductor and tensor. The most common type occurs when the paralyzed fold is fixed in the midline and does not abduct upon inspiration.

In unilateral abductor (posterior cricoarytenoid) palsy, the involved vocal fold is close to the midline and is not abducted on inspiration. Phonation and coughing need not be markedly affected since adduction is normal. Dyspnea (difficult respiration) is minor because the normal vocal fold is abducted in inspiration. The voice may be hoarse.

In bilateral abductor (posterior cricoarytenoid) paralysis, both vocal folds cannot be abducted. The voice may be hoarse, but phonation occurs since both folds can attain the adducted position. Coughing is normal. Although the expiratory phases are not affected, the close adduction on inspiration leads to severe dyspnea, with inspiratory stridor (noisy, difficult breathing with high-pitched sounds most distinct during inspiration, and indicative of airway obstruction).

In adductor muscle palsy the vocal folds adduct in coughing but not in phonation. Abduction, inspiration, and coughing are normal. There is no dyspnea or stridor. The voice is lost.

In bilateral thyroarytenoid paralysis there is some impairment of adductor function but only little difficulty with abduction. The glottis assumes an oval rather than a linear shape during phonation. There is no dyspnea or stridor. The voice is hoarse.

In cricothyroid paralysis the vocal fold tension is impaired, and the folds elongate in phonation. The result is a deep, hoarse voice, without high tones, and ready fatigability. There is no dyspnea or stridor, and inspiration is normal.

Laryngeal Dysfunction and Autonomic Nerves

The parasympathetic and sympathetic nerves travel to the larynx along with the vascular network and provide for secretion and vasomotor activity. Although autonomic nerves are not proved to be involved in muscle contraction and laryngeal motility, effects on phonation have been reported (Luchsinger and Arnold, 1965).

Nonspecific inflammation of one vocal fold (vasomotor monochorditis) is a sympatholaryngeal syndrome, produced by excessive use of a vocal fold already weakened.

Contact ulcers of the vocal folds are caused not only by mechanical trauma, as by forceful phonation, but also by emotional factors involving the autonomic nervous system (Wolcott, 1956).

Laryngeal Obstruction

The laryngeal mucous membrane is only loosely bound down except at the laryngeal surface of the epiglottis and the vocal ligaments. This facilitates obstruction following the accumulation of fluid in the loose areolar submucous tissue.

The lumen of the larynx may be obstructed from many causes including the traumatic crushing of cartilages, the pressure of growths, and the presence of foreign bodies. In the preimmunization days of diphtheria it was common to find a membrane which formed in the throat and spread to the larynx.

Laryngectomy

In the surgical treatment of the larynx, as in cancer, partial or total laryngectomy is done.

There are different methods of partial laryngectomy. *Laryngofissure,* or *thyrotomy,* allows access to a growth by splitting the thyroid cartilage. In *hemilaryngectomy* a partial or complete removal of one vocal fold is done. An *epiglottidectomy* is performed if the tumor is limited to the epiglottis.

Total laryngectomy, or complete removal of the larynx, may be indicated if there is fixation of one fold, extensive involvement in slow-growing tumors, subglottic extension of fast-growing tumors, or even involvement of an extrinsic part of the larynx. When growth has spread beyond the laryngeal boundaries, the removal of the lymph glands in the neck is also carried out. Where the pharynx also becomes involved, a partial *pharyngectomy* is carried out in the affected region. The total operation is a pharyngolaryngectomy.

In complete removal, the larynx may be excised from below the cricoid cartilage up to the hyoid bone, although the cricoid may remain attached to the trachea. The stump of the trachea is brought out anteriorly and sutured to the cervical skin so that breathing must take place through this new opening and no longer through the nose or the mouth. The opening of the pharynx into the larynx is closed, and the pharynx communicates at that region only with the esophagus. The reader is referred to Jackson and Jackson (1959) and Ballenger (1969).

The Asai operation is a three-stage procedure in which the trachea is loosened and elevated, the stoma placed higher, and, in a graft series, an air tube is constructed up the neck to the oral cavity so that sound can be produced on any exhalation. It is claimed that speech is immediate with postoperative recovery, even including regional accent qualities. Preoperative criteria, however, are lacking.

286

Speech without Vocal Folds

The production of a pseudovoice has become an integral part of the management of laryngectomies, and the orientation and training for this are instituted prior to surgery. The patient learns that the larynx is not absolutely essential to speech and that words can be formed in his supraglottic structures including the lips, tongue, cheek, and palate.

Several methods exist by which artificial voice (alaryngeal speech) is produced, and the best methods involve teaching the patient to use the remnants of his own speech apparatus. Artificial mechanical devices are best reserved for those who cannot master their own biologic structures.

Buccal Whisper

In a *buccal whisper* the air that is always accumulated in the mouth and pharynx is used instead of that ordinarily expelled from the lung passages. Quick articulatory movements are made. The method does not satisfactorily produce speech sounds. In many cases only the family or friends of the patient are able to understand his speech, which is of a Donald Duck variety.

Esophageal Voice

The method known as *esophageal* voice (or speech), if it can be learned, is preferable to other methods. Many patients master the technic within one or two months, although a fair number fail to master it and very few become proficient. Women dislike it because of the embarrassing "belch" quality. The voice is usually lacking in volume and rough because of inefficient control by the cricopharyngeal muscle (esophageal sphincter).

The patient must not revert to the buccal whisper; in esophageal speech the esophagus must be kept open, but in the former process voice is produced by the high pressure of air built up in the mouth with a tightly closed esophagus.

The essentials of sound production are somewhat similar in both normal and esophageal speech. In the former, exhaled pulmonary air passes through the narrow glottis between the vocal folds. In the latter, the air trapped in the upper esophagus, which acts as a substitute lung, is expelled through the closely approximated surfaces of the cricopharyngeal sphincter, or *pseudoglottis,* and in turn it is sent into the pharynx. The sound formed in this way is molded into speech by the lips, teeth, cheek, tongue, and palate.

In the early attempts to teach esophageal voice, the patient was instructed to swallow air and belch it forth. There is an objection to swallowing air to the degree that it travels as far down as the stomach because it is not readily erucated upon demand. Although a trained person manages to cease swallowing air, he can gain more by the use of pharyngeal and tongue movements. It thus became apparent that methods other than swallowing should be sought to continually replenish the air. Also, the vicarious "lung" should best be the esophagus.

In the method of *aspiration,* air is aspirated into the esophagus synchronously with the inspiratory phase of breathing. There is an exaggerated and rapid descent of the diaphragm. A disadvantage is that of having to pay considerable attention to breathing during early training.

In the method of *injection,* tiny quantities of air are injected into the esophagus from the mouth, prior to speech. With closed lips, along with some tension put upon the cheeks and tongue to elevate the soft palate, air is compressed within the mouth and pushed into the throat, during an inspiration preceding phonation (Snidecor, 1962). Although breathing and pseudovoice are coordinated, there are arguments against respiration and intrathoracic pressure playing a significant part in the production of the pseudovoice. Greene (1964) contends that esophageal voice occurs only during lung expiration, always being preceded by inspiration, and that these facts should form the basis of vocal training.

Pharyngeal Voice

It is possible to develop *pharyngeal voice* when the upper esophagus cannot be utilized as a vicarious lung. The air is harbored in the hypopharynx and sent upward by progressive sphincter activity about the pharyngeal space. The posterior pharyngeal wall and base of the tongue combine to act as a pseudoglottis.

The actual location of the pseudoglottis in laryngectomized persons varies according to many circumstances. In pharyngolaryngectomy, for example, where the upper esophagus and hypopharyngeal muscles have been removed, the air must be vibrated by a narrowing of the lower esophagus at some point. The precision of the voice is dependent upon the location of the pseudoglottis. The most advantageous site is above the esophagus, where the muscles and nerves can be adaptively managed for articulation (West and Ansberry, 1968).

Artificial Larynx

For those who cannot master esophageal speech, there are artificial larynges. An air-driven *reed* type, available since 1926 from the Bell Telephone System, is inefficient and destined for obsolescence, but there are models of improved design. The principle involves the use of a flexible rubber tube, attached at one end to the cannula of the tracheal opening and at the other end into the mouth. If the tracheal opening is manipulated by hand, the lung air can be directed into a reed which fits into the circuit just below the oral end of the instrument. This changes the upwardly directed air into a buzz or into tones within the normal voice range. The sounds are converted into speech by the existing natural resonators and articulators.

A preferable type of instrument is electrically driven. It consists of a battery-operated vibrator over which a diaphragm is stretched. The instrument is pressed against the outside of the throat at about the level of the excised thyroid cartilage. The diaphragm is made to vibrate, and it produces sound waves that pass through the throat tissues and into the mouth, where they are articulated by the lips and tongue. The voice is monotonous and unnatural.

The Bell Telephone Company has produced a transistorized electrolarynx, a small cylinder housing a modified telephone receiver or transducer that serves as a throat vibrator, a transistorized pulse generator with pitch control, and batteries. The cylinder is pressed against the throat, and speech is formed by movements of the vocal tract. The output of the instrument contains many inharmonic noises, not pure, periodic musical tones. From this the individual forms vowels, semivowels, nasal sounds, and a few consonants.

Other machines are under research and development. Intraoral types involve microtransmitters and loudspeakers housed in artificial dentures to emit audible sound waves.

10 THE VELOPHARYNGEAL MECHANISM: THE PALATE

The larynx produces audible sounds, but they do not constitute speech. Supra-glottic structures resonate characteristically to the laryngeal tones and add specific qualities to them. The tongue, lips, and teeth then shape the final sounds, and the individual voice acquires its unique quality.

In voice production the velum and the pharynx constitute a coupled velopharyn-geal mechanism in which the pharynx is significant in the activity called resonation. The velum is not a resonator per se but is classified with the articulators. How-ever, it helps regulate resonance in the oral and nasal cavities.

Resonance

The nature of resonance and its manner of production have been described in Chapter 2. It is pertinent to consider resonance again, from a somewhat different standpoint.

Definition

Borden and Busse (1929) define resonance as the reflection of the condensation phases of a large number of air waves such that they are focused at or close to the narrowed outlet of a cavity. The physical instruments or bodily structures used to intensify the sounds or produce a resonant quality are called resonators.

Anderson (1961) defines resonance as an action which develops the potentialities present in the laryngeal tone. There is such a reflection and concentration of sound waves that there is a significant increase in the energy output of the vibrating structures. Although the total number of overtones of a speech sound and their relation in pitch to the fundamental are chiefly a function of the basic structure of the vibrating body, the relative intensities of these overtones are greatly dependent upon resonance. Hahn et al. (1957) consider resonance as the process of reinforcement and amplification of the fundamental and its overtones.

Resonance may be physically defined in one way as the prolongation and intensification of sound caused by the transmission of its vibrations to a cavity. It is a drumlike reverberation obtainable from a cavity filled with air. It is a vibrant sound, as distinguished from a dull sound. The latter is a flat, colorless, uninteresting sound representing a decrease or absence of resonance. Physically, resonance in a single cavity is like the sound produced by blowing over the mouth of an empty bottle. In the speech apparatus we do not necessarily deal with single or empty cavities, and the statements made above do not adequately describe the biologic facts.

Resonance and quality are not synonymous; a voice having a disagreeable quality may not be lacking in resonance, although it may possess too much of the wrong kind.

290

Resonance and Amplification of Sound

Resonance produces significant amplification of the sound in addition to imparting a given shading to the quality of the resonated sound. Thus McBurney and Wrage (1953) state that without resonance the vocal fold tone would be inaudible even a short distance away. Berry and Eisenson (1956) caution against always relating resonance to increased vocal intensity and cite literature to the effect that the intensity of sound at the mouth is weaker than its value at the larynx, but this is at variance with the prevalent view that the tone at the laryngeal level is weak and requires strengthening by positive resonance. Westlake and Rutherford (1966) state that the intensity of the harmonics progressively diminishes in the vocal tract and only the lower harmonics would be audible if it were not for the supraglottic resonators.

It may be said that when the vocal tract is highly efficient in transferring the kinetic energy of the airstream into acoustic energy, or sound, resonance occurs and there is amplification of sound. If there is interference with the laryngeal vibrations, negative resonance, or *impedance,* exists and *attenuation* (weakening) of the voice occurs.

Attenuation may be due to absorption of the kinetic energy by the laryngeal walls, i.e., conversion to bound energy or heat, or to the fact that the response frequency of the vocal chambers does not match that of the laryngeal tone. The resonating structures can add discordant partials to the sound because of excessive tenseness in the mouth, nose, and throat.

Berry and Eisenson (1956) note that voice quality has a laryngeal and vocal tract dependency. The contribution of the latter is very great. As an illustration, voice communication from divers to persons on the surface of water is impaired due to poor quality. The essential problem is that the divers breathe a helium mixture, in which the velocity of sound exceeds that in air. This does not appreciably affect vocal cord frequency, but it affects the acoustic resonances of the vocal tract. Even though the fundamental voice pitch is unaltered, the amplitudes or loudness values of the harmonics change greatly.

Essentially, air is resonated much as organ pipes of various lengths resonate the sounds formed in their vibrational system. Reinforcement may occur when the laryngeal vibrations cause latent air in the supraglottic spaces to vibrate in tune with one or more partials of the incident waves. Damping occurs through selective absorption of the energy of certain tones by soft surfaces or else through neutralization of the energy by other movements in the same space. Most of the total energy of any speech sound lies in its fundamental and first harmonic (Heffner, 1960).

Nature of the Responsiveness: Formants

The vocal tract responds especially to those sounds which are at or near its own natural frequencies. These values for the tract change with its own changing shapes. In the highly mobile oral cavity the relative nature and strength of the partials are varied almost indefinitely.

The responsiveness of the vocal tract is clearly dependent upon its resonator activity. A resonator is a selective body that responds to a particular frequency, i.e., its resonant frequency. Actually, resonators respond to a narrow range of frequencies called the *bandwidth*. A formant expresses the bandwidth wherein a resonator responds to a given sound. In the body the formants refer to the resonants of the vocal tract, and characteristic formant frequencies are associated with any form assumed by the tract. The lowest formant frequency is called the first formant, the next higher is the second, and so on.

The effect of resonation is not to alter the frequency of the harmonics but rather to emphasize the amplitudes of certain harmonics.

Methods of Producing Resonance

Resonance has been discussed as being produced in three ways (Hahn et al., 1957; McBurney and Wrage, 1953), all methods operating independently or simultaneously.

In the first method, sound waves in a tube are reflected when hitting a surface, and the reflections change with the hardness and smoothness of the surface and also with the size of the tubal opening. This reflective resonance is effective in modifying the fundamental tone.

A second kind of resonance is that which occurs when sounds brought into contact with bodily structures produce a responsive vibration of these structures. This is forced or sounding-board resonation. Its role in speech appears to be minor.

A third method is that of sympathetic vibration. If two resonators are tuned to the same frequency and one of them is sounded in the vicinity of the other, the silent one will pick up the vibrations. In the vocal cavities an air column may vibrate in sympathy with a frequency sounded at the opening of the cavity. If the vocal cavities could assume only one particular form, they would vibrate sympathetically to a narrow range of frequencies. This modification would occur because their capacity to respond would be determined by the cavity volume and by the shape and size of its apertures. Since the mouth and pharynx have variable but controllable sizes and shapes, they can selectively respond to a broad range of overtones. This is less true for the relatively fixed nasal chambers.

Resonators in general are of two types, the cavity or the sounding-board type (Kantner and West, 1960). The latter may be represented by the piano or by placing a sounded tuning fork on a table; it is observed in the body by resonance in the chest walls, hard palate, bones of the cranium, and elsewhere. Cavity resonance is found in musical horns, and in the body it is produced as a tuned response in such cavities as the nose, mouth, pharynx, and larynx. Cavity resonance is the form usually meant when the unrestricted term resonance is employed.

292   Raubicheck (1952) says that faults in voice quality result from wrongly emphasized use of any one of the primary cavity resonators.

Akin (1958) calls the mouth, nasal passages and pharynx the primary cavity resonators and says that relaxed, open resonators generally produce a pleasant vocal effect.

The effects of the sounding-board type of resonance indicate that structures not usually designated as speech organs may contribute to speech (Fletcher, 1953). The ribs and sternum may be felt to vibrate and be heard by the stethoscope to do so during phonation. The facial bones are particularly active as sounding boards at medium and high frequencies, whereas the sternum and neighboring bones tend to vibrate at lower frequencies. The contribution of the chest at low frequencies is illustrated by the change of voice heard in an experimental subject placed knee-deep and then neck-high in water.

Moses (1954) lists the resonators for the voice as being in the mouth, nose, nasal sinuses, nasopharynx, pharynx, chest, and Morgagni's ventricles. He states that low tones receive their resonance low in the chest whereas the high tones find their resonator in the mouth, nose, or nasopharynx.

Resonance and Affective States

Resonance is influenced by emotions and other affective states. The nasal mucosa, which is important to resonance, is closely related to the swell bodies of the sex organs and shows functional changes in sexual activity, menstruation, pregnancy, and also in emotions apparently unrelated to sexual activity. Nasal mucosal swelling and discharge affect the voice. Recollections of emotional states may call forth such changes, and thus the neurotic may have vocal symptoms.

Resonance and Pitch

Resonation is involved in the concept of optimum pitch, which is the general pitch level of an individual at which he can best emit full, resonant, and rich tones. At the optimum pitch, phonation is very efficient, with a minimum of muscular action.

Velopharyngeal Activity and Culs-de-sac

The vibrations of the vocal folds, after being resonated, are collected within the restricted exit of the mouth or of the nose. The differential emphasis upon nasal or oral resonance is determined by whether the airstream can pass freely through the nose or the mouth or whether one of these chambers has been narrowed so that the stream is shunted through the path of least resistance. An individual learns to close his mouth or nose just to the proper degree for acceptable speech. Cerebrospinal control over the voluntary muscles in the involved areas, particularly the palatal muscles that raise or lower the velum, provides this facility.

The concept of the *cul-de-sac* is implied. If air is blown through a horn having a hollow diverticulum, the tone of the horn is altered. The diverticulum, or blind pouch, is the cul-de-sac. The sound emitted from such an instrument is blended from both the horn and the pouch. The same principle holds for the mouth and nose openings. Air from the pharynx is sent into either the mouth or the nose, depending on the muscular action, and it is fractionated in a specific ratio between the mouth and the nose.

In nasal sounds the fauces leading to the mouth is narrowed, and the mouth acts as the cul-de-sac. The nose becomes the cul-de-sac in sounds chiefly involving oral resonance. In cleft palate the speech is nasal because there is a change in the ratio between nasal and oral resonance.

In the oral (nonnasal) English sounds the soft palate is directed toward the pharyngeal wall. There is possibly a simultaneous protrusion of the pterygopharyngeal muscle (Passavant's cushion). The exhaled air is preferentially directed into the oral cavity. The closure of the nasopharynx is said to be produced by a palatopharyngeal sphincter. This mechanism involves the superior constrictor muscle of the pharynx, the levator palati muscle, and the glossopalatine and pharyngopalatine muscles of the palate.

Berry and Eisenson (1956) state that although the velum and pharynx close the entrance to the nose for all except nasal sounds, the closure is variable. In some bass resonant voices the nasopharynx could be kept open most of the time without producing nasality and, in fact, even enriching the timbre of the voice. Van Riper

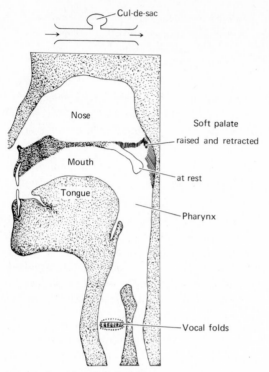

Figure 10-1 Diagrammatic sagittal view of pharyngeal area showing the changing positions of the soft palate at rest and when elevated. In the elevated position the nasal chambers are cut off to act as culs-de-sac (hidden recesses), and the airstream flows out almost entirely through the mouth.

294

and Irwin (1958) state that although one should not expect velopharyngeal closure to be airtight in nonnasal sounds, the degree of closure is important. Luchsinger and Arnold (1965) write that a distance of a few millimeters of the inferior margin of the velum from the posterior pharyngeal wall is physiologic but that when distances of 8 to 10 mm occur, increased nasality is expected. They note further that consonants usually require tight closure and that sibilants are most sensitive to nasal air escape.

Closure is much stronger in gagging or swallowing than in speech. The nature of the movements also differ, being sphincteric in swallowing and mostly elevating in speech. The last statement is controversial since although, in the classical view, the soft palate moves upward and rearward against the back wall of the pharynx (Murphy, 1964), the sphincteric concept of closure may adequately explain the process (Luchsinger and Arnold, 1965).

The Hard Palate

The hard palate is the bony **anterior** part of the partition which separates the oral and nasal cavities. It is **bounded** in front and on the sides by the alveolar and tooth-bearing arch of the upper jaw (maxilla) and in back by the pendulous **soft** palate. The boundary between the hard and soft palates is easily determined by pressing a finger against the **roof** of the mouth behind the central incisors and sliding the finger posteriorly until the roof tissue is found to yield. The hard palate is generally vault-shaped, and the **soft** palate is veillike.

Posteriorly, the hard palate **has a sharp** crescentic border on each side, separated by a median, posterior nasal spine. Its (superior) alveolar process is U-shaped, and has sixteen teeth when fully **developed**; its posterior end, the tuber maxillae, is free.

With the head erect, the hard **palate** is almost horizontal and is at the level of the atlas.

The hard palate is formed in **its anterior** two-thirds by the paired palatine **processes** of the maxillary bone and in **its posterior** one-third by the paired horizontal plates of the palatine bones. A transverse palatine suture marks the line of fusion of these bones.

The bony framework of the **hard palate** is penetrated by canals and foramina. The incisive canal is in the median **plane**, anteriorly. This canal connects the hard palate with the nasal cavity. **The** greater (major) palatine foramina are at the posterior corners of the hard **palate**, opposite the root of the last molar tooth on each side. They represent the **lower** part of the pterygopalatine canal, which is an extension of the pterygopalatine **fossa**. Nerves and blood vessels utilize these passageways.

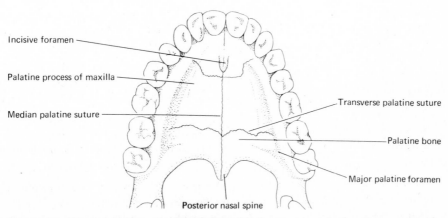

Incisive foramen

Palatine process of maxilla

Median palatine suture

Transverse palatine suture

Palatine bone

Major palatine foramen

Posterior nasal spine

Figure 10-2 The hard palate seen from below with the mucosa and other tissues removed.

The hard palate is covered by mucous membrane fused with the periosteal covering of the bone. In surgery of cleft palate the entire mucoperiosteum can be separated from the bone. The mucous membrane is continuous with that which lines the surrounding areas. It is very thick, especially at the alveolar margin, where it becomes continuous with the gums, or gingivae. The continuity facilitates the spread of dentoalveolar abscesses to the vault of the palate.

Sharp et al. (1956) divide the hard palate into three zones. There is a peripheral zone which is continuous with the dense gingiva and whose surface texture is firm, resistant, and smooth. A second, or central, zone extends along the center of the palate and covers the entire length of the structure. In the front part of the central zone irregular branching ridges, or rugae, cross the palate transversely. The rugae are composed of dense connective tissue overlaid by a cornified epithelium. Between the central and peripheral zones there is a third or intermediate zone, in which the mucosa is firmly adherent to the periosteum of the palate.

Functions are reflected in structure. A loose and movable mucosa would not favor crushing food between the palate and tongue. Anteriorly, the palatal rugae facilitate contact between the palate and the tongue. These ridges tend to disappear in old age.

The epithelial surface just behind the rugae is a region of considerable tactile sensibility which aids responses to taste upon tongue contact. Tactile sensitivity allows, through feedback into the nervous system, the accurate formation of speech sounds requiring palatal-tongue contact.

There are pinpoint orifices of ducts of glands everywhere over the hard (and soft) palates, and they give the hard palate an orange-skin cast. The ducts lead into mucous glands, which form a carpet under the mucous membrane.

Central to the alveolar arch, which provides sockets for the teeth, the hard palate is arched, with wide individual variations in height and breadth. The topography is important in that it is used in the description of many speech sounds. Oral resonance can be modified by a low or high, narrow vault. The density, rigidity, and tension of the palate also affect resonance.

The Soft Palate

The soft palate is the mobile and muscular posterior section of the partition between the oral and nasal cavities and between the mouth and pharynx. It is attached anteriorly (at its oral surface) to the hard palate and laterally to the side walls of the pharynx; it curves downward and backward into the pharynx.

The soft palate is variously called the velum palati, velum mobile, velum pendulum palati, septum palati, valvula palati, and claustrum of the palate. The velum is often synonymous with the soft palate, although it is more generally considered to be the lower portion of the soft palate that hangs down like an incomplete curtain.

The framework of the entire soft palate is the palatine aponeurosis, a fibrous sheet to which several muscles are attached. The aponeurosis is best developed in the anterior portion of the velum, where practically no muscle fibers exist.

Stratified squamous epithelium covers the oral surface of the soft palate, whereas ciliated columnar epithelium characteristic of the upper respiratory passages covers its nasal aspect.

Speech Function

The velum is of considerable importance in speech since it changes the size of the apertures between the pharynx and the mouth and between the pharynx and the nose. It can vary the degree of oral and nasal resonance. When it is relaxed, as in quiet respiration, it is obliquely dependent and partially obstructs the aperture between the pharynx and the mouth. This port can be narrowed further by the active contraction of the glossopalatal and pharyngopalatal muscles, which produce a riding-in of the palatal arches, or pillars of the fauces. For example, the velum is lowered in producing nasal tones, whereas it may be elevated by such actions as yawning or panting. Relaxation and depression of the arches may thus be opposed by tension and elevation.

The soft palate can rise variably with certain sounds. For example, it rises very little for the vowel /ɑ/ as in father and hardly touches the pharyngeal wall. It

297

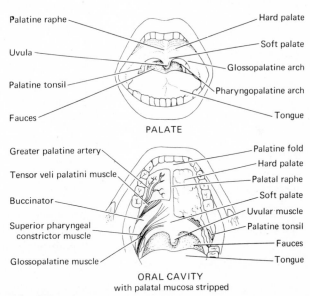

Figure 10-3 Top: Composition of the soft palate; Bottom: structures related to the hard palate as seen after removal of the mucosa.

rises progressively and hits the pharyngeal wall with increasing force for the vowels /o/ as in soap, /e/ as in ate, /i/ as in eat, and /u/ as in blue.

Uvula

The unpaired uvula is a cone-shaped structure of variable size, projecting downward from the center of the free lower border of the velum toward the fauces. It contains glands, connective tissue, and some muscle fibers. A definite uvula is present only in monkeys and man, although it appears in lower mammals.

The uvular or azygus muscle (musculus uvulae) is frequently paired and consists of slender slips which originate from the posterior nasal spine and the palatine aponeurosis. The fibers run through the soft palate. As they come in medially from both sides, they fuse before attaching to the mucous membrane of the uvula. The muscle shortens the uvula and brings the structure upward and backward.

The uvula is active in swallowing. Its movements are accessory to the ascent of the paired palatopharyngeal arches. Such movement shuts off the nasopharynx from the oropharynx, thus directing food downward.

The uvula is said to be important in helping the other parts of the palate protect the openings of the Eustachian tubes. It has been thought to direct mucous drainage from the nasal chambers toward the base of the tongue. Accumulated secretions on the nasal floor in acute infections are aided in expulsion into the mouth by uvular movement during expiration.

298

The uvula prevents excessive nasality of voice by controlling the resonance of the air column just over the larynx. It has attained phonetic significance in that it can be employed to make trilled sounds such as the uvular /r/ sound.

The uvula may be abnormally long, thick, or bifurcate (double). The long uvula can act as a foreign body and can impair the use of the soft palate in producing vowels. Van Riper and Irwin (1958) state that a long uvula is a rare cause of excessive nasality. The long, moist structure can cling to the rear of the tongue and be freed too slowly to prevent the air from being directed through the nasal chambers.

The long or redundant uvula is not ordinarily excised unless malignancy or protracted annoyance is present. In shortening an elongated uvula, care is taken to preserve the uvular muscle. Uvular resection (staphylectomy) may lead to disturbances of speech and deglutition.

All told, the uvula is functional, and it should not be regarded as a degenerate or vestigial remnant of vertebrate phylogeny. Actually, it has not made its biologic appearance until relatively recent time. It is absent in mammalian animals as high as the opossum.

The Fauces (Isthmus of the Fauces; Oropharyngeal Isthmus)

This is the port between the mouth and the pharynx. It is bounded superiorly by the velum, inferiorly by the root of the tongue, and laterally by the palatal arches.

Palatal Arches (Faucial Pillars)
The arches are important in speech because of their function in velopharyngeal closure and resonance. Their valvular effect is important to swallowing. They function in breathing in that their relaxation provides a free passage of air from the nose to the lungs.

The glossopalatal arches (anterior pillars of the fauces) are a pair of prominent folds located in the right and left lateral pharyngeal wall. Each contains a glosso-palatal muscle covered by mucous membrane.

The pharyngopalatal arches (posterior pillars) are directly behind the anterior arch on either side. Each contains a pharyngopalatal muscle covered by mucous membrane. The posterior arches diverge from the anterior arches to produce on each side triangular fossae, or depressions, in which the palatine tonsils are held.

Tonsils
The tonsils are lymphoid masses forming a discontinuous (Waldeyer's) ring, which surrounds the entrance to the oropharynx. Small collections of lymphoid tissue fill the intervals between the larger masses.

The *palatine* (faucial) tonsils are paired, soft, and bulging submucosal lymphoid masses enclosed between the anterior and posterior palatal arches on each side in a space called the tonsillar fossa. Their shape is variable but typically oval and flat. Their size is also variable. They are relatively (and in some instances actually) larger in children than in adults, but they shrink significantly after puberty.

299

A part of each tonsil is embedded, while the remainder projects and is visible upon inspection. The medial or pharyngeal surface is free except anteriorly. Mucous membrane covers the medial surface, and it presents twelve to fifteen orifices (fossulae tonsillares) leading into crypts that branch and penetrate the tonsillar substance. The cells of the surface, as well as those lining the crypts of the palatine tonsils, are stratified epithelium, like the cells that line the mouth. Mucous glands are abundant. Their ducts open onto the free surface and into the crypts.

The lateral surface of these tonsils is covered with a fibrous capsule, which is separated by connective tissue from the superior constrictor muscle of the pharynx, and to some extent from the palatopharyngeus muscle.

The palatine tonsils are the best-known members of the tonsillar ring and perhaps the most frequent cause of tonsillar pathology. These are the structures meant when the unrestricted term tonsils is used.

The unpaired *pharyngeal* tonsil (adenoid) is a lymphoid mass at the superior end of the pharynx, situated chiefly on its posterior aspect. This structure is most prominent in children, and it shrivels or disappears in adults. In the hypertrophied state it is called the adenoids (pleural).

The pharyngeal tonsil is composed of several lobules, which are particularly evident during its enlargement, but it has only one area of attachment, to the roof of the

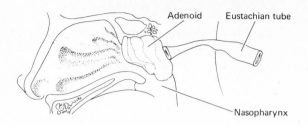

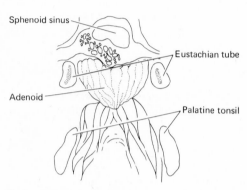

Figure 10-4 Top: Lateral view of the nasopharynx to show the pharyngeal tonsil; Bottom: the adenoid viewed directly after removing all structures anterior to it.

pharynx. Actually, this structure belongs to the pharynx. The cells of the surface of this tonsil and its follicles are ciliated columnar epithelium like the main part of the nose.

The *lingual* tonsil is a collection of lymph follicles covering the entire surface of the root of the tongue, lying directly below the mucous membrane and imparting a nodular appearance to this area. The lateral ends of each of these aggregations meet the lower poles of the palatine tonsils.

Just in front of the lingual tonsil is the foramen cecum; it marks the oral opening of the remnants of the thyroglossal duct, which in development led to the thyroid gland.

The lingual tonsils are not as large as the palatine tonsils, and they also do not have a complex crypt structure. They are rarely acutely infected concurrently with the palatine tonsils.

Functions and Pathology

The tonsillar ring is a first line of defense against bodily infection. Parts of this lymphoid ring affect the character of speech because of their active defense reactions which involve inflammation and edema.

The exact functions of the tonsils have never been proved, but several views exist: (1) they protect against bacterial invasion; (2) they are endocrine glands; (3) they are blood-forming organs; (4) they are exposed lymph nodes for secretion or excretion; (5) they provide antibodies; and (6) they protect the bronchial tubes against infection.

Hypertrophy (excessive size increase) of the palatine tonsils is perhaps the most common type of tonsillar pathology, especially in children. Excessive enlargement may partially occlude the mouth from the oropharynx. The next most common disorder is acute infection. Organisms and mucosal cells fill the follicles or crypts. Repeated attacks lead to infection in the Eustachian tube, middle ear, mastoid air cells, upper respiratory passages, brain, or even distant organs. This view of focal infection may not be as serious as was formerly believed.

Enlarged adenoids can block off the nasal cavity from the pharynx and distort nasal resonance. Snorting and snoring are characteristic sequelae. Enlarged adenoids may close the openings of the Eustachian tubes, with resulting inability to equalize pressure in the middle ear. The adenoids are said to contribute mechanically to distortion of the palate, narrowing and arching the vault of the mouth. Adenoids also encourage mouth breathing.

The problem of when tonsillectomy is indicated is far from solved. It depends primarily upon the seriousness of the infection and not upon the distortion of oral or nasal resonance. The tonsils and adenoids form part of a discontinuous ring, and the mere largeness of the components of this ring means nothing in itself. Throughout infancy and early childhood the incidence of respiratory infections is high, and if tonsillectomy is done then, it may unjustly be credited with reducing the frequency of such infections. It may be that the tonsils help establish immunity toward respiratory infections and recede when this has been accomplished.

Adenoids and tonsils differ considerably in their relative need for removal, and many of the reasons claimed for tonsillectomy are really reasons for adenoidectomy. Repeated earache, deafness, otitis media, and other symptoms of tubal blockage are relieved more by adenoidectomy than by removing the tonsils, which lie a little distance away.

During convalescence from tonsillectomy and adenoidectomy, the tonal quality of the voice can change but generally returns to normal. After adenoid removal there may be hyperresonance. This condition may require some relearning in the activity of the muscles involved. The situation can be complicated by taking a hyponasality problem due to adenoids and providing therapy to increase nasal resonance. Then postoperatively there may be an extreme hypernasality problem.

Pathology of the lingual tonsils is often overlooked. These tonsils also may become hypertrophied and in turn can influence the palatine tonsils above them and the epiglottis below them. If excessively large, the lingual tonsils interfere with deglutition and speech. Tremble (1957) asks for more attention to this area because of the possibility of malignancy.

Muscles of the Soft Palate

Muscles include depressor-relaxers (glossopalatinus and pharyngoplatinus), elevators (levator veli palatini and musculus uvulae), and an elevator-tensor (tensor veli palatini). Elevation is exemplified in swallowing in which the nasopharynx tends toward occlusion. Depression is exemplified in normal respiration in which the nasal port is kept open. The levator, tensor, and uvular muscles belong to the palate alone. The others are, in addition, a part of the lingual and pharyngeal mechanisms.

The *musculus uvulae* has already been described. It is coordinated with the levator and tensor muscles in elevating the posterior aspect of the uvula.

The paired *levator veli palatini* (soft palate elevator, levator palati) is a pencil-thick muscle located in the superior lateral pharyngeal wall lateral to each posterior naris, or choana. It originates from the petrous part of the temporal bone and the cartilage of the auditory tube. It passes downward and medially and attaches to the palatine aponeurosis, in which its fibers blend with those of the opposite side. It enlarges the fauces by lifting the soft palate upward and backward. It also elevates and widens the pharyngeal opening of the Eustachian tube during swallowing. This muscle forms the major mass of the soft palate.

The paired *tensor veli palatini* muscle (soft palate tensor, tensor palati) is a ribbon-like mass anterior and lateral to the palatal elevator. It arises at the base of skull, on the medial pterygoid lamina, on the inferior surface of the sphenoid, and on the cartilage of the Eustachian tube (see Figure 12–9 for an illustration of the sphenoid bone). The muscle passes downward and forward and ends in a tendon which goes medially into the soft palate. The fibers insert upon the posterior border of the palatine bone and fuse partly with the fibers on the other side. The muscle tenses the anterior portion of the soft palate, which then serves as a fixed band to which the other palatal muscles are attached. It assists the levator in raising the soft palate and in carrying it posteriorly to the pharyngeal wall. It also helps open the Eustachian tube by action on its cartilaginous wall. The tensor is relaxed in speech for all English sounds except the three nasal resonants.

The paired *glossopalatal* (palatoglossus) muscle is also called the constrictor of the fauces, and it extends between the soft palate and each side of the tongue. It forms with the mucous membrane the glossopalatine arch. It originates from the anterior aspect of the velum and goes downward, forward, and laterally. It inserts into the side and dorsum of the tongue. Diamond (1952) states that the fibers bend transversely to enter the median septum of the tongue, so that they aid in forming a more or less circular sphincter. The fibers are then said to continue as transverse intrinsic tongue fibers. The muscle may draw the tongue upward and backward. In reverse, it draws the glossopalatine arch down and medialward. These actions decrease the anterior aspect of the faucial port.

The paired *pharyngopalatus* (palatopharyngeus) is a long thin muscle forming with the mucous membrane the pharyngopalatal arch. It originates from the soft palate, passes laterally and downward, and inserts in common with the stylopharyngeus on the posterior border of the thyroid cartilage.

The chief action of the pharyngopalatal muscle is to bring together the pharyngopalatal arches, an action which depresses the soft palate and narrows the posterior faucial port. In reverse, the muscle raises the larynx and the lower larynx, as in the first stage of swallowing. This elevation is assisted by the stylopharyngeus muscle.

Salpingopharyngeus Muscle (paired) At the superior end of the pharyngopalatus muscle some fibers continue upward on each side as the salpingopharyngeus. The latter lies between the posterolateral aspect of the pharynx and the lower border of the Eustachian tube near its orifice. The muscle opens the Eustachian tube or elevates the pharynx while narrowing it from the sides.

In résumé, these muscles are important for speech. The soft palate becomes tensed. The levator veli palatini lifts the palate upward and backward and brings it close to the posterior pharyngeal wall. At the same time the superior constrictor muscle of the pharynx helps to constrict the pharyngeal lumen. The nasopharynx is narrowed to a degree varying with the sound. The elevation of the soft palate is also variable according to the sound, and it reaches maximum height during blowing movements. The details of the entire dynamics involved in velopharyngeal closure and relaxation are still to be clarified.

These activities help separate the oral from the nasal cavity, and they allow the oral pressure necessary for speech to be built up. In cleft palate the air pressure essential for plosive consonants, such as /p/, is unobtainable since the oral and nasal cavities cannot be separated.

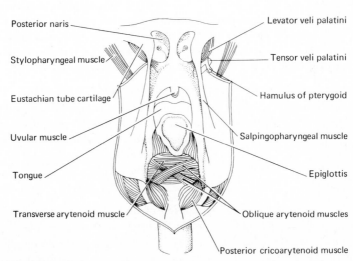

Figure 10-5 Muscles of the palate and pharynx as seen after reflection of the pharyngeal constrictors (posterior view).

The term *palatopharyngeal sphincter* is used to designate the action necessary during speech and blowing to obtain good efficiency with the least output of breath force while minimizing partial escape of the blast through the nose. The nasal resonants are exceptions to this statement.

Innervation and Blood Supply

The tensor veli palatini muscle is innervated by the internal pterygoid nerve, derived from the mandibular division of the trigeminal trunk. The uvular muscle is supplied by the spinal accessory nerve, which reaches the muscle by way of the pharyngeal plexus. The other muscles of the group may also be innervated by the spinal accessory, but this is not conclusive. These muscles are possibly also controlled through the sphenopalatine ganglion and the palatine nerves.

The nerves controlling the blood supply, sensation, and secretion for the palate go through the *sphenopalatine ganglion*. This is a nerve cell enlargement having sensory roots from the maxillary division of the trigeminal nerve and motor plus autonomic roots from the pterygoid or vidian nerve. The ganglion lies in the pterygopalatine fossa, a small triangular space deeply located among the facial bones directly below the apex of the orbit of the eye.

The sphenopalatine ganglion innervates the palate through several palatine nerves. The nasopalatines leave the pterygopalatine fossa through the sphenopalatine foramen and descend along the nasal septum. They penetrate the hard palate through the incisive foramen on each side, and they innervate the anterior section of the hard palate. The posterior palatal region and the entire soft palate receive three branches from the sphenopalatine ganglion; these nerves are the posterior palatine, the small posterior palatine, and the accessory posterior palatine. Since all the nerves from the ganglion contain somatic sensory fibers from the maxillary nerve, autonomic efferents from the facial nerve, and sympathetics from the superior cervical ganglion, the mucous membrane of the nose and palate has pathways to mediate general sensations of heat, cold, and pain; it also has secretory impulses for glandular activity and vasomotor impulses to control the diameter of its blood vessels.

The soft palate and the posterior section of the hard palate are supplied by the posterior or descending palatine arteries. These originate from the internal maxillary artery. The palatine vessels descend through the posterior palatine canals along with the posterior palatine nerves. They enter the palate through the greater palatine foramina and travel forward in the angle between the horizontal and vertical processes of the maxillary bones. The same arteries supply the tonsillar region.

The premaxillary, or front, portion of the hard palate obtains its blood from the anterior palatine arteries. These are terminal branches of the nasopalatine vessels, which in turn originate from the internal maxillary artery. The nasopalatines enter the nose from the pterygopalatine fossa through the sphenopalatine foramen and travel downward along the nasal septum to enter the oral cavity through the

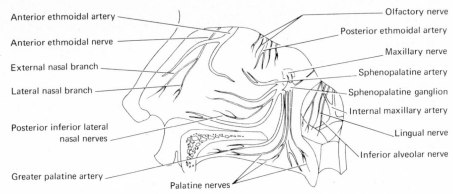

Anterior ethmoidal artery

Anterior ethmoidal nerve

External nasal branch

Lateral nasal branch

Posterior inferior lateral
nasal nerves

Greater palatine artery

Palatine nerves

Olfactory nerve

Posterior ethmoidal artery

Maxillary nerve

Sphenopalatine artery

Sphenopalatine ganglion

Internal maxillary artery

Lingual nerve

Inferior alveolar nerve

Figure 10-6 Vessels and nerves of the palatal area as seen in a sagittal section of the skull.

incisive (anterior palatine) canal. The nasopalatines supply the nose and paranasal sinus region before sending branches down into the anterior palatal area. These anterior palatine vessels anastomose with the anteriorly directed twigs of the posterior palatine arteries.

The veins of the palate follow the arteries, and they are tributaries of the pterygoid plexus.

The lymphatics drain the anterior portion of the hard palate by entering the anterior facial lymph vessels. These vessels in turn drain into the submaxillary and upper deep cervical nodes. The tongue uses the same route (Sharp et al., 1956). The lymphatics drain the hind part of the hard palate and the entire soft palate by taking a posterior route along the branches of the posterior facial vein into the anterior-superior deep cervical lymph nodes. The latter also drain the base of the tongue and the posterior sublingual area.

305

Developmental Anatomy

The stomodeum, or primitive mouth, is visible about the fourth week. It becomes surrounded by the frontonasal and the paired maxillary and mandibular processes.

The frontonasal process is above the mouth. It becomes separated by the appearance of paired olfactory pits into a lateral nasal process on the outer side of each pit and median nasal processes between the pits. The lateral nasal processes eventually form the lateral parts of the nose. The fusion of the two median nasal processes produces the septum and medial parts of the nose. The bridge of the nose comes from the frontal or upper part of the frontonasal process.

The median nasal processes help form the premaxillary region. A philtrum, or middle part of the upper lip, and also the upper incisor bony region will be produced when the median nasal processes fuse.

The maxillary processes produce the cheeks as well as the remainder of the upper lip not formed by the philtrum. They also form the floor of the nose, a considerable portion of the upper jaw, and most of the palatal region except for the premaxillary incisor area.

The mandibular processes give rise to the lower jaw and also to the lower lip. The maxillary processes and the mandibular processes merge with each other at the corners of the mouth.

The earliest fusion involves the median union of the paired mandibular processes late in the fourth week. In the sixth week, the frontonasal process has been separated by the developing olfactory pits into the median nasal processes and the lateral nasal processes. In the fifth and sixth weeks, the eyes are separated from the mouth by the central extensions of the maxillary processes. The maxillary processes then fuse with the lateral nasal processes. This joins the cheeks with the sides of the nose and, by forming a nasal floor, separates the stomodeum into nasal and oral chambers. Where the maxillary and lateral nasal processes fuse on each side, a nasolacrimal groove is seen. This later becomes a nasolacrimal, or tear, duct. It drains fluid from each eye into the nasal cavity.

In the seventh week, the median nasal processes fuse with each other in the midline and with the lower part of the maxillary processes laterally. The premaxillary bones bearing the incisor teeth form in that section of the upper jaw which is of medial nasal origin. The maxillary bones bearing all the other upper teeth form in that section of the arch coming from the maxillary processes. The arch of the upper jaw and also the palate are contributed to by both the medial nasal and maxillary processes. The original nasofrontal process contributes by the fusion of its nasal septal derivatives to the cephalic face of the palate.

In the sixth week the olfactory pits are shallow invaginations, but during the seventh week they are extended so that they open into the mouth just behind the premaxillary region. Their external openings are the nostrils, and their posterior openings are the choanae, or posterior nares.

The palate is coincidently being completed by a hard palate replacing the soft membranes. The activity involves a permant separation of the nasal from the oral cavities by the ingrowth of bones into the roof of the mouth. This is called secondary palate formation. This secondary roof of the mouth forces the choanae to open much more posteriorly so that the crossing of food and air, which is called the pharyngeal chiasm, is transferred from the mouth to the pharynx.

In this palatal formation, the premaxillary, maxillary, and palatine bones produce platelike extensions; these grow medially and meet in the midline. The hard palate begins in the sixth week with a central growth of palatal plates which have come from the maxillary process on each side. Fusion anteriorly with the premaxilla occurs in the seventh week, and complete midline closure occurs in the tenth week. The lower part of the nasal septum reaches the dorsum of the tongue until the sec-

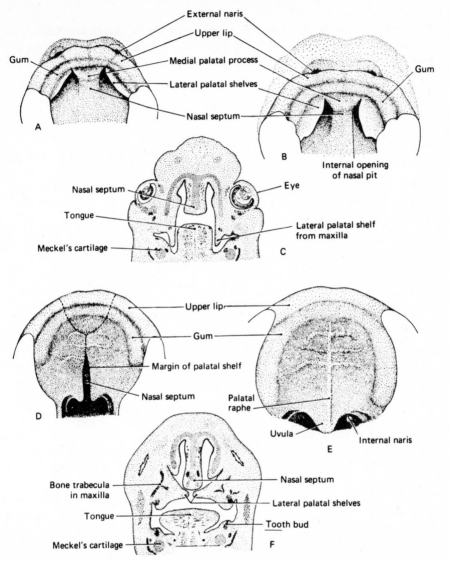

Figure 10–7 The development of the palate. (*a*) Upper jaw and roof of the mouth as seen from below in embryos a little over six weeks old (crown-rump length 14 to 15 mm). (*b*) Similar view in embryos of about seven weeks (crown-rump length 19 to 21 mm). (*c*) Projection drawing of a section through the head of a seven-week embryo showing how the palatal shelves at this stage are separated by the tongue. (*d*) The palate during the ninth week. Fusion of the lateral palatal shelves with each other is commencing rostrally and progressing toward the paired primordia of the uvula. Its extent is indicated by the median dotted line. The broken lines on either side indicate the part of the upper jaw, lip, and palate of nasomedial origin. (*e*) The palate in the last trimester of pregnancy. (*f*) Section of the head of an embryo late in the eighth week to show the change in relations of the palatal shelves to each other and to the nasal septum after the tongue moves down. (*From Bradley M. Patten, Human Embryology, 3d ed. Copyright 1968. McGraw-Hill Book Company. Used by permission.*)

ondary palatal plates fuse medially and separate these structures. The palatal plates fuse not only with the nasal septum, but their progressive median fusion continues posteriorly. At the ninth week, the anterior three-fourths of the septum are joined with the upper portion of the palate, and the posterior septal fourth is left free. In less than four months the nasal and oral cavities are completely separated by both hard and soft palates. The tongue first lies between the palatal shelves and then descends as the shelves grow in medially.

When the membranous ossifications of the secondary palate pushes inward to complete the definitive palate, the posterior part of the original maxillary mesoderm extends beyond the nasal septum and forms the soft palate (and uvula). Bone does not develop in these posterior structures.

There persists for a time in the median line between the original primitive palate and secondary bony maxillary palatal processes a small opening called the nasopalatine canal. Although this is obliterated by epithelial fusion, its position is represented permanently in the hard palate by the *incisive canals* (Hamilton et al., 1952).

The presence of the maxillary division of the trigeminal as the nerve supply to the palate is due to the fact that this was the innervation of the maxillary process which formed most of the sidewall of the original stomodeum. The latter represents the single nasal and oral cavities before the palate appears. The maxillary artery accompanies all the divisions of the nerve through the various apertures and canals. For a diagram illustrating the facial development, see Figure 13–2; Figure 10–7 illustrates palatal development.

The classical embryologic descriptions of facial development are changing. Anderson and Matthiesen (1967) state that the term "processes" is unfortunate because in the formation of the central face there are no processes which fuse by their forward growth. Instead, the processes result from localized mesenchymal proliferations which gradually make the lining epithelium protrude in relation to the surroundings and which are separated from each other by grooves, e.g., the nasal groove between the so-called median and lateral nasal process. A better term than processes would be localized swellings or prominences. We have retained the classical descriptions here, with the qualifications noted at this point.

Comparative Anatomy

In fishes and amphibians, the secondary palate of the higher vertebrates, which separates the oral cavity from the respiratory passage, is not present. A hard palate becomes a constant structure in reptiles, birds, and mammals, and the posterior nares open into the pharynx rather than into the mouth, as in fishes. The secondary palate begins in the turtle (Nelsen, 1953). Although well developed in crocodiles, it is less sturdy in birds.

In fishes, the nasal pits are blind and have no relation to a pharynx or to the function of breathing. In amphibians, the pharynx has made its appearance as a short and simple tube, called the pharyngeal chiasma, in which both food and air cross.

The velum has appeared in birds. Among mammals, there is a significant development of a movable velum. The highest mammalian order of primates acquires the soft palate pillars, or arches.

Pathophysiology

Disorders of resonance are common in palatal aberrations, although there may be factors operating as low as the larynx. There are also familial and emotional causes and those due to faulty learning, cultural influences, imitation, and carelessness of speech.

Hypernasality and Hyponasality

Hypernasality (open nasality, rhinolalia aperta, hyperrhinolalia, nasal speech, rhinophonia, rhinoglossia, nasalization, or palatal dysglossia) is one of the most common resonance disorders and involves any or all of the factors listed above. It may occur postoperatively after the removal of the tonsils or adenoids, or after paralysis of the soft palate musculature.

Soft palate paralysis produces undue patency of the posterior nares or the inability to separate the nasal from the oral cavity. All sounds may then display abnormal

309

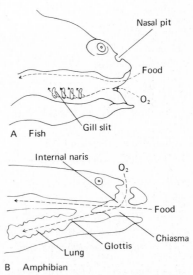

Figure 10-8 Diagrams of the evolution of the pharyngeal chiasma (crossing).

nasal resonance. There is considerable difficulty with velar sounds. There is also a weakening of lip and tongue sounds if much of the air used to produce such sounds escapes through the nose. The /b/ may become /m/, /d/ becomes /n/, and /k/ becomes /ŋ/. In the recumbent position, where the soft palate gravitationally falls back to occlude the nasopharynx, the distortions are less obvious.

The velopharyngeal mechanism should be evaluated for its role in causation. A paralysis limited to the pharynx would not produce the impairment described above.

Hyponasality (denasality, rhinolalia clausa) is a disorder both of articulation and resonance. This is seen in the substitution of one consonant for another and in the dull quality of the vowels and semivowels. The deficiency in the nasal resonance component may be due to obstruction of the nasal air passages, as in polyps, tumors, or a deviated septum, or else to the local effects of allergies and sinusitis.

House and Stevens (1956), in an attempt to determine the acoustic correlates of nasalization, have designed an electric analog of the nasal structures, combined it with an electric analog of the vocal tract, synthesized nasal vowels, and observed the activities of the acoustic systems. Coupling the nasal cavity to the vocal tract during vowel production produced a differential reduction in the amplitude of the first formant of various vowels, with increase in formant bandwidth and an upward shift in the center frequency of the formant. Nasality was perceived when the major effects on the spectrum of the acoustic output reached appropriate magnitudes. House (1957) has undertaken a similar study of the electric analogs of the nasal and vocal tracts to simulate the articulation of the three nasal consonants of "American" English.

Fant (1960) reviews the literature dealing with the acoustic bases of nasalization. He points up theories that a prominent feature for nasalized vowels is the intensity reduction of the first formant. There may also be antiresonance at certain frequencies. In regard to vocal tract regions involved in nasalization, the so-called nasal vowels, as in the French vowel system, are produced with specific tongue positions in addition to the expected elements of nasalization.

Anomalies of Development

Disorders of resonance are at times a result of embryologic deviations or failures.

One of the developmental abnormalities of the hard palate is an extremely high palatal arch. This may obstruct the nasal passages and produce an aberrant nasal quality of speech. If the tongue in a high palatal arch fails to contact the palate properly, or if air escapes from the sides, an influence would be exerted particularly on /s/, which might even be missing.

In a congenitally short soft palate there is not enough elevation and retraction to occlude the nasal port as needed, and excessive nasal resonance can result.

There may be an excess formation of bone in the midline of the hard palate, known as a torus palatinus, which is significant mostly because of dental difficulties in fitting an upper plate to the roof of the mouth.

Cleft Palates   These deviations constitute an important embryologic defect of the oropalatal region.   Although cleft palate is essentially an articulatory disorder, there are implications in regard to the adequacy of velopharyngeal closure (Mysak, 1966).

The cleft palate results from failures of unknown etiology occurring in embryonic development when many bilateral processes should have fused.   The failure occurs typically in the first twelve weeks of development, the most critical period being in the second month.

In pathogenesis the classical concept held that masses of ectoderm and mesoderm (termed maxillary, nasolateral, and nasomedian processes) in the early embryo were surrounded by free spaces, or clefts.   Any inhibition of the expansion and fusion of those processes was said to fix into permanency the pre-existing facial clefts.   Stark (1962) cites evidence against this explanation.   He notes that the primary and secondary palates form at different times and that aberrations in the mesoderm can produce an anomaly in either primary or secondary palate or in both.   Cleft lip and cleft palate are two different entities.

Facial processes in the palate must fuse if the palatal vault is to be intact.   Mesodermal deficiencies result in weakened soft palate musculature or in a frank submucous cleft.   Speech characteristic of cleft palate may occur without evidence of a cleft.   There is a developmental variation in the lip and premaxilla where the initial anlage of epithelium contains three mesodermal masses, each of which will expand and fuse with the others to produce a normal lip and anterior palate.   Any factor leading to the failure of appearance of one of these mesodermal masses will result in thinning of the epithelial wall, a subsequent rupture, and the production of a cleft.

Anderson and Matthiesen (1967) say that retardation of mesenchymal growth at an early stage is the direct cause of harelip and is responsible for certain cases of cleft palate.   Deficient vascularization, resulting in retarded mesenchymal proliferation, is a critical factor in cleft palate.

A cleft may involve the lip but not the palate, the palate but not the lip, or both. Any section of the palate may become cleft, and the abnormalities usually follow the lines of development.   A normal palate should complete itself by or before the twelfth fetal week.   If it does not do so, anomalies result.   Some of the causative factors may (with question) be failure in maternal nutrition, uterine conditions preventing joining of the palatal ridges, heredity (through recessive genes), heavy radiation during pregnancy, and deficient oxygen supply.   Berry and Eisenson (1956) state that 30 to 50 percent of the causes can be traced to genic factors.

The most frequent anomaly, i.e., the minimal lesion, is the single harelip, or cheiloschisis, which is generally on the left side. The failure is between the maxillary process and the lateral expansions of the median nasal process. The term harelip is a misnomer since the cleft of a hare is a midline one, whereas the human cleft is to one side of the midline. The double harelip is a common anomaly. It is called a wolf snout if it is accompanied by a palatal cleft and a projecting premaxilla.

In the more posterior failures, the hiatus (gap) is midline and involves the lack of median fusion of the lateral palatal shelves.

There is the rare failure of the median nasal processes to fuse together, resulting in a median cleft of the upper jaw. A similar median cleft may rarely occur in the mandible through lack of fusion of the paired mandibular arches.

A cleft lip and palate produces several major problems. (1) A very common difficulty is the retardation of certain consonant sounds. Thus, some prelanguage activity and good sound discrimination are lacking. (2) Speech with cleft palate is in a sense the opposite of that with nasal obstruction. In cleft palate the vowels and plosives become nasal, but the ordinarily nasal sounds are least affected. (3) Dental malformation and/or incorrect positioning of the tongue may develop prior to closure of the palate and produce articulatory disorders.

312

The details of surgery and the responsibilities of the physician, speech therapist, and parent are not within the scope of this text; the reader is referred to Koepp-Baker (1957), Pruzansky (1961), Levin (1962), Morley (1962), and to *The Cleft Palate Journal*.

II THE VELOPHARYNGEAL MECHANISM: THE PHARYNX

General Structure

The pharynx, or throat (throttle, gullet), is a single musculocutaneous tube common to the digestive and respiratory systems. It is situated posterior to the nose, mouth, and larynx and anterior to the cervical vertebrae. It is cone-shaped and about 14 cm (5½ in.) long. The funnel shape occurs as a result of the broadening of the nasopharynx above as the skull develops, along with a narrowing of the hypopharynx below as the larynx becomes an efficient pinchcock to separate the channels for air and food (Dolowitz, 1964). The upper end, or base, is just below the body of the sphenoid bone at the base of the cranium. The lower end, or apex, is continuous with the esophagus at the level of the lower border of the sixth cervical vertebra.

The tube is wider laterally than anteroposteriorly. The anteroposterior diameter is greatest in the nasopharynx (about 2 in.) just below the cranial base. The diameter lessens progressively and is only 1 in. at the junction of the pharynx with the esophagus. Although the anteroposterior diameter of the nasopharynx changes only very moderately from the child to the adult, its length doubles in the first 6 months after birth.

The pharynx has lateral and posterior walls but practically no anterior wall since it is directly continuous in front with the cavities of the nose, mouth, and larynx.

The lateral pharyngeal wall is attached above to the cartilaginous part of the Eustachian tube which enters the pharynx in that region. The lateral wall is attached in front from above down to the posterior border of the medial pterygoid process and its hamulus, the pterygomandibular raphe, the root of the tongue, inner aspect of the mandible, hyoid bone, and the thyroid and cricoid cartilages.

The posterior pharyngeal wall is attached above to the basilar part of the occipital bone and to the lower surface of the petrous part of the temporal bone. The posterior wall is separated from the prevertebral fascia covering the first six cervical vertebrae by loose fibrous connective tissue which forms a *retropharyngeal space*. This permits freedom of movement essential to pharyngeal function. This potential space is closed above by the base of the skull and on each side by the carotid sheath. It opens below into the superior mediastinum.

There is a *lateral pharyngeal space* on the lateral aspects of the pharynx lined with areolar fascia and containing fat as well as branches of the maxillary nerve and maxillary blood vessels. Its roof, where it is widest, is the base of the skull and the Eustachian tube. It extends down to an apex at the level of the hyoid bone.

The pharynx has three chief coats. The internal coat is a mucous membrane. The middle coat is fibrous and is called the pharyngeal aponeurosis (pharyngobasilar fascia or lamina). This layer is most definite in its uppermost part, where it is prominent in the posterior and lateral wall areas. The outermost coat is muscular, and on its external surface there is an indefinite fascial covering called the bucco-pharyngeal fascia.

314

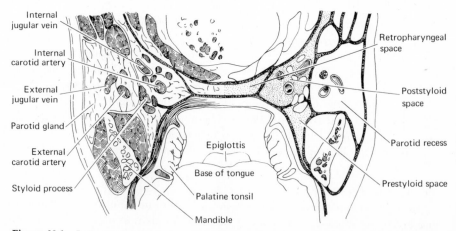

Figure 11-1 *Left:* transverse section through the pharynx; *right:* schematic arrangement of retropharyngeal and parapharyngeal fascial compartments (redrawn). (*By permission from F. L. Lederer, Diseases of the Ear, Nose and Throat, 6th ed., F. A. Davis Company, Philadelphia, 1952.*)

There are actually five histologic layers in the pharynx. The (1) internal mucous coat is surrounded by (2) a submucosa, which contains a rich venous plexus, and many lymph nodes and mucous glands. Outside of this is (3) a fibrous coat, or *pharyngobasilar fascia* (aponeurosis). This is firm material which fills in the gaps in the pharyngeal wall and which serves to anchor the pharynx to the medial pterygoid plate and basioccipital and petrous bone. Peripheral to this is (4) the muscular coat and finally (5) the areolar coat, or *buccopharyngeal fascia,* which lines the outside of the pharynx.

The tough, fibrous pharyngeal aponeurosis fills in the weak spot in the wall where the superior constrictor muscle fibers are absent. The aponeurosis disappears below as the muscles appear. The aponeurosis not only attaches the pharynx to the base of the skull but serves as a tendon of insertion for the constrictor muscles.

General Functions

The pharynx is a tube whose diameters can be actively changed. It is also subject to elevation and depression. The changing shape influences speech resonance (which may be considered as the selective support of certain desired partials in the complex sound wave). The sound is altered by varying not only the diameters but also the tension of the walls. Depending upon conditions at the places where the pharynx joins other cavities, its coupling with such cavities is affected, and an influence is brought to bear upon the resonance of the entire vocal system. The pharynx may be the principal resonator of the human voice.

315

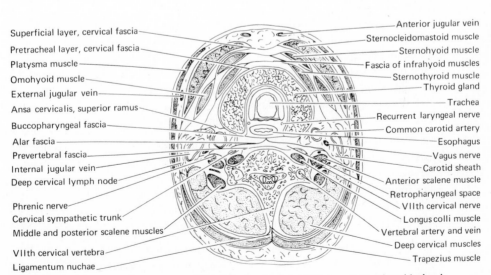

Figure 11-2 A cross section of the neck at the level of the isthmus of the thyroid gland. (*By permission from R. T. Woodburne, Essentials of Human Anatomy, 4th ed., Oxford University Press, New York, 1968.*)

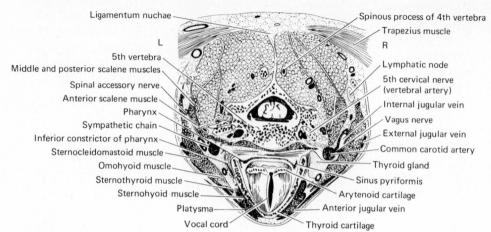

Ligamentum nuchae
Spinous process of 4th vertebra
Trapezius muscle
L
R
5th vertebra
Middle and posterior scalene muscles
Spinal accessory nerve
Anterior scalene muscle
Pharynx
Sympathetic chain
Inferior constrictor of pharynx
Sternocleidomastoid muscle
Omohyoid muscle
Sternothyroid muscle
Sternohyoid muscle
Platysma
Vocal cord
Lymphatic node
5th cervical nerve
(vertebral artery)
Internal jugular vein
Vagus nerve
External jugular vein
Common carotid artery
Thyroid gland
Sinus pyriformis
Arytenoid cartilage
Anterior jugular vein
Thyroid cartilage

Figure 11-3 Cross section through the neck at the level of the fifth cervical vertebra. *(Taken from K. von Bardeleben and H. Haeckel, Atlas of Applied Topographical Human Anatomy, Rebman Ltd., London, 1906.)*

316

The pharyngeal tube should be kept patent for proper resonance. Its effectiveness in collecting sound waves and directing them into the mouth is decreased by crowding backward the dorsum of the tongue or by producing excessive tension of the constrictor muscles which form the posterolateral pharyngeal walls. An elevated tongue dorsum can be one of the causes of a guttural quality of the voice. A narrowing of the palatal arches between the mouth and pharynx can produce a muffling effect in the vocal tone.

Gray and Wise (1959) emphasize the unlimited possibilities of tonal variations made feasible by the coupled resonating system of the mouth and pharynx. An open tube is adapted to the resonance of a wave whose fundamental is twice the length of the tube. A closed tube is adapted to a wavelength four times the length of the tube and of its odd-numbered partials. The larger the cavity of a resonator, the lower the pitch to which it is adapted; also, the larger the opening, the higher the pitch; and the longer the neck of the opening, the lower the pitch.

One then notes that the mouth can act either as a closed or open tube or that the pharynx can have one or two outlets, because the soft palate can open or close the pharyngeal connections with the nasopharynx. Since these adaptations are made more complex by alterations of tube length and diameter, aperture diameter, and length of neck of aperture, the number of different fundamentals and partials to which the pharynx is adapted for resonance is very great.

Anderson (1961) says that the role of the pharynx in resonation is more difficult to evaluate than that of the mouth or nose but that it is especially important to provide resonance for the fundamental and the lower overtones. This is said to give the voice a mellow, rich, and full quality.

The texture, as well as the size and shape, of the pharynx and its apertures affects speech quality. A hard-surfaced resonator emphasizes the higher partials, or overtones, so that a pharynx tightly constricted by its muscles takes on a metallic, strident, and tense tone. A soft surface, provided by relaxed throat muscles, increases the responsive range while damping the resonator. This gives relative prominence to the fundamental and lower partials.

Luchsinger and Arnold (1965) state that widening the pharynx increases resonance and describe the resulting sound as full, dark, strong, and resonant. The narrowing effect is associated with a voice described as thin, sharp, dampened, and throaty (guttural). In this terminology, "dark" refers to a predominance of low partial tones, and "sharp" indicates that the frequency region of 3,000 to 4,000 Hz is emphasized. (One may note the possibility of conflicting qualities within any one set of the results described.)

The pharynx has other functions more vital than resonance and speech. One is digestion. Of the three classically differentiated stages of swallowing food (deglutition), the second involves rolling the food into a bolus, or cohesive rope, and transmitting it through the pharynx. This is done by voluntary muscles which are activated reflexly through a deglutition center in the medulla. The pharynx is also a passageway for respiratory gases. The ciliated epithelial cells of the nasopharynx help keep the respiratory tract clear by pushing foreign material toward the mouth. The nasopharynx functions as a ventilator of the middle ear and the Eustachian tubes. It also serves as a drainage canal for the nose and lacrimal ducts.

Divisions of the Pharynx

Nasopharynx

The superior division, the nasopharynx, is a cube-shaped cavity just posterior to the nasal cavities and superior to the level of the soft palate. It has an average size about that of a walnut. It belongs with the nasal fossae as a part of the respiratory rather than the digestive system.

Unlike the remainder of the pharynx, its cavity is permanently open. During swallowing the nasopharynx is separated from the oropharynx by the soft palate and uvula, which are pushed against the contracting posterior pharyngeal wall. During speech the size of the velopharyngeal opening or closure has a correlation with the degree of nasal resonance (Murphy, 1964). Nonnasal sounds are also associated with some small velopharyngeal opening, thus permitting a moderate nasal resonance during speech.

Anteriorly, the nasopharynx communicates by the paired choanae with the nasal cavities. The choanae are rectangular apertures, which are about 1 in. long and ½ in. wide. The soft palate may be considered as furnishing a partial floor for the anterior section of the nasopharynx. The soft palate has lateral attachments to the walls of the pharynx and slopes inferiorly into it.

In the lateral walls of the nasopharynx there are the openings of the Eustachian tubes which lie almost in a direct line with the inferior nasal concha. The cartilage of the Eustachian tubes elevates the mucous membrane on each side into a cushion, or torus. The pharyngeal tonsil, or Luschka's tonsil, is a prominence on the posterior wall. Above the tonsil in the median line is a small diverticulum called the pharyngeal bursa. The tonsil throws the mucous membrane into many folds.

Just above the level of the nasal floor in the lateral walls of the nasopharynx is a distinct depression called the fossa of Rosenmüller. This is a landmark for the opening of each Eustachian tube, which lies both below and anterior to it. This pocket in the superior aspect of the nasopharynx is occasionally involved as a hidden trap because of its depth. Infection can arise therein, and it may be the origin of many head colds and nasopharyngeal infections. Malignant growths in the fossa metastasize (spread) rapidly.

The roof and posterior wall of the nasopharynx form a continuous arched wall. The roof passes backward from the superior border of the choanae to about the middle of the basilar aspect of the occipital bone. The posterior wall starts at this point and reaches down to the lower border of the anterior arch of the atlas.

The floor of the nasopharynx is incomplete and is formed by the posterosuperior aspect of the soft palate. An opening called the pharyngeal isthmus exists posterior to the floor. It is this space which is closed during swallowing and which tends to close in much speech activity. The pharyngeal isthmus is made smaller by the con-

318

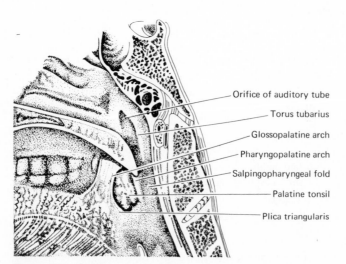

Figure 11-4 Structures in the pharynx, with particular reference to the auditory tube, palatine tonsil, and palatal arches (sagittal view).

tracting pharyngopalatines but is subsequently further decreased to closure by the levator palati muscles, which bring the upper surface of the soft palate to the wall of the narrowing pharynx. Lubricating mucus seals the isthmus and can make it airtight (Grant and Basmajian, 1965).

The nasopharynx is lined by pseudostratified ciliated columnar (respiratory) epithelium. This contrasts with the oropharynx, which is covered by stratified squamous epithelium. The linings are adapted to the differences in function.

Oropharynx
The middle pharyngeal division, called the oropharynx or mesopharynx, is directly below the nasopharynx and lies posterior to the mouth and tongue. It extends vertically from the soft palate and pharyngeal isthmus above to the level of the hyoid bone or pharyngoepiglottic folds below. Its posterior wall is in relation to the bodies of the second, third, and fourth cervical vertebrae. Anteriorly, it communicates through the fauces with the mouth. Below this region the anterior wall is formed by the root of the tongue.

The important structures within the oropharynx are the palatine tonsils and their pillars, the lingual tonsils, and the uvula. The epiglottis protrudes into it. The posterior wall becomes involved in inflammations, local muscle disturbances, and in abscesses within the retropharyngeal space.

The oropharynx, in conjunction with the laryngopharynx, serves as a respiratory passageway, a drainage channel from the nasopharynx, a pathway for food, and as a resonating chamber in voice production. The lymphoid tissue (in all areas of the pharynx) destroys and removes foreign material and participates in the formation of antibodies.

Laryngopharynx
The inferior subdivision, the laryngopharynx, decreases abruptly in width and becomes continuous with the esophagus at the level of the inferior border of the cricoid. Its anterior wall is formed partly by the posterior wall of the larynx, and it communicates with the larynx through the epiglottis. The aryepiglottic folds are its lateral boundaries, and the fifth and sixth cervical vertebrae are its posterior boundaries.

The uppermost part of the laryngopharynx is the locus of two spaces known as the *valleculae*. These are depressions produced on either side of a median glossoepiglottic ligament which runs from the base of the tongue to the epiglottis. The valleculae are thus in front of the epiglottis, or between the tongue and the epiglottis. The boundary of each lateral side of the vallecula is a lateral glossoepiglottic fold. In some individuals pills or other foreign bodies get lodged in these vallecular pockets.

There is a fairly deep *pyriform (piriform) sinus* in the laryngopharyngeal area, on either side of the larynx. Each recess lies between the arytenoid cartilages and aryepiglottic folds medially and the side wall of the pharynx laterally. The lateral wall of the pharynx in this area consists of the hyoid bone, thyrohyoid membrane, and the thyroid cartilage. The pyriform recesses are potential spaces therein which are formed by the bulk of the larynx dividing the laryngopharynx in two.

When the epiglottis deflects food or fluid to each side of itself, the material travels into the right and left pyriform sinus. Each sinus is like a trough, which can be eliminated when the larynx rises, as in swallowing.

The terminology of the pharyngeal divisions has been subject to change because of objections to static anatomic relationships (Bosma, 1957). The area above the palate is the epipharynx, that between the lower surface of the soft palate and the valleculae the mesopharynx, and that from the valleculae to the opening of the esophagus the hypopharynx. In this functional view, the boundaries shift with the position of the soft palate and the epiglottis.

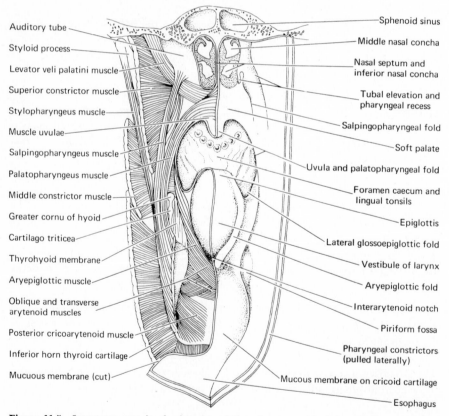

320

Figure 11-5 Structures seen in the interior of the pharynx, with the constrictors resected (posterior view). (By permission from R. C. Crafts, A Textbook of Human Anatomy, The Ronald Press Company, New York, 1966.)

Pharyngeal Muscles and Movements

Movements of the pharyngeal divisions and the neurophysiologic regulation of the movements have been described in some detail by Bosma (1957). Huber (1958) gives a concise description of the musculature. Motor performance in the pharyngeal area of several species of animals has been clarified by multiple-channel electromyography, among other technics (Doty and Bosma, 1956).

The pharynx is not a quiet, motionless passageway. Early in swallowing, it is pulled upward and dilated to receive the bolus of food. The active muscles are the palatopharyngeus (pharyngopalatine), stylopharyngeus, salpingopharyngeus, and the suprahyoid group of muscles. After receiving the bolus, the pharynx descends and constricts. This action pushes the bolus into the esophagus.

The constrictors contract energetically in orderly sequence, each for only about ⅓ sec in swallowing (Grant and Basmajian, 1965), but the contractions overlap.

Descent of the pharynx represents, to a great degree, relaxation of previously activated elevator muscles. Constriction results from active contraction of specific constrictor muscles.

Elevation of the organ narrows the opening through the epiglottis to help prevent food from entering the lung passages. The epiglottis also has some part in this action.

The muscles form much of the framework of the lateral and posterior walls of the pharynx. They are arranged in an outer and inner layer, which are not readily separable throughout. The outer layer is arranged circularly and comprises three constrictor muscles. These change the diameter of the tube. The inner layer is roughly longitudinal, and it includes the palatopharyngeus, salpingopharyngeus, stylopharyngeus, and other irregular muscle bundles. The inner muscles function in elevation, depression, expansion, and contraction of the pharynx.

The *superior pharyngeal constrictor* (paired) is a broad quadrilateral mass containing fibers which, for the most part, curve backward and upward. It has several origins including the pterygoid and hamular processes, the pterygomandibular raphe, the posterior end of the mylohyoid line on the medial area of the mandible, and the root of the tongue. The fibers run posteriorly and fuse at a median pharyngeal raphe with their fellows of the opposite side. The uppermost fibers fail to meet at the base of the skull, and the interval is filled by the pharyngeal aponeurosis.

At the level of the soft palate some of the uppermost constrictor fibers become intimately associated with the soft palate musculature. This forms a complex sphincter active in that region.

The superior constrictors do not have a broad attachment at the skull base, but they are suspended from a central area which is the pharyngeal tubercle on the

321

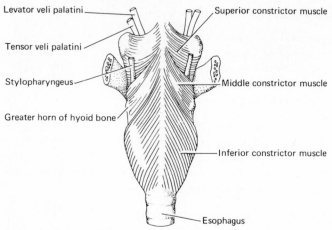

Figure 11-6 The intact pharyngeal musculature viewed from behind.

basilar part of the occipital bone. This leaves a variable free area on each side called the sinus of Morgagni. The levator and tensor veli palatini muscles and the cartilaginous part of the Eustachian tube run through this space.

The *middle pharyngeal constrictor* (paired) arises at the major and minor horns of the hyoid bone and along the adjacent part of the stylohyoid ligament. The fibers diverge widely from their origin as they curve backward and medialward to blend with those of the opposite side along the posterior median raphe. The upper fibers ascend obliquely to cover the superior constrictor muscle, the middle fibers course horizontally, and the lower ones run beneath the inferior constrictor.

There is a triangular gap, bounded anteriorly by the thyrohyoid muscle, between the lower edge of the middle constrictor and the upper edge of the inferior constrictor. The gap is occupied by the lower part of the stylopharyngeus muscle and the posterior part of the thyrohyoid membrane.

The *inferior pharyngeal constrictor* (paired) overlaps the middle constrictor posteriorly, and it is the broadest and thickest of the constrictors. It originates from the sides of the cricoid and thyroid cartilages, and its fibers curve backward and medialward to insert along the posterior median raphe. While the lowest fibers are horizontal, the highest ones rise obliquely to reach their insertion, which overlies much of the middle constrictor muscle.

The recurrent laryngeal nerves and associated blood vessels travel under cover of this muscle, coursing superiorly behind the cricothyroid joint to enter the larynx.

The obliquity of the pharyngeal constrictors in the position of rest is related to the gradual descent of the larynx through fetal and early postnatal life. When the pharynx elevates, the constrictor fibers become more circular and act as a sphincteric mechanism.

The *cricopharyngeus* muscle is important. Valsalva in 1717 applied this term to the horizontal muscle fibers arising from the cricoid cartilage at the lower end of the pharynx. Chevalier Jackson in 1915 referred to the structure as the cricopharyngeal pinchcock. Some investigators think of this muscle as an esophageal section of the inferior constrictor muscle (Batson, 1955; Palmer and LaRusso, 1965).

In normal swallowing the cricopharyngeus opens. Huber (1958) says that this muscle forms an annular bundle without a median raphe and blends to a variable extent with the circular fibers of the esophagus. The union of the cricopharyngeus fibers and esophageal elements closes the upper end of the esophagus over a distance of 1 to 3 cm, and this composite structure may be called the *upper esophageal sphincter* (Ingelfinger, 1958).

The sphincter is utilized in esophageal speech, as noted elsewhere in the text.

The sphincter is innervated by fibers from the nucleus ambiguus and dorsal vagal nucleus and carried by the vagus and to a lesser degree by the glossopharyngeal and spinal accessory nerves. Under their influence the sphincter opens for 0.2 to 0.3 sec after beginning a swallow, remains open for 0.5 to 1.2 sec, and then closes. The opening of the sphincter is ordinarily an involuntary act.

A zone of sparse musculature is present between the cricopharyngeus and the rest of the inferior constrictor muscle. This produces a localized, potentially weak area in the posterior wall of the pharynx (Huber, 1958). Another weak area in the posterior wall of the pharyngoesophageal junction occurs just below the inferior

323

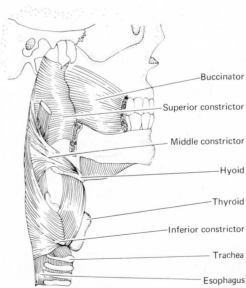

Figure 11-7 Relationships of the pharyngeal constrictors as seen in lateral view.

border of the cricopharyngeus muscle. In this region (Laimer's triangle) the posterior wall may be deficient because the longitudinal muscles of the esophagus diverge laterally to gain attachment to the cricoid.

The *stylopharyngeus* appears on the lateral wall of the pharynx as a long slender muscle that is cylindrical above but flattened below. It arises on the medial part of the base of the styloid process of the temporal bone. Its fibers travel down caudally and anteriorly between the external and internal carotid arteries. They enter the pharynx between the superior and middle constrictor muscles to insert partly in the constrictor musculature and the mucous lining of the pharynx. Some of the fibers join the pharyngopalatine muscle and insert on the superior and dorsal borders of the thyroid cartilage. Other fibers produce the pharyngoepiglottic fold, and still others travel to the posterolateral aspect of the pharynx and insert on the pharyngeal fibrous aponeurosis above the cricopharyngeus muscle.

The stylopharyngeus expands the pharynx laterally and also elevates the pharynx and larynx. The front to back dilation of the pharynx during its ascent is caused by the forward carriage of the larynx and the tongue. These actions are primarily to swallow food. The glossopharyngeal nerve on its way to the posterior part of the tongue innervates the stylopharyngeus.

Other muscles associated with the pharynx include the salpingopharyngeus and pharyngopalatine, which are especially important in deglutition. In brief, the chief pharyngeal muscles used in swallowing are the constrictors, stylopharyngeus, salpingopharyngeus, and pharyngopalatine.

324

Nerves and Vascular Supply of the Pharynx

Nerves
The motor supply appears to come chiefly through the pharyngeal branches of the vagus nerve. These rami generally include two on each side, originating from the nodose ganglion and running to the pharyngeal plexus on each side of the pharynx, adjacent to the middle constrictor. The plexus is formed by an intercommunication of the vagus pharyngeal rami with others from the glossopharyngeal nerve and from the laryngopharyngeal branch of the sympathetic nervous system. It is concerned with sensory, motor, and vasomotor control of the pharynx (Brantigan, 1963).

The plexus sends out motor fibers. Those going to the salpingopharyngeus and pharyngeal constrictors come through the vagus nerve, and those to the stylopharyngeus come through the glossopharyngeal nerve.

The autonomic nerve supply to the pharynx is through the greater superficial petrosal, vagus, and cervical sympathetic chain.

The sensory nerves from the mucous membrane of the pharynx come in through the pharyngeal plexus and are in part branches of the glossopharyngeal nerve.

The total sensory distribution of the glossopharyngeal nerve includes the root of the tongue, the posterior and lateral walls of the pharynx from the inferior part of the nasopharynx to the epiglottis, the glossopalatal and pharyngopalatal arches, the Eustachian tube apertures, the tympanic membrane, and parts of the soft palate and uvula. The nerve does not supply sensory fibers to the pharyngeal roof, the latter being innervated by pharyngeal branches of the maxillary division of the trigeminal. According to Boies et al. (1964), there is an innervation of the naso-pharynx from the greater superficial petrosal nerves (facial nerve origin) which send sensory fibers via the vidian nerves and the sphenopalatine ganglion.

The vagus, via the internal laryngeal nerve, carries sensory fibers from the hypo-pharyngeal region and the entrance to the larynx.

Crafts (1966) states that the mucous membrane is innervated also by autonomic nerves via the superior cervical ganglion. He regards the pharyngeal plexus located on the middle constrictor muscle as being made up from branches of the ninth and tenth cranial nerves and also from branches of the superior cervical ganglion.

Developmental anatomy explains the presence of more than one nerve in a small region. The hard and soft palates are peculiar to mammals and were necessary to separate the nose and nasopharynx from the mouth in evolving pulmonary respira-tion. This demanded modifications of preexisting muscles rather than the forma-tion of new ones. Certain muscles were locally available, e.g., those of the soft palate and the superior constrictor. These have a common nerve supply, involving the vagus and spinal accessory. A muscle coming in from a distance, e.g., the tensor palati, brought along its own nerve supply, which is the mandibular nerve via the otic ganglion.

325

Arteries
The chief arteries of the pharynx are the ascending pharyngeal and faucial branches of the external carotid and the superior palatine branch of the internal maxillary. The tonsillar artery, and sometimes the ascending palatine, supplies the soft palate and palatine tonsils. The tonsils may also be supplied by the ascending pharyn-geal, the dorsalis linguae, the small meningeal, and the descending or posterior palatine arteries. Writers differ about the arterial supply, probably because any one of the branches may be missing.

The internal carotid arteries pass lateral to the nasopharynx and send in no branches.

Veins
The drainage of blood from the head and neck is accomplished mainly by the internal jugular vein. Tributaries into it from the pharynx come chiefly from the pharyngeal plexus, an extensive vascular network on the pharyngeal wall. There is a direct flow from the plexus through short pharyngeal veins into the internal jugular vein. There is also an extensive connection of the pharyngeal plexus with the pterygoid plexus. The nasopharynx drains into the pterygoid plexus, which

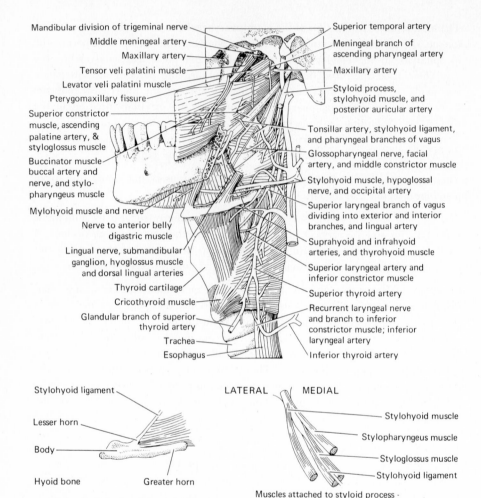

Mandibular division of trigeminal nerve
Middle meningeal artery
Maxillary artery
Tensor veli palatini muscle
Levator veli palatini muscle
Pterygomaxillary fissure
Superior constrictor muscle, ascending palatine artery, & styloglossus muscle
Buccinator muscle, buccal artery and nerve, and stylopharyngeus muscle
Mylohyoid muscle and nerve
Nerve to anterior belly digastric muscle
Lingual nerve, submandibular ganglion, hyoglossus muscle and dorsal lingual arteries
Thyroid cartilage
Cricothyroid muscle
Glandular branch of superior thyroid artery
Trachea
Esophagus

Superior temporal artery
Meningeal branch of ascending pharyngeal artery
Maxillary artery
Styloid process, stylohyoid muscle, and posterior auricular artery
Tonsillar artery, stylohyoid ligament, and pharyngeal branches of vagus
Glossopharyngeal nerve, facial artery, and middle constrictor muscle
Stylohyoid muscle, hypoglossal nerve, and occipital artery
Superior laryngeal branch of vagus dividing into exterior and interior branches, and lingual artery
Suprahyoid and infrahyoid arteries, and thyrohyoid muscle
Superior laryngeal artery and inferior constrictor muscle
Superior thyroid artery
Recurrent laryngeal nerve and branch to inferior constrictor muscle; inferior laryngeal artery
Inferior thyroid artery

326

Stylohyoid ligament
Lesser horn
Body
Hyoid bone
Greater horn
Origin of middle constrictor muscle

LATERAL   MEDIAL

Stylohyoid muscle
Stylopharyngeus muscle
Styloglossus muscle
Stylohyoid ligament

Muscles attached to styloid process - posterior view - left side

Figure 11-8 Blood and nerve supply to the pharynx and contiguous areas. (*By permission from R. C. Crafts, A Textbook of Human Anatomy, The Ronald Press Company, New York, 1966.*)

empties into the internal maxillary vein (Hollender, 1953). The latter vein joins with the superficial temporal vein to form the posterior facial vein. The posterior division of the latter fuses with the anterior facial vein to form the common facial vein that empties into the internal jugular system.

Lymphatics

The lymphatics follow in general the veins of the neck. The lymph nodes are separated into a superficial and a deep group. The chief nodes and vessels cluster about the internal jugular vein and follow it to drain into the thoracic duct near its union with the left internal jugular and subclavian veins or the right lymphatic duct where it joins the right internal jugular and subclavian veins.

The lymphatics are especially abundant in the upper pharynx and around Waldeyer's tonsillar ring. Those vessels located in the nasopharynx drain into lateral retropharyngeal nodes or into internal jugular vein nodes. They supply the pharyngeal tonsil, pharyngeal roof, posterior wall of the oro- and nasopharynx, and the uppermost lateral nasopharyngeal walls. The lymphatics of the hard and soft palates and of the middle region of the pharynx drain into retropharyngeal, deep lateral cervical, or submaxillary nodes. The lymphatics of the arches and faucial tonsils empty into the subdigastric or internal jugular nodes. These same nodes also receive the lymphatic drainage of the anterior portion of the lower pharynx, the posterior drainage of which goes into the lateral retropharyngeal or internal jugular nodes.

Passavant's Cushion

Passavant in 1869 described a cushion that projects forward into the pharynx originating from the posterior and lateral walls of the nasopharynx. Although he observed it in a patient with cleft palate, he stated that it is essential for normal speech.

The cushion, or bar, is formed at the level of the anterior aspect of the atlas by contraction of muscle fibers that course around the pharynx horizontally. These may be found in a sphincteric arrangement beginning at the posterolateral borders of the hard palate. The mass has the form of an anteriorly open semicircle.

The fibers are part of the palatopharyngeus muscle, which has fused posteriorly with the superior constrictor muscle. Greene (1964) states that such fibers should not be regarded as a part of the superior constrictor muscle, but Palmer and LaRusso (1965) state the opposite. Thus, although the fibers of the palatopharyngeus which encircle the upper portion of the pharynx are seen in all mammals, the chief difficulty has been to assign them to one definite muscle.

Passavant's bar appears considerably smaller in a normal person than it is in the individual with cleft palate. In the latter the closure of the nasopharynx is brought about by the strong contraction of muscles forming the palatopharyngeal sphincter. There is excessive obstruction to the oronasopharyngeal passage, and this alters breathing and resonance. In the normal person the closure of the nasopharyngeal valve is effected chiefly by the highly movable soft palate, so that the importance of Passavant's cushion is questionable.

In swallowing, palatal closure is brought about forcibly by several muscles, including the palatal levators, the superior constrictor muscle of the pharynx, and the palatopharyngeus muscle. In speech, the superior constrictor may possibly help to elevate the ridge of Passavant, narrowing the nasopharynx anteroposteriorly and laterally. Cessation of speech often is attended by a sensation of relaxation in the posterior pharyngeal wall.

Passavant's theory that the bulging of muscle on the posterior pharyngeal wall just above the level of the velum helps to produce a palatal flap necessary for intelligible speech has been both supported and denied (LeJeune and Lynch, 1955). Even the existence of Passavant's cushion has been questioned (Calnan, 1954) on the view that the level of the ridge anterior to the atlas is below the elevation of the velum required for speech. Hagerty et al. (1958) state that except when Passavant's phenomenon occurs as a process essential to closure, it is doubtful whether the forward movement of the posterior pharyngeal wall is significant in the production of speech sounds. These views do not invalidate the observations that a phenomenon of this kind apparently exists in association with a cleft palate. Also its formation is probable in such activities as swallowing, gagging, vomiting, or whenever it is advantageous to shut off the nasopharynx.

Microscopic Anatomy

The pharynx is divided to an epipharynx, mesopharynx, and hypopharynx, and each area may have some preferential functions correlated with the histologic specialization of its lining. Where blind pouches exist and there is need for cleaning machinery, a ciliated columnar epithelium tends to be laid down. The epipharynx and the ventricle of the larynx are blind pouches which must be kept clean. The mucous layer of the epipharynx is believed to be important in protecting the upper respiratory tract against infection. In areas of friction and movement, such as the mouth, most of the pharynx, and the vocal folds, a stratified squamous epithelium is laid down. Mucous glands predominate in the stratified squamous lining, but seromucinous glands are more common in the pseudostratified columnar epithelium.

In the epipharynx there is a pseudostratified ciliated columnar lining rich in mucous and seromucinous glands. This is also found on the nasal surface of the uvula. Where the function is not respiratory but one involving deglutition, the epithelium is nonciliated, stratified squamous in type. This variety is extended onto the oral surface of the uvula and variably onto the nasal or dorsal aspect of the soft palate, where friction occurs in swallowing.

There are age changes in histology which have an effect on processes involving the epipharynx. In young persons the mucosa of the anterior turbinal tips and the septal tubercle contains cilia, but in adults erosion of the membrane occurs (Hollender, 1953). The resulting tendency for particles to accumulate and adhere in the epipharynx forces the uvula into a more active role in the removal of foreign bodies.

All parts of the mesopharynx and hypopharynx retain the stratified squamous lining. The epiglottis has a mixed character such that squamous epithelium covers its anterior surface and the **upper half** of its posterior surface, while the lower half of its posterior aspect has a covering that is pseudostratified ciliated columnar.

The pharynx is a first line of defense against infection. This view is based upon the presence of many lymphocytic cells. These lie in a fibrous network of the reticuloendothelial system (Boies et al., 1964).

The pharyngeal mucosa is continuous with that of the nose, mouth, larynx, and Eustachian tubes.

Developmental Anatomy

In the early embryo the digestive tract appears as a tubular foregut and hindgut. The foregut dilates to form the pharynx, which is thus first a part of the digestive system. The respiratory relationships of the pharynx are seen about the fourth fetal week, when a series of ridges separated by grooves develops along each side of the head. The ridges have an evolutionary significance corresponding to the gill arches for breathing in fishes, and they are termed branchial arches.

As seen in fishes, outpocketings toward the surface from the sides of the pharynx occur, lined with endoderm. These are called pouches. There are corresponding invaginations from the external surface, lined with ectoderm, and known as branchial grooves. The deepening of both internal and external pockets continues until their walls meet, forming a plate consisting of two layers, endoderm and ectoderm. The plate breaks through, establishing communication between the interior of the pharynx and the external environment. This produces a series of openings, or gill slits, from the pharynx to the exterior. Their inner lining is endoderm, and their outer lining is ectoderm. The respiratory membranes, or gill filaments, develop from the inner walls of the gill slits.

329

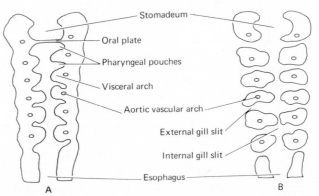

Figure 11-9 Diagram showing arrangement of the pharyngeal pouches in a generalized vertebrate animal: (*a*) during development; (*b*) after the gill slits have broken through and the oral plate is dissolved.

In reptiles, birds, and mammals, the allantois functions as the embryonic respiratory membrane, and gills are not needed. The human embryo does go through an eclipsed attempt to reproduce the gill apparatus in the form of pharyngeal pouches and branchial grooves, but the process is very incomplete. The furrows rarely perforate by inward extension. If they do, they produce a persistent fistula from the pharynx to the exterior through which fluid may drain.

In the human embryo of one month there are five pairs of branchial arches produced by thickening of mesenchyme in the lateral walls of the pharynx. Each arch has a cartilage framework upon which muscles and nerves develop. As seen externally on each side, furrows appear between each arch so that the arches are fairly distinct from one another.

The pharyngeal gill system would be of no use in pulmonary respiration. Since it is only an ontogenetic recapitulation of vertebrate evolution, it is transitory. Within perhaps two weeks the branchial arches disappear. The arches, pouches, and associated elements actually do not vanish but change into several structures modified for terrestrial rather than aquatic existence. There is some question about the exact fate of any given structure, and the following account is controversial.

In regard to the arches, the first forms the maxilla, the mandible, a portion of the tongue, and also the malleus and incus bones of the middle ear. The second arch forms the lesser cornua of the hyoid bone, the stapes, the styloid process, and perhaps the styloid ligaments. The third arch produces part of the epiglottis and the greater cornua of the hyoid. The fourth arch forms part of the epiglottis and also the arytenoid, corniculate, and cricoid cartilages of the larynx. The fifth arch may also contribute to the larynx.

The evaginating internal pharyngeal pouches, or grooves, which are formed in the late fourth week, also have many derivatives, some in common with the arches. The first pouch forms the paired middle ear chambers and possibly the Eustachian tubes, and it may contribute to the palatine tonsils. The second pouch also contributes to the palatine tonsils and to Waldeyer's ring. The third pouch produces the thymus gland and helps produce the parathyroids. The fourth pouch also contributes to the parathyroids. The fourth or fifth pouch produces the ultimobranchial bodies that either become enveloped by the thyroid gland or else atrophy completely.

The floor of the pharynx, like its lateral walls, produces or helps produce important structures, which include the thyroid bud, the tongue, and the glottis.

Prior to the bony development surrounding the pharyngeal area, a mass of glandular tissue appears, part of which remains in the vault of the pharynx to differentiate into the pharyngeal tonsil. The remainder is cut off from the pharynx and roof of the mouth by the growing sphenoid bone, whose body forms the superior boundary of the pharynx. This isolated glandular mass lies on the under surface of the brain, and it becomes a part of the pituitary gland.

The evolutionary attempts of the pharynx of the human embryo to form a fishlike respiratory apparatus do not end with the translation of the vestigial structures to other elements and purposes. During fetal development, even while the placenta is providing adequately for the exchange of respiratory gases, the pharynx is preparing for true postnatal breathing with lungs.

The lung first appears as a fingerlike diverticulum pushing out from the ventral floor of the posterior aspect of the pharynx. This outgrowth divides into a bilobed sac, and the division gradually becomes more definite. The sacs evolve into the two bronchi, leading to the right and left lungs. Further subdivisions occur within the lungs, so that the subdivisions, or bronchioles, terminate as alveoli (air sacs).

Comparative Anatomy

Lower animals up to mammals hardly show a definite pharynx, and the transition from mouth to esophagus is abrupt. This circumstance is partly explainable by the small size of the larynx and by the failure of the epiglottis and its folds to appear. Even in most mammals the pharynx is short. The human pharynx is relatively spacious, and this is related to the embryologic descent of the larynx.

In phylogeny, the pharynx changes more radically than any other bodily region. This is because of the transition of vertebrates from water to land with the corresponding loss in function of the pharyngeal gill slits.

In the lungfish, or Dipnoi, air is breathed in the dry season, and these animals develop a passageway from the external nares to the choanal openings leading to the pharynx. A pair of lungs forms, whose entrance is guarded by a sphincteric larynx. A glottis appears for the first time.

In the air-breathing amphibians, the glottis must be kept open. The pharyngeal gill arches become modified to supporting glottic cartilages. In newts, the cranial sector of the fifth gill arch becomes the arytenoids, which help open the laryngeal aperture. The caudal part becomes the cricoid cartilage, which keeps the larynx open.

The pharyngeal gill slits of snakes, birds, and mammals are visible as clefts only in embryonic life. The oral cavity achieves a sharp separation from the pharynx first in reptiles through development of the hard and soft palates. The mammalian pharynx is not very different from that of reptiles or birds.

A knowledge of developmental and comparative anatomy is highly relevant. The manner of evolution of the voice is closely dependent upon the emergence of animals from water to land.

Applied Anatomy and Physiology

Peripharyngeal Spaces

The anatomy of the space behind the pharynx, the retropharyngeal space, is of interest because of pathology. Abscesses occur there, especially in infants and children as a result of infection spreading through the posterior pharyngeal wall. The space separates the pharynx posteriorly from the vertebral column, and the loose connective tissue within the space permits the pharyngeal elevation and descent entailed in swallowing.

The original view that the area behind the pharynx is one space has been questioned. There appear to be four potential spaces called peripharyngeal, parapharyngeal, postvisceral, and prevertebral.

The retropharyngeal space is only a potential cavity, since the region is filled by the loose areolar tissue of the prevertebral fascia. Its vertical extent reaches from the base of the skull above to the farthest point of the cervical fascia below. Its anterior wall is the posterior wall of the pharynx. Posteriorly it is attached to the spine by connective tissue. Its lateral boundary is another compartment called the pharyngomaxillary fossa. The retropharyngeal space contains many lymph nodes, and their breakdown in lymphadenitis characterizes retropharyngeal abscess. These nodes tend to involute during childhood.

332

The pharyngomaxillary space (lateral, or parapharyngeal) is more often infected than the posterior retropharyngeal space (DeWeese and Saunders, 1964). This is a space only when filled with pus or tumor. It is a deep space, lying against the fascia of the parotid gland and internal pterygoid muscle laterally and against the fascia of the superior constrictor muscle medially. It connects with the retropharyngeal space posteriorly and extends inferiorly along the major cervical vessels into the superior mediastinum. It may be infected by needle contamination or by extension of an adjacent infection. Because the connective tissue in this series of spaces contains chiefly ground substance, infection is able to spread rapidly rather than being localized (Dolowitz, 1964).

Visualization of the Pharynx

Ordinarily, very little of the pharynx can be observed through the normal nasal passages. One can usually look posteriorly into the throat through a space close to the nasal floor. A test, which is especially valuable in children for visualizing the adenoids, is to have the patient say "twenty-five," during which the soft palate should rise and fall. Hypertrophied tissue is indicated if the palate fails to move or if its amplitude of motion is relatively small compared to normal controls.

The pharynx is often examined without using elaborate instrumentation. The posterior nasopharynx is conveniently studied with a nasopharyngeal mirror and reflected light. The midportion of the tongue is firmly held down with a tongue depressor, and the mirror is carefully introduced behind the soft palate, avoiding contact with the uvula, tongue, and posterior pharyngeal wall to prevent the gag reflex. The nasopharynx is brought into view by rotating the mirror so that its reflector surface is directed toward the subject's forehead. Where the gag reflex is too easily elicited, the uvula and soft palate are treated with a local anesthetic.

The pharynx can be visualized with the panendoscope, referred to in Chapter 9.

The pharynx can also be examined roentgenographically to demonstrate tumors and inflammatory lesions, since these alter the pharyngeal air shadows.

Diseases of the Pharynx

Several diseases of the pharynx are bacterial in origin. The pharynx can harbor potentially pathogenic microorganisms, and the nasopharynx and faucial tonsils may constitute the bacterial centers of the respiratory tract. The presence of pharyngeal anomalies, tumors, diverticula, etc., points up the presence of other categories of disease.

Inflammation of the mucous membrane and underlying tissues of the pharynx may produce pharyngitis (sore throat), which is a common cause of a harsh, husky voice or hoarseness. This is the most frequent disorder of this region. Since the lining membrane is one continuous sheet throughout, inflammation of one part of the pharynx is readily transferred to another part (Hall and Colman, 1967).

Acute pharyngitis may occur upon exposure to cold and wet, especially in debilitated persons. The infecting organism is bacterial or viral, but there can be other causes. There is irritation of the throat, the feeling of a lump in back of the throat, and an inflamed mucous membrane covered with whitish mucus.

Chronic pharyngitis may be a sequel to the acute form or a result of prolonged irritation from many causes, including excessive or faulty use of the voice. Neglect in treatment may lead to involvement of the Eustachian tubes, or it may heighten susceptibility to laryngitis, tracheitis, and bronchitis. There is persistent irritation and expectoration of mucus with voice fatigue and hoarseness. The throat shows venous engorgement and inflamed follicles.

Diseases of Waldeyer's ring are another aspect of pharyngeal pathology. The significance of these diseases in speech has already been discussed.

Motor Dysfunction

The motor aspects of function may also become deranged. Paralysis or weakness of the muscles of the pharynx, making complete closure of the nasopharynx difficult, has a diverse etiology. It is expressed primarily as a disturbance of swallowing or by a cough because of failure to propel food and secretions in the proper direction. The characteristic sign of organic pharyngeal lesions is painful swallowing, or dysphagia. In severe lesions of the hindbrain, dysphagia may be accompanied by paralysis of the muscles of the palate and pharynx and by alterations in the voice.

Glossopharyngeal Nerve Disorders

In disorders of the sensory fibers of this nerve, there may be several sequelae. Examples are hypersensitivity (hyperesthesia) with an excessive gag reflex, hyposensitivity (anesthesia) involving varying degrees of loss of pharyngeal sensation, or perverted sensations (parathesia) in which the patient often complains of bizarre stimulation of the pharyngeal area. Severe pain can attend a glossopharyngeal neuralgia, radiating from the throat to the ear along the course of the nerve.

Eustachian Tubes

The orifices of the Eustachian tubes are in the lateral nasopharynx behind the posterior ends of the inferior turbinates. The cartilage ridge, or torus tubarius, which bounds each orifice superiorly and posteriorly, can be seen shining through the mucosa of the tube openings in a mirror examination of the nasopharynx. One actually sees the reflection of the pharyngeal mucosa over the rounded protrusions of the cartilaginous portions of the Eustachian tubes.

Deep pharyngeal recesses, called the fossae of Rosenmüller, are located above and behind the openings of the tubes, and these fossae extend laterally beneath the petrous bone. This general region is of clinical significance because lymphoid tissue may proliferate and narrow the openings of the tubes. This could produce deficient ventilation of the middle ear.

In the infant, the Eustachian openings are level with the nasal floor, and they rise only later to a permanent site behind the inferior turbinates. Children are particularly susceptible to invasive nasopharyngeal infection since their tube openings are in a line with nasal secretions traveling posteriorly from the nasal floor.

12 THE NOSE AND SINUSES

The External Nose

The external nose is a triangular pyramid in shape. Its root is just below the fore-head, and its apex is its lower free end. The part extending from the root to the apex is called the *dorsum*. The superior aspect of the dorsum is composed of paired nasal bones and is called the *bridge*. The inferiorly placed nostrils (anterior nares) are separated from each other by a columella. Hairs protect the opening of the nostrils and decrease the incidence of foreign particles within the nasal chambers.

The nose has two lateral surfaces, each of which ends inferiorly in a rounded part, the ala nasi.

The framework of the external nose is made up of bones superiorly and laterally and cartilages and fatty tissue inferiorly. The bony area is immovable and the lower area movable.

The muscles of the external nose are small and ordinarily are not very important. One or more of them are occasionally absent. They lie in pairs on each side of the nose. The nasal muscles are included in the facial muscles of expression which form a part of the speech mechanisms. These muscles can become important in speech pathology because cleft palate children consistently develop their use in a vain attempt to provide anterior nasal closure to the escape of air past the palatal valve.

The primary muscles of the external nose are (1) the procerus, (2) nasalis, (3) depressor septi, and (4) dilator naris.

The *procerus* is an extension of the occipitofrontalis muscle over the bridge of the nose. It wrinkles the nasal skin over the root area.

A transverse part of the *nasalis* muscle originates in the maxilla superior to the incisor teeth and inserts in the dorsum of the nose. It compresses the sides of the nose. There is another, small component of this muscle, the alar part, found on the lateral sides of the nostril, which increases the transverse axis of the nostrils.

The *depressor septi* muscle originates in the incisor fossa of the maxilla and inserts on the ala and septum. It depresses the nose.

The *dilator naris* muscle is on the side of the nostril and dilates it. It is aided by a muscle of the mouth called the *levator labii superioris alaeque nasi,* which originates on the frontal process of the maxilla and inserts on the lip and the ala of the nose.

336 The entrance to the internal nose is the *vestibule.* It is seen as a large arc formed laterally by the encircling cartilages and supported medially by a T-shaped septal cartilage. The mobility afforded by the cartilages and muscles provides a pinchcock which determines the pattern of air currents entering the nose.

Skeletal Framework of the Nose

The nose is developed by the fusion of several bones and cartilages. The bones of the external nose are the nasals and the frontal processes of the maxillary bones. The maxillaries form not only the principal framework of the cheek but help form the lateral aspects of the external nose. When the small nasals undergo medial fusion, they produce the bridge of the nose in the superior facial region.

Cartilages

The nasal cartilages are prominent in the lower part of the external nose. They include the cartilage of the septum, the paired upper and lower lateral and paired major (greater) alar cartilages, and several minor (lesser) alar cartilages.

At the inferior section of the nasal septum there is a central post, or columella, which separates the right and left nostrils. The columella is developed in the embryo from a depressed part of the medial nasal process. The cartilages which enter into its construction include the lower part of the septal cartilage and the

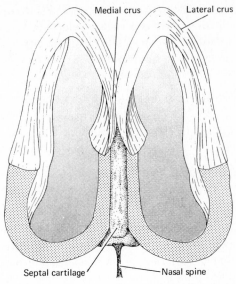

Figure 12-1 Nasal cartilages in anterior view.

medial parts of both greater alar cartilages. The bony anterior nasal spine also helps form the columella.

The cartilage of the septum fills in the anterior space left deficient by the recession of the perpendicular plate of the ethmoid bone. This cartilage fuses posteriorly with the ethmoid bone, connects above in front with the nasal bones and with the lateral cartilages, and meets the medial crura of the greater alar cartilages below. Its lower border connects with the vomer and the palatine processes of the maxillary bones.

The major alar cartilages shape the form of the nostrils and the nasal tip. Each major cartilage is a thin, flexible structure, so curved that it forms the medial and

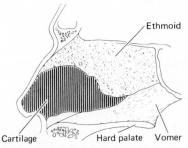

Figure 12-2 The septal cartilage and its relationships.

lateral nasal wall of its own side. There are thus the medial and lateral crura. The paired medial crura along with adjacent soft tissue form a movable structure, called the septum mobile nasi, in the lowest part of the nasal septum. The cartilage of the septum does not extend downward as far as this level. One can move the flexible septum mobile nasi voluntarily.

Stovin (1958) discusses the importance of the septum mobile nasi. It serves as a shock absorber for the lower nose. It is also concerned with the facial expressions elicited by speech and laughing, so that its mobility is important to facial appearance.

Each lateral crus of the major alar cartilages meets the frontal process of the maxillary bone in its posterior section. Within the membrane that connects the crus and the frontal process are several minor alar cartilage plates.

The lateral nasal cartilages are attached above to the nasal bones and to the frontal processes of the maxillary bones. They meet the greater alar cartilages below. The lateral cartilages are continuous above with the septal cartilage but slightly separated from it below.

Converse (1955) has briefly reviewed the anatomy of the nasal cartilages and their role in surgery. They are important in nasal physiology since their movements help maintain an adequate airway. Thus in facial paralysis, in which the cartilages are fixed, there is an inadequate airway on the paralyzed side.

338

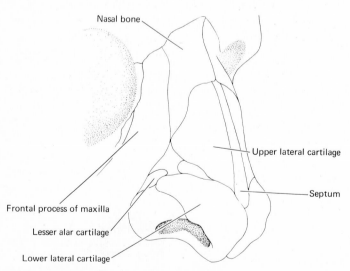

Figure 12-3 The external framework of the nose. (*By permission from H. C. Ballenger and J. J. Ballenger, Diseases of the Nose, Throat, and Ear, 11th ed., Lea & Febiger, Philadelphia, 1969.*)

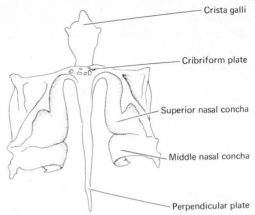

Crista galli

Cribriform plate

Superior nasal concha

Middle nasal concha

Perpendicular plate

Figure 12-4 The nasal septum in natural disarticulated appearance in the anterior view.

Bones of the Internal Nose

The nasal cavities, or fossae, are divided by a central structure called the nasal septum. It usually deviates, because of repeated trauma, toward one nasal cavity, generally to the left. This deviation can affect nasal resonance.

The anterior part of the septum, which is mainly cartilaginous, is received in a triangular wedge of bone. The crest of the nasal bone and the frontal spine help form the anterior aspect of the septum. The perpendicular plate of the ethmoid bone forms its middle section. The vomerine and the sphenoid bones form its posterior aspect. The perpendicular ethmoid section becomes fused below with the upper anterior border of the vomer. The vomer extends forward from this fusion, and this anterior extension fuses above with the lower margin of the septal cartilage of the nose. The septum nasi is completed below by the maxillary and palatine bones.

The ethmoid bone extends upward into the anterior part of the cranial cavity. This forms a projection resembling a cockscomb in the anterior cranial fossa, and it is thus called the crista gallae. A perforated sievelike area, the cribriform plate, surrounds this projecting spur and serves for the passage of the olfactory nerve from the upper olfactory areas of the nasal chambers into the rhinencephalic, or smell, areas of the forebrain.

The ethmoid bone is T-shaped, the upper horizontal cross limb being formed by the horizontal cribriform plate and its extensions. This constitutes the partition between the cranial and the nasal cavities.

The upper lateral extensions of the horizontal portion of the ethmoid bone appear on each side as a labyrinth or lateral mass. Each mass is a group of thin-walled

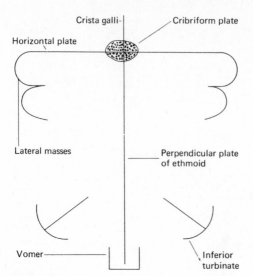

Crista galli-

Cribriform plate

Horizontal plate

Lateral masses

Perpendicular plate
of ethmoid

Vomer

Inferior
turbinate

Figure 12-5 The ethmoid bone and its extensions and relationships to other bones of the nasal septum (diagrammatic anterior view).

 340

cavities, arranged in an anterior, middle, and posterior group of ethmoidal cells, or paranasal sinuses. The labyrinth on each side folds in medially to produce a pair of oblique shelves, the upper and the middle turbinates, or conchae. Inferiorly on each side an independent bone, the inferior turbinate, similarly projects shelflike into the nasal cavity.

These three pairs of very light and spongy conchal processes divide each nasal chamber into three paired chambers, which extend from the front to the back of each nostril. The passages on each side are called the superior, middle, and inferior meati. Each meatus communicates with the air in front by an anterior naris and with the nasopharynx in back by a posterior naris, or choana. The meati receive, in localized regions, the canals which drain the various paranasal sinuses.

The turbinates increase the membrane surface within the small nasal chambers. Most of this surface deals with respiratory activity. In animals with considerable olfactory acuity, the turbinates may be greatly enlarged and are rolled up into scrolls.

Boundaries of the Nasal Cavity The *roof* of each nasal fossa is very narrow, being 1 to 2 mm wide through most of its length. Its most posterior section, however, which is formed by the lower surface of the body of the sphenoid, is about 10 mm wide. The bones constituting the roof are divisible into three sections from front to back, the frontonasal, ethmoidal, and sphenoidal.

The *floor* of the nose is smooth, almost horizontal anteroposteriorly, and slightly concave from side to side. It is about 10 to 12 mm wide, the greatest width being in its central portion.

The floor, which ordinarily is a complete partition between the nose and mouth, is formed by the maxillary and palatine bones. The maxillaries form the anterior section of the hard palate below and the floor of the nose above. The palatines form the posterior section of the hard palate below and the floor of the nose above. The maxillaries constitute approximately three-fourths of the floor.

The *lateral* wall, which is very irregular because of the three nasal conchae, is composed of the nasals, maxillaries, lacrimal, ethmoid labyrinth and turbinates, inferior turbinates, perpendicular part of the palatines, and the medial lamina of the pterygoid process. The order of placement of these bones is roughly in an anteroposterior direction. Below and lateral to each concha is a space called the superior, middle, and inferior meatus, respectively.

The *medial* wall is the nasal septum, already described.

Mucous Membranes

The membrane of the septum and of the nasal cavities generally contains many mucous glands. The upper third is the olfactory area, which contains the tiny filaments of the olfactory nerve. The lower two-thirds form respiratory epithelium, which contains a rich supply of glands. The respiratory lining is pseudostratified,

341

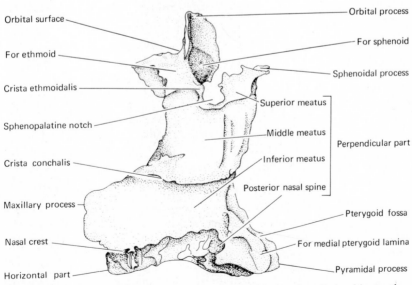

Orbital surface
For ethmoid
Crista ethmoidalis
Sphenopalatine notch
Crista conchalis
Maxillary process
Nasal crest
Horizontal part

Orbital process
For sphenoid
Sphenoidal process
Superior meatus
Middle meatus
Inferior meatus
Posterior nasal spine
Perpendicular part
Pterygoid fossa
For medial pterygoid lamina
Pyramidal process

Figure 12-6 Right palatine bone, medial aspect, showing its relationship to the boundaries of the nasal cavity.

ciliated, and columnar. The membrane is especially thick and vascular over the turbinates, somewhat less thick over the septum, and thin elsewhere including the inside of the paranasal sinuses.

In the more exposed parts of the nose, which include the anterior ends of the turbinates and the preturbinal regions, the epithelium loses its cilia, and squamous epithelium is seen.

In the olfactory region the cells are columnar and nonciliated. Supporting and olfactory cells occur. There are numerous serous glands of a simple tuboalveolar nature.

Blood and Nerve Supply

Blood and Lymph
The internal carotid sends branches through the ophthalmic artery. The external carotid utilizes its internal and external maxillary branches, chiefly the spheno-palatine branch of the internal maxillary artery.

The blood supply of the turbinates, meati, and septum comes from the spheno-palatine branch of the internal maxillary artery. The roof of the nose and the ethmoidal and frontal sinuses are supplied by anterior and posterior ethmoidal branches of the ophthalmic artery. The pharyngeal branch of the internal maxillary artery supplies the sphenoid sinus. A branch of the superior labial artery plus infraorbital and alveolar branches of the internal maxillary artery supply the maxillary sinus.

The facial artery, a branch of the external maxillary, travels along the sides of the nose and supplies its skin and dorsum. The nostrils receive blood from the facial artery and also from a septal branch of the superior labial artery.

The venous drainage exists under the mucous membrane as a cavernous plexus, emptying chiefly through the ophthalmic, anterior facial, and sphenopalatine veins. The swell bodies (erectile tissue on both sides of the septum which adjusts its thickness according to atmospheric changes) represent the venous plexus in full development over the lower septum and over the middle and inferior turbinates.

The nasal mucosa contains an abundant network of lymphatics which are continuous with the lymph vessels of the nasopharynx and soft palate. There is an anterior set of trunks which drain into the preauricular, facial, and the submaxillary nodes. Trunks in the Eustachian tube area drain a large segment of the nose and paranasal sinuses, and these in turn end in deep cervical and retropharyngeal nodes.

Lymphatics of the external nose, the vestibule and the mucosa of the anterior section of the nasal fossa travel up above the superior eyelid and drain into the parotid nodes. Other trunks from the sides and roof of the nose reach the parotid nodes by traveling across the lower eyelid. Still others from the front part of the septum and from the external nose drain into the facial or submaxillary nodes.

The lymph in the anterior third of the nose flows out to the external surface, but the lymph in the posterior two-thirds as well as in the sinuses flows toward the Eustachian region of the nasopharynx and eventually to deep cervical and retropharyngeal nodes.

Nerves
Several nerves innervate the nose. Somatic motor fibers to the muscles of the external nose are contained in the facial nerve.

The internal nose has a more complicated efferent supply, which is controversial. Efferent parasympathetic fibers for the nose and paranasal sinuses originate from cells in the reticular formation of the medulla, contiguous to the facial nerve nucleus. They pass from the medulla in the pars intermedia of the facial nerve and are distributed by the great superficial petrosal nerve to the sphenopalatine ganglion. Postganglionic fibers go from that ganglion to the mucosa, glands, and blood vessels of the nose, palate, tonsils, and lacrimal glands.

The complementary, or "opposing," sympathetic efferents originate in several segments of the thoracic spinal cord, typically 1-T to 5-T, and pass as preganglionics to the vertical sympathetic chain. They ascend to the superior cervical ganglion at the level of the thyroid cartilage. Postganglionics then go superiorly and form the deep petrosal nerve. This joins the greater superficial petrosal nerve (branch of the facial) to form the vidian nerve. The vidian nerve carries preganglionic parasympathetic fibers and postganglionic sympathetic fibers to the sphenopalatine ganglion.

The sympathetics are more vasoconstrictor than dilator, the latter tending to prevail in the parasympathetics of the pars intermedia. The erectile tissues of the nose are especially subject to vasodilation. The vasomotor nerves may produce immediate effects upon the diameter of the nasal passages and of the paranasal sinuses. Anger quickly produces swelling of the mucosa. Fear rapidly shrinks the membranes. These emotional effects are reflexly brought about by an action upon the vasomotor centers in the hindbrain.

The *sensory* innervation of the internal nose is complex. The ophthalmic and maxillary divisions of the trigeminal nerve innervate the nasal skin and mucosa for the general sensations of hot, cold, pressure, and pain. The anterior section of the septum and lateral wall of the nose receive the nasociliary branches of the ophthalmic nerve. The inferior turbinates and the inferior meati receive the anterior alveolar branches of the maxillary nerve. The posterior and superior aspects of the septum are supplied by the vidian nerve through the sphenopalatine ganglion.

The center of the septum receives the nasopalatine branches of the maxillary nerve. The innervation to the middle and superior turbinates comes from the posterior superior nasal branches of the maxillary.

The nose also receives the olfactory nerve for the special sensation of smell. This nerve leaves the sensory epithelium in the mucosa of the upper part of the nose. Its twigs penetrate the skull through the cribriform plate and reach the olfactory bulb. Central fibers pass from there to the smell areas of the cerebrum. It is claimed (Ballenger, 1969) that the olfactory nerve is distributed only to the mucous membrane covering the upper part of the superior turbinate and a corresponding part of the septum and that it does not innervate the middle turbinate and corresponding septal area, as formerly supposed.

Nasal Functions

The nose is involved in olfaction, respiration, and to some extent phonation. The entering air is modified by being moistened, warmed, and filtered. All these effects have an influence on speech.

Humidification

The nose can add moisture to the inspired air or remove moisture from it. Thus, the air reaching the pharynx is almost constant in water content. Ordinarily the seromucinous glands of the nasal mucosa may secrete as much as a liter of fluid per day.

The humidifying power of the nose is indirectly involved in modifying laryngeal function. In the dry larynx, or laryngitis sicca, the incident air has insufficient moisture. A lack of moisture is a factor in destroying the action of the nasal hairs, or cilia, which aid in the removal of dust and bacteria.

The humidity influences the resonating potential of the nasal cavities. This effect is reflected in the different degrees of swelling of the mucous membrane and turbinates.

In psychologic states such as fear, the mucous membrane may become dry, and the turbinates shrink. This suggests that voice problems with accompanying inflammatory changes may require psychic as well as medical consideration (Moses, 1954).

Heating Effect

The air is warmed by the radiator function of the mucosal blood vessels. The vessels open or close according to the air temperature, acting as a thermostat for the respiratory tract and perhaps allowing the paranasal sinuses to behave as heat insulators for surrounding cerebral structures. The turbinates have a rich capillary blood supply, and the associated erectile tissue can rapidly enlarge or contract. Regardless of the incident temperature, the nasopharyngeal temperature becomes fairly constant despite the fact that the passage of air over a journey of 4 in. from the nose to the nasopharynx takes only about ¼ sec (DeWeese and Saunders, 1964).

The air-conditioning activities of heat and moisture regulation represent the chief function of the two lower turbinates (Dolowitz, 1964). The lowest turbinate has the richest blood lakes, and it warms the air. The middle turbinate, which has fewer blood lakes, assists in warming the air but is the most important agency for moistening the air. The superior portion of the middle turbinate has olfactory epithelium and assists the superior turbinate in olfaction.

Filtering Activity

The cleansing action of the nose is linked to a great extent with the cilia of the respiratory epithelium and with the mucous coat that is seated above the cilia. The direction of mucus flow is generally posteriorly in the nose. Bacteria and other particulate matter are carried to the pharynx and then swallowed and destroyed by gastric juice.

The anterior third of the nose has squamous cells and no cilia. The remainder of the nose has ciliated, pseudostratified columnar epithelium. Each cell has twenty-five to thirty cilia which beat rhythmically about 250 times per minute in the direction of flow. The mucous coat is continuous throughout the nose, paranasal sinuses, pharynx, and tracheobronchial system. The mucus collects foreign particles, and eliminates them not only by the movements of the underlying cilia, but also because it contains lysozyme, which produces bacterial disintegration. A neutral pH is essential to both the ciliary and lysozyme action.

The importance of the cilia and mucus is seen by the fact that most clinical nasal complaints involve disorders of the epithelium. In atrophic rhinitis the ciliated cells become squamous, the turbinates atrophy, secretion dries, and crusting occurs. In asthma, the ciliated cells change to goblet cells and secrete a heavy mucus with no machinery for moving it. In the viral attack of a common cold, the injured epithelium loosens, and the ciliated cells float free in the secretion.

345

Endocrine Involvement of the Nasal Mucosa

The nasal mucosa is linked, although obscurely, with endocrine function. There is gonadotropic activity in extracts from the nasal mucosa and the paranasal sinuses of cattle. The erectile tissues of the nose develop in puberty. In animal castrates such tissues tend to involute. Endocrine influences are also suggested by the observation that menstruation and puberty may be associated with an increased incidence of nosebleeds.

Overall Importance in Speech

The nasal cavities are subdivided into many variably sized air spaces, and they should not be considered as a pair of large nasal chambers. The subdivisions of the nose tend to classify it as a multiple resonator. Its resonance cannot be readily varied since its upper bony walls are immovable. Its lower, fleshy walls can be moved, however, by external muscles. The posterior openings can be controlled by the velum and superior pharyngeal constrictor muscle. Also, changes in tuning follow swelling or shrinking of the nasal cavities from any causes.

The exact importance of the nose in speech is uncertain. In some regards it is less important than once thought. For example, the causes of nasality are not necessarily localized in the nasal chambers. Berry and Eisenson (1956) note that a discordant nasal twang may result from excessive tension of the pharyngeal constrictors, the pharyngeal arches, the levator palati muscles, or from tension anywhere in the supraglottal region.

On the other hand, the evidence of certain pathology indicates that the nose offers a relatively important contribution to speech. In the disorders, or dyslalias, caused by deformities of the nasal passages, distinct speech defects called rhinolalias are produced.

Hahn et al. (1957) state that the nasal cavities are the least adjustable and least versatile of the resonators. In an earlier edition they state that the nasal cavities may serve chiefly as supplemental sympathetic resonators for high-frequency overtones.

The Paranasal Sinuses

Four pairs of accessory sinuses, all called paranasal, drain into the nose. They include the frontal, maxillary, ethmoidal, and sphenoidal air cells. There is considerable variation in their shape and size among individuals.

All the sinuses are lined by a ciliated mucous membrane continuous with that of the nose and providing drainage into the nose. Because of the continuity, disease spreads rapidly from the nose to the sinuses. There are fewer glands in the sinus mucosa than there are in the nasal mucosa. Thus, most mucoid nasal discharge is referable to hyperplastic nasal rather than to sinus glands.

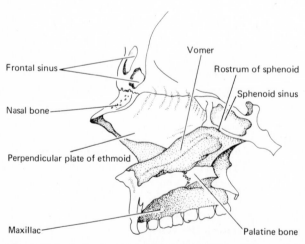

Figure 12-7 Sagittal section of the skull showing the frontal and sphenoid paranasal sinuses and a side view of the nasal septum.

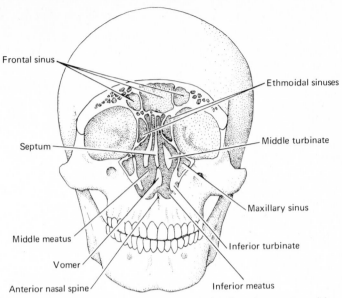

Frontal sinus

Ethmoidal sinuses

Septum

Middle turbinate

Maxillary sinus

Middle meatus

Inferior turbinate

Vomer

Anterior nasal spine

Inferior meatus

Figure 12-8 Anterior view of the skull showing the nasal cavities and paranasal sinuses.

The *frontal* sinus is an irregular cavity in the frontal bone, behind the superciliary arches. It occupies the space in the bone between the inner and outer tables. The paired sinuses are separated medially by a usually deviated bony septum. Each sinus drains by a frontonasal duct into the middle meatus, or passageway below the middle turbinate. In some individuals one frontal sinus is missing, and in others there are more than two, each with its own drainage canal.

The *ethmoidal* air cells are many, small, thin-walled, intercommunicating chambers in the labyrinth of the ethmoid bone between the orbit of the eye and the nasal cavity and just below the cranial cavity. The cells may pneumatize bones adjacent to the ethmoid. The ethmoid is separated from the orbit by a very thin plate, the lamina papyracea.

The number of ethmoid cells varies from three to eighteen. They are divided into anterior, middle, and posterior groups. The anterior and middle groups drain into the middle meatus, the middle by one or two openings. The posterior sinuses drain into the superior meatus by one or more apertures.

The *maxillary* sinus, or antrum of Highmore, is a pyramidal cavity occupying almost the entire body of each maxillary bone, in the cheek area. These are the largest paranasal sinuses. When fully developed, the floor of each space extends from the second premolar to the third molar tooth. The hard palate and alveolar process

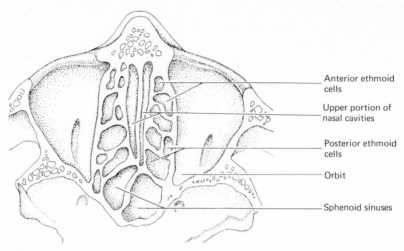

Anterior ethmoid
cells

Upper portion of
nasal cavities

Posterior ethmoid
cells

Orbit

Sphenoid sinuses

Figure 12-9 Horizontal section through the ethmoid labyrinth. (*By permission from H. C. Ballenger and J. J. Ballenger, Diseases of the Nose, Throat and Ear, 11th ed., Lea & Febiger, Philadelphia, 1969.*)

form its floor. Several conical processes corresponding to the roots of the teeth project into the floor. The medial boundary is the lateral nasal wall, and the lateral boundary is the maxilla. The sinus extends up to the floor of the orbit, which forms its roof. The sinus is occasionally divided by septa into two or more cavities.

The opening out of the maxillary sinus, which is on its medial side, drains into the middle meatus. There may be one or two drainage canals into the nose, and these are frequently higher than the sinus floor. This presents difficulty in drainage. The secretions of the mucous membrane are propelled toward the opening in the medial wall by cilia. It is during inflammation, when the cilia cannot keep up with the quantity of secretion formed, that the bottom of the sinus collects fluid.

The *sphenoidal* sinus is a large cavity within the body of the sphenoid bone. This bone occupies the central part of the base of the skull. The sinus is just above and behind the nasal cavities, and it is above and a little anterior to the nasopharynx. It is divided more or less completely into halves by a central bony septum. Each half may be considered to be an individual sphenoidal sinus. On each side a duct runs to the corresponding nasal cavity, terminating in the sphenoethmoidal recess of the nose, a space above the superior turbinates.

A *palatine* sinus may be present, lying within the orbital process of the palatine bone and opening either into the sphenoidal sinus or into a posterior ethmoidal sinus.

Functions of the Sinuses

Proetz (1953) states that the sinuses are developmental accidents which form as the facial bones grow away from the relatively stationary cranium. As an example, the maxilla grows inferolaterally to support the alveolar process, and the vacated space is filled by sucking in the nasal mucosa, which then lines the cavity so produced. This process could explain the position of the drainage opening in the upper medial part of the maxillary sinus. Boies et al. (1964) say that the sinuses have no physiologic function and are important primarily because of the complications of nasal disease originating in them.

The sinuses, on the other hand, have been claimed (without real proof) to do many things. Since they are cavities in the skull bones, they permit these bones to increase in size without adding too much weight. They add a mucous secretion to the nasal chambers, and they help moisten the incoming air. They equalize the barometric pressure of the air.

The direction of mucus flow in the sinuses is spiral (Boies et al., 1964), beginning at a region remote from the ostium. In approaching the ostium the rate increases, the mucus leaving the ostium in the form of a whirling tube. The gradient of speed increases from about 2 mm/min in the sinuses to 20 mm/min in the ostium.

The problem of the resonance function of the paranasal sinuses is still to be solved. There is little direct evidence that these cavities are important in resonance. A stuffy nose and sinuses will change voice quality. The greater nasal cavities seem to be the more important agents, since a loss of vocal resonance need not occur in a chronic sinus infection unless there is significant nasal involvement.

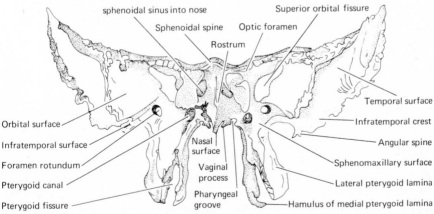

Figure 12-10 The sphenoid bone, disarticulated and seen from in front, showing position of sphenoid sinus within the bone and the relationship of the sphenoid to important foramina, fissures, and processes.

Greene (1964) differentiates the relative importance of the sinuses as resonators. The maxillary sinuses are stated to be important because they are large and open into the nose by fairly large orifices. The other sinuses, and also the Eustachian tubes and mastoid air cells, are small, closed in, and waterlogged. Since they have inadequate communication with the external air, their resonating function is problematical.

Some of the difficulty in analyzing the problem lies in the need to differentiate the part played by resonance due to forced vibrations occurring in bony and cartilaginous structures from the part played by cavity resonance which occurs within the known resonating chambers. The former have been termed universal and the latter selective resonators. Although the sinuses themselves may offer some relatively fixed contribution to resonance, the bones of the skull surrounding them are fairly thin and may add a forced vibration to the tones. Head resonance may be due to bone conduction (Luchsinger and Arnold, 1965).

Developmental Anatomy of the Nose and Sinuses

The earliest sign of the developing nose in the embryo is the olfactory placode, an oval thickening on each side of the front end of the head. About the fourth week a fold forms around the outer border of the olfactory placode, and small pits form in the surface. The pits deepen, move toward one another, and come to lie together except for a narrow separating band of tissue. The nostrils, or anterior nares, develop from the pits.

Simultaneously with the nasal changes, outgrowths called the maxillary processes appear. They grow forward and medialward to join the nasal structures and produce a primitive mouth and nose.

The nasal pits by the thirty-fifth day have deepened to blind pouches above the oral cavity. The pits grow posteriorly and become continuous with the throat through the posterior nares. Thickening of the walls above the mouth elevates the position of the nose. The nasal septum forms from the tissue between the nostrils.

By the end of the second month the external nose is broad and flat. The midline area develops early, and the inferior part descends to form the nasal tip.

The floor of the nose, or palate, develops as a part of both the face and the mouth (Chapter 10).

The paranasal sinuses begin in the fourth or fifth fetal month as small groups of cells which appear at different points in the mucous walls of the nasal fossae. The cells proliferate into the bones of the skull and form sacs at some distance from their origins, although they retain a permanent connection with the nasal chambers by one or more ducts. The mucous membrane of the nose continues along each duct as a lining of the sinuses.

The destruction of bone neighboring the nasal cavities, to make room for the expanding sinuses, occurs apparently under the influence of the lining epithelium (Arey, 1965). The epithelium proliferates at an equal pace with the destruction of bone.

The groove foreshadowing the maxillary sinus appears in the fourth fetal month, which is earlier than the other sinuses appear, but the structure is not fully developed until after the child gets its second dentition. The maxillary sinus at birth is represented only by a groove. According to Woodburne (1965), the maxillary sinus exhibits a definite cavity at birth, and it is the only one to do so. The floor of the sinus attains the same level as the floor of the nose only at about the ninth year, and the antrum is not completed until the twenty-third to the twenty-fifth year (Hall and Colman, 1967).

The rudiments of the sphenoidal sinuses appear in the fifth fetal month or later. They represent recesses of the nasal cavity which have been partly separated and enclosed within the sphenoidal conchae. The conchae comprise the anterior surface of the body of the sphenoid as well as the anterior part of its lower surface but not including its crest and rostrum. The sphenoidal rudiments actually do not extend into the body of the sphenoid until the seventh year or later. Although seen as minute cavities at birth, their chief development occurs after puberty.

The ethmoidal air sacs are present at birth, but they are very small. The frontal sinus first appears during childhood at about the fifth to the seventh years, when the air cells extend above the level of the supraorbital ridge. A recess in the anterior part of the nose pneumatizes the frontal bone superiorly and forms the frontonasal duct. The sinus enlarges in every direction within the frontal bone.

351

All the sinuses enlarge slowly until puberty, after which they expand and differentiate rapidly. Only the frontal and sphenoidal sinuses are radiologically visible at six or seven years of age.

Comparative Anatomy

In the most primitive vertebrates the only function of the nose is olfaction. The activity of warming inspired air for respiration is negated in that the temperature of the cold-blooded vertebrates is the same as that of their environment.

In typical aquatic forms the olfactory membranes line blind cavities in the head, communicating with the exterior by the anterior nares. In the terrestrial forms the nasal cavities break through internally into the pharynx, which adds a respiratory function. Among the fish, internal nares (choanae) are present in such atypical forms as the lungfish and hagfish.

In the amphibians the internal nares are present and open into the anterior region of the oral cavity. Air passes from the choanae into the mouth, then valves in the anterior nares are closed, the floor of the mouth is raised, and air is forced backward into the lungs.

As the terrestrial vertebrates arose, the more posterior position of the choanae allowed air to bypass the mouth and avoided exposing the oral mucosa to disastrous desiccation. In the reptiles this was effected by the appearance of a primitive type of hard palate and by carrying the choanae back to the pharynx.

The warm-blooded vertebrates encountered many unfavorable conditions for the olfactory mechanism in their diverse environments, and they adapted by developing mucous glands and capillary lakes. Increasing the internal functional surface areas and providing for moisture led to greater efficiency of the olfactory membranes. Mucous glands did not appear until the amphibians evolved. Much more elaborate evolutionary air-conditioning machinery arose in mammals. The carnivores reached a higher degree of such development than man did, and they obtained a more proper moisture saturation, essential to their greater olfactory acuity.

The olfactory mucosa tends to regress in the human species. The epithelium becomes restricted mostly to the superior turbinates in the upper angle of the nose and to the highest parts of the septum. The olfactory sense cells are true sensory nerve neurons, and the continuity of nerve fiber with the terminal cells is a primitive relationship reminiscent of the sense cells of the lower invertebrates. The arrangement suggests that the olfactory membrane is phylogenetically very old, and inherited from a remote invertebrate ancestor.

352   The paranasal sinuses increase the olfactory surface. In animals with the most elaborate nasal structures the sinuses are lined with olfactory mucous membrane and may even develop turbinates.

Except for special adaptations such as the tubular prolongations of the nostrils in certain fish and aquatic birds, an external nose as a separate organ is unique to mammals. In the anthropoids it reduces in size as the olfactory sense decreases in importance, but its muscles are very mobile and contribute markedly to facial expression. Although the human nose is more prominent than in most primates, the expressive functions of the nasal musculature are undergoing degeneration.

Pathophysiology of the Nose and Sinuses

There are a number of organic diseases of the nose and its sinuses which affect the quality of speech. The present discussion will be limited almost entirely to the deviation called nasality, certain aspects of which have already been considered.

Nasality

Nasality is one of the most frequent speech defects. This and nasal resonance are not synonymous. Nasal resonance is the normal resonance added by the nasal passages to the exhaled tone, whereas nasality implies too much nasal resonance. The opposite condition is called denasality.

The only English sounds primarily nasal are /m/, /n/, and /ŋ/. In American speech some nasal resonance may occur in all voiced sounds, so that the difference between the normal and the abnormal is one of degree rather than kind (Sokoloff, 1966). There is, for example, an *assimilation nasality,* where nasal emission occurs during the production of vowel sounds immediately preceded by or followed by nasal consonants. This may be a result of anticipating the lowering of the velum and relaxation of the velopharyngeal closure.

In nasality the subject seems to talk through his nose, and the vowels are over-nasalized. In denasality the vowels sound dull, and the nasal consonants show a lack of resonance, such as during speech with a head cold. The definition and acceptance of nasality are to a great extent subjective.

Nasality is in a sense a disorder of articulation, since the vowels are given distinctive qualities by the position of the articulators as well as by the size and shape of the resonating chambers. For example, the velum, which is an articulator, can lower improperly and permit nonnasal sounds to obtain nasal resonance.

Nasality or denasality are found under many circumstances. A point may be made here of their occurrence as sequelae of certain disorders involving excessive patency of the nasal passages (rhinolalia aperta) or excessive closure of the nasal passages (rhinolalia clausa).

Rhinolalia aperta (hyperrhinolalia) may result from cleft palate, holes in the hard or soft palate, soft palate paralysis, faulty habits in the use of the soft palate, etc. The voice is hypernasal.

Rhinolalia clausa (hyporhinolalia) has both anterior and posterior varieties. The anterior type is organic and involves different degrees of obstruction to the passage of air in the anterior part of the nose. There could be organic growths such as polyps. The voice may sound as though the person had a plugged nose or a head cold.

The posterior type may be associated with organic lesions such as adenoids or other growths in the nasopharyngeal region, or it may be functional. In the latter there may be permanent elevation of the soft palate during speech, along with contracted pharyngeal or tongue muscles.

The distortion of nasal sounds because of the absence of nasal resonance exemplifies denasality, or negative nasality, and it illustrates the fact that the voice without resonance is lifeless.

Some simple although inconclusive laboratory tests of nasal conditions may be tried. To check first for whether the air in a given person passes without obstruction through each nostril, hold a piece of paper so that its upper border is about 3 in. from his left nostril. Let him close his right nostril with a finger and gently exhale air for a few seconds through his open left nostril. If there is an unobstructed stream of air, the corner of the paper will be made to move visibly and smoothly. This procedure is repeated for the other nostril.

353

It may then be checked whether nasal resonance is being unduly involved in primarily nonnasal sounds. Cool a small mirror and dry it, then position it perhaps ¼ in. below the nostrils of a subject. Have him speak aloud a sentence in which nasal sounds are not emphasized. If an appreciable film of warm air condenses upon the mirror, there is too much nasal involvement in the emitted breath stream.

A modification may be tried to test whether sufficient nasal resonance is being imparted to what should be nasal sounds. Holding the cooled mirror below the nostrils and above the mouth, have the individual speak aloud a sentence in which nasal sounds predominate. The mirror should collect a more obvious film of condensed air.

The above tests must be interpreted with caution. Nasality can be fairly independent of the nasal emission. The nasal cavities could be occluded and still vibrate with sufficient intensity to produce audible sounds that are nasal.

Greene (1964) says that the most important factor causing nasality is not the degree of nasal air escape. Nasality is determined by the degree of tension found in the upper pharynx and also by the ratio of the size of the openings into the mouth and nose, relative to the size and shape of the air-filled cavities.

13 THE STRUCTURES FOR ARTICULATION

Definitions

Articulation in the broadest sense refers to the acceptability of sound to the listener. More restrictedly it refers to the activities of the supraglottic structures that modify the breath stream and produce meaningful sounds.

The terms speech and language may be differentiated at this point. Speech refers to meaningful sounds. When such sounds are used together in accepted ways, they constitute verbal language. The term verbal language pertains to the symbolic meanings associated with the sound groupings (Rousey and Moriarty, 1965). Hughes (1962) discusses the validity of several dictionary and linguistic definitions of language and suggests that language be defined as a system of arbitrary vocal symbols by which thought is transmitted among individuals.

McDonald (1964) considers language as an accumulation of concepts which exists in some symbolic form. Speech is one of several modalities through which language is utilized. Articulation is one of many interrelated processes by which speech is produced. In McDonald's definition of articulation, which stresses its dynamic nature, it is a series of overlapping ballistic movements which variably obstruct the exhaled airstream and also modify the size, shape, and coupling of the resonating chambers. In a ballistic movement the agonist, or primary muscle, contracts quickly, after which the structure moves as a result of its own momentum despite an absence of muscle contraction. The antagonist muscle group stops the movement.

The main division of the speech sounds is into consonants and vowels. Both are produced by the breath. Vowels are products of the vocalized breath traveling freely through the mouth with the speech organs positioned differentially. Consonants are produced by the speech organs positioned essentially to impede the passage of the outgoing breath (Colson, 1963).

Articulators are valves to stop the exhaled air completely or to narrow the space for its passage. They shape, fuse, and separate the sounds transmitted to them. Articulators include such structures as the lips, teeth, hard and soft palate, tongue, mandible, and posterior pharyngeal wall and probably should include the inner edges of the vocal folds. The hyoid bone may be classified as an articulator (Van Riper and Irwin, 1958) in view of the effects of its movements upon consonants and vowels. Some articulators, e.g., tongue, lips, velum, and mandible, are movable, whereas others, e.g., teeth, alveolar ridge, hard palate, and pharyngeal wall, are immovable.

In considering the teeth as articulators, the alveolar arch is significantly involved since the status of its cutting and shaping edge determines the characteristics of numerous fricatives. The mandibular arch is specifically an articulator since it moves against the upper lip in the sounds /f/ and /v/.

356

The tip of the tongue appears to be the fastest articulator, and the soft palate is probably the slowest. Perhaps the teeth and hard palate should be regarded as walls against which the articulators move. The soft palate is more a deflector than an articulator in that it differentially passes the airstream through the mouth and nose.

One should not get the impression that the articulatory configurations for speech sounds are restricted only to the structures listed above. Rather, they involve the entire vocal tract, which itself is in continuous change during the speech processes. Normal articulation depends upon the correlated activities of an enormous number of structures. The more immediate ones are discussed in this chapter, but there are also the problems of satisfactory intelligence, education and training, adequate hearing, proprioception, association pathways, and the integrity of all the brain structures and connecting pathways concerned.

The Mouth

Speech Activity

The structures of the mouth articulate recognizable sounds. They also provide the free passage necessary to build up tone by addition of volume and resonance. The mouth is not only an articulator but also the most movable and controllable of the resonators. This remarkable oral versatility is ascribable to the many associated structures within and about it such as the tongue, teeth, velum, pharyngeal walls, lips, cheeks, and mandible.

The muscles associated with the mouth continually alter their activity to modify the oral tone. In front, the orbicularis oris muscle of the lips alters oral resonance by pursing and retracting. Along the sides, the mouth is enlarged or constricted by the buccinator, platysma, risorius, and zygomaticus muscles. The posterior opening is constricted by the glossopalatal muscles.

Oral resonance is also influenced by the hard palate through the rigidity, density, and tension of its structure and also partly through its shape (low or high, narrow vault).

The mouth is important as a resonator in forming vowels. It changes its size and shape to amplify certain partials in the laryngeal tone, and it imparts to the tone a quality described as a vowel sound. Through the changes in tongue positions and in the shape of the lips, the tonal quality is altered, and another vowel sound is produced.

In the building up of mouth pressure the velum helps to dam up the air by aiding closure of the nasal passages. This action gives sufficient force to develop high-pressure consonant sounds, like /g/ or /k/.

The mouth may be said to form a natural amplifier, which collects sonorous vibrations and amplifies them during the external passage (Meano and Khoury, 1967).

357

Biologic Activity
The mouth has a primary role in the digestive function. It also is frequently involved in the mechanics of breathing. Oropharyngeal factors are important both in the identification of nutrients and as powerful loci of sensors involved as incentive devices for drinking and feeding (Epstein, 1967).

General Anatomy
The mouth is divided into a *buccal cavity,* which is the space external to all the teeth, and a larger *oral cavity* proper.

The buccal cavity is bounded externally by the lips and cheeks and internally by the outer aspect of the teeth and gums. Where there is a full dentition, the buccal and oral cavities in the resting position of the mandible communicate between the upper and lower teeth. In the occlusal position, when the teeth are in close contact, these cavities communicate through capillary clefts between the adjacent teeth in each jaw and also through a narrow opening behind the back teeth on each side.

The buccal cavity has many glands. The labial glands on the inner surface of the lip are mucous. Molar glands open from the cheeks to the buccal cavity opposite the back teeth. Stenson's ducts of the parotid salivary glands open opposite the second upper molar teeth.

The labial frenulum is a vertical fold of mucous membrane on the inside of the upper lip, and it connects the lip with the alveolar process. A similar but weaker structure is found in the inner median aspect of the lower lip.

In the oral cavity proper, the peripheral boundary is the alveolar process and the teeth. The roof is the hard palate. The floor is muscular, and it is occupied by the tongue. The posterior wall is the dependent section of the soft palate. The mouth communicates with the throat through the fauces.

The tongue is held down in the floor by the frenulum linguae, which is a distinct vertical fold of mucous membrane. Many of the ducts of Rivinus from the sublingual salivary glands empty into the oral cavity at the plica sublingualis, or elevated crest of mucous membrane produced by the projection of the gland on either side of the frenulum. Some of the sublingual ducts come together as a duct of Bartholin, which empties into the submaxillary duct. The ducts from the submaxillary salivary glands have a narrow opening into the sides of the frenulum linguae near the lower central incisors.

Mechanical Functions of Saliva

Oral lubrication from the salivary glands is important to speech as well as to mastication and deglutition. With a decreased salivary flow, the movements of the lips, tongue, and cheeks against the teeth are accomplished less smoothly and efficiently.

The maintenance of the pliability of the oral mucous membranes is an action somewhat different from lubrication. It is called an emollient action, and it is brought about by the mucin content of the saliva. It allows free movement without frictional injury to the surface of the moving structures. Abrasions, inflammations, and increased sensitivity of oral membranes tend to follow a long-standing decrease in mucin resulting from suppression of salivary flow. The protecting and soothing effects of saliva upon the surface membranes, in contrast to its softening property, is termed its demulcent action.

Prolonged speech activity can result in some deficiency of salivary flow. This failure is explained by nervous and endocrine influences or even by simple evaporation of water.

Mucous Membranes

There are three types of mucous membranes in the oral cavity. One type, which is sensory in nature, covers the dorsal surface of the tongue. A second variety lines the gingivae and the hard palate, and it is built to resist the strong pressures of mastication. The third type is an ordinary protective lining found in the lips, the cheeks, the alveolar processes peripheral to the gingivae proper, the floor of the mouth, the under surface of the tongue, and in the soft palate.

Oral Nerve Supply

The nerves are described with each organ. As a general statement, the motor nerves to the oral muscles include the facial nerve to the mimetic musculature, the mandibular division of the trigeminal nerve to the muscles of chewing, and the hypoglossal nerve to the tongue. On the afferent side, the oral mucosa, gums, teeth, and tongue are innervated by the trigeminal nerve for general sensation. Taste in the anterior tongue is mediated by the facial nerve and in the posterior tongue by the glossopharyngeal nerve. Distinct efferent autonomic fibers are carried in several nerves to the salivary glands and to the blood vessels and mucous glands.

Oral Blood and Lymph
The blood to the lips and cheeks comes chiefly from the external maxillary artery through its submental, superior, and inferior labial branches. There is a lesser contribution from the internal maxillary artery through its buccinator, infraorbital, and mental branches. The superficial temporal branch of the external carotid sends the transverse facial artery to the cheeks.

The blood supply to the gingivae and teeth of the lower jaw and also to the oral floor comes from the lingual, external, and internal maxillary arteries. The supply to the gingivae and teeth of the upper jaw and also to the roof of the mouth comes from the internal maxillary artery through the posterior and anterior alveolar, the greater palatine, and the long sphenopalatine branches.

The chief drainage is by way of the lingual veins into the anterior facial veins. In the upper mouth the pterygoid plexus drains into the internal maxillary veins.

Lymphatics in the anterior oral floor drain into the superior deep cervical nodes about the internal jugular veins or indirectly through the submental nodes into the deep cervical nodes. The lymphatics of the main oral floor drain into the submaxillary and upper deep cervical nodes.

359

Developmental Anatomy of the Facial Region
It has been noted that the essential elements for the formation of the face are usually present during the fourth week. Some additional details with particular reference to the mouth will be considered.

The anlage of the mouth appears in the ventral head region as an ectodermal pit called the stomodeum. This is bounded above by the projecting forebrain, laterally by the mandibular processes (and their developing extensions, the maxillary processes), and below by the mandibular processes. The pit is open in front, but it is closed in back by a buccopharyngeal membrane. This separates it from the foregut. During the third or fourth week the membrane, or stomodeal plate, ruptures at a point corresponding to the tonsillar region of the adult and forms the oral opening into the gut.

Several surrounding structures grow forward about the mouth to enclose it as the face and the jaws. At four weeks the stomodeum and the mandibular arch below it are the prominent landmarks of the face.

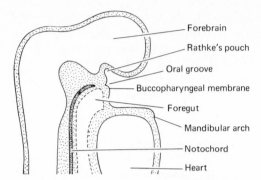

Forebrain
Rathke's pouch
Oral groove
Buccopharyngeal membrane
Foregut
Mandibular arch
Notochord
Heart

Figure 13-1 Median section through the head of a 3-mm human embryo. The oral groove is separated from the foregut by the buccopharyngeal membrane, or double layer of epithelium.

In the midline above the developing mouth there is an overhanging prominence. This is the frontonasal (nasofrontal) process, which projects from just below the forebrain to bound the upper border of the mouth. The process is derived from mesenchyme surrounding the cranial end of the notochord. The latter is a rodlike structure, ventral to the primitive nervous system of the embryo, which will define the primitive axis of the body and form vertebral elements.

360

A pair of olfactory pits, the primordia of the nostrils, divides the frontonasal process into a central section, the paired median nasal processes, which are between the developing nostrils, and the paired lateral nasal processes, which are lateral to the nostrils. This division occurs in the fifth week.

The maxillary processes, which have proliferated from the dorsal ends of the mandibular processes, grow inward toward the median line in the ventral aspect of the face. The medial tip of each maxillary process fuses with the lateral process on its own side. The combined processes are pushed medially. A fusion then occurs with the expansions called globular processes, which develop on each side of the median nasal processes. The maxillary process on each side also merges laterally with the section of the mandibular arch that is located at the corner of the mouth.

These fusions separate the oral pit from the olfactory pits. The olfactory pits will open later into the cavity of the oral pit by choanae, or posterior nares.

The anterior part of the mouth is bounded below by the mandible developing from fusion of the mandibular processes. It is bounded above by several fused processes. There are the median nasal processes and their paired globular process extensions in the midline. The lateral nasal processes are just lateral on each side. The fused maxillary and mandibular processes are forming the corners of the mouth.

In the second month, the frontonasal process has narrowed down to form the septum and bridge of the nose, and the face looks more human. The facial region is just about completed by the close of the third month.

The inward growth of the palatine extensions of the various processes to produce the secondary palate has been described in Chapter 10. This activity completes the midsection of the oral cavity. The hind part of the cavity of the oral pit then opens into the pharynx.

The upper lip develops from tissue covering the frontal and maxillary processes. The lower lip develops from tissue covering the mandibular arches.

In rare instances the mouth fails to develop, a condition called astomia. The essential failure occurs in the ninth and tenth week. An excessively large mouth, called macrostomia, is a result of incomplete fusion of the mandibular with the maxillary processes; if these fuse excessively, they produce a tiny mouth, or microstomia. Ordinarily, the paired mandibular processes fuse to form the mandible in the fourth or fifth week. An incomplete fusion may leave a median cleft in the lower lip.

Although the face is definitely human in form by the third month, there is significant growth and alterations in the proportionate size and position of the structures all through fetal life. The changes are ceaseless until adulthood, involving considerable forward and downward growth and having a relationship to tooth eruption and development. Knowing the normal changes is especially important in the management of cleft palate and other facial anomalies. For a concise treatment of the development of the oral and facial regions, the reader is referred to Orban (1962) and Patten (1968).

The Tongue, or Lingua 361

Functions
The tongue is the primary and the most important organ of articulation. It works in conjunction with the mandible and other articulators. By modifying the shape of the oral cavity, it also acts as a resonator. The tongue is the most mobile of the resonators. In order of speed come the tip of the tongue, the mandible, the back of the tongue, and the velum and lips equally.

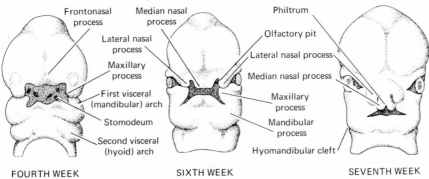

FOURTH WEEK   SIXTH WEEK   SEVENTH WEEK

Figure 13-2 Early development and fusion of the facial primordia.

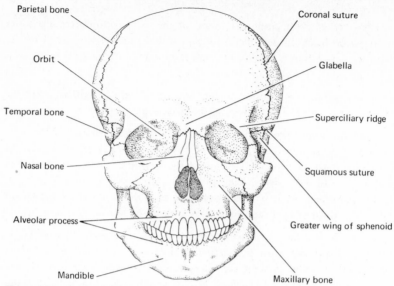

Figure 13-3 Bones of the skull viewed anteriorly.

During speech the tongue assumes positions that relate it to the language or dialect being spoken, and it produces most of the **phonemes**, or sound families, characteristic of connected speech. Many of the consonants are produced by movements of the tongue against the gums, palate, and teeth to cause friction or plosion. The tongue plays an essentially passive role in formation of the consonant sounds /p/, /b/, /m/, /f/, /v/, and /h/.

362

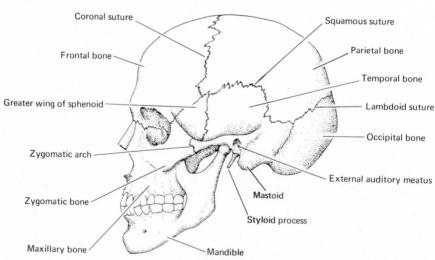

Figure 13-4 Bones of the skull viewed laterally.

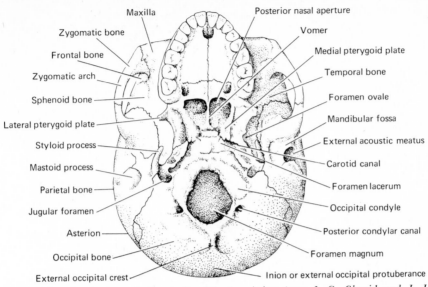

Figure 13-5 Basal view of the skull. (*By permission from J. G. Chusid and J. J. McDonald, Correlative Neuroanatomy and Functional Neurology, 13th ed., Lange Medical Publications, Los Altos, Calif., 1967.*)

The tongue has an important role in mastication, which is its chief biologic function. It transfers food to the occluding teeth surfaces and helps mix the particles with saliva. It removes from the teeth food that is ready for swallowing. It facilitates crushing by pressing the food against the hard palate. This action is aided by the roughness of the tongue dorsum because of its papillae and by the hard palate because of its rugae, which prevent the food from sliding. Following deglutition, the tongue removes particles much as a mechanical sweeper does. The dorsum of the tongue also functions for taste reception and for the selection of food through touch and temperature receptors.

The tongue moves most rapidly for protrusion and retraction and less rapidly for lateral motions. Adequate salivary lubrication increases its facility, a dry mouth being associated with slow and clumsy movements (O'Rourke and Miner, 1951).

Comparative Anatomy
The tongue varies greatly among animals. It first appears as a definite organ in fishes, where it is seen as an elevation of the oral floor. In fishes it contains no muscles but rather a cartilage or bony framework derived from the gills and covered by mucous membrane. There is little movement or prehensibility to this structure, although extrinsic muscles can cause it to vary its position and thus help in swallowing food.

A new tongue appears among amphibians in the more evolved salamanders, and it develops intrinsic muscles which bring about variations in shape. This tongue is

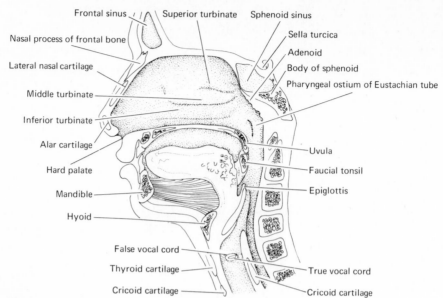

Frontal sinus   Superior turbinate   Sphenoid sinus

Nasal process of frontal bone

Lateral nasal cartilage

Middle turbinate

Inferior turbinate

Alar cartilage

Hard palate

Mandible

Hyoid

Sella turcica

Adenoid

Body of sphenoid

Pharyngeal ostium of Eustachian tube

Uvula

Faucial tonsil

Epiglottis

False vocal cord

Thyroid cartilage

Cricoid cartilage

True vocal cord

Cricoid cartilage

Figure 13-6   Medial view of structures in the head region.

protracted by the genioglossals and retracted by the hyoglossals. In the anuran frogs and toads, the tip of the tongue at rest is held posteriorly toward the pharynx, and it is quickly thrust out in capturing food.

In the reptiles, the tongue action ranges from very limited protraction in turtles to great protrusion in snakes. The carnivorous reptiles, such as crocodiles, have a flat, immobile tongue, since food is retained in the mouth only fleetingly.

The tongue of birds is well developed from vestiges of the nonfunctional embryonic gill arches. Extrinsic muscles are built upon the arch framework.

Among mammals, the anterior and posterior tongue divisions become distinguished by a V-shaped groove called the sulcus terminalis. At the center of the backward-pointed V lies a small pit, or foramen cecum. This marks the position of a thyroglossal duct through which, in the embryo, the thyroid gland is for a time continuous with the tongue.

The mammalian tongue is highly mobile and prehensile, and it serves many purposes. It is well formed and mobile in the carnivores, but it is best developed in the herbivores for grasping herbage. Although the oral cavity of man has suffered a relative decrease during phylogeny, the human tongue is relatively large. Whether or not this development is related to its activity in speech is speculative.

Developmental Anatomy

The anterior part of the tongue appears at about four or five weeks in front of the thyroglossal duct as a central swelling, or tuberculum impar, in the floor of the mouth. The inner aspect of the first (mandibular) arch on either side produces lateral lingual swellings which grow and entirely surround the central swelling. All these primordia form the anterior two-thirds of the tongue.

The posterior aspect of the tongue develops behind the thyroglossal duct, and it represents the primary tongue of the lower vertebrates. It arises from the ventro-medial ends of the second (hyoid) arches.

The paired second arches fuse to a single swelling called the copula, and this is the future root of the tongue. The mesoderm of the third arch contributes to the completion of the tongue.

The general connective tissue of the tongue is produced by the branchial mesoderm underlying the epithelium. The muscles seem to be formed by the ventral migration of muscle blocks (myotomes) from the occipital region. The overlying epithelium differentiates and becomes multilayered, in which process it develops the dorsal papillae containing taste buds.

General Anatomy

The tongue is a muscular organ located in the floor of the mouth to which it is attached at its base and at the central portion of its body. The root is connected with the hyoid bone, the epiglottis, the soft palate, and pharynx. The apex extends anteriorly to the lower incisor teeth. The inferior surface is connected with the mandible, and the mucous membrane is reflected from this surface to the floor of the mouth to form a median frenulum, which loosely binds down the tongue.

365

The upper surface, or dorsum of the tongue, is bisected by a longitudinal median sulcus which runs back to a pit, the foramen cecum. On either side of the pit a groove called the sulcus terminalis runs laterally and forward and separates the anterior two-thirds of the dorsum from the posterior one-third. The anterior section forms the body, or corpus, and the apex. The dorsum shows many punctiform (specifically positioned) projections, or papillae, which contain the taste buds. The

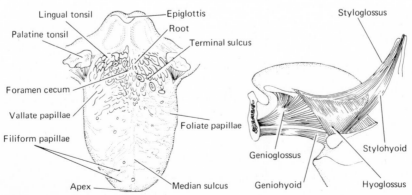

Figure 13-7 Structure of the tongue.

pharyngeal surface, or root dorsum, contains many prominences produced by accumulations of lymphatic tissue collectively constituting the lingual tonsils. The freely movable areas of the tongue include the apex, sides, dorsum, and a portion of the inferior surface.

The mucous membrane is stratified squamous epithelium. This is similar to that of the mouth in general. The mucosa is closely adherent to the underlying muscle on the anterior dorsum and on the free margins, but it is freely movable behind the sulcus terminalis.

Muscles

The directive movements of the tongue are produced by muscles. The muscles are described individually, but it is only through their combined actions that speech sounds are articulated.

There are factors in addition to muscles which determine the mobility of the tongue. The freedom of motion in the tip is determined by the frenulum. The neural capacity for precise regulation is also important.

The tongue muscles are extrinsic or intrinsic. The former originate from the skeleton, but the latter are located entirely within the tongue and produce internal changes in shape.

366

Detailed information is needed about how these muscles function in speech. The view that extrinsics govern tongue position and intrinsics govern tongue configuration may be an oversimplification (Huntington, 1968).

The intrinsic muscles are longitudinal, transverse, and vertical. The *superior longitudinal* muscle (unpaired) is a thin mass of longitudinal and oblique fibers that lie directly beneath the mucous membrane and extend throughout the dorsum from root to tip. It arises posteriorly from the septum and the submucosa, and it inserts in the skin along the borders and tip of the tongue. Its actual origins and insertions are indefinite. It works with the inferior longitudinal muscle to shorten the

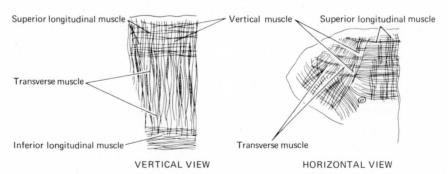

Superior longitudinal muscle — Vertical muscle — Superior longitudinal muscle

Transverse muscle

Inferior longitudinal muscle — Transverse muscle

VERTICAL VIEW   HORIZONTAL VIEW

Figure 13-8 Microscopic enlargement of intrinsic tongue muscles.

tongue, which becomes thicker and wider. The muscle can bulge the tongue upward in a longitudinal direction, and it can retract and curl the tongue tip.

The *inferior longitudinal* (paired) is a rounded muscle traveling longitudinally between the genioglossus and hyoglossus muscles through the lower and lateral tongue. It originates at the mucous membrane of the root of the tongue, and some of its fibers stem from the body of the hyoid bone. The fibers go downward and forward and converge to a bundle which goes apexward with the hyoglossus and styloglossus muscles. Most of the fibers pass forward to insert in the mucosa of the inferior lingual surface, but some go upward to the mucosa of the dorsum. The muscle shortens the tongue from front to back. It can also depress the tip if this has been elevated.

The *transverse* muscle (paired) forms much of the fleshy part of the tongue. It contains horizontal layers which fan out as they travel laterally toward the dorsum and to the lateral tongue margins. Some fibers originate from the dorsal septum, while others perforate it. The muscle does not reach either the dorsal surface or the tip of the tongue but inserts into the submucous fibrous tissue at the sides of the tongue.

The transverse muscle narrows the tongue and thereby protrudes it. It may bulge the organ upward. The lateral margins become lifted to help produce a tongue groove.

The *vertical* muscle (paired) constitutes with the transverse muscle much of the flesh of the tongue. The presence of vertical fibers has been questioned, and they may be localized to the borders of the anterior aspect of the tongue. They originate from the mucosa of the dorsum, whence they sweep downward and laterally to insert into the mucosa of the inferior surface. The muscle flattens and broadens the tongue.

There are several extrinsic muscles which act in synergism with the intrinsic ones to produce tongue mobility.

The *genioglossus* (paired) is a flat, triangular muscle which spreads fanlike toward its insertion. It is the strongest of the extrinsic muscles, and it forms most of the substance of the tongue. It originates from the mental tubercles at the posterior or inner aspect of the mandibular symphysis. The lowest fibers travel horizontally to the tongue base and insert into the body of the hyoid bone. Most of the fibers radiate to the dorsum, where their insertion extends from the tip to the base.

The middle and lower sections of the muscle are concerned primarily in protruding the tongue. The organ is also elevated. The upper fibers bring the tip back and down. The middle fibers can depress the median part of the tongue, making a concavity in its dorsum to receive food.

The *styloglossus* (paired) is an elongated muscle stretching from the styloid process to the apex of the tongue. It originates not only from the styloid process of the temporal bone but in small part from the stylomandibular ligament. It passes downward, medially, and somewhat anteriorly to end in the tongue near the base of the glossopalatal arch; there it turns almost horizontally and travels to the tip. An inferior group of fibers penetrates the hyoglossus fibers and goes medially into the substance of the tongue. The muscle retracts and elevates the whole tongue.

The *palatoglossus* muscle (paired) has been described as a depressor of the soft palate. Acting from a fixed soft palate, it elevates the posterior section of the tongue. The fibers of insertion of the palatoglossus and styloglossus are blended.

The *hyoglossus* muscle (paired) is a quadrilateral sheet of fibers which extends from the hyoid bone to the side of the tongue. It originates from the upper border of the greater hyoid cornua and from adjacent portions of the hyoid body. The fiber bundles go vertically up to the tongue and interlace en route with the horizontal fibers of the styloglossus muscle. Some writers call those fibers which originate from the lesser hyoid cornua the *chondroglossus* muscle.

The hyoglossus draws the tongue downward and backward. Acting in reverse, it can elevate the hyoid, but this is a secondary function. Note the antagonism between the depressor function of this muscle and the elevator activity of the other extrinsic muscles. In retraction, however, it can act with other muscles in opposition to protruding fibers of the genioglossus muscle.

Blood and Lymph Supply

The tongue blood comes chiefly from the lingual branch of the external carotid. There is a supplementary supply from the ascending pharyngeal and the external maxillary arteries. The lingual artery goes forward on each side on the deep surface of the hyoglossus muscle, and it ends as the *deep lingual* artery which reaches the tip of the tongue. A *dorsal lingual* branch supplies the dorsum and a *sublingual* branch supplies the sublingual gland.

The veins parallel the lingual artery as venae comitantes. Similar venous tributaries accompany the hypoglossal nerve. The veins join and drain into the facial vein or into the internal jugular vein.

The lymph vessels begin in a network in the submucous coat and in the muscles. Those in the anterior two-thirds drain into submaxillary and superficial cervical nodes. Those in the posterior third drain into the upper deep cervical and retropharyngeal nodes.

Nerve Supply

The tongue is innervated by the trigeminal, facial, glossopharyngeal, vagus, and hypoglossal nerves. The trigeminal nerve (lingual branch of the mandibular nerve) mediates general sensation. The glossopharyngeal nerve (lingual branch) mediates taste at the root, while the facial nerve (chorda tympani branch) does this at the body and apex. Small (questionable) taste areas on the cheeks and at the root are claimed to be innervated by the vagus nerve (superior laryngeal branch).

The lingual muscles proper, both intrinsic and extrinsic, receive motor fibers through the hypoglossal nerve. The palatoglossus muscle is innervated by the accessory nerve through the pharyngeal plexus; any involvement of the vagus nerve is problematical.

The hypoglossal fibers originate in the hypoglossal nucleus of the medulla and emerge from its ventral aspect. The rootlets unite in the anterior condylar foramen, and they leave the skull. In the neck the nerve travels downward and forward. In the region of the hyoid bone it turns medially and passes beneath the digastric and stylohyoid muscles. After going between the hyoglossus and mylohyoid muscles, it reaches the tongue.

The main trunk of the hypoglossal nerve gives off a descending ramus which runs down the neck with the vagus, meeting a cervical descending branch primarily from cervical nerves C-2 and C-3. This union forms a loop, or ansa hypoglossi, which supplies the omohyoid, sternohyoid, and sternothyroid muscles. Diamond (1952) says that the descending branches to the infrahyoid muscles are not produced from the XIIth nerve but from communicating branches of C-1 and C-2.

Technics of Analysis of Lingual Activity
Many technics have been evolved to study lingual dynamics. A citation of some pertinent literature is given by Steer and Hanley (1957), Fant (1964), and Huntington (1968).

Size, Shape, and Mobility Appropriate functioning of the tongue is associated to varying degrees with size, shape, and mobility. There are no conclusively established standards to evaluate these parameters in regard to the effect of their variations upon speech. Fairbanks and Bebout (1950) tried to correlate the size and

369

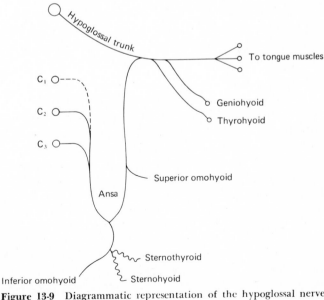

Figure 13-9 Diagrammatic representation of the hypoglossal nerve fibers to the tongue and neck muscles.

shape with superior and inferior speakers, but they could not find any real differences.

It may be noted that any gross movement of the tongue may be dependent upon the position and movement of the hyoid bone. In this sense the hyoid bone can be classified as an articulator. Although the hyoid has been considered to be one of the important speech derivatives of the primitive pharynx, originating from the second and third gill arches, the controversial (but not widely accepted) view has been expressed (Luchsinger and Arnold, 1965) that the hyoid has no distinct function of its own and is not followed by any symptomatology when it has to be surgically removed.

The hyoid can be elevated and simultaneously brought either forward or backward. It can be depressed and simultaneously tilted either forward or backward. It may possibly be pulled backward horizontally. Any one of these movements has an effect upon lingual sounds which is still to be definitely ascertained.

The mobility of the tongue is linked with the strength it has because of muscular development, and the physical ability has an effect upon the quality of speech (Luchsinger and Arnold, 1965). In the glossodynamometer technic a rubber balloon is pressed by the tongue against the palate, and the escaping air passes through a tube to a mercury manometer previously calibrated. The force exerted is read in pounds.

Motor Coordination The coordination of lingual activities is effected at the lower motor neuron level by the hypoglossal nerve.

Motor coordination has been tested in a crude way by kymography. The subject places his tongue against a Marey tambour, and then he rhythmically and rapidly protrudes and retracts his tongue. The movements are transmitted by the tambour to a moving kymograph drum or similar recorder. Normal records are compared with those of a subject with defective articulation and evaluated in terms of the rhythm, force, and ability needed to maintain the speed of motion.

Coordination of tongue movements is usually sufficiently obvious simply by listening to the articulated sounds. As an illustration, a complex integration of tongue movements is necessary in forming the sound /s/ and in making it different from /ʃ/ (sound of sh). The chief difference between these sounds is that whereas the point of articulation for /s/ is against the teeth ridge, that for /ʃ/ is a little farther back. The tongue is spread more for the latter than for the former phoneme, and the channel through which the air passes is wider. The nervous system has to control these precise articulatory activities to prevent confusion. A sigmatism, or the incorrect formation of the difficult to acquire /s/ sound, is of some interest in that it may be a relatively sensitive barometer of central nervous system damage.

Electromyography Using electromyography, MacNeilage and Sholes (1964) in a study of vowel articulation mapped the tongue surface and attempted to associate the muscle activity involved in the differential EMG patterns.

Palatography For many speech sounds the tongue and palate come into contact. The nature of this contact is visualized by palatography. In the direct method a visualizable substance is placed on the tongue, a given sound is made, and the disposition of the substance is observed and sketched. In the indirect method a thin, powdered artificial palate is fitted to the roof of the mouth, an isolated sound is produced, then the artificial palate is examined to find where the surface powder has been removed by contact with the wet tongue.

The palatograms are individualized, capable of being accurately duplicated, and provide the basis for describing specific sounds in terms of a geographic site of action within the oral cavity. There is the limitation resulting from foreign substances within the mouth.

The fact that the tongue may act in conjunction with the palate can be illustrated in the phonetic analysis of consonants such as /g/ and /k/. Cleft palate patients have difficu˙ · with these sounds, and they are termed posterior linguapalatal sounds to indicate that the back of the tongue rises against a depressed soft palate when the sound is started. They are produced abruptly with pressure from a closed position, /g/ being voiced and /k/ voiceless. To sound /k/ the back of the tongue becomes lowered and the soft palate raised. In sounding /g/ the vocal folds force a short vibration against the /k/ position, with subsequent blending into the succeeding vowel. In both consonants the tongue is primary and the soft palate secondary.

371

X-ray Photography The relative positions of the articulatory organs have been studied by x-ray photography. An early attempt to ascertain the forms and sizes of the speech cavities and to determine the positions and relations of the various structures as they appear during vocal activity was that of Russell (1931), who obtained a comprehensive series of x-rays as well as data from a laryngoperiscopic study of the vocal fold and of internal laryngeal function.

Carmody (1941) studied by x-ray films the positions of the tongue in relation to the palate during speech, and he concluded that there is a mean anatomic position for each speech sound. He extended this study to the pharyngeal region and established tables giving the length and breadth of the pharynx for the vowels and consonants.

X-ray studies are providing data on the dimensions of various articulatory contacts and the diameters of the vocal tract (Moll, 1960; MacNeilage and Scholes, 1964). Because of instrumentation the measurement of the vocal tract is becoming increasingly precise. Similar quantitation is developing also for dynamic events including pressures and velocities.

Sensory Feedback Studies Another technic involves the study of sensory feedback of the articulators (Ringel and Fletcher, 1967). Speech defective adolescents have been compared to normal speakers in the ability of various articulation regions to sense differences in the grains per inch of grits of sandpaper, and speech defectives with "functional" problems were found to be significantly inferior.

Sensory feedback studies have showed that tactile, proprioceptive, auditory, and visual stimuli are all important in modulating correct articulation.

The Mandible

The mandible, or lower jaw, is an important determinant of the growth and form of the facial skeleton. The growth of the upper and lower jaws anteroposteriorly gives the needed space for the temporal eruption of the back teeth. The growth in height of the jaws, stimulated by vertical growth of the mandibular ramus, is required for the free vertical eruption of the teeth. As bone develops in the jaws, it acts as a force to produce eruption. Mandibular growth at the condylar cartilage is necessary for the vertical growth of the upper face. Thus, disorders of mandibular growth contribute to facial disturbances.

The mandible is one of the primary articulators, but it also influences resonance. A "tight" jaw adds to tonal flatness. Because the elevator muscles are stronger than the depressors, there may be a tendency to speak with a closed mouth or with muffled resonance. In cerebral palsy the jaw action may be ungraded and unpredictable, producing a distorted oral resonance.

372

Comparative Anatomy

The evolutionary history of the mandible is remarkable, involving transformations of the gill arches of fish that were no longer necessary when the terrestrial vertebrates arose.

In the dogfish and its relatives the jaws are modifications of the first splanchnic arches. The upper jaw on each side is called the *pterygoquadrate,* and the lower jaw is called *Meckel's cartilage.* The latter cartilage of the primitive jaw becomes encased during evolution by several investing bones. Certain of the bones, e.g., the *dentaries,* eventually bear the teeth, and Meckel's cartilage then loses this function.

In reptiles, as seen in the alligator, the investing bones are distinct. In man these bones have undergone fusion in each jaw, and they have also been joined by an anterior attachment to become the unpaired mandible.

The increasing phylogenetic importance of the investing bones is accompanied by a disappearance of the encased Meckel's cartilage. Its vestige remains as a hollow space in the ossified proximal end of the mandible. In reptiles, this bony end becomes the *articular* bone. In mammals, including man, it is transformed into the *malleus,* which moves up into the middle ear.

The importance of understanding the present form of the bony jaw or of the entire skull through evolution is brought out in the writings of Weidenreich (Washburn and Wolfson, 1949). Although such factors as an abundance of iodine, calcium, and other materials influence the skull and the form of the mandible, the ultimate cause is more general. The history of the human skull is determined by the expansion of the brain and independently by the adaptation to erect posture. The size of the face reduces as the braincase expands. The adoption of erect posture changes the form of the skull base. Brachycephalization, or the increase of the brain case in width observed in modern man, indicates a better adjustment of the skull to upright posture through the adoption of a more complete globular form. Some caution is needed in the tendency to ascribe too much to evolutionary causes. The prognathism of the jaw may result from relatively immediate factors.

Osteology

The body, or corpus, of the jaw is a roughly U-shaped arch, and the arch represents the fusion of two embryonic cartilage bones at the mandibular symphysis. The upper surface of the body carries the alveolar process. The arch continues on each side upward and backward into the mandibular ramus, and the two sides of the arch become widely separated posteriorly. The posterior border of the ramus meets the inferior border of the body at the angle of the mandible. The most anterior part of the body elevates externally in the midline to a prominence called the mental protuberance, or bony chin. An opening called the mental foramen lies just posterolateral to the chin, and it allows blood vessels and the mental nerve to pass from a canal inside the bone to the external surface on each side.

On the inner or medial aspect of the body, a crest called the mylohyoid line runs diagonally downward and forward to the region of the chin. This crest gives origin to the mylohyoid muscle, which forms the floor of the mouth. Just behind the symphysis there are one or two mental spines (genial tubercles) for the origin of the genioglossus muscles above and the geniohyoid muscles below.

373

The alveolar process on the upper border of the body consists of two bony plates, external and internal, which fuse and form the sockets for the teeth.

Each ramus is a quadrilateral and somewhat perpendicular plate which extends upward from the posterior part of the body. The superior border of each ramus

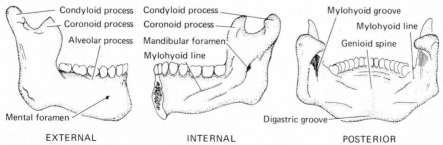

Figure 13-10 The lower jaw seen in different aspects.

displays two prominent projections, the anterior coronoid process and the posterior condyloid process, which are separated by a semilunar (sigmoid, mandibular) notch.

The coronoid process is a triangular spicule of bone which terminates in a spike or in a backward-curved hook. It is convex forward and concave backward. The temporalis muscle inserts upon it.

The condyloid process is the mandibular head (condyle, capitulum), which fits into the mandibular fossa (depression) of the temporal bone of the skull to form the temporomandibular joint. The condyle sits upon the neck of the condyloid process, and it is bent forward so that its articulating surface faces anteriorly and superiorly.

The ramus is overlaid by the masseter muscle on its external surface. It contains on its internal surface a mandibular canal, which houses the inferior alveolar nerve and the blood vessels to the teeth. This canal begins proximally at the mandibular foramen and then travels downward and forward, becoming horizontal in its course under the roots of the molars. At the bicuspid region the canal divides, and a narrow channel continues toward the symphysis, while a wider mental canal goes laterally upward and backward to open at the mental foramen.

Developmental Anatomy

The growing bony mandible encases and then replaces Meckel's cartilage. Mandibular development is very incomplete at birth, and growth is not completed until the approach of adulthood.

The bony changes of the mandible with age are externally conspicuous. The body of the bone at birth is simply a shell with incompletely partitioned sockets for the incisor, canine, and deciduous molar teeth, and the ramus is at an obtuse angle. In the first year the two separate arches fuse at the symphysis; then each arch elongates and deepens, while the ramus becomes less obtuse. In the adult the ramus has become nearly vertical, and the alveolar and subdental parts of the arch are of approximately equal depth so that the mental foramen is about equidistant from the top and bottom of the bone. The alveolar process regresses with the loss of teeth in senescence, and the mandibular canal with its mental foramen is brought up near the top of the body. The ramus again becomes oblique, the angle measuring about 140°, the neck of the condyle is inclined somewhat backward, and the jaw becomes protruded.

Muscles

The mandible is important primarily in mastication, or chewing, and only secondarily in speech.

The muscles of the mandible operate in functional groups, just as they do elsewhere in the body. The chief movements are elevation and depression. The mandible can also be protruded and slightly retracted, and it has obliquely lateral motions. The last variety is for grinding food.

The four muscles chiefly responsible for chewing movements and generally classified as muscles of mastication include the masseter; temporalis; external, or lateral, pterygoid; and internal, or medial, pterygoid.

The mandible is elevated by the masseter, temporalis, and internal pterygoid muscles.

The *masseter* muscle (paired) is the most superficial and stretches as a thick, flat quadrilateral mass over the outer surface of the mandibular ramus. The muscle is incompletely divided to a superficial and deep part, both originating on the zygomatic arch and inserting upon the ramus or upon the angle of the mandible.

This muscle not only powerfully elevates the lower jaw, but it puts pressure upon the teeth, particularly in the molar area. The deep part of the muscle can retract as well as elevate, since its fibers go downward and forward when the mandible is protruded. The superficial part helps to protrude the mandible as well as elevate it.

The *temporalis* muscle (paired) is a triangular sheet originating from a large area on the side of the skull called the temporal fossa. The muscle travels deep to the zygomatic arch and converges toward the coronoid process of the mandible upon which it inserts as far down as the ramus of the jaw. Although the muscle is chiefly an elevator, its posterior fibers travel downward and forward, and they possess a retracting function. The retraction of the mandible may be accomplished primarily by the temporalis, although the digastric, geniohyoid, and other muscles contribute (Huber, 1958).

375

The *internal pterygoid* muscle (paired) is a thick, quadrilateral muscle roughly paralleling the masseter but lying on the medial surface of the mandibular ramus.

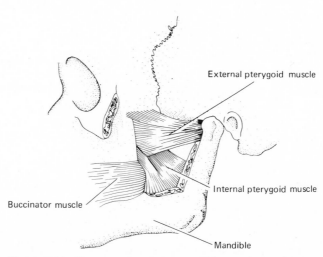

Figure 13-11 Deep muscles of the mandible seen by cutting out a section of the bone.

It is somewhat weaker than the masseter. It originates mainly in the pterygoid fossa of the sphenoid bone, although its inner fibers originate from the medial surface of the lateral pterygoid plate. All the fibers run downward, backward, and slightly outward to insert upon the medial surface of the mandible near its angle. The muscle acts with the masseter to elevate the lower jaw. It can also help to protrude the jaw. Acting unilaterally, it pulls the mandible to one side.

The depressors include the mylohyoid, geniohyoid, anterior belly of the digastric, and external pterygoid muscles. The first three have been mentioned among the suprahyoid extrinsic muscles as raising the laryngeal apparatus when the mandible is fixed. When the hyoid bone is immobilized by the infrahyoid muscles, the suprahyoid muscles will depress and retract the lower jaw.

The *external pterygoid* (paired) is a thick triangular muscle located deep to the temporalis. It originates in two heads. The larger inferior head arises from the lateral pterygoid plate, and the smaller superior head arises from the infratemporal surface of the greater wing of the sphenoid bone. Although the two heads are separated anteriorly, they fuse as they pass in front of the temporomandibular joint. The fibers travel backward and outward to insert upon the condyloid process of the mandible and also upon the capsule and articular disk of the temporomandibular joint. The muscle protrudes the lower jaw by pulling the mandibular head and articular disk forward, downward, and inward. When acting unilaterally, it draws the mandible outward.

376

The muscles of protrusion and retraction have been anticipated. The primary protruder is the external pterygoid. It is assisted by other muscles, including the internal pterygoid and the superficial part of the masseter.

The retractors have been described. They include the deep section of the masseter, the posterior fibers of the temporalis, and the suprahyoid muscles (mylohyoid, geniohyoid, and anterior belly of the digastric).

The grinding movements of the mandible require compounded movements. To a

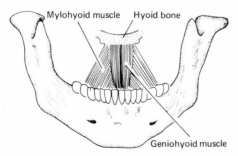

Figure 13-12 The mandible and the muscular oral floor.

great extent, they are accomplished by the external pterygoid and the posterior fibers of the temporalis.

Nerve Supply

The nerve supply to certain structures in and directly about the mandible involves branches of the third, or mandibular, division of the trigeminal nerve.

The mandibular division is primarily sensory to the mandibular teeth, but it gives off motor branches to the elevator muscles of chewing. The division originates in the semilunar ganglion of the Vth nerve. After giving off several branches, the mandibular division splits to an anterior and posterior trunk.

The largest branch of the posterior trunk is the *inferior alveolar* nerve. This is sensory to the mandibular teeth and cutaneous aspects of the chin and lower lip. Just before the inferior alveolar nerve enters the mandibular foramen, it gives off the *mylohyoid nerve* to the mylohyoid and digastric muscles. The main inferior alveolar trunk proceeds forward and gives off *dental branches* to the molar and premolar teeth. Continuing forward, it terminates by dividing to two branches. The *incisive branch* goes to the canine and incisor teeth. The second branch is the *mental nerve,* which emerges from the mandibular canal through the mental foramen. The mental nerve sends fibers to supply the skin of the chin and the skin and mucous membrane of the lower lip.

377

Several branches originate from the anterior trunk of the mandibular division of the trigeminal nerve. These branches are the *masseteric* nerve to the masseter muscle, the *buccal, anterior,* and *posterior deep temporal* nerves to the temporalis muscle, the *internal pterygoid* nerve to the internal pterygoid muscle, and the *external pterygoid* nerve to the external pterygoid muscle. All these nerves carry both motor and proprioceptive fibers.

Blood Supply

The blood supply to certain structures in and directly about the mandible comes from branches of the maxillary artery, which itself is one of the two terminal branches of the external carotid artery.

The maxillary artery splits to mandibular, pterygoid, and pterygopalatine divisions.

One of the large branches of the mandibular arterial division is the *inferior alveolar* artery, which travels with the inferior alveolar nerve into the mandibular canal and supplies the mandibular teeth. Just before entering the mandibular foramen, the inferior alveolar vessel splits off a *mylohyoid* artery to the mylohyoid muscle.

The pterygoid division of the maxillary artery produces *deep temporal* arteries to the temporalis muscle, *pterygoid* branches to the pterygoid muscles, a *masseteric* artery to the masseter muscle, and a *buccal* artery to the buccinator muscle.

The pterygopalatine division of the maxillary artery supplies structures in facial and upper jaw regions above the mandible and need not be described.

Temporomandibular Joint

The mandibular articulation is a freely movable joint (diarthrosis) between the capitulum (condyle) of the mandible and the mandibular fossa and articular tubercle of the temporal bone.

A fibrous disk within the joint separates the head of the condyloid process from the temporal bone. The disk divides the joint into upper and lower sections, each lined by a synovial membrane. The disk functions to adapt the bony surfaces to each other, particularly in the forward position of the jaw when the convex condyle approaches the convex articular tubercle. The joint is seen from the above to have two distinct parts. One articulation is between the condyle and the articular disk, and the other is between the disk and the mandibular fossa.

The joint is enclosed by an articular capsule which is fairly lax but strengthened on its lateral side by a temporomandibular ligament. A stylomandibular ligament goes from the styloid process to the ramus of the mandible just above its angle. A sphenomandibular ligament goes from the sphenoid bone above to structures about the mandibular foramen below.

378

The joint is a modified ginglymus, permitting a hinge motion and gliding. When the upper and lower teeth are brought into contact, the hinge effect occurs in the lower area of the joint, between the disk and condyloid process. The upper part of the joint also enters the action if the mandible is protruded or lowered beyond the resting point. The condyloid head and disk are drawn forward toward the temporal eminence. When the mandible is retracted, the disk and head slide backward into the fossa.

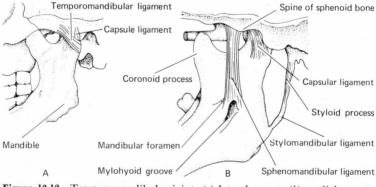

Figure 13-13 Temporomandibular joint: (*a*) lateral aspect; (*b*) medial aspect.

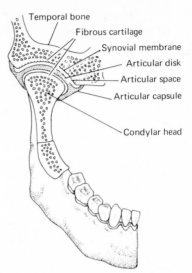

Depression of the mandible alters the angle between the upper and lower jaws. The importance of this angle for the formation of speech sounds, especially vowels, has been a subject of discussion among phoneticians (Heffner, 1960). Although vowels may be pronounced acceptably at various jaw angles, it may be that compensatory movements are the explanation.

A greater variety of movements occurs during mastication than during speech, but the louder the speech, the more extensive the movements (Balber et al., 1962).

The Teeth

Structure

A tooth is composed of a crown, which projects above the gums; a root, embedded in the jaw socket; and a neck, or region of transition, between the crown and root. Each tooth contains a hollow pulp cavity which admits blood vessels and nerves. This cavity eventually narrows, and the growth of the tooth ceases.

Most of the solid part of a tooth is a very dense tissue, called the dentine, which deposits around embryonic cells termed odontoblasts. A solid layer of enamel covers over the dentine in the crown region. The protective coat around the dentine in the root area is a hard cement.

Number and Succession

The number of teeth is definite, limited, and differentiated according to position and function. The front teeth, which are incisors and canines, serve for gripping and tearing; the back teeth, which are premolars (bicuspids) and molars, serve for grinding and crushing.

The above facts are conveniently illustrated in a dental formula in which the adult or permanent dentition is expressed as $\frac{2.1.2.3.}{2.1.2.3.} \times 2$. The figures in the numerator from left to right indicate respectively the number of incisors, canines, premolars, and molars on the right side of the upper jaw, and the figures in the denominator show the corresponding teeth in the right lower jaw.

The child has a temporary or deciduous set of twenty teeth, which are gradually replaced from about six years of age by the thirty-two permanent teeth. The first set of teeth has erupted by the second year of life. The permanent teeth originate with the first molars, which erupt just behind the last deciduous teeth. The permanent teeth are essentially established about the twelfth year.

The time of dental maturation has been used in speech therapy as one index of physiologic maturity. In many cases the general bodily structures have not matured enough to make meaningful speech possible. Cretins and other feeble-minded children are physiologically retarded, and their dental development is similarly delayed.

380

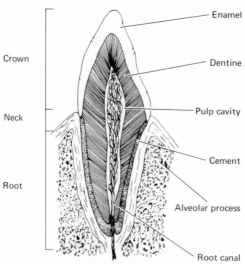

Figure 13-15 Diagrammatic microscopic enlargement of a tooth.

APPROXIMATE AGES FOR TOOTH ERUPTION

DECIDUOUS	MONTHS	PERMANENT	YEARS
Lower central incisors	6–9	First molars	6
Upper incisors	8–10	Central incisors	7
Lateral incisors and first molars	15–21	Lateral incisors	8
Canines	16–20	First premolars	9
Second molars	20–24	Second premolars	10
		Canines	11–12
		Second molars	12–13
		Third molars	17–25

Usually the dental status is not a practicable method of diagnosing maturity until at least seven years of age. For a schedule of dental maturation, the reader is referred to Scott and Symons (1967).

Relationship of Dental Arches in Occlusion

The relation of the upper and lower teeth to each other upon closing the jaws is called occlusion; this relation during movements of the mandible is called articulation. In occlusion there is a maxillary overbite, since the upper arch has a greater diameter. The upper incisors and canines bite labial to (outside) the lower teeth, while the upper bicuspids and molars are shifted buccally. Normally the distal overlap of the upper teeth nearly disappears at the posterior part of the arches. In the temporary dentition the occlusal relationships are essentially similar to those of the permanent teeth.

381

The relationships of the jaws in occlusion are described in the universally accepted classification devised by Angle in 1899. Malocclusions are grouped into three classes, based on the relations of the jaws in the sagittal plane.

In class I the dental arches are in proper anteroposterior relation to each other. This normal occlusion is called neutrocclusion. If the lower jaw is retruded in relation to the upper jaw, the condition is placed in class II. The term distocclusion applies to receding teeth and the lower jaw. Where the lower jaw is protracted, the condition is placed in class III. The term mesiocclusion refers to protruding teeth and the lower jaw.

Although Angle believed the mandible to be responsible for the deviations, this concept is untenable because maxillary and other facial bone development is also variable. Thus malocclusions may result from several causes (Moorrees, 1968).

The normal developmental relationships of the jaws have important implications for speech, and any disturbances in these relationships are of particular concern to workers dealing with cleft palate and the various facial anomalies. It has been commonplace to associate malformed jaws and gross malocclusion with the aftereffects of surgical treatment for cleft lip and cleft palate. The approach in dentistry was to regard the treatment of these clefts as an exacting prosthetic problem. It is becoming increasingly realized, however, that the emphasis should be on the encouragement of adequate growth and development of the jaws.

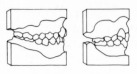

Class I   Class II, division 1   Class II, division 2   Class III

Figure 13-16 The anteroposterior relationships of the dental arches, following Angle's classification, seen in diagrammatic sagittal section: class I: neutrocclusion, or normal (one or more teeth, however, may be in malposition); class II: retrusive position of the mandible and its dental arch (these are malpositions of one or more teeth; in division 1 the maxillary incisors are inclined labially, and in division 2 the maxillary incisors are inclined palatally); class III: protrusive position of the mandibular dental arch (malpositions of one or more teeth).

The severity of the abnormal appearance associated with the cleft lip and palate is related to the faulty development of the upper jaw. In the retruded upper jaw and lip, at times with overclosure of the mandible, the basic cause is a failure of the upper arch to grow downward and forward. Secondary pressure effects of the outer muscle sphincter of the mouth and cheeks influence the upper-arch form. The congenital deformity is superimposed upon the inherited skeletal and soft tissue patterns.

Although the maxillas and mandible develop individually, their growth must be integrated, or malocclusion will result. The mandibular growth rate normally exceeds that of the maxillas. Since the jaws are the structures upon which the teeth rest, the final maturation of the jaws occurs when the teeth are erupted and in position. When the teeth do erupt, an occlusion begins to be established. Thereafter, the jaws, dental arches, and teeth are subjected fully to environmental factors, such as muscular forces, eruptive forces, and masticatory stresses upon the teeth, all contributing to occlusion or malocclusion (Goldman et al., 1968).

Crossbites; Open and Closed Bite These states are related to speech. *Crossbite* refers to any departure from a normal buccolingual or labiolingual relation of the upper to the lower teeth. One or more of the upper incisors may close lingual to the lower ones (incisor crossbite). One or more of the upper teeth may be positioned such that the buccal cusps of the upper teeth occlude between the buccal and lingual cusps of the lower teeth. Upper posterior teeth may be entirely lingual (or buccal) to the lower teeth. Crossbites in the bicuspid and molar regions are fairly common. A crossbite narrows the dental arch and interferes with oral developmental processes.

In the vertical plane an anterior overbite indicates the distance by which the upper incisors overhang the lower ones. It can vary from no contact (*open bite*) to a state where the upper anterior teeth entirely obscure the lower ones when the jaws are approximated (completely *closed bite*). The open bite may be a part of an oral habit pattern whereas a closed bite may indicate retarded development. The deep overbite is common in any class of occlusion and may retard tooth development.

382

Individual tooth displacements may upset speech, and such terms as rotation, labioversion, linguaversion, and mesioversion may be encountered in speech pathology. The rotation of teeth is among the causes of loss in arch length, or a crowded arch may lead to rotation.

Agencies Influencing Tooth Development

Teeth, especially in the developmental stages, are affected by many agencies. The minerals and vitamins A, C, and D are important for development, although the teeth are less sensitive to these factors than many other tissues. Although teeth are not overly responsive to vitamin A deficiency, they may suffer hypoplasia if there is deficiency of members of the vitamin B complex.

Some of the disorders of the softer oral tissues are nutritional. Swollen gingivae may result from ascorbic acid deficiency and swollen tongue from a reduction of nicotinic acid. A loss of riboflavin can produce glossitis (tongue inflammation) or cheilosis (fissures at the mouth angles with lip desquamation).

The physical character of the diet influences the teeth and their supporting tissues. Diet has an effect of massage upon local circulation and brings about growth and keratinization of gingival epithelium from frictional contact.

Hormones have a marked influence upon the teeth. In hypothyroidism there may be a small dental arch, a poorly developed mandible, and delayed eruption. In the hypopituitary dwarf there may be delayed eruption, loss of teeth, faulty dental arches, and malocclusion. In hyperpituitary acromegaly and giantism, the tongue enlarges, and the lower jaw may become prognathic. The mandible is a bone which seems to be able to grow even in an adult.

The parathyroid hormone may play a role during tooth calcification. Injection of this hormone softens the alveolar bone and produces drifting of teeth with subsequent malocclusion.

Many pregnant women develop a gingivitis with bleeding and edema. The hormonal changes are speculative, but they probably involve the sex hormones of pregnancy.

The premature loss of the first teeth or the retarded development of the second teeth produces faulty development and function of the jaws. The results are malpositions and disturbances of the eruption of teeth.

In cleft lips or palate the deciduous and permanent teeth in or about the pathologic process may be deformed or missing. The premaxillary support of the incisors can be weakened in bilateral clefts of the lip and palate.

Phylogeny

The masticatory apparatus is suffering progressive reduction. There is frequent absence of the third molars (wisdom teeth) and the upper lateral incisors. Where the molars of primitive man increased distally, they now decrease in size distally.

With the reduced dental arches there has appeared a shortening of the jaws and an expansion of the brain and its capsule. A concomitant reduction has occurred in the supraorbital ridges and in the prominent facial processes which once served for attachment of the larger chewing musculature.

Man is unique among the primates in that there is a marked reduction of the canine teeth, which are prominent especially in most primate males. All human teeth show an evenness in height and width. This structural characteristic is the prerequisite for the production of spirant sounds, e.g., /f/, /v/, /s/, /ʃ/ or /ʒ/, and /θ/ or /ð/ (Lenneberg, 1967).

Lips, Cheeks, and the Muscles of Expression

The Lips, or Labia

The lips encircle the mouth orifice as a pair of fleshy folds whose contents include blood vessels, nerves, labial glands, and areolar connective tissue. They are covered externally by integument and internally by mucous membrane. There are glands directly underneath the mucous membrane. The connection between the lips is made at the corner of the mouth on each side by a thin fold called the labial commissure.

384

The skin of the lips terminates in a sharp line where a transitional area, the red or vermilion zone, lies between the skin and the mucous membrane. The vermilion epithelium is thin, and the cells contain eleiden. This substance increases their transparency so that the underlying capillaries show up with a red hue. The red zone may contain sebaceous glands but neither sweat glands nor hairs.

The external integument and the internal mucosa are so tightly bound to the fascia over the great orbicularis oris muscle, or fleshy substance of the lips, that these membranes follow the muscle movements without folding. In the male the skin is thicker and firmer, which especially restricts upper lip mobility. In the resting mandibular position the lips are loosely approximated.

The lips of all mammals except monotremes are mobile, perhaps because of the primitive function of suckling. They are well developed in marsupials, which in later fetal life attach by their lips to the maternal mammae. There are no movable lips in the egg-laying fishes or in the reptiles and birds.

The lips have other functions. They are very sensitive to touch and temperature, and these sensations help in the rejection of unsuitable material. They aid in transferring food and water into the mouth and prevent the escape of food during mastication.

The lips are important articulators. They form speech sounds such as the labial consonants, /p/, /b/, /m/, /w/, /f/, and /v/. They also form certain vowels and diphthongs. Sounds would suffer a loss in quality if the lips were flaccid and immobile. Fairbanks and Green (1950) were unable to relate the dimensions of the lips and the size of the mouth opening to articulatory ability.

A few examples may be cited to illustrate labial activity in speech. The full closure of the lips followed by their immediate separation produces the sounds /p/ and /b/. The velum assists the action by closing the nasal port. In lip closure without velar action, /m/ is articulated. The /p/, /b/, and /m/ are generally among the earliest and the easiest sounds to produce. They are primitive compared with the high-frequency sounds like /s/, /z/, /ʃ/ or /ʒ/, /θ/ or /ð/, and /tʃ/. In stutterers these primitive sounds can be troublesome. In a rounding motion with the velum blocking the nose, /w/ and /hw/ are sounded. To produce /v/ and /f/, the lower lip presses lightly against the upper front teeth and interferes with the exhaled air, the nares being simultaneously closed. There is a difference, however, between the processes used to form /v/ as compared with /f/. Both are continuant fricatives, which means that they take an appreciable amount of time to be produced and also that a pressure and friction are set up which result in a rushing sound. However, /f/ is a breath, or voiceless, consonant, whereas /v/ is vocalized and produces a vibration which can be sensed by placing the fingers upon the throat.

The lips should not be considered essential to the formation of all consonants. /s/ and /z/ are tongue and teeth consonants and do not require lip activity. In some cases, as in the /r/ sound, the tongue is the primary agent and the lips are secondary. In the consonant /l/, which is formed essentially by the tongue, the lips only shape the vowel that directly follows. If the lip movements are substituted for the normal tongue movements, trouble with the /l/ usually arises. Tongue-tip movements have been substituted for labial movements in facial paralysis.

Lip action is tested very simply by pursing and retracting the lips, by moving the right and then the left lip corners, and by smiling.

A method to test the strength and rhythm of lip movements is described by Froeschels (1952). This is only an approximation in that the influence of extraneous muscles cannot be eliminated. In this procedure a glass tube fixed to a small rubber ball, such as an eyedropper, is attached at its free end to rubber tubing which is connected in turn to a Marey tambour that is free to write on a kymograph drum. The subject places the ball between his lips and compresses it rhythmically, which produces a rhythmic rise and fall of the tambour lever. This is a convenient ergometer which could allow rough comparisons of the lip movements of normal subjects and those with dysarthric (spastic) speech. This procedure is also feasible for testing the tip of the tongue, but in this instance the ball is inserted just behind the upper incisors.

The Cheeks, or Buccae
The buccae, or cheeks, form the lateral aspects of the face. They are a fleshy mass composed chiefly of the buccinator, platysma, risorius, and zygomaticus muscles. Their external boundary is the integument. Their internal boundary is mucous

membrane, which fuses above and below with the gingivae or gums and behind with the mucosa of the soft palate. The mucous membrane is firmly attached to the buccinator fascia, and it thus closely follows the muscular movements.

The mucous membrane contains fairly thick epithelium, which is stratified squamous and nonkeratinizing. This type occurs typically on wet surfaces, where there is no absorption but where destruction of cells is favored because of continual friction. The deeper epithelial cells have to divide very rapidly to compensate for the cell losses.

Buccal glands are found between the buccinator muscle and the mucous lining. The ones which drain their secretion into the mouth in the region of the last molar tooth are called molar glands.

The duct of the parotid gland opens into the cheek opposite the second upper molar tooth, and a raised papilla usually marks the orifice.

Sebacious glands may occur posterolateral to the mouth angles. They occasionally enlarge in older people, in which case they are seen as yellowish structures through the mucous membrane.

The buccal fat pad of Bichat (suckling pad) fills in the area between the buccinator and the chewing muscles. It is extensively developed in the infant, and it has been questionably implicated in suckling movements. It is more likely a mechanical cushion.

In the lower animals the mouth is large, but the cheeks are deficient. The necessity of keeping the mouth closed and the loss of food minimized becomes associated with the appearance of cheeks. Whereas there are no cheeks in fishes and only rudimentary ones in reptiles and birds, the cheeks are well developed in monkeys, higher apes, and man. The phylogenetic appearance of the cheeks is also related to the muscular apparatus for chewing, which the cheeks assist by retaining food between the grinding teeth. Chewing is exclusively a mammalian property.

The cheeks are not very important in mastication. In the speech function they are used, like the lips, chiefly to articulate the labial consonants.

The Muscles of the Lips and of Expression
The muscles acting upon the lips and cheeks are part of the apparatus for facial expression, although additional muscles specifically performing the mimetic functions lie in other regions of the face and allow one to express such states as anger, contempt, disdain, disgust, fear, sadness, surprise, and other affective reactions.

Facial expression as an independent activity can have an influence upon articulation and tone. Changes in the tenseness of the muscles involved may interfere with tone by influencing oral resonance (Moses, 1954).

The facial expressions can be more important than words in social interaction. Typical facies have commonly been associated with specific diseases, such as the characteristically chronic anxiety expression of the child who has severely infected pharyngeal tonsils.

Human expressions can be traced back to reflex responses of animals. Andrew (1963) writes that facial expressions in subhuman primates are produced neither by specific conditions or drives nor by pleasant or unpleasant feelings, although they convey the motivation of the organism which displays them. Facial expressions may have evolved from such sources as responses through which vulnerable areas are protected, responses associated with vigorous respiration, and grooming responses. The facial expressions retain something of the causation of the early responses from which they originate.

The various muscles of expression have in common their relatively superficial position in the subcutaneous fascia. This position contrasts with the deeper one of most other muscles. Also, these muscles have an attachment to, or an influence upon, the skin. They are highly variable in extent, shape, and strength among individuals and are difficult to isolate because of fusions and interlacing of fibers. Although small, they are among the strongest muscles in the body.

There are several muscles of the face which are classified as muscles of expression. Except for the circular muscle of the lips, all are paired. The muscles of the nose may be included in the expressive groups (Mosher, 1951). The expressive muscles do not include the intrinsic muscles of the eye or the muscles of mastication (temporal, internal and external pterygoids, masseter, and anterior digastric).

387

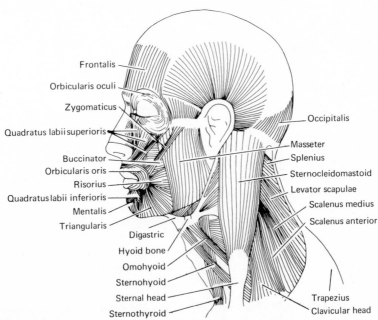

Figure 13-17 Superficial muscles of the face viewed from the side.

The facial muscles are arranged in separate groups. One group is composed solely of the platysma muscle. A second set occurs around the eyelids, a third around the ear, a fourth around the scalp, and a fifth around the mouth and nostrils. The muscles of the lower third of the face are often used to express sadness, anger, and aggression, unlike those of the middle third, which express happiness, joy, contentment, and peace (Conley, 1968).

The *platysma* (paired) is a wide, quadrilateral muscle covering most of the anterolateral surface of the neck, and it extends from the chest to the face, always lying between the superficial and the deep fascias. Its origin is from the skin and the superficial fascia in the superior chest and deltoid regions. It travels upward and forward. Some of its fibers attach to the lower border of the mandible and connect with the quadratus labii inferioris and triangularis muscles. The remainder of the fibers pass up into the face, and at the level of the lower lip these fibers cross each other. The most anterior and posterior fibers end in the lower lip, while the middle ones reach the upper lip.

The fibers ending in the mandible probably have very little influence in depressing the jaw. The muscle tends to draw the angle of the mouth downward and laterally, which changes the facial expression. Acting reversely, it elevates and wrinkles the skin over the clavicle and the deltopectoral region.

Most of the facial muscles act directly upon the lips, the most mobile part of the face. Changes in the shape of the lips affect oral resonance, and they also help complete the articulation of sounds. One set of lip muscles consists of parts of the orbicularis muscle, and it acts to adduct the lips. The other set separates the lips, and it is superficial or deep. The superficial activators of the upper lip are the quadratus labii superioris and the zygomaticus, while the deeper muscle of this region is the caninus.

In the lower lip the superficial muscle is the triangularis, and the deep muscles include the mentalis and the quadratus labii inferioris. The risorius and the buccinator muscles extend between the upper and lower lips to the mouth angle, the buccinator being the deeper.

The *orbicularis oris* (unpaired), or oral sphincter, is an oval ring of muscle located within the lips and completely encircling the mouth. It has no direct attachment to the skeleton. It contains upper and lower fibers which are limited to one side, but these interlace with the opposite fibers at the midline.

The muscle primarily adducts the lips, but it can narrow them while pressing them against the teeth. It can also protrude the lips and draw the lower lip up or the upper lip down. Pouting is an expressive result. The muscle can perform these several actions because it is actually a collection of independent units and also acts in conjunction with other lip muscles.

The *quadratus labii superioris* (paired) is a flat, triangular muscle located above the lateral portion of the upper lip. It is formed of three heads. Each of these has an independent origin which extends from the side of the nose to the zygoma (cheek bone).

The *angular* head originates from the infraorbital margin and the frontal process of the maxilla. Its fibers run downward and somewhat laterally to insert at the ala nasi (wings of the nose) and the orbicularis oris.

The *infraorbital* head originates from the infraorbital margin. Its fibers converge as they run downward to insert into the skin, in which they travel almost to the vermilion lip region. Many of these fibers interlace with the orbicularis oris muscle.

The *zygomatic* head originates on the facial surface of the zygomatic bone. It travels downward and medially to insert into the skin of the upper lip and into the orbicularis oris.

Although in most cases the three heads are separated, their fibers of insertion converge near the mouth angle. Their common action is to raise the upper lip and also to elevate the corner of the mouth and the wing of the nose. The nostril is widened. Contraction particularly of the infraorbital head produces an expression of sadness. Contraction of the entire muscle produces an expression of disdain and contempt.

The *zygomaticus* (paired) is a flat, oblong muscle located superficial to the maxillary and zygomatic bones. It is one of the most developed and constant muscles of the middle face. It originates from the temporal process of the zygomatic bone and travels downward and medially to insert into the orbicularis oris and the skin at the mouth angle. It pulls the corner of the mouth upward and laterally. This expresses smiling or laughing.

389

The *caninus* (paired) is a flat, triangular muscle above the corner of the mouth. It is deep to the middle quadratus labii superioris. Its origin, just below the infraorbital foramen, is at the canine fossa on the superficial surface of the maxilla. It goes downward and laterally toward the corner of the mouth, where some fibers insert; others end in the skin and mucous membrane of the lower lip. It elevates the corner of the mouth and may also help to close the mouth by elevating the lower lip. A sneering expression is ascribable to caninus activity.

The *risorius* (paired) is a flat muscle lateral to the mouth and superficial to the platysma. It is highly variable, and it may often be reduced to a few bundles or may even be missing. It originates in the fascia over the masseter muscle and crosses horizontally and superficially to the corner of the mouth. Most of the fibers insert into the skin and mucosa of the upper lip and also into the mucosa directly lateral to the mouth angle. A few bundles terminate in the lower lip. The muscle retracts the corner of the mouth and produces an expression of grinning, threatening, or sneering. When contracted strongly, the muscle produces an expression of tenseness and strain.

The *buccinator* (paired) is the principal muscle of the cheek. It forms the lateral wall of the mouth and is deep to the remainder of the oral musculature. It arises

(1) from the outer alveolar border of the maxilla in the molar region, (2) from the pterygomandibular raphe, and (3) from the outer alveolar border of the mandible in the molar region. Its fibers go forward to the corner of the mouth and enter both the upper and lower lips, in which they interlace with those of the opposite side. The middle fibers decussate at the mouth angle in such a manner that the lower set goes to the upper lip and the upper set goes to the lower lip. The muscle is covered posteriorly by the masseter and anteriorly by the muscles which converge upon the mouth angle.

The buccinator pulls the mouth angle laterally and posteriorly. It keeps the cheek stretched during any phase of oral activity. If it is paralyzed by a nerve lesion, the mucous membrane of the cheek cannot be tensed and becomes lacerated during chewing. The muscle can narrow the mouth opening and press the lips and cheeks against the teeth. This activity has given it the name of the "bugler's muscle."

The *quadratus labii inferioris* (paired) is a flat, quadrangular muscle located below the lateral portion of the mouth. It originates on the outer surface of the mandible between the symphysis and the mental foramen. It travels upward and medially into the orbicularis oris and into the skin of the lower lip. The deep fibers insert into the mucosa of the lower lip. There are some fibers which insert into the integument of the chin. The muscle draws the lower lip downward and slightly lateralward. This action produces an expression of irony.

The *triangularis* (paired) is a flat, triangular muscle located superficial and slightly lateral to the quadratus labii inferioris. It originates from the oblique line on the outer surface of the mandible. Along its origin, the fiber bundles alternate with those of the platysma. The fibers converge as they ascend to the corner of the mouth. They insert partly into the skin of the mouth angle and partly into the integument of the upper lip. The muscle pulls the mouth angle down. When both sides function together, the mouth is closed because of a depression of the upper lip. The expression of contempt is mediated.

The *mentalis,* or chin muscle (paired), originates from the incisive fossa of the mandible, just above the mental tuberosity. The medial fibers pass centrally and cross the midline to interlace with those of the contralateral muscle. They finally insert into the integument of the chin. The lateral fibers terminate in the skin on the same side. The uppermost fibers course superiorly to reach the lower part of the orbicularis oris muscle.

The muscle raises and wrinkles the integument of the chin. It also protrudes the lower lip and turns it outward. The expression of doubt or disdain exemplifies this activity.

Certain muscles of expression are on the forehead and scalp. The *corrugator* muscle originates from the medial aspect of the superciliary arch and inserts into the skin of the forehead. It wrinkles the forehead skin vertically, as in frowning.

The *epicranius,* or *occipitofrontalis,* muscle is comprised of the occipitalis muscle which covers the occiput and the frontalis which covers the front of the skull. A

390

thin aponeurosis, the galea aponeurotica, which lies over the entire upper cranium, connects the two muscles.

The occipitalis muscle originates from the occipital bone and from the mastoid part of the temporal bone and inserts into the aponeurosis. The muscle draws the scalp backward.

The frontalis muscle originates from the anterior border of the aponeurosis and inserts into the corrugator and orbicularis oculi muscles. The frontalis draws the scalp forward, elevates the eyebrows in the expression of surprise, and throws the skin of the forehead into horizontal wrinkles. Exaggerated frontalis action with the occipitalis fixed wrinkles the forehead to produce an expression of fright or horror.

The Nerve Supply of the Face

Facial Nerve

The innervation of the muscles of expression is from the *facial* nerve.

The facial nerve proper is primarily motor and goes to all the superficial muscles of the scalp, face, and neck and also to some of the deep muscles in this area. The trunk includes a smaller division called the intermediate nerve (of Wrisberg). This division mediates taste from the anterior two-thirds of the tongue, and it also sends autonomic efferents by way of the sphenopalatine, otic, and submaxillary ganglia to the lacrimal gland and to the submaxillary and sublingual salivary glands. The sensory fibers traveling in the intermediate nerve are received in the geniculate ganglion.

The facial nerve originates in cells near the junction of the medulla and pons. It emerges from the brain and enters the internal auditory canal, where it sends out branches. It then passes through the facial canal in the petrous area of the temporal bone, where it presents an oval swelling called the geniculate ganglion. From this ganglion three small nerves arise. These are (1) the great superficial petrosal, which becomes joined by the great deep petrosal; (2) the small superficial petrosal, which is joined by a nerve from the tympanic branch of the glossopharyngeal; and (3) the external superficial petrosal, which is an inconstant branch that enters the sympathetic plexus surrounding the middle meningeal artery.

In the lower part of the facial canal, the facial nerve gives off branches to the stapedius muscles and to the auricular branch of the vagus. It also produces the chorda tympani, which contains parasympathetic salivary fibers and other fibers mediating taste.

The facial nerve subsequently emerges from the base of the skull through the stylo-mastoid foramen and passes forward through the parotid gland to supply the muscles of the face. Within the parotid gland there is an indefinite split to an upper temporofacial and a lower cervicofacial division.

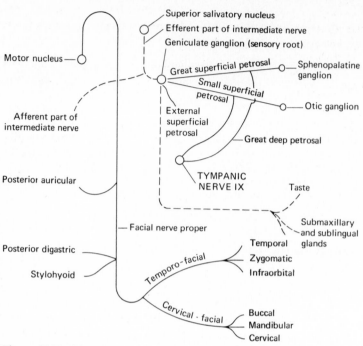

Figure 13-18 Diagrammatic representation of the main branches of the facial nerve.

When the facial nerve is subject to an extensive lesion, there is little or no power to raise the eyebrow, lip, cheek, and the skin of the forehead. There is also no ability to whistle or to close the eyelids firmly. All these defects are on the affected side.

Trigeminal Nerve

This supplies sensory innervation to the face and head, and it also provides motor fibers to muscles of chewing.

The trigeminal motor root fibers arise from a superior, or mesencephalic, nucleus in the cerebral aqueduct and an inferior nucleus in the upper pons. The sensory root fibers arise from the semilunar, or gasserian, ganglion located near the apex of the petrous part of the temporal bone. All fibers unite to one trunk and then subdivide to three great divisions, the ophthalmic, maxillary, and mandibular.

The ophthalmic division is the smallest and is sensory. It innervates the cornea, ciliary body, iris, lacrimal gland, and conjunctiva. It goes to the skin of the eyebrow, eyelid, forehead, and nose, and it supplies part of the mucous membrane of the nasal cavity.

The maxillary division is sensory. It innervates the dura mater, forehead, lower eyelid; the lateral aspect of the orbit, upper lip, gums, and teeth of the maxillary jaw; and the skin and mucous membrane of the cheek and nose.

The mandibular division is sensory and motor. It innervates the auditory pinna, cutaneous temporal region of the face, lower lip and face, mandibular gums and teeth, mucous membrane of the anterior aspect of the tongue, and the muscles of chewing.

The Blood Supply of the Face

Arteries supplying the superficial parts of the head region originate from the external or internal carotids.

The internal carotid artery gives off the supratrochlear, supraorbital, palpebral, dorsal nasal, and external nasal branches. These provide blood for the eyelids, nose, and anterior parts of the scalp as far back as the vertex.

The external carotid artery gives off several branches. The superficial temporal branch supplies the lateral parts of the scalp and the posterior aspect of the face. The posterior auricular branch supplies the scalp region posterior to the ear. The occipital branch supplies the posterior aspect of the scalp. The facial branch plus

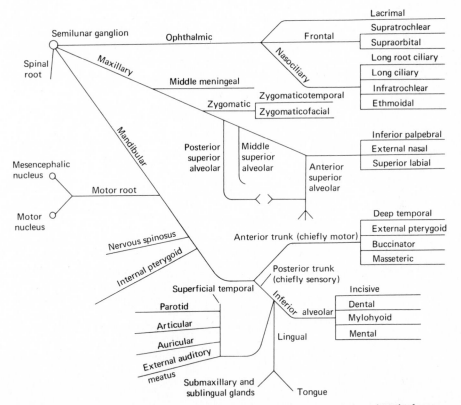

Figure 13-19 Diagrammatic representation of the main branches of the trigeminal nerve.

a small buccal branch supplies the entire anterior region of the face. There are also small arteries which enter the face through every foramen. Of the above vessels, the facial artery and transverse facial branch of the superficial temporal artery are the most important. The facial artery coils as it loops around the mandible, which avoids severe stretch when the mouth is opened.

For drainage, the supraorbital and supratrochlear veins leave the anterior surface of the scalp, fusing to a facial vein. The latter runs inferiorly, receiving tributaries from the eyelids, nose, and lips, and it finally drains into the internal jugular vein.

The posterior aspects of the scalp are drained by the occipital vein. This empties into the suboccipital venous plexus in the suboccipital triangle.

All other superficial parts of the head and face are drained by the superficial temporal and posterior auricular veins. The superficial temporal joins with the maxillary vein to form the retromandibular vein. The latter joins with the posterior auricular vein to form the external jugular vein, which empties into the subclavian system.

Phylogeny of Speech

The racial history of speech and particularly the role of the articulatory structures are entirely speculative. As Keleman (1958) has pointed out, this study interests the biologist not purely from a taxonomic standpoint but in his attempt to ascertain the origins of speech, its present status in the evolutionary scale, and the directions

394

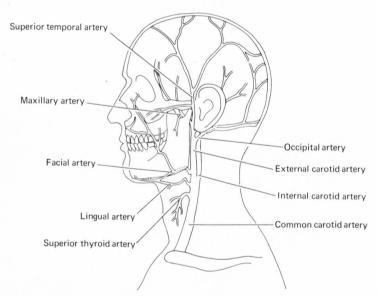

Figure 13-20 Facial arteries, mainly superficial.

it may take in the future. Evolution has tried endless combinations in structure and function, and these attempts may be revealed in a survey of the phonetic elements and processes of present-day species.

According to Froeschels and Jellinek (1941), phonetic utterances made while chewing are formed into articulated speech. They based this theory on the assumption that primitive man produced sounds while eating and that the connection between the vocal activity and the chewing function did not disappear in phonetic utterances. In animals and primitive tribes chewing is accompanied by various sounds.

Among the linguistic theories, it has been proposed that language or speech imitates naturally occurring sounds, e.g., the barking of dogs or the howling of jungle animals. Language has also been envisioned as an emotional outlet for pain or pleasure. There is also the view of a mystic harmony between sound and sense. It has further been propounded that language is linked with strong muscular effort, work being associated with vocal expressions. Meaningless humming may have taken place during collective group activity and a chant became identified perhaps with a victory. A gestural theory identifies language as a substitute for bodily actions; speech was useful in suggesting the movements of running or the actions of an enemy. All the views in this entire group fail to provide an adequate basis for the complexity of primitive languages. Over thousands of years a kind of simplification evolved, with words signifying both concrete objects and general concepts.

Montagu (1963) proposes a hunting theory of speech origin which suggests that when man began to hunt in groups, the tendency to produce sounds was strong. Such cries could then become identified with a specific context. This could influence success and the ability to survive and bear progeny. The view at least includes the criteria necessary for evolutionary success, i.e., an origin rooted in necessity and a development and survival fostered by natural selection.

Critchley (1967) presents some interesting concepts about the origin and development of speech. Marx (1967) briefly discusses the biologic basis of language.

Information Theory

The need to develop the relationships from the generated sound to the physiologic response appears to be a central problem in speech. Much more will have to be known about the anatomy and the exact changes in the vocal and auditory systems before strict relations can be established.

Many quantitative as well as qualitative facts concerning the acoustic signal have been derived from use of the information theory. The reader is referred to papers by Miller (1951) and Licklider and Miller (1951) and to Wiener's presentation (1961) of the relation of time series to information and communication. A major problem in communication involves the amount of information conveyed by speech and the efficiency of the average speaker in producing the information. Fant (1964) notes that the relatively low rate of information flow in speech messages may be contrasted with the great complexity of the specification necessary for the faithful description of the corresponding speech wave. A reduction of redundancy, i.e., how the complexity of signal descriptions matches the complexity of a speech message from a structural linguistic standpoint, is an important objective of the communication engineering involvement in speech research.

The speech musculature has been said to produce about 5 syllables, or 12.5 speech sounds per second. If any one of 39 different speech sounds were randomly generated at 12.5 phonemes per second, the speaker is estimated to produce any one of 10^{19} different sequences of sounds per second, and a perfectly efficient listener could select any one of the possible referents. There are factors, however, which reduce the amount of information. The speaker is relatively inefficient in that (1) motivation may be limited; (2) not all speech sounds are articulated with equal ease or frequency; and (3) the speech mechanism cannot select many words per second. Another set of limiting factors depends upon the construction of the spoken language, in that (1) phonemes and different words are not emitted equally often; (2) there is a sequential dependency of phonemes; and (3) the verbal context restricts the number of words which may be chosen.

In a fully developed speech message individual words have a meaning only in context. The unit of meaning is one or more sentences. In isolation a single word has a meaning; it is an auditory or visual symbol of an object, with a meaning of an elementary nature. Meanings are also communicated otherwise, as through gestures, exemplified in the manual speech of the deaf and dumb. The term propositional speech was coined by Hughlings Jackson to differentiate the communication of meanings from the expression of feelings, which have no propositional value. Logical abstract thought may also require concomitant internal verbal formulations, but this may not be needed for the more simple mental processes. Brain (1955) defines speech as the entire process by which meanings are comprehended and expressed in words, whereas articulation is a motor activity in which the formulated words are changed into sounds. A disorder of articulation would involve no derangement in the correct formulation of words, but it would in the machinery of verbal sound production.

Travis (1957) discusses factors governing the accuracy and validity of the information derived from central nervous system automatons in terms of the cybernetic reactions involved. Speech lapses are said to be rarely the failure of pure automatisms but a result of breakdown of some speech synergy or an interference with such a synergy by the entrance of an automatism into the efferent circuit which frees the lower motor neurons of articulation.

The cybernetic analysis of speech may provide significant contributions. It is one way in which the activity of nerve fibers can be quantitatively treated, by the analogy that the nervous system operates similarly to an electronic calculating machine. Since neurons and synapses act as relays which are either on or off, the Boolean algebra of classes (particularly the algebra of propositions, which is based upon the choice between yes or no, on or off) is especially applicable to treating information. Simplification is made possible by using binary arithmetic with a scale of 2 instead of the decimal scale of 10, since the number of alternatives presented at each choice is two.

One must be aware of oversimplification. The nervous system can apparently use frequency-modulation coding in addition to binary coding. If the mathematical precision of the nervous system is assumed to be inferior to computerlike function, then other nonbinary forms may be operating. Also, unlike binary-function systems, the nervous system has a great structural margin of safety and can suffer extensive structural loss without corresponding functional loss.

Instrumentation for General Articulatory Dynamics

In the noninstrumental subjective examination of articulation, the subject's spontaneous speech in normal conversation may be observed. The subject may be asked to read some printed matter aloud, with observations taken of the mode and character of enunciation, the rate of talking, and the pitch, rhythm, and stress of pronunciation. Abnormalities such as stuttering, slurring, or other articulatory disorders are observed. Test phrases, weighted words, rapid counting, and other evaluative items are used.

The development of machines for the analysis and synthesis of speech sounds may be noted. The reader is referred to a brief account by Carroll (1955) of some devices which are helping to establish a field of experimental phonetics. This instrumentation is illustrative of the entrance of communication engineering into the field of speech. For example, the sound spectrograph measures variations in vowel quality among dialects and permits the phonetic range of variation of a phoneme to be estimated. The speech stretcher plays back speech at a changed utterance rate without changing the original pitch. The electrical vocal tract synthesizes vowel sounds, which are quite naturalistic. Machines to convert speech to writing and to translate languages are in the making.

Speech elements have been artificially varied independently of one another to test the specific role played by each in speech by a device called the vocoder, first demonstrated by the Bell Telephone Laboratories in 1939. An oscillator replaces the larynx, and electrical filters replace the vocal resonators. The spectrum of the desired sound is obtained by filters, and the oscillators are converted to audible sound waves. Such parameters as the pitch can be varied at will.

Van Riper and Irwin (1958), in discussing the treatment of voice disorders, review a number of instrumental methods used to improve voice quality. These methods make such factors as pitch variation visible and make the correct control of pitch possible. Nasality can be indicated and controlled and intensity levels can be analyzed and corrected.

A presentation by Fant (1964) shows how the earlier kymograph studies have been supplanted by spectrographic analysis technics, multichannel oscillographic displays of subglottal activities, segmentation methods, vocal tract models, and speech synthesis technics.

The sound spectrograph electronically records sound waves. Objective correlates of the auditory sensation are registered in terms of frequency, intensity, and duration. The result is a "picture" of the sound wave which can be correlated with the subjective impression of the sounds and with the articulatory descriptions given to them (Dinneen, 1967).

Huntington (1968) cites new instrumentation for continuous recording of articulatory data, including electromyography, recording of tongue-palate contacts, and improvements in high-speed photography, stroboscopy, and roentgenography.

General Involvement of Articulation in Speech

There are minimum essentials of speech sound formation to produce intelligibility. Any sound, whether in isolation or in context, should be supported by adequate breath pressure and should be correctly formed. There must also be a sharp release or movement into the next sound formation. The clearness necessary for intelligibility is provided by the consonants, while much of the tonal quality of speech is given by the vowels. A dominant role is assumed by the articulators in shaping all consonants. They also assist in forming some of the vowel phonemes.

398

Some phonemes, especially vowels, are primarily resonance phenomena. Other phonemes, like the unvoiced consonants, are mouth noises which bear no relationship to the laryngeal note. Still other phonemes, such as most voiced consonants, combine the mouth noises of their respective unvoiced partners with a laryngeal note.

In the formation of consonants, the breath stream is interrupted to variable degrees in the mouth or diverted through the nose. The air does not flow through a wide-open mouth. The consonant machinery includes the mandible, lips, tongue, and velum. There are movements such as approach and recession of the jaws, protrusion of the lips, and approximation of the lower lip to the upper teeth. The tongue moves toward or to the teeth, palate, velum, or alveolar ridge. The velum rises or falls.

Voiced sounds are produced by the airstream when the glottis is narrowed and the vocal folds approach each other or touch lightly. The sounds travel variably through the mouth or nose. The spectral composition of these sounds is a resultant of the laryngeal tone and the supraglottic modifications on the amplitude and phase of the frequency components.

Unvoiced (voiceless) sounds are produced while the glottis is open for outgoing breath. The sounds are made by articulatory closure or constrictions at one or more places through which the airstream travels. The spectral composition is subjected to change by the activities in the tract lying between the constriction and the mouth opening.

Although all vowels are voiced, which implies activity of the larynx, consonants can be voiced or voiceless. The latter term negates laryngeal activity. A changing relative importance of phonation and articulation in the formation of sounds is therefore indicated. Humming with the mouth open is solely phonation. Whispering involves articulation. In English, whispering is almost fully as intelligible as loud speech, which implies that phonation is adjunctive, providing such parameters of speech as amplification, emotional setting, and inflection. In a language where inflection is necessary for intelligibility, whispering is not effective.

Classification of Sounds

In the description of the articulation of sounds, a simplifying system of classification had to be established. This is the province of phonetics. There have been three main approaches to this problem (Kantner and West, 1960). In the acoustic approach, sounds are classified by their effect upon the auditory mechanism in terms dealing with auditory sensation. Thus there are the vowels, semivowels, diphthongs, and consonants. The consonants in turn are subdivided to sonants and surds, and these are further subdivided into fricatives, sibilants, etc. The vowels, which are less clearcut, are described by such terms as long, short, high or low pitched, stressed or unstressed, strong or weak, more or less resonant, and more or less sonant.

In the placement or positional approach the geographic places of the articulators in producing the given sound are described. Thus there are front, mid-, and back vowels, and there are palatal, velar, various labial, and other varieties of consonants. The emphasis is placed upon anatomy.

In the kinesiologic approach, the positions of the articulators are similarly determined, but the movements of the machinery to accomplish such positions are also emphasized. The neuromuscular apparatus is brought into the description. Such terms as stop, glide, and continuant suggest movement rather than position or auditory sensation. They also suggest persistence, or duration, whose value is indicated as a continuant or a stop. A continuant sound is continuable as long as the breath holds out, but a stop (plosive) is instantaneous and finished.

Consonants
It is customary to divide oral speech sounds into two primary categories, vowels and consonants, but this division is somewhat arbitrary (Huntington, 1968). The reader is referred to standard textbooks dealing with phonetics for a comprehensive discussion.

The sound /p/ involves closure of the lips and subsequent sudden opening of the mouth. This sound is called an unvoiced bilabial plosive, or stop. The release, or explosion, follows the increase in oral air pressure, or implosion. The /p/ sound could also be described by stating that the exhaled air is stopped completely. This would then be a stopped consonant.

The involvement of the soft palate in articulation can be illustrated in the plosives. The increasing air pressure in the mouth is made possible not only by a closed oral port but also by closure of the posterior nares through elevation of the soft palate. Perhaps the first stage in the formation of such sounds is this velopharyngeal closure.

We can similarly describe the sounds /f/ and /v/. These are called labiodentals from the fact that the lower lip lightly meets the upper incisors and sharply withdraws. The lip is the active agent; /f/ is unvoiced, and its cognate, /v/, is voiced. From another standpoint, /f/ and /v/ are fricatives, or the air escaping through the mouth is only partially stopped with the velopharyngeal valve closed. These sounds are also called oral continuants.

Air stoppage depends upon the velopharyngeal mechanism. If oral escape is minimized or prevented, the sound stream is directed through the nasal passages. The entire relatively immovable nasal chambers, because of limited resonance, tend to produce a sameness to all the nasal sounds. The distinctiveness imparted to the sounds is ascribed to differential activities within the oral cavity.

The nasal family of sounds in English consists of /m/, /n/, and /ŋ/. They may be regarded in one sense as nasal consonants (continuants), but they stand between the consonants and vowels. Although vowels tend to be emitted through the oral cavity, the nasal sounds act like the vowels in having laryngeal and resonance features and in being voiced.

For the /m/, the lips are closed, and the entire oral cavity contributes to the resonance qualities. For the /ŋ/, the tongue and posterior aspect of the palate form the closing partition, and there is less oral resonance. For the /n/, the size of the oral resonator is somewhere between that for the other two sounds. In none of these instances is the position of the velopharyngeal valve one of nasal closure.

In the /s/ and /z/ phonemes, air is forced through a narrowed oral port. These are continuant fricatives, which are sounds that have encountered an obstruction to passage, with the resulting production of friction sounds. If the airstream has been vibrated by the larynx, the friction sounds are components of the final *voiced* sound. If the airstream has not been excited to vibration, only the friction wave components will produce the final acoustic effect, the voiceless sound. /s/ is an unvoiced fricative, and its cognate, /z/, is a voiced fricative. These sounds are also called hissing sounds or sibilants.

/s/ and /z/ can be described anatomically. The tongue is the primary articulating agent. The velopharyngeal mechanism first closes. Then the mandible rises to approximate the upper and lower teeth. The lips retract, and the tongue tip is free, although the sides of the tongue occlude with the lateral dental surfaces as far forward as the labial incisors. This action allows air to travel in a small channel over the tip as well as through the narrow opening between the central incisors.

In consonant formation, the partial or total stoppage of air or its direction of flow are not the only variables. The time taken to dissipate the augmented air pressure is another factor. Thus in /dʒ/, as in judge, or /tʃ/, as in church, which are called affricatives, the air is partially stopped, but it need not be quickly released. For all sounds the time order of muscle contractions is vital (Judson and Weaver, 1965). This involves an orderly sequence of dynamic events, subject to control by yet undetermined centers.

Dynamic bodily changes and movements, involving the activity of muscle groups and studied as the science of kinesiology, are of considerable importance in the explanation of how the individual phonemes are produced. As a single example of this approach, in the voiceless th or theta (symbol is θ) the genioglossus muscle flattens and protrudes the tongue postdentally or intradentally, along with the cooperation of the verticalis muscle, while the genioglossus thrust is opposed by muscles including principally the hyoglossus. There is complete velar pharyngeal closure. One must always be aware, however, of the danger of stating that a sound is made in a certain way when differing contexts make for thousands of permutations. The /r/ by itself has a great number of combinations. Nevertheless, the advantages of systematic description seem to outweigh the dangers. The investigations of muscular movements in articulation, including electromyographic technics, are numerous, and are best discussed in courses dealing with phonetics. There is no question that a major section in a textbook of anatomy could be directed toward evaluating the contributing muscles to each of the major phonemes.

401

Semivowels

Certain sounds, e.g., /w/ and /j/, as in way and yes, are called semivowels because they partake of the nature of both vowels and consonants. They are sounds of a gliding type in that the articulatory structures are positioned for one vowel and at once pass to another vowel position. These sounds need to be pronounced with force.

The semivowels /w/, /j/, /r/, and /l/ and diphthongs (double vowels in a stereotyped combination, e.g., oil) are classified as *vowel glides*, or methods of beginning, connecting, or ending vowel sounds.

Vowels

The articulatory adjustments for vowel phonemes are less precise than for consonants. In the vowels the mouth is relatively open, yet there are constrictions of the mouth and throat which modify the volume of these chambers and the size of their openings. In the front vowels the anterior part of the mouth narrows between the tongue blade and the hard palate while the pharynx widens. In the back vowels the lips narrow, the tongue dorsum elevates toward the soft palate, and the cavity of the pharynx enlarges. In the neutral vowels the tongue is in a "resting" position.

Vowel production is particularly linked with resonation, which may be the chief factor in differentiating the vowels. Although vowels are produced by vocal fold vibration, it is possible to replace the laryngeal sound. Thus, vowels can be produced by whispering or be formed even in laryngectomized subjects. To produce vowels, several conditions are ordinarily needed. The vocal folds vibrate. The velum rises against the posterior pharyngeal wall. There must be a relatively open passage from the vocal folds through the lips, and movements of the articulators must change the size and shape of the oral cavity.

For each vowel, the mouth, nose, and pharyngeal resonators take a given position and shape which permit selection and exaggeration of specific overtones. Lip shaping is essential, especially to certain vowels, but vowels may be recognizable by compensating with different tongue positions (Colson, 1963). The length of time a vowel is sustained depends upon its position in the word.

The *quality* of vowels has been described both from the articulatory and acoustic standpoints. In the former the position of the tongue has been analyzed during the pronunciation of vowel sounds and diagrams made (Mase, 1962; Ladefoged, 1967). The cardinal vowel system, first developed in 1917, was a marked step in that direction. Ladefoged (1967) emphasizes that vowels used in ordinary speech are not sufficiently equivalent phonetically to use for specifying or comparing vowel quality.

402   Daniel Jones devised a system involving the use of the so-called cardinal vowels. These are sounds equivalent in phonetic quality to the corresponding cardinal vowels produced by Jones or by phoneticians who can duplicate the exact quality of the original cardinal vowels.

Standard reference sounds were designed supposedly to have a quality independent of language or any dialect. All vowels would then be describable from this schema

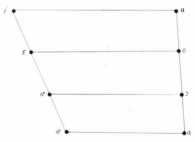

Figure 13-21 Schematic vowel quadrilateral diagram showing the outer limits of the tongue positions for articulating the eight primary cardinal vowels. The articulatory tongue positions of other English vowels are not shown.

in terms of tongue positions, as higher, lower, farther front, or farther back than the corresponding cardinal vowels.

The existing cardinal vowel system does not fully specify the vowels or allow for exact reproduction of the vowel qualities. The precise difference between two vowel sounds can be conveyed only if there are equally precise reference points. The cardinal vowel system should be retained for this purpose until it is possible to make acoustic measurements which are more accurate for specifying vowels of all types.

Vowels from the acoustic standpoint may be described in terms of *formants,* a development accelerated by the sound spectrograph (Ladefoged, 1967). The rationale of specification by formants is that each vowel is a complex vibration containing a fundamental tone and a series of harmonics (Fletcher, 1962). The vocal resonators accentuate some of the overtones and attenuate others, resulting in a prominence of certain regions of frequency, termed formants.

Malmberg (1963) states that the timbre of vowels is due essentially to two formants, one low and the other high, and that for some vowels a third formant is important. In what is considered by many writers to be an undue simplification, the two formants correspond to the two important resonators, the pharynx and mouth, and it is by tongue movements that the resonance effects of the two cavities are varied.

One of the difficulties in relating formants to vowel quality is in giving a good operational definition of a formant. The term is often applied to a frequency region in which the sound is more intense than elsewhere in the spectrum. The reinforced frequencies which constitute a formant are harmonics of the fundamental tone, and a vowel formant in speech is not a single tone but a range of frequencies. Each vowel is associated with such a specific region, but the center of a formant is not always easy to locate.

A number of vowels cannot be adequately specified in terms of their formant frequencies. In addition, even if the specification of the formant frequencies accounted for the main spectral characteristics of the sound, it does not explain the chief auditory attributes of the sound. Heffner (1960) says that the existence of formants should not be denied but their adequacy to describe a vowel must be challenged.

There have been several theories of vowel production. In the harmonic, or relative-pitch, theory (Fletcher, 1953), the vocal folds are said to produce a compound wave containing a fundamental and many harmonics, and the component frequencies are exact multiples of the fundamental. The bodily resonators magnify frequencies to which they are tuned, and this in turn determines the vowel quality. This is a steady-state theory, in which the waves pass in regular succession for short periods of time.

In the inharmonic view, the vocal folds serve to excite transient frequencies characteristic of the vocal cavities. Irregular or nonperiodic puffs of glottic air excite the supraglottic air. In this second, cavity-tone, or fixed-pitch, theory (see Judson and

Weaver, 1965), the vowel is made up of a tone produced at the glottis plus a tone produced by the vocal cavities which is not necessarily related to, or dependent upon, the glottal tone. In both theories, the vocal quality depends upon the natural periods and damping of the vocal cavities. A brief historical survey of theories of vowel production is given by Chiba and Kajiyama (1958).

There is a school of thought (McDonald, 1964) which deemphasizes the previous classifications and holds that speech is not a succession of sounds in which each sound implies a specific corresponding position of the speech organs. Heffner (1960) says that speech is a continuum of movements and the isolated sounds and positions represent ranges of variation rather than fixed entities. The same sound is produced inconstantly; conversely, different sounds can be elicited by the same articulation. Sound is learned and expressed as a unit resulting from considerable integrated bodily activity. Even in the earlier literature it was emphasized that it is inadvisable in therapy to reeducate only a limited group of muscles. The important goal is to establish a new total-reaction pattern.

Rousey and Moriarty (1965) make the statement that any belief that anatomy and physiology are sufficient for the study, diagnosis, and rehabilitation of persons with speech disorders is a gross oversimplification of a very complex problem. There is little doubt of the validity of these contentions, but it is also true that speech is inescapably bound to a unique human structure and its correlative activities. Lenneberg (1967) emphasizes that although anatomy does not explain the origin of language or man's capacity for it, the sounds of language are intimately dependent upon the morphology of the vocal tract. All biologic activities are more complex and dynamic than previously supposed, but the importance of their correlates in structure is in no wise diminished by this knowledge. We are simply confronted with the necessity of adding additional technics of analysis to our investigative armamentarium.

404

Articulatory Pathophysiology: General

The largest percentage of speech disorders are those of articulation. West and Ansberry (1968) differentiate the term *speech disorder* from *speech defect*. The former term considers the causative factors and the acoustic result, whereas the latter considers only the acoustic end result.

Classification

The classification of speech disorders is somewhat chaotic. The term *dyslalia* has been used frequently as one of the blanket words to cover disorders of the articulatory mechanisms caused by structural anomalies of the organs of articulation and/or disorders of hearing. There are many kinds of dyslalias. Some examples include low intelligence, auditory defects, motor deficiencies, cleft palate, retarded speech, irregular teeth, inactive tongue, and social and psychological causes. In the dyslalic individual the sounds are improperly produced, replaced by others, or entirely lacking.

The term *dysarthria* is also used to identify persons with imperfect articulation of speech (Meano and Khoury, 1967). It signifies a faulty pronunciation of certain sounds or groups of sounds, especially consonants (Brain, 1965; DeParrel, 1965) but also vowels. Examples of common dysarthrias are sigmatism (lisping or the erratic pronunciation of /s/), and rhotacism (incorrect use or overuse of /r/). Greene (1964) states that dysarthrias are caused by lesions in the central or peripheral nervous system which produce motor impairment of the muscles of articulation. The term is not used to include damage to the language areas of the cerebral cortex.

Dysphonia refers to a voice deviating from an acceptable normal. Whispering and pitch abnormalities are examples. The term does not refer to complete absence of voice (aphonia). Dysphonia was defined previously under laryngeal pathophysiology, where it is more relevant.

Dysrhythmia includes stuttering and cluttering. The cluttered speech is slurred, hasty, inaccurate, uncontrolled, and may contain substitutions, transpositions, omissions, inversions, and other distortions. The differences between cluttering and stuttering are important from a practical standpoint (see Luchsinger and Arnold, 1965).

Dsyphemia is a term for speech disorders that have an etiology in psychopathology. Another speech disorder that results from a psychopathologic condition of the individual is *dyslogia*, which is a disorder of words or of language.

405

Mase (1962) states that disorders of articulation are commonly classified in a generalized way as substitutions, omissions, additions, or distortions and that an individual may display any or all of these errors. This classification is based on the listener's interpretation rather than upon etiology.

This discussion of terminology leads to the comment that there is a movement away from the European mélange of pseudo-Latin and of other pseudomedical nomenclature such as dyslalia, dyslogia, gammacism, sigmatism, and similar types of terms. Some words, e.g., dysarthria, dysphasia and dysphonia, are retained.

Anatomic Structure and Articulatory Disorders

Whether persons have real differences in anatomic structure at the basis of their articulatory disorders remains uncertain. In functional articulation disorders, no systematic differences in the lips, palate, or tongue have been proved. Better instrumentation and technics are beginning to reveal differences in coordination, movement and sensory patterns, however, if one excludes the somewhat ambivalent "mild" category of disorders.

In disorders of the dominant cerebral hemisphere, there may be thick and slurred speech as a result of hemiplegia of such articulator organs as the cheeks, lips, and tongue.

Basal ganglia disturbances affect articulation. In progressive lenticular degeneration (Wilson's disease), the hypertonus and stiffness of all muscles, including those of the mandible, lips, pharynx, and tongue, lead to faulty articulation. The patient with Parkinson's disease usually has a slow and hesitating speech. The individual with chorea may have explosive and arrhythmic speech along with irregularities in respiration.

In a cerebellar lesion, phonation may suffer more than articulation. There is a lack of rhythmic correlation of respiration with speech, and even the strength of the breath stream suffers. The speech is labored, many syllables tend to be explosive, and facial grimaces are common.

When the articulator muscles become paralyzed, as in progressive atrophy of the motor neurons of the cranial nerves leaving the brain stem (progressive bulbar paralysis), the speech becomes labored and eventually unintelligible.

When phonetic lapses are traceable to disorders of the articulatory muscles or of their lower motor neurons, it is useful to list the difficulty according to the fairly distinct neuromuscular unit involved in producing the given sound. The variety of the phonetic failure would help to diagnose the lesion. In this grouping, the labial sounds are articulated by facial muscles innervated by the facial nerve. The lingual group is articulated by lingual muscles and the hypoglossal nerve. The nonnasal group, requiring velar closure, is supplied by palatal and pharyngeal muscles through the glossopharyngeal and spinal accessory nerves. The guttural group involves the palatopharyngohyoid musculature, supplied by the glossopharyngeal, vagus, spinal accessory, and the first three cervical nerves. The mandibular group, requiring either a wide or a narrow spread of the mandible, uses the muscles of mastication and the trigeminal nerve. Finally, all voiced sounds involve laryngeal muscles and the vagus nerve.

Phonetic Alphabet

In a phonetic alphabet speech sounds are represented by special phonetic symbols instead of conventional letters or orthographic symbols. This alphabet ideally attempts to have one symbol for one speech sound. This is an efficient device because if the alphabet had a sign for each word or each syllable, one would have to reckon with thousands of words or hundreds of syllables. Since words and syllables are composed of individual sounds which rarely exceed sixty to seventy in number, an alphabetic system can use the minimum units to express every possible utterance in the language (Hughes, 1962; Judson and Weaver, 1965). The phonetic alphabet can logically supplant the existing English alphabet in which the letters, or visual symbols, have failed to keep pace with the continuously changing auditory symbols, or speech sounds.

The plan of a phonetic alphabet allows for a very efficient reduction in the number of symbols, although in practice the assumption is not generally true that one sound has one symbol and vice versa. For example, what is exactly heard as a t depends upon how it has been generated. If the tongue tip is placed in different positions in the oral cavity, the sound quality will vary. The symbol /t/ can be used to represent all the variations. This "family" of sounds, which includes the various acoustically perceived variations (within the limits that the sound is still perceived), in this case as *t,* is called a *phoneme.* A simplified phonetic alphabet presents one symbol per phoneme without consideration of all the variations within the limits of recognition of that sound. If a sound were specified within brackets, it could stand for a single, distinct variant, which is called a *phon.*

Several factors produce variations in sounds. Significant examples include the inability to replicate speech patterns exactly, the influence of the preexisting position of the speech organs, individual variations, and the tendency to repeat environmental speech sounds. There is a definite position of the tongue, teeth, and lips for every sound, and these positions vary in accordance with the real nature and form of the sounds as they are spoken. The phonetic alphabet, which is based upon describable structural positions, can aid in correctly producing the acceptable sound of words. Although ordinary spelling emphasizes only one pronunciation of a word, the phonetic alphabet shows the variant pronunciations. It is applicable for teaching a foreign language or correcting an unwanted accent because it can designate any position of the articulatory organs. Although the phonetic alphabet is not the alphabet of any given language, it can be a system in which any language can be written. Its symbols are essentially a formula expressing how a sound is produced by the vocal tract.

By using a phonetic alphabet, the vowels, diphthongs, consonants, and consonant blends can be tested and a systematic phonetic inventory of an individual's speech can be made (Powers, 1957).

A very widely used system is the International Phonetic Alphabet (IPA), although there are other systems. The symbols used are not in many instances readily recognizable by a layman or by one just beginning the study of the science of speech. Readers outside the speech field are referred to standard textbooks of phonetics.

Phonetics has a very vital place in anatomy, and a logical direction of attack might well have been in an "anatomy of misarticulations." Thus, what anatomic pattern must be broken down and retrained if a person repeatedly mispronounces certain sounds? Malformations are responsible for only a small proportion of speech defects, and most cases are due to bad habits set up in childhood and are curable. In correction, one must have an exact knowledge of the formation of speech sounds, as well as being capable of recognizing the wrong sound.

The inattention of anatomists to speech disorders is almost parallel to the relationship of anatomy to kinesiology, where the latter science has had to assume the professional role and answer the applied questions about muscle involvement in specific physical exercise tasks.

Northampton Chart of Symbols A simplified Northampton Chart (Yale, 1946), which is practicable in teaching the deaf and uses symbols recognizable by the layman, may give an elementary concept of the number of English speech sounds and

SIMPLIFIED NORTHAMPTON CHART*

	1	2	3	4	5	6	7	8	9
	CONSONANTS					VOWELS			
	Breath sounds	Voiced sounds	Nasal sounds						
1	p	b–	m						
2	t	d–	n	l	r				
3	k	g–	ng						
4	t^1h	t^2h							
5	f	v							
6	s	z							
7	sh	zh							
8	ch	j–							
9	wh	w							
10	h–								
					y–	ee	o^1o	a(r)	i–e
					x = ks	–i–	o^2o	wr	a–e
					qu = kwh	a–e	o–e	–u–	o–e
						–e–	–o–		u–e
						–a–	aw		ou
									oi

* A dash after a letter in the consonant chart signifies that the sound is initial in a word or syllable.

SOURCE: By permission, The Clarke School for the Deaf, Northampton, Mass. As found in Caroline A. Yale, *Formation and Development of Elementary English Sounds*, Metcalf Printing and Publishing Company, Inc., Northampton, Mass., 1946.

how they are formed in isolation. The symbols used represent the most frequent spellings.

In column 1 the vocal folds are in open position, but in column 2 they are vibrating. The sounds of column 3 are nasal, and they are the only English sounds having an open nasopharyngeal port. The sounds of column 6 are associated with extended lips and sounds at the front of the tongue while phonated air passes freely through the mouth. In column 7 there is emphasis upon the back of the tongue, and the lips are rounded. The sounds of column 8 are misfits. In column 9 the sounds are diphthongs, or combinations of two vowels.

Other similarities among speech sounds are illustrated in the horizontal rows. In row 1 the lips are closed. In row 2 the tongue tip in most cases reaches the hard palate. In column 3 the back of the tongue touches the hard palate, or it rises in the posterior part of the mouth. In row 4 the tongue tip goes between the teeth. In row 5 the superior border of the lower lip meets the inferior borders of the upper teeth. In row 6 frictional noises at the edges of the front teeth produce a part of the sound. In row 7 similar events occur, but the medium groove of the tongue is wider and forms more posteriorly. In row 8 the tongue tip drops or explodes into positions such as those of row 7. In row 9 the lips are rounded. The /h/ of 10 is without its own position and takes that of the succeeding sound, e.g., the /o/ of hole.

Pathophysiology of Articulation: Special Organs

The Tongue
O'Rourke and Miner (1951) emphasize that apart from local causes the tongue expresses many disorders of systemic origin. These conditions include blood diseases, metabolic disorders, etc. In this sense the tongue is a barometer of much internal function. Locally, when the teeth deteriorate, the tongue is adaptively set into greater compensatory activity. This is carried on in a medium favoring local lesions of the organ.

In hypothyroid states, such as myxedema, the tongue may enlarge, and this may be accompanied by a slow, thick speech. A large tongue may be found in severe cervical infections. It may also be enlarged congenitally, and this is called *macroglossia*. In a rare developmental anomaly called *microglossia* the tongue is excessively small. At least one record exists of the congenital absence of a tongue, *aglossia* (Bloomer, 1957; Shafer et al., 1963). The difficulties with eating and speech are obvious.

A cleft or bifid tongue is a rare developmental anomaly, resulting from failure of the paired lateral primordia to fuse.

In hemiplegia, the tongue when protruded deviates markedly to one side. This is observed similarly in lesions of the hypoglossal nucleus or of the nerve trunk, such as in bulbar paralysis. Unilateral paralysis need not impair articulation.

A tongue displaying tremor may indicate such conditions as nervousness, alcoholism, hyperthyroidism, and dementia paralytica. If the tremor is hesitating, it is suggestive of prolonged infection, debilitating conditions, or senescence.

A tongue that cannot protrude beyond the teeth even by force is not free enough for proper speech. In a tongue-tied individual, where the frenulum is binding down the tongue, there is an especial effect upon a sound such as /s/. In correct articulation the tip of the tongue is raised so as to almost touch the teeth ridge, leaving a narrow channel through which air passes. In lisping, the tip of the tongue is placed between the teeth or against the edge of the upper front teeth. This position produces a frontal or lingual lisp, which is the usual type. In the lateral lisp, air escapes from the sides of the tongue. There is faulty use of the lingual muscles.

Lisping is a disorder of the sibilant consonants, and /s/ and /z/ are sounded incorrectly. It is common for /θ/ to be substituted for /s/, and /ð/ to be used instead of /z/. Sometimes /ʃ/ and /ʒ/ and also /dʒ/ and /tʃ/ are sounded incorrectly.

The Lips
Of the two lips the upper one is more often defective. A congenital cleft affects the upper lip. Paralysis of one or both lips may interfere with air flow and the labial sounds.

Harelip is a congenital anomaly seen in the upper lip and resulting from failure of the structures forming the lip to fuse properly during fetal development. The globular aspect of the median nasal process is improperly joined with the lateral nasal and maxillary processes. The defect is unilateral or bilateral, but it is not a midline one since the line of union and fusion normally occurs on either side of the midline. If a part of the median nasal process is absent, however, the cleft could appear in the midline (Shafer et al., 1963).

The failure shows several variations, such as a small fissure in the vermilion border of the lip, an extension of the cleft to the nostril, or a continuation of the fissure with an anteroposterior cleft through the hard palate. The term harelip is frequently applied to all varieties of cleft lips. The sounds distorted are characteristically those involving the upper lip.

Heredity is an important factor in harelip, and nutritional disturbances are also of importance. The lip cleft occurs more frequently in males and on the left side. Facial clefts may occur anywhere on the face where developmental processes join, but the cleft lip is the most important of the facial clefts.

There is a rare, mandibular type of cleft lip, seen in the midline of the lower lip and originating from failure of the mandibular processes to fuse medially. Sometimes the jaw as well as the lip is involved.

410   There is an uncommon condition of unknown etiology, called *cheilitis glandularis aspostematosa*, in which the lower lip becomes enlarged, firm, and everted. A chronic condition, similar in clinical appearance but apparently unrelated, is *cheilitis granulomatosa*, in which there is diffuse swelling, especially in the lower lips. Fairbanks and Green (1950) measured lip dimensions in a variety of subjects and conclude that the dimensions are not causally related to articulatory efficiency.

The Mandible

There are developmental disturbances of the mandible. In *agnathia,* which is very rare, neither the mandible nor maxilla develops. Partial or unilateral absence of the mandible may occur. In *micrognathia,* which may be hereditary or acquired (Shafer et al., 1963), the jaw is small or abnormally positioned, and there is marked retrusion of the chin. In *macrognathia* the upper or lower jaws, or both, are abnormally large.

If the muscles of the lower jaw do not function properly, mandibular action is distorted. The malfunction is observable in the instance where the jaw sags and saliva drools out of the mouth. The fault may reside in the muscles closing the lips as well as in the elevators of the jaw. The cause may also reside in a spasm of certain depressor muscles, like the digastric.

Difficulty with the motions of the mandible is also seen in pathology of the temporomandibular joint. Severe discomfort follows overclosure or any displacement of the mandible, and a loss of hearing acuity may result. Condylar displacement at the joint may produce pain and other symptomatology by a degenerative arthritis rather than by any compression of the auriculotemporal or chorda tympani nerve fibers within the joint region. Overclosure disturbs muscular coordination, which in turn produces the chronic joint trauma.

The up and down motions are important in speech, and their function is tested by having an individual very rapidly and repeatedly open and close his mandible. About 5 cycles per second in rhythm is a normal expectation.

There is a disorder termed an open bite in which the molar teeth occlude prior to approximation of the incisor teeth. The airstream is not correctly impeded in front, and the sibilants are distorted. The handicap is often spontaneously palliated by blocking the opening with the tip of the tongue. The specific effect of an open bite upon speech would depend upon the size of the residual opening and also upon mandibular or maxillary prognathism.

A recessive mandible affects sounds requiring the proper position of the lips, incisors, and tongue. These sounds include /p/, /b/, /m/, /s/, /z/, /θ/ and its voiced analog /ð/.

Prognathism has a similar effect. Bloomer (1957) states that mandibular protraction may produce no speech difficulty if the condition is relatively mild and that even a marked deformity may not produce an articulatory defect if the lips and tongue can effect adequate substitution.

411

Dental Defects

The proper shape of the dental arches and the correct occlusion of the teeth may be essential for proper speech. There seems to be considerable difference of opinion about this statement. Carrell (1936) studied children with speech defects and said that they showed no real differences from the normal children in dental abnormalities or palatal malformations. Fymbo (1936) related the severity of speech defects to malocclusion. In another study inferior speakers were found to have a greater incidence of dental abnormalities (Fairbanks and Lintner, 1951). Bloomer (1957) says that although structural defects in teeth occur more frequently in persons with speech defects, this does not prove that dental abnormalities are primary causes of speech disturbances. Bloomer discusses the relation of orofacial abnormalities to speech and makes a plea for a genetic approach because it can help the speech clinician understand the problems and the limitations of treatment.

The teeth obstruct the free passage of air in certain sounds. When the upper incisors protrude and rest upon the lower lip so that both lips approximate with difficulty, the labial sounds such as /p/, /b/, and /m/ can be distorted. The quality of /s/ is changed by protrusions of the upper teeth and by dental gaps.

Speech defects seem to be produced by the absence of teeth. In a loss of the upper incisors or in an open bite where the upper teeth do not touch the lower lip, /f/ and /v/ are distorted. If the lips do not come into contact, /b/ and /m/ are not sounded and even /s/ and /z/ can be difficult. Although the four pairs of incisors participate in forming the hissing noises of the sibilant sounds and lisping can result from missing or maloccluded incisors, other factors are more important in leading to this defect (Luchsinger and Arnold, 1965).

The faulty position of even one tooth seems to be able to interfere with the position of the tongue. If one incisor is pulled backward, there may be hissing or whistling upon attempting to articulate certain sounds, for example, /d/ and /t/.

Orthodontic appliances and dentures have produced distortions of speech. Subsequently there is the necessity to form new speech habits, especially those involving the tongue. Dentures that are too thick in the rugae area prevent the tongue from making a small air space.

The effect of distorted teeth upon the personality is emotionally linked with speech. Although difficult to assess, it produces feelings of inferiority which lead to functional vocal disturbances.

14 THE EAR AS A SOUND RECEPTOR

The External Ear

Sound is produced by a body vibrating in a medium such as air. When a sounding body like a tuning fork vibrates, alternate condensations and rarefactions of the air, called sound waves, radiate out from it. The waves may reach the external ear.

Auricle

The auricle, or pinna, is a concave cartilaginous structure which directs sound waves to the external auditory meatus, or canal. Its significance in man may be negligible, although it has been said to help localize sound and to have most of its effect on tones of high pitch. The stereophonic hearing effect of two ears, which allows judgment of the direction of a sound, may result from the difference in the phase of the vibration as it reaches the two ears and also from the differences in intensity and quality, because sound must go around the corner in the far ear. It is possible that the auricular shape aids in differentiating acoustic vibrations coming directly from behind and directly in front.

Perhaps the human auricle is best considered a vestigial structure. Its muscles,

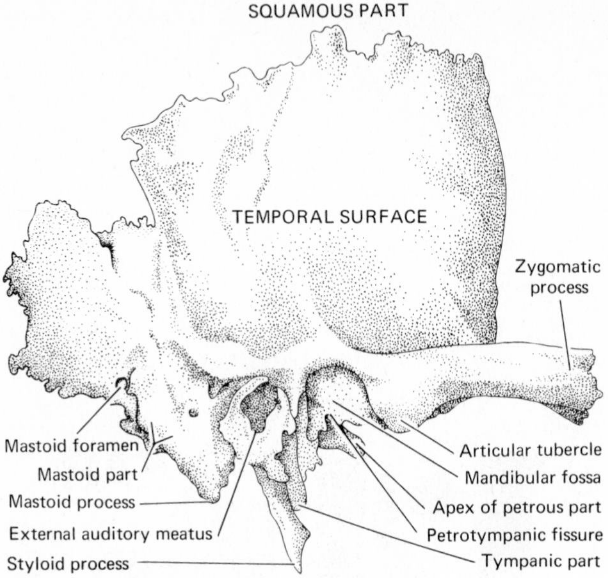

SQUAMOUS PART

TEMPORAL SURFACE

Zygomatic process

Mastoid foramen
Mastoid part
Mastoid process
External auditory meatus
Styloid process

Articular tubercle
Mandibular fossa
Apex of petrous part
Petrotympanic fissure
Tympanic part

Figure 14-1 The right temporal bone, external aspect.

414

which in lower animals direct the ears to the source of sound, are still present in man, but they are rarely functional.

The auricle develops essentially from six primordia, which accounts for the wide diversity in its shape. The primordia are mesenchymal derivatives of the first and second branchial arches.

External Auditory Meatus

The external canal, about $1\frac{1}{4}$ in. long, is entirely closed medially by the drum, or tympanic membrane. The canal is an oval cylinder whose widest region is at the external orifice. It forms an S-shaped curve, whose direction is downward and backward at its lateral aspect but almost horizontal at its medial end.

The lateral third of the canal is movable and formed of cartilage that is continuous with the cartilage of the auricle. The medial two-thirds constitute a bony canal in the temporal bone.

The epidermal lining, which is a continuation of the epidermis of the auricle, is thin and tightly adherent to the walls of the canal. Many hairs are present, and there are numerous modified sweat glands that produce cerumen, or earwax.

There are two sources of the sensory nerve supply to the canal. One is the auriculotemporal branch (mandibular division) of the trigeminal nerve. The other, which is the auricular branch of the vagus, or Arnold's nerve, supplies part of the bony meatus and possibly includes a small sensory branch from the facial nerve (Hall and Colman, 1967).

Developmental Anatomy Although the canal is present at birth, it is then only an imperfect ring, which has come from a cartilaginous primary auditory meatus and also from an inner incomplete meatal plate. In the early embryonic stages an epithelial tube grows inward. The tube comprises the hollow primary meatus and the solid meatal plate, the latter being an extension of the former. The cartilaginous external canal develops from the primary meatus. The inner part of the canal comes from the meatal plate, which develops a lumen. The tympanic membrane comes from tissue located between the cavities of the meatal plate and the middle ear.

The front and lower walls of the external meatus develop from the tympanic bone, while the back and upper walls develop from the mastoid process and the zygomatic arch. The elements fuse to a great extent in the second year of life, and the canal attains its definite form.

Functions The auditory canal not only transmits sound waves, but as a consequence of its being an acoustic resonator it can amplify those sound waves whose frequencies are near its resonant frequency. This makes the pressure at the tympanic membrane for tones about 3,000 to 4,000 Hz two or four times greater than that prevailing at the lateral orifice of the canal (Denes and Pinson, 1963). The inner position of the membrane is therefore fortunate in that some sound waves would be imperceptible if it were laterally placed.

415

The canal serves also to shelter the tympanic membrane and to maintain the relatively constant conditions of temperature and humidity necessary to preserve the

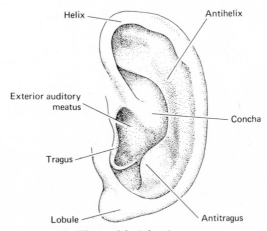

Figure 14-2 The auricle (pinna).

membrane's elasticity. The stiff hairs in the canal and the cerumen secreted by the wax glands protect the membrane.

The Tympanic Membrane

This is a thin parchmentlike membrane of a pearly gray color, which closes the inner end of the external auditory canal and forms the lateral wall of the middle ear. The terms eardrum, drum membrane, drumhead, or tympanic membrane are in common use.

The membrane consists of three layers, an outer single layer of epithelium continuous with that lining the external canal, a middle connective tissue framework of yellow elastic fibrous tissue, and an inner layer of mucous membrane. The membrane is not more than 0.1 mm thick, and it is almost round, with approximate dimensions of 8 mm wide and 9 mm high. It is funnel-shaped, with the concavity facing the external canal. Its direction is obliquely downward and inward. The membrane is supported around its periphery by a bony annulus, forming a ring which is deficient in a small upper sector called the notch of Rivinus.

The upper part of the membrane is the pars flaccida, or Shrapnell's membrane. It is delicate and has no connective tissue, unlike the remainder of the drum. The lower part comprises most of the drum and is called the pars tensa. The manubrium (handle) of the malleus is prominent, observable as a white streak running down through the pars flaccida to the approximate center of the drum. Since the handle is attached to the membrane, both vibrate together.

The blood vessels enter about the periphery. This explains the fact that the earliest sign of acute inflammation is enlarged vessels encircling the tympanic membrane (Dolowitz, 1964). The arteries to the external surface come from the deep auricular branch of the maxillary. Those to the inside surface come from the stylomastoid branch of the posterior auricular and the tympanic branch of the maxillary. The nerves to the external tympanic surface come from the auriculo-

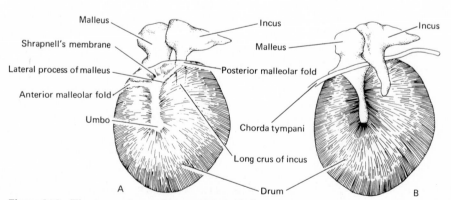

Figure 14-3 The tympanic membrane: (*a*) lateral view; (*b*) medial view.

temporal branch of the trigeminal and the auricular branch of the vagus. The nerves to the internal surface come from the tympanic branch of the glossopharyngeal.

Functions The drum is extremely sensitive to sound waves, and it transmits all audible sound frequencies. Its vibrations are at the same frequencies as those of the sounding body, and the middle ear bones in turn faithfully follow these frequencies. The tympanic membrane thus does not have its own vibration rate but is aperiodic. As stated previously, there are three layers in this very thin membrane, but the middle one may be chiefly responsible for the aperiodicity. This layer has circular and radial fibers; their tension varies at different regions because the malleus handle pulls the membrane inward to give it the shape of a hollow cone whose apex is below its true center. These properties not only produce aperiodicity but prevent the vibrations from persisting after the incident sound ceases.

A simple rupture of the tympanic membrane could impair sound transmission, although perhaps not as much as once thought. Sometimes an extensive hole in the drum causes only a slight loss in hearing (Fowler, 1947). A few exceptional individuals who have lost the membrane as well as the malleus and incus retained hearing intensity within 20 to 30 dB of normal.

It has been contended that the tympanic membrane is not elastic enough to obey Hooke's law, which states that within limits displacement is directly proportional to the displacing force. The auditory response may thus fail to be linear, which results in the production of aural harmonics, or overtones. These are lower in intensity than the fundamental and may become masked, but they can modify the sound quality. Despite these statements, it is generally agreed (Wever, 1949), that except for high intensities of sound the drum does not significantly distort the form of the incident sound waves.

The tympanic membrane ordinarily works like the diaphragm of a microphone. The amplitudes of its vibrations are extremely small. During ordinary conversation the displacement of the drum may be only the diameter of a molecule of hydrogen (Myers et al., 1962). This indicates the human sensitivity for intensity perception. The supposed superiority of auditory acuity in animals is not due to greater sensitivity of intensity perception but to an extended frequency range. In addition, animals tend to have a sound localizing-amplifying ability in "adjustable" external ears, and they do not suffer the same traumatic losses typical of man.

The tympanic membrane not only functions to receive vibrations, but it is a barrier to protect the delicate structures of the middle ear. It affords an acoustic dead space so that air vibrations in the middle ear will be broken up and dissipated by the irregular walls, epitympanic recess, and mastoid cells. This avoids any pressure against the round window which might compete with opposing vibrations originating from the oval window. This might also be considered in terms of phase relationships (DeWeese and Saunders, 1964). If a wave entered both windows simultaneously, the likelihood of mutual cancellation would be significant.

The Middle Ear

The middle ear is an efficient instrument to direct sound energy to the oval window, to match the impedance of the air to the inner ear, and to protect the inner ear from intense sounds.

Fallopius in the sixteenth century termed the middle ear chamber the tympanum. The chamber may be said to encompass the tympanic cavity, the antrum, and the Eustachian tube.

The tympanic cavity is an irregular space in the petrous bone. Its anteroposterior and vertical dimensions are each about 15 mm. Its transverse measurement is 2 mm at its narrowest portion at the level of the tympanic membrane and about 6 mm at its uppermost end. It extends upward into an epitympanic space which contains the head of the malleus and the body of the incus. This space, or attic, is separated from the middle cranial fossa on the inner aspect of the skull by a thin bone called the tegmen tympani.

The aditus, which is a recess in the posterior wall of the attic, connects the main chamber with a passageway called the antrum. The middle ear communicates by way of the antrum with the air sacs of the mastoid process. The antrum develops before birth as an air sac produced by expansion of the tympanic cavity. The sac in turn proliferates small, hollow cells which project backward into the mastoid region. The antrum and air cells become lined with a mucous membrane which is continuous with the membrane of the tympanic cavity.

Although the air space of the middle ear is in continuity with the air spaces of the many bony cells contained in the mastoid process, this relationship does not have the same functional implications as that of the middle ear and Eustachian tube. The fact of continuity is of importance in pathology, however, where infection travels from the tympanic cavity to the mastoid.

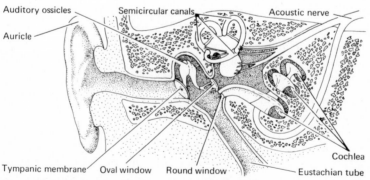

Figure 14-4 Diagrammatic view of the entire auditory mechanism within the temporal bone.

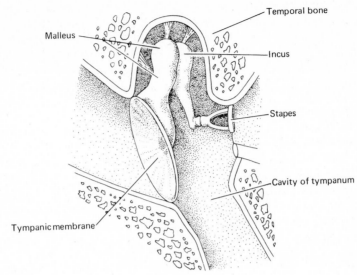

Labels on figure:
- Malleus
- Temporal bone
- Incus
- Stapes
- Cavity of tympanum
- Tympanic membrane

Figure 14-5   The middle ear chamber.

Vessels and Nerves

The tympanic branch of the maxillary artery supplies the tympanic membrane. The stylomastoid branch of the posterior auricular artery supplies the back part of the middle ear chamber and the mastoid. There are also lesser arteries, including (1) the petrosal branch of the middle meningeal, (2) the tympanic branch of the internal carotid, (3) a branch from the ascending pharyngeal artery, and (4) a branch from the artery of the pterygoid canal. The last two branches travel with the Eustachian tube.

The veins drain into the pterygoid plexus and the superior petrosal sinus.

The middle ear, except for its muscles, receives its nerve supply through the tympanic plexus. Branches of the plexus innervate the mucous membrane, fenestra vestibuli, fenestra cochleae, and auditory tube. The tympanic plexus is formed by (1) the caroticotympanic nerves, (2) the smaller petrosal nerve, (3) a branch that joins the greater petrosal, and (4) the tympanic branch of the glossopharyngeal nerve.

Eustachian (Auditory; Pharyngotympanic) Tube

This is an air duct from the nasopharynx. It enters the anterior wall of the middle ear cavity at its lowest point on each side, traveling along an approximately 37-mm (1½-in.) course. It is developmentally continuous with the middle ear cavity and mastoid antrum, and this explains its direction backward, laterally, and somewhat upward toward the mastoid process.

The anterior (pharyngeal) two-thirds is partly cartilaginous and partly fibrous, whereas the posterior third is surrounded by the temporal bone. The bony part is triangular in cross section. The tube is flared out at both pharyngeal and middle ear openings. The middle ear orifice is too high to permit effective drainage of that chamber, but it can be drained with the patient prone (lying on the abdomen), which places the anterior wall of the tube in a dependent position.

The pharyngeal end of the cartilage is just inside the mucosa of the nasopharynx. In that area it produces an elevation behind the pharyngeal opening of the tube called the torus tubarius. The place where the narrowest part of the tube is located in the temporal bone is called the isthmus. Clearly the tubal bore changes, narrowing down from a 9 mm diameter at the pharyngeal end to a constricted zone where the cartilage changes to bone. The lumen at this point is only 2 to 3 mm high and 1 to 1.5 mm wide. Then the tube reexpands to the flared orifice in the middle ear. The Eustachian tube of the infant is about half as long and is straighter.

The tube is lined by a mucosa which is continuous with that of the nasopharynx and of the tympanic cavity. It is a pseudostratified, ciliated columnar epithelium which contains a rich supply of mucous glands in the pharyngeal sector, especially near the tubal orifice. The pharyngeal part is also well supplied with lymphatic tissue and is sometimes called the tubal tonsil.

420

The tube permits the middle ear air to be equalized in pressure with that of the outside. This is necessary for proper movements of the drum membrane and for sound transmission. Thus, in an airplane ascent the drop in pressure may produce a temporary deafness which can be alleviated by opening the entrance to the canal through swallowing or yawning. Air blockage as a complication of inflammation, as it occurs in a head cold, may result in air absorption from the chamber. The inequality of external and internal pressures causes the drum to be pushed inward tightly, which may produce hearing impairment. Transmission of high tones seems

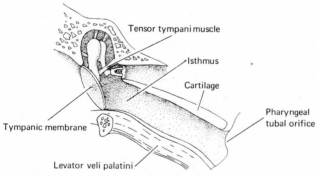

Figure 14-6 The Eustachian tube, showing its flared ends.

to be especially impaired in the occlusion of the Eustachian tube, although not necessarily at first.

The Eustachian tube also functions to protect the middle ear cavity against foreign bodies and nasopharyngeal infection. It accomplishes this by remaining variably closed except in activities such as coughing, deep breathing, sneezing, swallowing, and yawning. Actually the osseous portion is always open. If the cartilaginous sector of the tube fails to open when it should, deafness and retraction of the drum may follow. Sometimes the tube is chronically patent. This condition may not affect hearing, but the voice may seem to the patient to have a disagreeable reverberation. In some instances the protective function of the tube is pathologically stressed in that the mucosa in the cartilaginous area may be thrown into folds which act like valves and obstruct the passage of air.

The drainage of normal and abnormal secretions out of the middle ear is still another function of the Eustachian tube.

It is noted above that the Eustachian tube is ordinarily closed at one end and that it opens with yawning, swallowing, and with the contraction of muscles. The muscles involved are still open to question, and some different views follow.

Guild (1955) describes the probable machinery of Eustachian tube movements, and he involves the elastic tissue present in the tube in such movements. This tissue is said to counterbalance the action of the tensor veli palatini muscles, the latter serving to pull the lateral wall of the tube away from its medial wall and thereby open the tubal lumen. Closure has usually been regarded as a passive event which is caused by the pressure of neighboring structures. In Guild's view, closure is associated with active rebound of the elastic tissue.

Keogh (1957) describes the opening and closing of the Eustachian tube as being brought about chiefly by contraction and relaxation of the palatal levators, assisted by the tensors and by the salpingopharyngeus muscle. When the levators contract, their structure rises in the opening of the tube and plugs its lumen. When the levators relax and the soft palate is depressed by the tensors, there is a transient opening of the valvelike slit in the anterior part of the tube. The suction caused by contraction and relaxation of the levators is a factor in draining the auditory tube of mucus.

The tube has been said to be opened, as during swallowing, by the salpingopharyngeus and dilatator tubae muscles. The salpingopharyngeus muscle originates from the inferior aspect of the tube close to its orifice and descends to fuse with the posterior portion of the pharyngopalatine muscle, which controls the opening between the mouth and throat. The dilatator tubae muscle originates from the cartilage sector of the Eustachian tube and passes downward to fuse with the tensor veli palatini muscle, which tenses the soft palate.

The muscles of the tube usually operate on an unconscious level, but the individual can open the tube at will. This can be accomplished by swallowing. Grant and

Basmajian (1965) cite literature that in the awake state swallowing occurs once a minute, but this slows during sleep to once in 5 minutes, thus making it advisable to remain awake during ascent or descent in a plane.

If the tube cannot be opened for equalization of pressure, a transudate collects in the middle ear to fill the partial vacuum, and the stage is set for infection or scarring (Dolowitz, 1964). The reader is referred to Donaldson (1970) for a symposium on Eustachian tube problems.

Middle Ear Bones
The three bones, or ossicles, of the middle ear are the malleus, incus, and stapes, which stretch in that order from the tympanic membrane to the oval window. They are interconnected by small ligaments and covered by mucous membrane which is continuous with that of the main chamber.

The oval window is on the medial wall of the middle ear at the entrance to the scala vestibuli of the inner ear. The stapes sends a footplate into the oval window which can push inward to displace the liquid, or perilymph, in the scala vestibuli. Because stapes fixation is stronger on one side than the other, its movement is not like that of a piston in a cylinder but rather like a pivot whose axis of rotation is at the lower posterior pole.

The ossicles vibrate as a single compound lever with a small amplitude. The fulcrum of the lever is in the incus. When the malleus handle moves inward, the malleus head and the greater part of the incus move outward; the long process of the incus and the stapes attached to its end move inward. Because the lever arm on the malleus side is about 1.3 times that on the stapes side, the excursion of the stapes is less than that of the malleus handle. The thrust on the perilymph at the oval window, however, is magnified. The greater force, whose increase is a factor of about 1.3, is necessary to produce pressure waves in the cochlear fluid, which possesses considerable inertia. The increased power is essential when a wave passes from air, which is a lighter conducting medium, to the perilymph fluid. The ossicles are thus seen to change high-amplitude low-pressure sound waves into those of lower amplitude and higher pressure.

422

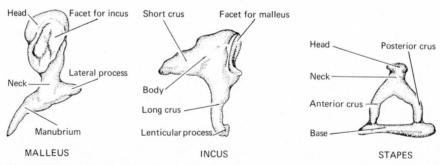

Figure 14-7 The form of the disarticulated ossicles.

The increase in the amount of energy transferred is effected not so much by the gain due to leverage but by a second factor, which involves the relative areas of the tympanic membrane (55 mm²) and stapedial footplate (3.2 mm²). This is a 17 to 1 advantage. The combined effect of the two factors produces an approximately twenty-two fold greater pressure on the fluid of the inner ear than is found at the tympanic membrane. Thus, much weaker sounds are perceived than would be the case if the vibrations passed through the middle ear with the tympanic membrane missing. At a lever ratio of 22 to 1, the intensity advantage may be as much as 26 dB (Ronis, 1962). This gain is necessary to compensate for the tremendous loss of energy suffered when sound pressure is transferred from the gaseous medium of air to the liquid medium of the endolymph. Taking an analogy, it was observed by Wever and Lawrence (1954) that men talking in a boat do not disturb the fish in the water below, because over 99 percent of the sound energy is reflected from the water to the air.

There is still a third gain factor, which is an inner ear phenomenon but which might nevertheless logically be considered here while analyzing the transformer activities of the ear. In the inner ear the pressure on the basilar membrane is converted to shearing forces several times greater than the incident forces. These forces can more readily activate the extremely sensitive hair cell receptors.

The ossicles serve to deliver sound energy preferentially to the oval window. Otherwise, sound waves would enter the inner ear through the round window, and since in this instance they would hypothetically reach the sensory mechanisms in opposite phase to the waves entering through the oval window, they would reduce the effectiveness of the ossicle-borne waves. In this sense the round window decreases the maximum effectiveness of the auditory processes.

The ossicles protect the inner ear against loud, low tones while still allowing passage of faint low-frequency tones.

There is also a protective mechanism inherent in the normal air cushion of the middle ear. It guards against sudden large pressure changes or against loud low-frequency sounds. This buffering effect, which is maintained by several factors, is known as the acoustic impedance of the ear. The stapes in loud sounds dissipates some energy by rotation on its transverse axis. Excessive vibration of the ossicles is moderated by muscle action as well as by the elastic cushion effect of the air within the chamber.

Attenuation of vibrations through fusion of the ossicles to an immovable joint leads to deafness. These bones can be bypassed in cranial bone conduction, in which instance the waves travel directly to the inner ear.

The stapes is the primary bone concerned in conduction hypacusis, which is a shift in the hearing threshold that can be corrected. Otosclerosis is the common cause. Disorders of the stapes usually involve its footplate. Lesions of the malleus and incus are much less common.

That hearing could occur without the chain of ossicles does not deny their importance. Without them sound waves in the air space would be almost entirely reflected from the hard surfaces encountered.

Muscles of the Middle Ear

The actions of the two intrinsic striated muscles of the middle ear may not be essential to the auditory process, but they are of value to the optimal functioning of this chamber.

The *tensor tympani* muscle was first described by Eustachius in 1564. It is slender, spindle-shaped, with many short parallel fibers, and is 22 to 25 mm long. It goes from the upper edge of the orifice of the Eustachian tube to the handle of the malleus. It brings the handle of the malleus inward and pulls the tympanic membrane in with it. This activity is linked with maintaining tension of the membrane.

The presence of abundant amounts of fat in this muscle has no known functional significance. The rich presence of elastic tissue in the tendons of both tensor tympanic and stapedius muscles may serve to damp the vibrations of the ossicles and also to make muscular traction less abrupt (Jepsen, 1963). The encasement of both muscles in canals or subcavities throughout their length may serve to minimize muscular vibrations that could interfere with sound transmission. Both muscles provide strength and rigidity to the ossicular chain.

The tensor tympani is relaxed during silence. If the tympanic membrane is slack, movements of peripheral portions of the membrane will not affect the malleus. Transfer of energy from the tympanic membrane to the malleus involves a tensing of the membrane.

The muscle apparently protects the ear from excessive amplitude of vibrations. This may be its only function. Boies et al. (1964) state that both muscles decrease the sensitivity to low tones. There is a statement that the tensor tympani heightens the sensitivity of the ear to high frequencies.

The motor nerve supply of the tensor tympani is a branch of the internal maxillary division of the trigeminal. Proprioceptive afferent fibers are also present.

The *stapedius* muscle was first accurately described by Varolius in 1591. It has short parallel fibers, with an average length of just over 6 mm, making it the smallest muscle in the body. It runs from the posterior tympanic wall to the posterior surface of the neck of the stapes. It pulls the stapes downward and outward and puts the oval window under tension. This is a protective function. Neither of the two muscles produces any real net change in the position of the tympanic membrane.

The stapedius is derived from the second branchial, or hyoid arch, and is innervated by the facial nerve which originally supplied the arch.

Acoustic reflexes, including middle ear muscle reflexes, have assumed an importance in the diagnosis of certain auditory disturbances. Their most appropriate stimulus is sound. The reader is referred to Jepsen (1963).

Developmental Anatomy

Some points should be brought out about the middle ear. The gill arch system of aquatic vertebrates is deeply involved in providing the evolutionary material, and the embryology roughly recapitulates the evolution.

When vertebrates took to land and the elements of their respiratory gill system were no longer necessary, the parts became transformed into useful derivatives including the auditory structures. Thus, in man the middle ear and the Eustachian tube are derived from the first pair of lateral pharyngeal evaginations called pouches, with a small contribution from the second pharyngeal pouches. These pouches originate from the embryonic germ layer called entoderm. In fishes each pouch would have pushed laterally to fuse with the correspondingly medially directed ectoderm of the arch. Their fusion and the subsequent dissolution of the intervening plate would have produced a branchial groove, or gill slit. In man the first and second pouches dilate, and they reach the outer ectoderm only fleetingly. The proximal stalk of each of these pouches narrows at approximately the second month, and this narrowed region forms the Eustachian tube, which gradually elongates. The dilated distal pouch is the forerunner of the middle ear chamber on each side.

425

Posteriorly located skeletal parts of the first and second arches form the auditory ossicles. In lower vertebrates the malleus and incus are drawn into the construction of the upper and lower jaws, but in human embryology they are removed from their chewing function and serve for sound transmission. The second (hyoid) arch produces hyomandibular and hyoid pieces. It is the former which attaches the jaws to the skull in fishes, but in amphibians, reptiles, and birds it forms the columella, which carries sound impulses across the middle ear. In mammals the hyomandibular piece produces the stapes, which is the evolutionary homologue of the columella.

The middle ear and the Eustachian tube make their first appearance in the higher anuran orders of amphibians. The Eustachian tube is variably developed in reptiles, and it is a bony structure in birds. Mammals below man generally have a wide and patent tube, and, as in man, the tube tends to be differentiated into bony and cartilaginous sections.

The Inner Ear

The inner ear in its embryology is derived from a placode, or thickened plate, of ectoderm, which early in development sinks below the surface on each side to form an otic pit. This pit deepens to a vesicle from which all structures of the membranous labyrinth develop.

The internal ear grows as a labyrinthine series of membranes into the petrous portion of the temporal bone. The membranes proliferate into the temporal bone as a cast into a mold. The central or entrance section of this structure is the vestibule. The membranous vestibule divides to a saccule and utricle, which remain connected by Hensen's duct, or the ductus reuniens. From the utricle three semicircular canals develop. Since these are organs of equilibrium and not of hearing, they will not be discussed further. The cochlea develops as an extension of the saccule.

The blood supply of the cochlea is from the cochlear branch of the internal auditory artery. The latter is a branch of the basilar artery or anterior inferior cerebellar artery. The veins leave the base of the modiolus and unite with the internal auditory veins, which drain into the transverse, or superior, petrosal sinus.

The cochlea has the shape of a snail's shell, or spiral structure, which has approximately 2½ turns. The outside of this spiral contains a horizontal membranous partition which divides the cochlea along most of its length into two parallel circular stairways (scalae). The upper stairway on the oval window side of the partition is the scala vestibuli, while that on the round window side is the scala tympani. Both regions contain perilymph. Since the scala vestibuli and scala tympani are in direct communication with the subarachnoid space around the brain, the compositions of the perilymph and cerebrospinal fluid are almost identical.

426

The interior of the cochlear partition forms a third, wedge-shaped compartment, called the scala media or *cochlear duct*. This constitutes the membranous labyrinth, which is separated from the osseous labyrinth around it by membranes. The *vestibular* (Reissner's) *membrane* separates it from the scala vestibuli, and the *basilar membrane* separates it from the scala tympani. The term scala vestibuli is used at times to include the cochlear duct because the vestibular membrane is so delicate that it conceivably allows the two regions to behave as a single tube in the transmission of sound.

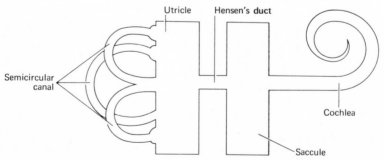

Figure 14-8 The vestibule of the inner ear and its diverticula (diagrammatic).

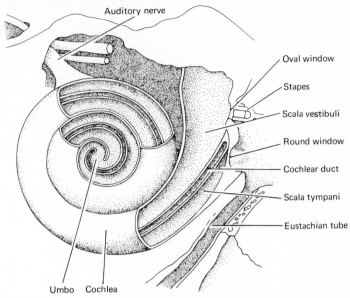

Figure 14-9 The cochlea of the internal ear, showing the arrangement of its chambers.

The endolymph, or fluid within the scala media, has a higher specific gravity than the perilymph and is secreted from the vessels called the stria vascularis surrounding this chamber. Whereas the perilymph contains considerable sodium and low levels of potassium, the endolymph has the opposite conditions. The continuous secretion of positive potassium ions into the endolymph produces an *endocochlear potential,* of perhaps 80 millivolts, between the positive scala media and negative perilymphatic chambers. The significance of the potential will be considered later.

The endolymph is the only source of nourishment to the hair cells since there is no direct blood supply. A possible reason for the isolation of the organ of Corti from the blood supply is that the noise produced by ordinary vascular flow would be intolerable (DeWeese and Saunders, 1964).

At the apex of the cochlea there is a space called the helicotrema, which permits passage of perilymph from the scala vestibuli to the scala tympani. There is no direct communication in the cochlea between the endolymph and perilymph, however, since the cochlear duct is closed at the helicotrema.

In diagrams of the cochlea, its long axis is usually drawn as vertical with the scala vestibuli lying above the scala tympani. The cochlea is actually a flattened cone with a central core called the modiolus. Around this core a hollow spiral tube about 32 mm long makes 2½ turns. The apex of the cochlea faces forward and laterally, while the base goes backward and medially. The scala vestibuli is placed

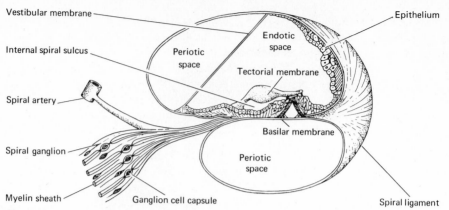

Figure 14-10 The cochlea of the internal ear in diagrammatic section, showing its internal membranes and the auditory nerve fibers.

anteriorly and the scala tympani posteriorly, with the scala media between. Spiral canals in the modiolus transmit the cochlear nerve fibers. The base of the bony cochlea opens into the vestibule, into the round window, and also into the perilymphatic duct to make connections with the subarachnoid space.

In its spatial relationship the saccule connects with the medial wall of the middle ear. On this wall the oval window is adjacent to the scala vestibuli, and the round window is adjacent to the scala tympani.

General Function
The middle ear bones vibrate, and the footplate of the stapes thrusts against the oval window, which transmits the incident pressure to the perilymph of the scala vestibuli. Since the bony labyrinth is inextensible, the waves travel a variable length up the scala vestibuli and then down the scala tympani to terminate in the membrane of the round window. This so-called *secondary drum membrane* is thrust back into the middle ear, and equilibrium is restored. Whether the pressure waves will travel up the scala vestibuli all the way to its apex (helicotrema) depends upon the frequency of the tones. Low tones approach the apex, whereas high-frequency vibrations short-circuit the length of the cochlea and cross at the basal end, producing local vibrations of the basilar membrane during their passage from the scala vestibuli to the scala tympani.

As explained later, the place of deformation of the basilar membrane is involved in auditory analysis in the inner ear. At any frequency of sound a given sector of the membrane vibrates more strongly than other sectors. Very high frequencies produce resonance pressure nodes near the base of the cochlea, while intermediate frequencies excite the membrane at about the middle of the cochlea. These points are called the resonant nodes for such frequencies. The position of resonance on the membrane is determined primarily by the fibers of the basilar membrane. The greater elasticity of the basal fibers plus the small inertia of the fluid at the base determine the fact that high-frequency sounds will be resonated at the base. This fact accords with the principle that the frequency of vibration varies directly with the elastic coefficient of the system and inversely with the inertia of the system. High fluid inertia and a lower elastic coefficient at the apex of the cochlea bring about resonance of low tones there. The position of resonant nodes on the basilar membranes is approximately known for each frequency (Guyton, 1966).

The round window is of considerable importance because the elastic thrust of its membrane into the middle ear allows pressure equalization within the inner ear. Any rigidity of this membrane has been claimed, controversially, to hinder the vibration of the relatively incompressible perilymphatic fluid and thus impair hearing. The round window is not importantly concerned with the forward conduction of sound waves into the inner ear, although even this view is controversial.

The vibrations of the round window coincide with those of the oval window, except that they occur a fraction of second later and in opposite direction. The function of the round window apparently is to provide "give" in a rigidly encased cochlea. Deformation is essential for stimulation of the hair cells. If deformation is to occur, the basilar membrane must move, even though very minutely, and the membrane of the round window must bulge to effect this.

The Vibrating Membranes

The fluid-pressure vibrations in the perilymph excite the production of electrical potentials in the organ of Corti. This organ is situated upon the basilar membrane, and it is bathed by the endolymph of the scala media. It is built up as a series of arches, or pillars, arranged in series along the length of the basilar membrane. Supporting cells and sensory hair cells lie between these arches. The hair cells contain hairs, or cilia, which project from their free surface. There is a row of inner hair cells on one side of the inner rod, which is a limb of the arch, and there are several rows of outer hair cells on the side of the outer rod, which completes the arch. The total number of inner hair cells is about 7,000 and of outer hair cells about 24,000. A colloidal semifluid tectorial membrane rests upon the hair cells. At their basal ends the cells are connected with the terminal twigs of nerve fibers which combine to form the main bundle of the cochlear nerve.

The *basilar membrane* is about 0.04 mm wide at the basal end of the cochlea and is stiff and light there. It is about 0.5 mm wide at the apical end, where it is also massive and most flexible. The manner of its response, i.e., the appearance of a traveling wave, will be seen to depend upon this differential structure as well as the fact that the membrane is a continuous structure and each element is intimately coupled to its neighbor.

The response of the basilar membrane to sine wave excitation emphasizes the relationship between structure and the nature of the response. The entire cochlear

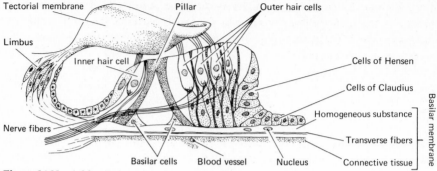

Figure 14-11 A histologic concept of a section of the organ of Corti.

partition is activated, but the amplitude of vibration at specific places along the partition varies with the incident frequency. In high frequencies it is greatest near the oval window, where the basilar membrane is very light and stiff. In lower frequencies the region of greatest amplitude shifts toward the broader, more elastic end. Thus, the basilar membrane promotes spatial separation of the maximum response at various frequencies. This view is expressed by Békésy and Rosenblith (1951) and by Davis (1961*b*) in their statements that the cochlea acts as a mechanical acoustic analyzer and that the place of greatest mechanical activity on the basilar membrane changes as a function of frequency.

When the stapes vibrates, it seems clear that the basilar membrane vibrates correspondingly. How the vibrations are transmitted to the hair cells is uncertain. They may be carried through the rods forming the arches of Corti and agitate the endolymph of the scala media. This activity may in turn excite the hair cells by way of their cilia, which project up into the endolymph. There is no proof that this is actually the manner of transmission. We shall consider this question again, with reference to the tectorial membrane.

Another membrane of uncertain significance is the vestibular (Reissner's) membrane, which is much more delicate than the basilar membrane. It separates the scala vestibuli from the scala media. Myers et al. (1962) state that vibrations are transmitted through the vestibular membrane to the endolymph and thence through the basilar membrane to the scala tympani, where they pass downward to the round window.

Guyton (1966) states that the vestibular membrane is too weak to resist the passage of sound waves from the scala vestibuli to the scala media. Each time that the fluid impinges upon the membrane, the structure moves along with the fluid. The result is a forward movement of the endolymph of the scala media. Because of this the membrane may be ignored in auditory function. Perhaps it serves only to separate the fluids of the scala vestibuli and scala media. The need for fluid separation is obscure.

430

The *tectorial membrane* in the scala media lies above the hairlike processes of the sensory cells and is possibly in contact with them. It is a nearly structureless, jelly-like membrane, which is attached at one margin to the spiral lamina, or limbus, and is free at the other end.

The tectorial membrane may act as a damper to suppress excessive and continued vibrations, or possibly it may be activated by the stapes and in turn stimulate the hair cells (Kostelijk, 1950). The stimulus is initiated, at least partly, because the cilia of the hair cells are distorted or twisted from their points of attachment to the tectorial membrane. This shearing action may trigger the neuron discharge. Because the basilar membrane is hinged at the bony spiral lamina and the tectorial membrane is hinged at the limbus, the different points of attachment result in different axes of rotation. This permits a sliding action between the tectorial membrane and the hairs of the hair cells. Whether the resultant neural discharge comes from direct electrical stimulation of the endings or by a chemical process is still uncertain.

Neuroanatomic Pathways

The auditory pathways involve a succession of at least four groups of neurons from the cochlea to the temporal cerebrum. Since some neurons may not end in the relay stations, some tracts are more direct, suggesting that many impulses arrive at the cerebrum in advance of others.

The first-order neurons have their cell bodies in the spiral ganglion, which is located in the modiolus, or hollow core of the cochlea, and whose course is parallel with that of the organ of Corti. Their axons travel as the cochlear nerve within the modiolus. The dendrites of the neurons receive impulses from the sensory hair cells. The inner hair cells are served usually by only one neuron and the outer hair cells by several. This overlapping of connections may provide flexibility of function and also the power to compensate for injury to single hair cells or neurons.

There are 29,000 or more fibers in the cochlear nerve, which is the same as the estimated number of hair cells (see previous estimate), despite an overlapping. Possibly some of these fibers are returning signals from the brain to the organ of Corti to provide adaptive feedback. Efferent fibers have been found throughout the auditory pathway (Ballenger, 1969).

The cochlear nerve trunk leaves the temporal bone through the internal auditory meatus. This division joins the vestibular division, with about 20,000 fibers then being added from that source. An approximately 50,000-fiber nerve trunk is not great when compared with the optic nerve, which contains over a million fibers.

The fibers may be systematized in that tones are transmitted by different groups among them according to the sound frequencies. In this view spatial orientation occurs within the cochlear nerve.

The central auditory pathways are discussed in standard textbooks of physiology or neuroanatomy. In the typical, four-neuron pathway the first-order neurons enter the dorsolateral border of the pons where it joins the medulla. The entering neuron bifurcates, one branch ending in the dorsal cochlear nucleus and the other in the ventral cochlear nucleus. The second-order neurons have their cell bodies in these nuclei, while their axons form a discrete bundle, called the lateral lemniscus, on each side.

The decussating fibers of the ventral nucleus loop below the superior olivary nucleus of the pons, or else go through it, and form a transverse bundle called the trapezoid body. Many second-order neurons from the dorsal nucleus cross over, and some or all of these neurons synapse with the contralateral cells of the superior olivary nucleus. The uncrossed second-order fibers ascend in the lateral lemniscus of the same side, but eventually cross over to end with the crossed fibers in the inferior colliculus, a lower auditory center in the midbrain.

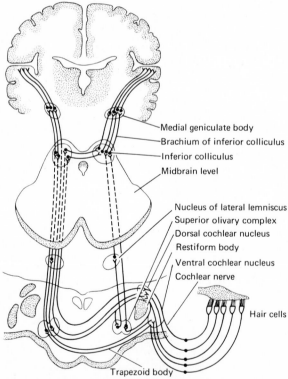

Medial geniculate body
Brachium of inferior colliculus
Inferior colliculus
Midbrain level

Nucleus of lateral lemniscus
Superior olivary complex
Dorsal cochlear nucleus
Restiform body
Ventral cochlear nucleus
Cochlear nerve

Hair cells

Trapezoid body

Figure 14-12 The neuroanatomic acoustic system (redrawn). *(By permission from The Ciba Collection of Medical Illustrations, vol. 1, Nervous System, by Frank H. Netter, Ciba Pharmaceutical Products, Summit, N.J., 1953.)*

Third-order neurons ascend in the lateral lemniscus to another auditory center called the medial geniculate body, which is in the posterior part of the thalamus.

Many collaterals of the ascending systems travel into the reticular system of the brainstem. They may then be relayed diffusely upward to the cerebrum and downward into the spinal cord.

Cerebral Auditory Endings

The final, thalamocortical radiation ascends chiefly to Heschl's convolution located in the superior temporal (anterior transverse) cerebral gyrus. This reception region involves areas 41 and 42 of Brodmann in the inferior wall of the sylvian fissure. The impulses may spread over the lateral border of the temporal lobe, much of the insular cortex, and into the parietal operculum. The temporal lobe proper contains a wide expanse to which no definite auditory or other function can be assigned.

Because almost 50 percent of the nerve fibers travel upward ipsilaterally from the cochlear nuclei, the impulses from each ear reach both the right and left cerebral cortex. The cochlea is bilaterally represented in the cerebral cortex. None of the impulses crosses above the thalamus. It is thus understandable that the removal of one temporal lobe does not cause deafness in either ear but only a small hearing loss. There is a factor of dominance, however, and the removal of the dominant temporal lobe impairs associations and decreases the ability to interpret the meaning of sounds despite the persistence of sound reception.

433

There appears to be a cortical area, or *primary auditory cortex,* which is also called a *short latency area.* This is activated by fibers from the medial geniculate body. There is a *secondary auditory cortex,* or *long latency area,* which can be excited either from the primary area or directly from the medial geniculate body. The short latency area is a receptive area whereas the long latency area is an interpretive area allowing synthesis of intelligible sounds.

Topographical Organization

In the process of impulse transmission from ear to brain, the number of nerve impulses progressively decreases. This decrease indicates that the temporal cortex is not concerned with all auditory processes. The lower nuclei perhaps act as filters which adjust the impulses and relay only certain ones to the cerebrum. The lower centers are also relay nuclei which can send adjusted impulses to other bodily areas for quick adaptive responses to sound. The medial geniculate bodies of the thalamus may be able to generate a crude consciousness of the various qualities of sound. This possibility is suggested by the ability to perceive intense sounds after the removal of both primary temporal cortices.

The medial geniculates appear to be systematized, in that each point on the organ of Corti has a corresponding point there. Also the geniculates may have a systematized projection upon the ipsilateral temporal cortex. Local destruction of the geniculates can be followed by localized destruction in the temporal cortex. This is a logical extension of the place-mechanism theory of hearing, in which the pitch heard depends upon the area of the cochlea stimulated and which cells in the cerebrum are activated.

Theories of Hearing

In considering the physiologic basis of specific kinds of consciousness, it is not yet possible to know how the "causal" relationship between excitatory neural patterns and the development of conscious perceptions comes about (Hess, 1967). In conversation, the listener is unaware of the pressure changes in his eardrum, he does not perceive their transmission upon the sensory surface within the organ of Corti, and he is also unaware of the nerve impulses sent to the auditory centers of the brain. Yet he can understand the meaning of a spoken message. No road to a full understanding of the process of transformation seems open at present. Nevertheless, great strides have been made in the comprehension of many peripheral processes, and this is the subject of the present discussion.

The outstanding psychologic characteristics of sound are pitch, loudness, and timbre. Other sensations include density, volume, and duration. In physics there are sound parameters, or dimensions, such as frequency, intensity, and others.

The Perception of Pitch
Most theories concerning the function of the inner ear have emphasized the perception of pitch (Békésy and Rosenblith, 1951). Pitch is a consciousness of the highness or lowness of tones.

Resonance Theory
It was stated in Germany by the physicist Ohm in the early nineteenth century that the hearing mechanism of the ear can analyze a complex sound into its frequency components, or pure tones. The first rational theory to account for such pitch perception was formulated by Helmholtz, in 1863. This is the resonance theory of hearing, one of the *place* theories.

In the resonance theory the analysis of sound, especially for pitch perception, is a function particularly of the cochlea rather than of the cerebrum. The basilar membrane is considered to contain a series of tightly stretched transverse fibers, or resonators, whose natural periods correspond with the range of frequencies in the audible spectrum. The system is one of tuned elements that resonate such that a definite unit at a given place along the basilar membrane is most vigorously stimulated by a given frequency. The basilar membrane has a sinusoidal pattern of vibration, being equally displaced first in one direction and then in the other. A different nerve fiber discharges more actively for each frequency in the range of hearing. This differential discharge is recognized by the cerebral cortex as a given pitch. Low tones are analyzed at the apex and high tones at the base of the membrane. For a compound wave a given region responds to the fundamental and other regions to the overtones.

Pitch in the original resonance concept is a psychologic sensation corresponding to the physical dimension of frequency. These dimensions are differentiated in that frequency can be regarded as the number of incident sound waves reaching the ear in a given time, whereas pitch is the tone as perceived. In high intensities there can be a relative change in pitch without a change in frequency, so that these two parameters of sound are not always in correspondence.

Helmholtz stated that the segments of the basilar membrane could be brought into vibration only when the tension in the transverse direction greatly exceeded the tension in the direction of their length. However, Békésy asserts that the basilar membrane has no tension and acts like a gelatinous layer and also that the tension in a transverse direction is no different from that in a longitudinal direction. These objections seriously weaken one of the cardinal tenets of the resonance theory. Also, calculations indicate that the resonance theory can account for only 4½ of the 10½ octaves sensed by the human ear (Ruch and Fulton, 1960).

A paradox exists in the resonance theory, in that the cochlea seems to possess both high selectivity and almost critical damping. These qualities are antagonistic, since a critically damped system loses its characteristic frequency, and this effect exerted upon a set of such systems does away with their functioning as a harmonic analyzer (Kostelijk, 1950).

435

Another of the many objections to the resonance theory has been that the basilar fibers are embedded in a homogeneous ground substance which binds them into a continuous structure and prevents them from vibrating separately as a selective series of resonators. The concept of the place of maximum stimulation has been proposed to meet this objection to the resonance view. Sound activates not only the basilar fibers in tune with it but also and less forcibly the fibers on each side of the tuned resonators. A given set of fibers vibrates maximally, and others vibrate progressively less as their distance increases from the central disturbance. Only the vibrations of maximal amplitude effectively stimulate the nerve endings and become associated with the discrimination of pitch.

Wever and Bray Volley Theory
Wever (1949) discusses theories which have gradually evolved, such as place and frequency theories. The place theories are subdivided into resonance and non-resonance (wave) theories. The frequency theories are subdivided into telephone (nonanalytic) and pitch (analytic) types. Wever accepts elements of the place and frequency views in helping to synthesize a resonance-volley theory.

If any view held rigidly that the frequency of impulses in each nerve fiber increases to discriminate pitch, the theory would be weakened by the fact that an auditory nerve fiber can follow the frequency of stimulus only up to 900 to 1,000 Hz. The

Wever and Bray volley theory attempts to explain transmission of higher frequencies by postulating rational activity of individual fibers at higher frequencies. A bundle of fibers delivers a volley of impulses at a higher frequency than is possible for one fiber. At a given frequency one group of fibers might respond to every second pulse, and the remaining fibers might respond to the alternate ones. At higher frequencies a group of fibers could respond to every third, fourth, or successively higher wave. High frequencies can have synchronous volleys fired by dividing all the available fibers into progressively smaller squads. Galambos and Davis (1943) estimate about 400 Hz as the point at which fiber rotation begins. The smaller the squads, the more the volleys must decrease in size, and there is some evidence to bear this out (Fulton, 1955).

One objection to the volley theory is that the secondary and tertiary neurons of the auditory path follow the stimulating frequency even less well than the primary neurons do, and the central auditory areas may follow the frequency with even less success. Above 3,000 to 4,000 Hz, rotation of fibers becomes inadequate to explain sound transmission.

In a later view, called the resonance-volley theory, all tones are said to affect the entire cochlea, but high tones have their maximum effect at the base and low tones at the apex. The form of the patterns determines pitch, in that high tones give sharp, peaked curves and low tones give broad, sloping curves. Intensity is said to depend upon the voltage output of each hair cell, and this output varies with the amplitude of output at a given place.

Nonresonance Place Theory (Traveling Wave)

This kind of theory refers pitch discrimination to the results of maximum vibration of a given place on the basilar membrane. It involves the concept of traveling waves or basilar membrane displacement and the capacity of the cochlea to analyze specific frequencies. It does not demand the existence of resonating structures on the cochlea.

The place theories have shed some light on the problems left unanswered by other viewpoints. The salient features of a place theory are now reviewed.

There are perhaps as many as 29,000 to 30,000 individual basilar fibers in the basilar membrane. The same number of nerve fibers travel from the hair cells above the basilar fibers into the spiral ganglion of Corti. These fibers in turn enter the cochlear nuclei of the brainstem. Each area on the basilar membrane connects with a given area in the cochlear nuclei. The neurons retain their relative positions, and the stimulus pattern is possibly carried through to higher levels of the brain.

The incident sound waves are said to stimulate a specific area of the basilar membrane. The vibrations of the basilar membrane will have a maximum at some region even though a large segment of its length can be thrown into vibrations by a pure tone. The nerve fibers originating from the region of maximum response will discharge at maximum level, and the pitch is then sensed through evaluation

436

of the maximum level. Alteration of the pitch implies shifting in the locus of the point of maximum along the basilar membrane. In the event that there is enough intensity to a tone, probably the whole basilar membrane responds. This kind of theory supports the resonance view that the cochlea can separate sounds into the individual frequencies of the complex waveform.

In a place theory there is no sharp, selective mechanical responsivity of the basilar membrane to different vibration frequencies, as postulated in the resonance theory. Rather, excitation produces large movements along appreciable lengths of the membrane. A traveling wave, resulting from a given frequency, has a crest producing a greater displacement at one place. There is a gradation of stiffness with a degree of localization at the crest of the traveling wave (Ochs, 1965). The localization of the crest can be sensed within a relatively narrow range.

The basilar membrane, which is displaced at the crest, apparently produces a shearing deformation of the hair cells above the membrane. The events leading to the transmission of impulses from the deformed hair cells to the cochlear nerve endings in contact at their base have posed another important problem that has involved the analysis of the electric currents in the cochlea.

The emphasis in a place theory is that the frequency of the stimulus is transformed into a place of maximum vibration. Also, the perception of pitch depends partly on the assumption that only certain fibers carry the impulses to the brain. A given fiber responds most readily to the frequency giving the strongest response at a place on the organ of Corti from which the fiber originates.

437

The selectivity of nerve fiber response should not be too greatly emphasized. It holds only variably both for the acoustic nerve and for the central neurons of the higher auditory pathways.

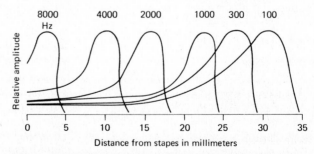

Figure 14-13 Traveling-wave theory of basilar membrane movement. Low-frequency vibrations are associated with maximal amplitude of basilar membrane vibration near the apex of the cochlea. The higher frequencies shift toward the cochlear base. The pattern of movement is like that of an arterial pulse wave. The figure shows shifting of amplitude maxima on the basilar membrane for selected tones between 100 and 8,000 Hz.

Place theories in themselves only partly explain sound analysis; for example, pitch is altered by a change in intensity. In the resonance-volley theory low tones are represented by frequency, high tones by place, and other tones by a combination of frequency and place.

Standing-wave Theory
The sinusoidal vibrations of the basilar membrane may be attended by the formation of nodes and antinodes. The distance between the nodes decreases as the vibrational frequency increases. The membrane is displaced maximally at the nodes, and this sets off the nerve impulses. The parameters of the perceived sound are dependent upon the pattern of activity in the nodes and internodes. The resistance to such vibration because of the stiffness of the basilar membrane offers one objection to this concept.

Space- Time-pattern Theory
In the space- time-pattern theory of Fletcher (1953) the pitch is sensed not only by its place of maximum stimulation on the cochlea but also by the time pattern transmitted to the cerebrum. Time is more important for low tones and place for high tones. The time pattern in the air is translated to a space pattern on the basilar membrane; the space pattern upon reaching the brain produces similar right and left cerebral patterns, and the time of maximum stimulation in each patch of structures involved on the basilar membrane is detectable. Thus, in binaural hearing four space patterns are produced in the brain, and each carries some sort of time pattern. Fletcher holds that the recognition of the changes of these patterns accounts for all the phenomena of hearing. The space- time-pattern theory explains loudness by the number of nerve impulses reaching the brain each second and also by the extent of the stimulated patch on the basilar membrane. The length of the stimulated patch produces a definite size for the portion of the brain excited. This delineation in turn gives a sensation of extension or volume.

Davis (1961 *b*) also emphasizes the time component in stating that the systematic time differences between impulses in basal and apical fibers resulting from the delay of traveling waves on the cochlear partition assists in pitch discrimination of low frequencies.

Telephone Theory
There is a body of theory which denies the selective action of the basilar membrane. The Rutherford telephone theory (1886) asserted that the membrane vibrates as a whole, like the diaphragm of a microphone, and that the differentiation of the various frequencies of the waveform is not a resonance property of the cochlea. Pitch was said to depend upon the frequency of the impulses transmitted over each auditory nerve fiber and received by the auditory centers. Wrightson (1918) proposed what is essentially a telephone concept in his modification of Rutherford's contentions. The telephone theories have suffered from the knowledge that there is no close relation between sound frequency and action currents in the acoustic nerve.

438

As a general statement, the crude response to pitch is perhaps made peripherally, whereas the finer discrimination is a function of the cerebrum.

The Subjective Analysis of Pitch

The theories of hearing are greatly concerned with the mechanisms for frequency analysis. Pitch is the psychologic sensation especially associated with frequency. Pitch depends also on intensity, especially for pure tones at very high or very low frequencies. In complex periodic waveforms the pitch is often determined by the lowest frequency.

Frequency is used as a psychologic, intensive scale to judge pure tones of fixed intensities, the sensation of pitch varying directly with the frequency.

In numerical scales the *mel* is the unit of pitch. If 1,000 mels is taken as the pitch of a 1,000-Hz tone, 500 mels is the pitch of a tone that sounds half as high, but the 500-mel tone does not have a corresponding frequency of 500 Hz.

Electrical Activity of the Cochlea

Wever and Bray in 1930 performed an experiment which was eventually used to support modified resonance ideas (resonance-volley theory). Their work also contributed greatly to the knowledge of the electrical activity of the cochlea. The voice, as spoken into the ear of an anesthetized cat, and pure tones up to 20,000 Hz were reproduced after the impulses were led off the cochlea, amplified, and sent into a loudspeaker.

439

The Wever-Bray phenomenon at first seemed to substantiate a telephone theory, in which the basilar membrane acting as a diaphragm was following the high-frequency 20,000-Hz impulses. The Helmholtz resonance view appeared to be untenable except for the lower frequencies, since the auditory nerve did not have a refractory period brief enough to allow it to conduct the higher frequencies. The intrinsic operations occurring in the nerve were made doubtful, because the high frequencies were reproduced, although for a brief period, even after the death of the experimental animal. Because the phenomenon did later disappear after death, Wever and Bray concluded that it was biologic in nature.

Two processes are involved in the explanation, (1) a cochlear response and (2) the VIIIth nerve response. In the former, electric *cochlear potentials (microphonics)* are generated through conversion of pressure vibrations in nonnervous structures to electrical impulses, perhaps as a summation of the output of the hair cells. The origin of the microphonics has been referred to the external hair cell. This is analogous to a piezoelectric effect, and these impulses can be recorded from any tissue, such as the round window. Cochlear potentials are said by some workers to represent the form in which the stimulus is received and altered by the peripheral auditory machinery. The cochlear microphonic potential is so named because it seems to originate in the cochlea and because it resembles the oscillations of a microphone whose membrane is displaced by sound waves. This potential does not appear when the system is at rest.

Cochlear microphonics should not be confused with the electrical action potentials that arise in the acoustic nerve. Both result from sound waves activating the cochlea, and the cochlear microphonics can mask the action of the acoustic nerve potentials unless suitable instrumental detection is enlisted. The microphonics are artifacts which precede the true action potentials, although it has even been contended that they are the stimulus for the nerve endings on the hair cells. Thus, it has been stated that the cochlear microphonic potential is formed by more than one wave (Eyzaguirre, 1969). One of the waves persists after death and may be a piezoelectric effect. The other wave is a neural component, which does not persist after death, and which may possibly be biologic.

The cochlear microphonic potentials are still of obscure significance, and they may be incidental by-products of activity. They have been studied intensively, however, in auditory physiology, since they indicate that sound has stimulated the organ of Corti. They are also useful in localizing the site of a lesion in the cochlea. The microphonics can reproduce the frequency, amplitude, and form of the sound waves that stimulate the cochlea, and they are an important tool to measure cochlear function during life.

440

The electrical phenomenon that is called the true *acoustic (action) potential* of the VIIIth cranial nerve has been claimed by some workers to be activated by the liberation of a chemical substance, such as acetylcholine, from the hair cells. This potential can be obtained at the round window, the VIIIth nerve, or within the cochlea and does not occur in the resting system.

The hypothesis that chemical mediators may stimulate the nerve fibers has the advantage that the latent period of the nerve impulses can be simply explained. A latency of 0.7 msec or more showed by the auditory nerve impulses has been an objection to the view that the electrical potential stimulates the nerve. In the chemical theory the latency expresses the time needed for some substance to cross the cell membranes and excite the nerve fibers. The mediator is possibly acetylcholine. This substance could also be the mediator between the hair cells and the sensory nerve fibers.

The action potential is produced by axons of the VIIIth nerve and represents the total reaction of the neurons involved in the discharge produced by sound stimulation.

Resting dc potentials (endocochlear potentials) may be considered as a third distinct electrical phenomenon that can be recorded from the ear. This represents a positive polarization of the endolymph in the scala media and is not the same as cochlear microphonics or acoustic action potentials. The resting dc potentials are large. According to Ruch and Fulton (1960), if the fluid of the scala vestibuli is considered as a zero point, the fluid of the scala media has a positivity of 50 millivolts, whereas the organ of Corti has a negativity of 50 millivolts. Some other values for these endocochlear voltages will be given later. On the supposition that the mechanical energy of sound cannot supply all the electrical energy of the microphonic potential, the dc potential may be the source of the increment. It appears to be generated in the stria vascularis and is somehow modulated by movements of the cochlear structures.

Manner of Stimulation of the Nerve Fibers

It is seen that the machinery of how hair cell deformation is transduced to acoustic nerve impulses is not yet satisfactorily answered. When the hairs of the hair cells move back and forth, they produce an alternating potential across the surface of the cells. This is the *receptor*, or *generator, potential*. Whether it stimulates nerve endings by direct electrical excitation or by chemical mediation is obscure.

Some investigators believe that the cochlear microphonic potential is the key to the transduction process. In this regard, the microphonic potential is stated by Ochs (1965) to be produced by a steady potential (endocochlear voltage) of +80 millivolts inside the scala media. This adds to the membrane potential of the hair cells to give 140 to 150 millivolts (Ochs, 1965; Guyton, 1966) acting across the hair cell membranes. When the hair cells are deformed, the relatively large voltage changes of the microphonic potentials are produced. This may sensitize the hair cell and increase its ability to respond to slight movement of its hairs.

The distinct discharge activity in the acoustic nerve fibers is called a *summating potential*. These and the microphonic potentials are both classified as receptor potentials from their origin in hair cell deformation followed by depolarization of the auditory nerve endings. Davis (1960, 1961b) thinks that the cochlear microphonics are generated by deformation of the external hair cells and the summating potential by the internal hair cells.

441

The Perception of Loudness

Loudness is a subjective sensation, or psychologic attribute of the sound. It expresses the judgment of the strength of the sensation, i.e., loud or soft.

Loudness has some correlation with the amplitude of the sound wave. The amplitude is roughly indicative of the intensity, the latter being proportional to the square of the amplitude. The term intensity actually refers to energy flux density, but in acoustics it commonly refers to power or energy. When the incident sound waves have greater intensity, as evidenced by their amplitude, the number of nerve impulses increases. The total number of nerve impulses generated, however, is determined by the general activity of structures in the cochlea.

Frequency as well as amplitude influences the loudness of a sound. As the frequency of nerve impulses increases, the sound becomes louder. If a nerve fiber from the basilar membrane is stimulated at low frequency, the sensation is one of a weak sound, whereas stimulation of the same fiber at high frequency produces a louder sound. It may be well to remind the reader that the frequency of the nerve impulses is not necessarily the same as the frequency of the incident sound.

Loudness appears to depend not only upon the intensity of the waves and the frequency of the nerve impulses, but also upon the number of nerve fibers involved in carrying the impulses, although the numerical relations are not simple. Finally, it involves subjective judgment.

Although loudness increases with the intensity of a pure tone, a given intensity may sound much louder near the midpoint of the audible range of frequencies than at very high or very low frequencies.

In regard to the responses of the basilar membrane, the region of maximum stimulation does not shift if a tone rises in intensity while remaining fixed in frequency. However, the extent or magnitude of the local response increases.

Measures of Loudness

There are intensive subjective scales that allow the ranking of loudness in order of increasing magnitude. The *phon* is a unit of loudness based on a subject's own value judgment. For a given tone it is the intensity, in decibels, of a 1000-Hz tone that is sensed as being as loud as the given tone. If two tones greatly different in frequency are each adjusted to the same loudness, expressed in phons, an attenuation of volume will differentially change the loudness of each tone. At the point where the loudness of the two tones are made equal, the intensities are different. Also, when the intensities of two equally loud tones are changed, there is a differential change in their loudness.

Another scale of loudness expresses how many times louder one tone is than the other. The arbitrary unit is the *sone,* which is the loudness of a 1,000-Hz tone at a 40-dB intensity level. A 2-sone sound is sensed as being twice as loud as a 1-sone sound.

There is logic in developing the sone as a unit. Although the logarithmic phon scale covers the dynamic range of the ear (120 dB), it does not fit a subjective loudness scale. The difficulty is that a noise that sounds twice as loud as another does not measure twice the number of phons. The sone scale, however, does correspond closely to the subjective sensation of loudness. Thus, where the comparison between a jet takeoff and quiet talking is 3 to 1 (120 to 40) in phons, it is more realistically 64 to 1 (256 to 4) in sones.

Accurate measurements of loudness must take into account the spectral distribution of the sound and relate it to empirically determined critical bandwidths. Broadband sounds, like those of jet aircraft, are sensed as much louder than narrow-band noise of the same sound pressure level. This has been handled by a *bark* scale.

There is a significant difference between objective and subjective measures of loudness when two sounds are presented to the ear simultaneously. If they are widely separated in frequency, their partial loudnesses sum to a total loudness. If not separated by a critical bandwidth, one sound masks the other.

An individual's estimate of the *distance* of sounds is partly associated with loudness at given distances and, to a lesser extent, with the fact that distant sounds change their quality through reflection and refraction.

The Perception of Quality

A distinct parameter of sound is its quality, or special nature, called timbre. The quality is determined by the frequency, strength, and number of partials present. Musical instruments might be indistinguishable if only their fundamental tones were sounded, and this is true for the voice. Timbre is associated with the complexity of the waveform. Two identical sounds of the same fundamental pitch may have unlike waveforms.

The auditory mechanism can discriminate the separate simple tones of a complex waveform, provided the sound is neither very intense nor has many overtones. A trained person can differentiate all the instruments in an orchestra. This is referred to as the analytical capacity of the ear.

443

The timbre of the voice sounds is related to the vibrations of the vocal folds, the size and shape of the air column, and the texture (tenseness and tonus) of the pharyngeal walls.

The qualities called consonance and dissonance are explainable through processes occurring in the basilar membrane. The pleasant sensation of a musical chord arises when the frequencies of simultaneous tones have simple mathematical ratios to one another and their overtones are in mutual support. In this instance the basilar membrane is said to display discrete nodes of activity at regular intervals while other areas along it are quiescent. In discordance the sounds do not support one another and produce generalized activity along several areas of the basilar membrane with fewer discrete nodes.

Beats result from summation and interference of sound waves. For example, if two tones with similar but not identical frequencies, such as 2,000 and 2,003 Hz, reach the ear simultaneously, the sound perceived may be periodically strengthened and weakened. The result is pulsations, or beats. Reinforcement occurs when the sounds reach the ear in the same phase, and a mutual weakening occurs when they are in opposite phases.

It is known that a pure tone may sound differently to different individuals (Fowler, 1947). This is a result of anatomic variations. Cochleas are not identical, and the same is true for the higher centers. No one knows what the exact quality of a sound is in another person.

The Perception of Volume and Duration

Pitch, loudness, and timbre are not the only parameters of sound; volume and duration are some others. Volume implies massiveness, or the filling of space by sound, and it is a subjective rather than a physical measure of the extensiveness of the incident sound. Rather than being dependent upon a specific mechanism for its production, it is a function of pitch and intensity, varying with the amplitude and approximately inversely with the frequency, or pitch (Osgood, 1956). The volume increases with increasing areas of stimulation of the cochlea. Loudness is closely related to volume but not synonymous in cause or effect.

Time is involved in the psychologic interpretation of sound. It is expressed in the duration of tones and also in the frequency and duration of the pulses between tones.

Van Riper and Irwin (1958) discuss the factor of time in relation to such phenomena as the sound duration, the time qualities of the syllable, the time values of the pause, the sound unit, and the word. They use certain terms in this connection. Pitch/time is the judgment of the frequency of vocal fold vibrations. Loudness/time is a quality judgment of the incident sound intensity at a given time, and it is related to complex laryngeal mechanisms. Quality/time is the listener's perception of the frequencies and their relative intensities, and it, too, is a complex function of several laryngeal mechanisms.

Sound Localization

There is an auditory perspective which consists of recognizing the direction of sound. The time of arrival in each ear is an important determinant. Ordinarily, the ear which first receives the sound makes one localize the sound on the corresponding side. When both ears are simultaneously excited, the source seems to be in the median plane of the listener. If a sound is heard with greater intensity in one ear, one tends to localize it on the corresponding side.

In continuous sounds of low pitch the phase of the waves is important. Movements of a sound wave resemble those of a pendulum. The particle of air vibrating is displaced in one direction then returns and becomes displaced in an opposite direction. Finally it returns to its resting position. Sound waves are localized in the median plane when they arrive in both ears in the same phase. If they reach the ear in different phases, the sound is localized where the crest of the wave arrives first.

A sound lateral to the ears is more easily localized than one from above. Also, intermittent sounds are more easily localized than continuous ones.

The location of the brain centers for finding sound direction is uncertain. Because of the rapidity of the reactions, lower centers in the brainstem are probably operative. Nuclei therein are also involved in responsive eye and general body movements. It has been suggested that the ability to localize sound is partly dependent upon mechanisms in the accessory nucleus of the superior olive (Ballenger, 1969). The cerebral cortex may be the primary center that finally discriminates the direction of sound. Decorticate animals do not localize short, rapid sounds and only roughly localize persistent sounds.

The Biologic Significance of Speech Sounds

A system of sounds is available as language in man, and it is also used as a primitive code of communication in animals. There are vast possibilities of variation because of such differences as occur in the pitch of tones, in the patterns of overtones, in the great range of noises of varied pitch, and in the changes in volume.

Most vertebrates produce no noise. The large class of fishes is dumb except for a few species. The development of voice has been closely dependent upon the emergence of animals from an aquatic to a terrestrial existence.

445

Many animal sounds are purposeless, such as those resulting from movement of limbs. Some sounds, such as sneezing, are not for communication. In time, purposeless sounds may have become biologically adaptive and eventually used for social communication.

Sound in animals is used primarily for its survival value, as in offense, defense, food, and sex. It is generally the male who calls to the female in courtship phonation. Animals also use calls to keep together or to signal impending danger.

Many parts of the animal body have been put to use to produce sound. Some insects rub one part of the integument against another. The porcupine rattles its quills. The transmission of the most complicated messages, however, makes use of parts of the respiratory apparatus. The development of the vocal folds in mammals becomes the most efficient adaptation.

Sound can be produced with a fairly simple vocal mechanism. However, the presence of an adequate phonating structure is not enough for meaningful sound production. Animals with similar structures may be contrastingly vocal and mute. An animal such as the rabbit uses its larynx only in extreme circumstances, screaming, for example, when struggling against an enemy or subjected to severe stress. A deer or giraffe is notably silent but not because of laryngeal defection. The use of sound may be tied up with intelligence, the free use of the extremities, and the manner of life.

Sound and language in animals may be more related to the degree of development of the brain than to the structure of the larynx. Charles Darwin had the view that the higher apes have no speech because they lack sufficient intelligence. Darwin's view has been contested on the basis of animal experimentation. The voice has been studied particularly in the chimpanzee. Keleman (1948), after such an anatomic study, concluded that a hypothetical animal with a human brain and chimpanzee larynx could not produce any other phonetic effect than that animal now does. A human variety of speech would fail in spite of the animal's rich scale of phonetic possibilities.

The primitive sense organ for receiving sound messages was probably a vibration receptor, such as the lateral line organ of fishes. Sounds of very low pitch seem to be sensed in fishes.

Applied Anatomy and Physiology

Informational Feedback

Fry (1957) discusses the dependence of speech upon hearing through natural feedback controls. In any speech sequence the information concerning the progress and bodily effects of the sound transmission is simultaneously relayed to the brain of the sender, and such information is used to control subsequent speech and adjunctive activity. The main servomechanism is the auditory feedback, although there are in addition tactual and kinesthetic circuits. Much of this information is stored in memory circuits, and the speaker can draw upon this in future speech activity. Informational feedback will also enable him to control speech movements even in the temporary absence of the auditory feedback.

Fatigue

All sense organs are subject to fatigue. The ear has the power of rapid recovery from fatigue in spite of continuous stimulation. High tones in particular increase the duration of fatigue. A common measurement is to contrast the intensity threshold of a tone which has been sounded continuously for some time with the resting threshold.

Prolonged stimulation by noise produces general bodily disorders such as an increase of the energy required for cardiac and respiratory activity, a jump in the metabolic rate, and psychologic disturbances. Very high sound frequencies, known as supersonics, can cause severe damage to many animal cells or even the death of the animal. The chief cause of death is cavitation. This process involves the appearance of submicroscopic bubbles in tissue fluids, and the pathologic effects are immediate.

If one ear is subjected to stimulation, the other ear may suffer a decrease in auditory acuity (Houssay, 1955). This suggests a central factor in fatigue and it makes it difficult to assign a given role to the receptor in the origin of fatigue.

Fatigue should not be confused with another auditory property called adaptation. When stimulation begins, the rate of the nerve discharges is high but decreases rapidly. As seen in the electrical responses of single nerve fibers, the voltage (spike height) also decreases. There is thus an adaptation in both rate and amplitude, and it is similar to adaptation in other varieties of sensory fibers.

Speech Intelligibility

The range of hearing is roughly from 20 to 20,000 Hz, but the upper limit decreases with age. In normal speech, frequencies from approximately 250 to 4,000 Hz are readily differentiated.

The intensity of a sound is another factor which determines whether it will be perceived. Speech is fully recognizable at a distance of 3 ft at an average intensity of 30 to 40 dB stronger than 10^{-16} watt/cm^2 (the absolute threshold of hearing). The range of intelligibility encompasses about 80 dB between the threshold and disagreeable sensation.

Even when we speak at a fairly uniform intensity, certain speech sounds are more easily heard. Every sound is linked by its method of phonation and resonation with a certain speech power. For a table of the relative powers of the speech sounds in order of strength, consult Akin (1958). The frequency region in which the greatest energy of each of the speech sounds lies is also given. Denes and Pinson (1963) have a brief, clear review.

447

In addition to the acoustic clues, such factors as expectations, familiarity with the subject matter, and knowledge of the rules of grammar and semantics add to the intelligibility.

Conduction Routes and Hearing Impairment

Deafness as a term is confusing in that it may imply hearing deficits covering a wide range of intensities, perhaps from a small 15-dB loss to a total loss at the 100-dB level. More descriptive terms have come into usage. A loss that is innately restorable or subject to correction by prosthetic means is a hypacusis. People who are hard of hearing may be described as being mildly or moderately hypacustic. If a person has a more profound loss or an ear nerve disorder which cannot be restored to a reasonable level of hearing, the term anacusis applies. When the defect is central and includes psychogenic types and the aphasias, the term dysacusis is applicable.

In general, hearing losses can be classified into two types, conductive and sensorineural. A conductive loss is caused by a defect in the mechanism that transmits sound to the inner ear. The lesion may occur in the external auditory canal, tympanic membrane, middle ear space, ossicles, or the oval window. A sensorineural loss is caused by a lesion in the inner ear, acoustic nerve, or the central neural pathways.

A loss of hearing that is less than 15 dB may be considered to be within the normal range of hearing speech sounds. Low-intensity sounds may be hard to hear when the loss is between 15 and 30 dB. The difficulty in hearing conversation increases when the hearing loss exceeds 30 dB. Between a loss of 45 to 60 dB the individual is generally incapable of ordinary speech communication, and beyond 65 dB the hearing loss is severe.

External and Middle Ear Deafness This category includes conduction-transmission disorders and involves interference with the passage of sound waves through the external or middle ear.

Sound waves may pass through these chambers by several routes. The first one has already been described and is the *physiologic,* or *ossicular, route.* The round window is the terminal structure involved in this process.

There is a second, or direct, *air route* through the middle ear. Since the oval window is covered by the stapes, and especially so in stapes ankylosis, the air route is one involving chiefly the round window. Because of the thinness of its membrane, the latter can respond to the vibrations. This is an inefficient mechanism.

In otosclerosis the stapes becomes fixed in the oval window and the ossicular route of conduction with its amplification factors is lost. The substituted round window, however, does not provide enough "give" to produce optimal vibrations of the basilar membrane and deformation of the hair cells.

448

Surgery for otosclerosis was first attempted in the late nineteenth century, and it involved mobilization or removal of the stapes. The operations were performed by incisions made into the tympanic membrane. From 1897 to 1922 procedures were developed to create a new window (fenestra) in the surgically accessible horizontal semicircular canal, but failures occurred through infection and osteogenetic closure of the fenestra.

In 1938, Lempert of New York City developed a single-staged fenestration operation, creating a new window in the horizontal semicircular canal so as to short-circuit the stapes (Lempert, 1950; DeWeese and Saunders, 1964). The perilymph connects as the oval window does with the scala vestibuli, and vibrations travel through normal physiologic routes. Thousands of such operations were performed in the next twenty years. Unfortunately, the patient is left with a mastoidectomy cavity that requires internal care, and there is a persisting conductive hearing defect. Subsequent closure of the fenestra is a frequent problem.

Stapes surgery (stapes mobilization), developed by Rosen (1952), avoids the foregoing problems. This is a procedure performed under local anesthesia through the external auditory canal. The dramatic hearing improvement is usually temporary, however, because of refixation of the stapes. Many people with sensorineural losses have worse hearing postoperatively, even though their acuity is better, because amplification brings more distortion and/or recruitment problems.

The stapes mobilization technic has been supplanted by the stapedectomy operation of Shea (1958). The stapes is replaced with a venous graft and polyethylene strut, and hearing is restored to the full sensorineural potential in most patients. The hearing gain is claimed to be stable (Schuknecht and Applebaum, 1969).

There are transmission defects in the middle ear other than otosclerosis. Blocked Eustachian tubes are frequent and may be caused by enlarged adenoids or by infections. The absorption of air in the middle ear decreases sound transmission. In otitis media, resulting from infection, the products of inflammation may rupture the drum membrane, and the scar tissue produced in healing may decrease the responsiveness of the drum and cause deafness.

Rohan (1957) reviews the history of the attempts to make artificial tympanic membranes. These devices are particularly applicable in chronic suppurative otitis media. In 1640 Marcus Banzer attempted to close the perforated eardrum with pig bladder fixed to the end of an ivory rod. Interest waned during the early twentieth century and is being revived. One device is dried human amniotic membrane, but it falls off too easily and it is readily infected. Polyethylene lamellae are more easily sterilized, are more resistant, and can be cut into any shape. To keep the lamellae in place, the natural cerumen plus electrical forces may suffice. Mawson (1958) has found skin grafting to be fairly satisfactory for repairing defective drum membranes. The problem is chiefly one of maintaining the blood supply.

Schuknecht and Applebaum (1969) note that the early enthusiasm for artificial prostheses as ossicular substitutes has waned because of occasional extrusion of these devices. It is better to use ossicular transplants or grafts of cartilage or bone.

Internal Ear Deafness This type of deafness includes nerve (perceptive) disorders, such as lesions in the organ of Corti and in the efferent cochlear nerve. The auditory receptors may be damaged congenitally or from explosive noises, trauma, and infections. The cochlea and cranial nerve VIII may be involved in syphilis and meningitis. Tumors also can destroy nerve fibers. Drugs, such as streptomycin, may be toxic to the static labyrinth and to the VIIIth cranial nerve nuclei. Decreased acuity of hearing is also a complication of the aging process.

Ménière's disease is a nerve or perceptive deafness in which the pathologic process affects chiefly the cochlea and the saccule, with increased pressure in the labyrinth. There may be vertigo, tinnitus, nausea, vomiting, nystagmus, and variable hearing loss.

Central Deafness This type of deafness involves the auditory tract and the cerebral endings in the auditory cortex.

Bone Conduction A third route of conducting sounds through the ear may be considered. This is the *osseous route,* by bone conduction. The middle ear is bypassed, and the sound waves travel through the skull bones. There is considerable energy loss as the vibrations pass from air to a solid medium, which makes this route unimportant in normal hearing.

The tiny movements of the skull bones produce normal, downward movements of the basilar membrane due to the lesser resistance of the round window and its bulging into the middle ear. The round window movements are favored because the stapes and cochlear fluids are prevented by inertia from following exactly the skull bone oscillations.

The two modes of cochlear stimulation involved in bone conduction are *inertial* and *compressional* conduction. In the inertial type the middle ear ossicles, which are not rigidly attached to the skull, vibrate with an inertial lag behind the vibrations of the skull. This occurs at low frequencies, and the movement of the stapes is the same as though it had been energized through ordinary air conduction.

In the compressional type, which occurs at higher frequencies, inertia is a less significant factor. The skull vibrates in sections separated by nodes, allowing the establishment of compressional or flexural forces within the walls both of the skull and the inner ear. With the stapes footplate being less mobile than the oval window, the forces can produce basilar membrane deformation and cochlear stimulation. The compression of the fluids on the vestibular aspect of the basilar membrane during bone conduction enhances the displacement effect.

There are other processes which occur during bone conduction. The inertia of the mandible allows a motion relative to the adjacent articular surface, resulting in deformation of the cartilaginous external auditory canal and transmission of airborne sound vibrations. This is an osseotympanic factor. Naunton (1963) discusses these modes of transmission, noting that a theory is rational when it involves a unitary mode of stimulation whose efficiency varies with impedance changes anywhere in the conducting system.

Hearing Tests

There are many tests, varying from qualitative to quantitative. In view of the availability of the instruments and the relative ease of conducting the tests, it is suggested that they be incorporated into a laboratory course that might be developed as part of a basic preclinical science in speech pathology and audiology.

In the historical development of tests, the whispered and spoken voice tests, watch-tick tests, and coin-click tests were important screening technics. They are now known to be inaccurate and inadequate, and they are no longer of practical interest.

Tuning-fork Tests Conductive and sensorineural hearing losses can be differentiated by comparing auditory acuity for sound transmitted by air and by bone. The tuning-fork tests are particularly suitable for such comparisons. If the thresholds are the same, no conductive loss is present. If, however, the auditory acuity by bone transmission is better than that for air transmission, the hearing loss is conductive in type. The 512-Hz fork is preferred because lower-frequency forks produce a strong vibratory sensation, but forks of other frequencies are used, depending upon the test. The use of tuning forks is becoming a lost art, despite their value.

The Weber test compares the bone conduction of both ears to find whether a monaural defect has a sensorineural or conductive cause. A sounded 256-Hz tuning fork is placed in the midline upon the vertex, forehead, teeth, or chin. The subject is asked to state in which ear he hears the fork better. If he hears it more clearly in the diseased ear, the bone conduction is greater in that ear and a conductive type of deafness exists. If he hears the sound better in the normal ear, the hearing defect of the diseased ear is of the sensorineural type.

In the Rinne test, the duration of bone conduction is compared with that of air conduction for each ear. The shank of a vibrating 512-Hz fork is placed against the subject's mastoid until it is no longer sensed, then the prongs are held about 1 in. lateral and broadside to the external ear.

If the hearing is normal, or if there is a sensorineural hearing loss, the tuning fork is heard longer and louder when held near the ear than when placed firmly over the mastoid bone. This is called a positive Rinne test. If the fork is heard longer and louder when placed over the mastoid, this indicates a conductive loss (negative Rinne test). If one ear is totally deaf, a false negative result occurs in the deaf ear because the bone-conducted sound is heard in the opposite ear.

In the Schwabach test, forks such as 512-, 1,024-, and 2,048-Hz are successively used. The fork is sounded, and the time is recorded until the subject can no longer hear the sound. The shank of the vibrating fork should be placed on the subject's mastoid, and the test repeated on the mastoid of the examiner (whose hearing should be normal). In conduction deafness the sound through the cranial bones persists longer than normal. Equal decrease in both air and bone conduction, as compared to that in a normal individual, indicates sensorineural deafness.

Pure-tone Audiometry The development of audiometry was stimulated by the earlier inadequate testing methods, and it was important in turning the measurement of auditory acuity into an exact science. The audiometer is an important diagnostic instrument to provide intensities at controlled frequencies of sound. It evaluates the auditory sensitivity within the audible range of frequency as a function of the intensity of sounds.

Intensity is conveniently measured in decibel units. The decibel, as already stated, is the logarithmic ratio of the intensity of two sounds. It may be thought of as the smallest change of intensity that is perceptible.

The *pure-tone* audiometer is the basic instrument. It consists essentially of an electronic oscillator which generates pure and constant tones whose frequency and intensity can be varied over a large range. The output of the oscillator is fed to earphones, which must be comfortably fitted to the subject. The use of a masking noise generator in the circuit will exclude the ear not being tested and reduce confusion in the interpretation of results.

The intensity of each tone can be increased or decreased in steps from a zero level. For instance, if the intensity must be increased 20 dB for audibility, then the hearing loss for that tone is 20 dB. Several frequencies covering the auditory range are tested to find the hearing loss for each tone in each ear.

The subject is seated in a room specially controlled for minimizing disturbing background noise. This can avoid apparent hearing loss, especially for the lower tones. If the subject hears the test sound, he signals by a simple response device, e.g., raising a finger.

In the procedure involving *pure-tone air-conduction* audiometry, a 1,000-Hz tone is presented to the "better" ear. The threshold at this frequency (1,024 when based on a musical notation that middle C is 256 Hz) is thought to be the most stable in the scale. The signal is presented at a strong intensity based upon the apparent hearing loss. The intensity is decreased in steps of 5 (or 10) dB until no response is elicited. As an example, if 40 dB is first used and the subject responds, the hearing level may be set to 30 dB. If the subject responds, the level is set to 20 dB, and so on until the subject fails to respond. The intensity is then increased, in 5-dB steps, until the tone is heard. The threshold is the lowest intensity or hearing level at which there is a response two or three times out of three trials, or two or more times out of four trials, or three or more times out of five trials.

Examiners may prefer to test the sensitivity for the higher frequencies first on the claim that the ascending threshold is the more precise.

Air conduction (AC) thresholds are plotted at 125, 250, 500, 1,000, 2,000, 4,000, 6,000 and 8,000 Hz (and higher) in octave and half-octave intervals. The intensities range from 10 above to 100 dB below the zero axis in steps no greater than 5 dB. The intensity (loss in decibels) increases downward on the audiogram.

In the procedure involving *pure-tone bone-conduction* audiometry, a bone oscillator is used which produces mechanical vibration of the skull. The instrument is firmly pressed against the forehead (or mastoid).

Bone conduction (BC) thresholds are plotted from 250 to 4,000 Hz. The intensities range from 10 above to 60 dB below the zero axis in 5-dB steps. The procedure used to find each threshold is the same as that used in air conduction.

Because contralateralization of sound by transcranial bone transmission is very frequent, the elimination of the opposite ear by masking (with noise) becomes more urgent than in air conduction.

Persons with normal air conduction should also have normal bone conduction. It is possible for a patient with a severe hearing loss for bone-conduction sound to respond to the vibrator by vibration sense before the bone conduction threshold is stimulated, producing a spurious result.

The audiometric curve is constructed by marking a point for each threshold determination on a chart called an audiogram. Frequencies are read on the abscissa and intensities on the ordinate. For air conduction, a cross is used as a symbol for the left ear and a circle for the right ear. For each ear the points found are connected by straight lines. In the grid used, the "zero" line must be defined. International reference levels for pure-tone audiometers have been agreed upon (Glorig, 1965) and recommended by the International Organization for Standardization (ISO). In bone conduction, certain designations are different than for air conduction. In the former, each point is represented by the signs [or <, the concavity turning toward the right for the right ear and toward the left for the left ear.

The *AC audiogram* measures the sensitivity of the entire auditory mechanism, including the ear and the auditory nerve. If there is considerable difference between threshold levels in the two ears, for example, 30 to 50 dB, the sound presented to the poorer ear may be heard in the good ear because of air or bone transmission. One cannot then be certain in which ear the subject is hearing the tone. It is preferable to mask out the better ear by noise when testing the poorer ear, entering the noise level used on the audiogram form.

The *BC audiogram* is used to measure the sensitivity of the sensorineural mechanism. Tones are presented to the skull with a bone-conduction vibrator, placed best on the forehead rather than the mastoid of the test ear. Also, whereas masking of the nontest ear may not be necessary in AC audiometry, because of a 40- to 50-dB attenuation between the test and nontest ears, masking may well be necessary in BC testing because there is little or no attenuation between the two ears and both may be stimulated about equally by the vibrator. The question of the optimal amount of masking needs more study.

453

A significant advance in conventional audiometry was the introduction of the self-recording, or semiautomatic, audiometer by Békésy. In this technic both the frequency and intensity of the test signal are motor-operated. The subject records his threshold by controlling the direction of intensity change.

For a discussion of audiometers and procedures in audiology, the reader is referred to Jerger (1963; 1968), Newby (1964), Glorig (1965), O'Neill and Oyer (1966), and Sataloff (1966).

Speech Audiometry The pure-tone audiometer, as described above, quantifies the thresholds for air conduction or bone conduction and permits screening the level of hearing as well as an estimation of the speech discrimination ability of an individual. It does not test overall hearing activity. To do this tests are available to measure the ability to understand speech, and they use speech rather than pure tones as the stimulus. The speech audiometer can utilize a standardized record, or it can deliver a live voice at controlled intensities. There are two kinds of measurements, one concerned with sensitivity and the other with understanding.

The *Speech Reception Threshold Test* (SRT) is a sensitivity test that measures the threshold intensity of speech at which the subject discriminates half the test matter given. This arbitrarily expresses the threshold of intelligibility of speech. Isolated words, connected speech, or spondee words (two-syllable words, each of equal

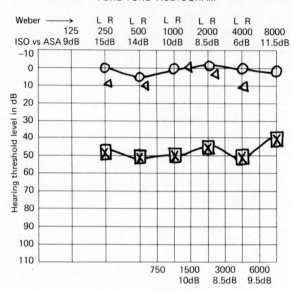

Weber ⟶	L R	L R	L R	L R	L R	L R	
125	250	500	1000	2000	4000	8000	
ISO vs ASA 9dB	15dB	14dB	10dB	8.5dB	6dB	11.5dB	

	750	1500	3000	6000
	10dB	8.5dB	9.5dB	

Legend

Ear	AC	AC mask	BC	BC mask	Audiom. limits	Sound field
Right ear	O—O	⊡—⊡	>—→	▷—▷	Q	∪
Left ear	X—X	⊠—⊠	←—<	◁—◁	X	

Level of masking

Frequency tested		250	500	1000	2000	3000	4000
Air cond	Testing RE LE masked						
	Testing LE RE masked	70	70	70	70	—	70
Bone cond	Testing RE LE masked						
	Testing LE RE masked	60	60	60	60	—	60

To convert ISO readings to ASA readings subtract appropriate "difference in dB" at each frequency

To convert ASA readings to ISO readings add appropriate "difference in dB" at each frequency

This Audiogram is plotted on: (check one)

ISO 1964 ✓

ASA 1951 ☐

Southern Illinois University
Clinical Center

Figure 14-14 Audiogram, showing conduction loss in left ear. (*Courtesy of Dr. Alfred Copeland, Southern Illinois University.*)

454

acoustic power) may be used as the stimulus. The test can be given with a stand-ardized record or by live voice.

There is an audiometer, the VASC (visual auditory screening for children), which can do SRT tests in small groups of children, and it is portable so that it can be used in public schools.

The threshold of intelligibility is closely linked with another physiologic attribute called speech discrimination. This involves the use of PB (phonetically balanced) word lists, containing lists of single words representative of conversational speech. When presented at suprathreshold levels, the percentage of correct responses (discrimination score) indicates how well the individual understands conversational speech. The percentage of incorrect responses is the discrimination loss. The use of PB word lists for this testing has been questioned as predicators of a person's ability to understand actual running speech.

Auditory Testing of Children The testing of children has involved successful revision of adult procedures, and neonate testing as well as that of the very young child is common.

One approach involves sending pure tones from 500 through 4,000 Hz through loud-speakers at 85 to 95 dB above normal threshold. These elicit an auropalpebral reflex during the first two weeks of life.

At sixteen weeks, high-intensity sounds typically elicit eye movement in the horizontal plane (auditory oculogyric response). At about twenty-six weeks there is localization of sound sources at lower intensity levels. Auditory symbols are well comprehended by the average child at one year of age. At about twenty-two months, it is possible to obtain pure-tone audiometric thresholds, and at three years of age conventional adult audiometry is applicable.

Masking
The masking effect of sound is obvious in trying to interpret conversation in noisy surroundings. When two tones are sounded together, one may raise the threshold of the other. The closer the tones coincide in pitch, the greater the masking effect. Also, two tones reaching the same ear are more likely to produce masking of one than if such tones arrive at opposite ears.

The decrease in the neural response to one sound by simultaneous stimulation with another is linked with the refractory period of nerve fibers. A second tone produces impulses in fibers whose refractory states are such that the first tone does not get through. Apparently the stimuli are competing for the same fibers. It is of interest that although action potentials show masking, the cochlear microphonics summate (add) the impulses. This fact reveals a basic difference in the nature of these two varieties of current.

In practice, noise (from different kinds of generators) is used to mask a pure tone or speech, because in an attempt to mask pure tones by pure tones, distortion products can develop. White noise is commonly used. This is a sound whose frequency spectrum is continuous (no frequencies missing in the included range) and uniform (all frequencies having the same average intensity). White noise and random noise are not the same.

The amount of masking is the number of decibels by which the threshold is raised. That produced by a noise is dependent on the noise level and also on the threshold (in quiet) of the subject for the sound to be masked.

It is occasionally desirable to have masking occur. For example, a tone sensed in one ear may be not less than 50 dB or so weaker in the opposite ear, under the best sealing. The sound can cross the base of the skull by transcranial bone conduction. If the acuity is still greater, one must put a masking noise into the more sensitive ear to obtain a valid audibility threshold measurement (in audiometric measurements) on the less sensitive ear.

Because of the development in the inner ear of aural harmonics of the noise band, a narrow band of noise will mask tones above it in frequency when the intensity of the masking noise is raised. Even the lower frequencies can become masked when the masking noise attains very high intensities. At the cause, there is distortion in the inner ear. Also, there is an auditory reflex whereby the middle ear muscles contract with the incident high-intensity sound, thus affecting the transmission of low-frequency tones in both ears. A false high hearing level may be reported (Glorig, 1965).

In considering the practicable masking intensity to be used, the masking noise should strive to exclude the influence of the ear not being examined, and it should leave intact the hearing of the ear under examination.

Recruitment

This is a clinical term used to denote an auditory response characterized by an abnormally rapid increase in loudness. It is sometimes associated with elevated thresholds of hearing, and it is typical of the temporary losses produced by exposure to noise.

Because recruitment does not occur if the decreased sensitivity results from a conductive (transmission) failure through the middle ear, tests for recruitment are thus valuable in the differential diagnosis of middle ear from inner ear pathology.

In a unilateral cochlear disease, e.g., Ménière's disease, sounds of equal intensity, given at threshold levels, will be heard by the good ear only. When the intensity is raised sufficiently for the recruiting ear to hear, recruitment becomes apparent. A very small increase in intensity at which this ear first hears raises the loudness to that of the normal ear. There may even be hyperrecruitment, and the rapid increase in loudness becomes unpleasant. A subject with an inner ear hearing loss has a very narrow range of tolerance between the threshold intensity for hearing and that intensity where the sound is distressingly loud. This makes a hearing aid a difficult prosthetic choice in many instances.

Hypothetically, recruitment indicates degeneration of a number of hair cells or cochlear fibers. Although it would thus be impossible to hear weak signals, strong ones may saturate the system abruptly by way of the healthy fibers.

457

APPENDIX: TABULAR REVIEW OF MUSCLES DESCRIBED IN TEXT

MUSCLES OF THE ANTERIOR ABDOMINAL WALL

NAME	ORIGIN	INSERTION	INNERVATION	ACTION
External abdominal oblique	Lower 8 ribs	Linea alba, iliac crest, inguinal ligament	Iliohypogastric, ilioinguinal, intercostals 8–12	Draws ribs downward, decreases volume of thorax, compresses abdomen, flexes and rotates vertebral column
Internal abdominal oblique	Thoracolumbar fascia, iliac crest, inguinal ligament	Lower 3–4 ribs, linea alba, pubis	Iliohypogastric, ilioinguinal, intercostals 8–12	Draws ribs downward, decreases volume of thorax, compresses abdomen, flexes and rotates vertebral column
Transversus abdominis	Thoracolumbar fascia, lower 6 ribs, iliac crest, inguinal ligament	Linea alba, pubis, inguinal ligament	Intercostals 7–12, iliohypogastric, ilioinguinal	Compresses abdomen

NAME	ORIGIN	INSERTION	INNERVATION	ACTION
Rectus abdominis	Pubis	Xiphoid, fifth to seventh costal cartilages	Lower 6 intercostals	Flexes vertebral column and pelvis, depresses thorax

MUSCLES OF THE BACK

NAME	ORIGIN	INSERTION	INNERVATION	ACTION
Latissimus dorsi	Lowest 6–7 thoracic vertebrae, thoracolumbar fascia, lowest 3–4 ribs, iliac crest	Intertubercular groove of humerus	Thoracodorsal from brachial plexus	Elevates lowest 3–4 ribs if arm is fixed
Quadratus lumborum	Iliac crest, iliolumbar ligament	Lowest rib, transverse processes of upper 4 lumbar vertebrae	Twelfth thoracic and first lumbar	Fixes ribs 11–12 in forced expiration; depresses twelfth rib or laterally flexes vertebral column
Erector spinae (sacrospinalis complex)	Lumbar vertebrae, sacrum, posterior sacroiliac ligament, iliac crest, thoracolumbar fascia	Ribs	Posterior rami of spinal nerves at various levels of spinal cord	Depresses or elevates ribs, depending on segment in action
Trapezius	Superior nuchal line, external occipital protuberance, ligamentum nuchae, spines of vertebrae C-7 through T-12	Spine of scapula, acromion process, lateral third of clavicle	Spinal accessory nerve, C-3 and C-4	Extends neck and assists action of sternomastoid; fixes shoulder girdle and assists pectoral muscles

MUSCLES OF THE EUSTACHIAN (AUDITORY) TUBE

NAME	ORIGIN	INSERTION	INNERVATION	ACTION
Salpingopharyngeus	Inferior aspect of auditory tube near its orifice	Fuses with posterior portion of palatopharyngeus	Through pharyngeal plexus from pharyngeal branches of vagus which consist chiefly of spinal accessory fibers	Weakly opens auditory tube and raises pharynx during swallowing
Dilatator tubae	Fused with tensor veli palatini muscle	Hook of the cartilage and membranous part of auditory tube	Pharyngeal plexus	Opens auditory tube during swallowing
Levator veli palatini	Palatine aponeurosis	Petrous part of temporal bone, cartilage of auditory tube	Spinal accessory through pharyngeal plexus	Elevates and widens pharyngeal opening of auditory tube during swallowing; elevates soft palate and draws it backward; elevates pharynx

MUSCLES OF THE EUSTACHIAN (AUDITORY) TUBE (Cont'd)

NAME	ORIGIN	INSERTION	INNERVATION	ACTION
Tensor veli palatini	Palatine aponeurosis	Medial pterygoid plate, spine of sphenoid bone, cartilage of auditory tube	Mandibular nerve	Tightens soft palate as in blowing, and may open auditory tube

MUSCLES ACTING ON THE HYOID BONE OR THYROID CARTILAGE

NAME	ORIGIN	INSERTION	INNERVATION	ACTION
Digastric anterior belly	Inner surface of mandible	Intermediate tendon and body of hyoid	Mylohyoid (V₃) branch of inferior alveolar nerve	With mandible fixed it elevates hyoid and draws it forward
Posterior belly	Mastoid process of skull	Hyoid body via an intermediate tendon	Facial	Elevates, retracts, and tilts hyoid
Stylohyoid	Styloid process of temporal bone	Between body and greater cornu of hyoid bone	Facial	Elevates, retracts, and tilts hyoid
Mylohyoid	Mylohyoid line of mandible	Median tendinous raphe; posterior fibers end in body of hyoid	Mylohyoid branch of inferior alveolar nerve	With fixed mandible it elevates and draws forward the hyoid and raises tongue; in reverse it depresses lower jaw as in chewing or speech
Geniohyoid	Symphysis of mandible; inferior genial tubercle	Body of hyoid	Hypoglossal plus C-1	With fixed mandible it elevates and protrudes hyoid and tongue
Genioglossus	Superior genial tubercle on inner surface of symphysis of mandible	Lower fibers insert on hyoid; middle and upper fibers go to under side of tongue from root to apex	Hypoglossal	Lower fibers can elevate hyoid
Hyoglossus	Body and greater cornua of hyoid	Posterolateral areas of tongue	Hypoglossal	Depresses side of tongue, or may raise hyoid
Middle pharyngeal constrictor	Posterior median septum of pharynx	Greater cornua of hyoid, stylohyoid ligament	Pharyngeal plexus	Weak elevator and retractor of hyoid
Sternohyoid	Manubrium sterni, clavicle, sterno-clavicular ligament	Body of hyoid	Ansa hypoglossi containing fibers from C-1, C-2, C-3	Depresses hyoid
Omohyoid inferior belly	Scapula upper border, often from suprascapular ligament	Intermediate cervical tendon	Ansa hypoglossi containing fibers from C-1, C-2, C-3, for both bellies	Acting from the scapula, the muscle as a whole depresses and retracts hyoid, larynx

461

NAME	ORIGIN	INSERTION	INNERVATION	ACTION
Superior belly	Intermediate cervical tendon	Lower border of hyoid body	Ansa hypoglossi containing fibers from C-1, C-2, C-3, for both bellies	Acting from the scapula, the muscle as a whole depresses and retracts hyoid, larynx
Sternothyroid	Sternum and variably from upper costal cartilages	Lamina of thyroid cartilage	Ansa hypoglossi containing fibers from C-1, C-2, C-3	Depresses thyroid cartilage
Thyrohyoid	Lamina of thyroid	Major cornu and body of hyoid	Descendens hypoglossi plus C-1 and C-2	Depresses hyoid, or with fixed hyoid it elevates thyroid cartilage; it may tilt hyoid backward

INTRINSIC MUSCLES OF THE LARYNX

NAME	ORIGIN	INSERTION	INNERVATION	ACTION
Posterior cricoarytenoid	Posterior surface of cricoid	Muscular process of arytenoid	Recurrent laryngeal branch of vagus	Rotates arytenoids outward and widens glottis
Transverse arytenoid	Muscular process and lateral border of arytenoid cartilage	Lateral border of opposite arytenoid cartilage	Recurrent	Draws arytenoids medially and approximates vocal folds
Oblique arytenoid	Lower posterior surface of each arytenoid cartilage (muscular process)	Apex of opposite arytenoid cartilage	Recurrent	Approximates vocal folds; weak sphincter for superior opening of larynx
Aryepiglottic	Extension upward of some fibers of oblique arytenoid muscle	Epiglottis, quadrangular membrane	Recurrent	Weak depressor and retractor of epiglottis; sphincter
Lateral cricoarytenoid	Arch of cricoid cartilage	Front part of muscular process of arytenoid cartilage	Recurrent	Rotates muscular process forward and inward, thus approximating vocal folds
Thyroarytenoid	Posterior surface of thyroid cartilage, conus elasticus	Lateral edge and muscular process of arytenoid cartilage	Recurrent	Sphincter of superior part of larynx; adducts and shortens vocal folds; affects tension of folds
Cricothyroid	Lower border and outer surface of cricoid arch	Anterior section goes to thyroid cartilage lamina, posterior section to inferior cornu of thyroid cartilage	Superior laryngeal branch of vagus	Anterior section tilts front part of thyroid cartilage down, or in reverse elevates cricoid toward thyroid; tenses vocal folds; posterior section

462

NAME	ORIGIN	INSERTION	INNERVATION	ACTION
				pulls thyroid cartilage forward and elongates vocal folds; affects tension; muscle is an external adductor of arytenoids
Vocalis	Posterior aspects of thyroid cartilage angle; conus elasticus; medial but fused to thyroarytenoid; not attached to vocal ligament	Vocal process and lateral surface of arytenoid cartilage	Recurrent laryngeal	May shorten folds; modifies inner margin of folds and contour of glottis; changes vibrational mode of folds and determines the register
Thyroepiglottic	Inner surface of thyroid cartilage near its angle	Aryepiglottic fold and margin of epiglottis	Recurrent laryngeal	Depresses epiglottis; widens upper laryngeal opening; is part of upper sphincteric ring

MUSCLES OF THE LIPS AND OF FACIAL EXPRESSION

NAME	ORIGIN	INSERTION	INNERVATION	ACTION
Platysma	Skin and superficial fascia on chest and deltoid regions	Lower border of mandible; skin and muscles around the mouth	Facial	Draws corner of mouth downward and outward; very weak depressor of mandible
Orbicularis oris	Various muscles acting on the lips	Ends as fibers producing an oral sphincter; fibers proper to lips pass obliquely from skin to mucous membrane	Facial	Closes, narrows, protrudes lips; draws lower lip up or upper lip down
Quadratus labii superioris	Infraorbital margin and frontal process of maxilla, zygomatic bone	Ala nasi, skin of upper lip, orbicularis oris	Facial	Raises upper lip, corner of mouth and wing of nose; widens the nostrils
Zygomaticus	Temporal process of zygomatic bone	Orbicularis oris, skin of corner of mouth	Facial	Pulls corner of mouth upward and laterally; laughing
Caninus	Canine fossa of maxilla	Corner of mouth; skin and fascia of lower lip	Facial	Elevates corner of mouth; helps close mouth by elevating lower lip; sneering

NAME	ORIGIN	INSERTION	INNERVATION	ACTION
Risorius	Fascia over masseter muscle	Skin and mucosa of upper lip and a few fibers in the lower lip; corner of mouth	Facial	Retracts corner of mouth; grinning, threatening, sneering
Buccinator	Outer alveolar border of maxilla and mandible in molar region, pterygomandibular raphe	Corner of mouth, upper and lower lips, orbicularis oris	Facial	Pulls mouth angle laterally and posteriorly; narrows mouth opening and presses lips and cheeks against teeth; keeps cheeks taut
Quadratus labii inferioris	Outer anterolateral surface of mandible	Orbicularis oris, mucosa of lower lip, integument of chin	Facial	Draws lower lip downward and slightly lateralward; irony
Triangularis	Outer surface of mandible	Skin of mouth angle and of upper lip	Facial	Pulls mouth angle down; closes mouth; contempt
Mentalis	Incisive fossa of mandible	Orbicularis oris, integument of chin	Facial	Raises and wrinkles integument of chin; protrudes lower lip; doubt, disdain

464

MUSCLES CONTROLLING THE MANDIBLE

NAME	ORIGIN	INSERTION	INNERVATION	ACTION
Masseter	Zygomatic arch	Ramus or angle of mandible on lateral aspect	Mandibular division of trigeminal (masseteric nerve)	Elevates mandible and can retract or protrude it
Temporalis	Temporal fossa of skull	Coronoid process of mandible	Mandibular division of trigeminal	Elevates and retracts mandible
Internal (medial) pterygoid	Pterygoid fossa of sphenoid, lateral pterygoid plate	Inner surface of ramus of mandible	Mandibular division of trigeminal	Elevates and protrudes mandible; acting unilaterally, it pulls mandible to one side
External (lateral) pterygoid	Lateral pterygoid plate, greater wing of sphenoid	Condyloid process of mandible, area of temporomandibular joint	Mandibular division of trigeminal	Protrudes mandible and pulls it to one side; can depress mandible
Mylohyoid	Inner surface of body of mandible	Hyoid; most fibers end in median tendinous raphe	Mylohyoid branch of inferior alveolar nerve	Can depress mandible and retract it
Geniohyoid	Inferior mental spine of mandible	Hyoid (front of body)	Hypoglossal (includes branches from C-1 and perhaps C-2)	Can depress mandible and retract it; protrudes hyoid
Digastric, anterior belly	Digastric fossa of mandible	Intermediate tendon making connections with hyoid bone	Mylohyoid branch of inferior alveolar nerve	Can depress mandible and retract it; supports hyoid

MUSCLES OF THE MIDDLE EAR

NAME	ORIGIN	INSERTION	INNERVATION	ACTION
Tensor tympani	Upper edge of orifice of Eustachian tube (cartilaginous sector)	Handle of malleus	Tensor tympani branch of trigeminal; mandibular nerve	Brings handle of malleus inward and increases tension on tympanic membrane; heightens sensitivity; protective against excessive amplitude of vibrations
Stapedius	Posterior tympanic wall	Posterior surface of neck of stapes	Facial	Pulls stapes laterally; puts oval window under tension; protective

MUSCLES OF THE NECK

NAME	ORIGIN	INSERTION	INNERVATION	ACTION
Platysma	Subcutaneous tissues of pectoral region and neck	Mandible, skin of cheek, of chin, and corner of mouth	Facial	Depresses mouth angle, wrinkles cervical skin
Sternocleidomastoid	Manubrium, clavicle (medial third)	Mastoid, superior nuchal line of occipital bone	Spinal-accessory plus C-2 and C-3	With head fixed, it raises sternum, clavicle, and indirectly the ribs
Scalenus anterior	Transverse processes of cervical vertebrae 3–6	First rib	Lower cervicals	Elevates first rib if cervical spine is fixed
Scalenus medius	Transverse processes of lower 6 cervical vertebrae	First rib	Lower cervicals	Elevates first rib
Scalenus posterior	Transverse processes of lowest 2 or 3 cervical vertebrae	Second rib	Lower cervicals	Elevates second rib if cervical spine is fixed

MUSCLES OF THE PALATE

NAME	ORIGIN	INSERTION	INNERVATION	ACTION
Musculus uvulae	Posterior nasal spine, palatine aponeurosis	Mucous membrane of uvula	Spinal accessory nerve through pharyngeal plexus	Shortens uvula, bringing it upward and backward
Levator veli palatini	Petrous part of temporal bone and cartilage of auditory tube	Palatine aponeurosis and muscle of opposite side	Spinal accessory nerve through pharyngeal plexus	Lifts soft palate upward and backward, elevates and widens pharyngeal opening of Eustachian tube during swallowing

465

MUSCLES OF THE PALATE (Cont'd)

NAME	ORIGIN	INSERTION	INNERVATION	ACTION
Tensor veli palatini	Medial pterygoid lamina, inferior surface of sphenoid, cartilage of Eustachian tube	Posterior border of palatine bone and palatine aponeurosis	Internal pterygoid branch of mandibular division of trigeminal	Tenses anterior part of soft palate; assists levator in raising soft palate; opens auditory tube
Palatoglossus	Anterior aspect of velum (palatine aponeurosis)	Side and dorsum of tongue	Spinal accessory nerve through pharyngeal plexus	Draws glosso-palatine arch downward and medialward
Palatopharyngeus	Posterior border of bony palate and palatine aponeurosis	Posterior surface of thyroid cartilage and into side of pharynx and esophagus	Spinal accessory through pharyngeal plexus	Depresses soft palate and narrows posterior faucial port

MUSCLES OF THE PECTORAL REGION

NAME	ORIGIN	INSERTION	INNERVATION	ACTION
Pectoralis major	Medial half of clavicle; sternum, costal cartilages 2–7	Intertubercular sulcus of humerus	Medial and lateral anterior thoracic	Elevates ribs if shoulder girdle is fixed, but perhaps only during forced inspiration
Pectoralis minor	Ribs 3–5	Coracoid process of scapula	Medial and lateral anterior thoracic	Weakly elevates ribs if shoulder girdle is fixed, only during forced inspiration
Subclavius	First rib	Under surface of clavicle	Subclavius	Weakly elevates first rib if clavicle is fixed
Serratus anterior	Vertebral border of scapula	Upper 8–9 ribs	Long thoracic	Elevates ribs if shoulder girdle is fixed (also claimed not to be a muscle of respiration)

MUSCLES OF THE PHARYNX

NAME	ORIGIN	INSERTION	INNERVATION	ACTION
Superior pharyngeal constrictor	Pterygoid and hamular processes, pterygomandibular raphe, mylohyoid line of mandible, root of tongue	Posterior median raphe and in aponeurosis attached to pharyngeal tubercle on basilar part of occipital bone	Vagus through pharyngeal plexus	Constrictor of pharynx; active in swallowing
Middle pharyngeal constrictor	Hyoid cornua, stylohyoid ligament	Posterior median raphe	Vagus through pharyngeal plexus	Constrictor of pharynx; active in swallowing

MUSCLES OF THE PHARYNX (Cont'd)

NAME	ORIGIN	INSERTION	INNERVATION	ACTION
Inferior pharyngeal constrictor	Sides of cricoid and thyroid cartilages	Posterior median raphe	Vagus through pharyngeal plexus; other branches from external and recurrent laryngeal nerves	Constrictor of pharynx; active in swallowing
Stylopharyngeus	Styloid process of temporal bone	In constrictor musculature and in posterior surface of thyroid cartilage	Glossopharyngeal	Expands pharynx laterally; elevates pharynx and larynx
Palatopharyngeus	Posterior border of bony palate and palatine aponeurosis	Posterior surface of thyroid cartilage	Spinal accessory through pharyngeal plexus	Elevates larynx and pharynx; swallowing
Salpingopharyngeus	Auditory tube near its orifice	Posterior fasciculus of palatopharyngeus, walls of the pharynx	Spinal accessory through pharyngeal plexus	Elevates upper and lateral parts of pharynx; swallowing
Suprahyoid muscles*				Elevate pharynx; swallowing

* See description of muscles of larynx.

DEEP MUSCLES OF THE THORAX

467

NAME	ORIGIN	INSERTION	INNERVATION	ACTION
Diaphragm	Xiphoid, lower 6 ribs and costal cartilages, first few lumbar vertebrae	Central tendon	Phrenic	Expands thorax; compresses abdomen
External intercostals	Under surface of all ribs except last	Upper surface of next lower rib	Intercostal or thoracoabdominal nerves	Elevate ribs and enlarge all diameters of thorax
Internal intercostals	Under surface of all ribs except last	Upper surface of successively lower ribs	Intercostal or thoracoabdominal nerves	Elevate ribs (controversial); lower sections may be expiratory
Transversus thoracis (triangularis sterni or sternocostalis)	Body and xiphoid process of sternum	Costal cartilages 2–6	Intercostals 2–6	Depresses ribs (some claim action is uncertain)
Serratus posterior superior	Last cervical and upper 2 thoracic vertebrae, ligamentum nuchae	Ribs 1–4 or 2–5	Intercostals 1–4	Elevates upper ribs
Serratus posterior inferior	Last 2 thoracic and upper 2 lumbar vertebrae, supraspinal ligament	Ribs 9–12	Intercostals 9–12	Depresses lower 4 ribs and pulls them laterally in expiration

NAME	ORIGIN	INSERTION	INNERVATION	ACTION
Levatores costarum	Transverse processes seventh cervical and first 11 thoracic vertebrae	Next lower rib, usually, between tubercle and angle	Eighth cervical and first to eleventh thoracic nerves	Elevate ribs and rotate, extend, or laterally flex vertebral column
Subcostals	Inner surfaces of several ribs	Deep surfaces of ribs a few segments above their origin	Intercostal or thoracoabdominal nerves	Depress ribs when the last rib is fixed by the quadratus lumborum; controversially said to elevate ribs

MUSCLES OF THE TONGUE

NAME	ORIGIN	INSERTION	INNERVATION	ACTION
Superior longitudinal	Posterior origin from septum and submucosa	Skin along borders and tip of tongue	Hypoglossal	Shortens tongue, bulges it upward longitudinally, and retracts and curls tongue tip
Inferior longitudinal	Mucous membrane of root of tongue on inferior surface	Mucosa of inferior lingual surface, and some fibers to mucosa of dorsum of tongue; extends from root to apex	Hypoglossal	Shortens tongue from front to back and depresses the previously elevated tip, making the dorsum convex
Transverse (transversus linguae)	Lateral margins and dorsal septum	Areas near dorsal surface or tip of tongue; submucous fibrous tissue at sides of tongue	Hypoglossal	Narrows, protrudes, and may bulge tongue upward
Vertical (verticalis linguae)	Mucosa of dorsum. Occurs only at borders of anterior part of tongue	Mucosa of inferior surface	Hypoglossal	Flattens and broadens tongue
Genioglossus	Superior mental spine on inner aspect of mandibular symphysis	Lowest fibers go to tongue base and body of hyoid bone; most fibers to dorsum, from tip to base	Hypoglossal	Middle and lower sections protrude and elevate tongue; middle fibers depress median part of tongue; upper fibers bring tip back and down
Styloglossus	Styloid process of temporal bone, stylomandibular ligament	Tip and substance of tongue	Hypoglossal	Retracts and elevates tongue
Palatoglossus	Anterior part of velum	Side and dorsum of tongue	Spinal accessory through pharyngeal plexus	Draws tongue upward and backward

468

NAME	ORIGIN	INSERTION	INNERVATION	ACTION
Hyoglossus	Greater cornu and body of hyoid; travels almost vertically upward	Side of tongue between stylo-glossus and infe-rior longitudinal	Hypoglossal	Draws tongue downward and backward
Chondroglossus	Lesser cornu and body of hyoid bone	Intrinsic muscular fibers of tongue	Hypoglossal	Draws tongue downward and backward

469

GLOSSARY

abdominal aponeurosis The conjoined tendon of the oblique and transverse muscles on the abdomen.

abduct To draw away from the median line.

abscess A localized mass of pus walled off in a cavity produced by disintegrating and defensive cells.

abscissa The horizontal axis of a mathematical graph, as contrasted with the vertical axis, or ordinate.

acetylcholine The mediator of nerve impulses in parasympathetic nerves, in preganglionic sympathetics, and in cerebrospinal fibers.

acinus 1. A small lobule of a compound gland. 2. The air sac of the lung. 3. The glandular type may have a nar-row lumen in contrast to the free lumen of the alveolus.

acoustic Pertaining to sounds, especially their perception.

acoustic impedance The buffering effect of the air in the middle ear against sudden, large pressure changes or loud low-frequency sounds.

acoustic nerve The VIIIth cranial nerve, having a cochlear branch to the organ of Corti and a vestibular branch to the postural receptors in the vestibule and semicircular canals.

acoustic power The time rate of expenditure of acoustic energy; energy divided by time, expressed in watts.

acromegaly Chronic enlargement of the bones and soft parts of the hands, feet, and face due to excessive secretion of growth hormone of the anterior pituitary.

action current A transmitted electric current set up in active tissue, the active part being electronegative.

adduct To draw toward the median line.

adenoids The hypertrophied pharyngeal tonsil. Luschka's tonsil.

adiadochokinesia A failure in timing of muscle impulses to the appropriate muscles, so that activities such as pronation vs. supination or flexion vs. extension are interfered with.

adipose tissue A variety of connective tissue serving preferentially for the deposit of fat cells.

aditus laryngis The superior aperture of the larynx.

adrenalin A hormone secreted by the medulla of the adrenal gland, technically called epinephrine.

adrenergic Designating the sympathetic nerves which secrete a mixture of adrenalin and noradrenalin.

adrenogenital syndrome The condition in which the female shows excessive secondary sexual characteristics of the male because of hyperadrenal activity.

afferent Coming in, as opposed to efferent, or going out. May be sensory or nonsensory.

affricative A speech sound that begins with a stop and ends with a fricative. For example, /tʃ/ as in church begins like /t/ and ends like /ʃ/.

afterdischarge A series of repetitive responses from one afferent stimulus. May be due to central reverberating circuits.

aglossia Congenital absence of the tongue.

agnathia Congenital absence of the mandible.

agnosia Failure to recognize objects in general.

agonist A prime mover, opposed in action by another muscle called the antagonist.

agraphia Inability to express thoughts in writing, caused by a lesion in the central nervous system.

alexia Failure to comprehend the written word.

all-or-none Pertaining to the general property of nerves and muscles whose individual fibers react maximally or remain inactive.

alveolar 1. Pertaining to an alveolus, or tooth socket. 2. Referring to the air sac of the lung.

alveolus 1. The socket of a tooth. 2. The air sac of the lung. 3. The acinus of a gland.

ambilaterality Lack of marked dominance of either hand or other ordinarily unilateralized structure.

amphiarthrosis A somewhat movable joint in which the opposing structures are connected by disks of fibrocartilage. Ordinarily there is no joint cavity.

amplitude The distance from crest to trough in a given wave. The amount of contraction and expansion as represented by the deviation of the curve from the base line.

amygdala A lobule on the lower surface of each cerebellar hemisphere.

anacusis A profound hearing loss or ear nerve disorder which is not restorable to a reasonable level of hearing.

analytical capacity of the ear The capacity to differentiate all the distinct qualities or frequencies in a complex waveform.

anastomose To join with one another, as blood vessels do. Noun is anastomosis.

androgens Male sex hormones.

aneurysm A sac caused by the dilatation of the walls of a blood vessel and filled with blood.

angular gyrus An area near the junction of the occipital, parietal, and temporal lobes in which the brain synthesizes many diverse impulses into integrated concepts.

ankylosis Abnormal immobility and consolidation of a joint.

anlage The embryonic region in which evidence of a structure first appears.

anomaly A marked deviation from the normal.

anomia Inability to name objects or to recall or recognize names.

anoxia State without oxygen. The more usual state is hypoxia, or a given degree of oxygen lack.

ansa hypoglossi A U-shaped nerve loop on each side of the neck, formed by a branch of the hypoglossal nerve joining with branches from the first few cervical nerves.

antagonist See agonist.

anterior poliomyelitis Inflammation of the ventral horns of the gray matter of the spinal cord.

aperiodic waves Those which have components at all frequencies and not restricted to components at multiples of a fundamental frequency.

aphasia A defect in symbolization of objects. Defective expression in speech, writing, or signs. Failure to comprehend spoken or written language.

apnea Suspended respiration, usually from washing out of carbon dioxide from the blood.

aponeurosis A broad flat tendon investing muscles or connecting muscles with the structures they move.

areolar tissue A variety of connective tissue in which bundles of elastic and inelastic fibers produce an open meshwork in the ground substance.

articulation 1. A joint. 2. The enunciation of words and sentences.

articulators Valves to stop the exhaled air completely or to narrow the space for its passage.

aryepiglottic folds Bilateral folds of tissue that help form the upper open-ing of the larynx. They extend from the epiglottis to the arytenoids.

assimilation The effect of one speech sound upon another uttered in close sequence, such that the sounds become more like each other.

astasia Loss of steadiness. Motor incoordination with inability to stand.

asthenia Loss of muscle force. Asthenic is the adjective.

ataxia Irregularity of muscle action due to faulty timing and coordination of muscle agonists and antagonists. A drunken gait. Asynergia.

athetoid movements Aimless, slow, twisting movements and facial grimaces considered to be release phenomena and referable to basal ganglia disorders.

atonia Absence of tone or state of partial tension, referable chiefly to muscles.

atresia Absence or closure of a normal aperture.

atrophy A wasting away of a cell, tissue, or organ through a decrease in protoplasm. A diminution in size.

audiology The science of hearing, including structure, function, disorders, education, and treatment.

audiometer An instrument to measure auditory sensitivity within the audible range of frequency as a function of the intensity of sounds. An instrument incorporating an audiofrequency oscillator, an amplifier, and an intensity-controlling attenuator, connected in sequence to a telephone type of receiver held to the ear.

auditory perspective The recognition of the direction of sound.

auricle The external, visible part of the ear; pinna.

average speech power The totality of all speech sound energy emitted in a complete speech, divided by the total time for that activity. Expressed in microwatts.

axillary Pertaining to the armpit.

axon A process of a neuron that trans-

473

mits the impulse away from the neuron cell body.

bandwidth The operative range of frequencies within which a resonator will respond effectively.

basal ganglia Subcortical nuclei relaying impulses through the extrapyramidal tracts. The term includes the caudate, putamen, globus pallidus, and the amygdaloid nuclei.

basal metabolism The lowest energy expenditure in the waking state compatible with life. Preferably called standard metabolism.

basilar membrane A membrane of the inner ear which supports the organ of Corti.

beats Throbs, or pulsations, resulting from the summation and interference of sound waves.

bel The logarithm of the ratio of the energy of two sounds.

Betz cells Large pyramidal cells in one or more of the layers of the principal motor area of the gray matter of the cerebrum.

bifid Split into two parts.

bifurcate Divide into two parts.

bilabial A term describing consonants produced by the action of both lips.

B.N.A. Basle Nomina Anatomica A system of anatomic terminology adopted by an international convention in 1895 at Basle, Switzerland.

bolus A cohesive, sticky mass of food prepared for swallowing by the salivary glands and by the action of the tongue and palate.

bone The substance of most of the skeleton. It is connective tissue, whose substrate is ossein impregnated with calcium salts.

brachial Pertaining to the arm.

brainstem The midbrain, hindbrain, and medulla, not including the cerebellum.

branchial (visceral) arches Bars of cartilage on each side of the neck of the fetus which in evolution served as a framework for the blood vessels (aortic arches) and gill-breathing apparatus of water-living vertebrates.

branchial pouch A pocketlike finger thrust out bilaterally in the throat of the fetus from the entodermal lining of its digestive tract. In fishes these pouches meet inpushing ectodermal pockets from the body surface to produce gill slits between each skeletal gill arch.

breathiness The effect produced by the escape of unvocalized air so that the voice sounds as if a whisper were added to the tone.

breath stream The exhaled air released from the lungs and used to activate the vocal folds.

Broca's area Area 44 in the frontal lobe of the cerebrum in the left inferior frontal convolution. Originally said to control the formation of words.

Brodmann's area Discrete small regions generally in the neocortex of the cerebrum which are numbered.

bronchiole A fine division of the arborized bronchial tree. It has no serosal capsule, and the muscular layer is exposed.

bronchus One of the two sections into which the trachea divides.

buccal cavity The irregular space between the teeth and the cheeks. Distinct from the oral cavity, which is bounded externally by the teeth.

buccal whisper Sound produced by accumulation of air in the mouth and pharynx which is used instead of that ordinarily expelled from the lung passages.

bulbar Pertaining to the hindbrain, or medulla oblongata.

bulbar palsy A paralysis due to destruction of motor cells in the medulla oblongata. Poliomyelitis. Progressive bulbar paralysis.

474

canaliculus Any small canal or channel.

carious Pertaining to decay, or caries, of a bone or tooth.

carotid sinus A dilatation at the beginning of the internal carotid artery which is stimulated by changes in blood pressure.

cartilage The gristle or white elastic substance attached to articular bone surfaces and forming certain parts of the skeleton. A variety of connective tissue with cells arranged in groups and buried in cavities within a ground substance or matrix.

cathode-ray oscilloscope An instrument in which waves impinging on a sensor are translated to electrical oscillations; when amplified, the oscillations make a stream of electrons display a picture of such waves on a fluorescent screen.

caudal See cephalic.

celiac plexus A great, paired ganglionated neural mass just under the diaphragm which receives the vagus and splanchnic nerves and distributes these fibers to visceral structures.

cephalic Toward the head. Cranial. Often called anterior in animals. Superior in man. The opposite is caudal, inferior, or posterior in animals.

cerebellum A division of the brain in the dorsal rhombencephalon, behind the cerebrum and above the pons and fourth ventricle, functioning in the coordination of movements.

cerebral dominance The state in which one hemisphere takes the lead in controlling bodily processes.

cerebral palsy A special paralysis affecting control of the motor system, due to lesions in various parts of the brain. A result of birth injury or prenatal brain defects.

cerebral peduncle A white bundle forming the ventral part of the midbrain and passing from the upper margin of the pons to the optic tract; crus cerebri.

cerumen Ear wax from sebacious gland secretion.

chest pulses Rapid-breath pulse movements produced by costal muscles.

choanae The posterior pair of nasal openings, which lead into the pharynx. Singular is choana, or posterior naris.

cholinergic Designating parasympathetic nerves which secrete acetylcholine.

chondrification Transformation into cartilage.

chorea A convulsive nervous disease displaying involuntary and irregular jerky movements. An example is St. Vitus's dance.

choreiform movements Aimless and abruptly changing movements and facial grimaces possibly referable to disorder of the corpus striatum. A release phenomenon.

chondroblasts Cells producing cartilage.

chondrocyte A cartilage cell.

cilia Minute hairs on the free borders of cells which move in synchronism and propel materials in a given direction.

cinefluorography Moving pictures made by fluoroscopy.

cineradiography Making moving pictures by x-rays.

clavicular breathing Raising the clavicle and sternum excessively during inspiration.

cleft palate Congenital failure of fusion of primordia in the roof of the mouth and soft palate, at times extending through the premaxilla and upper lip.

clonus Spasm in which rigidity and relaxation alternate in rapid succession.

cluttering Rapid nervous speech characterized by dropping of sounds or syllables.

cochlear duct A portion of the membranous labyrinth, forming with the

475

semicircular ducts, saccule, and utricle a closed system filled with endolymph and containing on its floor the basilar membrane and the organ of Corti with its sensory auditory cells. The cochlear duct starts at its base as the ductus reuniens and ends distally as a blind pouch near the helicotrema.

cochlear microphonics A piezoelectric effect in the cochlea, where pressure vibrations in nonnervous as well as nervous structures can be converted into electrical impulses. These microphonics simulate the true action potentials generated in the hair cells and transmitted to the auditory cortex for hearing.

cogwheeling A state of altered inhibitory control over the stretch reflex such that a rigid limb does not produce resistance over the full range of a passive movement but responds as a series of catches and gives, sensed by the examiner as a jerkiness when he moves a muscle about a joint.

collagen A protein occurring in bones, cartilage, and white fibrous connective tissue.

collaterals Shunts or side branches.

colliculi The paired superior and inferior colliculi are nuclei in the dorsal midbrain which collectively constitute the corpora quadrigemina. The superior pair are lower visual centers, and the inferior pair are lower auditory centers.

colloidal Pertaining to basic particles, such as those of proteins, etc., whose size is between that of large particles (like sand) held in suspension and microscopic particles of molecular size. Because of relatively large particle size, colloidal solutions are cloudy.

commissure A fiber or fibrous tract connecting the right and left sides of the nervous system.

compression A state in which air particles are closer together than normal; condensation.

conditioned reflex Behavioral learning by associating an indifferent or unlearned stimulus with a stimulus which ordinarily evokes a given reaction.

conductive deafness Partial or total loss of hearing due to some abnormality in the bony chain of the middle ear.

condyle A rounded surface at the articular end of a bone.

congenital Existing at or before birth. Not necessarily hereditary.

connective tissue Supporting or uniting tissue of the body.

consonance A pleasant sensation which results when the frequencies of simultaneous tones in a musical chord have simple mathematical ratios to one another and their overtones are in mutual support.

consonant A voiced or voiceless speech sound that serves to link vowels together.

contralateral Relating to different sides. Opposite is ipsilateral.

conus elasticus The lateral section of the cricothyroid membrane, whose free border forms the vocal ligament, or platform for the construction of the vocal folds.

copula A median ventral swelling on the embryonic tongue formed by fusion of the paired hyoid branchial arches. The copula forms the root of the tongue.

corniculate cartilage One of a pair of cartilages in the larynx, situated like a grain of corn on top of each arytenoid cartilage.

cornified 1. Changed to tissue resembling horn. 2. Epithelium converted to a stratified squamous type.

corpus callosum A great white band of commissural fibers connecting the right and left cerebral hemispheres.

corpus striatum A subcortical mass of gray and white matter in front of the thalamus in each cerebral hemisphere.

corticofugal Directed outward or away from the cortex.

cretin An individual with congenital lack of thyroid secretion, associated with hyponormal physical and mental development.

cricoid cartilage A ringlike cartilage of the larynx, just below the thyroid cartilage and filling in the gap between the thyroid horns posteriorly.

cricopharyngeal sphincter A sphincter of the esophagus or an esophageal section of the inferior constrictor muscle. Also called the cricopharyngeus muscle or the pinchcock at the lower end of the pharynx.

crus The stalk or leg of any structure. Plural is crura.

crustomy Bilateral interruption of the pyramidal tracts in the crura of the midbrain.

cul-de-sac A blind pouch, or hollow diverticulum, of the main passage.

cuneiform cartilage An inconstant wedge-shaped cartilage in the lower posterior part of each aryepiglottic fold, perhaps giving some support to these folds.

cybernetics The study of regulatory mechanisms including governors, thermostats, feedback, and reverberating circuits.

cyst A normal or abnormal sac containing fluid or a semisolid.

cytogenetics The study of the structure and numerical characteristics of the chromosomes.

cytology The study of the fine structure of cells.

cytoplasm The protoplasm of a cell, excluding that within the nucleus.

damping A lessening of the incident energy. In damping of partials in resonating cavities, the energy of some of the tones is selectively absorbed by soft surfaces or neutralized by opposing movements in the same space.

decibel A quantitative unit of sound intensity bearing a logarithmic relationship to the amplitude of the sound. One-tenth of a bel.

deciduous Temporary. The first set of teeth.

decorticate Pertaining to animals with their cerebral cortex surgically removed.

decussate To cross over; used of muscle fibers, and of nerve fibers crossing from one side to the other of the central nervous system.

deglutition Swallowing.

dementia paralytica Chronic result of syphilis, showing progressive mental deterioration and generalized paralysis. General paresis.

demulcent An agent which protects and soothes a surface.

dendrite A short but extensively branched set of processes of a neuron. It receives impulses and sends them to the neuron cell body.

dentine The chief substance of a tooth. It surrounds the pulp and is covered by enamel on its exposed part, or crown.

desmocyte See fibroblast.

desquamation Sloughing off of tissue cells.

diaphragmatic breathing Protrusion of the anterior abdominal wall with each inspiration. Abdominal breathing, as contrasted with costal breathing seen more in the female and characterized by activity predominantly of the ribs.

diarthrosis A freely movable joint having a joint cavity.

dichotomize Split into two.

diffraction The modification of light or other radiation when it passes the edge of an opaque body or is sent through small apertures, resulting in dark and light bands, or an interference pattern.

digastric triangle A triangular space in the lateral aspect of the neck, bounded

477

above by the mandible, anteroinferiorly by the anterior belly of the digastric muscle, and posteroinferiorly by the posterior belly of the digastric muscle.

diphthong 1. Two contiguous vowel phonemes in the same syllable. 2. A vowel sound that ends so unlike its beginning that it requires two letters to represent it adequately.

diplophonia The production of double vocal sounds.

dissonance An inharmonious combination of musical sounds, in contrast with consonance.

diverticulum An offshoot of the main chambers or tube.

dominance, cerebral The implication that most or all neurally regulated functions will be governed by one hemisphere.

dura mater The outermost sheath of the three sheaths, or meninges, covering the brain and spinal cord.

dyne A unit of force. The force needed to produce an acceleration of 1 centimeter per second in a 1-gram mass.

dysacusis Hearing defect which is central in origin, including psychogenic types and the aphasias.

dysarthria Imperfect articulation in speech.

dyskinesia Impairment of the capacity for voluntary movement, resulting in abnormal movements.

dyslalia Disorders of articulation in which sounds are improperly produced, replaced by others, or entirely lacking.

dyslexia A variety of dysphasia characterized by inability to read. Alexia is a complete inability to read.

dysphemia Stammering or other speech disorder, perhaps due to psychoneurosis.

dysphonia plicae ventricularis The con-dition in which the false vocal folds phonate in place of the true folds.

dyspraxia A variety of dysphasia characterized by an inability to make directive movements, as in the use of tools or instruments. A complete failure is apraxia.

edema Excessive collection of tissue fluid in locations such as in the spaces around the cells, causing swelling or dropsy.

efferent Going out, as opposed to afferent, or coming in.

elastic tissue Connective tissue having a predominance of yellow elastic fibers.

electrical vocal tract A device to synthesize vowel sounds simulated to be natural.

electroencephalogram An electrical record of brain waves occurring normally and abnormally. Action currents are the source of the waves.

electromyography The testing of action potentials from muscles.

eleiden A substance similar to keratin, occurring in the cells of the stratum lucidum of the skin.

embryology The science of the genesis and development of the embryo.

emollient A softening or soothing agent.

encephalization The shifting in evolution of important functions to the cerebrum.

endocochlear potential A cochlear microphonic potential of about +80 millivolts found inside the scala media and produced by the stria vascularis in the wall of the scala media. It adds its voltage to the membrane potential of the hair cells to produce about 140 millivolts acting across the membranes of the hair cells. It is classed as a receptor potential because it arises from deformation changes in the hair cells, which in turn depolarize the auditory nerve endings. The endocochlear voltage is distinct from the summating potential that is related to discharge processes in the auditory nerve fibers.

endoplasmic reticulum Fine canal systems throughout the cytoplasm of cells, revealed by the electron microscope, and serving essentially for transportation.

energy The capacity for doing work, expressed in foot-pounds, ergs, joules, or other units in which work is expressed.

eosinophile A variety of white blood cell susceptible to staining with acid dyes; acidophile.

epiglottis The lidlike structure covering the entrance to the larynx.

epimysium The fibrous sheath of a muscle.

epithelium The covering of the skin and mucous membranes, consisting entirely of cells of various forms and arrangements.

erg A unit of work in the decimal system. The work done by a force of 1 dyne acting through a distance of 1 centimeter.

ergometer A device to measure mechanical output or work done.

esophageal speech Speaking by expelling air trapped in the esophagus through the adducted surfaces of the cricopharyngeal sphincter or pseudoglottis.

estrogens Female sex hormones derived from the follicles containing the ova, or eggs, within the ovary.

etiology Cause or origin of a disease.

eunuch A castrated male.

eunuchoid Having the major characteristics of a eunuch. Functionally but not organically a male castrate.

eupnea Quiet, normal breathing.

Eustachian tube The auditory tube, or channel, connecting the middle ear with the pharynx.

evaginate To grow outward. Opposed to invaginate, or to grow inward.

eversion A turning outward. Opposed to inversion, or a turning inward.

exteroceptor Sense organ, such as pressure and other receptors, located on the surface of the body.

extrapyramidal tracts A loose system of nerve fibers ultimately controlled by the premotor cortex working through the basal ganglia. Fibers not pyramidal which help regulate postural and mass movements of voluntary muscles.

extrinsic Refers to muscles originating outside of the structure upon which they act. An intrinsic muscle originates and inserts within the part.

exudate Waste products in solution to be excreted from the blood to the kidney, skin, etc. To be distinguished from a transudate, which is a fluid that normally crosses cell membranes for vital purposes.

facies The expression of the face.

falsetto An unnaturally or artificially high-pitched voice or register, especially in the adult male.

fascia Fibrous connective tissue covering the body just below the skin; also covering the muscles and certain organs.

fasciculus Mixed nerve tracts running together in the white matter. A cluster of muscle fibers.

fauces The opening between the mouth and the pharynx.

fenestration The Lempert operation, in which a new window is made into the internal ear to short-circuit the stapes.

fibrillar Containing threads, or fibrils.

fibroblast A connective tissue cell, forming fibrous tissues, tendons, aponeuroses, supporting, and binding tissues. Also called fibrocyte and desmocyte.

fibrocartilage An elastic cartilage whose matrix contains an abundance of white fibrous tissue.

fibrocyte See fibroblast.

fibrous membrane Fibrous connective

tissue that connects adjacent structures or forms capsules around organs.

fissure of Rolando A vertical cut in the brain, extending from the apex of each cerebral hemisphere down toward the horizontal fissure of Sylvius and dividing the principal motor area in front from the somesthetic area behind.

fissure of Sylvius A deep, rather horizontal cut which separates the anterior and middle lobes of the cerebrum.

fistula A deep ulcer which may lead into an internal hollow organ.

flaccidity A state of marked hypotonus of muscles.

fluoroscopy Examination of deep structures by x-rays, using a fluorescent screen covered with crystals of calcium tungstate.

formant For vowels and resonant consonants it implies a frequency region in which a relatively high degree of acoustic energy is concentrated. In a sound spectrogram it refers to the concentration of spectral energy in a frequency region.

formant frequencies Resonant frequencies.

fossa of Rosenmüller A deep pocket in the upper part of the nasopharynx on each side of the opening of the Eustachian tube.

frenum A fold of the integument or mucous membrane that limits the movements of a structure, e.g., the lingual frenum under the tongue. A small frenum is a frenulum.

frequency The number of waves passing a given point in a unit of time, usually 1 sec.

frequency of a vibrating string

$$F = \frac{1}{2L} \sqrt{\frac{T}{M}}$$

where L = length of string
M = mass per unit length of string
T = applied force or tension

fricative A noise produced by forcing air through an opening, as in /f/, /v/, /s/.

fundamental The lowest tone in a series of vibrations produced by a generator.

funiculus A column within the dorsal, lateral, or ventral regions of the white matter of the spinal cord.

galvanic current A direct current as contrasted with an alternating current.

gametogenesis Development of the sex cells to a sperm or an egg in the testis or ovary.

ganglion A collection of nerve cell bodies lying outside the brain or spinal cord. The dorsal root ganglion contains the cell bodies of afferent neurons.

general senses. Those senses from the general body, such as pain, heat, cold, touch, and proprioception. To be distinguished from the special senses of taste, smell, vision, and hearing.

gestalt A pattern involving relationships with a whole rather than isolated actions.

gingiva The gum. Plural is gingivae.

gingivitis Inflammation of the gums.

globus pallidus The interior, or the lenticular nucleus, of a basal ganglion called the corpus striatum.

glossal Pertaining to the tongue.

glossitis Inflammation of the tongue.

glottal click A plosive sound produced by impounding the breath stream below the closed vocal folds and then suddenly releasing the air.

glottal tone The laryngeal tone, originating from the vibratory activity of the vocal folds when energized by the subglottal breath stream.

glottis The variable space between the vocal folds.

glycogenolysis The breakdown of glycogen, or animal starch, into simpler products, the end product being the sugar glucose.

480

goiter Enlargement of the thyroid gland, visible as a swelling in the front of the neck.

gomphosis An articulation in which a conical process is received in a socket, as teeth in the maxillary bone.

gonadotropic hormones Chemicals which control puberty, lactation, growth of the sexual tract, and the secondary sexual characters.

gonads Testes or ovaries.

granuloma A tumor composed of granulation tissue, which is connective tissue involved in the healing of wounds.

gravid Pregnant.

gyrus A hill, or convolution, of the cerebral cortex, as opposed to sulcus, or depression.

hamulus Any hook-shaped process. The pterygoid hamulus is a paired process of the pterygoid bone.

hard palate The bony front part of the partition which separates the oral and nasal cavities.

harelip A congenital defect of the upper lip in which a cleft occurs because the structures forming the lip do not fuse.

harmonics In sound, the simplest mode of vibration, where the generator vibrates as a whole, is the first harmonic, and it produces the fundamental tone. Integral multiples of the first harmonic produce higher-frequency audible components called overtones. Thus the second harmonic evokes the sensation of the first overtone, and so on.

harmonics in vibrating air columns 1. Closed pipes: odd-numbered harmonics only. 2. Open pipes: all possible harmonics may be present.

Haversian canals Freely intercommunicating canals of the compact tissue of bone. They contain blood vessels and nerves.

helicotrema An opening in the basilar membrane at the apex of the cochlear canal allowing communication between the scala vestibuli and scala tympani.

hematoma A mass, or tumor, containing blood that has come out of its vessel.

hemiballismus Violent jerking and twitching movements on one side of the body.

hemilaryngectomy Surgical removal of one-half of the larynx.

hemiplegia Paralysis of one side of the body.

Heschl's convolution An auditory projection terminal in the superior temporal gyrus of the cerebral cortex.

hiatus A gap or fissure.

hippocampus A gyrus on the floor of the middle horn of the lateral ventricle, forming a considerable part of the olfactory region of the cerebral cortex.

hirsutism Excessive hairiness, especially in the female.

histology The science of the study of cells and tissues as seen under a microscope.

hoarseness A rough, harsh quality of the voice that is relatively low in pitch.

homeostasis The preservation of the steady state of the internal processes of an organism.

homologue The evolutionary descendant of a previous structure.

hormone A chemical messenger formed in a ductless gland and delivered through the blood stream to target organs.

humerus The bone of the arm.

hyaline Transparent or nearly so, as in the matrix of hyaline cartilage.

hyoid bone A U-shaped bone in the neck, acting as support for the tongue root above and as a suspension for the larynx below.

hypacusis A hearing loss that is innately restorable or correctible by prosthetic devices.

hyperkinesia Excessive movement.

hyperplasia An abnormal cell division

or cell multiplication in a given structure.

hypertrophy The pathologic enlargement of an organ or structure resulting from an increase in the size of its cells.

hyponasality See nasality.

hypophysectomy Surgical removal of the pituitary gland.

hypoplasia Faulty or incomplete development.

hypophysis cerebri The pituitary gland, which is an endocrine organ extending downward from the diencephalon of the brain.

hypothalamus An area of the diencephalon forming the floor and part of the lateral wall of the third ventricle. It includes the infundibulum, mammillary bodies, neurohypophysis, and tuber cinereum.

hypoxia See anoxia.

hysteria A psychoneurosis involving poor control of acts and emotions, anxiety, excessive self-consciousness and self-concern, and simulation of many diseases.

ideomotor area A cerebral area, usually unilateralized, anterior to the angular gyrus. It is a quick and automatic selector of words needed in an appropriate sequence for conversation.

impedance, vocal The quantitative resistance to the transmission of air, to the flow of an alternating current, or to other vibratory phenomena.

incisive foramen A funnel-shaped aperture centrally located in the hard palate just behind the incisor teeth. It opens into paired incisive canals, which transmit the descending palatine artery and the nasopalatine nerve.

incus The middle of the three ossicles of the middle ear, shaped like an anvil.

inertia A resistance to a change in the state or position in space of a body.

inflammation A reaction of tissues to injury, involving heat, pain, redness,

swelling, and variable loss of function.

inguinal Pertaining to the groin.

innervation The distribution of nerves to a structure.

integument Outer surface of the body; skin in man.

intensity The time rate of energy flow per unit of intercepted area, expressed in watts per square centimeter.

internal capsule An area bounded by elements of the corpus striatum and carrying tracts to and from the brain.

internuncial neuron An associative or connecting neuron between afferent and efferent neurons. A type II Golgi cell restricted to the gray matter of the brain or cord.

interstitial Situated in the interspaces of a tissue; between the cells.

intrapulmonic pressure The pressure in the lungs and air passages; pulmonary pressure.

intrathoracic pressure The pressure in the thorax outside of the pulmonary spaces; intrapleural pressure.

invaginate To grow inward. Opposed to evaginate, to grow outward.

inversion A turning inward. Opposed to eversion, a turning outward.

involute To regress.

ipsilateral Relating to the same side; opposite is contralateral.

irritability The capacity of protoplasm to react to a stimulus.

karyosome A discrete mass of chromatin in the nucleus of cells.

keratinization Making a tissue horny by deposition of a protein called keratin.

kinetic energy The energy of motion, as in the dynamic movement of muscles.

labial Pertaining to the lips. Noun is labium, plural is labia. In phonetics it implies involvement of lip articulation, as /p/, /v/, /m/.

labiodental Pertaining to the lips and

teeth. The lower lip touches the upper front teeth, as in /f/ or /v/.

lacrimal Pertaining to the tears and the system for lubricating the eyeball surface.

lacuna A hollow, depression, or lake. A blood-filled space.

lamella A thin plate, as of bone.

lamina A flat plate, as one of the two plates forming the anterolateral structure of the thyroid cartilage.

language Communication by voice in a uniquely human manner, using arbitrary auditory signals in conventional ways with conventional meanings.

laryngitis Acute or chronic inflammation of the larynx, with dryness and soreness of the throat, hoarseness, cough, and painful swallowing.

laryngitis sicca Chronic inflammation of the larynx, with dryness of the mucosa.

laryngocele An abnormal air sac connecting with the laryngeal cavity. It produces a tumorlike mass seen externally on the neck.

laryngoperiscope A self-illuminating laryngoscopic mirror.

laryngoscope An instrument for visual examination of the larynx.

larynx The voicebox, or musculocartilaginous organ with a mucous lining extending from below the hyoid bone to the top of the trachea.

lemniscus A fiber tract within the central nervous system. The lateral lemniscus carries up auditory impulses. The medial lemniscus transmits pressure, pain, heat, cold, taste, temperature, and other impulses.

lingual Pertaining to the tongue.

lisping A disorder of the sibilant (hissing or whistling) consonants. /s/ and /z/ are particularly affected, and /θ/ is substituted.

lobotomy Disconnection of lobes of the cerebral cortex from the remainder of the brain. Frontal and temporal lobotomies are examples. Surgical excision of a lobe is lobectomy.

localization, cerebral Association of specific bodily functions with definite areas of the cerebral cortex.

longitudinal wave A vibratory disturbance involving the transmission of a pulse of compression (condensation) and expansion (rarefaction), moving away from the center of the disturbance. Example is a sound wave, in which there is transmission of a disturbance through a medium such as air without permanent displacement of the molecules of air. The particles vibrate to and fro in the direction of the wave movement.

loudness An intensity dimension of hearing dependent upon the amplitude of the incident sound waves and also upon the number and the frequency of nerve impulses.

lower motor neuron The anterior horn cells of the brain and spinal cord and the axonal nerve fibers to the effectors.

lumbodorsal fascia A combined lumbar and dorsal aponeurotic fascia in the middle of the back, for attachment of several posterior muscles.

lumen Cavity or space. Plural is lumina.

lymph A colorless fluid derived from the blood, acting chiefly to drain wastes from the tissue cells and bring such wastes back to the blood.

lymphadenitis Inflammatory reaction in lymph glands.

lymph nodes Glands or filtering stations for microorganisms, placed at strategic areas along the lymphatic vessels. They produce lymphocytes.

lymphopenia Reduction in the count of the white blood cells called lymphocytes.

macrostomia Excessively large and wide mouth caused by incomplete fusion of the mandibular and maxillary processes. Contrasted with microstomia, or tiny mouth, and astomia, or no mouth.

male climacteric Cessation of sexual activity and regression of secondary sexual characters in the male.

malleus The most lateral, hammer-shaped ossicle of the middle ear, attached laterally to the tympanic membrane and medially by a club-shaped head to the incus.

malocclusion A failure of the maxillary and mandibular teeth to meet such that the upper incisors overlap the lowers, the canines meet point to point, and the molars meet cusp to pit.

mandible The lower jaw.

mechanoreceptors Receptors responding to pressure, stretch, and mechanical forces.

Meckel's cartilage The first visceral arch of the embryo, which forms the primitive cartilaginous mandible; also called mandibular cartilage. It gradually becomes encased within outer and inner dermal bones, which then bear the teeth and form the definitive mandible. The first visceral arch in evolution served as a bearer of gills for aquatic respiration.

medial longitudinal fasciculus An extension into the brainstem of the anterior and lateral ground bundles on each side of the spinal cord.

mediastinum The central area of the thorax between the lungs and their pleural investments.

medulla The central part of an organ as contrasted with the external region. Also the medulla oblongata, or hindbrain.

mel A unit of pitch scale used in constructing a scale for the subjective sensory experience of pitch; 1,000 mels is the pitch of a 1,000-Hz tone sounded at 40 dB above threshold for normal listeners. The pitch function in mels varies as a power function of

sound frequency except at the low-frequency end of the audible range.

Ménière's disease Deafness, dizziness, and ringing in the ears associated with nonsuppurative disease of the otic labyrinth.

meningitis Inflammation of the meninges, or coverings, of the brain and cord.

mesenchyme The connective tissue of the embryo. A derivative of a germ layer called the mesoderm functioning particularly to produce connective tissues, blood vessels, and lymph vessels.

metabolism The sum total of the energy exchanges occurring in the body at a given time.

mimetic Pertaining to simulation. Also applies to muscles of expression.

mitochondria Organelles in the cytoplasm of cells functioning as powerhouses to deliver energy released by oxidative processes.

modality A separate sense, such as hearing or vision. Experiences in a given modality can be arranged in a continuum.

modiolus The central pillar, or columella, within the cochlea.

modulate To alter the voice adaptively during speech; to vary the tone volume.

monaural Designating one ear, as contrasted with binaural, or both ears.

mucoperiosteum Periosteum with a mucous surface.

mucopurulent Containing both mucus and pus.

mucous Resembling mucus, which is a viscid secretion that covers mucous membranes.

mucous membrane Epithelium upon a basement membrane with a subcutaneous tissue. It lines canals and cavities, such as the Eustachian tube and alimentary canal, which communicate with the external environment.

music A sensation resulting from a pleasing succession or combination of different tones, and the arrangement of such tones to form a structure of acceptable melody, harmony, and rhythm.

mutation In speech, a change in the character and quality of the voice, ascribable to the biologic processes of puberty.

myelencephalon The most caudal division of the embryonic brain. That part of the rhombencephalon which gives rise to the medulla oblongata.

myelin The inner fatty covering of a typical neuron; medullary sheath.

myoneural junction A specialized area or motor end plate between a nerve and a muscle.

myotactic Pertaining to the proprioceptive sense of muscles.

myotatic Produced or induced by stretching or extending a muscle.

myotome An embryonic muscle block.

myxedema An abnormal hypothyroid condition in an adult, characterized by retardation of vital processes.

nasality A speech defect of varying degrees in which the nasal chambers are used as resonators and as channels to emit sounds that should not ordinarily have such nasal emphasis. In the negative condition, or hyponasality, there is interference with flow through the nasal passages or failure to make the adjustments necessary to produce the nasal sound.

nasal resonance The normal resonance added by the nasal passages to the tone.

natural period The inherent power of a vibrating body to go into free oscillation with regard to frequency.

neoplastic Pertaining to a new and abnormal growth, such as a tumor.

nerve impulse The disturbance propagated along a nerve fiber, probably electrochemical in nature.

neuralgia Pain expressed along the course of one or several nerves.

neuritis Inflammation of a nerve.

neuroblasts Embryonic cells which produce neurons.

neurogenic Seated in the nervous system.

neuron A nerve cell. The basic unit of structure and function of the nervous system.

nodes The point of minimum displacement (ideally zero) of an oscillating mass. The region of maximum amplitude of displacement is the antinode. Seen typically in the stationary wave pattern of a vibrating string.

noise A complex sound having many frequencies not in mutual harmonious relation. A white noise contains all frequencies in the sound spectrum.

nucleotides An end product of the splitting of nucleic acid by nuclease.

nucleus of the tractus solitarius An ending nucleus of the facial, glossopharyngeal, and vagus nerves. The nucleus extends the whole length of the medulla on each side. The nucleus is especially concerned with taste.

obturator A plate which closes an opening.

occiput Back of the head. Occipital region. The basiocciput is the basal section of the occipital bone.

occlusal Pertaining to closure with reference to the chewing surfaces of molar and bicuspid teeth.

octave The interval between two notes whose frequency ratio is 1 to 2.

odontoblast A connective tissue cell which produces the outer surface of the dental pulp contiguous to the dentine.

olfaction Smell.

ontogenetic Embryologic.

optimum pitch The general level of pitch in an individual at which he can best emit rich, full, and resonant tones.

ordinate The vertical axis of a mathematical graph, as contrasted with the horizontal axis, or abscissa.

organelles Vital bodies in the cytoplasm of cells that are actively engaged in some specialized activity of the cell. Distinct from inclusions, which are end products of cell metabolism or distribution.

organ of Corti The end organ of hearing situated on the basilar membrane in the internal ear and containing the hair cells that respond to sound waves in a crudely analytic manner.

orthodontic Pertaining to the prevention and correction of irregular teeth and malocclusions.

ossicles The chain of three bones (malleus, incus, and stapes) in the middle ear, stretching as a compound lever from the eardrum to the oval window.

ossification Conversion into bone or a bony substance.

osteoid Resembling bone.

osteology The study of the bones.

otitis media Inflammation of the middle ear.

otosclerosis Appearance of spongy bone in the capsule of the auditory labyrinth.

ovariectomy Surgical removal of the ovaries.

overtone A multiple of the fundamental, which is the lowest frequency tone for a vibrating structure.

palate The roof of the mouth, or partition that mostly separates the oral and nasal cavities. The term includes the anterior bony hard palate and the posterior fleshy soft palate.

palatal arches The right and left dependent fleshy sections of the soft palate, each containing the glossopalatal muscle in front, the palatopharyngeal muscle behind, and an intervening palatine tonsil.

palatography Making graphic records of the movements of the palate in the process of speaking.

palatopharyngeal sphincter The levator veli palatini and superior pharyngeal constrictor muscles, acting to narrow the passage between the nose and pharynx.

palliate To relieve symptoms.

palpate To obtain knowledge of a structure from touch and pressure.

papilla A pimple, or nipple-shaped elevation. Plural is papillae.

parameters Dimensions. Arbitrary constants whose values characterize the quantitative expressions into which they enter. Pitch and volume are parameters of sound.

paranasal sinuses Cavities in the interior of skull bones, all of which drain into the nose.

parasympathetics The cranial or sacral part of an involuntary or autonomic nervous system, the other part of which is sympathetic or thoracolumbar.

parathyroid gland Any one of four small glands, one on the lateral and one on the mesial aspect of each thyroid lobe.

Parkinson's disease Paralysis agitans. A disorder of the basal ganglia in which release phenomena occur, such as tremors, postural inadequacies, and hypertonicity of muscles.

partial A fundamental and its overtones. A segmental vibration. In a fundamental of 100 Hz and an overtone of 200 Hz, the fundamental is the first partial, and 200 is the second partial (or first overtone).

Passavant's cushion The highest part of the superior constrictor muscle of the posterior pharyngeal wall. The pterygopharyngeal muscle fusing posteriorly with superior constrictor muscle fibers.

past pointing The inability to bring a

486

finger to a predesignated mark unless the eyes are kept open.

patent Open.

PB words A phonetically balanced list of words used in articulation tests. Two-syllable words, with equal stress on both syllables (spondee words) are spoken, and the response of the listener in terms of the correct percentage of words recognized is taken as a measure of speech intelligibility.

pendulous Loosely hanging.

perception A consciousness that is the result of a complex pattern of stimulation plus the effect of experience and attitudes. This is in contrast to a sensation, which is very dependent upon specific sense-organ stimulation.

perichondritis Inflammation of the perichondrium.

perichondrium The white fibrous tissue sheath covering the surface of cartilage.

perimysium A delicate sheath of connective tissue surrounding a muscle and sending fibrous septa into the muscle to divide it into bundles called fasciculi.

period The period of a vibration is the time taken to complete one cycle of the vibration. It is the reciprocal of the frequency.

periosteum The fibrous membrane that ensheaths a bone.

phagocyte A scavenging cell that ingests other cells or microorganisms. Macrophage; polymorphonuclear leucocyte.

phagocytosis The ingestion of microorganisms or other particles by specialized active cells called phagocytes.

pharyngitis Inflammation of the mucous membrane and deeper tissue of the pharynx.

pharyngomaxillary fossa A space forming each lateral boundary of the retropharyngeal space.

pharyngostome Window into the pharynx.

pharynx The throat, or pouchlike structure, between the base of the skull and the sixth cervical vertebra. It is a common digestive and respiratory passageway.

phase A given stage in a cycle. For example, in a 60-Hz alternating current, each phase is 1/120 sec.

phasic activities Voluntary isolated movements of skeletal muscle.

phon A unit of subjective loudness based on the observer's own value judgment. Phon and decibel values differ sharply except at a reference 1,000-Hz point, where they are identical.

phonation The utterance of vocal sounds, resulting from vibrating activity of the vocal folds.

phoneme A family of speech sounds.

phonetics The study of speech sounds.

phrenicectomy Surgical division of the phrenic nerve. Phrenectomy.

phylogenetic Pertaining to phylogeny, the evolution, or ancestral history, of a race or group.

physiologic breathing Respiration for gas exchange without reference to speech. Biologic breathing.

piezoelectricity Electricity produced by mechanical pressure. It occurs in crystals which are compressed along certain axes. The mechanical stress generates an electromotive force, by transduction of one form of energy into another.

pineal gland A cone-shaped body in the epithalamus (roof of the diencephalon), nonneural in structure and thought to be an endocrine gland.

pinna The external, visible part of the ear; auricle.

pitch A qualitative dimension of hearing related to the highness or lowness of tones and correlated with the fre-

487

quency of the sound waves making up the stimulus. Higher frequencies yield higher pitches.

place-theory In hearing, pitch is associated with a place on the basilar membrane where maximal activation occurs.

placode A plate of ectoderm which, in the embryo, indicates the anlage of an organ.

pleural cavity A potential space in the double-walled sac surrounding and enclosing each lung.

plexus A network of nerves or of veins.

plosive A sound involving oral closure followed by abrupt opening through air pressure with the posterior nasal and other openings obstructed. A stop.

pneumograph An instrument to visualize respiratory movements on a kymographic drum or other recording device.

polyp A smooth growth from a hypertrophied mucous surface. It is attached by a stalk.

pons A bridge in the ventral hindbrain connecting the cerebrum, cerebellum, and medulla.

postcentral convolution A region in the parietal cerebral cortex posterior to the fissure of Rolando and encompassing the somesthetic area.

precentral convolution A region of the cerebral cortex anterior to the vertical fissure of Rolando and above the horizontal fissure of Sylvius, encompassing the principal motor area.

preganglionics Neurons that connect the autonomic system with the brain or spinal cord. The postganglionics leave the primary autonomic ganglion and travel toward the visceral effector.

prevertebral fascia The anterior part of the great vertebral fascia, which encloses the vertebral column and its muscle masses.

primordia Original structures; anlages.

procerus The pyramidalis muscle.

progesterone Female sex hormone derived from the corpora lutea in the ovary.

prognathic Marked projection of the lower jaw.

prognosis The probable course and outcome of a disease.

projection area A region on the cerebral cortex where a function is localized.

propositional speech The communication of meanings, as contrasted with the expression of feelings.

proprioceptor Sense organ for detecting the position and spatial relations of a muscle, located in the muscles or tendons.

prosencephalon The most anterior of the three primary embryonic vesicles of the brain. The developing forebrain. This area divides to a cranial section called the telencephalon and a section just caudal called the diencephalon.

prosthetic Pertaining to artificial organs, parts, and devices.

prosthodontist Prosthetic dentist, who makes appliances and substitutes for oral structures.

protoplasm The material of the body cells which displays the properties of life.

protract To push forward, as contrasted with retract, or pull backward.

pseudovoice Voice produced in an unusual manner, as by discrete spurts of air released through the upper esophagus.

pseudostratified epithelium Epithelium which appears to consist of two or more layers but does not. It enters into the lining of the upper respiratory tract where it has goblet cells and cilia to catch and remove dust.

pterygoid processes Paired medial and lateral winglike processes of the sphenoid bone, which project down from the bone like a pair of legs. Between the lateral and medial processes is the pterygoid fossa.

pterygomandibular raphe A tendinous structure between the buccinator and superior pharyngeal constrictor muscles. It gives origin to the middle part of both muscles. The pterygomandibular ligament.

pterygopalatine A space deeply located in the facial bones just below the apex of the eye socket.

pterygoquadrate A derivative of the first visceral (branchial) arch of the embryo. This is the primordium of the upper jaw. The cartilage becomes encased by investing bones (palatines and pterygoids). The quadrate portion of the cartilage migrates to the middle ear to become the incus bone. As the palatines and pterygoids eventually migrate to new positions and functions, the premaxillaries and maxillaries, each bearing teeth, are added to the outside of the original upper jaw and take over the functions of the pterygoquadrate. In man, the premaxillaries disappear by fusion with the maxillaries.

puberty The period of reproductive and associated mental and physical maturation in either sex.

putamen The outer part of the lenticular nucleus of a basal ganglion called the corpus striatum.

pyramidal tract The corticobulbar and corticospinal fibers passing from the motor cerebrum to the nuclei of cranial and spinal nerves. The upper motor neuron which regulates voluntary motion.

pyriform sinus A depression on each side of the larynx external to the aryepiglottic folds.

ramus A branch of a vessel or nerve. Also a section of a bone. Plural is rami.

raphe A line of union between the members of a bilaterally symmetrical structure.

rarefaction The separation of air particles by more than the usual distance.

rectus sheath The sheath encasing the rectus abdominis muscle, produced by the splitting of the tendon of the internal oblique muscle of the abdomen.

reflex A fundamentally involuntary response to an afferent stimulus.

reflection of waves The sending back of sound or other waves, either in a diffuse or in a regular direction.

refraction The bending of sound (or light) waves in passing into a medium of altered density.

refractory period The time of depressed irritability during the activity of a protoplasmic structure.

register, vocal An arbitrary division of the range of pitch in music, such as head and chest registers.

reinforcement Increase in the intensity of the incident vibrations. It occurs for laryngeal vibrations when supraglottic air vibrates in tune with one or more partials of the incident wave.

Reissner's membrane The vestibular membrane of the cochlea which separates the scala vestibuli from the scala media. Its functions are speculative.

Renshaw cells Nuclei located in the medial part of the ventral horns of the gray matter of the spinal cord. They send axons to neighboring motor neurons and inhibit their activity, thus providing for purposeful limitation and localization of activity in other discrete motor neurons.

resonance 1. The vibrant sound of ordinary speech as contrasted with dull or flat sound. 2. Selective support of certain desired partials in the complex sound wave. 3. Sympathetic vibration of bodies coupled sufficiently close together in space.

resonant nodes The places on the basi-

489

lar membrane excited by the sound waves.

resonator An instrument that intensifies sounds.

reticular activating system A group of neural cells regulating sleep and wakefulness. It directs attention to the events of the environment. The system extends from the lower brainstem up through the midbrain and thalamus and terminates by diverse pathways in all parts of the cerebral cortex.

reticular formation A collection of neurons diffusely spread throughout the medulla, pons, midbrain, and into parts of the diencephalon. It is continuous below with the internuncial cells of the spinal cord. It is for the most part excitatory and concerned in maintaining the body posture against gravitational forces.

reticuloendothelial system Cells in different organs showing a common phagocytic behavior toward dyes.

retrograde Directed backward or in a course contrary to the usual direction.

retropharyngeal space The region behind the pharynx which is subdivided to four potential spaces: peripharyngeal, parapharyngeal, postvisceral, and prevertebral. The space is also called the retropharyngeal fascial cleft.

reverberation Multiple echoes produced when the source of sound is located between two parallel sound-reflecting surfaces. The roll of thunder occurs by repeated reflections of the original burst between the earth and the clouds or between neighboring clouds.

rhinencephalon The smell brain, or discrete cell bodies on the cerebral cortex. The archipallium. Distinguished from the nonolfactory neocortex.

rhinitis A symptom complex in which nasal secretions are increased and the nasal mucosa is swollen.

rhinolalia aperta Excessive nasality of

voice through undue patency of the posterior nares.

rhinolalia clausa A nasal quality of the voice from excessive closure of the nasal passages.

ribonucleic acid RNA in small amounts is associated with the chromosomes and is the prime nucleic acid of the nucleolus. RNA is characteristic of the cytoplasm and transmits to it information coded in the nucleus by DNA. The formation of RNA is the principal function of the nucleus in the resting cell. There are three types of RNA: ribosomal, messenger, and transport.

ribosomes Particles in the cell cytoplasm that line the canal system called endoplasmic reticulum. RNA is the main constituent of these particles. The ribosome is the locale of protein synthesis.

rima glottidis The glottis, or variable space between the vocal folds.

Rinne test The duration of bone conduction is compared with that of air conduction for each ear, using a tuning fork.

roentgenography The study of x-rays.

rostrum A beak, such as the beak of the sphenoid bone. Rostral may indicate the cranial as opposed to the caudal end.

sacculus An upward, hollow projection from the roof of the ventricle of Morgagni.

sagittal A median longitudinal plane through the body dividing it into right and left halves.

sarcolemma A thin elastic sheath encasing every voluntary muscle fiber.

sarcomere The sarcostyles, or bundles of fibrils of striated muscle, are made up of segments, the sarcomeres. Each of these is separated from the next by an impermeable Krause's membrane, the Z disk. Krause's membranes of contiguous sarcostyles are joined together and finally insert in the sarco-lemma. The sarcomere gives a fiber its cross-striated appearance.

sarcoplasm Muscle protoplasm.

Schwabach test The shank of a vibrating tuning fork is placed on the patient's mastoid until no longer heard, then placed on the examiner's mastoid. The results are recorded in plus or minus seconds.

sebaceous glands Glands which secrete an oily lubricating fluid called sebum.

secondary palate The final palatal structures which complete the floor of the nasal cavity and the roof of the mouth.

secretion A substance put out by any gland and serving a useful purpose, as distinguished from an excretion.

selective permeability The quality of a cell membrane which allows only certain substances to cross in or out of it.

semivowel A vowellike sound, low in phonetic carrying power, produced by the articulatory organs moving to change the dimensions of the emitting orifice and to change the resonance of the sound. Sounds which, while vowellike, act as consonants do to initiate, join, and terminate vowels. Examples are /r/, /l/, /w/.

sensation A change in awareness or consciousness resulting from a discrete sensory stimulation.

sepsis Infection.

sequelae Results of an action or disease.

seromucinous Partly serous and partly mucous. Also called seromucous.

serosa Any serous membrane.

serous Resembling serum in physical consistency. Watery.

serous membrane Connective tissue lining any of the major splanchnic or lymph cavities. Peritoneum, pleura, pericardium.

sigmatism Incorrect, difficult, or excessive use of the /s/ or /z/ sounds.

sine wave A wave showing a positive displacement, or upper loop, above an undisturbed or reference position and a negative displacement below the reference position. In sound, positive displacements occur during condensations and negative displacements during rarefactions. The maximum displacement is the amplitude and the number of complete condensation-rarefaction patterns, or cycles per second, is the frequency of the wave. See sinusoidal.

singer's nodules Fibrous nodes between the anterior third and middle of the vocal folds. Screamer's nodes.

sinus A cavity, recess, or hollow space. It may contain air or fluid.

sinusitis Inflammation of a sinus.

sinusoidal The waveform of a pure tone, as emitted by a tuning fork or pure-tone audiometer.

soft palate The mobile and muscular posterior sections of the partition between the nasal and oral cavities and between the mouth and pharynx.

somatic Pertaining to the body. Also implies voluntary as contrasted with autonomic.

somesthetic area Discrete areas on the parietal cerebral cortex including areas 3, 1, 2, 5, and 7 for three-dimensional reasoning about projected sensations, such as pain, hot, cold, and muscle sensation.

sonant 1. Voiced or having sound. 2. A sound which in itself makes a syllable or subordinates to itself the other sounds in the syllable.

sone A unit of loudness.

sonorous Loud; having phonetic power or volume.

sound 1. An auditory sensation which ceases when the ear is withdrawn from the scene. 2. The energy reaching the ear from outside, continuing to be propagated even if no ear is present to detect it, or though present, cannot detect it.

sound quality The unique pattern of speech sound, based physically on waveform and mode of vibration and making recognition of the speaker or instrumental generator possible. A function of the blend of various overtones.

sound spectrograph A machine to obtain visible records of the frequency, intensity, and time of samples of speech.

sound waveform The character of the sound vibrations, determined by the number and relative intensities of the various harmonics present.

spasticity A state of marked hypertonus of muscles.

spatial summation Two subthreshold stimuli applied simultaneously to two different locations on the body may elicit a reflex response. There is an irradiation and overflow of impulses providing for reinforcement.

spectrogram A "voice print" containing information about the frequency components of speech and the patterns of voice energy.

speculum An instrument for bringing into view a bodily passage or chamber.

speech Oral communication. Expression of human thought and emotions by speech sounds and gesture. A meaningful utterance.

speech defect A significant deviation from an assumed normal speech pattern, or a deviation which significantly interferes with communication.

speech deviation Any demarcation from an assumed normal speech pattern.

speech stretcher A device to play back speech sounds at a changed utterance rate without changing the original pitch.

sphenopalatine foramen A space between the orbital and sphenoid processes of the palatine bone. It goes from the pterygopalatine fossa into the superior meatus of the nose and carries sphenopalatine vessels, nasopalatine nerves, and superior nasal nerves.

sphincter A muscle arranged around an opening to constrict or dilate the passageway. May be smooth or skeletal muscle.

spinal accessory nerve The XIth cranial nerve, running from the hindbrain and spinal cord to the pharynx and larynx.

spirometer An instrument to measure the volumes of air respired under many conditions. The data are in the science of spirometry.

splanchnic Pertaining to the abdominal viscera.

spondee Two equally accented syllables.

stapes The stirrup-shaped innermost ossicle of the middle ear, joined at its head with the incus and inserting at its base into the oval window.

stapes mobilization A method to treat otosclerosis by exposing the lenticulocapitular joint and applying instruments on parts of the stapes. The method preserves and uses the middle ear bones and does not change the structure of the external or middle ear.

stenosis Narrowing of a duct or canal.

stereognosis Three-dimensional reasoning about an object by means of touch, pressure, and muscle sensibility. Opposed to astereognosis or agnosia.

stimulus Any change in the internal or external environment which can elicit a response or protoplasmic change.

stomodeum The embryonic anlage of the mouth. The ectodermal portion that invaginates.

stratified squamous epithelium This lining has several layers to withstand wear and tear, but the depth of cells prevents them from functioning in absorption and secretion. Flat cells.

stretch reflex Myotactic or proprioceptive reflex. The feedback of information from muscle receptors concerning

492

the tensions of these muscles and the adaptive change in the tone of the same muscles.

stridency A harshness for tones of high pitch. Any creaking sound.

stridor A harsh and high-pitched respiratory sound often heard in an acute laryngeal obstruction.

stroboscope An instrument which furnishes an intermittent light of adjustable pulse frequency, which can be used to illuminate the vibrating vocal folds, "slowing down" their movements so that the successive phases of the movements can be followed.

stuttering Repetitious speech, as compared with stammering, or hesitant speech.

styloid process A downward projecting spur from the temporal bone serving for the origin of muscles and ligaments

substantia nigra A region of gray matter dorsal to the basis pedunculi (cerebral peduncles containing descending fibrous tracts).

subthalamus The ventral thalamus. A lower portion of the diencephalon lying between the thalamus and the tegmentum (covering) of the mesencephalon.

sulcus A depression of the cerebral cortex, as opposed to gyrus, or hill.

superciliary Pertaining to the region of the eyebrow. The arch is the visible prominence.

supersonics High-frequency sound waves above 20,000 Hz.

suppressor areas Regions of the brain that can inhibit motor activity.

suppurative Producing pus.

surd A voiceless consonant. Opposite to sonant.

surfactant A lipoprotein secreted by the alveolar epithelium into the alveoli and respiratory passages. It acts as a detergent, decreasing the surface tension of fluids and permitting adequate lung expansion. Lack of surfactant in infants induces hyaline membrane disease involving inadequate breathing.

suture The line of union of adjacent cranial or facial bones.

sympathetic vibration Resonance. If two bodies of the same natural period (capacity for free vibration) are close to each other and one is put into vibration, the other will also go into vibration, or resonate with the first.

sympathectomized Designating the removal of the thoracolumbar or sympathetic section of the autonomic nervous system.

symphysis A line of fusion between bones that were originally separate. Example is pubic symphysis.

synapse Synaptic junction, or physiologic but not physical contact, between the axon of the preceding neuron and the dendrites of the successive neuron. A one-way valve for electrochemical impulses.

synarthrosis An immovable joint, having no tissue between the articular bony surfaces.

synchondrosis A joint in which the bones are joined by fibrous or elastic cartilage.

syndesmosis A fixed joint between bones whose opposing surfaces are joined by fibrous tissue.

syndrome A symptom complex which is the total of the signs of any morbid condition.

synergism State of cooperation with another agent such that the total action is greater than the single ones. Synergy.

synovial membrane A membrane lining the interior of the capsule surrounding a freely movable joint and capable of secreting a watery or synovial fluid to lubricate the joint surfaces.

systemic Pertaining to the general bloodstream.

tachycardia Excessively fast pulse rate.

493

taxonomy The science of classification of animals and plants.

tectorial membrane A membrane within the scala media, spreading like a lid over the organ of Corti. It may possibly act to dampen aftervibrations of the auditory hair cells. Its movements may be related to the generation of electric impulses in the hair cells.

tegmentum The upper covering of the crura cerebri, or cerebral stalks. The upper and larger portion of the two major portions of each cerebral stalk.

telencephalon That part of the embryonic forebrain, or prosencephalon, which will form the cerebral hemispheres, corpora striata, and smell brain (rhinencephalon).

temporal summation If a subthreshold stimulus is repeated in rapid succession, nerve impulses are generated and a reflex response occurs. Local excitatory states are summed to a threshold level.

tendon A connective tissue band which connects a muscle with a bone.

tetanus A fusion of discrete individual muscular contractions. The verb is to tetanize. The condition is usually normal.

tetany A disorder involving generalized intermittent muscular contractions and muscle pain. Often caused by hypoparathyroidism and calcium deficiency.

thalamus A part of the forebrain, or diencephalon, containing many nuclei which principally mediate and adjust impulses arriving from discrete sense organs below. A center of crude consciousness.

throatiness A guttural quality in which the voice seems to fall back into the throat and become harsh and raspy.

thymus A gland in the front part of the neck or in the upper mediastinum which may be endocrine and which, if enlarged, can mechanically affect speech.

thyroglossal duct A duct of the embryo extending from the posterior area of the tongue to the thyroid gland. The vestigial opening after birth is the foramen cecum.

thyroid A large ductless organ in front of and on either side of the trachea composed of two lateral lobes and an isthmus connecting them.

tic A habit spasm. A twitching as of the face.

tidal volume The volume of air inhaled or exhaled in quiet breathing.

timbre The quality of sound. The differentiation of tones of a given pitch in different instruments or sources.

tinnitus Ringing sensation in the ears.

tongue-tied Designating an adherent tongue with too little mobility, tied too closely by the frenulum to the floor and sides of the mouth.

tonsil A circumscribed mass of lymphoid tissue, but particularly those between the arches of the soft palate in the passageway called the fauces.

topical Pertaining to a localized area.

topically Locally. On a particular region.

torpid Sluggish.

torus tubarius The projecting posterior lip of the Eustachian tube in the pharynx. The Eustachian cushion.

trachea The windpipe extending from the pharynx to the bronchi.

tracheostomy Making a window in the trachea to insert a cannula.

tracheotomy Making an opening into the trachea.

transillumination Examination of the interior of a cavity by an intense beam of light directed into it from outside its walls.

trapezoid body A decussating group of fibers in the hindbrain which represents the second order of neurons of the auditory tract. These fibers transmit impulses from the cochlear nuclei to somewhat higher auditory relay centers.

tremolo A tremor of the voice. An exaggerated vibrato. Used often in the expression of emotions.

tremor An involuntary trembling.

trigeminal nerve The trifacial, or Vth cranial, nerve, sensory and motor, with three major branches: ophthalmic, maxillary, and mandibular.

turbinate Any one of three bones (a concha, plural conchae) extending downward into each nasal fossa from the lateral walls of the nasal chamber.

tussive Pertaining to or caused by a cough.

tympanum The middle ear.

ulcer A loss of cells on a cutaneous or mucous surface, resulting in disintegration and necrosis of tissue.

ultimobranchial bodies Diverticula of the fourth branchial pouches or derivatives of the fifth pouches. They are surrounded by the lateral lobes of the thyroid gland and may completely atrophy.

upper motor neurons The neurons of the pyramidal or corticospinal tract, traveling down to the anterior horn cells of the spinal cord.

upper premotor neurons The axons of neurons having an ultimate origin in the premotor cortex and relayed as extrapyramidal fibers through the basal ganglia.

uvula A cone-shaped structure projecting downward from the center of the free lower border of the velum.

vagal centers Individual cell bodies of axons belonging to the afferent and efferent systems of the vagus nerve. The term embraces the dorsal nucleus, the nucleus ambiguus, and also the jugular and nodose ganglia.

vagus The pneumogastric, or Xth, cranial nerve.

vallecula 1. Any depression. 2. A pair of depressions between the lateral and median glossoepiglottic folds.

vasoconstriction The narrowing of the bore, or lumen, of a blood vessel, as opposed to opening, or vasodilation.

vasomotor Pertaining to nerves which control the diameter of blood vessels, and therefore the blood pressure.

velopharyngeal mechanism The machinery of the velum and pharynx to partition the phonated air properly between the oral and nasal passages, thus providing appropriate resonance.

velum The lower portion of the soft palate that hangs down like an incomplete curtain.

ventricle of Morgagni The middle division of the internal laryngeal chambers.

ventricular ligament The framework of the false vocal folds or the free border of the quadrangular membrane.

vertex The crown or top of the head. A summit or apex.

vesicle A small sac, or bladder, containing fluid.

vestibule The entrance cavity of the internal ear, forming the approach to the cochlea and to the organs of equilibrium.

vestigial A remnant of a more functional structure in racial evolution.

vibrato The periodic, usually consciously regulated rise and fall in pitch and volume of the voice, at about 6 to 10 Hz.

virilism 1. Masculinity. 2. The development of masculine traits in the female.

viscera Internal soft organs in the body cavities. Singular is viscus.

visible speech Visual patterns of speech transduced from the original audible laryngeal waveforms.

vital capacity The largest volume of air that can be put out in a forced

495

expiration after the deepest inspiration. The respiratory capacity.

vocal attack The configuration of the vocal tract just preparatory to the utterance of sounds. Refers especially to the morphodynamic "set" of the vocal folds.

vocal ligament The skeleton and medial part of the vocal fold. It represents the free border of the conus elasticus.

vocal process A small protuberance on the anterolateral aspect of each arytenoid cartilage, serving for attachment of the vocal ligament and the vocalis muscle.

voice The sounds uttered through the mouth, especially of human beings typically in speaking or singing.

voiceless consonant Uttered without tonal vibration of the vocal folds. Thus, /p/, /f/ and /s/ are voiceless. A surd in phonetics.

volley theory Wever and Bray's modified frequency theory in which the stimulus frequency is represented in fiber bundles of the auditory nerve acting somewhat independently so that higher frequencies are represented by a composite volley.

volume Massiveness, or the filling of space by sound. A subjective sensation dependent upon intensity, frequency, and the overtone pattern of the sound.

vowel A speech sound articulated so that there is a clear channel for the voice through the middle of the mouth.

Waldeyer's ring A discontinuous ring of tonsillar masses that surrounds the entrance to the oropharynx.

Weber test A tuning-fork test to compare the bone conduction in both ears, for evaluating conduction vs. perception deafness.

Wernicke's area An auditory center in the left superior temporal gyrus and the adjacent part of the middle temporal gyrus. Its destruction may involve failure to understand the spoken or written word.

Wever and Bray effect The electric activity of the cochlea, specifically the microphonic response, which is a piezoelectric transduction of mechanical pressure to electric current. Not true action currents of the VIIIth nerve, which can be recorded separately.

white noise A waveform displaying a number of frequencies combined randomly. There is a superposition of sinusoids of all frequencies with random phases. The so-called power spectrum is uniform over an extended range of frequencies.

zygomatic arch The prominent bone of the side of the face, or cheek, produced by the zygomatic process of the temporal bone fusing anteriorly with the zygoma, or malar bone.

BIBLIOGRAPHY

Akin, J.: *And So We Speak: Voice and Articulation,* Prentice-Hall, Inc., Englewood Cliffs, N.J., 1958.

Anderson, H., and M. Matthiesen: "Histochemistry of the Early Development of the Human Central Face and Nasal Cavity with Special Reference to the Movements and Fusion of the Palatine Processes," *Acta Anat.,* 68:473–508, 1967.

Anderson, V. A.: *Training the Speaking Voice,* Oxford University Press, New York, 1961.

Andrew, R. J.: "Evolution of Facial Expression," *Science,* 142(3595):1034–1041, 1963.

Ardran, G. M., F. H. Kemp, and L. Mannen: "Study of the Alterations in the Lumen of the Larynx during Breathing and Phonation," *Brit. J. Radiol.,* 26:497–509, 1953.

Arey, L. B.: *Developmental Anatomy,* W. B. Saunders Company, Philadelphia, 1965.

Arnold, G. E.: "Physiology and Pathology of the Cricothyroid Muscle," *Laryngoscope,* 71:687–753, 1961.

Arnold, M.: *Reconstructive Anatomy,* W. B. Saunders Company, Philadelphia, 1968.

Asherson, N.: "Large Cysts of the Epiglottis: A Classification and Case Records," *J. Laryng.,* 71:730–743, 1957.

Baker, A. B. (ed.): *Clinical Neurology,* vol. 1, 2d ed., Paul B. Hoeber Inc., medical book department of Harper & Row, Publishers, Incorporated, New York, 1962.

Balber, G., F. Coret, R. Litowitz, A. E. Rosenthal, and J. Seitlin: "Dento-Facial Aspects of Speech Disturbances," pp. 729–742, in N. M. Levin (ed.), *Voice and Speech Disorders: Medical Aspects,* Charles C Thomas Company, Springfield, Ill., 1962.

Ballenger, J. J. (ed.): *Diseases of the Nose, Throat and Ear,* 11th ed., Lea & Febiger, Philadelphia, 1969.

Barbara, D. A.: *New Directions in Stuttering,* Charles C Thomas, Springfield, Ill., 1965.

Barnes, J.: "Vital Capacity and Ability in Oral Reading," *Quart. J. Speech Educ.,* 12(3):176–182, 1926.

Basmajian, J. V.: *Muscles Alive,* The Williams & Wilkins Company, Baltimore, 1962.

Bastian, H. D.: *The Brain as an Organ of the Mind,* Kegan Paul, Trench, Trubner & Co., Ltd., London, 1880.

Batson, O. V.: "The Cricopharyngeus Muscle," *Ann. Otol.,* 64:47–54, 1955.

Bay, E.: "The History of Aphasia and the Principles of Cerebral Localization," pp. 43–65, in G. Schaltenbrand and C. N. Woolsey (eds.), *Cerebral Localization and Organization,* The University of Wisconsin Press, Madison, 1964.

Békésy, G. V., and W. A. Rosenblith: "The Mechanical Properties of the Ear," pp. 1075–1115, in S. S. Stevens (ed.), *Handbook of Experimental Psychology,* John Wiley & Sons Inc., New York, 1951.

Berry, M. F., and J. Eisenson: *Speech Disorders,* Appleton-Century-Crofts, Inc., New York, 1956.

Blewett, J. E., and A. M. Rackow: *Anatomy and Physiology for Radiographers,* Butterworth & Co. (Publishers), Ltd., London, 1966.

Bloomer, H. H.: "Speech Defects Associated with Dental Abnormalities and Malocclusions," pp. 608–652, in L. E. Travis (ed.), *Handbook of Speech Pathology,* Appleton-Century-Crofts, Inc., New York, 1957.

Bocock, E. J., and R. W. Haines: *Applied Anatomy for Nurses,* E. and S. Livingstone, Ltd., London, 1954.

Bogert, B. P., and G. E. Peterson: "The Acoustics of Speech," pp. 109–173, in L. E. Travis (ed.), *Handbook of Speech Pathology,* Appleton-Century-Crofts, Inc., New York, 1957.

Boies, L. A., J. A. Hilger, and R. E. Priest: *Fundamentals of Otolaryngology,* 4th ed., W. B. Saunders Company, Philadelphia, 1964.

Bolt, R. H., F. S. Cooper, E. E. David, P. B. Denes, J. M Pickett, and K. N. Stevens: "Identification of a Speaker by Speech Spectrograms," *Science,* 166:338–343, 1969.

Borden, R. C., and A. C. Busse: *Speech Correction,* F. S. Crofts & Co., New York, 1929.

Bosma, J. F.: "Deglutition: Pharyngeal Stage," *Physiol. Rev.,* 37:275–300, 1957.

Brain, R.: *Diseases of the Nervous System,* 5th ed., Oxford University Press, London, 1955.

Brain, L.: *Speech Disorders,* 2d ed., Butterworth, Inc., Washington, 1965.

Brantigan, O. C.: *Clinical Anatomy,* McGraw-Hill Book Company, New York, 1963.

Brewer, D. W.: *Research Potentials in Voice Physiology,* State University of New York, Syracuse, 1964.

Broca, P.: "Remarques sur le siège de la faculté du langage articulé suive d'une observation d'aphémie," *Bull. Mém. Soc. Anat. Paris,* 36(2):331, August, 1861.

Brock, S., and H. P. Krieger: *The Basis of Clinical Neurology,* The Williams & Wilkins Company, Baltimore, 1963.

Brutton, E. J., and D. J. Shoemaker: *The Modification of Stuttering,* Prentice-Hall, Inc., Englewood Cliffs, N.J., 1967.

Bucy, P. C.: "Is There a Pyramidal Tract?" *Brain,* 80:376–392, 1957.

Burns, G. W.: *The Science of Genetics,* The Macmillan Company, New York, 1969.

Calnan, J.: "The Error of Gustav Passavant," *Plast. Reconstr. Surg.,* 13:275–289, 1954.

Campbell, C. J., and J. A. Murtagh: "Electrical Manifestations of Recurrent Nerve Function," *Ann. Otol.,* 65: 747–765, 1956.

Campbell, E. J. M.: *The Respiratory Muscles and the Mechanics of Breathing,* The Year Book Publishers, Inc., Chicago, 1958.

Carmody, F. J.: "An X-ray Study of Pharyngeal Articulation," *Univ. Calif. Pub. Mod. Philo.,* 21(5):377–384, 1941.

Caro, C. G.: *Advances in Respiratory Physiology,* The Williams & Wilkins Company, Baltimore, 1966.

Carrell, J. A.: "A Comparative Study of Speech Defective Children," *Arch. Speech,* 1:179–203, 1936.

————: *Disorders of Articulation,* Prentice-Hall, Inc., Englewood Cliffs, N.J., 1968.

Carroll, J. B.: *The Study of Language,* Harvard University Press, Cambridge, Mass., 1955.

Cates, H. A., and J. V. Basmajian: *Primary Anatomy,* 3d ed., The Williams & Wilkins Company, Baltimore, 1955.

Cecil, R. L., and R. F. Loeb: *Textbook of Medicine,* W. B. Saunders Company, Philadelphia, 1955.

Chiba, T., and M. Kajiyama: *The Vowel: Its Nature and Structure,* Phonetic Society of Japan, Tokyo, 1968.

Chvapil, M.: *Physiology of Connective Tissue,* Butterworth and Co. (Publishers), Ltd., London, 1967.

Cleary, J. A.: "On the Ary-epiglottic Folds," *Ann. Otol.,* 63:960–979, 1954.

Collins, V. C.: *Principles of Anesthesiology,* Lea & Febiger, Philadelphia, 1966.

Colson, G.: *Voice Production and Speech,* Museum Press, Ltd., London, 1963.

Conley, J.: *Face-lift Operation,* Charles C Thomas, Springfield, Ill., 1968.

Converse, J. M.: "The Cartilaginous Structures of the Nose," *Ann. Otol.,* 64:220–229, 1955.

Cotes, J. E.: *Lung Function,* F. A. Davis Company, Philadelphia, 1965.

Crafts, R. G.: *A Textbook of Human Anatomy,* The Ronald Press Company, New York, 1966.

Critchley, E.: *Speech Origins and Development,* Charles C Thomas, Springfield, Ill., 1967.

Crosby, E.: "Neurophysiology: Anatomical Considerations," pp. 43–60, in D. W. Brewer (ed.), *Research Potentials in Voice Physiology,* State University of New York, Syracuse, 1964.

Cruickshank, W. M.: *Cerebral Palsy,* rev. ed., Syracuse University Press, Syracuse, N.Y., 1966.

Curtis, J. F.: "Acoustics of Speech Production and Nasalization," pp. 27–60, in D. C. Spriesterbach and D. Sherman (eds.), *Cleft Palate and Communication,* Academic Press Inc., New York, 1968.

Darley, F. L.: *Diagnosis and Appraisal of Communication Disorders,* Prentice-Hall, Inc., Englewood Cliffs, N.J., 1964.

Davis, H.: "Mechanism of Excitation of Auditory Nerve Impulses," pp. 21–39, in G. L. Rasmussen and W. F. Windle (eds.), *Neural Mechanism of the Auditory and Vestibular Systems,* Charles C Thomas, Springfield, Ill., 1960.

————: "Some Principles of Sensory Receptor Action," *Physiol. Rev.,* 41:391–416, 1961a.

————: Peripheral Coding of Auditory Information," pp. 119–141, in W. A. Rosenblith (ed.), *Sensory Communica-*

tion, The M.I.T. Press, Cambridge, Mass., 1961*b*.

Dejerine, J.: *Anatomie des centres nerveux*, J. Rueff, Paris, 1901, vol. II.

——: "L'Aphasie sensorielle: sa localization et sa physiologie pathologique," *Presse méd.*, 14:437–439; 453–457, 1906.

De Jong, R. N.: *The Neurologic Examination*, 3d ed., Harper & Row, Publishers, Incorporated, New York, 1967.

Denes, P. B., and E. N. Pinson: *The Speech Chain*, Waverly Press, Baltimore, 1963.

Denhoff, E.: "Cerebral Palsy: Medical Aspects," pp. 24–100, in W. M. Cruickshank (ed.), *Cerebral Palsy*, rev. ed., Syracuse University Press, Syracuse, N.Y., 1966.

Denny-Brown, D., and J. Pennybacher: "Fibrillation and Fasciculation in Voluntary Muscle," *Brain*, 61:311–334, 1938.

DeParrel, S.: *Speech Disorders*, Pergamon Press, New York, 1965.

DeWeese, D. D., and W. H. Saunders: *Textbook of Otolaryngology*, 2d ed., The C. V. Mosby Company, St. Louis, 1964.

Diamond, M.: *Dental Anatomy*, 3d ed., The Macmillan Company, New York, 1952.

Dinneen, F. P.: *An Introduction to General Linguistics*, Holt, Rinehart and Winston, Inc., New York, 1967.

Dolowitz, D. A.: *Basic Otolaryngology*, McGraw-Hill Book Company, New York, 1964.

Donaldson, J. A. (ed.): *Symposium on Eustachian Tube Problems*, Otolaryngologic Clinics of North America, W. B. Saunders Company, Philadelphia, February, 1970.

Doty, R. W., and J. F. Bosma: "An Electromyographic Analysis of Reflex Deglutition," *J. Neurophysiol.*, 19:44–61, 1956.

Draper, M. H., P. Ladefoged, and D. Whitteridge: "Respiratory Muscles in Speech," *J. Speech Hearing Res.*, 2(1): 16–27, 1959.

Eisenson, J.: "Aphasia in Adults," "Correlates of Aphasia in Adults," "Therapeutic Problems and Approaches with Aphasic Adults," pp. 450–467, in L. E. Travis (ed.), *Handbook of Speech Pathology*, Appleton-Century-Crofts, Inc., New York, 1957.

Eldridge, M.: *A History of the Treatment of Speech Disorders*, E. and S. Livingstone, Ltd., Edinburgh, 1968.

Epstein, A. N.: "Oropharyngeal Factors in Feeding and Drinking," pp. 197–218, in C. F. Code and H. Werner (eds.), *Handbook of Physiology*, Physiological Society, Washington, 1967.

Eyzaguirre, C.: *Physiology of the Nervous System*, Year Book Medical Publishers, Inc., Chicago, 1969.

Faaborg-Andersen, F.: "Electromyographic Investigation of Intrinsic Laryngeal Muscles in Humans," *Acta Physiol. Scand.*, 41, suppl. 140:1–149, 1957.

——: "Electromyography of the Laryngeal Muscles in Man," pp. 105–140, in D. W. Brewer (ed.), *Research Potentials in Voice Physiology*, State University of New York, Syracuse, N.Y. 1964.

Fairbanks, G., and E. M. Green: "A Study of Minor Organic Deviations in Functional Disorders of Articulation 2. Dimensions and Relationships of the Lips," *J. Speech Hearing Dis.*, 15: 165–168, 1950.

—— and B. Bebout: "A Study of Minor Organic Deviations in Functional Disorders of Articulation 3. The Tongue," *J. Speech Hearing Dis.*, 15: 348–352, 1950.

—— and M. V. Lintner: "A Study of Minor Organic Deviations in Functional Disorders of Articulation 4. The Teeth and Hard Palate," *J. Speech Hearing Dis.*, 16:273–279, 1951.

Falck, F. J.: *Stuttering; Learned and*

500

Unlearned, Charles C Thomas, Springfield, Ill., 1969.

Fant, G.: *Acoustic Theory of Speech Production,* Mouton and Company, The Hague, 1960.

———: "Phonetics and Speech Research," pp. 199–239, in D. W. Brewer (ed.), *Research Potentials in Voice Physiology,* State University of New York, Syracuse, 1964.

Farnsworth, D. W.: "High-speed Motion Pictures of the Human Vocal Cords," *Bell Lab. Rec.,* 18:203–208, 1940.

Fink, B. R., and M. Basek: "The Mechanism of Opening of the Human Larynx," *Laryngoscope,* 66:410–425, 1956.

Fletcher, H.: *Speech and Hearing in Communication,* D. Van Nostrand Company, Inc., Princeton, N.J., 1953.

Fletcher, W. W.: "Physical and Physiological Nature of Normal Voice and Speech," pp. 57–89, in N. M. Levin (ed.), *Voice and Speech Disorders: Medical Aspects,* Charles C Thomas, Springfield, Ill., 1962.

Fowler, E. P.: *Medicine of the Ear,* 2d ed., Thomas Nelson & Sons, New York, 1947.

Freedman, A. O.: "Diseases of the Ventricle of Morgagni," *Arch. Otolaryng.,* 28:329–343, 1938.

French, J. D.: "The Reticular Formation," pp. 232–238, in J. L. McGaugh, N. M. Weinberger, and R. E. Whalen (eds.), *Psychobiology,* W. H. Freeman and Company, San Francisco, 1967.

Freund, E. D.: "Voice and Breathing," *Arch. Otolaryng.,* 67:1–7, 1958.

Freund, H.: *Psychopathology and the Problems of Stuttering,* Charles C Thomas, Springfield, Ill., 1966.

Friedhoff, A. J., M. Alpert, and R. L. Kurtzberg: "An Electro-acoustic Analysis of the Effects of Stress on Voice," *J. Neuropsychiat.,* 5:266–272, 1964.

Froeschels, E.: *Dysarthric Speech,* Expression Company, Magnolia, Mass., 1952.

——— and A. Jellinek: *Practice of Voice and Speech Therapy,* Expression Company, Boston, 1941.

Fry, D. B.: "Speech and Language," *J. Laryng.* 7:432–452, 1957.

Fulton, J. F.: *A Textbook of Physiology,* 17th ed., W. B. Saunders Company, Philadelphia, 1955.

Furstenberg, A. C., and J. E. Magielski: "A Motor Pattern in the Nucleus Ambiguus: Its Clinical Significance," *Ann. Otol.,* 64:788–793, 1955.

Fymbo, L. H.: "The Relation of Malocclusion of the Teeth to Defects of Speech," *Arch. Speech,* 1:204–216, 1936.

Galambos, R., and H. Davis: "The Response of Single Auditory-nerve Fibers to Acoustic Stimulation," *J. Neurophysiol.,* 6:39–57, 1943.

Gillilan, L. A.: *Clinical Aspects of the Autonomic Nervous System,* Little, Brown and Company, Boston, 1954.

Gisselsson, L.: "Dislocation of the Larynx," *Laryngoscope,* 60:117–120, 1950.

Glorig, A.: *Audiometry: Principles and Practice,* The Williams & Wilkins Company, Baltimore, 1965.

Goerttler, K.: "Die Anordnung, Histologie und Histogenese der quergestreiften Muskulatur im menschlichen Stimmband," *Z. Anat. u. Entwicklungsgesch,* 115:352–401, 1951.

Goldman, H. M., S. P. Forrest, D. L. Byrd, and R. E. McDonald (eds.): *Current Therapy in Dentistry,* vol. 3, The C. V. Mosby Company, St. Louis, 1968.

Goldstein, K.: "Ueber Aphasie," *Schweiz. Arch. Neurol.,* 19:3–38, 1926.

———: *Aftereffects of Brain Injuries in War,* Grune & Stratton, Inc., New York, 1942.

———: *Language and Language Disturbances,* Grune & Stratton, Inc., New York, 1948.

Graham, E. C.: *The Basic Dictionary of*

501

Science, The Macmillan Company, New York, 1966.

Grant, J. C. B., and J. V. Basmajian: *Grant's Method of Anatomy,* 7th ed., The Williams & Wilkins Company, Baltimore, 1965.

Gray, G. W., and C. M. Wise: *The Bases of Speech,* 3d ed., Harper & Brothers, New York, 1959.

Gray H.: *Anatomy of the Human Body,* 28th ed., Lea & Febiger, Philadelphia, 1966.

Greene, M. C. L.: *The Voice and Its Disorders,* J. B. Lippincott Company, Philadelphia, 1964.

Grollman, S.: *The Human Body,* The Macmillan Company, New York, 1964.

Guild, S. K.: "Elastic Tissue of the Eustachian Tube," *Ann. Otol.,* 64: 537–545, 1955.

Guthrie, D., and A. Milner: "Discussion on Functional Disorders of the Voice," *J. Laryng.,* 54:261–272, 1939.

Guyton, A. C.: *Textbook of Medical Physiology,* 3d ed., W. B. Saunders Company, Philadelphia, 1966.

Hagerty, R. F., M. J. Hill, H. S. Pettit, and J. J. Kane: "Posterior Pharyngeal Wall Movement in Normals," *J. Speech Hearing Res.,* 1:203–210, 1958.

Hahn, E., C. W. Lomas, D. E. Hargis, and D. Vandraegen: *Basic Voice Training for Speech,* 2d ed., McGraw-Hill Book Company, New York, 1957.

Haines, R. W., and A. Mohiudden: *Handbook of Human Embryology,* 4th ed., E. and S. Livingstone, Edinburgh, 1968.

Hall, S. I., and B. H. Colman: *Diseases of the Nose, Throat and Ear,* 8th ed., E. and S. Livingstone, Edinburgh, 1967.

Hamilton, W. J., J. D. Boyd, and H. W. Mossman: *Human Embryology,* The Williams & Wilkins Company, Baltimore, 1952.

Hast, M. H.: "The Respiratory Muscle of the Larynx," *Ann. Otol.,* 76(2):489–497, 1967.

Head, H.: *Aphasia and Kindred Disorders of Speech,* 2 vols., The Macmillan Company, New York, 1926.

Heffner, R. M. S.: *General Phonetics,* The University of Wisconsin Press, Madison, 1960.

Henderson, I. F., and W. D. Henderson: *Dictionary of Scientific Terms,* D. Van Nostrand Company, Inc., Princeton, N.J., 1949.

Hess, W. R.: "Causality, Consciousness and Cerebral Organization," *Science,* 158(3806):1279–1283, 1967.

Hiroto, I., M. Hirano, and H. Tomita: "Electromyographic Investigation of Human Vocal Cord Paralysis," *Ann. Otol.,* 77(2):296–304, 1968.

Holinger, P. H., and K. C. Johnson: "Congenital Anomalies of the Larynx," *Ann. Otol.,* 63:581–606, 1954.

Hollender, A. R.: *The Pharynx,* Year Book Publishers, Inc., Chicago, 1953.

Hollien, H.: "Some Laryngeal Correlates of Vocal Pitch," *J. Speech Hearing Res.,* 3:52–58, 1960.

———: "Vocal Fold Thickness and Fundamental Frequency of Phonation," *J. Speech Hearing Res.,* 5(3):237–243, 1962.

——— and J. F. Curtis: "Laminagraphic Study of Vocal Pitch," *J. Speech Hearing Res.,* 3:361–371, 1960.

Hollinshead, W. H.: *Anatomy for Surgeons,* Paul B. Hoeber, Inc., medical book department of Harper & Row, Publishers, Incorporated, New York, 1954.

Holmes, F. L.: *A Handbook of Voice and Diction,* F. S. Crofts & Co., New York, 1940.

Holt, G. H.: *The Vagi in Medicine and Surgery,* Charles C Thomas, Springfield, Ill., 1968.

Hopp, E. S.: "The Development of the Epithelium of the Larynx," *Laryngoscope,* 65(7):475–499, 1955.

——— and H. F. Burns: "Ground Substance in the Nose in Health and Infection," *Ann. Otol.,* 67:480–490, 1958.

502

Hoshiko, M. S.: "Sequence of Action of Breathing Muscles during Speech," *J. Speech Hearing Res.*, 3(3):291–297, 1960.

Hough, J. N.: *Scientific Terminology*, Rinehart & Company, Inc., New York, 1953.

House, A. S.: "Analog Studies of Nasal Consonants," *J. Speech Hearing Dis.*, 22:190–204, 1957.

———— and K. N. Stevens: "Analog Studies of the Nasalization of Vowels," *J. Speech Hearing Dis.*, 21:218–232, 1956.

Houssay, B. A.: *Human Physiology*, 2d ed., McGraw-Hill Book Company, New York, 1955.

Huber, J. F.: "Anatomy of the Mouth," *Clin. Sympos.*, 10(3):67–94, 1958.

————: "Anatomy of the Pharynx," *Clin. Sympos.*, 10(4):117–128, 1958.

Hughes, J. P.: *The Science of Language*, Random House, Inc., New York, 1962.

Hull, H., and B. Bryngelson: "A Study of Respiration of Fourteen Spastic Paralysis Cases during Silence and Speech," *Speech Monogr.*, 8:114–121, 1941.

Huntington, D. A.: "Anatomical and Physiological Bases for Speech," pp. 1–25, in D. C. Spriestersbach and D. Sherman (eds.), *Cleft Palate and Communication*, Academic Press Inc., New York, 1968.

Husson, R.: "Étude stroboscopique des modifications réflexes de la vibration des cordes vocales declenchées par des stimulations expérimentales du nerf auditif et du nerf trijumeau," *C. R. Acad. Sci.*, 232:1247–1249, 1951.

————, E. J. Garde, and A. Richard: "Étude de la vibration des cordes vocales et de la couverture du son sur le mi 3 sous cocainisation profonde des thyro-arytenoidiens internes," *C. R. Acad. Sci.*, 230:999–1000, 1950.

Ingelfinger, F. J.: "Esophageal Motility," *Physiol. Rev.*, 38(4):533–584, 1968.

Jackson, C., and C. L. Jackson: *Diseases of the Nose, Throat and Ear*, 2d ed., W. B. Saunders Company, Philadelphia, 1959.

Jenkins, G. N.: *The Physiology of the Mouth*, 2d ed., Blackwell Scientific Publications, Ltd., Oxford, 1960.

Jepsen, O.: "Middle Ear Muscle Reflexes in Man," pp. 193–239, in J. Jerger (ed.), *Modern Developments in Audiology*, Academic Press Inc., New York, 1963.

Jerger, J.: *Modern Developments in Audiology*, Academic Press Inc., New York, 1963.

————: "Review of Diagnostic Audiometry," *Ann. Otol.*, 77(6):1042–1053. 1968.

Johnson, W., J. J. Curtis, C. W. Edney, and J. Keaster: *Speech Handicapped School Children*, Harper & Brothers, New York, 1956.

Judson, L. S. V., and A. T. Weaver: *Voice Science*, 2d ed., Appleton-Century-Crofts, Inc., New York, 1965.

Kantner, C. E., and R. West: *Phonetics*, Harper & Brothers, New York, 1960.

Karlin, I. W.: "Stuttering: The Problem Today," *JAMA*, 143:732–736, 1950.

Keenan, J. S., and G. C. Barrett: "Intralaryngeal Relationships during Pitch and Intensity Changes," *J. Speech Hearing Res.*, 5(2):173–178, 1962.

Keleman, G.: "The Anatomical Basis of Phonation in the Chimpanzee," *J. Morph.*, 82(2):229–256, 1948.

————: "Physiology of Phonation in Primates," *Logos*, 1:32–35, 1958.

Keogh, C. A.: "The Neurology and Function of the Pharynx and Its Powers of Compensation in Paralysis," *Ann. Otol.*, 66:416–439, 1957.

Kirchner, J. A., and B. D. Wyke: "Electromyographic Analysis of Laryngeal Articular Reflexes," *Nature (London)*, 203(4951):1243–1245, 1964.

————: "Afferent Discharges from Laryngeal Articular Mechanoreceptors," *Nature (London)*, 205(4966):86–87, 1965a.

503

————: "Articular Reflex Mechanisms in the Larynx," *Ann. Otol.*, 74:749–768, 1965*b*.

Knowles, J. H.: *Respiratory Physiology and Its Clinical Application,* Harvard University Press, Cambridge, Mass., 1959.

Koepp-Baker, H.: "Speech Problems of the Person with Cleft Palate and Cleft Lip," pp. 597–607, in L. E. Travis (ed.), *Handbook of Speech Pathology,* Appleton-Century-Crofts, Inc., New York, 1957.

Kostelijk, P. J.: *Theories of Hearing,* Leiden University Press, Leiden, 1950.

Kreig, W. J. S.: *Functional Neuroanatomy,* McGraw-Hill Book Company, New York, 1942.

Ladefoged, P.: "The Regulation of Subglottal Pressure," *Folia Phoniat.*, 12: 169–175, 1960.

————: *Elements of Acoustic Phonetics,* The University of Chicago Press, Chicago, 1962.

————: *Three Areas of Experimental Phonetics,* Oxford University Press, London, 1967.

Lassek, A. M.: "Human Pyramidal Tract; Numerical Investigation of Betz Cells of Motor Area," *Arch. Neurol.*, 44:718–724, 1940.

———— and G. L. Rasmussen: "Human Pyramidal Tract: Fiber and Numerical Analysis," *Arch. Neurol.*, 42:872–876, 1939.

LeJeune, F. E., and M. G. Lynch: "Review of the Available Literature on the Pharynx and Pharyngeal Surgery for 1954," *Laryngoscope,* 65(11):1005–1031, 1955.

Lempert, J.: "Analytical Survey of Evolutionary Development of Fenestration Operation," *Ann. Otol.*, 59:988–1019, 1950.

Lencione, R. M.: "Speech and Language Problems in Cerebral Palsy," pp. 195–276, in W. M. Cruickshank (ed.), *Cerebral Palsy,* Syracuse University Press, Syracuse, N.Y., 1966.

Lenneberg, E. H.: "A Laboratory for Speech Research at the Children's Hospital Medical Center," *New Eng. J. Med.*, 266(8):385–392, 1962.

————: *Biological Foundations of Language,* John Wiley & Sons, Inc., New York, 1967.

Levin, N. M.: *Voice and Speech Disorders: Medical Aspects,* Charles C Thomas, Springfield, Ill., 1962.

Lewis, R. S., S. R. Mawson, W. G., Edwards, and H. Ludman: *Essentials of Otolaryngology,* William Heinemann Medical Books, London, 1967.

Licklider, J. C. R., and G. A. Miller: "The Perception of Speech," pp. 1040–1074, in S. S. Stevens (ed.), *Handbook of Experimental Psychology,* John Wiley & Sons, Inc., New York, 1951.

Lieberman, P.: "Vocal Cord Motion in Man," pp. 28–41, in A. Bouhuys (ed.), *Sound Production in Man, Ann. N.Y. Acad. Sci.*, 155(art. 1):1–381, 1968.

Lindsley, D. B.: "Emotion," in S. S. Stevens (ed.), *Handbook of Experimental Psychology,* John Wiley & Sons, Inc., New York, 1951.

Lippold, O: *Human Respiration: A Programmed Course,* W. H. Freeman and Company, San Francisco, 1968.

Luchsinger, R.: "Voice Disturbances on an Endocrine Basis," pp. 410–428, in N. M. Levin (ed.), *Voice and Speech Disorders: Medical Aspects,* Charles C Thomas, Springfield, Ill., 1962.

———— and G. E. Arnold: *Voice—Speech —Language,* Wadsworth Publishing Company, Belmont, Calif., 1965.

Luhman, J. A.: *Neurology,* The Williams & Wilkins Company, Baltimore, 1968.

MacNalty, S. A.: *Butterworth's Medical Dictionary,* Butterworth & Co (Publishers), Ltd., London, 1965.

MacNeilage, P. F., and G. N. Sholes: "An Electromyographic Study of the Tongue during Vowel Production," *J. Speech Hearing Res.*, 7:209–232, 1964.

Malmberg, B: *Phonetics,* Dover Publications, Inc., New York, 1963.

Marie, P.: "La troisième circonvolution frontale gauche ne joue aucun role spécial dans la fonction du langage," *Semaine Méd.,* 26:241–247, 1906.

————: "Que faut-il penser des aphasies sous-corticales (aphasies pures)?" *Semaine Méd.,* 26:493–500, 1906.

Marx, O.: "The History of the Biological Basis of Language," pp. 443–469, in E. H. Lenneberg (ed.), *Biological Foundations of Language,* John Wiley & Sons, Inc., New York, 1967.

Mase, D. J.: "Disorders of Articulation," pp. 604–637, in N. M. Levin (ed.), *Voice and Speech Disorders: Medical Aspects,* Charles C Thomas, Springfield, Ill., 1962.

Mawson, S. R.: "Myringoplasty," *J. Larnyg.,* 73:56–66, 1958.

McBurney, J. H., and E. J. Wrage: *The Art of Good Speech,* Prentice-Hall, Inc., Englewood Cliffs, N.J., 1953.

McDonald, E. T.: *Articulation Testing and Treatment: A Sensory-motor Approach,* Stanwix House, Pittsburgh, 1964.

McLean, F. C.: "The Ultrastructure and Function of Bone," *Science,* 127(3296): 451–456, 1958.

Meano, C., and A. Khoury: *The Human Voice in Speech and Song,* Charles C Thomas, Springfield, Ill., 1967.

Meschan, I.: *Normal Radiographic Anatomy,* 2d ed., W. B. Saunders Company, Philadelphia, 1959.

Meyers, R.: "Physiological and Therapeutic Effects of Bilateral Intermediate Crusotomy for Atheto-dystonia (17 Cases)," *Surg. Forum,* 6:486–488, 1955.

————: "Results of Bilateral Intermediate Midbrain Crustomy in Seven Cases of Severe Athetotic and Dystonic Quadriparesis," *Amer. J. Phys. Med.,* 35: 84–105, 1956.

Michel, R.: "Die Bedeutung des Musculus Sternothyroideus für die Rahmenmodulation der menschlichen Stimme," *Folia Phoniat.,* 6(2):65–100, 1954.

Milisen, R.: "The Incidence of Speech Disorders," "Methods of Evaluation and Diagnosis of Speech Disorders," pp. 246–312, in L. E. Travis (ed.), *Handbook of Speech Pathology,* Appleton-Century-Crofts, Inc., New York, 1957.

Milner, B.: "Laterality Effects in Audition," pp. 177–195, in V. B. Mountcastle (ed.), *Interhemispheric Relations and Cerebral Dominance,* The Johns Hopkins Press, Baltimore, 1962.

Miller, G. A.: "Speech and Language," pp. 789–810, in S. S. Stevens (ed.), *Handbook of Experimental Psychology,* John Wiley & Sons, Inc., New York, 1951.

Mills, C.: "Aphasia and the Cerebral Zones of Speech," *Amer. J. Med. Sci.,* 16:375–377, 1904.

Moll, K. L.: "Cinefluorographic Techniques in Speech Research," *J. Speech Hearing Res.,* 3:227–241, 1960.

Montagu, A.: "A New Theory Concerning the Origin of Speech," *JAMA,* 185(13) : 109–110, 1963.

Montreuil, F.: "Bifid Epiglottis: Report of a Case," *Laryngoscope,* 59: 194–199, 1949.

Moore, P.: "Voice Disorders Associated with Organic Abnormalities," pp. 653–703, in L. E. Travis (ed.), *Handbook of Speech Pathology,* Appleton-Century-Crofts, Inc., New York, 1957.

———— and H. von Leden: "Dynamic Variations of the Vibratory Pattern in the Normal Larynx," *Folia Phoniat.,* 10:205–238, 1958.

Moorrees, C. F. A.: "Orthodontics," *New Eng. J. Med.,* 279(13): 689–695, 1968.

Morley, M. W.: *Cleft Palate and Speech,* 5th ed., The Williams & Wilkins Company, Baltimore, 1962.

Morris: *Human Anatomy,* 12th ed., B. J. Anson (ed.), McGraw-Hill Book Company, Inc., New York, 1966.

Morrison, W. W.: *Diseases of the Ear, Nose and Throat,* Appleton-Century-Crofts, Inc., New York, 1955.

Moses, P. J.: *The Voice of Neurosis,* Grune & Stratton, Inc., New York, 1954.

Mosher, H. D.: "The Expression of the Face and Man's Type of Body as Indicators of His Character," *Laryngoscope,* 61:1–38, 1951.

Mountcastle, V. B. (ed.): *Interhemispheric Relations and Cerebral Dominance.* The Johns Hopkins Press, Baltimore, 1962.

————: *Medical Physiology,* 12th ed., The Johns Hopkins Press, Baltimore, 1968.

Müller, J.: *Handbuch der Physiologie des Menschen für Vorlesungen,* vol. 2, J. Hülscher, Coblenz, 1834–1840, pp. 133–245; quoted from Leden, H.: "The Mechanism of Phonation: A Search for a Rational Theory of Voice Production," *Arch. Otolaryng.,* 74: 660–676, 1961.

Murphy, A. T.: *Functional Voice Disorders,* Prentice-Hall, Inc., Englewood Cliffs, N.J., 1964.

Myers, D., W. D. Schlosser, and R. A. Winchester: "Otologic Diagnosis and the Treatment of Deafness," *Clin. Sympos.,* 14(2):1–73, 1962.

Mysak, E. D.: "Phonatory and Resonatory Problems," pp. 150–181, in R. W. Rieber, and R. S. Brubaker (eds.), *Speech Pathology,* North-Holland Publishing Company, Amsterdam, 1966.

Naunton, R. F.: "The Measurement of Hearing by Bone Conduction," pp. 1–29, in J. Jerger (ed.), *Modern Developments in Audiology,* Academic Press Inc., New York, 1963.

Negus, V. E.: *The Mechanism of the Larynx,* William Heinemann, Ltd., London, 1929.

————: *The Comparative Anatomy and Physiology of the Larynx,* Grune & Stratton, Inc., New York, 1949.

————: "The Mechanism of the Larynx," *Laryngoscope,* 67:961–986, 1957.

Nelsen, O. E.: *Comparative Embryology of the Vertebrates,* McGraw-Hill Book Company, New York, 1953.

Neuroscience Research Symposium Summaries, The M.I.T. Press, Cambridge, Mass.

Newby, H. A.: *Audiology,* Appleton-Century-Crofts, Inc., New York, 1964.

Noback, C. R.: *The Human Nervous System,* McGraw-Hill Book Company, New York, 1967.

Ochs, S.: *Elements of Neurophysiology,* John Wiley & Sons, Inc., New York, 1965.

O'Leary, J. L., and L. A. Coben: "The Reticular Core: 1957," *Physiol. Rev.,* 38:243–276, 1958.

O'Neill, J. J., and H. J. Oyer: *Applied Audiometry,* Dodd, Mead & Company, Inc., New York, 1966.

Orban, B. J.: *Oral Histology and Embryology,* 5th ed., The C. V. Mosby Company, St. Louis, Mo., 1962.

O'Rourke, J. T., and L. M. S. Miner: *Oral Physiology,* The C. V. Mosby Company, St. Louis, Mo., 1951.

Osgood, C. E.: *Method and Theory in Experimental Psychology,* Oxford University Press, New York, 1956.

Palmer, J. M., and D. A. LaRusso: *Anatomy for Speech and Hearing,* Harper & Row, Publishers, Incorporated, New York, 1965.

Patten, B. M.: *Human Embryology,* 3d ed., McGraw-Hill Book Company, New York, 1968.

Patton, F. E.: "A Comparison of the Kinesthetic Sensibility of Speech-defective and Normal-speaking Childen," *J. Speech Hearing Dis.,* 7:305–310, 1942.

Peele, T. L.: *The Neuroanatomical Basis for Clinical Neurology,* 2d ed., McGraw-Hill Book Company, New York, 1961.

Penfield, W., and T. Rasmussen: *The Cerebral Cortex of Man: A Clinical*

Study of Localization of Function, The Macmillan Company, New York, 1950.

———— and L. Roberts: *Speech and Brain-mechanisms,* Princeton University Press, Princeton, N.J., 1959.

Perkins, W. H.: "The Challenge of Functional Disorders of Voice," pp. 832–874, in L. E. Travis (ed.), *Handbook of Speech Pathology,* Appleton-Century-Crofts, Inc., New York, 1957.

————: "Stuttering: Some Common Denominators," pp. 16–30, in B. A. Dominick (ed.), *New Directions in Stuttering,* Charles C Thomas, Springfield, Ill., 1965.

Peterson, G.: "Changes in Handedness in the Rat by Local Application of Acetylcholine to the Cerebral Cortex," *J. Comp. Physiol. Psychol.,* 42:404–412, 1949.

Portmann, G.: "The Physiology of Phonation," *J. Laryng.,* 71:1–15, 1957.

Potsaid, M. S.: "Kineradiography," *New Eng. J. Med.,* 264(4):178–184, 1961.

Potter, R. K., G. A. Kopp, and H. G. Kopp: *Visible Speech,* Dover Publications, Inc., New York, 1966.

Powers, M. H.: "Clinical and Educational Procedures in Functional Disorders of Articulation," pp. 769–804, in L. A. Travis (ed.), *Handbook of Speech Pathology,* Appleton-Century-Crofts, Inc., New York, 1957.

Pressman, J. J.: "Physiology of the Vocal Cords in Phonation and Respiration," *Arch. Otolaryng.,* 35:355–398, 1942.

————: "The Sphincters of the Larynx," *Trans. Amer. Acad. Opthal.,* 57:724–737, 1953.

————: Sphincters of the Larynx," *Arch. Otolaryng.,* 59:221–236, 1954.

———— and G. Kelemen: "Physiology of the Larynx," *Physiol. Rev.,* 35:506–554, 1955.

Proetz, A. W.: *Applied Physiology of the Nose,* Annals Publishing Company, St. Louis, Mo., 1953.

Pruzansky, S.: *International Symposium on Congenital Anomalies of the Face and Associated Structures,* Charles C Thomas, Springfield, Ill., 1961.

Rasmussen, T., and W. Penfield: "Further Studies of the Sensory and Motor Cerebral Cortex of Man," *Fed. Proc.,* 6:452–460, 1947.

Raubicheck, L.: *Speech Improvement,* Prentice-Hall, Inc., Englewood Cliffs, N.J., 1952.

Rieber, R. W., and R. S. Brubaker: *Speech Pathology,* North-Holland Publishing Company, Amsterdam, 1966.

Ringel, R. L., and H. M. Fletcher: "Oral Perception: III. Texture Discrimination," *J. Speech Hearing Res.,* 10(3): 642–649, 1967.

Robbins, S. D.: *A Dictionary of Speech Pathology and Therapy,* Expression Company, Boston, 1951.

Roberts, A. C.: *The Aphasic Child,* Charles C Thomas, Springfield, Ill., 1966.

Roche, A. F., and D. H. Barkla: "The Level of the Larynx during Childhood," *Ann. Otol.,* 74(3):645–654, 1965.

Rogers, W. P., C. Reynolds, and M. Yatsuhashi: "Cancer of the Larynx," *New Eng. J. Med.,* 274(11):596–599, 1966.

Rohan, R. F.: "Artificial Tympanic Membranes: Old and New," *J. Laryng.,* 71:605–615, 1957.

Ronis, B.: "Tympanoplasty," pp. 140–168, in N. M. Levin (ed.), *Voice and Speech Disorders: Medical Aspects,* Charles C Thomas, Springfield, Ill., 1962.

Rosen, S.: "Preparation of Stapes for Fixation: Preliminary Procedures to Determine Fenestration Suitability in Otosclerosis," *Arch. Otolaryng.,* 56: 610–615, 1952.

Rossier, P. H., A. A. Buhlmann, and K. Wiesinger: *Respiration,* The C. V. Mosby Company, St. Louis, Mo., 1960.

Rousey, C. L., and A. E. Moriarty: *Diagnostic Implications of Speech Sounds,*

Charles C Thomas, Springfield, Ill., 1965.

Rubin, H. J.: "The Neurochronaxic Theory of Voice Production: A Refutation," *Arch. Otolaryng.*, 71:913–920, 1960.

———, C. C. Hirt, and M. LeCouer: "The Falsetto: A High Speed Cinematographic Study," *Laryngoscope* 70 (9):1305–1324, 1960.

Ruch, T. E., and J. F. Fulton: *Medical Physiology and Biophysics*, W. B. Saunders Company, Philadelphia, 1960.

Ruedi, L.: "Some Observations on the Histology and Function of the Larynx," *J. Laryng.*, 73:1–20, 1959.

Russell, G. O.: *Speech and Voice*, The Macmillan Company, New York, 1931.

Sataloff, J.: *Industrial Deafness*, Mc-Graw-Hill Book Company, New York, 1957.

———: *Hearing Loss*, J. B. Lippincott Company, Philadelphia, 1966.

Saunders, J. B. de C. M., C. Davis, and R. Miller: "The Mechanism of Deglutition (Second Stage) as Revealed by Cine-radiography," *Ann. Otol.*, 60: 879–916, 1951.

Schaltenbrand, G., and C. N. Woolsey: *Cerebral Localization and Organization*, The University of Wisconsin Press, Madison, 1964.

Schuknecht, H. F., and E. L. Applebaum: "Surgery for Hearing Loss," *New Eng. J. Med.*, 280(21):1154–1160, 1969.

Scheer, B. T.: *Animal Physiology*, John Wiley & Sons, Inc., New York, 1963.

Scott, J. H., and N. B. B. Symons: *Introduction to Dental Anatomy*, E. and S. Livingstone, Ltd., London, 1967.

Shafer, W. G., M. K. Hine, and B. M. Levy: *A Textbook of Oral Pathology*, W. B. Saunders Company, Philadelphia, 1963.

Sharp, G. S., W. K. Bullock, and J. W. Hazlet: *Oral Cancer and Tumors of the Jaws*, McGraw-Hill Book Company, New York, 1956.

Shea, J. J.: "Fenestration of Oral Window," *Ann. Otol.*, 67:932–951, 1958.

Slonim, B. N., and J. L. Chapin: *Respiratory Physiology*, The C. V. Mosby Company, St. Louis, Mo., 1967.

Smith, S.: "Remarks on the Physiology of the Vibrations of the Vocal Cords," *Folia Phoniat.*, 6:166–178, 1954.

Snidecor, J. C.: *Speech Rehabilitation of the Laryngectomized*, Charles C Thomas, Springfield, Ill., 1962.

Sokoloff, M.: "Phonatory and Resonatory Problems," pp. 321–336, in R. W. Rieber and R. S. Brubaker (eds.), *Speech Pathology*, North-Holland Publishing Company, Amsterdam, 1966.

Solomon, A.: "An Unusual Receptive Aphasia as a Manifestation of Temporal-lobe Epilepsy," *New Eng. J. Med.*, 257:313–317, 1957.

Sperry, R. W.: "The Great Cerebral Commissure," pp. 240–250, in J. L. McGaugh, N. M. Weinberger, and R. E. Whalen (eds.), *Psychobiology*, W. H. Freeman and Company, San Francisco, 1967.

Spriestersbach, D. C., and G. R. Powers: "Articulation Skills, Velopharyngeal Closure, and Oral Breath Pressure of Children with Cleft Palates," *J. Speech Hearing Res.*, 2(4):318–325, 1959.

Starbuck, H. B., and M. D. Steer: "The Adaptation Effect in Stuttering and Its Relation to Thoracic and Abdominal Breathing," *J. Speech Hearing Dis.*, 19(1):440–449, 1954.

Stark, R. B.: "Embryology, Etiology and Pathogenesis of Cleft, Lip and Palate," pp. 743–760, in N. M. Levin (ed.), *Voice and Speech Disorders: Medical Aspects*, Charles C Thomas, Springfield, Ill., 1962.

Steer, M. D.: "A Qualitative Study of Breathing in Young Stutterers," *Speech Monogr.*, 2:152–156, 1935.

———, and T. D. Hanley: "Instruments of Diagnosis, Therapy and Research," pp. 174–245, in L. E. Travis (ed.), *Handbook of Speech Pathology,* Appleton-Century-Crofts, Inc., New York, 1957.

Stetson, R. H.: *Motor Phonetics,* North-Holland Publishing Company, Amsterdam, 1951.

Stovin, J. S.: "The Importance of the Membranous Nasal Septum," *Arch. Otolaryng.,* 67:540–541, 1958.

Taub, S.: "The Taub Oral Panendoscope: A New Technique," *Cleft Palate J.,* 3:328–346, 1966.

Thomson, W. A. R.: *Black's Medical Dictionary,* Barnes & Noble Inc., New York, 1967.

Timcke, R., H. von Leden, and P. Moore: "Laryngeal Vibrations: Measurements of the Glottic Wave," *Arch. Otolaryng.,* 68:1–19, 1958.

Tonndorf, W.: "Die Mechanik bei Stimmlippenschwinzungen und beim Schnarchen," *Z. Hals- Nasen- Ohrrenheilk,* 12:241–245, 1925.

Travis, L. E. (ed.): *Handbook of Speech Pathology,* Appleton-Century-Crofts, Inc., New York, 1957.

Triboletti, E.: "Unusual Congenital Anomaly Involving the Larynx, Trachea and Esophagus," *New Eng. J. Med.,* 258(20):1002–1003, 1958.

Turner, C. D.: *General Endocrinology,* W. B. Saunders Company, Philadelphia, 1966.

Tuttle, W. W., and B. A. Schottelius: *Textbook of Physiology,* 15th ed., The C. V. Mosby Company, St. Louis, Mo., 1965.

van den Berg, J.: "Myoelastic-aerodynamic Theory of Voice Production," *J. Speech Hearing Res.,* 1(3):227–244, 1958.

Van Riper, C., and J. V. Irwin: *Voice and Articulation,* Prentice-Hall, Inc., Englewod Cliffs, N.J., 1958.

Vinken, P. J., and G. W. Bruyn (eds.): *Handbook of Clinical Neurology,* vols. 1–6, Interscience Publishers, a division of John Wiley & Sons, Inc., New York, 1969.

Vogel, P. H.: "The Innervation of the Larynx of Man and the Dog," *Am. J. Anat.,* 90:427–447, 1952.

von Leden, H.: "The Mechanism of Phonation: A Search for a Rational Theory of Voice Production," *Arch. Otolaryng.,* 74:660–676, 1961.

Walter, H. E., and L. P. Sayles: *Biology of the Vertebrates,* 3d ed., The Macmillan Company, New York, 1949.

Washburn, S. L., and D. Wolffson: *Anthropological Papers of Franz Weidenreich, 1939–1948: A Memorial Volume,* The Viking Fund, Inc., New York, 1949.

Weiss, D. A.: "Discussion of the Neurochronaxic Theory," *Arch. Otolaryng.,* 70:607–618, 1959.

Weisskopf, A., and H. F. Burns: "The Ground Substance of the Nasal Turbinates," *Ann. Otol.,* 67:292–304, 1958.

Wepman, J. M.: *Recovery from Aphasia,* The Ronald Press Company, New York, 1951.

Wernicke, C.: *Der aphasische Symptomcomplex,* Breslau, 1874.

West, R.: "The Neurophysiology of Speech," pp. 72–90, in L. E. Travis (ed.), *Handbook of Speech Pathology,* Appleton-Century-Crofts, Inc., New York, 1957.

———, M. Ansberry, and A. Carr: *The Rehabilitation of Speech,* Harper & Brothers, New York, 1957.

——— and ———: *The Rehabilitation of Speech,* 4th ed., Harper & Row, Publishers, Incorporated, New York, 1968.

Westgate, H., and D. Rutherford: *Cleft Palate,* Prentice-Hall, Inc., Englewood Cliffs, N.J., 1966.

Wever, E. G.: *Theory of Hearing,* John Wiley & Sons, Inc., New York, 1949.

——— and M. Lawrence: *Physiological Acoustics,* Princeton University Press, Princeton, N.J., 1954.

Widdicombe, J. G.: "The Regulation of Bronchial Calibre," pp. 48–82, in C. G. Caro (ed.), *Advances in Respiratory Physiology,* The Williams & Wilkins Company, Baltimore, 1966.

Wiener, N.: *Cybernetics,* 2d ed., John Wiley & Sons, Inc., New York, 1961.

Wilson, W. A.: "Essay Review: Higher Cortical Functions in Man," *Amer. Sci.,* 54(4):465–470, 1966.

Winckel, F.: "Phoniatric Acoustics," pp. 24–55, in R. Luchsinger and G. E. Arnold (eds.), *Voice—Speech—Language,* Wadsworth Publishing Company, Belmont, Calif., 1965.

Wolcott, C. C.: "Contact Ulcer of the Larynx," *Ann. Otol.,* 65:816–819, 1956.

Woodburne, L. S.: *The Neural Basis of Behavior,* Charles E. Merrill Books, Inc., Columbus, Ohio, 1967.

Woodburne, R. T.: *Essentials of Human Anatomy,* Oxford University Press, New York, 1965; 4th ed., 1969.

Wright, S.: *Applied Physiology,* Oxford University Press, New York, 1961.

Wyatt, G. L.: *Language Learning and Communication Disorders in Children,* The Free Press, New York, 1969.

Wyke, B. D.: "Effects of Anaesthesia upon Intrinsic Laryngeal Reflexes: An Experimental Study," *J. Laryng.,* 82 (7):603–612, 1968.

Yale, C. A.: *Formation and Development of Elementary English Sounds,* Metcalf Printing and Publishing Company, Northampton, Mass., 1946.

Zenker, W.: "Vocal Muscle Fibers and Their Motor End-plates," pp. 7–19, in D. W. Brewer (ed.), *Research Potentials in Voice Physiology,* State University of New York, Syracuse, 1964.

INDEX

Myoelastic (tonic) theory of phonation, 256
Myxedema and voice, 282, 409

Nasality and nasal resonance, 345, 346, 352, 353
    assimilation, 353
Nasofrontal process (*see* Frontonasal process)
Nasolacrimal duct, 306
Nasopalatine canal, 308
Nasopharynx, 317–319
Negative feedback, 142
Nerve of Cyon, 188
Nerve impulse:
    conduction across synapses, 66
    inhibition of, 67
    nature of, 64–66
    summation of, 66
    transmission of, 65, 66
Nerves:
    cranial, 68–74
    spinal, 68
Neuroblasts, 90
Neurochronaxic (clonic) theory of phonation, 254, 255
Neuron:
    axon of, 63
    cell bodies of, 63, 64
    classification of, 63
    coverings of, 64
    impulses in, 64–66
    involvement of, in reflexes, 84
    neurofibrils of, 64
    Nissl bodies of, 64
    origin of, 63
Neuron components, 136
Nissl, Franz, 64
Nissl bodies, 64
Nodose ganglion, 233–235, 324
Nodules of vocal folds, 282
Noise, 20, 281, 446, 449, 455, 456
    examples of, 20
    white, 456
Norepinephrine, 148

Nose:
    blood and lymph of, 342, 343
    boundaries of, 340, 341
    evolution of, 351, 352
    functions of, 344, 345
    importance of, in speech, 345–346
    mucous membranes of, 341, 342, 345
    muscles of, 335, 336
    nerve supply of, 343, 344
    pathophysiology of, 352, 353
    skeletal framework of, 336–341
        bones in, 339–341
        cartilages in, 336–338

Occlusion:
    Angle's classification of, 381
    crossbite in, 382
    effects of, on speech, 381, 411
    open bite in, 411
Oculomotor nerve (*see* Cranial nerves)
Olfactory nerve (*see* Cranial nerves)
Olfactory pits, 306, 350, 360
Olfactory placode, 350
Olivocerebellar tract, 117
Olivospinal tract, 83
Open bite (*see* Occlusion)
Open quotient, 263
Ophthalmic nerve, 392
Optic nerve (*see* Cranial nerves)
Optimum pitch, 266, 293
Oral cavity (*see* Mouth)
Oral manometry, 199
Organ of Corti, 7, 427, 429
Organs of body, 58
Oropharynx, 319
Ossicles of middle ear, 422–424
Otic ganglion, 325, 391
Otitis media, 449
Otosclerosis, 423, 448, 449
    Lempert operation for, 448
    stapedectomy for, 449
    stapes mobilization for, 448
Oval window, 422, 423, 426, 428–430
Ovaries (*see* Gonads)
Overtones (*see* Harmonics)

Speech range, audiologic, 265
Speech reception threshold test, 453, 454
Speech sounds:
  biologic significance of, 445
  classification of, 356, 399
  consonants, 5, 356, 385, 398–400
  diphthongs, 384, 399, 401
  intensity of, 26–28
  semivowels, 399, 401
  vowels, 9, 251–260, 264, 265, 356, 398,
    399, 401–404
Sphenopalatine ganglion, 304, 325, 343,
  391
Sphincter, upper esophageal, 323
Spinal accessory nerve (see Cranial
  nerves)
Spinal cord, 77–84
  ascending tracts in, 79–81
  coverings of, 78
  descending tracts in, 81–84
  general structure of, 77–79
  nerve plexes of, 78
Spindles:
  of muscles, 75, 76
  of tendons, 77
Spirants, production of, 384
Spirometry, 195–199
Stapedectomy, 449
Stapedius muscle, 391, 424
Stapes mobilization, 448
Stenson's duct, 357
Stereognosis, 80
Sternum, 163–165
Stomodeum, 305, 359
Stretch reflexes:
  afterdischarge in, 87
  clasp-knife reaction in, 87
  cogwheeling in, 87
  gamma neurons in, 77
  muscle spindles in, 75–77
  receptors for, 3
  relation of spasticity to, 88
Stria vascularis, 427, 441
Stridor of voice, 271, 280, 284
Stroboscopy of larynx, 278
Stuttering, 127–129
Subarachnoid space, 94, 95

Subglottal air pressure, 259, 272
  in singing, 272
Submaxillary ganglion, 391
Substantia nigra, 107, 109, 119
Subthalamus, 107
Summating potential in acoustic nerve,
  441
Summation, 66
Superior cervical ganglion, 138, 325,
  343
Superior olivary nucleus, 432
Supraglottis, 215
Supramarginal gyrus, 81
Surds, 399
Surfactant, 161
Sutures, 51
Sympathetic nerves, 137, 138
Sympathetic vibration, 22, 292
Sympathetico-adrenal system, 133
Sympathin, 140
Symphyses, 51
Synapse, 66
  inhibition at, 67
Synarthrosis, 51
Synchrondrosis, 51
Synchronstroboscope, 263, 278
Syndesmosis, 51
Syrinx, 241
Systems of body, 58

Tabes dorsalis, 85
Tectorial membrane, 429, 431
Tectospinal tract, 83
Teeth:
  abnormalities of, and speech, 383
  articulator function of, 356
  crossbites of, 382, 383
  factors influencing development of,
    383
  number and succession of, 380, 381
  occlusion of, 381–383
  phylogeny of, 383, 384
  structure of, 379, 380
Telephone theory of hearing:
  Rutherford, 438
  Wrightson, 438